A GENERATION OF CHANGE

A GENERATION OF CHANGE
A Profile of America's Older Population

Jacob S. Siegel

CONTRIBUTING AUTHORS

Murray Gendell
Sally L. Hoover

for the
National Committee for Research
on the 1980 Census

RUSSELL SAGE FOUNDATION / NEW YORK

The Russell Sage Foundation

The Russell Sage Foundation, one of the oldest of America's general purpose foundations, was established in 1907 by Mrs. Margaret Olivia Sage for "the improvement of social and living conditions in the United States." The Foundation seeks to fulfill this mandate by fostering the development and dissemination of knowledge about the political, social, and economic problems of America.

The Board of Trustees is responsible for oversight and the general policies of the Foundation, while administrative direction of the program and staff is vested in the President, assisted by the officers and staff. The President bears final responsibility for the decision to publish a manuscript as a Russell Sage Foundation book. In reaching a judgment on the competence, accuracy, and objectivity of each study, the President is advised by the staff and selected expert readers. The conclusions and interpretations in Russell Sage Foundation publications are those of the authors and not of the Foundation, its Trustees, or its staff. Publication by the Foundation, therefore, does not imply endorsement of the contents of the study.

Library of Congress Cataloging-in-Publication Data

Siegel, Jacob S.
   A generation of change : a profile of Ameria's older population /
Jacob S. Siegel.
      p.   cm.—(The Population of the United States in the 1980s)
   Includes bibliographical references and index.
   ISBN 0-87154-789-9
   1. Aged—United States—Social conditions.   2. Aged—United
States—Statistics.   3. Age distribution (Demography)—United
States.   4. United States—Population—Statistics.   I. Title.
   II. Series.
   HQ1064.U5S534   1993
   305.26'0973—dc20   91-42772
                                                                                              CIP

RUSSELL SAGE FOUNDATION
112 East 64th Street, New York, New York 10021

10 9 8 7 6 5 4 3 2 1

FTW
AEK 3252

The National Committee for Research on the 1980 Census

Foreword

A Generation of Change: A Profile of America's Older Generation is one of an ambitious series of volumes aimed at converting the vast statistical yield of the 1980 census into authoritative analyses of major changes and trends in American life. This series, "The Population of the United States in the 1980s," represents an important episode in social science research and revives a long tradition of independent census analysis. First in 1930, and then again in 1950 and 1960, teams of social scientists worked with the U.S. Bureau of the Census to investigate significant social, economic, and demographic developments revealed by the decennial censuses. These census projects produced three landmark series of studies, providing a firm foundation and setting a high standard for our present undertaking.

There is, in fact, more than a theoretical continuity between those earlier census projects and the present one. Like those previous efforts, this new census project has benefited from close cooperation between the Census Bureau and a distinguished, interdisciplinary group of scholars. Like the 1950 and 1960 research projects, research on the 1980 census was initiated by the Social Science Research Council and the Russell Sage Foundation. In deciding once again to promote a coordinated program of census analysis, Russell Sage and the Council were mindful not only of the severe budgetary restrictions imposed on the Census Bureau's own publishing and dissemination activities in the 1980s, but also of the extraordinary changes that have occurred in so many dimensions of American life over the past two decades.

The studies constituting "The Population of the United States in the 1980s" were planned, commissioned, and monitored by the National Committee for Research on the 1980 Census, a special committee appointed by the Social Science Research Council and sponsored by the Council, the Russell Sage Foundation, and the Alfred P. Sloan Foundation, with the collaboration of the U.S. Bureau of the Census. This committee includes leading social scientists from a broad range of fields—

demography, economics, education, geography, history, political science, sociology, and statistics. It has been the committee's task to select the main topics for research, obtain highly qualified specialists to carry out that research, and provide the structure necessary to facilitate coordination among researchers and with the Census Bureau.

The topics treated in this series span virtually all the major features of American society—ethnic groups (blacks, Hispanics, foreign-born); spatial dimensions (migration, neighborhoods, housing, regional and metropolitan growth and decline); and status groups (income levels, families and households, women). Authors were encouraged to draw not only on the 1980 census but also on previous censuses and on subsequent national data. Each individual research project was assigned a special advisory panel made up of one committee member, one member nominated by the Census Bureau, one nominated by the National Science Foundation, and one or two other experts. These advisory panels were responsible for project liaison and review and for recommendations to the National Committee regarding the readiness of each manuscript for publication. With the final approval of the chairman of the National Committee, each report was released to the Russell Sage Foundation for publication and distribution.

The debts of gratitude incurred by a project of such scope and organizational complexity are necessarily large and numerous. The committee must thank, first, its sponsors—the Social Science Research Council, the Russell Sage Foundation, and the Alfred P. Sloan Foundation. The long-range vision and day-to-day persistence of these organizations and individuals sustained this research program over many years. The active and willing cooperation of the Bureau of the Census was clearly invaluable at all stages of this project, and the extra commitment of time and effort made by Bureau economist James R. Wetzel must be singled out for special recognition. A special tribute is also due to David L. Sills of the Social Science Research Council, staff member of the committee, whose organizational, administrative, and diplomatic skills kept this complicated project running smoothly.

The committee also wishes to thank those organizations that contributed additional funding to the 1980 census project—the Ford Foundation and its deputy vice president, Louis Winnick, the National Science Foundation, the National Institute on Aging, and the National Institute of Child Health and Human Development. Their support of the research program in general and of several particular studies is gratefully acknowledged.

The ultimate goal of the National Committee and its sponsors has been to produce a definitive, accurate, and comprehensive picture of the U.S. population in the 1980s, a picture that would be primarily descriptive but also enriched by a historical perspective and a sense of the challenges for the future inherent in the trends of today. We hope our readers will agree that the present volume takes a significant step toward achieving that goal.

CHARLES F. WESTOFF

Chairman and Executive Director
National Committee for Research
on the 1980 Census

For Lorise

Acknowledgments

Preparation of this monograph was supported in part by a grant from the Russell Sage Foundation joined by the Social Science Research Council and its National Committee for Research on the 1980 Census. These organizations were supported in this project by the National Institute of Aging of the U.S. National Institutes of Health. It is a pleasure to acknowledge also the contribution of many individuals who aided in the completion of this monograph. Dr. Charles F. Westoff, executive director of the National Committee for Research on the 1980 Census, read and offered insightful comments on the various chapters. Several members of the staff of the U.S. Bureau of the Census were helpful in providing data or comments. Cynthia Taeuber provided comments on the drafts of many of the chapters, and comments on individual chapters were given by Campbell Gibson, Gregory Spencer, Arlene Saluter, Leonard Norry, and others. Enrique Lamas, Edward Welniak, Tom Palumbo, John Priebe, and Gregory Robinson made available unpublished data and answered many questions relating to the census data. Persons in other government agencies or private organizations who provided unpublished data or advice are Ira Rosenwaike, University of Pennsylvania; Alice J. Wade, Office of the Actuary, Social Security Administration; Lester R. Curtin, National Center for Health Statistics; and Howard Fullerton, Bureau of Labor Statistics.

The monograph benefited greatly from the writing contributions of two associates. They helped to expand the scope and depth of the monograph in the areas of their special interests. Murray Gendell, Georgetown University, developed much material on work and retirement used for Chapter 7. Sally L. Hoover, United Way of Los Angeles, provided the first draft of Chapter 9.

A special debt is owed to the Department of Demography, Georgetown University, my "home base" during the preparation of the monograph, for its administrative support. Grants from the provost's office of the university helped to defray some of the expenses of publication. The

Department of Rural and Development Sociology, College of Agriculture and Life Sciences, Cornell University, and the Graduate Group in Demography, University of California, Berkeley, provided auxiliary administrative support during my brief tours at these institutions.

Wendy E. Williams, a "whiz" on the word processor, translated many rough drafts into finished typed text and tables. Kathryn Murray of Words and Numbers Ltd. and Lucy Cunnings provided additional assistance on the word processor, as did Tracy Manbeck and Melissa Jones. Sandor Toth assisted in carrying out necessary calculations and in locating appropriate reference materials.

Much of the supporting technical work in the later period of preparation was done by Donald S. Akers and Rose Varon Siegel. Don Akers compiled and checked much of the tabular material in the book. Rose Siegel assisted in selecting and designing some of the tabular material as well as in providing assistance with the myriad management tasks that attend the preparation of such a work.

In preparing this monograph, I drew heavily on two previous publications: "Demographic and Socioeconomic Aspects of Aging in the United States" (with Maria Davidson), U.S. Bureau of the Census, *Current Population Reports*, Series P-23, No. 138, August 1984, and "Demographic Dimensions of an Aging Society" (with Cynthia Taeuber) in: Alan Pifer and Lydia Bronte (editors), *The Aging Society: Paradox or Promise*, W.W. Norton and Company, New York, 1986.

Finally, my thanks go to the publication staff at the Russell Sage Foundation for their patience and dedication—from Lisa Nachtigall to Charlotte Shelby, Anna Marie Muskelly, and Sylvia Newman.

It is my hope that those who use this volume will find that it fills an important academic and practical need. I alone should be held responsible for any deficiencies the work may have in meeting these goals.

JACOB S. SIEGEL

Preface

The elderly population of the United States grew from 12.5 million in 1950 to nearly 30 million in 1987, with prospects for continuing rapid growth to the fourth decade of the next century. More significantly, the proportion of elderly has grown from 8 percent in 1950 to 12 percent in 1987 and is expected to grow to 22 percent in 2030. Demographic changes of this kind will be accompanied by many social and economic changes and political problems, which will require new policy formulations. This volume brings together a wide body of demographic facts regarding aging and the elderly population necessary to identify the policy options. It describes and analyzes the residential and migration patterns of the elderly, their length of life and health conditions, living arrangements and family status, educational level, work and retirement characteristics, income and wealth, and finally, their housing conditions, mainly for the period from 1950 to 1985.

In this analysis, a life-course perspective was applied to the demographer's grist. It asked the question: How did a particular demographic characteristic or event evolve as cohorts aged from youth or midlife to old age? The life-course perspective has tremendous implications for public policy since the character of life in the older years is strongly influenced, if not often closely determined, by experiences in earlier years. Particular emphasis is placed on cohort/cross-sectional comparisons to elucidate the difference between the variations over the age scale that the population displays in a particular year and the age variations that it experiences over its lifetime and to identify the emerging characteristics of the elderly more adequately.

The relative numbers of the elderly and various other age segments of the population have important social and economic implications. Accordingly, the numbers of the elderly in relation to the working-age population and in relation to the number of their children receives special attention. The sharp rise in the so-called burden of older persons on society and the family in the next century will be associated with numerous policy issues, particularly those relating to long-term care and Social Security funding.

The attributes of the elderly population have been highlighted by contrasting them with the attributes of the younger population or the total population, from which they often differ notably. Much attention is also given here to the variation in the characteristics of the age groups that make up the elderly population. This variation is considerable since, at the least, a wide span of years is included. Like many others before it, this study emphasizes the diversity of the older population, with the hope that policy formulations will take this diversity into account.

Although this volume is included in the 1980 Census Monograph Series, it makes liberal use of other sources of demographic data in addition to the 1980 decennial census. These include not only the censuses of 1950, 1960, and 1970 but also the Current Population Survey, the National Health Survey, the population estimates and projections of the U.S. Bureau of the Census, vital statistics data and life tables of the National Center for Health Statistics, and other appropriate sources. The recourse to multiple sources made possible a greater currency in the analysis and wider coverage of demographic topics and issues pertaining to the elderly than the 1980 census alone would have afforded.

GENERAL NOTES

This study relates principally to the United States as a whole. It is the geographic area referred to unless another area, such as a geographic subdivision of the United States or a foreign country, is specifically identified.

Much of the data presented in this monograph are sample data, whether from the census or sample surveys. These data and the differences between them are, therefore, subject to sampling error. Confidence intervals corresponding to the sample data and their differences are not given, however. The author has been careful not to refer to differences between the sample data unless such differences would be supported by a complete census.

The following standard symbols are employed in the various tables:

X   Not applicable

NA   Not available, or not computed because the basic data are not available.

B   Base is too small to produce reliable results. Base required is given in each table.

—   Value is zero or rounds to zero (0 or 0.0).
    The value may be an absolute number or a percentage.

Contents

List of Tables

List of Figures

BASIC DIMENSIONS OF AN AGING POPULATION

THE CHARACTER of the era since the end of World War II has been shaped greatly by the so-called baby boom: the 75 million births that occurred from mid 1945 to mid 1965.[1] The number born during the period exceeded the number born during the preceding two decades by 70 percent. As the birth group has moved up the age ladder, it has had a powerful influence on the institutions of our society, especially through the competition for resources between the age segments of the population and the special shape it has given to many of the issues facing our aging society.

Although the elderly population actually grew at a faster pace than the child population as a whole from 1950 through the mid 1970s and important social programs in support of the elderly were implemented during this period, the attention of American society was focused on the baby-boom cohorts—first as babies and then as school-age children and teenagers. The size of the elderly population was small relative to the size of the baby-boom cohorts and much of society's resources, particularly private and familial resources, were devoted to the young. By the mid 1980s, however, the front-runners of the baby-boom cohorts were

[1]The baby-boom period is arbitrarily considered to be July 1, 1945, to July 1, 1965, rather than 1946 to 1964—the period often used—to simplify correspondence with population projections for midyear quinquennial dates.

TABLE 1.1

Population Aged 65 and Over and Annual Average Increase: 1950–2050
(numbers in thousands; figures as of July 1)

Year	Population	Average Annual Increase in Preceding Period	
		Amount	Percent
1950	12,397	X	X
1965	18,451	404	2.7
1985	28,530	504	2.2
Projections[a]			
Middle Series			
1995	33,887	536	1.7
2010	39,196	354	1.0
2030	64,580	1,269	2.5
2050	67,412	142	0.2
Highest Series			
1995	34,618	609	1.9
2010	42,067	497	1.3
2030	72,587	1,526	2.7
2050	82,744	508	0.7
Lowest Series			
1995	33,127	460	1.5
2010	36,547	228	0.7
2030	58,085	1,077	2.3
2050	56,336	−87	−0.2

SOURCES: Based on U.S. Bureau of the Census, *Current Population Reports*, series P-25, nos. 311, 519, 917, 952, and 985.

NOTES: Minus sign denotes a decrease. X = not applicable.

[a] Definitions of series are: middle series—middle fertility, middle mortality, middle immigration; highest series—high fertility, low mortality, high immigration; lowest series—low fertility, high mortality, low immigration. The projections are not affected by fertility until after 2047.

facing middle age and attention was turning more and more to their future needs as an older population.

From 1985 until 2010, the population aged 65 and over will continue to increase, but not dramatically (Table 1.1). This period provides an opportunity to prepare for the years after 2010, when the baby-boom cohorts begin to reach age 65 and cause an elderly boom. Then, growth is expected virtually to halt for every age group except the elderly, and their number will jump from 39 million to 65 million in only 20 years, according to the Census Bureau's middle-series projections. By 2030, the elderly population will be at least 2.5 times larger than it was in 1980.

After 2030, when the elderly boom becomes the older-aged boom, there will be major growth only among the "oldest old." One American in 5 will be aged 65 and over and 1 in 19 will be 85 and over in 2050.

The elderly are different from the rest of the population in many ways. Although we cannot predict closely how existing differences will change in the future, we should be aware of the current differences and try to anticipate possible changes as we design public policy for the elderly as well as for the other age segments of our population. Planning efforts should go beyond devising ways of providing for the burgeoning elderly group, however: They should recognize the implications of a much older age structure for all age segments of our population and for the whole range of our social institutions.

The influence of a large, elderly population on the character of the twenty-first century will be profound. To assess this influence, we consider not only the size of that population, as we do in this chapter, but also its characteristics and its changes over the life course, as we do in later chapters. In this connection, we will look both backwards to the 1950s and forward to the twenty-first century. In this chapter, I discuss various concepts and measures of aging, the numbers and proportions of older persons in the past and future, and the role of demographic factors in these changes.

Concepts and Measures of Aging

Definitions of the Older Population

The present monograph focuses on the older population—namely, those aged 60 and over, and particularly those 65, 75, and 85 and over, but it also deals with persons of these ages in terms of the changes they have experienced over the entire age range or a large part of it. At the older ages the impact of aging in the form of changes in the individual's physical condition (e.g., health) and social and economic characteristics (e.g., labor force participation, income, living arrangements) or in a population's characteristics (e.g., sex ratio, proportion of households maintained by females) is most pronounced and of special public concern. The individual changes are collectively reflected in the data on the demographic and socioeconomic characteristics of the population.

The older population is a demographically heterogeneous population; a wide range of ages is included and sharp variations occur in the characteristics of persons in the component ages. In addition, there is rapid turnover in this population, mortality rates being relatively high and past fertility rates being variable. As time passes, a younger group enters the elderly age range; and the survivors of each age group among the elderly move up to occupy a new and higher age category as the former occupants age or die. These new members may have quite different characteristics from those they replace. Variations in initial size, the level of survival rates, and the share of immigrants also distinguish each cohort.

As a result, substantial shifts in the size and characteristics of each constituent age group and of the elderly population as a whole occur over time. In fact, shifts in numbers, age distribution, sex composition, health status, marital status, and economic characteristics may be considerable. The degree to which health deteriorates with age, for example, affects the shifts in other demographic, social, and economic characteristics, and shifts in these other characteristics exert an influence on the mortality and health of older people.

Since the older population is so demographically heterogeneous, this analysis often considers the broader group in terms of component age groups. We distinguish at times the older population (60 and over), the elderly (65 and over), the aged (75 and over), the older aged (85 and over), and the extreme aged (90 and over). Other ages and age bands have special significance and are sometimes referred to in the monograph. For example, age 62 is the age of eligibility for reduced Social Security benefits. The age group 80 and over has often been used by gerontologists to identify the "frail elderly" since a substantial share of persons in this age band are dependent on others for their care. The age band 60 and over is separately identified in the Older Americans Act of 1965 as the population eligible for receipt of various benefits.

For convenience and simplicity in the discussion, as well as its general appropriateness as a definition of the older population, however, the single broad age group 65 and over is most often selected in this monograph for detailed consideration. The attainment of age 65 marks the point of retirement for many workers and the point of qualification for full Social Security benefits and for Medicare coverage. Age 65 figures in several other important pieces of legislation affecting the older population, including federal and state tax laws. Beginning at age 65, many characteristics of the older population change very rapidly (e.g., sex composition, health conditions, work participation, living arrangements) and hence differ greatly from those for younger ages or the oldest ages.

Population Aging Versus Individual Aging

It is important to distinguish between the aging of individuals and the aging of populations. Although the summary measures of individual aging and population aging usually move together today, the two processes are essentially independent. In the United States currently, population aging is associated with low and declining mortality, but this association is not necessary or intrinsic.

Individual aging focuses on the aggregate experience of individuals, as units in a population, with respect to survival and longevity. This experience is reflected in such measures as life expectancy at birth and at other ages, the probability of survival from birth to a later age or from one age to another, person-years lived in an age interval, and percentage of potential years of life lost. Aging of this kind is a function purely of changes in death rates at each age of life.

In demographic as well as biological terms, the aging of individuals marks the inexorable running out of the biological time clock for the individual, given the presumably limited life span of roughly 95–105 years for the human species. Although changes linked to aging go on steadily throughout life, the term "aging" most commonly refers to the changes in later life, following the reproductive age period. Aging proceeds at different rates for different individuals in its physiological, psychological, behavioral, or sociological manifestations. In chronological terms it proceeds at the same pace for everyone. Physiologists will look for signs of aging in the loss of functional efficiency of various bodily organs. Psychologists will look for signs of aging in the decline in neuromuscular skills, learning ability, memory, and sensory acuity. Behavioral scientists and sociologists will look for signs of aging in the individual's disengagement from social roles and growing inability to live independently. The signs of physiological deterioration or the inability to function independently come earlier for some than for others, but they inevitably appear for all as time passes. Demographically, aging of individuals is defined in terms of chronological age. For large populations, chronological age follows functional age and physiological age closely. The demographic approach avoids the problem of fixing the onset of aging in the individual case, a task faced by the biological and behavioral sciences and beset with grave difficulties.

The aging (or younging) of a population refers to the fact that a population, as a unit of observation, is getting older (or younger). Population aging may be measured variously in terms of the median age, the mean age, the proportion of persons aged 65 and over, the ratio of persons aged 65 and over to persons under 18, the slope of a regression line fitted to the age distribution, and similar measures.[2] The various measures of

[2]H. S. Shryock, Jr., J. S. Siegel, and Associates, U.S. Bureau of the Census, *The Methods and Materials of Demography* (Washington, DC: U.S. Government Printing Office, 1980), pp. 234–235; T. Kii, "A New Index for Measuring Demographic Aging," *Gerontologist* 22 (4) (August 1982):438–442.

aging may indicate different degrees or even directions of aging for the same population during a particular period. (See Figure 1.1.) The aging or younging of populations results from the changes in their fertility, mortality, and migration rates, but under most conditions fertility is the dominant factor, as explained further below. For this monograph, aging will generally be defined as a rise in the proportion of the population aged 65 and over.

Two related measures—the age corresponding to some stated life expectancy, say 10 or 15 years, and the proportion of the total population above that age—are discussed later in the chapter.

Period Analysis Versus Cohort Analysis

In the analysis of aging and the characteristics of the older population, we are often concerned with the underlying pattern of variation of some demographic or socioeconomic event (e.g., migration) or characteristic (e.g., marital status) according to age. We may get a misleading impression as to the nature of this variation by merely examining the age variation in a particular year. To deal with this problem, the data must be compiled and analyzed for birth cohorts—that is, groups of persons born in the same calendar years who are followed with respect to their experience regarding some event (e.g., migration) or characteristic (e.g., marital status) over later calendar years as they grow older.[3] In this monograph we deal often with the difference in the variation of some demographic characteristic over the age scale in 1980 or other recent year from its variation for relevant birth cohorts.

Cohort analysis reflects the age variation in demographic events or characteristics more realistically than cross-sectional or period analysis—the analysis of the data for the same calendar year. The use of cohort analysis is also based on the fact that the demographic events experienced by individuals in later life are influenced by their previous experience of these events. Cohort analysis also avoids certain gross distortions in interpretation which could occur with period analysis (e.g., that educational attainment declines with age). It has, however, the disadvantages that the experience of a birth cohort has no simple time reference, that a large number of years have to pass before a record of lifetime experience can be secured, and that its experience is influenced at

---

[3]See, for example, N. B. Ryder, "The Cohort as a Concept in the Study of Social Change," *American Sociological Review* 30 (6) (December 1965): 843–861; "The Process of Demographic Transition," *Demography* 1 (1964):74–82.

FIGURE 1.1

Comparison of Various Measures of Population Aging in the Form of Indexes:
1920–2020

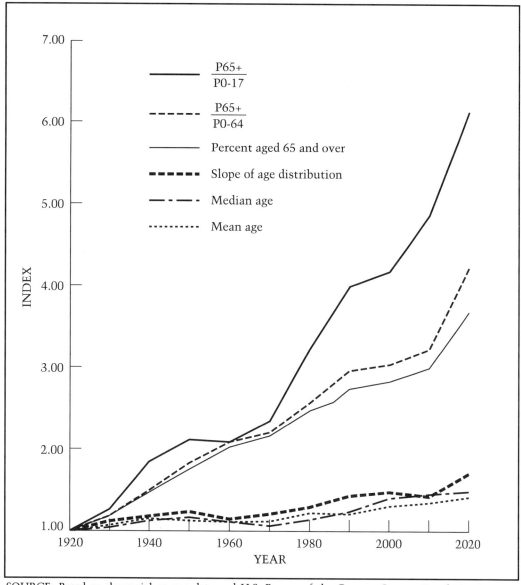

SOURCE: Based on decennial census data and U.S. Bureau of the Census, *Current Population Reports*, series P-25, nos. 952 and 985.

NOTE: Base of index = 1920. Points are plotted at 10-year intervals and for 1985. Projections are from the middle series.

different stages in the life cycle by the various historical events occurring in particular years over its lifetime.

The age data for a single year consist of "slices" of the experience of a large number of real cohorts. All of the cohorts represented are influenced by the socioeconomic, environmental, and historical events of the year in question. The influence of some external events, such as an economic depression, tends to be pervasive over the age span, even though these events do not affect all the ages equally and the response varies with the previous cohort experience of each age group.

Age Cycle, Cohort, and Period Effects

We may view the pattern of age variation of a demographic or socioeconomic event or characteristic in a particular year, or the changes in the age pattern between two years, as the joint product of three general factors or components: the general age pattern of a particular event or characteristic for population cohorts in a given era (age cycle effect), the changing historical-sociocultural conditions to which the various cohorts constituting the age groups of the particular year are exposed as they move through the age cycle (period effect), and the distinctive demographic and other properties of each of these several birth cohorts (cohort effect).[4] The first refers to the general succession of events or statuses characterizing the life course as the members of a cohort grow older (e.g., the rise, leveling off, and decline of labor force participation of men). The historical-sociocultural conditions producing period effects include the level of technology, the state of the economy, social norms, and so on, as they vary from year to year. Finally, birth cohorts vary with respect to initial size, proportions of births surviving to older ages, sex balance, and so on; large cohorts tend to have very different life course economic experiences from small cohorts, for example.

Various efforts have been made to disentangle age cycle, period, and cohort effects in age data in a given year or over some period or to measure the variation imposed on the age cycle by period and cohort effects. A general solution to disentangling age cycle, period, and cohort effects may not be possible, however, without imposing rather restrictive as-

[4]See also J. Hobcraft, J. Menken, and S. Preston, "Age, Period, and Cohort Effects in Demography: A Review," *Population Index* 48 (1) (Spring 1982):4–43; and S. E. Fienberg and W. M. Mason, "Identification and Estimation of Age-Period-Cohort Models in the Analysis of Discrete Archival Data," in K. F. Schuessler, ed., *Sociological Methodology* (San Francisco: Jossey-Bass, 1979).

sumptions. I consider this problem to a limited degree, deriving generalized cohort age cycles for a number of characteristics for comparison with the corresponding generalized period age cycles.

Numbers of Older Persons
Past and Prospective Trends

The older population of the United States is sizable. There were 39.5 million persons aged 60 and over, 28.5 million 65 and over, 11.5 million 75 and over, and 2.7 million 85 and over in 1985 (Table 1.2). Since 1950 the older population has shown an impressive growth. The age group 60 and over more than doubled in size between 1950 and 1985. Census Bureau population projections indicate that the older population will continue to grow at least to 2030.[5] The decennial growth rate for the population aged 60 and over approximated 29 percent between 1950 and 1960, but then it began a general declining trend which is expected to bring it down to about 7 percent in the decade 1990–2000. Decennial growth rates in subsequent decades will rise sharply, reaching 29 per-

[5]The basic assumptions underlying the three principal series of Census Bureau population projections—the middle, highest, and lowest series—are as follows:

Series	Fertility (Ultimate Lifetime Births per Woman)	Mortality (Life Expectancy in 2050)	Net Immigration (Annual)
Middle	1.9	79.6	450,000
Highest	2.3	83.3	750,000
Lowest	1.6	76.7	250,000

Appendix 1A gives a detailed description of the assumptions employed in developing the population projections. This monograph employs the population projections issued by the U.S. Bureau of the Census: "Projections of the Population of the United States, by Age, Sex, and Race: 1983 to 2080," by Gregory Spencer, *Current Population Reports*, series P-25, no. 952 (May 1984). These projections are based on current population estimates for July 1, 1982. The Census Bureau prepared some 30 series of population projections on the basis of alternative assumptions of fertility, mortality, and net immigration.

More recent population projections are available from the U.S. Bureau of the Census: *Current Population Reports*, series P-25, no. 1018 (January 1989), but it was not feasible to substitute them for the projections shown. The differences are not significant. See Appendix 1-A.

TABLE 1.2

Population in the Older Ages and Decennial Percent Increases,
for Cumulative Age Groups: 1950–2040
(numbers in thousands; estimates and projections as of July 1)

Year and Series	Ages 60 and Over		Ages 65 and Over		Ages 70 and Over	
	Number	Percent Increase[a]	Number	Percent Increase[a]	Number	Percent Increase[a]
Estimates						
1950	18,500	X	12,397	X	7,348	X
1960	23,828	28.8	16,675	34.5	10,394	41.5
1970	28,783	20.8	20,107	20.6	13,080	25.8
1980	35,849	24.5	25,704	27.8	16,893	29.2
1985	39,527	X	28,530	X	19,100	X
Projections[b]						
Middle Series						
1990	42,315	18.0	31,697	23.3	21,701	28.5
2000	45,408	7.3	34,921	10.2	25,825	19.0
2010	55,219	21.6	39,196	12.2	27,492	6.5
2020	71,213	29.0	51,422	31.2	34,802	26.6
2030	81,827	14.9	64,580	25.6	46,447	33.5
2040	83,073	1.5	66,988	3.7	52,086	12.1
Highest Series						
1990	42,675	19.0	31,989	24.5	21,914	29.7
2000	46,943	10.0	36,246	13.3	26,936	22.9
2010	58,596	24.8	42,067	16.1	29,916	11.1
2020	77,206	31.8	56,332	33.9	38,810	29.7
2030	91,224	18.2	72,587	28.9	53,003	36.6
2040	96,276	5.5	78,558	8.2	62,030	17.0
Lowest Series						
1990	41,902	16.9	31,353	22.0	21,415	26.8
2000	43,900	4.8	33,621	7.2	24,716	15.4
2010	52,080	18.6	36,547	8.7	25,264	2.2
2020	66,109	26.9	47,135	29.0	31,297	23.9
2030	74,304	12.4	58,085	23.2	41,070	31.2
2040	73,045	−1.7	58,116	0.1	44,417	8.1

SOURCES: U.S. Bureau of the Census, *Current Population Reports*, series P-25, nos. 311, 519, 917, 985, and 952.

NOTES: X = not applicable. Minus sign denotes a decrease. Base date of projections is July 1, 1982.

[a] For preceding decade.
[b] Based on alternative assumptions of fertility, mortality, and immigration. The projections for ages 60 and over are not affected by fertility until 2042. Definitions of series are: middle series—middle fertility, middle mortality, middle immigration; highest series—high fertility, low mortality, high immigration; lowest series—low fertility, high mortality, low immigration.

| Ages 75 and Over | | Ages 80 and Over | | Ages 85 and Over | | Ages 90 and Over | |
Number	Percent Increase[a]	Number	Percent Increase[a]	Number	Percent Increase[a]	Number	Percent Increase[a]
3,904	X	1,749	X	590	X	151	X
5,621	44.0	2,541	45.3	940	59.3	234	55.0
7,613	35.4	3,742	47.3	1,430	52.1	397	69.7
10,052	32.0	5,224	39.6	2,270	58.7	733	84.6
11,535	X	6,040	X	2,711	X	984	X
13,662	35.9	7,402	41.7	3,313	45.9	1,156	57.7
17,244	26.2	9,949	34.4	4,926	48.7	1,901	64.4
18,877	9.5	12,095	21.6	6,551	33.0	2,795	47.0
21,567	14.3	12,743	5.4	7,081	8.1	3,494	25.0
30.045	39.3	17,426	36.7	8,611	21.6	3,814	9.2
37,716	25.5	23,871	37.0	12,834	49.0	5,822	52.6
13,807	37.4	7,504	43.6	3,379	48.9	1,190	62.3
18,133	31.3	10,619	41.5	5,387	59.4	2,155	81.1
20,896	15.3	13,726	29.3	7,755	44.0	3,531	63.9
24,778	18.6	15,278	11.3	9,016	16.3	4,828	36.7
35,187	42.0	21,345	39.7	11,417	26.6	5,664	17.3
45,994	30.7	30,373	42.3	17,568	53.9	8,924	57.6
13,428	33.6	7,228	38.4	3,202	41.1	1,104	50.6
16,331	21.6	9,247	27.9	4,444	38.8	1,645	49.0
17,023	4.2	10,611	14.8	5,486	23.4	2,181	32.6
18,803	10.5	10,619	0.1	5,532	0.9	2,504	14.8
25,800	37.2	14,273	34.4	6,490	17.3	2,549	1.8
31,338	21.5	18,942	32.7	9,391	44.7	3,771	47.9

cent in 2010–2020. In 2010, we may expect about 55 million persons in these ages (middle series), or about 40 percent more than in 1985.[6]

The numbers in all of the component cumulative age categories within age 60 and over will be substantially or considerably larger by the end of this century and will continue to grow at least for the first three decades of the next century. The population aged 65 and over numbered 12.4 million in 1950. By 1985 this age group had more than doubled in size to 28.5 million. In 2010 we may expect about 39.3 million persons aged 65 and over (middle series), or nearly 40 percent more than in 1985. Further massive increases are expected to bring the figure to 65 million in 2030, when the elderly will number nearly four times the 1960 figure. The alternative lowest and highest population projections for 2030, representing a possible 90 percent confidence range around the middle projections, are 58 million and 73 million.

The population aged 65 and over increased rapidly during the 1970–1980 period (28 percent), much more rapidly than the population as a whole (11 percent) but far less rapidly than the group representing the first wave of the baby boom, the group aged 25–34 (49 percent). (See Tables 1.2 and 1.3 and Figure 1.2.)[7] The growth rate of the population aged 65 and over during the 1960s (21 percent) again greatly exceeded that of the total population (13 percent). The recent growth rates of the elderly population stand in contrast to the consistently sizable growth rates of the decades before 1960 (about 35 percent).

According to the Census Bureau's middle series of projections, the population aged 65 and over will show an increase of 23 percent during the 1980s, an increase somewhat similar to those in the previous two decades. We can then expect a sharp drop in the rate of increase lasting about two decades (10 percent for 1990–2000 and 12 percent for 2000–2010) and a sharp rise lasting about two decades (31 percent for 2010–2020 and 26 percent for 2020–2030). The elderly population as a whole never grows as rapidly as the 10-year age group carrying the first wave

[6]The projected numbers of older persons cited here should serve as good approximations because they are unaffected by future fertility. The people who will be aged 60 and over in 2010 or even 2040 are now all living. Their future size is determined by the current size of the cohort (which is essentially known), future mortality, and future net immigration. While future changes in the base population have to be predicted, this is quite different from predicting the entire population, which has to be done for age groups born after the base date. The latter involves prediction of fertility as well as mortality and net immigration; and fertility has tended to fluctuate widely and to elude close prediction. The highest population and lowest population series may be interpreted as providing an approximation of the range of uncertainty to the middle series. It is not possible to state precisely the probability associated with the uncertainty range given, but the figures for the older populations may be considered roughly as delimiting an 85–95 percent confidence interval.

[7]See Appendix 1B for a discussion of the quality of census data on the elderly.

TABLE 1.3

Decennial Percent Increase of the Population for Broad Age Groups: 1950–2020

Decade	All Ages	Age									
		Under 5	5–14	15–24	25–34	35–44	45–54	55–64	65–74	75–84	85–94[a]
1950–1960	18.7	24.0	45.3	9.9	-4.6	11.9	17.9	16.6	30.1	41.2	59.3
1960–1970	13.5	-15.6	14.1	48.7	10.5	-4.4	13.3	19.6	13.0	32.1	51.5
1970–1980	11.1	-4.1	-14.5	17.0	48.6	11.7	-2.4	16.5	25.3	25.9	56.5
Projections											
Middle Series											
1980–1990	9.6	16.6	1.5	16.8	15.7	46.3	11.6	3.3	15.2	33.0	42.2
1990–2000	7.3	-8.2	8.2	1.5	16.3	15.6	46.1	12.9	-2.0	19.0	45.7
2000–2010	5.7	2.0	-7.1	8.0	1.5	15.9	15.7	46.6	14.9	0.1	28.1
2010–2020	4.7	2.1	3.8	-6.9	7.7	1.6	-15.8	15.6	46.9	17.5	2.4
Highest Series											
1980–1990	11.6	25.3	3.8	15.7	17.8	47.8	12.4	-2.6	16.2	34.0	44.7
1990–2000	10.8	-0.4	16.9	4.0	14.6	18.0	47.8	14.3	-0.4	22.2	54.8
2000–2010	10.1	11.6	0.8	16.3	3.9	14.0	18.2	48.6	16.9	3.1	36.4
2010–2020	9.9	11.0	13.3	0.8	15.4	3.8	13.8	18.3	49.0	20.0	7.5
Lowest Series											
1980–1990	7.9	6.4	-0.1	-17.6	14.7	45.2	10.9	-3.9	14.5	31.4	37.7
1990–2000	4.2	-14.7	-2.4	-0.3	-17.5	14.4	44.8	11.6	-3.5	16.2	37.2
2000–2010	2.1	-4.3	-12.8	-2.3	-0.2	-17.3	14.4	45.1	12.9	-2.9	20.6
2010–2020	0.5	-5.8	-3.3	-12.6	-2.3	-0.2	-17.2	14.2	45.1	15.0	-2.8

SOURCES: U.S. Bureau of the Census, *Current Population Reports*, series P-25, nos. 311, 519, 917, 985, and 952.

[a] Population aged 85–94 estimated for July 1, 1950, to July 1, 1980, on the basis of adjusted census data.

NOTES: Minus sign denotes a decrease. Periods extend from July 1 of initial year to June 30 of terminal year. Based on total population including armed forces overseas, except for 1950. Base date of projections is July 1, 1982. Diagonal lines link birth cohorts.

FIGURE 1.2

Decennial Percent Increase of the Population Aged 65 and Over: 1950–2050

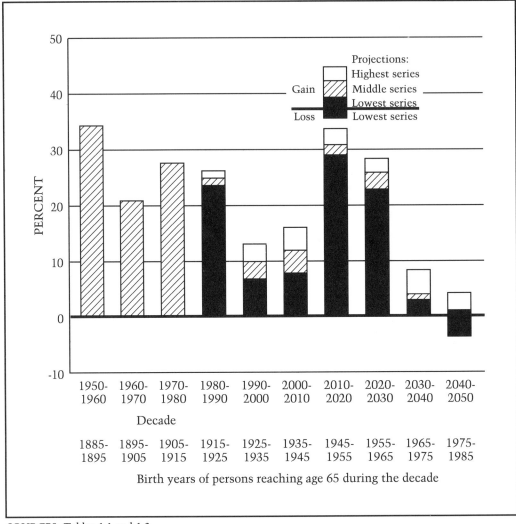

SOURCES: Tables 1.1 and 1.2.

of the baby-boom cohorts, however. During the period 2010–2020, when the latter group, aged 65–74, will grow about 47 percent, the population aged 65 and over will grow only two thirds as fast.

In 1985, the group aged 85 and over numbered 2.7 million; in 1950, it numbered 590,000. Older-aged persons have been recording the largest percent increases of all age segments in the decades since 1950 (Tables 1.2 and 1.3). Moreover, among the elderly the older the age group, the greater is the growth rate. The latter pattern is apparent from data for the period 1950–1980; and it is expected to continue for the period 1980–2010, albeit at much reduced levels:

	Percent Increase			
Period	Ages 65 and Over	Ages 65–74	Ages 75–84	Ages 85 and Over
1950–1980	107	84	135	285
1980–2010	53	30	56	199

The population aged 85 and over grew by nearly 300 percent between 1950 and 1980 while the group aged 65–74 grew by a "mere" 84 percent. Estimates of population changes at the highest ages (85–89, 90–94, and 95 and over) based on Medicare enrollments confirm the pattern of rising percent changes with rising age (Table 1.4).

In future years, the age groups 75 and over and 85 and over will show fluctuations in decennial growth rates similar to those in the population aged 65 and over, but with a lag of 10 and 20 years, respectively. Accordingly, the population aged 75 and over will grow very rapidly after 2020 and the population aged 85 and over will advance sharply after 2030, following a decade or two of slower growth. Some 38 million persons are expected to be aged 75 and over in 2040, after the various waves of the baby-boom cohorts have arrived. A decennial increase of about 50 percent between 2030 and 2040 will bring the group aged 85 and over to nearly 13 million in the later year.

The Role of Demographic Factors

The influential role of fertility in the decennial changes in the number of elderly persons is suggested by the fact that the fluctuations in the percent growth of the elderly population roughly parallel the fluctuations in the percent increase in births 65–84 years earlier. The general rise in the number of births in the latter part of the nineteenth century and in the first two decades of this century largely accounts for the rapid increases in the number of elderly persons between 1950 and 1985. (The rise in the number of births was occurring in this period even while the birth rate was falling, because of the rapid increase in the size of the population.)

Future shifts in the number of elderly persons largely reflect the trend of births since World War I. The sharp drop in the increase of the population aged 65 and over expected from about 1985 to 2005 is attributable in large part to the net decline or stability in the number of births

TABLE 1.4

Percent Increase in Persons Aged 85 and Over Enrolled in the Medicare Program, by Age and Sex: January 1, 1970, 1976, and 1982

Age	Medicare Population (in thousands)[a]			Percent Increase	
	1970	1976	1982	1970–1976	1976–1982
Both Sexes					
85 and Over	1,379	1,852	2,459[b]	34.4	32.7
85–89	1,021	1,319	1,683	29.2	27.6
90–94	294	429	606	45.9	41.3
95 and Over	63	104	169	65.2	63.2
Male					
85 and Over	471	585	718[b]	24.2	22.6
85–89	359	429	512	19.4	18.3
90–94	93	128	164	37.7	27.6
95 and Over	18	28	42	51.4	51.8
Female					
85 and Over	908	1,267	1,741[b]	39.6	37.4
85–89	612	890	1,171	34.5	31.5
90–94	201	301	443	49.7	47.1
95 and Over	45	76	127	71.0	67.4

SOURCES: U.S. Social Security Administration and U.S. Health Care Financing Administration (unpublished tabulations). Cited by I. Rosenwaike, "A Demographic Portrait of the Oldest Old," *Milbank Memorial Fund Quarterly* 63 (2) (Spring 1985): 187–205. Copyright © 1985. The Milbank Memorial Fund. Reprinted by permission.

[a] Data exclude persons tabulated at ages 120 and over.
[b] Estimates for January 1, 1982, consistent with 1980 census counts, are 2,413,000 (both sexes), 716,000 (male), and 1,697,000 (female).

during the 1920–1930 and 1930–1940 decades. The births of the postwar baby boom, extending from mid 1945 to mid 1965, will have their direct impact on the size of the elderly population after about 2010. As the first members of the postwar birth cohorts attain age 65, the number of elderly persons will rise sharply. The direct effect of the baby boom on the number aged 65 and over will run about 20 years, from 2010 to 2030. Thereafter, as the smaller birth cohorts of the later 1960s and the 1970s reach age 65, the growth rate of the elderly will begin a sharp decline.

Mortality and immigration, particularly the former, have had an important effect on the size of the elderly population also. Deaths reduce the size of the initial cohort of births, and net immigration typically increases it. Mortality rates have fallen rather steadily through most years of this century, and as a result larger and larger shares of the initial cohorts of births have been surviving to age 65 or ages 65–84 as the decades passed. About 43 percent of births survive to ages 65–84 according to the U.S. life table for 1949–1951, and 57 percent according to the life table for 1985. The middle series of the Census Bureau's mortality projections implies that about 68 percent of the births of 1955–1975 will survive to ages 65–84 in 2040.

While the declines in death rates have contributed to the increase in the number of older persons in this century, the contribution of declining mortality has generally been much less than the rise in the number of births. Some illustrative data on the relative contribution of births and deaths to the change in the population aged 60–69 for 1950–2010 are shown in Table 1.5. It may be seen that, for the most part, the percent changes in births greatly exceed the percent changes in survival rates. Furthermore, the absolute shifts in the percent changes of the population and of births from decade to decade are virtually identical; that is, the patterns of fluctuations in the rate of population growth and the rate of change in births are nearly the same. On the other hand, the contribution to the percent change in the population aged 60–69 in recent decades, of factors other than births, has clearly increased and exceeds the contribution of births.

Table 1.6, relating to the population aged 85–94, presents the results of allocating the population change among births, deaths, and net immigration for 1900–1980, with a partial allowance for the interaction between them. Tables 1.5 and 1.6 together inform us that the relative roles of births and deaths in the change of the older population have been shifting. Prior to 1950, births had a quite dominant influence, but more recently death rates have fallen rapidly at the higher ages, particularly at the very old ages, so that the relative influence of births has been declining. The extent of the decline varies directly with age and the recency of the period. The contribution of births to "natural increase" at ages 60–69 was still quite dominant in the 1950–1980 period (70 percent), but the contribution of births to change in the population aged 85 and over in this period was only 41 percent.

Period	Ages 60–69	Ages 65–84	Ages 85 and Over
1900–1940	NA	NA	.86[a]
1950–1980	.70[b]	.54[a]	.41[a]
1980–2010[d]	.60[b]	.68[c,e]	NA

NOTE: NA = not available.

[a]Based on Table 1.6.
[b]Based on Table 1.5.
[c]Based on data in text and Table 1.5.

[d]Middle series of mortality projections.
[e]Figure is for 1980–2040.

TABLE 1.5

Illustrative Estimates of the Contribution of Births and Deaths to the Decennial Percent Change in the Population Aged 60–69: 1950–2010

Year or Period	Population Aged 60–69			Births 60–69 Years Earlier			Survival Rate, Birth to Ages 60–69 [d]	
	Number (thousands)	Percent Increase in Preceding Decade [a]	Absolute Increase [a,b]	Number [c] (thousands)	Percent Increase in Preceding Decade [a]	Absolute Increase [a,b]	Rate	Relative Percent Change
1950	11,152	X	X	21,193	X	X	.672	X
1960	13,434	20.5	X	23,923	12.9	X	.707	5.2
1970	15,688	16.8	-3.7	26,215	9.6	-3.3	.716	1.3
1980	18,939	20.7	3.9	28,557	8.9	-0.7	.762	6.4
1990	20,645 [e]	9.0	-11.7	27,826	-2.6	-11.5	.801	5.1
2000	19,604 [e]	-5.0	-14.0	24,162	-13.2	-10.6	.817	2.0
2010	27,699 [e]	41.3	46.3	32,008	32.5	45.7	.823	0.7
1950–1980	X	69.8	X	X	34.7	X	X	13.4
1980–2010	X	46.3	-23.5	X	12.1	-22.6	X	8.0
1950–2010	X	149.4	X	X	51.0	X	X	22.5

SOURCES: Based on U.S. Bureau of the Census, Current Population Reports, series P-25, nos. 519, 917, and 922; A. J. Coale and N. W. Rives, Jr., "A Statistical Reconstruction of the Black Population of the United States, 1880–1970: Estimates of True Numbers by Age and Sex, Birth Rates, and Total Fertility," Population Index 39(1) (January 1973): 3–36; A. J. Coale and M. Zelnik, New Estimates of Fertility and Population in the United States (Princeton, NJ: Princeton University Press, 1963); U.S. National Center for Health Statistics, U.S. Life Tables: 1959–61, and U.S. Decennial Life Tables: 1969–71; U.S. Social Security Administration, Office of the Actuary, "Life Tables for the United States, 1900–2050," by J. F. Faber, Actuarial Study, no. 87 (September 1982). Originally published as Table 2-3 in U.S. Bureau of the Census, Current Population Reports, Series P-25, no. 138 (1984).

NOTES: X = not applicable. Minus sign denotes a decrease. The contribution of net migration is not shown and cannot be closely inferred as a residual from these data since changes in the population and in the components are not entirely consistent.

[a] Increase also shown for broad periods.
[b] Absolute increase between entries in column "Percent Increase in Preceding Decade."
[c] White and black births only. Figures are adjusted for underregistration.
[d] Rates are only illustrative since they are derived from current life tables.
[e] Middle population series.

TABLE 1.6

Components of Increase in the Population Aged 85–94: 1900–1940 and 1940–1980

Components	1900–1940 Change			1940–1980 Change		
	Number (thousands)	Percent of Total	of Native	Number (thousands)	Percent of Total	of Native
Total Increase	233	100	X	1,731	100	X
In Native Population	183	79	100	1,436	83	100
Increase in births	158	68	86	570	33	40
Decrease in mortality	25	11	14	866	50	60
In Foreign-born Population	50	21	X	295	17	X

SOURCE: Adapted from I. Rosenwaike and A. Dolinsky, "The Changing Demographic Determinants of the Growth of the Extreme Aged," *Gerontologist* 27 (3) (June 1987): 275–280, Table 4. Copyright © The Gerontological Society of America. Reprinted by permission.

NOTE: X = not applicable.

Although the contribution of births to population growth at ages 60–69 (60 percent) is expected to exceed the contribution of mortality (40 percent) in the 1980–2010 period, its contribution will have fallen substantially. The relative contribution of mortality declines to the growth of the older population will necessarily increase if death rates decline mainly at the older ages and if fertility remains low, as is assumed in the Census Bureau's population projections. The influence of fertility will experience a resurgence after 2005 or 2010 as the baby-boom cohorts enter the older ages. It is important to note, however, that because deaths number far fewer than births, are distributed over all ages (unlike births), and are subject to less fluctuation than births, the *potential* role of fertility in changes in the size of the older population will always greatly exceed the *potential* role of mortality, as has been the case in the past.[8]

Somewhat greater increases in the elderly population, and a greater influence of mortality in elderly population growth, than are shown by the Census Bureau's middle series of population projections could occur if the low mortality path is followed. For example, the projection of the population aged 65 and over is larger by about 2.4 million, or 6 percent, for 2010, and by 5.9 million, or 9 percent, for 2030 in the low series than in the middle series. Age-specific death rates are assumed to decline between 1981–1982 and 2050 at a rate 75 percent faster in the low series than in the middle series. Alternatively, if the high series of mortality projections prevails, there would be 2.1 million, or 5 percent, fewer persons aged 65 and over in 2010, and 5.0 million, or 8 percent, fewer in 2030, than if the middle series prevails. Age-specific death rates are assumed to decline between 1981–1982 and 2050 one half as rapidly in the high series as in the middle series.

The extent to which immigration contributes to the size of the older population depends on the age distribution of immigrants and the fluctuations in the volume of immigration. Immigration has sometimes resulted in a rise in the growth rates for the elderly and at other times in a decline in the rates. The large and increasing volume of young immigrants prior to World War I contributed greatly to the increase in the number of persons aged 65 and over up to 1960. Between 1895–1899 and 1905–1909 the numbers of immigrants rose from 1.4 million to 4.9 million, and over three fourths of the immigrants were aged 15–45. Because of the general falling off of immigration since World War I, however, this factor has been much less important in contributing to the

[8]D. McFarland, "The Aged in the 21st Century: A Demographic View," in L. E. Jarvik, ed., *Aging into the 21st Century: Middle-Agers Today* (New York: Gardner Press, 1978), esp. p. 21.

rise of the elderly population since 1960. Between 1950 and 1960, about 2.4 million foreign-born immigrants in the United States reached age 65, but between 1970 and 1980 the number was only 1.5 million. The actual net additions to the population through net immigration *at ages 65 and over* in these decades (allowing for immigrants reaching age 65, and immigration, emigration, and deaths at ages 65 and over) were far smaller, however, mainly because of deaths.

Immigration is expected to play a minor role in the growth of the elderly population in the future. For example, the middle allowance for net immigration (450,000 persons of all ages per year) from 1982 on adds only 0.8 million persons, or 2 percent, to the middle projection series for the population aged 65 and over in 2010, and 3.1 million persons, or 5 percent, in 2030.

Net and Gross Changes

Because of the relatively high death rates of the older population, membership in the group is, on the average, relatively short in duration. Population turnover in this group over a decade may be measured simply on the basis of the percentage of the total population aged 65 and over at the end of the decade falling in the 65–74 age group, that is, the proportion of the total elderly population who are surviving new entrants. Of the population aged 65 and over in 1985, 60 percent will have joined the group after 1975. According to this measure, turnover has been declining. The 10-year entering share in 1960 was 66 percent.

The turnover of the elderly population may be measured also by the ratio of the net change in the population aged 65 and over to the gross change in this age group (i.e., the sum of the components of change without regard to sign). The lower the ratio is, the greater the turnover is and the less "efficient" the demographic changes are. For the 1970–1980 decade this ratio was 0.18; that is, there was a net addition to the population aged 65 and over of only 18 persons for every 100 demographic events affecting that age group (Table 1.7). The figures for the decades since 1950 imply that turnover has been considerable but has changed little. The ratio was 0.14 in 1960–1970 and 0.18 in 1950–1960.

Turnover of the elderly population may also be measured in terms of the gross gain, gross loss, and net gain of the group during a specified period. The rate of gross gain during the decade 1970–1980, calculated as the number of persons reaching age 65 during the decade (17.9 million) plus the number of (net) immigrants during the decade (0.1 million) per 100 persons aged 65 and over in 1970 (20.1 million) was 89 percent. The rate of gross loss—the number of deaths of persons aged 65 and over

TABLE 1.7

*Estimates of the Demographic Components of Change in the Population Aged 65
and Over: 1970–1980, 1960–1970, and 1950–1960*
(numbers in thousands)

Item and Period	July 1, 1970–July 1, 1980	April 1, 1960–April 1, 1970	April 1, 1950–April 1, 1960
Population Aged 65 and Over, Terminal Date	25,707	19,972	16,560
Population Aged 65 and Over, Initial Date	20,107	16,560	12,295
Net Increase [a]			
Amount	5,600	3,412	4,265
Percent	27.9	20.6	34.7
Number Reaching Age 65	17,897	14,388	12,564
Net "Migrants" Aged 65 and Over	53	68	62
Deaths Ages 65 and Over	12,442	10,979	8,714
Deaths to initial population aged 65 and over	10,051	8,833	6,636
Deaths to persons reaching age 65	2,391	2,146	2,078
Gross Change [b]	30,393	25,435	21,340
Ratio, Net Change to Gross Change	.181	.137	.183
Rate of Gross Gain [c]	89.3	87.3	102.7
Rate of Gross Loss [d]	61.9	66.3	70.9
Rate of Net Gain	27.4	21.0	31.8
Ratio, Gross Loss Rate to Gross Gain Rate	.693	.759	.690
Mortality Rate of Population Aged 65 and Over [e]	32.7	35.5	35.1
Mortality rate of initial population aged 65 and over (per 100)	50.0	53.3	54.0
Mortality rate of persons reaching age 65 (per 100)	13.4	14.9	16.5

SOURCES: Population data are from the U.S. Bureau of the Census, *Current Population Reports*, series P-25 and 1970, 1960, and 1950 Censuses of Population; and mortality and migration statistics are from unpublished Census Bureau records. (Adapted from Table 2-4 in U.S. Bureau of the Census, *Current Population Reports*, series P-25, no. 138 (1984).

[a] Represents the difference between the census counts, including the "error of closure," the residual representing the difference between net increase based on the census counts, and net change based on the components of change (4.8 million for all ages, 1970–1980, 0.3 million for 1960–1970, and 0.4 million for 1950–1960).
[b] Represents the sum of persons reaching age 65, net "migrants," and deaths ages 65 and over. It does not include the "error of closure."
[c] Number reaching age 65 plus net "migrants" per 100 initial population.
[d] Total deaths per 100 initial population.
[e] Deaths ages 65 and over per 100 initial population aged 65 and over plus persons reaching age 65 during the period.

during the decade (12.4 million) expressed as a percentage of the population aged 65 and over in 1970—was 62 percent. Accordingly, the rate of net gain—the difference between the gross gain rate and the gross loss rate—was 27 percent.

About 50 percent of the initial population cohort aged 65 and over (i.e., persons aged 65 and over in 1970) died during the 1970–1980 decade. In addition, the new arrivals in the group (i.e., persons reaching age 65 during the decade) sustained a loss of 13 percent between 1970 and 1980. The resulting average gross loss rate through death for the initial population and the new arrivals combined is 33 percent.

During the prior decade, 1960–1970, the rate of gross gain (87 percent) and the rate of gross loss (66 percent) of the population aged 65 and over were, respectively, slightly lower and somewhat higher than the same measures for the 1970–1980 period (Table 1.7). Accordingly, the rate of net gain for 1960–1970 (21 percent) was somewhat lower than for 1970–1980 (27 percent). The rate of gross gain and the rate of gross loss were substantially greater in the 1950–1960 decade than in the subsequent decades. A rate of gross gain of 103 percent was mostly offset by a rate of gross loss of 71 percent, with a residual net gain of 32 percent. Mortality rates fell over the three decades, but the decline in death rates was not strong enough to assure a consistent reduction in the turnover of the elderly population over this period, as shown by the fluctuations in the ratio of the gross loss rate to the gross gain rate. On balance, little net change in turnover would be expected between 1950–1960 and 1970–1980 since both the "birth" rate (number reaching age 65 per 1,000 mid-decade population) and the death rate fell in this period by about the same percentage (i.e., 10 percent). (See Table 1.8.)

TABLE 1.8

"Birth" Rates and Death Rates for the Population Aged 65 and Over:
1970–1980, 1960–1970, and 1950–1960

Component Rate[a]	1970–1980	1960–1970	1950–1960
Net Growth Rate[b]	24.0	19.0	27.1
"Birth" Rate[c]	78.1	78.8	87.1
Death Rate	54.3	60.1	60.4
Net Immigration Rate	0.2	0.4	0.4

[a] Rates per 100 mid-decade population, derived as the average of figures for the beginning and end of the decade.
[b] Net growth is based on the component data.
[c] Numbers reaching age 65 during the decade represent births.

The Proportion of Older Persons
Past and Prospective Trends

The unbroken rise in the proportion of the population aged 65 and over between 1920 and 1985 is one numerical measure of the fact that the population has been aging steadily for many decades. In fact, the share of the population aged 65 and over in the total population has been rising from the earliest years of the nation and is expected to go on rising at least for the next several decades.[9] Percentages from 1920 to 2050 are as follows:

				Percent	
Year (July 1)	Percent	Year (July 1)	Middle[a]	Highest Population[b]	Lowest Population[c]
Estimates		Projections			
1920	4.6	1990	12.7	12.6	12.8
1930	5.4	2000	13.0	12.9	13.1
1940	6.8	2010	13.8	13.6	14.0
1950	8.1	2020	17.3	16.7	17.8
1960	9.3	2030	21.2	19.7	22.4
1970	9.9	2040	21.7	19.8	23.4
1980	11.3	2050	21.8	19.4	24.0
1985	11.9				

SOURCE: U.S. Bureau of the Census, *Current Population Reports*, series P-25, no. 952 (May 1984) and other nos.

[a]Middle fertility, middle mortality, and middle immigration.
[b]High fertility, low mortality, and high immigration.
[c]Low fertility, high mortality, and low immigration.

The proportion aged 65 and over rose from 8.1 percent to 11.3 percent between 1950 and 1980. (See also Table 1.9.) The rate of aging should decelerate between 1980 and 2010 and then accelerate again between 2010 and 2040. According to the middle population series, the proportion will rise by 2.5 points to 13.8 percent in 2010 and then will leap upward by 7.9 points to 21.7 percent in 2040. Under alternative assumptions, the proportion may rise more slowly to 19.8 percent in 2040, as in the highest population series, or more rapidly to 23.4 percent, as in the lowest population series.[10] The actual decennial increases in the

---

[9]During the 1950–1960 decade the population "aged" and "younged" simultaneously, since the proportion of elderly persons and the proportion of children both increased at the same time.

[10]The range defined by the percentages aged 65 and over corresponding to the highest population series and the lowest population series is believed to understate the uncertainty to be associated with the middle series. The combination of fertility, mortality, and immigration producing a maximum range in the total population (high fertility/low mortality/high immigration and low fertility/high mortality/low immigration) does not produce a maximum range in the proportion of elderly persons. In each of these series, the directional effect of mortality on the proportion aged 65 and over tends to offset the directional effect of fertility. The lowest proportions aged 65 and over, obtained from the high fertility/high mortality/high immigration series, and the highest proportions, obtained from the low fertility/low mortality/low immigration series, provide a much wider range of uncertainty. The lowest and highest percentages for 1985–2050 are as follows:

Year (July 1)	Lowest[a]	Highest[b]
1985[c]	11.9	11.9
1990	12.4	13.0
2000	12.2	13.9
2010	12.3	15.5
2020	14.7	20.1
2030	17.2	25.5
2040	16.5	27.6
2050	15.6	29.3

SOURCE: U.S. Bureau of the Census, *Current Population Reports,* series P-25, no. 952 (May 1984) and other nos.

[a]High fertility, high mortality, high immigration.
[b]Low fertility, low mortality, low immigration.
[c]Current estimate.

The range defined by these percentages is believed to overstate the uncertainty associated with the middle series. An appropriate range of uncertainty in the proportion of elderly may be represented by percentages midway between the two sets just presented.

Year (July 1)	Percent		
	Middle	Low	High
1985[a]	11.9	11.9	11.9
1990	12.7	12.5	12.9
2000	13.0	12.6	13.5
2010	13.8	13.0	14.8
2020	17.3	15.7	18.9
2030	21.2	18.4	23.9
2040	21.7	18.1	25.5
2050	21.8	17.5	26.6

[a]Current estimate.

This set of percentages is more useful for applications of projections that focus on the age structure of the population than the first or second set of figures presented. (Consider, for example, applications in programs calling for the maximum or minimum reasonable proportion of elderly, such as funding for Social Security.)

TABLE 1.9

*Percentage of the Total Population in the Older Ages, for Cumulative Age Groups:
1950–2020 (figures as of July 1)*

	Age					
Year and Series	60 and Over	65 and Over	70 and Over	75 and Over	80 and Over	85 and Over
Estimates						
1950	12.1	8.1	4.8	2.6	1.1	0.4
1960	13.2	9.3	5.8	3.1	1.4	0.5
1970	14.0	9.8	6.4	3.7	1.8	0.7
1980	15.7	11.3	7.4	4.4	2.3	1.0
1985	16.5	11.9	8.0	4.8	2.5	1.1
Projections[a]						
Middle Series						
1990	16.9	12.7	8.7	5.5	3.0	1.3
2000	16.9	13.0	9.6	6.4	3.7	1.8
2010	19.5	13.8	9.7	6.7	4.3	2.3
2020	24.0	17.3	11.7	7.3	4.3	2.4
Highest Series						
2020	22.7	16.5	11.4	7.3	4.5	2.6
Lowest Series						
2020	25.2	17.9	11.9	7.2	4.0	2.1

SOURCE: U.S. Bureau of the Census, *Current Population Reports*, series P-25, nos. 311, 519, 917, 952, and 985.

NOTE: Based on the total population including armed forces overseas, except for 1950.

[a]Base date is July 1, 1982. Percentages for the highest and lowest population series do not represent a range (i.e., confidence interval) around the percentages for the middle series. See text for explanation. Definitions of series are: middle series—middle fertility, middle mortality, middle immigration; highest series—high fertility, low mortality, high immigration; lowest series—low fertility, high mortality, low immigration.

proportion aged 65 and over may fluctuate greatly, as in the past, but barring a marked upward shift in fertility, such as is not now envisaged, the proportion will maintain an upward course. (See Figure 1.3.)

Relatively more rapid growth than for the total population is characteristic of all age segments of the elderly population. This is reflected in the steady increase in the proportion aged 75 and over, 80 and over, and 85 and over, as well as 60 and over and 65 and over, from 1950 to 2020, shown in Table 1.9. The proportion of persons aged 75 and over, like that for persons 65 and over, has been rising very rapidly since 1950. By 1980 the proportion aged 75 and over had nearly caught up with the proportion 65 and over in 1920; and by 2030 the proportion aged 75 and over will have caught up with the proportion 65 and over in 1970. The

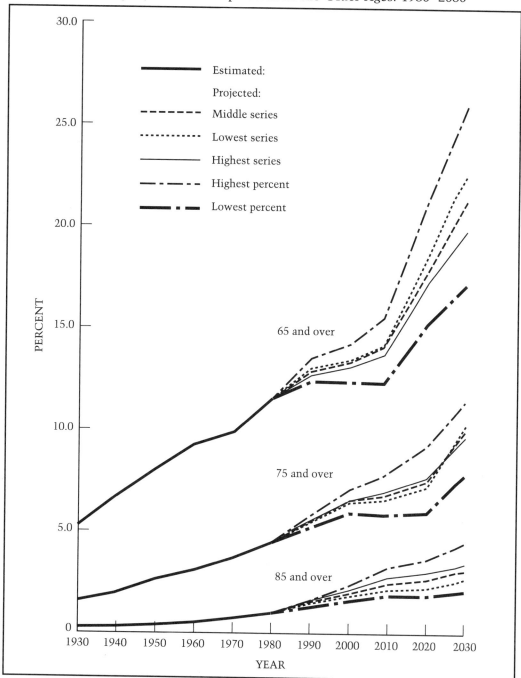

FIGURE 1.3

Percentage of the Total Population in the Older Ages: 1930–2030

Estimated:
Projected:
Middle series
Lowest series
Highest series
Highest percent
Lowest percent

65 and over

75 and over

85 and over

PERCENT

YEAR

SOURCES: Tables 1.2 and 1.9.

NOTES: Estimates and projections as of July 1. Points are plotted for years ending in zero.

27

proportion aged 75 and over is expected to rise steadily from 4.4 percent in 1980 to 6.7 percent in 2010 and to 12 percent in 2040—that is, nearly to treble between 1980 and 2040.[11]

Year (July 1)	Percent	Year (July 1)	Percent		
			Middle[a]	Highest[b]	Lowest[c]
Estimates		Projections			
1920	1.4	1990	5.5	5.5	5.5
1930	1.6	2000	6.5	6.5	6.4
1940	1.4	2010	6.7	6.9	6.5
1950	2.6	2020	7.3	7.4	7.1
1960	3.1	2030	9.8	9.6	9.9
1970	3.7	2040	12.2	11.6	12.5
1980	4.4	2050	12.0	11.4	12.4
1985	4.8				

SOURCE: U.S. Bureau of the Census, *Current Population Reports*, series P-25, no. 952 (May 1984) and other nos.

[a] Middle fertility, middle mortality, and middle immigration.
[b] High fertility, low mortality, and high immigration.
[c] Low fertility, high mortality, and low immigration.

The population of the United States is moving toward and will attain zero population growth (ZPG) about the middle of the next century under conditions of continuing subreplacement fertility (1.9 children per woman), moderate net immigration (450,000 per year), and moderately declining mortality. These assumptions correspond to those of the middle

[11] As suggested earlier, the range of uncertainty in the middle projected proportions aged 75 and over may not be adequately represented by proportions from the highest and lowest population series. Projections of minimal and maximal percentages, based on alternative high and low assumptions of fertility, mortality, and immigration for 1990–2050, are as follows:

Year (July 1)	Lowest[a]	Highest[b]
1985[c]	4.8	4.8
1990	5.3	5.6
2000	5.9	7.0
2010	5.7	7.8
2020	5.8	9.0
2030	7.5	12.6
2040	8.7	16.5
2050	7.9	17.6

SOURCE: U.S. Bureau of the Census, *Current Population Reports*, series P-25, no. 952 (May 1984).

[a] High fertility, high mortality, high immigration.
[b] Low fertility, low mortality, and low immigration.
[c] Current estimate.

series of the Census Bureau projections. Under these circumstances, as we noted, the proportions of persons aged 65 and over in the population and those aged 75 and over would rise steadily until about 2040, when persons at these ages would constitute about 22 percent and 12 percent of the total population, respectively.[12]

The lowest population series would reach ZPG even earlier, about 2015, when elderly persons would make up about 16 percent of the population. The total population would then turn downward as the number of deaths exceeds the number of births and net immigration. The percentage of elderly persons would continue to rise because of continuing low fertility, continuing declines in mortality at the older ages, and the entry of the baby-boom cohorts into the elderly age range.

Even as the general population has been aging, the elderly population itself has been aging (Table 1.10). This was implied earlier by the data showing larger percent increases for the older segments of the elderly population than for the younger segments. The proportion aged 65–74 of the group aged 65 and over is now falling while the proportion aged 75 and over is rising. In 1950, the proportion aged 75 and over of the total aged 65 and over was 31 percent; by 1985, the proportion had risen to 40 percent; and in 2000 and 2010 we may expect almost 50 percent. This trend is temporary and will continue only through the first decade of the next century. After 2010, the aging trend of the elderly population should reverse itself because of the sharp shift in the trend of fertility after World War II. By 2020, the older share is expected to fall back to 42 percent.

Preferred projections of the proportions aged 75 and over, derived by averaging the two series just given, are as follows:

Year (July 1)	Percent		
	Middle	Low	High
1985[a]	4.8	4.8	4.8
1990	5.5	5.4	5.6
2000	6.5	6.2	6.7
2010	6.7	6.3	7.1
2020	7.3	6.6	8.0
2030	9.8	8.5	11.2
2040	12.2	10.1	14.5
2050	12.0	9.6	15.0

[a] Current estimate.

[12]Note that in a stationary population (i.e., a population with ZPG and unchanging numbers at each age), subject to the middle death rates of 2050, replacement level fertility (2.1 children per woman), and no net immigration, 22 percent of the population would also be aged 65 and over and 12 percent would also be aged 75 and over.

TABLE 1.10

Percent Distribution of the Population Aged 65 and Over, by Age: 1950–2020
(estimates and projections as of July 1)

Year and Series	Total, Ages 65 and Over	Ages 65–69	Ages 70–74	Ages 75–79	Ages 80–84	Ages 85 and Over
Estimates						
1950	100.0	40.7	27.8	17.4	9.3	4.8
1960	100.0	37.7	28.6	18.5	9.6	5.6
1970	100.0	34.9	27.2	19.3	11.5	7.1
1980	100.0	34.3	26.6	18.8	11.5	8.8
1985	100.0	33.1	26.5	19.3	11.7	9.5
Projections[a]						
Middle Series						
1990	100.0	31.5	25.4	19.7	12.9	10.5
2000	100.0	26.0	24.6	20.9	14.4	14.1
2010	100.0	29.9	22.0	17.3	14.1	16.7
2020	100.0	32.3	25.7	17.2	11.0	13.8
Highest Series						
2020	100.0	31.1	24.9	16.9	11.1	16.0
Lowest Series						
2020	100.0	33.6	26.5	17.4	10.8	11.7

SOURCES: U.S. Bureau of the Census, *Current Population Reports*, series P-25, nos. 311, 519, 917, 985, and 952.

[a]Base date is July 1, 1982. Definitions of series are: middle series—middle mortality, middle immigration; highest series—low mortality, high immigration; lowest series—high mortality, low immigration. The fertility assumption has no effect on the data.

The Role of Demographic Factors

As has been stated, the general rise in the numbers of births up to the early 1920s, the marked declines in death rates over the last century, and the heavy volume of young immigrants prior to World War I have contributed directly to the increase in the number of persons aged 65 and over since 1950. We have noted the predominant influence of the fluctuations in the number of births in accounting for shifts in the number of persons aged 60 and over in this century and the increasing role of mortality declines in these shifts.

Reductions in death rates may contribute to an increase in the *number* of elderly persons over some period and, even more broadly, to an increase in the numbers at other ages, with the net effect of retarding the increase in the *proportion* of elderly persons. Between 1900 and 1960, on balance, the changes in mortality contributed to a slight reduction in the proportion of elderly persons (i.e., a "younging" of the population), as Hermalin's analysis suggests.[13] Relative increases in survival rates were greater in this period at the younger ages than at the older ages. While a decline in fertility always contributes to a rise in the proportion of the older population, declines in death rates do not cause a rise in the proportion of older persons unless the declines are concentrated at the older ages or, prospectively, the late middle ages.[14] In the period 1960–1985, especially since 1968, improvements in survival rates at the older ages have exceeded those at the younger ages. Hence, in this period, mortality has been contributing to the aging of the population.[15]

Immigration acts like mortality in its effect on age composition; that is, it tends to reduce the proportion of older persons unless the migrants are concentrated in the older ages or, prospectively, in the late middle ages. The analysis by Hermalin also showed that immigration contributed to younging the population in the first 60 years of this century.[16] It may be shown that immigration tended to reduce the proportion of the population aged 65 and over in the period 1960–1985 as well as in the period 1900–1960.

The principal factor contributing to the increase in the proportion of the elderly from 1960 to 1985 has apparently been the general decline in mortality. The effect of the decline in the birth rate, extending up to the mid 1970s, has been reinforced by the sharp decline in mortality at the older ages since the 1960s. An analysis of the contribution of the demographic components of change to the aging of the population has been carried out by Preston, Himes, and Eggers in terms of the extent to which the birth rate, death rate, and immigration rate retard the natural tendency for the mean age of the population to rise, and to which changes

[13]A. I. Hermalin, "The Effect of Changes in Mortality Rates on Population Growth and Age Distribution in the United States," *Milbank Memorial Fund Quarterly* 44 (4) (October 1966):451–469.

[14]Uniform percentage changes in *survival rates* in some period (i.e., changes that do not modify the age pattern of survival rates) would have no effect on the age structure of the population and, hence, on the proportion of the elderly. Uniform percentage reductions in age-specific *death rates* would, however, correspond to greater relative increases in survival rates at the older ages and, hence, would contribute to a rise in the proportion of older persons. See also A. J. Coale, "The Effects of Changes in Mortality and Fertility on Age Composition," *Milbank Memorial Fund Quarterly* 34 (1) (January 1956):79–114.

[15]Data for this period combine different mortality "experiences"; between 1954 and 1968 little change in age-specific death rates occurred, whereas there were pronounced declines in death rates before and after these years.

[16]Hermalin (1966), p. 461.

in births, deaths, and migration contribute to change in the mean age of the population.[17] For 1980–1985 they obtained the following results:

	Male	Female
Average Annual Change in Population Mean Age	.146	.154
Contribution of Change in Births	.061	.073
Deaths	.095	.103
Immigration	−.010[a]	−.022[a]

[a] A negative sign indicates retardation of aging.

About 60–66 percent of the increase in mean age in this period was due to mortality decline and the remainder to changes in fertility. Net immigration had a slightly retarding effect. Preston et al. conclude that the dominant factor in current aging is mortality. The principal reason that the population is aging is that mortality declines are causing relatively greater increases in the growth rate of the elderly population than in the growth rate of the nonelderly population.

Analysis of the alternative series of population projections of the Census Bureau suggests that fertility will continue to be the principal determinant of the general age structure of the population and, specifically, of the proportion of the population in the older ages, in future years as it has in the past.[18] Mortality will play an important contributory role, however, since reductions in mortality will be mainly confined to the older ages and may be relatively large. To evaluate the relative role of fertility, mortality, and immigration in the change in the proportion of elderly persons shown by the Census Bureau projections, we compare those series of projections in which only one of the components is subject to variation. An indication of the effect on the proportion aged 65 and over of variations in the level of mortality is given by a comparison of the three series based on middle fertility, middle immigration, and high, middle, or low mortality (Table 1.11). The effect of variations in fertility is shown by proportions computed from the three series based on middle mortality, middle immigration, and high, middle, or low fertility (Table 1.12).

The assumptions on mortality allow for considerable variation in relation to their potential range while the assumptions on fertility are rather narrow by the same standard. Yet, by the early part of the next

[17]S. H. Preston, C. Himes, and M. Eggers, "Demographic Conditions Responsible for Population Aging," *Demography* 26 (4) (November 1989):691–704.
[18]See McFarland (1978).

TABLE 1.11

Projections of the Percentage of the Population Aged 65 and Over, According to
Middle Fertility, Middle Immigration, and Alternative Assumptions of Mortality:
1990–2040

Year	High Mortality	Middle Mortality	Low Mortality	Range, Low-High Mortality
1990	12.6	12.7	12.8	0.2
2000	12.7	13.0	13.4	0.7
2010	13.2	13.8	14.5	1.3
2020	16.5	17.3	18.3	1.8
2030	20.0	21.2	22.6	2.6
2040	20.1	21.7	23.6	3.5

SOURCE: U.S. Bureau of the Census, *Current Population Reports*, series P-25, no. 952, Tables 7, 8, and 9; projection series 23, 14, and 5.

NOTE: Estimated proportion for 1985 is 11.9 percent.

TABLE 1.12

Projections of the Percentage of the Population Aged 65 and Over, According to
Middle Mortality, Middle Immigration, and Alternative Assumptions of Fertility:
1990–2040

Year	High Fertility	Middle Fertility	Low Fertility	Range, Low-High Fertility
1990	12.6	12.7	12.8	0.2
2000	12.8	13.0	13.4	0.6
2010	13.3	13.8	14.5	1.2
2020	16.1	17.3	18.6	2.5
2030	19.0	21.2	23.5	4.5
2040	18.6	21.7	25.0	6.4

SOURCE: U.S. Bureau of the Census, *Current Population Reports*, series P-25, no. 952, Table 8; projection series 15, 14, and 13.

NOTE: Estimated proportion for 1985 is 11.9 percent.

century, the range of variation in the proportion aged 65 and over resulting from the variation in fertility assumptions clearly exceeds the
range of variation in the proportion resulting from the variation in mortality assumptions. The estimated range in 2030 as a result of fertility
variation, at the middle mortality level, is from 19.0 percent (high fertility) to 23.5 percent (low fertility), while the estimated range in 2030
as a result of mortality variation, at the middle fertility level, is from

20.0 percent (high mortality) to 22.6 percent (low mortality). In later years the excess in the fertility range over the mortality range grows wider.[19]

The net immigration anticipated in future years will have a slightly minifying effect on the proportion of the population in the older ages. For example, the proportion aged 65 and over in 2000 assuming middle fertility and mortality will be 13.4 percent for the population without immigration compared with 13.1 percent for the population with middle immigration (450,000 per year). The difference of 0.3 percentage point in 2000 grows to only 1.2 percentage points in 2030:

	Percentage Aged 65 and Over (Middle Fertility, Middle Mortality)			
Year	Zero Immigration	Low Immigration	Middle Immigration	High Immigration
2000	13.4	13.2	13.1	12.8
2010	14.4	14.0	13.9	13.5
2030	22.3	21.5	21.1	20.4

SOURCE: Based on U.S. Bureau of the Census, *Current Population Reports*, series P-25, no. 952 (May 1984).

The high, middle, and low series of fertility projections incorporated in the Census Bureau's population projections posit a total difference in completed fertility of only 0.7 child per woman, and all three fertility series imply low fertility approximating replacement level (2.1 children per woman).This is consistent with the prevailing view of demographers today that although fertility levels of the future may fluctuate somewhat, they will remain low indefinitely. Westoff points, for example, to the changed status and roles of women, the changed attitudes of women toward marriage, childbearing, housekeeping, and work, and the improvements in the technology of fertility control.[20] Small families are more compatible with the newly sought and achieved economic independence of women. Like Westoff's sociologically oriented view, the more economically oriented theories offered by Becker and by Butz and Ward also support the prospect of continuing low fertility. Only Easterlin's theory calls for rising fertility in the coming decades.[21]

[19]The effect of fertility variation on the projected proportions aged 65 and over at the low and high mortality levels shows only a slight or small difference from the variation at the middle mortality level.

[20]C. F. Westoff, "Some Speculations on the Future of Marriage and Fertility," *Family Planning Perspectives* 10 (2) (March–April 1978):79–83; "Fertility Decline in the West: Causes and Prospects," *Population and Development Review* 9 (1) (March 1983):99–105.

[21]G. S. Becker, *A Treatise on the Family* (Cambridge, MA: Harvard University Press, 1981); W. P. Butz and M. P. Ward, "Will U.S. Fertility Remain Low? A New Economic

International Variations

The population aged 65 and over is currently growing rapidly in the world as a whole and in nearly every region, with the rate of growth for the less developed regions (Africa, Asia except Japan, and Latin America) far outstripping the rate for the more developed regions (Europe, Northern America, USSR).[22] (See Table 1.13.) The largest regional increases are occurring in South Asia and Africa. Moreover, the growth *rate* of the less developed regions' elderly population is also rising. From 1965 to 1985, the less developed regions' population aged 65 and over increased by four fifths, and from 1985 to 2005 it is expected to increase by nearly nine tenths. These marked past and prospective increases in the numbers of elderly people are primarily a result of continuing high fertility rates in earlier years reinforced by declines in death rates. With each passing year high fertility adds a larger number of births to the total population and, later, a larger number of persons to the elderly population.

Aging of the populations of the world's regions is also nearly universal. Yet, the population aged 65 and over in some less developed regions still makes up a relatively small proportion of the total population (e.g., 3 percent in Africa in 1985). In contrast, the proportions for Northern America and Europe (12 and 14 percent, respectively) are quite high. The proportion of persons aged 65 and over in the United States is exceeded by the proportions in most countries of Western Europe. Sweden, France, Belgium, Austria, Norway, Denmark, Great Britain, and West Germany, for example, all have much higher proportions—most as high as 16 percent.

The relative youth of the less developed regions is a consequence of the coexistence of high fertility and low survival to old age. The relative agedness of the more developed regions is associated with a pattern of continuing low fertility, past rises in the number of births followed by declines, and continuing low mortality, with substantial declines in death rates at the later stages of life. The principal demographic factor that accounts for the wide difference in age structure is fertility, however. Fertility is extremely low in most countries of Western Europe. In these countries, as in the United States, substantial declines in death rates have occurred at the older ages in recent decades.

Interpretation," *Population and Development Review* 5 (1979):663–688; R. A. Easterlin, "What Will 1984 Be Like? Socioeconomic Implications of Recent Twists in Age Structure," *Demography* 15 (4) (1978):397–432.

[22]J. S. Siegel, "Demographic Background for International Gerontological Studies," *Journal of Gerontology* 36 (1) (January 1981):93–102; and J. S. Siegel and S. L. Hoover, "Demographic Aspects of the Health of the Elderly to the Year 2000 and Beyond," *World Health Statistics Quarterly* 35 (3-4) (1982):134–202.

TABLE 1.13

Estimates and Projections of the Percentage of the Population Aged 65 and Over,
1950–2020, and of the Percent Increase in Population Aged 65 and Over,
1965–2025, for Selected Areas

Area	Percent Aged 65 and Over			Percent Increase in Population Aged 65 and Over		
	1950	1985	2020[a]	1965–1985	1985–2005[a]	2005–2025[a]
World	5	6	9	64	63	74
More Developed Countries	8	11	17	49	38	38
Less Developed Countries	4	4	7	79	86	97
Africa	3	3	4	78	81	106
Europe	9	13	19	11	55	29
United Kingdom	11	15	19	28	29	3
Federal Republic of Germany	9	15	22	27	24	16
Sweden	10	18	23	52	−2	30
United States	8	12	17	55	23	68

SOURCE: Based on United Nations, *Global Estimates and Projections of Population by Sex and Age: 1988 Revision* (New York: United Nations, 1989).

[a] Medium variant. Base date is 1985.

The more developed regions also have a greater share of *aged* persons among the older population than do the less developed regions. In Europe, for example, about two fifths of the population aged 65 and over is 75 and over compared with only one quarter in South Asia and Africa. In most regions, as in the United States, the older segment of the elderly population has been increasing at a faster pace than the younger segment.

In the more developed regions, low fertility and low mortality are giving rise to populations that are not growing (ZPG) and to age structures that are approaching stationarity (i.e., unchanging numbers at each age). Fertility and mortality are both lower in many countries of Western Europe than in the United States. Several are now losing population (e.g., West Germany, Denmark, Great Britain) and will soon reflect the higher percentages of elderly persons shown by stationary populations with high life expectancies (e.g., 18 percent aged 65 and over when life expectancy at birth is 75 years).

Population Age Ratios

Public policy issues affecting the elderly arise often from the changing balance of the numbers of elderly and the numbers in other age groups.

One measure of this balance, reflecting broad variations in the age structure, is the elderly dependency ratio, which shows the number of persons aged 65 and over per 100 persons of working age (18–64). A contrasting measure is the child dependency ratio, or the number of persons
under age 18 per 100 persons aged 18–64. Age dependency ratios are
measures of age structure and hence do not measure economic dependency per se. Many people in the so-called working ages, especially
women, are not in the labor force and many older persons in the so-
called dependent ages, especially the young-elderly (65–74), are economically active. Age dependency ratios do indicate how changes in age
structure may affect economic dependency and hence are useful in interpreting measures of economic dependency, such as those employing
labor force data.

At present, there are about 19 persons aged 65 and over for every
100 persons of working age but, by 2030, after the baby-boom cohorts
have all joined the elderly group, this ratio is expected nearly to double
(Table 1.14). At the same time, the child dependency ratio is expected
to show a moderate decline from its current level of 43. As a result of
these divergent trajectories and amounts of change, by 2030 the elderly
dependency ratio and the child dependency ratio may be approximately
equal (38 vs. 37) for the first time in our history. (See Figure 1.4.)

The net effect of the rapid rise in the elderly dependency ratio and
the smaller decline in the child dependency ratio is a substantial rise in
the total dependency ratio from 62 per 100 persons aged 18–64 in 1985
to 75 in 2030. Nevertheless, the total dependency ratio is likely to remain lower during the next three decades than it was during the three
decades following World War II. The highest and lowest population series show trends similar to the middle series. For 2030 the elderly dependency ratio varies from 36 (highest series) to 38 (lowest series) and
the total dependency ratio varies from 69 (lowest series) to 82 (highest
series).[23]

The rising trends in elderly dependency ratios have implications for
shifts in the demand for services on the part of the elderly and in the
costs of supporting the elderly by the working-age population through
public funds. The moderately rising trend expected in the total dependency ratio provides a rough indication of the shift in the combined
demand for services on the part of both children and the elderly.

A more realistic view of the shifts in the dependency of the elderly
may be obtained by an examination of dependency ratios for specific
groups aged 65 and over and by an allowance in the ratios for the greater

---

[23]A much wider range in the elderly dependency ratio in 2030 is given by the high
fertility/high mortality/high immigration series (31) and the low fertility/low mortality/
low immigration series (44), but the values for the total dependency ratio in these series

needs of the very old. Dependency ratios for the aged (75 and over) have been increasing far more rapidly than those for the young elderly (65–74) and will continue to do so for the next several decades (Table 1.15). To illustrate how the burden on the working-age population would be affected by an allowance for the greater needs of the very old, the overall elderly dependency ratios were recomputed using a weight of 1.0 for the dependency ratio at ages 65–74 and weights of 1.5 and 2.0, respectively, for the dependency ratios at higher ages, 75–84 and 85 and over. The elderly dependency burden now shows a much steeper rise over time as a reflection of the more rapid rise of the aged population than of the young elderly.

Later chapters will consider special variations and extensions of general age dependency ratios that take into account sex and race composition and labor force participation.

Years Until Death

Two other measures—one of old age and population aging and the other of population aging only—are considered next. The first measure is the age corresponding to some stated life expectancy and defines old age in terms of a specified number of years until death. This method of measuring old age has been referred to as "counting backward from

have a much narrower range because of the offsetting effect of child dependency ratios and elderly dependency ratios with opposite rank orders:

Year and Series[a]	Total Dependency		Child Dependency		Elderly Dependency	
	Ratio	Rank	Ratio	Rank	Ratio	Rank
1985	62.0	X	42.7	X	19.3	X
2030						
LF, LM, LI	75.2	3	30.7	5	44.5	1
LF, HM, LI[b]	69.2	5	31.0	4	38.2	2
MF, MM, MI[c]	74.8	4	37.8	3	37.0	3
HF, LM, HI[d]	82.1	1	46.4	2	35.7	4
HF, HM, HI	77.4	2	46.7	1	30.7	5

SOURCE: Based on data in U.S. Bureau of the Census, *Current Population Reports*, series P-25, no. 952 (May 1984).

NOTE: X = not applicable.

[a]L = low, M = middle, H = high; F = fertility, M = mortality, I = immigration.
[b]Lowest population series.
[c]Middle population series.
[d]Highest population series.

TABLE 1.14

Societal Age Dependency Ratios: 1950–2030

Year	Total Dependency[a]	Child Dependency[b]	Elderly Dependency[c]
1950	64.4	51.1	13.4
1960	81.6	64.9	16.8
1970	78.0	60.6	17.5
1980	64.6	46.0	18.6
1985	62.0	42.7	19.3
Projections			
Middle Series			
1990	62.5	41.9	20.6
2000	61.8	40.7	21.1
2010	58.1	36.2	21.9
2020	65.6	36.9	28.7
2030	74.8	37.8	37.0
Highest Series			
1990	63.5	42.9	20.6
2000	65.3	44.0	21.3
2010	63.7	41.5	22.2
2020	72.7	44.2	28.6
2030	82.1	46.4	35.7
Lowest Series			
1990	61.3	40.7	20.6
2000	57.5	36.8	20.7
2010	52.6	31.3	21.3
2020	59.2	30.7	28.5
2030	69.2	31.0	38.2

SOURCES: Based on U.S. Bureau of the Census, *Current Population Reports*, series P-25, nos. 311, 519, 917, 952, and 985.

NOTE: Figures as of July 1, including U.S. armed forces overseas. See text for explanation of middle, highest, and lowest series of projections.

[a] $\dfrac{\text{Population under aged 18 + population aged 65 and over}}{\text{Population aged 18–64}} \times 100.$

[b] $\dfrac{\text{Population under age 18}}{\text{Population aged 18–64}} \times 100.$

[c] $\dfrac{\text{Population aged 65 and over}}{\text{Population aged 18–64}} \times 100.$

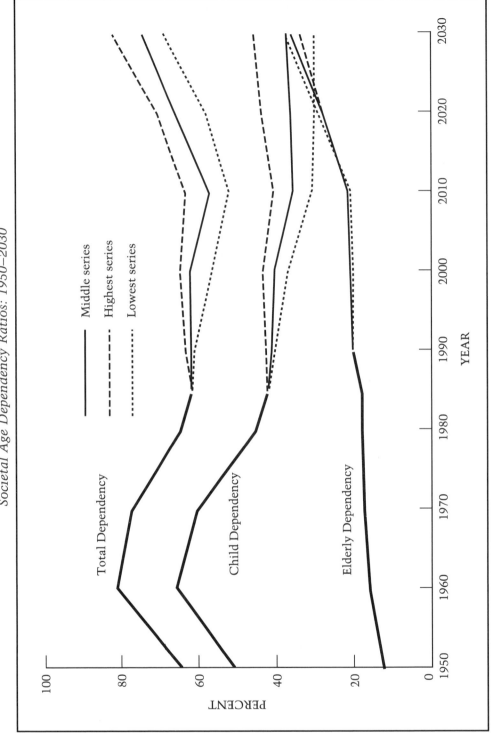

FIGURE 1.4

Societal Age Dependency Ratios: 1950–2030

SOURCE: Table 1.14.

NOTE: Points are plotted at decennial years, with current observations for 1985.

40

TABLE 1.15

Unadjusted and Adjusted Societal Elderly Dependency Ratios: 1950–2030
(figures as of July 1, and including U.S. armed forces overseas)

Year	Unadjusted Ratios				Adjusted Ratios[a]	Indexes (1984 = 100)	
	$\frac{65+}{20-64}$	$\frac{65-74}{20-64}$	$\frac{75-84}{20-64}$	$\frac{85+}{20-64}$		Unadjusted Ratios	Adjusted Ratios
1950	14.1	9.6	3.8	0.7	16.6	69	65
1960	17.6	11.7	5.0	1.0	21.1	87	83
1970	18.7	11.6	5.7	1.3	22.9	92	90
1980	19.8	12.1	6.0	1.8	24.6	98	97
1984	20.3	12.1	6.2	1.9	25.4	100	100
1990	21.6	12.3	9.1	2.3	27.4	107	108
2000	22.1	11.2	7.8	3.1	29.1	109	115
2010	22.9	11.8	7.2	3.8	30.3	113	119
2020	29.9	17.4	8.4	4.1	38.2	147	151
2030	38.7	20.7	12.8	5.2	50.3	191	198

SOURCE: Based on U.S. Bureau of the Census, *Current Population Reports*, series P-25, nos. 311, 519, 917, 952, and 985.

NOTES: Denominator of all ratios is the total population aged 20–64. Projections are from the middle series. Ratios expressed per 100.

[a] Adjusted ratios were obtained by weighting the original ratios for ages 65–74, 75–84, and 85 and over by the factors 1.0, 1.5, and 2.0, respectively.

death."[24] The period of 10 or 15 years is arbitrarily selected as the duration of old age, and the age corresponding to a life expectancy of 10 or 15 years is identified as the lower bound of old age. The age of onset of old age fluctuates in accordance with the level of death rates at the older ages. As life expectancy at the older ages rises, the period of old age begins at a progressively later age. Old age would begin at higher ages for population groups that have comparatively low death rates at the older ages (e.g., females) than for population groups that have comparatively high death rates in the older ages (e.g., males).

The age corresponding to a life expectancy of 10 years advanced from 70.0 years in 1940 to 76.2 years in 1985 (Table 1.16). Thus, an increase of 6.2 years in the age at which the average person had 10 years to go was recorded in the 45 years from 1940 to 1985. A choice more concordant with the public's current view of old age would designate the last 15 years of life as the period of old age; thereby, old age begins earlier and lasts longer. According to this definition, the lower bound of the period of old age rose from 61.4 years in 1940 to 63.1 years in 1950 and 67.7 years in 1985, and an increase of 6.3 years was recorded for the 45-year period.

The concept of years until death could serve as the basis for a new measure of individual and population aging. Specifically, the demarcation line for old age could be a variable line which moves upward as life expectancy increases. While this measure has serious limitations as a general measure of old age and population aging, it has several potential administrative and legal uses.[25] Such a linkage of the definition of old age to changing longevity may, for example, be a basis for defining old age in programs where the financial viability of the program is affected by the length of life (e.g., the Social Security retirement program).

The proportion of the actual population above the age corresponding to a life expectancy of 10 or 15 years may be considered as an alternative measure of population aging, based on the concept of years until death. From 1940 to 1985 the proportion of the population above the age corresponding to a life expectancy of 10 years remained nearly unchanged, even though the proportion rose and fell somewhat in the interim. About 4 percent of the population was above age 76.2 in 1985, the age corresponding in that year to a life expectancy of 10 years. In 1940, 4 percent of the population was also at an age above that corre-

[24]N. Ryder, "Notes on Stationary Populations," *Population Index* 14 (1) (January 1975):3–28, esp. pp. 16–17.
[25]L. D. Cain, "Counting Backward from Projected Death: An Alternative to Chronological Age in Assigning Status to the Elderly," paper presented at the Policy Center on Aging, Syracuse University, March 22, 1978; L. D. Cain, "Aging and the Law," in R. H. Binstock and E. Shanas, eds., *Handbook of Aging and the Social Sciences* (New York: Van Nostrand Reinhold, 1976), pp. 342–368.

TABLE 1.16

Age at Which Average Remaining Life Equals 10 or 15 Years and the Percentage of the Total Population Above This Age: 1940–2030

Year	10 Years of Average Remaining Life		15 Years of Average Remaining Life	
	Age at Which Average Remaining Life Equals 10 Years	Percentage of Total Population above This Age	Age at Which Average Remaining Life Equals 15 years	Percentage of Total Population Above This Age
1940[a]	70.0	4.0	61.4	9.4
1950[a]	71.7	3.9	63.1	9.6
1960	72.5	4.2	64.0	10.0
1970	73.7	4.4	65.0	9.8
1980	75.9	4.0	67.3	9.4
1985	76.2	4.2	67.7	9.7
Increase, 1940–1985	6.2	0.2	6.3	0.3
Projections[b]				
1990	77.4	4.2	69.4	9.1
2000	78.5	4.5	70.5	9.3
2010	79.1	4.7	71.1	9.0
2020	79.7	4.5	71.7	10.1
2030	80.3	5.5	72.3	12.7
Increase, 1985–2030	4.1	1.3	4.6	3.0

SOURCES: Based on various official U.S. life tables and U.S. Social Security Administration, Office of the Actuary, *Life Tables for the United States: 1900–2050*, by J. F. Faber and A. H. Wade, *Actuarial Study*, no. 89 (December 1983); population data from *Current Population Reports*, series P-25, nos. 311, 519, 917, 952, and 982.

[a] Conterminous United States (excluding Alaska and Hawaii).
[b] Middle mortality and middle population series.

sponding to a life expectancy of 10 years (70.0 years). A roughly similar pattern is observed when 15 years of remaining life is chosen as the threshold of old age. In 1940 and 1985 the proportions of the population above the ages at which average remaining lifetime is 15 years, 61.4 years, and 67.7 years, respectively, were nearly the same, about 9.5 percent, although the proportion rose and fell slightly in the intervening years.

This measure of population aging links shifts in mortality with the actual population, but it is still heavily dependent on changes in mortality, as is the underlying measure, the age corresponding to a life expectancy of 10 or 15 years. It may fluctuate erratically, and has actually done so over the 1940–1985 period.

Summary

The definitions of "old," "elderly," "aged," and related terms are difficult to establish because the various aspects of a person—physiological, psychological, behavioral, and so on—suggest different criteria. While a demographic criterion, such as assigning a fixed, arbitrary initial age like 65, is often convenient, there are alternative demographic definitions, varying not merely in the choice of a fixed age but in the way old age is measured. Life expectancy at birth and the age at which a population has a specified number of years until death according to current life tables represent two possibilities involving shifting ages. In fact, a life expectancy of 15 years came at age 61 in 1940 and at age 68 in 1985. The concept of old age in terms of a specified number of years until death may have important administrative and legal applications.

The elderly population, defined for this monograph as the population aged 65 and over, is a demographically heterogeneous population whose characteristics are steadily and rapidly changing. The component age groups show sharp variations in their characteristics, whether demographic, economic, social, or physical. The characteristics of each new birth cohort, both initially and subsequent to birth, have much influence on the characteristics of the group when it reaches age 65 and later ages. The characteristics of the new entrants are likely to differ from those of the cohorts they replace and the new entrants tend to constitute a large share of the total population aged 65 and over after a brief period.

An age distribution in a single year represents a combination of many birth cohorts. An analysis of age variation in some characteristic in a single year—that is, a cross-sectional analysis—cannot faithfully represent the experience of a real cohort. Cross-sectional age variation reflects jointly cohort effects, period effects, and age cycle effects. Any individual birth cohort is influenced by period effects over its lifetime as well as the unique characteristics of the cohort and the underlying age cycle. For many characteristics this monograph attempts to determine a generalized postwar age cycle essentially excluding period and cohort effects.

The number of elderly persons (aged 65 and over) has more than doubled since 1950 to about 29 million in 1985, and the number of the older aged (85 and over) has more than quadrupled since 1950 to 2.7 million in 1985. The older the age group among the elderly, the higher the growth rate has been and promises to be in the next few decades. The older aged are currently the fastest growing age segment of the population. With the arrival of the baby-boom cohorts at age 65, the number of elderly persons will rise dramatically between 2010 and 2030, from 39 million to 65 million, following a 25-year period (1985–2010) of sustained but moderate growth. The growth of the group aged 85 and over will parallel that of the group aged 65 and over 20 years later.

Concomitantly, the share of the elderly in the total population has been rising steadily. From only 8 percent in 1950, the percentage elderly climbed to 12 percent in 1985. By 2030, it is expected that about 21 percent of the total population will be aged 65 and over. A sustained rise in the proportion of the population aged 65 and over is a characteristic of an aging society, but the rise from 2010 to 2030 will be dramatic. Furthermore, the elderly population has itself been aging and by 2005 about one half of the population aged 65 and over will be 75 and over.

The degree of population aging is influenced by changes in fertility, mortality, and migration. Potentially, fertility is always the principal determinant of the age structure of populations and, in fact, it tended to be the dominant influence in the aging of the population up to a few decades ago. Its influence is now less prominent, however, and sharp declines in mortality, concentrated at the older ages, particularly the more advanced ages, are exerting a stronger influence. In recent decades these declines in mortality have contributed greatly to the rise in the number and proportion of the elderly as the size of cohorts reaching age 65 has diminished and even stopped its steady increase and fertility rates have remained low. With the advent of the baby-boom cohorts of the 1945–1965 period at ages 65 and over after 2010, fertility will once again be the major factor in the rapid growth of the number and proportion of elderly. The continuation of population aging is predicated on the assumption that fertility will remain low and/or that substantial mortality reductions at the older ages will continue, as is widely expected.

The past and prospective trends in the number of elderly persons in relation to the number of working-age persons are reflected in shifts in elderly dependency ratios. A slow, steady rise has been occurring since 1950 and is expected to continue until about 2010, when dependency ratios will begin to rise sharply. On the other hand, child dependency ratios have been falling since 1960 and are expected to continue falling until 2010. As a consequence, the total dependency ratio, which has been showing a steady, usually moderate decline, should rise steeply after 2010, when the trend of elderly dependency "overwhelms" the trend of child dependency. While age dependency ratios inform us only about age structure and not economic dependency, the implications of this shift in age structure and intergenerational numbers are pervasive and profound, particularly with respect to the financing of programs for the elderly and the delivery of services to them.

Appendix 1A. A Note on the National Population Projections

The national population projections presented in Chapters 1 and 2 of this monograph are consistent with the population projections published by the U.S. Bureau of the Census in *Current Population Reports,* series P-25, no. 952 (May 1984). The Census Bureau report presents projections of the population of the United States for age, sex, and race groups to 2080. These figures are consistent with the 1980 census counts in level and coverage except for the principal races.

The definitions of the races employed in the projections differ from the definitions used in the 1980 census. They conform to the definitions used in the 1970 census and in the postcensal estimates following both the 1970 and 1980 censuses. In the 1980 census the approximately 6.5 million persons of Spanish origin who failed to report a specific race in response to the question on race and reported "other" race were left classified as "other" race. For the preparation of current estimates and projections, the race tabulations in the 1980 census were modified to reassign most Hispanics who reported "other" race to a specific race. The net effect of the shift was to increase the white population in 1980 by 6,438,000, increase the black population by 135,000, and reduce the population of other races by 6,574,000.

After the initial draft of the text and tables of this monograph was completed, the U.S. Bureau of the Census issued a revised set of population projections in *Current Population Reports,* series P-25, no. 1018. Their issuance in January 1989 made it impractical and imprudent to incorporate the new projections into the main body of the monograph. The methodology employed in preparing these projections was virtually identical to that employed in preparing the prior set, that is, the one incorporated in the main text of this study. In the revision the base date was brought forward from July 1, 1982, to July 1, 1986, and the principal assumptions were slightly modified. The revised assumptions are summarized in Table 1A.1.

Selected figures based on the two sets of projections are given in Table 1A.2. The figures shown relate mainly to the population aged 65 and over for 1990 and 2030. Differences for intermediate years would tend to be of intermediate magnitude. It is apparent that the revised figures are not essentially different from the projections incorporated in the main text of this monograph, except for the steeper rise in the sex ratio shown by the revised figures. Replacement of the earlier figures would serve the theoretical goals of statistical currency and neatness, but would not substantially modify the analysis and conclusions.

TABLE 1A.1

Alternative Assumptions of Fertility, Mortality, and Net Immigration Employed in Census Bureau Population Projections

Series	Fertility Assumption: Lifetime Births per Female	Mortality Assumption: Life Expectation[a]		Immigration Assumption: Annual Net Immigration
		2050	2080	
Projections Issued January 1989 Current Estimate 1986	1.82[a]	75.0		662,000
Projections				
Middle	1.80	79.9	81.2	500,000
High	2.20	77.0	78.0	800,000
Low	1.50	85.0	88.1	300,000
Projections Issued May 1984 Current Estimate 1982	1.83[a]	74.5		450,000[b]
Projections				
Middle	1.90	79.6	81.0	450,000
High	2.30	76.7	77.4	750,000
Low	1.60	83.3	85.9	250,000

[a] Period (or calendar-year) measures.
[b] 1973–1982 average.

Appendix 1B. Accuracy of Census Counts of the Population Aged 65 and Over

The age classification in the decennial census is based on the age of a person in completed years as of the date of the census. In 1980, the data on age represent the difference between date of birth and April 1, 1980. In each census since 1940, the Census Bureau has assigned the age of a person when it was not reported. The allocation procedure was based on information reported for another person with characteristics similar to those of the person for whom allocation was necessary. Substitution

TABLE 1A.2

Selected Projections and Derived Measures Relating to the Population Aged 65 and Over Based on the Two Most Recent Sets of Census Bureau Population Projections

Projection Set, Year, and Race	Population Aged 65 and Over Number (in thousands)	Population Aged 65 and Over Percentage of Total	Population Aged 85 and Over Number (in thousands)	Population Aged 85 and Over Percentage of Total	Median Age	Elderly Dependency Ratio[a]	Sex Ratio, Ages 65 and Over[b]
Projections Issued January 1989							
1990							
Total[c]	31,559	12.6	3,254	1.3	33.0	20.4	68.7
White	28,344	13.5	2,962	1.4	33.9	18.3	68.7
Black	2,612	8.4	251	0.8	28.1	1.7	67.4
2030							
Total[c]	65,604	21.8	8,129	2.7	41.8	38.0	77.3
White	54,460	23.2	6,923	2.9	43.0	31.5	78.1
Black	7,784	17.5	788	1.8	37.4	4.5	76.2
Projections Issued May 1984							
1990							
Total[c]	31,697	12.7	3,313	1.3	33.0	20.6	66.3
White	28,597	13.6	3,019	1.5	33.9	18.3	66.7
Black	2,579	8.2	257	0.8	27.7	1.7	60.8
2030							
Total[c]	64,580	21.2	8,611	2.8	40.8	37.0	71.5
White	54,299	22.6	7,156	3.1	42.1	31.1	73.0
Black	7,305	15.3	831	1.7	35.5	4.2	63.2

[a] Persons aged 65 and over of given race per 100 persons of all races aged 18–64.
[b] Males per 100 females.
[c] All races combined, including races other than white and black.

NOTE: Middle population series.

of a whole array of characteristics was also necessary at times when census schedules or interviews could not be obtained.

Errors in the census count of an age group include errors of coverage of the age group and errors of misreporting age or of misassigning age when it is not reported. Measures of the extent of age assignment and of the net undercount (i.e., the combined effect of coverage errors and age reporting errors) of the older population are available for age groups for 1980 and earlier censuses.

Age was assigned to a disproportionate share of the population aged 65 and over. Age assignments amounted to 5.5 percent for this age group, 4.7 percent for the population aged 55–64, and 4.4 percent for the population as a whole. Age assignment at the extreme ages was expectedly great. A substantial share of the population aged 85 and over live in nursing homes and their true ages are often unknown or are taken from records that may be incorrect.

The effect of the assignment of ages on the age distribution was small. Some 11.1 percent of the total population was aged 65 and over before the assignment of missing ages and 11.3 percent was aged 65 and over after the assignment. For ages 55–64 the share was 9.6 percent both before and after the assignment of unreported ages.

The U.S. Bureau of the Census has estimated a net undercount of the population aged 65 and over in the 1980 census amounting to 0.3 percent—a quite small net error (Table 1B.1). The population aged 65

TABLE 1B.1

Estimated Net Census Percent Errors for the Population Aged 55 and Over: 1950–1980
(percentage of estimated population)

Age	1980	1970	1960	1950
All Ages	−1.4	−2.9	−3.3	−4.4
55–59	−1.2	−3.5	−2.8	−8.7
60–64	−0.8	−2.7	−5.5	−7.9
65 and Over	−0.3	−2.7	−2.5	−2.7
65–69	+1.3	−1.4	−2.9	NA
70–74	+0.4	−2.0	−0.4	NA
75 and Over	−2.2	−4.4	−3.8	NA
75–79	+0.1	−6.1	NA	NA
80–84	−4.1	−3.7	NA	NA
85 and Over	−4.6	−0.4	NA	NA

SOURCES: U.S. Bureau of the Census, "The Coverage of Population in the 1980 Census," by R. E. Fay, J. S. Passel, and J. G. Robinson, *Evaluation and Research Reports*, series PHC80-E4 (February 1988); and unpublished tabulations.

NOTE: NA = not available.

and over was understated at a nearly consistent 2.5 percent in the preceding three censuses. There is a notable variation around the 1980 figure for the component age groups. The net overcounts at ages 65–69 and ages 70–74 are small or minor, but there is a moderate net undercount of 2.2 percent at ages 75 and over, apparently concentrated at ages 80–84 (4.1 percent) and 85 and over (4.6 percent). The estimated net undercounts for the extreme ages must be viewed as very rough. The estimates at the older ages are based on Medicare enrollments.

Population increases between 1970 and 1980 tend to be overstated because of the relatively greater net underenumeration in the 1970 census. A comparison of the reported percentage changes between 1950 and 1980 in the older ages and the changes adjusted for net census errors shows that the reported changes reflect the estimated changes reasonably well:

| | Percent Increase | | |
Age	1950–1960	1960–1970	1970–1980
Adjusted			
All ages	17.2	12.9	9.7
65 and over	34.3	20.9	24.8
65–74	NA	13.0	22.0
75 and over	NA	36.2	29.4
Unadjusted			
All ages	18.5	13.4	11.4
65 and over	34.7	20.7	27.9
65–74	30.4	13.2	25.2
75 and over	44.0	35.4	32.3

SOURCE: Based on U.S. Bureau of the Census, *Evaluation and Research Reports*, PHC80-E4 (February 1988), Tables A.80.3, A.70.3, A.60.2, and A.50.1.

NOTE: NA = not available.

The number of persons aged 100 and over cannot be satisfactorily approximated by the census. Estimates of this population indicate that the number of centenarians has been greatly overstated in recent censuses. The census of 1980 reported 32,194 centenarians while an independent analytic estimate of the number of centenarians in 1980 prepared at the Census Bureau showed 14,000. The only other source of information currently available is the Social Security rolls, which carried approximately 15,000 persons aged 100 and over in 1980. Prior to the allocation of ages, 23,000 persons were reported to be aged 100 and over in the 1980 census. The Census Bureau has adopted 14,000 as an estimate of the number of centenarians in 1980 for its postcensal population estimates and projections program.

The centenarian population was more grossly overstated in the 1970 census, apparently because of a misunderstanding by some persons in filling in the age portion of the census questionnaire. Estimates of the population aged 100 and over in 1970 range from 3,000 to 8,000 persons compared with the 106,441 persons shown by the census. The preferred estimate derived by averaging several analytic estimates and adopted by the Census Bureau is 4,800. The correction of the census figure on centenarians in 1970 calls for a large downward adjustment of the census count for the total aged 85 and over, 90 and over, and so on. In 1960, the tabulated census figure of 10,369 centenarians was approximately double the highest available independent estimate. For a discussion of the number of centenarians in the 1950, 1960, and 1970 censuses and of the derivation of estimates for this age group, see J. S. Siegel and J. S. Passel, "New Estimates of the Number of Centenarians in the United States," *Journal of the American Statistical Association* 71 (355) (September 1976):559–566.

2

SEX, RACE, AND
ETHNIC COMPOSITION

T HE TWO sexes and the various racial/ethnic groups in the population differ in their demographic, social, and economic characteristics in both early and later life and in the ways they deal with the major transitions in the life course, in their knowledge of English, and in their attitudes vis-à-vis having children, engaging in work and leisure, living with relatives, pursuing educational goals, remarrying, accepting public services, and so on. As a consequence, the sexes and the racial/ethnic groups differ in their need for and use of community services. In this chapter we consider the basic demographic differences between the groups and in later chapters we consider their social and economic differences. Although the treatment of racial/ethnic group differences is necessarily limited, I wish to stress the great heterogeneity in the racial/ethnic background of the older population and the need to design programs for the elderly that take it into account.

Sex Composition

A large majority of older persons are women. The characteristic pattern of variation of sex ratios (males per 100 females) over the age scale today is a generally progressive decline from a small excess of boys among young children to a massive deficit of men in extreme old age (Table 2.1

TABLE 2.1
Males per 100 Females for the Total, Black, and Hispanic Populations, by Age: 1985 and 1950

Age	1985[a]				1950[b]			
	Total	White	Black	Hispanic	Total	White	Black[c]	Hispanic[d]
Total, All Ages	95.1	95.7	90.6	101.1	98.6	99.0	93.7	103.1
0–4	104.8	105.4	102.6	104.6	103.9	104.4	100.5	102.6
5–14	104.9	105.5	102.6	104.0	103.6	104.1	99.3	102.5
15–24	102.9	103.5	98.2	107.1	97.6	98.7	88.7	97.6
25–34	100.5	102.3	90.0	108.8	95.3	96.1	86.4	102.9
35–44	97.3	99.3	84.0	97.3	97.5	98.0	89.8	105.7
45–54	94.3	96.2	81.3	92.6	99.6	99.6	96.6	115.2
55–64	88.7	89.6	82.1	88.6	100.6	100.2	104.1	110.4
65–74	78.4	78.8	73.3	75.9	92.9	92.7	91.5	102.0
75–84	59.4	59.0	⎰ 61.1		⎱ 85.1	84.3	⎰ 95.5	
85 and Over	39.9	39.1	⎱ 46.4	67.0	⎰ 69.6	69.5	⎱ 64.2	91.3
65 and Over	67.8	67.7	67.0	72.4	89.6	89.1	90.8	98.8
75 and Over	54.3	53.8	57.4	67.0	82.6	81.9	89.0	91.3

SOURCES: Based on U.S. Bureau of the Census, *Current Population Reports*, series P-25, no. 985 (April 1986); unpublished tabulations consistent with *Current Population Reports*, series P-20, no. 403 (December 1985); and 1950 Census of Population, *U.S. Summary*, Tables 38 and 97; and *Special Reports*, "Persons of Spanish Surname," Table 2, and "Puerto Ricans in Continental United States," Table 2.

[a]Figures relate to July 1 and to the total population including armed forces overseas.
[b]Figures relate to April 1 and to the resident U.S. population.
[c]20 percent sample data.
[d]Represents white persons of Spanish surname in five southwestern states and persons of Puerto Rican birth or parentage.

and Figure 2.1). The Census Bureau's estimates for 1985 show 105 boys per 100 girls under age 5, 99 men per 100 women aged 30–34, 81 men per 100 women aged 65–69, and only 53 men per 100 women aged 80–84.

Only 55 or so years earlier, in 1930, equal numbers of males and females were reported at ages 65 and over, but since that time there has been a steadily growing deficit of men at these ages. As of 1985, the ratio of males per 100 females among the elderly was 68 (Table 2.2). According to the Census Bureau population projections, the sex ratio of the population aged 65 and over will continue to fall in the near future, but much more slowly than in the past, reaching 65 in the year 2000; and then it will return to its mid 1970s level of 70 by 2020.

Data on sex ratios for age groups in a particular year, such as those for 1985, tend to overstate or understate the fall in the sex ratio with age experienced by real birth cohorts. Generally, in the past the reduction has been much more pronounced in cohort data than in cross-sectional data for the birth year of the cohort. The cohorts born in 1875–1880 showed a sex ratio of 103 at ages 0–4 in 1880, 97 at ages 65–69 in 1945, and 73 at ages 80–84 in 1960. Thus, there was a 30-point fall in the sex ratio of the cohorts from ages 0–4 to ages 80–84 compared with a 16-point fall between these ages in calendar year 1880. Immigration usually accounts for rises or sharply diminished falls in the sex ratio. The sex ratio for the cohorts born in 1915–1920 dropped from 103 for ages 0–4 in 1920 to 82 for ages 65–69 in 1985. In calendar year 1920 there was a 7-point rise between ages 0–4 and 65–69. The declines have tended to grow larger for the more recent birth cohorts reaching old age.

The changes for cohorts reaching old age in the future reflect particularly the mortality assumptions used in preparing the projections. The cohorts born in 1930–1935 begin with a sex ratio of 103 at ages 0–4, show a ratio of 82 at ages 65–69 in 2000, and end up with a ratio of 57 at ages 80–84 in 2015. A 46-point cumulative drop from ages 0–4 is indicated for these cohorts, while the data for the calendar year 1935 show a drop of 15 points between these same age groups. The cohorts born in 1980–1985 are expected to show a sex ratio of 90 at ages 65–69 in 2050 and of 65 at ages 80–84 in 2065 (Figure 2.1). The drop from ages 0–4 to ages 80–84 for the cohort data is 40 points compared with 52 points for calendar year 1985. The sex ratios for future cohorts drop less sharply than those for past ones.

More realistic indications of the level and age-to-age variation in sex ratios, both for particular calendar years and for birth cohorts, are given by figures adjusted for errors in the basic census data (i.e., coverage error plus age reporting errors). (See Appendix Table 2A.1.) The demonstrated excess omission of males in censuses assures us that the adjusted sex ratios and the corresponding age at which numerical equality

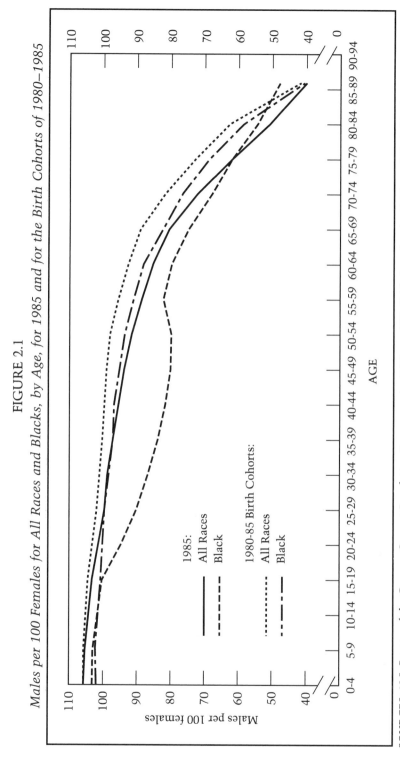

FIGURE 2.1

Males per 100 Females for All Races and Blacks, by Age, for 1985 and for the Birth Cohorts of 1980–1985

SOURCES: U.S. Bureau of the Census, *Current Population Reports*, series P-25, no. 985, Table 1, and series P-25, no. 952, Table 6.

NOTES: Points for five-year age groups are plotted over the mark for the five-year group. The point for ages 85 and over is plotted at age 88.8.

TABLE 2.2
Males per 100 Females for the Total and Black Populations Aged 60 and Over, by Cumulative Age Groups: 1950–2020

Race and Age Group	1950[a]	1960	1970	1980	1985	2000 Middle Series	Projections 2020 Middle Series	Projections 2020 Highest Series	Projections 2020 Lowest Series
All Races									
60 and Over	93.0	85.1	76.4	72.5	72.8	69.8	75.8	76.1	75.5
65 and Over	89.5	82.6	71.9	67.6	67.8	65.0	70.2	70.5	69.9
70 and Over	86.6	79.6	67.6	61.8	61.5	59.7	63.3	63.4	63.0
75 and Over	82.6	75.0	63.3	55.2	54.4	53.2	54.8	54.7	54.7
80 and Over	76.9	69.2	58.4	48.8	46.9	45.7	46.1	45.7	46.2
85 and Over	70.0	63.8	53.1	43.5	40.0	37.8	37.8	37.3	38.0
90 and Over	62.2	56.4	48.9	39.4	35.3	30.4	30.7	30.3	30.8
Black									
60 and Over	98.8	87.9	78.5	71.3	70.8	59.1	64.9	66.0	63.7
65 and Over	95.8	86.7	76.2	68.2	67.0	55.2	58.2	59.2	56.9
70 and Over	97.2	85.1	74.4	64.7	62.1	51.2	51.2	51.8	50.0
75 and Over	93.2	82.6	70.7	60.2	57.4	47.1	43.9	44.0	42.9
80 and Over	82.6	78.0	65.1	55.3	51.6	41.8	37.3	37.0	36.6
85 and Over	70.4	73.7	60.9	50.0	46.4	36.4	31.4	30.6	30.9
90 and Over[b]	57.3	61.5	58.7	47.6	43.1	31.7	26.7	25.5	26.1

SOURCES: U.S. Bureau of the Census, *Current Population Reports*, series P-25, nos. 311, 519, 917, 985, and 952. Age group 90 and over, 1950–1980: census data as reported or modified.

NOTES: Figures as of July 1, except for age group 90 and over, which refers to April 1, 1950–1980. Figures for 1960 and later years include armed forces abroad.

[a] Races other than white shown for "black," based on 100 percent census data.
[b] Races other than white for 1950, 1960, and 1970.

of the sexes is attained will tend to be higher than the reported values. The adjusted sex ratios for the total population including armed forces overseas in 1980 cross the balance point of 100 at about ages 45–49. The age groups at which the crossover in the balance of the sexes occurs in the census years since 1950 and in 1985, for the total, white, and black populations (including armed forces overseas), are as follows:

Population	1950[a]	1960	1970	1980[b]	1985[b]
Total	20–24	35–39	40–44	40–44 45–49	40–44 45–49
White	20–24	35–39	40–44	45–49	45–49 50–54
Black	20–24	35–39	20–24	25–29	25–29 30–34

[a] Resident population, excluding armed forces overseas.
[b] First ages in a pair have equal numbers of men and women.

The age of the crossover has been steadily rising for whites but has shown no steady progression for blacks over the 1950–1985 period. It is lower for blacks than for whites in recent censuses. The sex ratios of the birth cohorts of 1980–1985 are expected to fall more slowly with advancing age than those of calendar year 1985, crossing 100 at ages 45–49 instead of ages 30–34, as in the unadjusted estimates for 1985, or ages 40–44, as in the adjusted estimates for 1985 (Figure 2.1 and Table 2.1).

The decline in sex ratios *over the age cycle* for a particular birth cohort and the decline in sex ratios for a *specific age group over time,* particularly an older age group, call for somewhat different, but related, explanations. The sex ratio of an age group is determined by three basic factors: the sex ratio at birth, differences between the sexes in rates of survival from birth, and the balance of males and females among net immigrants (including the net movement of citizens). The sex ratio in a broad age group, such as the group aged 65 and over, is also affected by the distribution of the population by age within the group. Finally, the sex ratio of an age group as enumerated is affected by sex differences in errors of coverage and age reporting in the census data. These factors operate on specific cohorts of births as the cohorts progress from birth to extreme old age and ultimate extinction. We consider these factors further below.

A higher crossover age reflects a higher sex ratio of births, a smaller gap between male and female survival rates, or net immigration with a larger proportion of males. The black-white difference in crossover age is especially affected by the lower sex ratio of births among blacks. The adjustment for the undercount of young black men could also be too low.

The pattern of variation of sex ratios with age noted reflects mainly the persistent excess of boys among newborn infants (e.g., 5.1 percent in 1982, 5.1 percent in 1965, and 5.5 percent in 1940) and the progressive effect of higher death rates for males than for females over the age range. An excess of male mortality has prevailed since the beginning of this century at most or all ages. It largely explains the low sex ratios of the older population in any particular recent year.

The decline in the sex ratio of the older population over time at the same age is mainly due to the fact that males have benefited much less than females from the historical decline in death rates. (See Chapter 4.) As the female mortality advantage has increased, there has been a more rapid reduction in the sex ratio over the age range from birth to old age in recent cohorts than in earlier ones. The effects of the excess mortality of World War II on the sex ratio are not readily discernible, even in the cohorts most involved (e.g., ages 60–64 and 65–69 in 1985). The limited impact of the war was due to the relatively low casualty rate and the dispersion of the casualties over several years and many ages. As we have seen, the change in the sex ratio of births has been negligible, so that we can dismiss it as a factor in the decline of the sex ratio of the older population over time.

Net immigration has always had a rather limited *direct* effect on the sex distribution of the older population since only a small share of immigrants has been aged 60 and over. The *indirect* impact of the large pre–World War I and post–World War I immigration on the sex balance of the older population has been considerable, however. The diminution, with increasing age, of the sex ratios of the cohorts born before 1900 was greatly retarded or even reversed by the heavy, predominantly male immigration before World War I. This immigration wave was still reflected in the sex ratio of the population aged 65 and over in 1980, but its influence was modest, except for those aged 75 and over. Changes in immigration policy in 1930 gave preference to spouses and dependent children of U.S. citizens in the implementation of the immigration laws. As a result, the share of females among immigrants rose before declining again; it ranged from a high of 61 percent in the 1940s to a low of 53 percent in the 1970s.[1] The change in the sex balance of immigrants in the 1930s and later contributed little to the reduction of the sex ratio

---

[1]M. Houston, R. G. Kramer, and J. M. Barrett, "Female Predominance of Immigration to the United States Since 1930: A First Look," *International Migration Review* 18 (4) (1984):908–963.

of the elderly, however, mainly because the volume of immigration relative to population was small.

The general level and pattern of changes in the sex ratios at ages 65 and over in 1985 are hardly affected by an adjustment of the data for net census errors, but there are notable deficits at ages 55–59 and 60–64 (Appendix Table 2A.2). For older blacks, substantial deficits at ages 55–64 turn into substantial excesses at ages 80 and over.

Calculations made by the author demonstrate the overwhelming importance of the factor of mortality in the decline of the sex ratio of the population at ages 65 and over. Mortality accounts for four fifths of the decline in the sex ratio at ages 65 and over between 1950 and 1985 (from 88 to 68). Aging into the age group ("births") accounts for a negligible part of the change, and net immigration at ages 65 and over and data errors account for about one sixth of the decline.[2]

The survival advantage of females appears to be diminishing somewhat and the relative difference in the numbers of elderly men and women has ceased growing (Table 2.2 and Figure 2.2). The continuation of the decline in the sex ratio of the population aged 65 and over as a whole to the year 2000, shown by the projections of population, results partly from the aging of the elderly population; aging gives increasing weight to the lower sex ratios at the higher ages.

These factors are also reflected in the much more rapid growth of the female population aged 65 and over than of the male population at these ages (Table 2.3): Between 1970 and 1980 the female population grew more than one third more rapidly than the male population. It grew two and a half times as rapidly during the 1960–1970 decade and nearly two fifths more rapidly during the 1950–1960 decade. At the same time, the growth rates for the total (all ages) population of the two sexes were more nearly equal. As a result, the proportion aged 65 and over among females has moved well above that among males (Figure 2.3). While the proportions for the two sexes were nearly the same in 1930 (about 5.5 percent) and only moderately different in 1950, by 1985 the proportions had moved far apart (14 percent and 10 percent). (See Table 2.4.) The excess of the female proportion is expected to become even greater in the future. The middle, or most probable, projection series shows 16 percent for females and 11 percent for males in 2010.

The current difference between the sexes in the proportions aged 65 and over can also be explained by considering the male and female pop-

---

[2]For the method of derivation, including the general formula used, See H. S. Shryock, Jr., J. S. Siegel, and Associates, *The Methods and Materials of Demography* (Washington, DC: U.S. Government Printing Office, 1980), p. 195. The population estimates were adjusted for net undercounts in the censuses of 1950 and 1980.

FIGURE 2.2

Males per 100 Females in the Older Ages: 1930–2030

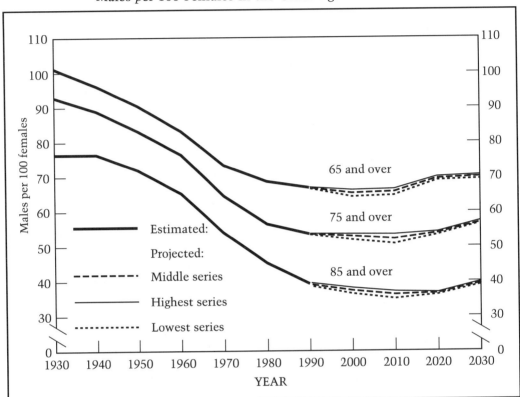

SOURCES: Table 2.2 and U.S. Bureau of the Census, *Current Population Reports*, series P-25, nos. 311 and 952, Table 6.

NOTES: Estimates and projections as of July 1, except for ages 85 and over, 1920 and 1930, which relate to April 1. Points are plotted for years ending in zero.

ulations as two separate populations, with their own birth rates and death rates. The higher male birth rate tends to raise the share of male children and depress the share of elderly men, and the higher male mortality means a relatively low number of survivors at the older ages. The birth rate of the male population[3] has exceeded the birth rate of the female population[4] since at least 1950, and the relative excess has grown through most of this period.

[3]Male births per 1,000 male population.
[4]Female births per 1,000 female population.

| | Births per 1,000 Population | | | | |
Sex	1950	1960	1970	1975	1982
Male	24.6	24.6	19.3	15.4	16.7
Female	23.1	22.7	17.3	13.8	15.1
Percent Excess, Male over Female	6.2	8.1	11.2	11.1	11.2

The high sex ratio at birth is a factor in the higher male birth rate; as mentioned, an excess of boys among births of about 5 percent is the rule. The excess of the male birth rate is also a result of the declining

FIGURE 2.3

Percentage of the Total Population Aged 65 and Over, by Sex: 1930–2030

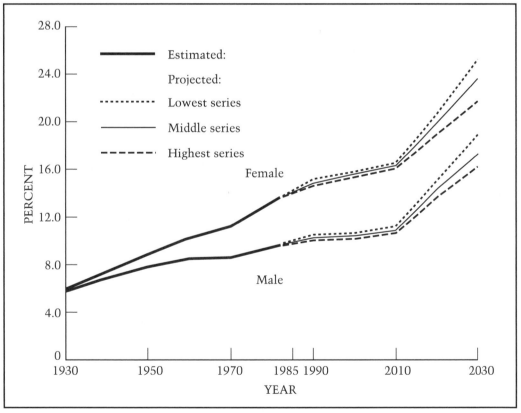

SOURCES: Table 2.4 and U.S. Bureau of the Census, *Current Population Reports,* series P-25, nos. 311; and 952, Table 6.

TABLE 2.3
Decennial Percent Increase of the Population in the Older Ages, by Sex and by Race: 1950–2020

Sex, Race, and Age	1950–1960	1960–1970	1970–1980	1980–1990	1990–2000	Projections[a] 2000–2010	Middle Series	2010–2020 Highest Series	Lowest Series
Male									
55–64	12.6	16.7	15.2	-2.8	16.0	48.1	16.8	24.0	11.7
65–74	25.5	6.3	24.3	15.8	-1.2	16.8	48.8	75.2	39.8
75–84	34.1	19.9	17.5	32.6	19.6	0.8	20.7	34.1	9.0
85–89	56.4	30.2	31.8	33.2	41.3	25.7	-1.7	16.5	-18.2
90 and Over	48.9	49.3	62.2	34.5	59.9	47.0	26.1	72.5	-9.5
55 and Over	20.1	14.1	19.1	9.8	10.9	28.7	25.8	28.9	23.5
65 and Over	28.8	11.4	23.2	22.1	8.6	12.8	35.5	38.8	32.8
75 and Over	36.4	22.3	21.2	33.9	24.6	7.7	16.9	21.5	12.5
85 and Over	50.6	35.8	33.6	39.5	46.9	30.2	7.1	36.9	-15.0
Female									
55–64	20.7	22.0	17.6	-3.3	11.7	45.0	14.4	20.3	10.1
65–74	34.5	18.7	26.0	15.0	-2.6	12.9	45.2	51.9	39.2
75–84	47.3	40.8	31.5	31.7	18.2	-1.0	15.2	24.0	6.8
85–89	67.2	56.2	59.0	48.1	39.8	23.5	-5.7	9.3	-19.9
90 and Over	61.3	77.0	98.0	67.9	66.1	47.1	24.6	72.7	-10.8
55 and Over	30.1	25.1	25.0	12.7	11.4	24.0	22.0	24.8	20.1
65 and Over	39.6	27.9	31.2	24.8	11.3	11.6	27.8	30.3	25.9
75 and Over	50.2	44.8	39.1	38.1	27.0	10.4	12.3	16.8	8.5
85 and Over	65.4	62.9	69.5	51.3	49.4	33.7	7.8	37.9	-15.8

White

55–64	14.5	18.8	15.4	−4.8	11.0	44.3	12.7	17.5	8.7
65–74	30.0	11.4	24.4	15.1	−3.9	12.9	44.7	51.5	38.1
75–84	40.4	31.2	24.0	30.9	18.2	−2.4	15.6	24.6	6.5
85–89	61.6	44.7	49.0	37.2	39.3	23.5	−7.0	7.6	−21.1
90 and Over	59.9	67.1	85.3	60.8	61.8	46.3	23.3	69.8	−11.3
55 and Over	24.0	19.0	21.3	10.4	9.7	23.8	21.3	23.7	19.4
65 and Over	34.2	19.2	26.7	23.1	8.9	10.3	28.7	31.1	26.6
75 and Over	43.3	34.5	30.6	35.4	25.5	7.8	11.9	16.1	8.1
85 and Over	59.7	51.2	59.3	44.7	47.2	31.9	5.4	34.1	−16.9

Black

55–64	45.3	25.4	18.7	4.3	17.6	59.0	36.2	43.9	29.7
65–74	29.3	27.6	28.7	10.8	7.4	20.4	60.6	71.8	50.2
75–84	49.8	34.2	45.5	39.8	16.1	11.3	23.8	36.0	11.4
85–89	85.5	42.6	40.9	72.0	45.3	20.8	9.9	28.1	−9.3
90 and Over	40.3	41.0	88.7	37.1	90.6	47.5	31.0	78.7	−7.5
55 and Over	40.1	28.0	26.6	14.3	16.4	36.8	39.5	42.4	37.4
65 and Over	34.8	30.9	34.9	23.3	15.5	19.3	43.0	46.4	40.3
75 and Over	49.0	38.0	47.5	45.7	26.5	17.8	22.1	27.6	17.4
85 and Over	68.1	42.1	55.3	58.6	60.3	32.6	18.9	50.5	−8.5

SOURCES: Based on U.S. Bureau of the Census, *Current Population Reports*, series P-25, nos. 311, 519, 624, 917, and 952. Data for ages 85–89 and 90 and over in 1950, 1960, 1970, and 1980 obtained from appropriate censuses.

NOTES: Periods extend from July 1 of initial year to June 30 of terminal year. Minus sign denotes a decrease. Base date of projections is July 1, 1982.

[a] Projections given are for the middle series, except where indicated otherwise.

TABLE 2.4

Percentage of the Total Population in the Older Ages, by Sex and by Race: 1950–2030 (figures as of July 1)

Sex, Race, and Age	1950	1960	1970	1980	1985
Male					
60 and Over	11.8	12.4	12.6	13.6	14.3
65 and Over	7.7	8.5	8.5	9.4	9.9
70 and Over	4.5	5.2	5.3	5.8	6.2
75 and Over	2.3	2.7	3.0	3.2	3.5
80 and Over	1.0	1.2	1.4	1.6	1.7
85 and Over	0.3	0.4	0.5	0.6	0.7
Female					
60 and Over	12.5	14.1	15.6	17.8	18.7
65 and Over	8.6	10.0	11.2	13.1	13.9
70 and Over	5.2	6.3	7.5	9.0	9.6
75 and Over	2.8	3.5	4.4	5.6	6.1
80 and Over	1.3	1.6	2.3	3.0	3.4
85 and Over	0.5	0.6	0.9	1.4	1.6
White					
60 and Over	12.6	13.7	14.6	16.6	17.5
65 and Over	8.4	9.6	10.2	11.9	12.7
70 and Over	5.0	6.0	6.7	7.9	8.5
75 and Over	2.7	3.3	3.9	4.7	5.2
80 and Over	1.2	1.5	1.9	2.5	2.6
85 and Over	0.4	0.5	0.7	1.1	1.2
Black					
60 and Over	8.2	9.2	10.1	11.1	11.5
65 and Over	5.7	6.3	6.8	7.8	8.1
70 and Over	3.0	3.7	4.1	4.9	5.2
75 and Over	1.6	1.9	2.2	2.8	3.0
80 and Over	0.8	0.9	1.1	1.4	1.5
85 and Over	0.3	0.4	0.5	0.6	0.7

SOURCE: U.S. Bureau of the Census, *Current Population Reports*, series P-25, nos. 311, 519, 614, 917, 952, and 985.

NOTES: Based on the total population including armed forces overseas. Base date of projections is July 1, 1982. Projections are for the middle series, except as shown for 2030. Percentages for the highest and lowest projection series do not represent a range (i.e., uncertainty interval) around the percentages for the middle series. See text of Chapter 1 for explanation.

				Projections		
					2030	
1990	2000	2010	2020	Middle Series	Highest Series	Lowest Series
14.5	14.3	16.8	21.2	23.8	21.9	25.6
10.4	10.5	11.2	14.6	18.2	16.9	19.4
6.7	7.4	7.4	9.2	12.4	11.7	13.0
3.9	4.6	4.7	5.2	7.5	7.2	7.6
2.0	2.4	2.7	2.8	3.9	3.9	3.8
0.8	1.1	1.3	1.3	1.7	1.8	1.5
19.4	19.5	22.1	26.7	29.7	27.3	31.9
14.9	15.5	16.4	20.0	24.0	22.2	25.5
10.6	11.8	12.0	14.1	17.9	16.8	18.7
7.0	8.3	8.6	9.3	12.1	11.7	13.3
4.0	5.1	5.9	5.9	7.4	7.5	7.2
1.9	2.7	3.4	3.5	3.9	4.3	3.5
18.1	18.1	20.8	25.5	28.4	26.3	30.5
13.6	14.0	14.9	18.6	22.6	21.1	24.0
9.3	10.4	10.5	12.7	16.4	15.5	17.1
5.9	7.0	7.3	7.9	10.7	10.3	10.8
3.2	4.1	4.7	4.7	6.3	6.4	6.0
1.5	2.1	2.6	2.7	3.1	3.4	2.7
11.3	11.3	12.9	16.9	20.3	18.5	21.9
8.2	8.4	8.9	11.6	15.4	14.2	16.4
5.6	6.0	6.1	7.4	10.4	9.8	10.9
3.5	3.9	4.1	4.5	6.4	6.2	6.5
1.8	2.3	2.6	2.7	3.5	3.6	3.4
0.9	1.2	1.4	1.5	1.7	1.9	1.5

balance of males to females in the total population brought about mainly by the excess mortality of males. Life expectancy at birth for females exceeded that for males in 1985 by 7 years, for example, and there were 5 percent fewer males than females in the population in that year.

In 1985, the excess of elderly females, numbering 5.5 million, was 19 percent of the total population aged 65 and over. In 1950, the excess was relatively small: 0.7 million, or 5.5 percent of the total aged 65 and over. The excess is expected to grow as the elderly population grows. According to the Census Bureau population projections (May 1984), a quarter century hence, in 2010, the excess will grow to a huge 8 million, or 20 percent of the total population aged 65 and over. The excess of women increases greatly, in spite of the moderate change in the sex

FIGURE 2.4

Percentage of the Total Population Aged 65 and Over, by Race: 1930–2030

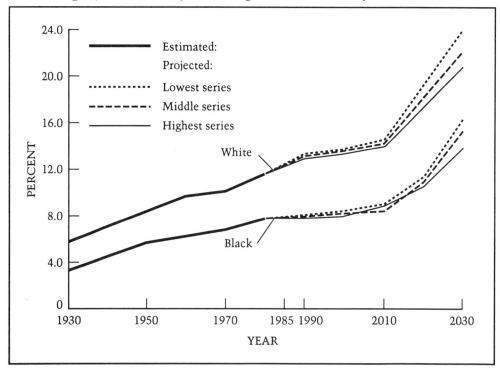

SOURCES: Table 2.4 and U.S. Bureau of the Census, *Current Population Reports*, series P-25, nos. 311; and 952, Table 6.

NOTE: Black and other races, 1930 and 1940.

ratio projected, because the elderly population will be far larger. The great imbalance of the sexes at the older ages has numerous, pervasive, and profound implications which will often be referred to in later chapters.

Race Composition

Black-White Differences in Age Structure

A much smaller proportion of the black population than of the white population is aged 65 and over (8.1 percent vs. 12.7 percent in 1985). (See Table 2.4 and Figure 2.4.) The difference has been steadily widening as the white population has been aging more rapidly than the black population. The census of 1950 recorded a difference of 2.6 points between the two race groups in the percentage aged 65 and over (5.8 percent and 8.4 percent) compared with 4.6 points in 1985. The difference results primarily from the higher fertility of the black population and secondarily from the higher mortality of blacks at the adult ages below 65 (which reduces the number of survivors at the older ages). The relatively greater concentration of declines in mortality at the younger ages among blacks than among whites and the relatively greater immigration of young whites several decades ago have also contributed to the difference.

The difference in fertility may be illustrated on the basis of various measures for 1982 and 1980.

Race	Birth Rate[a]	Total Fertility Rate[b]	Children Ever Born per 1,000 Women[c]
Black	21.4	2,188	3,545
White	14.9	1,742	2,807
Percent Excess, Black over White	43.6	25.6	26.3

SOURCE: U.S. National Center for Health Statistics, "Advance Report of Final Natality Statistics, 1982," *Monthly Vital Statistics Report* 39 (6), supplement 2 (September 1984); U.S. Bureau of the Census, 1980 Census of the Population, *U.S. Summary: Detailed Characteristics*, PC80-1-D1-A, Table 270.

[a]Births per 1,000 population, 1982.
[b]The total number of births that 1,000 women would have in their lifetime according to the age-specific birth rates of 1982, assuming that none of the women die before the end of the childbearing period.
[c]Children ever born per 1,000 women aged 40–44, 1980.

The continuing wide gap between the fertility of the races is a strong factor inhibiting the convergence of the proportions aged 65 and over for the races. The trend of the excess of black over white fertility for recent decades suggests that the proportions will remain far apart for many years.

| | Percent Excess | |
Year	Birth Rate	Total Fertility Rate
1950[a]	44.8	32.0
1960	40.5	28.6
1970	45.4	29.9
1975	52.2	33.0
1980	48.3	29.6
1985	42.6	25.2

[a]Excess of black and "other races" over white.

The gap in the mortality of the races, especially at the middle adult ages, is also associated with the tendency for the race gap between the proportions aged 65 and over to widen. Much smaller proportions of blacks than whites survive to old age, but survival within old age, on the average, is more similar for the two races. For example, according to life tables for 1985, 80 percent of whites survive from birth to age 65 compared with 67 percent of blacks, but the percentages surviving from age 65 to age 85 were 38 and 30, respectively. Life expectancies at birth of whites and blacks have converged sharply in the last half century, but the convergence of death rates was essentially confined to the ages under 65. Life expectancies at age 65 have moved *pari passu* at about the same level for the races.

The widening of the gap between the proportions of elderly whites and elderly blacks has been accompanied by a more rapid growth of elderly blacks (Table 2.3). The excess of the decennial growth rates of elderly blacks over elderly whites since 1950 varies from a negligible amount (1950–1960) to nearly 12 percentage points (1960–1970), with the difference in the 1970s being intermediate. This seeming contradiction is explained by the fact that the black population under age 65 has also been growing much more rapidly than the corresponding white population.

Changes in the proportions aged 75 and over and 85 and over give similar indications of the relatively greater aging of whites than blacks as the proportions aged 65 and over (Table 2.4). Data for these older ages taken in combination also document the fact that the black *elderly* population tends to be younger than the white *elderly* population and that both the white and black elderly populations have been aging rapidly. For example, the shares of the white and black populations aged 65 and over that are 75 and over rose by 9 to 10 percentage points from 1950 to 1985.

Race	1950	1985	Increase: 1950–1985
Total	31	40	9
White	32	41	9
Black	28	38	10

Black-White Differences in Sex Composition

The age patterns of sex ratios for the two racial groups are roughly similar, but the decline with age is more irregular for blacks, possibly because of sex differences in census coverage. (See Table 2.1 and Figures 2.1 and 2A.1.) Differences in the sex ratios of the races at the various ages are affected not only by the differences in the sex ratio at birth but also by differences between the races in the sex balance of death rates and immigrants. The sex ratios at the younger ages are lower for blacks than for whites, largely because the sex ratio of births is lower for blacks (e.g., 102.8 in 1983 and 102.6 in 1940) than for whites (e.g., 105.7 in 1983 and 106.0 in 1940). Since the figures for the races fall at different rates with increasing age, they converge, cross (at about ages 70–74), and diverge again.

The sex ratio of elderly blacks had been substantially higher than that of elderly whites for many decades, but as the figures for both blacks and whites fell, the difference has been diminishing. It was quite small in 1985; the comparative figures for ages 65 and over were 67.0 and 67.7 (Table 2.2). In contrast, the sex ratio in 1985 for the population aged 80 and over was much higher for blacks. Factors contributing to this reversal include the narrower gap between male and female mortality rates for blacks at these ages and the relatively greater coverage of black males than of black females in the census at the higher ages. When the 1980 census data are adjusted for net undercounts, the sex ratios at the older ages for whites and blacks are more alike (Appendix Table 2A.2 and Figure 2A.1).

Other Racial Groups

To consider the principal aging characteristics of the major racial group other than white and black, the remaining population was subdivided into two racial subgroups: Asian and Pacific Islanders (API) and

American Indians/Eskimos/Aleuts.[5] These groups had small proportions aged 65 and over in 1980, even smaller proportions than blacks: 6 percent and 5 percent, respectively (Table 2.5). The elderly of both groups together represent only 1 percent of all persons aged 65 and over.

The API population has been aging, but more slowly than the white or black populations. The elderly API population has also been aging; the share of the population aged 65 and over that is 75 and over increased from 27 percent in 1950 to 36 percent in 1980. On the other hand, the share of elderly American Indians has not been increasing and there is no evidence of aging within the elderly group.[6]

Today the API group, like whites and blacks, has deficits of men in the older ages, but the deficits are far smaller. In fact, in comparison with the general population, the API group has a sex ratio at ages 65 and over that is roughly in balance, with 91 men per 100 women.

Age	Asian and Pacific Islanders		All Races	
	1980	1950	1980	1950
Sex Ratio				
65 and Over	91	191	68	90
75 and Over	82	157	55	83
85 and Over	62	129	44	70
All Ages	95	130	95	99
Population				
65 and Over	287,000	37,000	25,429,000	12,257,000

At the highest ages substantial deficits of men occur, but the balance is much more favorable than for the general population. In 1950, massive deficits of women characterized the API group. This is a consequence of the great predominance of males among Chinese and Japanese immigrants arriving before 1920. In 1950 nearly four fifths of all API elderly persons were foreign-born, and 65 percent of these were male. In 1980 two thirds were foreign-born, but only 41 percent of these were male.

[5]The statement is consistent with the classification of the human species into three major races, Caucasoid, Negroid, and Mongoloid, following widely accepted anthropological practice. The further subdivision into various racial subgroups follows ethnic and "nationality" lines. Asian and Pacific Islanders includes principally Japanese, Chinese, Filipinos, Hawaiians, Koreans, Asian Indians, and Vietnamese. Some groups such as Asian Indians and Hawaiians do not fit the broader classification as given. Note that the census uses a social definition of race, which is currently self-reported on the basis of specified categories.
[6]The 1980 and the 1950 census data on American Indians are so grossly inconsistent as to preclude a meaningful interpretation of the change. Persistently high fertility and persistently high mortality below age 65 have contributed to the apparent lack of aging.

TABLE 2.5

Percentage Aged 65 and Over, for Race Groups and the Hispanic Population, by Age: 1980 and 1950

Race/ Hispanic Origin	1980			1950		
	Age 65 and Over	Age 75 and Over	Age 85 and Over	Age 65 and Over	Age 75 and Over	Age 85 and Over
Total	11.3	4.4	1.0	8.2	2.6	0.4
White[a]	11.9	4.7	1.1	8.4	2.7	0.4
Black[a]	7.8	2.8	0.6	5.8	1.6	0.3
American Indian/ Eskimo/Aleut	5.3	1.9	0.4	5.3	1.9	0.3
Asian and Pacific Islander	6.0	2.1	0.4	5.0	1.0	
Hispanic Origin[b]	4.9	1.7	0.3	3.3	1.0	NA

SOURCES: Based on U.S. Bureau of the Census, *Current Population Reports*, Series P-25, no. 965, Table 4; 1980 Census of Population: *U.S. Summary: General Population Characteristics*, Table 43; and 1950 Census of Population, *U.S. Summary: Detailed Characteristics*, Table 97; and *Special Reports*, "Nonwhite Population by Race," Tables 1, 2, and 3; "Persons of Spanish Surname," Table 2; and "Puerto Ricans in Continental United States," Table 2.

NOTE: NA = not available.

[a]Census data as enumerated in 1980 have been adjusted to include an estimate of white or black persons of Hispanic origin or descent who did not report a specific race.
[b]Persons of Hispanic origin or descent for 1980; white persons of Spanish surname in five southwestern states and persons of Puerto Rican birth and Puerto Rican parentage in 1950.

Sex-Race Differences

Gross and Net Changes

The changes in the male and female populations and in the white and black populations that occurred during recent decades have been described in their simplest terms as net changes. Net changes mask the actual processes of change and the rapidity with which membership in the various groups shifts. The changes may be analyzed further in terms of gross changes (i.e., in terms of demographic components) or measures of population turnover.

Population turnover among the elderly is impressively high for each sex-race group. Most measures show that it is greater for blacks than for whites and for males than for females. Of the white males aged 65 and over in 1980, 65 percent joined the elderly population after 1970 compared with 57 percent of white females (Table 2.6).[7] Of black males aged 65 and over in 1980, 67 percent joined the elderly population after 1970, and of black females 62 percent joined after 1970. The rates of gross gain and gross loss in the population during the 1970–1980 decade were also larger for males and blacks than for females and whites, respectively.[8] The higher these measures, the greater is the population turnover.

The growth-effectiveness ratio—the ratio of net to gross change— shows that population turnover is more pronounced for males than for females, but slightly less for blacks than for whites.[9] The growth-effectiveness ratio for the white female population during the 1970–1980 decade was much greater than for the white male population (.222 vs. .131), and the growth-effectiveness ratio for black males was slightly greater than for white males (.143 vs. .131). The lower the ratio, the greater is the population turnover. These measures showed the same general levels and patterns of turnover for the sex-race groups in the 1960–1970 period as in the 1970–1980 period. The differences between the sexes result mainly from the much higher mortality of males. The smaller differences between the races result almost entirely from different rates of entry into the group.

---

[7] The percentage aged 65–74 of those 65 and over may be viewed as the percentage of the elderly population who are surviving new entrants to the group.

[8] The rate of gross gain is the number of persons reaching age 65 during the decade plus the number of (net) immigrants at ages 65 and over expressed as a percentage of the initial population. The rate of gross loss is the number of deaths at ages 65 and over during the decade expressed as a percentage of the initial population.

[9] The growth-effectiveness ratio is the ratio of the net increase in the population aged 65 and over to the gross change in this age group (i.e., the number reaching age 65 plus deaths plus net immigrants).

Societal Age Dependency

Use of dependency ratios may be extended to sex and race groups to reflect the age factor in economic dependency for these groups. Inasmuch as the societal support population is not limited to persons of a particular sex or race group, sex- or race-specific dependency ratios have been based on the entire population of working age, not merely the population of one sex or race group.

Elderly dependency ratios for women (women aged 65 and over/total population aged 18–64 per 100) consistently exceed those for men (men aged 65 and over/total population aged 18–64 per 100), as would be expected from the excess of women over men at ages 65 and over (Table 2.7). Dependency ratios for females grew much more rapidly than those for males in the years since 1950, so that the excess was considerable by 1984 (12.1 vs. 8.2). In the several decades to come, however, the rapid rise in the "burden" of females is likely to be matched by an even more rapid rise in the "burden" of males. The index of change from 1984 to 2030 is 197 for males and 186 for females. The age-sex structure of the population implies that elderly women constitute a disproportionate share of the potential economic burden on the working-age population and that they will continue to do so.

Dependency ratios for blacks are low (1.0 and 1.7 for 1950 and 1984). They have gradually risen in relation to the figures for whites (13.0 and 18.3) and are expected to continue doing so. The indexes in Table 2.7 indicate that, as a result of age shifts in the future, blacks will constitute a steadily rising but relatively small share of the potentially dependent elderly population. The dependency ratios expected in 2030 are 4.4 for blacks and 32.7 for whites.

Years Until Death

Since the passage of the Social Security Act in 1935, and particularly since the late 1960s, death rates at the older ages have declined notably. As a result, the ages at which the population has 10 or 15 years to live according to current life tables have risen substantially for each sex-race group, especially white females (Table 2.8). The figures suggest a rising threshold of old age for each sex-race group. As a result of the shifts in the relative levels of death rates at the older ages for the sexes, favoring females over males, the ages at which females show an average remaining lifetime of 10 or 15 years have been rising faster than those for males. Females now show an average remaining lifetime of 10 or 15 years at a much higher age than do males. As a result of shifts in death

TABLE 2.6

*Estimates of the Demographic Components of Change in the Population Aged 65
and Over, by Race and Sex: 1970–1980 and 1960–1970*
(numbers in thousands)

Item and Period	White		Black	
	Male	Female	Male	Female
July 1, 1970–July 1, 1980				
Population Aged 65 and Over, 1980	9,358	13,932	852	1,252
Population Aged 65 and Over, 1970	7,655	10,734	674	885
Net Increase	1,703	3,198	178	367
Number Reaching Age 65	7,321	8,769	715	916
Net "Migrants" Aged 65 and Over	—	5	3	7
Deaths Ages 65 and Over	5,687	5,653	524	507
Deaths to initial population aged 65 and over	4,433	4,809	392	415
Deaths to persons reaching age 65	1,254	844	132	93
Gross Change[b]	13,007	14,427	1,242	1,430
Rate of gross gain[c]	95.6	81.7	106.5	104.2
Rate of gross loss[c]	74.3	52.7	77.7	57.3
Population Aged 65–74 as Percentage of Population 65 and Over, 1980	65.4	57.3	66.7	62.3
Ratio, Net Change to Gross Change[b]	.131	.222	.143	.256
Mortality Rate of Population Aged 65 and Over[d]	38.0	29.0	37.7	28.2
Mortality rate of initial population aged 65 and over[e]	57.9	44.8	58.2	46.9
Mortality rate for persons reaching age 65[e]	17.1	9.6	18.5	10.1

SOURCES: Population data are from U.S. Bureau of the Census, 1960–1980 Censuses of Population and estimates of the number reaching age 65, deaths, and migration are from unpublished Census Bureau records. This table corresponds to Table 3-5 in U.S. Bureau of the Census, "Demographic and Socioeconomic Aspects of Aging in the United States," by J. S. Siegel and M. Davidson, *Current Population Reports*, series P-23, no. 138 (August 1984).

NOTES: — = rounds to zero. Figures from the 1980 and 1970 censuses have been adjusted for the "misclassification" of persons of Spanish origin as black and other races, rather than white. Figures from the 1970 census have been adjusted for the overstatement of centenarians.

[a]Black and other races for the 1960–1970 period.
[b]Gross change represents the sum of persons reaching age 65, net migrants, and deaths ages 65 and over. It does not include the "error of closure," the residual (4.8 million for all classes, 1970–1980, and 0.3 million for 1960–1970), representing the difference between net increase based on the census counts and the net change based on the components of change. "Net increase" in the table represents the difference between census counts, including the "error of closure."
[c]Per 100 initial population aged 65 and over.
[d]Per 100 initial population aged 65 and over plus persons reaching age 65 during the decade.
[e]Per 100 persons reaching age 65 during the decade.

Item and Period	White		Black[a]	
	Male	Female	Male	Female
April 1, 1960–April 1, 1970				
Population Aged 65 and Over, 1970	7,615	10,657	752	949
Population Aged 65 and Over, 1960	6,908	8,396	595	661
Net Increase	707	2,261	157	288
Number Reaching Age 65	6,044	7,009	636	699
Net "Migrants" Aged 65 and Over	22	38	3	5
Deaths Ages 65 and Over	5,254	4,848	468	409
Deaths to initial population aged 65 and over	4,115	4,127	310	281
Deaths to persons reaching age 65	1,139	721	158	128
Gross Change[b]	11,320	11,895	1,107	1,113
Rate of gross gain[c]	87.8	83.9	107.4	106.5
Rate of gross loss[c]	76.1	57.7	78.7	61.9
Population Aged 65–74 as Percentage of Population Aged 65 and Over, 1970	64.7	59.8	68.5	66.2
Ratio, Net Change to Gross Change[b]	.062	.192	.158	.273
Mortality Rates of Population Aged 65 and Over[d]	40.6	31.5	38.0	30.1
Mortality rate of initial population aged 65 and over[c]	59.6	49.2	52.1	42.5
Mortality rate for persons reaching age 65[e]	18.8	10.3	24.8	18.3

TABLE 2.7

Societal Elderly Dependency Ratios, by Sex and by Race: 1950–2030
(figures relate to July 1 and include U.S. armed forces overseas)

	Sex		Race	
Measure and Year	Male	Female	White	Black
Ratios				
1950	6.6	7.4	13.0	1.0
1960	8.0	9.7	16.3	1.3
1970	7.8	10.9	17.1	1.4
1980	8.0	11.8	18.0	1.6
1984	8.2	12.1	18.3	1.7
1990	8.6	13.0	19.5	1.8
2000	8.4	13.4	19.7	1.9
2010	9.1	13.8	20.1	2.1
2020	12.3	17.6	25.8	3.0
2030	16.2	22.6	32.7	4.4
Indexes				
(1984 = 100)				
1950	81	61	71	63
1960	98	80	89	75
1970	95	90	93	87
1980	98	98	98	98
1984	100	100	100	100
1990	106	107	107	105
2000	106	110	107	113
2010	111	114	109	125
2020	151	145	141	178
2030	197	186	179	262

SOURCES: Based on U.S. Bureau of the Census, *Current Population Reports*, series P-25, nos. 311, 519, 917, 952, and 985.

NOTES: Denominator of all ratios is the total population aged 20–64. Numerator of ratios is the population aged 65 and over for a specified sex or race group. Ratios expressed per 100. Middle series projections.

rates for the races, blacks show an average remaining lifetime of 10 or 15 years at an age only slightly below whites, except for males with 15 years of expected life.

If the age at which a population has 10 years of remaining lifetime is arbitrarily designated as the point of entry into old age, according to data for 1985 males reach old age at 73—five years before females (78), and blacks and whites reach old age at 75 and 76, respectively. The proportions of persons falling in the old-age group in the actual population will vary on the basis of these threshold ages. About the same proportion of the male population (4.8 percent) and the female population (4.6 percent) falls in the old-age group (Table 2.8). However, a larger propor-

TABLE 2.8

Age at Which Average Remaining Life Equals 10 or 15 Years and Percentage of the Total Population Above These Ages, by Sex and by Race: 1940–1985

| | Age at Which Average Remaining Life Equals 10 or 15 Years | | | | Percentage of Population Above Specified Age | | | |
| | White | | Black[a] | | White | | Black | |
Year	Male	Female	Male	Female	Male	Female	Male	Female
10 Years								
1940[b]	68.8	70.9	70.3	74.5	4.6	3.9	2.4[c]	1.4[c]
1950[b]	70.1	72.9	71.9	75.4	4.6	3.9	2.4[c]	1.5[c]
1970	70.8	75.4	71.1	77.1	5.1	4.5	3.1	1.8
1985	72.8	77.8	71.8	77.0	4.9	4.8	3.5	2.9
Increase, 1940–1985	4.0	6.9	1.5	2.5	0.3	0.6	1.1	1.5
15 Years								
1940[b]	60.1	62.9	58.6	62.5	10.6	8.8	8.2	5.4
1985	64.4	70.0	61.8	68.1	11.0	10.3	8.7	7.2
Increase, 1940–1985	4.3	7.1	3.2	5.6	0.4	1.5	0.5	1.8

SOURCES: Ages based on official U.S. life tables; population data for calculating percentages are from U.S. Bureau of the Census, *Current Population Reports*, series P-25, nos. 311, 519, 917, and 985.

[a] Black and "other races" life table for 1950.
[b] Conterminous United States (excluding Alaska and Hawaii).
[c] Black and "other races" population.

tion of whites (4.8 percent) than blacks (3.1 percent) falls in the old-age group. These differences mainly reflect the fact that while the female population has a larger share of persons aged 70 or 77 and over than the male population, the shares become nearly equal for the two sexes when the age bands for males are widened.

With 15 years until the age of death as a criterion, old age would begin at age 64 for males and age 70 for females; these figures imply a difference of 6 years in the age of transition to old age. The transition to old age would occur at age 68 for whites and at age 66 for blacks. The proportion of the population of each sex-race group over the threshold has remained relatively unchanged since 1935. At least for the recent past, a shifting start of dependent old age for each sex-race group is consistent with support for a relatively unchanging share of the population above this age.

The experience of real cohorts will follow more closely the pattern shown by the data in Table 2.9. The cohort of males born in 1920 had 15 years to live when it reached age 66 in 1986, while the cohort of females born in 1920 will have 15 years left at age 73 in 1993. For the cohort born in 1970 old age will not come until age 69 in 2039 for males and until age 77 in 2047 for females. Recent historical and prospective progress in late-life mortality reduction is about the same for these cohorts of men and women, so that the difference between the sexes in the age of onset of old age changes little.

Accordingly, men become old several years before women, while blacks and whites become old at about the same age. By extension, per-

TABLE 2.9

Age at Which Average Remaining Life Equals 10 or 15 Years, by Sex, for Birth Cohorts: 1900–1970

Year of Birth	10 Years Remaining		15 Years Remaining	
	Male	Female	Male	Female
1900	72.6	78.9	62.4	70.1
1920	75.2	81.6	65.8	73.3
1940	76.5	82.9	67.2	74.7
1950	77.2	83.6	67.8	75.3
1960	77.8	84.3	68.3	75.9
1970	78.5	84.9	68.9	76.6

SOURCE: Based on unpublished generation life tables provided by the U.S. Social Security Administration, Office of the Actuary. See "Life Tables for the United States, 1900–2050," by J. F. Faber and A. H. Wade, *Actuarial Study*, no. 89 (December 1983).

sons with certain chronic illnesses reach old age before those free of these conditions. Such findings may have significant legal and administrative implications. If the years-until-death concept of old age is sustained in the courts and becomes embedded in statutory and administrative law, there could be important changes in the benefits awarded to various classes of persons designated as old in various laws or public programs.

Ethnic Composition

Hispanic Population

The Hispanic population[10] has a very low proportion at ages 65 and over even though it has been aging like the non-Hispanic population. The figure for 1985 is 5.0 percent compared with 12.5 percent for the non-Hispanic population.

Hispanic Origin	1950	1985	2020
Hispanic	3.4	5.0	10.6
Non-Hispanic	8.0	12.5	18.7

One factor explaining the low share of elderly Hispanics relative to that of non-Hispanics is their higher fertility. The relative level of fertility of the Hispanic and non-Hispanic populations is illustrated by a comparison based on various measures of fertility in 1980 and 1982.

Hispanic Origin	Crude Birth Rate: 1982[a]	General Fertility Rate: 1982[a,b]	Children Ever Born Rate: 1980[c]
Hispanic	23.9	96.1	3,491
Non-Hispanic	15.3	65.0	2,880
Percent Excess	56.2	47.8	21.2

SOURCES: U.S. National Center for Health Statistics, "Births of Hispanic Parentage, 1982," *Monthly Vital Statistics Report* 34 (4), supplement (July 1985), Table 5; U.S. Bureau of the Census, 1980 Census of the Population, *U.S. Summary: Detailed Characteristics*, PC80-1-D1-A, Table 270.

[a] Hispanic origin of mother. Total of 11 selected states.
[b] Births per 1,000 women aged 15–44.
[c] Children ever born per 1,000 women aged 40–44 for 50 states and District of Columbia.

[10]The Hispanic population consists of persons who reported that they or their antecedents came from a Spanish-speaking country. They may be of any race.

A continuing large volume of immigration, consisting disproportionately of young people from Mexico, also contributes to depressing the percentage of the elderly among Hispanics. As reported in the 1980 census, 77 percent of all Hispanic immigrants between 1970 and 1980 (excluding those who died or emigrated by 1980) were under age 35, while 71 percent of the entire Hispanic population and 73 percent of all immigrants between 1970 and 1980 were under age 35. In addition, many young immigrants entered illegally and were not enumerated in the census. The role of mortality is indeterminate because of the lack of exact information on the mortality of Hispanics; it appears to approximate the level for non-Hispanics.

The Hispanic population has a relatively high sex ratio at ages 65 and over (72 males per 100 females in 1985) compared with the sex balance for the white and black populations (Table 2.1). We turn to the sex ratios of births, immigration, and deaths for some explanation. According to tabulations of births of Hispanic parentage for 23 states and the District of Columbia, the sex ratio at birth of Hispanics is intermediate between the ratios of whites and blacks. The figures for 1981 and 1983 are 104.8 and 105.1, respectively. Males appear to outnumber females slightly among immigrants of Hispanic origin, as suggested by census data on foreign-born Hispanics, Immigration and Naturalization Service data on immigration from Latin American countries, and estimates of illegal immigrants in the 1980 census. The very high sex ratios at ages 15–34 imply, however, that the young immigrants were heavily male. The relatively high sex ratios at the older ages are consistent with the possibility that the male disadvantage in survival for Hispanics is less than the male disadvantage for non-Hispanics.

Nativity

The age distribution of the foreign-born population and its share of the elderly population reflect the immigration policies of the past century. Until a few years after World War I, immigration from abroad was essentially unrestricted. Then it was sharply curtailed. As a result of this change in immigration policy, there is at the present time a relatively high concentration of foreign-born persons in the extreme old ages, which is greatly attenuated for the elderly population as a whole. The peak was in the past, however. In 1950, of all foreign-born persons, 26 percent were aged 65 and over, and of all persons aged 65 and over, 22 percent were foreign-born. In 1970, the corresponding percentages were 32 and 15.

Since 1970, aging, mortality, and additional immigration have tended to reduce these proportions. According to the July 1975 Current Population Survey (CPS), the November 1979 Ancestry and Language Survey, and the 1980 census, the concentration of the elderly among the foreign-born and the concentration of the foreign-born among the elderly fell appreciably after 1970. In 1975 about 25 percent of the foreign-born population was aged 65 and over and the foreign-born constituted 12 percent of those aged 65 and over. The 1980 census recorded 21 percent and 12 percent, respectively.

The foreign-born population is now twice as likely as the native population to be aged 65 and over (Table 2.10). In 1950, when the aging of the general population had progressed far less than now, the foreign-born were nearly four times as likely as the native population to be aged 65 and over. The decline in this ratio is an indication that the survivors of the massive pre–World War I immigration are passing from the scene

TABLE 2.10

Percentage Aged 65 and Over, for Race Groups and the Hispanic Population, by Nativity: 1980 and 1950

Race/Hispanic Origin and Nativity	1980	1950
All Races	11.3	8.2
Native	10.6	6.8
Foreign-born	21.2	26.3
White and Other Races	11.7	8.4
Native	11.0	7.0
Foreign-born	22.0	26.5
Black	7.8	5.7
Native	7.8	5.7
Foreign-born	7.2	11.9
Hispanic	4.6	3.4
Native	3.1	2.0
Foreign-born	8.3	11.2

SOURCES: Based on U.S. Bureau of the Census, 1980 Census of Population, *U.S. Summary*, Table 253; 1950 Census of Population, *U.S. Summary*, Tables 96 and 97, and *Special Reports*, "Nonwhite Population by Race," Tables 3, 26, 27, and 28; "Persons of Spanish Surname," Table 5; and "Puerto Ricans in Continental United States," Table 2.

NOTES: "Other races" comprises mainly American Indians and Asian and Pacific Islanders. Census data for whites, as enumerated in 1980, exclude an estimated 214,000 persons aged 65 and over of Hispanic origin or descent who did not report a specific race in the census and, hence, were tabulated as "other races."

and are not being fully replaced. This pattern of change in the shares of elderly for nativity groups describes not only the white population but blacks and Hispanics as well. For these groups, too, as the native population was aging, the elderly share of the foreign-born population was diminishing sharply.

Examining the data from a different focus, we note a decline of about 50 percent in the foreign-born share of the elderly population between 1950 and 1980 (from 22 percent to 12 percent). (See Table 2.11.) The

TABLE 2.11

Percentage Foreign-born of the White, Black, and Hispanic Populations Aged 65 and Over, by Age: 1980 and 1950

Race/Hispanic Origin and Age	Number, 1980 (in thousands)	Percent	
		1980	1950
All Races			
65 and Over	2,980	11.7	22.2
65–74	1,408	9.0	22.3
75–84	1,166	15.1	21.6
85 and Over	407	18.6	24.2
White and Other Races			
65 and Over	2,922	12.5	23.8
65–74	1,373	9.6	24.0
75–84	1,147	16.1 ⎫	
85 and Over	402	19.7 ⎭	23.6
Black			
65 and Over	58	2.8	1.6
65–74	34	2.6	1.8
75–84	19	3.2 ⎫	
85 and Over	5	3.4 ⎭	0.9
Hispanic			
65 and Over	348	51.8	51.1
65–74	213	48.8	50.4
75–84	109	57.1 ⎫	
85 and Over	26	58.3 ⎭	52.7

SOURCES: Based on U.S. Bureau of the Census, 1980 Census of Population, *U.S. Summary*, Table 253; 1950 Census of Population, *U.S. Summary*, Tables 96 and 97; and *Special Reports*, "Nonwhite Population by Race," Tables 2 and 26; "Persons of Spanish Surname," Table 5; and "Puerto Ricans in Continental United States," Table 2.

NOTES: "Other races" comprises mainly American Indians and Asian and Pacific Islanders. Census data for whites, as enumerated in 1980, exclude an estimated 214,000 persons aged 65 and over of Hispanic origin or descent who did not report a specific race in the census and, hence, were tabulated as "other races." The combination of whites and other races is not affected by this reporting anomaly.

TABLE 2.12

Percentage Foreign-born of Persons Aged 65 and Over, by Race Group and Hispanic Origin: 1980 and 1950

Race/Hispanic Origin	1980	1950
Total	11.7	22.2
White	11.7[a]	23.7
Black	2.8[a]	1.6
American Indian/Eskimo/Aleut	3.6	3.3
Asian and Pacific Islander	65.2	78.8[b]
Hispanic Origin[c]	51.8	51.1

SOURCES: Based on U.S. Bureau of the Census, 1980 Census of Population, *U.S. Summary*, Table 253; 1950 Census of Population, *U.S. Summary*, Tables 96 and 97, and *Special Reports*, "Nonwhite Population by Race," Tables 3, 26, 27, and 28; "Persons of Spanish Surname," Table 5; and "Puerto Ricans in Continental United States," Table 2. See also U.S. Bureau of the Census, *Current Population Reports*, series P-25, no. 965, Table 4.

[a]The white and black populations as enumerated in 1980 exclude an estimated 214,000 and 5,000 persons aged 65 and over of Hispanic origin who did not report a specific race, respectively. As a result, the percentages shown for 1980 are believed to be biased slightly downward.
[b]Other races, representing the total excluding white, black, and American Indian.
[c]Persons of Hispanic origin or descent for 1980; white persons of Spanish surname in five southwestern states and persons of Puerto Rican birth and Puerto Rican parentage in 1950.

relative decline in the percentages varied inversely with age, with the result that in 1980 the share of foreign-born among those aged 85 and over (19 percent) was twice as great as the share for those aged 65–74 (9 percent), in contrast to the similarity of the shares in 1950. The share at the oldest ages will diminish further in the future as the younger, "less foreign-born," population moves up in age.

This pattern mainly describes the white population. In contrast, the tiny share of foreign-born among the older black population has been rising. The share for the Hispanic population has been changing little, but more than one half of Hispanics aged 65 and over and nearly three fifths of those aged 75 and over are foreign-born. The foreign-born share among elderly Asian and Pacific Islanders is even higher, with two thirds foreign-born (Table 2.12).

In 1980, the great majority (82 percent) of the elderly foreign-born were naturalized citizens, and these elderly citizen immigrants made up a large share (34 percent) of all naturalized citizens. This suggests that the elderly are not much less assimilated than younger persons. A similar degree of assimilation is suggested by a comparison of the share of elderly persons who speak a language other than English at home (13 percent) and the share for the entire population aged 5 and over (11 percent). On the other hand, so large a share of elderly persons, especially Hispanics and Asians and persons aged 85 and over, are foreign-born, and so large a share of the foreign-born population, especially particular white ethnic groups, are aged 65 and over, that the question of their ability to take advantage of available services and of the need to provide special services for them must be considered. (See the discussion below.)

Country of Birth

There is a wide variation in the share of elderly among foreign-born persons according to period of immigration and country of birth. One third (33 percent) of the foreign-born population of 1980 that had arrived in the United States before 1970 was aged 65 and over compared with 3 percent of the foreign-born arriving between 1970 and 1980 (Table 2.13). Only immigrants from Cuba (14 percent), China (10 percent), and the Philippines (6 percent), among the principal countries of origin, showed proportions of elderly that substantially exceeded the overall proportion for immigrants arriving between 1970 and 1980. Older immigrants from these countries appear to be joining their relatives, since so large a share arrived in recent years. The figures for elderly immigrants from Africa, Mexico, India, and Vietnam are especially low, even though impressively large shares of immigrants have arrived from these areas since 1965 (Table 2.14).[11] In 1970, a year for which detailed age data on the foreign-born according to country of birth are available from the census reports, there were some countries (e.g., Italy and Poland) for which almost one half of the total foreign-born were aged 65 and over, others (e.g., in Asia and Latin America) for which one tenth or less fell in this age band, and one (USSR) for which almost two thirds of the total foreign-born were elderly. The detailed age data in Table 2.15 reflect the aging of both the total foreign-born population and the foreign-born population from most major countries of immigration, as well as the aging of the foreign-born elderly population, between 1950 and 1970.

Country differences are reflected also in data for 1980 on the proportion of persons aged 65 and over who speak a language other than English at home. For example, this proportion is 25 percent or more for German, Italian, and Polish, but is only 5 percent and 8 percent for Spanish and Chinese, respectively. Since immigrants tend to move when they

---

[11]These patterns are corroborated by data on immigrants admitted between July 1978 and June 1988 compiled by the Immigration and Naturalization Service (*1988 Statistical Yearbook of the U.S. Immigration and Naturalization Service*, August 1989). In this decade 3.7 percent of immigrants admitted were aged 65 and over.

TABLE 2.13

Percentage Aged 65 and Over and Males per 100 Females Aged 65 and Over, for the Foreign-born Population, by Country of Birth for Persons Immigrating Between 1970 and 1980: 1980

Period of Immigration and Country of Birth	Percentage of Total	Males per 100 Females	Period of Immigration and Country of Birth	Percentage of Total	Males per 100 Females
Total, Foreign-born	21.2	69.7	Total, North and Central America	2.5	57.6
Immigrated Between 1970 and 1980[a]	3.2	61.9	Canada	3.6	77.3
			Cuba	13.8	63.3
Total, Europe	4.4	62.2	Dominican Republic	2.8	64.3
Greece	3.6	61.9	Haiti	2.7	34.3
Italy	4.1	66.2	Jamaica	2.9	43.6
Portugal	3.8	61.1	Mexico	1.1	59.7
United Kingdom	3.5	57.2			
Total, Asia	3.2	69.7	South America	2.3	42.8
China	9.7	74.1			
India	1.6	95.4	Africa	1.2	67.1
Korea	2.6	48.9			
Philippines	6.0	69.6	Immigrated before 1970	32.9	70.2
Vietnam	1.7	62.8			

SOURCE: U.S. Bureau of the Census, 1980 Census of Population, *U.S. Summary*, Chapter D, Table 253.

[a]Constitutes only 5.9 percent of the total foreign-born population.

TABLE 2.14

Distribution of Foreign-born Persons, by Year of Immigration, for Selected Countries of Birth: 1980 (numbers in thousands; includes countries with 200,000 or more foreign-born)

Country of Birth	Total Number	Total Percent	1965–1980	1950–1964	Before 1950
Total	14,080	100	52	23	25
Europe	4,743	100	26	31	44
Germany	849	100	19	45	36
Greece	211	100	52	24	24
Italy	832	100	22	26	52
Poland	418	100	17	27	56
United Kingdom	669	100	30	29	40
USSR	406	100	27	16	58
Asia	2,540	100	81	12	6
China	286	100	65	21	15
India	206	100	92	7	1
Japan	222	100	56	34	10
Korea	290	100	93	7	—
Philippines	501	100	81	11	8
Vietnam	231	100	99	1	—
North and Central America	4,665	100	63	23	15
Canada	843	100	24	30	46
Mexico	2,199	100	71	19	10
Cuba	608	100	59	38	3
South America	561	100	77	19	4
Africa	200	100	77	15	8
All Other Countries	79	100	65	16	19

SOURCE: U.S. Bureau of the Census, 1980 Census of Population, *U.S. Summary*, Chapter D, Table 254.

NOTES: Total includes "country of birth not reported." Dash denotes that figure rounds to zero.

are relatively young, these country-to-country differences reflect in large part the periods during which immigrants from the various countries entered the United States, with the high proportions of foreign-born and of speakers of a foreign language in old age corresponding to immigration of a more distant period and the low proportions corresponding to immigration of a more recent period.

TABLE 2.15

Percentage of the Foreign-born Population Aged 55 and Over, by Age, for Specified Countries of Birth: 1970 and 1950 (numbers in thousands)

Year and Country of Birth	All Ages		Ages 55 and Over	Ages 55–64	Ages 65–74	Ages 75 and Over	Ages 65 and Over
	Number	Percent					
1970							
All Countries[a]	9,619	100.0	46.9	14.9	17.9	14.1	32.0
United Kingdom	686	100.0	49.5	15.2	19.4	14.9	34.3
Ireland	251	100.0	61.5	19.9	23.0	18.6	41.6
Germany	833	100.0	45.2	15.1	17.7	12.4	30.1
Poland	548	100.0	69.3	20.4	24.4	24.5	48.9
USSR	463	100.0	84.6	20.7	37.4	26.5	63.9
Italy	1,009	100.0	63.6	16.9	25.3	21.4	46.7
Canada	812	100.0	42.6	18.1	14.4	10.1	24.5
Mexico	760	100.0	26.8	12.4	9.9	4.5	14.4
1950[b]							
All Countries[a]	10,095	100.0	52.8	26.1	18.4	8.3	26.7
England and Wales	585	100.0	53.6	20.8	21.0	11.9	32.9
Ireland	506	100.0	57.0	22.0	22.1	12.9	35.0
Germany	983	100.0	54.0	18.1	20.6	15.2	35.8
Poland	860	100.0	59.6	36.7	17.9	5.0	22.9
USSR	854	100.0	58.3	32.3	20.0	6.0	26.0
Italy	1,419	100.0	54.8	31.4	17.9	5.5	23.3
Canada	990	100.0	40.0	16.2	14.9	8.9	23.9
Mexico	451	100.0	24.5	14.0	7.3	3.2	10.5

SOURCES: U.S. Bureau of the Census, 1970 Census of Population, *Subject Reports*, "National Origin and Language," PC(2)-1A (1973), Table 10; 1950 Census of Population, *Subject Reports*, "Nativity and Parentage," P-E, no. 3A (1954), Table 14 and Table 3.

NOTE: Includes countries with 450,000 or more foreign-born.

[a]Includes countries of birth not listed and "country of birth not reported."
[b]White population only.

Foreign Stock and Ancestry

The discussion so far has been limited to the first-generation population. The foreign stock (i.e., the foreign-born population and the native population of foreign or mixed parentage) is less directly affected by the timing of immigration than the foreign-born population alone and shows much lower shares of elderly persons, while aging more rapidly (Table 2.16). In 1950, 14 percent of the foreign stock was aged 65 and over, and by 1970 the percentage had mounted to 21. The Italian and Polish populations will serve as illustration for particular foreign stocks: The shares more than doubled from 8 percent to 16 percent or more in these 20 years. The immigrants and their children are both aging without substantial replacement.

As a country largely peopled by immigrants, the United States contains within it many ancestry groups but, as we have seen, for many of these groups the years of heavy immigration are long past and the immigrants are well along in years. Persons reporting specific ancestries tend to be first-, second-, or perhaps third-generation persons. According to the 1980 census and the Ancestry and Language Survey conducted by

TABLE 2.16

Percentage Aged 65 and Over and Males per 100 Females Aged 65 and Over, by Country of Origin, for the Foreign Stock: 1970 and 1950

Country of Origin	Percent Ages 65 and Over		Males per 100 Females	
	1970	1950[a]	1970	1950
All Countries[b]	20.8	14.3	75.3	89.8
United Kingdom	26.6	21.7[c]	66.8	79.6[c]
Ireland	32.2	23.9	58.4	64.9
Germany	35.2	24.5	71.8	81.0
Poland	18.2	8.0	71.5	111.1
USSR	24.7	9.7[d]	82.6	107.5[d]
Italy	16.0	7.7	95.6	136.3
Canada	18.1	13.3	64.7	76.4
Mexico	6.1	4.3	93.0	96.2

SOURCES: U.S. Bureau of the Census, 1970 Census of Population, *Subject Reports,* "National Origin and Language" PC(2)-1A, (1973), Table 10; 1950 Census of Population, *Subject Reports,* "Nativity and Parentage," P-E, no. 3A (1954), Tables 4 and 14.

NOTE: The foreign stock comprises the foreign-born population and the native population of foreign or mixed parentage.

[a]White population only.
[b]Includes all other countries in adddition to those listed.
[c]England and Wales only.
[d]Excludes the Ukraine.

TABLE 2.17

Percentage Aged 65 and Over and Males per 100 Females Aged 65 and Over, by Age, for Specified Ancestry Groups: 1980 (numbers in thousands)

Ancestry	Number[a]	All Ages Percent or Ratio	Ages 65 and Over	Ages 65–74	Ages 75–84	Ages 85 and Over
Ages 65 and Over						
English	23,749	100.0	15.3	8.9	4.9	1.5
German	17,943	100.0	15.6	8.8	5.3	1.6
Irish	10,337	100.0	15.6	9.4	5.0	1.3
Italian	6,883	100.0	15.6	10.3	4.2	1.1
Polish	3,806	100.0	18.0	12.4	4.3	1.3
French	3,069	100.0	14.0	8.1	4.6	1.2
Males per 100 Females						
English	12,059	96.9	67.6	79.1	58.2	40.6
German	8,892	101.8	73.5	86.0	64.3	46.3
Irish	5,394	91.6	62.9	73.3	52.8	38.0
Italian	3,452	99.4	79.1	82.8	71.5	75.7
Polish	1,958	94.4	70.3	79.5	54.6	48.1
French	1,601	91.7	62.1	71.6	53.6	39.5

SOURCE: U.S. Bureau of the Census, 1980 Census of Population, *U.S. Summary: General Characteristics,* PC80-1-C1, Table 172.

[a] Total of all ages shown for "percentage aged 65 and over" and females of all ages shown for "males per 100 females."

the Census Bureau in November 1979 as a supplement to the CPS, several ancestry groups had quite high proportions of elderly persons. Among the single ancestry groups with at least 2 million persons reporting, the Polish had the largest proportion of elderly (18 percent), followed by the Irish, German, and Italian (16 percent each) and the English (15 percent). (See Table 2.17.) Several less numerous groups had higher proportions (e.g., Russian and Swedish, 27 percent each). The high proportions of elderly persons of Russian, Swedish, and Polish ancestry are due to their immigration in large numbers into the United States before 1924, the subsequent falling off of the volume of immigration because of restrictive legislation, and the aging of their children. The high proportions of elderly persons of English and Irish ancestry are due primarily to limited immigration in this century (most immigrant ancestors of these groups having arrived in the nineteenth century) and progressively lower fertility.

Among the more numerous multiple-ancestry groups, only "Scottish and other" had a relatively high proportion of elderly (13 percent) compared with the entire U.S. population (11 percent). "English and other," "German and other," and "Irish and other," three numerically important ancestry groups, had relatively low proportions of elderly (10 percent, 6 percent, and 9 percent, respectively), as was the case for all multiple-ancestry groups taken together (8 percent). To explain variations in the percentage of elderly among groups with multiple ancestries, patterns of ethnic intermarriage as well as of fertility and immigration have to be taken into account.

Ability to Speak English

Older persons who speak a language other than English at home are not as likely to speak English, or speak English as well, as younger persons who speak a language other than English at home. In 1980, among persons aged 65 and over in households speaking a language other than English at home, 22 percent did not speak English well or at all (Table

TABLE 2.18

Ability to Speak English, for Persons Aged 65 and Over Who Speak a Language Other than English at Home: 1980 (numbers in thousands)

Age and Ability to Speak English	Speaks a Language Other than English at Home	Speaks Spanish at Home	Speaks Another Language at Home
65 and Over			
Total Persons[a]	3,092	628	2,464
Total Percent	100.0	100.0	100.0
Speaks English			
Very Well or Well	77.8	53.0	84.1
Speaks English			
Not Well	14.4	22.9	12.3
Speaks English			
Not at All	7.7	24.1	3.6
5 and Over			
Total Persons[a]	22,433	10,870	11,562
Total Percent	100.0	100.0	100.0
Speaks English			
Very Well or Well	81.6	75.6	87.3
Speaks English			
Not Well	13.1	16.0	10.4
Speaks English			
Not at All	5.3	8.4	2.4

SOURCE: U.S. Bureau of the Census, 1980 Census of Population, *U.S. Summary: Detailed Characteristics*, PC80-1-D1-A, Table 258.

[a] Persons resident in households who speak a language other than English at home.

TABLE 2.19

Distribution of Persons Aged 65 and Over, by Use of English and by Language, for Persons Who Speak a Language Other than English at Home: 1980
(numbers in thousands)

Language Spoken	Ages 65 and Over	Percentage of All Ages [a]	Percentage of Total Ages 65 and Over	Percentage of Total Non-English Speakers
Total	25,498	11.3	100.0	X
Speak only English at Home	22,225	11.1	87.2	X
Speak a Language Other than English at Home [b]	3,273	12.8	12.8	100.0
French	259	15.3	1.0	7.9
German	424	24.8	1.7	13.0
Italian	515	30.2	2.0	15.7
Polish	281	32.9	1.1	8.6
Spanish	648	5.1	2.5	19.8
Chinese	53	7.7	0.2	1.6
Other	1,094	17.3	4.3	33.4

SOURCE: Based on U.S. Bureau of the Census, 1980 Census of Population, *U.S. Summary: Detailed Characteristics*, PC80-1-D1-A, Table 256.

NOTE: X = not applicable.

[a] Children under age 5 were assigned the language of the parent.
[b] Languages listed have 650,000 or more speakers at all ages.

2.18); among persons aged 5 and over, only 18 percent did not speak English well or at all.

Elderly persons who speak Spanish at home, as do the great majority of elderly Hispanics, are particularly likely to be unable to speak English. Nearly half of them do not speak English well or at all. They make up one fifth of all elderly persons who do not speak English at home (Table 2.19). Elderly persons who speak a language other than Spanish or English at home are far more likely to be effective in the use of English. Only 4 percent of them did not speak English at all (Table 2.18).

These data suggest that a small portion of the elderly household population—two thirds of a million, or 3 percent of the total—may have excessive problems in taking advantage of available services because they have more limited facility in English than the elderly population in general or than younger persons who speak a language other than English at home. Among these, there is a heavy concentration of persons of Hispanic origin. The task of service providers is made correspondingly more difficult, especially when working on behalf of Hispanic elderly.

Summary

Higher death rates of males than of females throughout the age span steadily reduces the initial numerical advantage (about 5 percent) of males at birth. The numbers of men and women cross in the 40s, diverge sharply in the older ages, and by the advanced ages show a massive excess of women. Moreover, the declines in the sex ratio over the age span have tended to grow larger for the more recent birth cohorts reaching old age. The sex ratios at the older ages have been falling steadily since at least 1950, as the gap between age-specific death rates at these and earlier ages for the two sexes has widened. The influence of immigration on the sex balance of the population is generally minor now, except at the extreme old ages, where in 1985 we see the residual effect of the large, mainly male immigration of the pre-1924 years. The demographic, social, and economic consequences of low sex ratios at the older ages are numerous, pervasive, and profound.

The sex balance among the black population is affected by the low sex ratio of births (about 103), the wide gap between male and female death rates, and the new net immigration from Africa and the Caribbean. The reported figures are also depressed by a relatively large omission of young-adult and middle-aged black males from the census counts. Black sex ratios at most ages are low compared with those of whites, but the two sets of sex ratios converge and then cross at about age 75. Nevertheless, the sex balance of blacks, like that of whites, falls to extremely low levels at the older ages. By ages 85 and over, the sex ratio of blacks is only 50; that is, only one third of the population is male.

Increasingly lower female mortality has contributed to a much more rapid growth of the female population aged 65 and over than of the male population at those ages. As a result, the share of the total female population that is aged 65 and over (14 percent in 1985) greatly exceeds the share of males aged 65 and over (10 percent). The difference will increase from 4 percentage points in 1985 to 5 percentage points in 2010 according to the Census Bureau's middle series of projections. The excess of females will then amount to a huge 8 million.

The proportion of the elderly among whites (12 percent) is well above that among blacks (8 percent), who, in turn, have a larger proportion of elderly than Asian and Pacific Islanders, American Indians, and Hispanics. Higher fertility and lower adult survival to age 65 among blacks account for the white-black difference. The shares of elderly for the race/ethnic groups other than American Indians have been rising since at least 1950. The problems of the elderly among these groups arise not from their great shares or numbers of elders, but from their greater poverty (blacks, Hispanics, American Indians), geographic isolation (American Indians), recency of immigration (Asian and Pacific Islanders), or cultural/linguistic separateness (especially Hispanics).

Blacks constitute a majority of the 3.7 million nonwhite and Hispanic population, followed by Hispanics, Asian and Pacific Islanders, and American Indians. The vast majority of elderly Hispanics, Asian and Pacific Islanders, and blacks live in urban areas. Most elderly blacks who are urban dwellers live in the North, and the bulk of the few elderly rural blacks live in the South.

Most indexes of population turnover for the elderly population reflect a greater turnover for elderly men than women and for elderly blacks than whites. Differences in death rates at the older ages account for most of the difference in turnover between the sexes, but differences in the ratios of new entries to the population account for nearly all the difference in turnover between the races.

If the age of entry into old age is set as the age at which life expectancy is exactly 15 years, men and blacks reach old age at an earlier point in the life cycle than women and whites, respectively. The sex difference is pronounced, but the race difference is small.

Elderly dependency ratios for women, which relate the number of elderly women to the total population of working age, are much higher than for men, since such a large share of the elderly are women. Dependency ratios for each sex have followed the same general course upward over the last several decades, but the ratios for females have grown more rapidly than those for males. They are expected to continue a slow, steady climb until about 2010, when they will start to leap upward as a result of the accession of the baby-boom cohorts to age 65. Elderly dependency ratios for blacks, which relate the number of elderly blacks to the total population of working age, are relatively low since blacks constitute only a modest share of the elderly population. The black dependency ratio will follow a course similar to that of whites, though it is expected to rise more rapidly. Like the white dependency ratio, the black dependency ratio will rise sharply after 2010, when the baby-boom cohorts begin to reach age 65.

Higher proportions of the elderly than of younger age groups have foreign backgrounds, typically eastern and southern European, and such persons tend to have limited use of English. A large share of elderly Hispanics also do not speak English well or at all. This fact suggests the need for recognizing cultural differences among elderly clients and for outreach programs in the provision of services to them. The prospects are for a sharp increase in the share of the elderly who belong to racial minorities or are of Hispanic origin. In 1985 1 in 8 persons aged 65 and over was other than white-non-Hispanic, but in 2020 it is expected that about 1 in 4 persons aged 65 and over will be in this group. The emphasis in programs for the elderly will clearly need to shift.

Appendix 2A. Accuracy of Census Counts of the Older Population for Age, Sex, and Race Groups

According to estimates of net census errors (net coverage errors plus net age reporting errors) in the 1980 census prepared at the Census Bureau by the method of demographic analysis, the net errors for males and females aged 65 and over as a whole were near zero (Table 2A.1). Substantial net undercounts—about 3 to 4 percent—occurred for women aged 65 and over in each of the three previous censuses, while net undercounts for men in this age range amounted to only 1 or 2 percent. Some of the component ages showed somewhat larger net undercounts; for example, those for women aged 80 and over in 1980 and 75 and over in 1970 and 1960 were of the order of 4 to 5 percent.

Net census errors for blacks were typically larger than for all races combined and for whites. Blacks aged 65 and over as a whole showed a small net overcount in 1980 (0.8 percent). All the censuses from 1950 to 1980 showed a net overcount at ages 65–69 or 65–74 and a net undercount at ages 55–59 and 60–64, suggesting age misreporting out of the younger ages into the older ages. In 1980 the net overcounts extended from ages 65–69 to 75–79, and the net undercounts from ages 55–59 to 60–64, and 80–84 to 85 and over, where the deficits were considerable. The net errors for older blacks are small or moderate compared with the massive errors for young adult and middle-aged black males, reaching 16 to 18 percent at ages 35–54. There has been a general tendency for the quality of the data for older blacks, both males and females, to improve from one census to another.

Adjustment of the population counts in 1980 for net census errors hardly modifies the level and pattern of the sex ratios of the older population for all races combined or for whites, but has a pronounced effect on the level and pattern of the sex ratios for blacks in these ages (Table 2A.2). Adjustment of the census data for all races combined reduces the sex ratio for ages 65 and over as a whole by only 0.3 per 100 females and modifies the sex ratios for most five-year age groups 55 and over by only small amounts. When the data for blacks are adjusted, however, the sex ratios assume a sharper downward slope with increasing age, as a result of an upward adjustment of 8 points at ages 55–59 and a downward adjustment of 5 points at ages 85 and over (Figure 2A.1). The sex ratio for the total aged 65 and over is shifted downward by only 0.8 per 100 females.

TABLE 2A.1

Estimated Net Census Percent Errors for the Population Aged 55 and Over, by Age, Sex, and Race: 1950–1980

Year and Age	All Classes			Black		
	Both Sexes	Male	Female	Both Sexes	Male	Female
1980						
All Ages	-1.4	-2.4	-0.4	-5.9	-8.8	-3.1
55–59	-1.2	-3.1	+0.6	-6.1	-10.8	-1.8
60–64	-0.8	-2.1	+0.4	-3.2	-6.7	-0.4
65–69	+1.3	+0.5	+1.9	+5.0	+2.9	+6.6
70–74	+0.4	+0.3	+0.5	+2.2	+1.8	+2.4
75–79	+0.1	+0.5	-0.1	+2.6	+4.4	+1.4
80–84	-4.1	-2.6	-4.8	-12.2	-8.2	-14.4
85 and Over	-4.6	-2.1	-5.6	-8.9	-2.7	-11.7
65 and Over	-0.3	—	-0.5	+0.8	+1.4	+0.3
75 and Over	-2.2	-0.9	-2.9	-4.3	-0.6	-6.4
1970						
All Ages	-2.9	-3.7	-2.2	-8.0	-10.6	-5.6
55–59	-3.5	-3.9	-3.2	-8.8	-10.2	-7.5
60–64	-2.7	-2.7	-2.7	-7.4	-8.9	-6.2
65–69	-1.4	-1.5	-1.3	+3.6	+1.9	+4.9
70–74	-2.0	-1.1	-2.7	-3.3	-1.6	-4.7
75 and Over	-4.4	-2.8	-5.4	-3.9	+1.2	-7.2
65 and Over	-2.7	-1.8	-3.3	-0.8	+0.7	-1.9

TABLE 2A.1 (continued)

Year and Age	All Classes			Black		
	Both Sexes	Male	Female	Both Sexes	Male	Female
1960						
All Ages	-3.3	-3.8	-2.8	-8.3	-10.4	-6.2
55–59	-2.8	-1.4	-4.1	-10.6	-8.6	-12.4
60–64	-5.5	-4.2	-6.7	-16.8	-16.5	-17.1
65–69	-2.9	-1.8	-3.8	+2.3	+1.6	+3.0
70–74	-0.4	+1.8	-2.1	+6.0	+10.1	+4.3
75 and Over	-3.8	-1.7	-5.3	+7.4	+11.0	+4.6
65 and Over	-2.5	-0.7	-3.9	+5.1	+6.6	+3.8
1950						
All Ages	-4.4	-4.8	-4.1	-9.6	-11.6	-7.6
55–59	-8.7	-7.4	-9.9	-20.5	-18.3	-22.8
60–64	-7.9	-6.4	-9.4	-19.1	-17.0	-21.0
65 and Over	-2.7	-1.7	-3.6	+16.0	+14.4	+17.4

SOURCES: U.S. Bureau of the Census, "The Coverage of Population in the 1980 Census," by R. E. Fay, J. S. Passel, and J. G. Robinson, *Evaluation and Research Reports*, series PHC80-E4 (1988); and unpublished tabulations.

NOTES: Minus sign denotes net census undercount and plus sign denotes net census overcount. Dash denotes that figure rounds to 0.0.

TABLE 2A.2

Comparison of "Enumerated" and Adjusted Sex Ratios for the Population Aged 55 and Over, by Age and Race: 1980 and 1950

Year and Age	All Classes			Black		
	Adjusted	Enumerated	Excess or Deficit	Adjusted	Enumerated	Excess or Deficit
1980						
All Ages	96.4	94.5	−1.9	95.2	89.6	−5.5
55–59	92.8	89.4	−3.4	90.1	81.8	−8.3
60–64	88.4	86.2	−2.2	84.6	79.2	−5.4
65–69	81.1	80.0	−1.1	77.2	74.5	−2.7
70–74	72.4	72.3	−0.1	71.5	71.1	−0.4
75–79	62.3	62.7	+0.4	63.2	65.1	+1.9
80–84	52.0	53.2	+1.2	56.0	60.0	+4.0
85 and Over	42.2	43.7	+1.6	45.4	50.0	+4.6
65 and Over	67.3	67.6	+0.3	67.5	68.3	+0.8
1950						
All Ages	99.5	98.8	−0.8	98.7	94.3	−4.4
55–59	98.0	100.8	+2.7	99.4	105.2	+5.8
60–64	97.4	100.7	+3.3	96.3	101.2	+4.9
65 and Over	88.0	89.7	+1.7	94.7	92.3	−2.4

SOURCES: U.S. Bureau of the Census, "The Coverage of Population in the 1980 Census," by R. E. Fay, J. S. Passel, and J. G. Robinson, *Evaluation and Research Reports*, series PHC80-E (1988); and unpublished tabulations.

NOTE: Males per 100 females.

98

FIGURE 2A.1

Comparison of "Enumerated" and Adjusted Sex Ratios for the Total and Black Populations, by Age: 1980

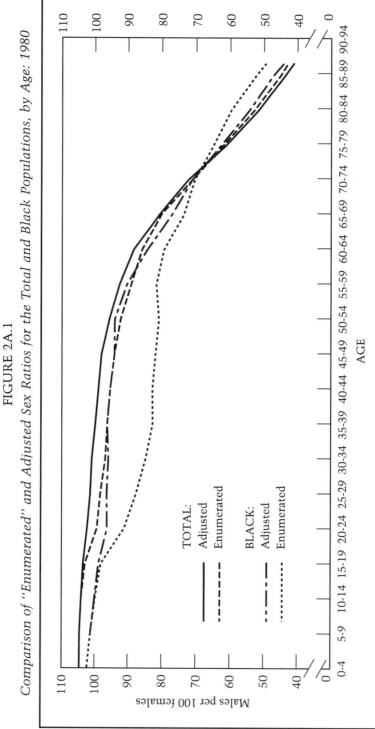

SOURCE: U.S. Bureau of the Census, "The Coverage of Population in the 1980 Census," by R. E. Fay, J. S. Passel, and J. G. Robinson, *Evaluation and Research Reports*, series PHC80-E (1988).

NOTES: Points for five-year age groups are plotted over the mark for the five-year age group. The point for ages 85 and over is plotted at age 88.8.

3

GEOGRAPHIC DISTRIBUTION AND RESIDENTIAL MOBILITY

State and County Variations in Numbers and Proportions

State Variations

ELDERLY persons tend to be most numerous in the most populous states and in Florida. In 1985, California and New York, together with Florida, had the largest numbers of people aged 65 and over, with more than 2 million each (Table 3.1), followed by Pennsylvania, Texas, Illinois, Ohio, and Michigan. Each of these five states also has over 1 million people aged 65 and over. Together these eight states account for 49 percent of the elderly population in the United States. This proportion is close to the proportion which the total population of these eight states, taken as a group, makes up of the national total (48 percent).

The number of persons aged 65 and over increased in every state between April 1, 1970, and July 1, 1985.[1] Florida added 1,016,000, California, 974,000, and Texas, 550,000. Since California's elderly population in 1970 was nearly twice as great as that of Florida, its growth rate

[1]The amounts and rates of population growth for states, 1970–1980 and 1970–1985 are affected by the apparently much greater completeness of coverage of the population in the 1980 census than the 1970 census.

TABLE 3.1

Change in the Population Aged 65 and Over, by State: 1960–2000
(population as of April 1, 1960, 1970, and 1980, and July 1, 1985 and 2000)

Region, Division, and State	Population (in thousands)				Percent Increase[a]		
	1970	1980	1985	2000	1960–1970	1970–1985	1985–2000
United States	19,972	25,549	28,540	34,882	20.6	42.9	22.6
Regions							
Northeast	5,176	6,072	6,584	7,348	15.1	27.2	11.6
Midwest[b]	5,703	6,692	7,285	7,914	12.3	27.7	8.6
South	6,014	8,488	9,642	12,809	31.2	60.3	32.8
West	3,060	4,298	5,029	6,812	28.3	64.3	35.5
Northeast							
New England	1,264	1,520	1,668	1,883	12.7	32.0	12.9
Middle Atlantic	3,911	4,551	4,916	5,466	15.8	25.7	11.2
Midwest[b]							
East North Central	3,793	4,493	4,942	5,400	13.0	30.3	9.3
West North Central	1,909	2,199	2,343	2,513	11.0	22.7	7.3
South							
South Atlantic	2,922	4,367	5,097	7,185	39.2	74.4	41.0
East South Central	1,263	1,657	1,815	2,148	20.1	43.7	18.3
West South Central	1,828	2,464	2,730	3,478	27.8	49.3	27.4
West							
Mountain	692	1,061	1,298	1,815	31.3	90.3	39.8
Pacific	2,389	3,237	3,740	4,995	27.5	56.6	33.6
New England							
Maine	114	141	154	172	7.5	35.1	11.7
New Hampshire	78	103	116	149	11.7	48.7	28.4
Vermont	47	58	63	71	6.8	34.0	12.7
Massachusetts	633	727	782	849	11.2	23.5	8.6

TABLE 3.1 (continued)

Region, Division, and State	Population (in thousands)				Percent Increase[a]		
	1970	1980	1985	2000	1960–1970	1970–1985	1985–2000
Rhode Island	104	127	139	154	15.6	33.7	10.8
Connecticut	286	365	413	485	17.0	44.1	17.4
Middle Atlantic							
New York	1,951	2,161	2,258	2,472	16.2	15.7	9.5
New Jersey	696	860	968	1,175	24.5	39.1	21.4
Pennsylvania	1,267	1,531	1,700	1,819	12.7	34.2	7.0
East North Central							
Ohio	993	1,169	1,296	1,441	11.3	30.5	11.2
Indiana	492	585	645	717	10.8	31.1	11.2
Illinois	1,089	1,262	1,366	1,459	12.2	25.4	6.8
Michigan	749	912	1,019	1,127	18.0	36.0	10.6
Wisconsin	471	564	616	656	17.4	30.8	6.5
West North Central							
Minnesota	407	480	520	579	15.5	27.8	11.3
Iowa	349	388	411	387	6.7	17.8	-5.8
Missouri	558	648	686	764	11.5	22.9	11.4
North Dakota	66	80	87	86	11.9	31.8	-1.1
South Dakota	80	91	97	102	11.1	21.2	5.2
Nebraska	183	206	216	227	12.2	18.0	5.1
Kansas	265	306	326	358	10.8	23.0	9.8
South Atlantic							
Delaware	44	59	70	90	22.2	59.1	28.6
Maryland	298	396	459	608	32.2	54.0	32.5
District of Columbia	70	74	76	83	1.9	8.6	9.2
Virginia	364	505	588	790	26.6	61.5	34.4
West Virginia	194	238	257	255	12.1	32.5	-0.8
North Carolina	412	603	708	991	32.7	71.8	40.0
South Carolina	190	287	343	456	26.5	80.5	32.9
Georgia	365	517	593	828	26.1	62.5	39.6
Florida	985	1,688	2,003	3,069	78.2	103.4	53.2

TABLE 3.1 (continued)

Region, Division, and State	Population (in thousands)				Percent Increase[a]		
	1970	1980	1985	2000	1960–1970	1970–1985	1985–2000
East South Central							
Kentucky	336	410	442	494	15.4	31.5	11.8
Tennessee	382	518	577	710	24.3	51.0	23.1
Alabama	324	440	486	584	24.9	50.0	20.2
Mississippi	221	289	310	361	16.8	40.3	16.5
West South Central							
Arkansas	237	312	338	386	22.7	42.6	14.2
Louisiana	305	404	443	518	26.9	45.2	16.9
Oklahoma	299	376	405	449	20.5	35.5	10.9
Texas	988	1,371	1,543	2,125	33.2	56.2	37.7
Mountain							
Montana	68	85	97	102	6.2	42.6	5.2
Idaho	67	94	109	121	17.2	62.7	11.0
Wyoming	30	37	42	41	15.4	40.0	−2.4
Colorado	187	247	286	388	19.0	52.9	35.7
New Mexico	70	116	139	203	39.2	98.6	46.0
Arizona	161	307	392	655	78.9	143.5	67.1
Utah	77	109	130	155	30.0	68.8	19.2
Nevada	31	66	93	140	72.2	200.0	50.5
Pacific							
Washington	320	432	505	596	15.4	57.8	18.0
Oregon	226	303	353	372	23.4	56.2	5.4
California	1,792	2,414	2,768	3,822	30.9	54.5	38.1
Alaska	7	12	17	46	36.0	142.9	170.6
Hawaii	44	76	99	177	51.7	125.0	78.8

SOURCES: U.S. Bureau of the Census, Current Population Reports, series P-25, no. 1024 (May 1988), and no. 1017 (October 1988); 1970 Census of Population, U.S. Summary: General Population Characteristics, PC[1]-B1, Table 62.

[a] Minus sign denotes a decrease.
[b] Formerly the North Central region.

in the 1970–1985 period was far smaller (54 percent) than Florida's (103 percent). All of the states with high growth rates of the elderly are in the South or West.[2] Very rapid growth of elderly persons between 1970 and 1985 occurred in Arizona, Nevada, New Mexico, South Carolina, Alaska, and Hawaii, as well as Florida. Each of these states experienced a gain of over 75 percent in its population aged 65 and over in the 1970–1985 period compared with 43 percent for the entire country. Other states with high growth rates (over 55 percent) in the 1970–1985 period were Delaware, Texas, Georgia, North Carolina, Utah, Virginia, Idaho, Washington, and Oregon—all in the South or West. Slow growth of the elderly (under 25 percent) was experienced by Massachusetts, New York, Iowa, Missouri, South Dakota, Nebraska, Kansas—all in the Northeast region or the West North Central Division—and the District of Columbia. All four geographic divisions in the North had growth rates of the elderly during the 1970–1985 period well below the national average, and all five divisions of the South and West, especially the South Atlantic Division and the Mountain Division, had growth rates above the national average.

The geographic patterns of the changes in the elderly population were roughly similar in the 1970–1985 period, the 1960–1970 period, and the 1950–1960 period. In the 1960s also, the South, especially the South Atlantic states, and the West had growth rates well above the national average (21 percent), and the Northeast and Midwest[3] had growth rates well below the national average. Many of the same states as later showed relatively high growth rates of the elderly in the 1960s (above 30 percent): Maryland, North Carolina, Florida, Texas, New Mexico, Arizona, Nevada, California, Alaska, and Hawaii. Many of the same states as later showed relatively low growth rates in the 1960s (below 12 percent): Maine, Vermont, District of Columbia, Massachusetts, Iowa, Indiana, Illinois, Missouri, South Dakota, and Kansas.

The current population of most states may be described as mature if we employ 10.0 percent or more elderly persons as the measure of maturity. All but 10 states met this condition in 1985. In that year the share of elderly persons in the states varied from 3.3 percent (Alaska) to 17.6 percent (Florida), but the figures for half of the states fell within one percentage point of the national average (12.0 percent). Several midwestern states, constituting much of the midwestern farm belt, namely, Iowa, Nebraska, South Dakota, and Missouri, as well as Florida, Rhode Island, Pennsylvania, and Arkansas, showed percentages of elderly per-

---

[2]See Table 3.1 for the definition of each of the geographic divisions and regions in terms of states.

[3]The North Central region has been renamed the Midwest by the Census Bureau. The Far West continues to be referred to as the West.

sons of 13.5 percent or more in 1985 (Table 3.2 and Figure 3.1). Heavy outmigration of young persons, relatively low fertility, and, for Florida in particular, heavy inmigration of older persons are the principal factors that have contributed separately or jointly to the relatively large proportions of older persons in these states. The effect of the heavy immigration from abroad in the years prior to World War I has by now almost completely dissipated except in a few states (e.g., New York, Connecticut, and, indirectly, Florida). Attracted by the favorable climate, many elderly, especially the more affluent, have been migrating to retirement homes in Florida and Arizona, but they have also relocated in various remote communities of the North, such as in the northern parts of Maine, Wisconsin, and Michigan.

States with relatively low proportions (under 10.5 percent) of elderly persons in 1985 are located mainly in the South and West. The list includes several states that have relatively high fertility (i.e., Louisiana, South Carolina, Georgia, New Mexico, Utah, and Wyoming) and several states that have been experiencing a large net inmigration of persons under age 65 (i.e., Texas, Wyoming, Nevada, and Colorado), as well as Maryland, Virginia, California, and the outlying states of Alaska and Hawaii.

The aging of the nation's population since 1950 is reflected in the record of nearly all the states. With the exception of Alaska, all the states show a net rise in the proportion of elderly persons between 1950 and 1985, and in all but five states the rise was continuous. Several states mirrored the amount of increase in the proportion aged 65 and over shown by the United States as a whole in the last few decades. One fifth of the states showed increases from 3.5 to 4.4 percentage points between 1950 and 1985, near the U.S. figure of 3.8. Eight states aged very slowly, showing increases of less than 2.5 percentage points, and eight aged very rapidly, showing increases in excess of 5.5 percentage points.

Change in Percent: 1950–1985	Number of States
Total	51[a]
Under 2.5	8
2.5–3.4	15
3.5–4.4	10
4.5–5.4	10[a]
5.5 and Over	8

[a]Includes the District of Columbia.

TABLE 3.2

Percentage Aged 65 and Over and 75 and Over, by State: 1950–2000

| Region, Division, and State | Ages 65 and Over | | | | | Ages 75 and Over | | | | | |
| | Percentage of Total | | | | Change in Percent[a] | Percentage of Total | | | As Percentage of Ages 65 and Over | | |
	1950	1970	1985	2000	1950–1985	1950	1985	2000	1950	1985	2000
United States	8.2	9.9	12.0	13.1	3.8	2.6	4.8	6.5	31	40	50
Northeast	8.7	10.6	13.2	14.8	4.5	2.7	5.4	7.5	31	41	51
New England	9.7	10.7	13.2	14.3	3.5	3.3	5.5	7.4	34	42	51
Maine	10.2	11.6	13.1	13.5	2.9	3.7	5.8	6.8	36	44	50
New Hampshire	10.8	10.6	11.6	11.7	0.8	3.9	4.8	5.6	36	41	48
Vermont	10.5	10.7	11.8	12.0	1.3	3.8	5.0	5.9	37	43	49
Massachusetts	10.0	11.2	13.4	14.7	3.5	3.3	5.7	7.6	33	42	52
Rhode Island	8.9	11.0	14.4	15.9	5.5	2.9	6.0	8.5	32	42	53
Connecticut	8.9	9.5	13.0	15.2	4.2	2.8	5.2	7.9	32	42	52
Middle Atlantic	8.4	10.6	13.2	14.9	4.8	2.6	5.3	7.7	30	40	52
New York	8.5	10.9	12.7	13.9	4.2	2.5	5.3	7.0	30	42	50
New Jersey	8.1	9.4	12.6	14.5	4.5	2.5	4.9	7.3	30	39	50
Pennsylvania	8.4	10.8	14.3	16.3	5.9	2.6	5.6	8.5	31	39	52
Midwest[b]	8.9	10.1	12.3	13.0	3.4	2.9	5.2	6.6	33	42	51
East North Central	9.5	9.5	11.9	12.9	3.4	2.7	4.8	6.5	32	40	51
Ohio	8.9	9.4	12.1	13.9	3.1	2.9	4.8	6.5	32	40	51
Indiana	9.1	9.5	11.7	13.2	2.6	3.1	4.8	6.7	33	41	51
Illinois	8.7	9.8	11.9	12.3	2.2	2.7	4.8	6.3	31	41	51
Michigan	7.3	8.5	11.2	12.2	4.0	2.2	4.4	6.1	31	39	50
Wisconsin	9.0	10.7	12.9	12.9	3.9	3.0	5.5	6.4	33	43	50
West North Central	9.8	11.7	13.4	13.1	3.6	2.4	6.0	6.7	24	45	51
Minnesota	9.0	10.7	12.4	12.0	3.4	3.0	5.6	6.1	33	45	51
Iowa	10.4	12.4	14.3	13.6	3.9	3.7	6.5	7.1	35	45	52
Missouri	10.3	12.0	12.7	14.4	3.4	3.5	6.0	7.2	34	44	50
North Dakota	7.8	10.7	13.7	11.8	4.9	2.4	5.5	6.0	31	44	50
South Dakota	8.5	12.1	13.5	13.4	5.2	2.7	6.2	7.0	32	45	52
Nebraska	9.8	12.4	13.3	13.0	3.7	3.4	6.3	6.6	34	47	51
Kansas	10.2	11.8	13.3	13.4	3.1	3.5	6.0	6.8	35	45	51

TABLE 3.2 (continued)

Region, Division, and State	Ages 65 and Over					Ages 75 and Over					
	Percentage of Total				Change in Percent[a]	Percentage of Total			As Percentage of Ages 65 and Over		
	1950	1970	1985	2000	1950–1985	1950	1985	2000	1950	1985	2000
South	6.9	9.6	11.8	13.8	4.9	2.1	4.7	6.6	30	40	48
South Atlantic	6.6	9.6	12.7	15.9	6.1	2.0	4.9	7.7	30	39	48
Delaware	8.3	8.8	11.3	14.8	3.0	2.7	4.3	7.6	33	39	51
Maryland	7.0	7.6	10.4	12.7	3.4	2.2	4.0	6.4	32	38	50
District of Columbia	7.0	9.4	12.1	13.8	5.1	2.2	4.8	6.4	31	40	46
Virginia	6.5	7.9	10.3	11.9	3.8	2.0	3.9	5.8	31	38	49
West Virginia	6.9	11.1	12.3	13.7	6.4	2.1	5.3	7.2	31	40	52
North Carolina	5.5	8.1	11.3	14.4	5.8	1.6	4.3	7.1	29	38	49
South Carolina	5.4	7.4	10.2	13.0	4.8	1.5	3.7	6.2	27	36	48
Georgia	6.4	8.0	9.4	11.8	3.0	1.8	3.8	5.8	29	38	49
Florida	8.6	14.6	17.6	21.5	9.0	2.5	7.1	10.1	30	40	47
East South Central	7.2	8.9	12.0	13.0	4.8	2.2	4.9	6.3	31	41	49
Kentucky	8.0	10.5	11.9	12.4	3.9	2.6	4.9	6.1	33	41	49
Tennessee	8.1	9.8	12.1	13.3	5.0	2.2	4.9	6.5	31	40	49
Alabama	6.5	9.5	12.1	13.6	5.6	1.9	4.8	6.5	29	40	48
Mississippi	7.8	10.1	11.9	12.6	4.8	2.1	4.9	6.0	30	41	48
West South Central	7.1	9.5	10.3	10.8	3.2	2.2	4.2	5.2	31	41	48
Arkansas	7.8	12.3	14.3	14.8	6.5	2.4	5.9	7.1	30	41	48
Louisiana	6.6	8.5	9.8	11.0	3.2	1.9	3.8	5.3	29	39	48
Oklahoma	8.7	11.7	12.3	12.4	3.6	2.9	5.3	6.1	33	43	49
Texas	6.7	8.9	9.4	9.9	2.7	2.1	3.8	4.7	31	40	48
West	8.0	8.9	10.5	11.0	2.5	2.5	4.1	5.4	31	39	49
Mountain	7.1	8.4	10.1	10.7	3.0	2.2	3.8	5.1	31	38	48
Montana	8.6	9.9	11.9	10.9	3.2	2.5	4.1	5.5	29	39	50

TABLE 3.2 (continued)

Region, Division, and State	Ages 65 and Over					Ages 75 and Over					
	Percentage of Total				Change in Percent[a]	Percentage of Total			As Percentage of Ages 65 and Over		
	1950	1970	1985	2000	1950–1985	1950	1985	2000	1950	1985	2000
Idaho	7.4	9.5	10.8	11.6	3.4	2.2	4.2	5.8	30	39	50
Wyoming	6.3	9.1	8.3	8.4	2.0	1.8	3.4	4.1	29	41	49
Colorado	8.7	8.5	8.8	8.5	0.1	2.9	3.6	3.9	33	40	46
New Mexico	4.9	6.9	9.6	12.1	4.7	1.5	3.7	6.1	31	38	50
Arizona	5.9	9.1	12.3	15.1	6.4	1.7	4.5	7.3	29	37	48
Utah	6.2	7.3	7.9	6.4	1.7	1.9	3.1	2.9	31	39	45
Nevada	6.9	6.3	9.9	12.5	3.1	1.9	3.1	6.0	28	31	48
Pacific	8.4	9.1	10.7	11.1	2.3	2.6	4.2	5.6	31	40	50
Washington	8.9	9.4	11.5	10.7	2.6	2.7	4.5	5.4	31	40	50
Oregon	8.7	10.8	13.2	10.9	4.4	2.7	5.3	5.5	31	40	50
California	8.5	9.0	10.5	11.4	2.0	2.6	4.2	5.7	31	40	50
Alaska	3.7	2.3	3.3	3.9	-0.4	1.0	1.0	1.8	28	29	46
Hawaii	4.1	5.7	9.4	9.9	5.3	1.2	3.4	4.8	29	36	48

SOURCES: U.S. Bureau of the Census, *Current Population Reports*, series P-25, no. 1024 (May 1988), and no. 1017 (October 1988); 1950 Census of Population, 1970, *U.S. Summary: General Population Characteristics*, PC(1)-B1.

[a] Difference in percentage points between percentage in 1985 and percentage in 1950.
[b] Formerly the North Central region.

FIGURE 3.1

Percentage Aged 65 and Over of the Total Population of States: 1985

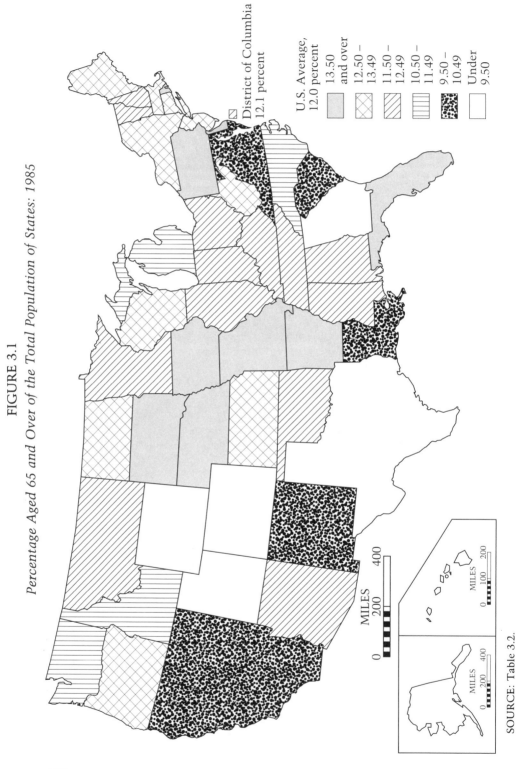

SOURCE: Table 3.2.

Special interest lies in the most rapid gainers: Florida, Arkansas, Rhode Island, Arizona, Pennsylvania, North Carolina, Alabama, and West Virginia. Many of the rapid gainers had below-U.S.-average proportions aged 65 and over in 1950 and above-U.S.-average proportions in 1985. The variation in the growth of the shares of elderly for states between 1950 and 1985 increased the similarity in the shares of elderly persons among the states in this period. In 1985 the relative deviation from the national average proportion was only three quarters as great as in 1950.

The more rapid national growth of the population aged 75 and over than of the population aged 65 and over and the even more rapid growth of the population aged 85 and over between 1970 and 1985 are reflected in the individual regions, divisions, and states, with the possible exception of the Mountain and Pacific states (Table 3.3). Without exception, the elderly population of every state has been aging and is expected to continue aging. Every state showed a net rise in the share which the 75-and-over group constituted of the 65-and-over group between 1950 and 1985, and is expected to show a further rise to 2000 (Table 3.2). By 1985 seven states had in excess of one half million persons aged 75 and over and in excess of 100,000 persons 85 and over (Table 3.3).

County Variations

Counties show a much wider variation in the proportion of elderly persons than states. Many counties with extremely high proportions of persons aged 65 and over may be found in the West North Central Division and the West South Central Division. In over half of the 619 counties in the West North Central Division and in over two fifths of the 470 counties in the West South Central Division, 15 percent or more of the total population was aged 65 and over in 1980 (the U.S. average being 11.3 percent). Over one quarter of the counties in Kansas and over one fifth of the counties in Texas and Missouri had proportions aged 65 and over of 20 percent or more in 1980. In six midwestern and southwestern states (Arkansas, Iowa, Missouri, Nebraska, Kansas, and Oklahoma), approximately half or more of the counties had proportions in excess of 20 percent aged 60 and over (the U.S. average being 15.7 percent). These are usually small counties, that is, counties with no place over 25,000.

Florida is a special case among the states. It is exceptional not only for having a uniquely high share of elderly persons, but also for having more counties than any other state with over one quarter of the population aged 65 and over. In 1980, over one fifth of the counties in Florida had proportions aged 65 and over of 20 percent or more, eight counties

TABLE 3.3

Change in the Population Aged 75 and Over, 1970–2000, and in the Population Aged 85 and Over, 1970–1985, by State (population as of April 1, 1970, and July 1, 1985 and 2000)

Region, Division, and State	Ages 75 and Over					Ages 85 and Over	
	Population (in thousands)			Percent Increase		Population (in thousands), 1985	Percent Increase, 1970–1985
	1970	1985	2000	1970–1985	1985–2000		
United States	7,631	11,531	16,639	51	44	2,695	78
Regions							
Northeast	1,962	2,679	3,567	37	33	641	71
Midwest[a]	2,277	3,051	3,899	34	28	755	66
South	2,194	3,831	5,965	75	56	838	93
West	1,199	1,970	3,209	64	63	461	88
Northeast							
New England	506	696	940	38	35	176	72
Middle Atlantic	1,455	1,983	2,628	36	33	465	70
Midwest[a]							
East North Central	1,485	2,005	2,630	35	31	484	66
West North Central	793	1,047	1,268	32	21	272	66
South							
South Atlantic	1,043	1,983	3,363	90	70	427	115
East South Central	471	736	1,009	56	37	163	68
West South Central	679	1,112	1,594	64	43	248	78
West							
Mountain	264	490	838	86	71	108	105
Pacific	934	1,480	2,370	58	60	353	83
New England							
Maine	47	66	85	40	29	17	70
New Hampshire	31	48	70	55	46	12	83
Vermont	19	27	35	42	30	7	63
Massachusetts	255	330	432	29	31	85	65
Rhode Island	40	58	77	45	33	14	83
Connecticut	114	166	240	46	45	42	85

TABLE 3.3 (continued)

Region, Division, and State	Ages 75 and Over					Ages 85 and Over	
	Population (in thousands)			Percent Increase		Population (in thousands), 1985	Percent Increase, 1970–1985
	1970	1985	2000	1970–1985	1985–2000		
Middle Atlantic							
New York	716	939	1,175	31	25	226	69
New Jersey	257	374	549	46	47	86	80
Pennsylvania	482	670	904	39	35	153	67
East North Central							
Ohio	393	519	702	32	35	125	60
Indiana	195	265	349	36	32	64	59
Illinois	421	556	707	32	27	133	64
Michigan	286	401	544	40	36	95	75
Wisconsin	189	264	328	40	24	66	76
West North Central							
Minnesota	169	232	292	37	26	62	85
Iowa	150	186	209	24	12	51	61
Missouri	223	299	374	34	25	71	55
North Dakota	27	38	44	41	16	10	69
South Dakota	34	44	53	29	20	12	80
Nebraska	78	100	116	28	16	27	66
Kansas	112	147	181	31	23	38	61
South Atlantic							
Delaware	17	27	46	59	70	7	96
Maryland	108	176	279	63	59	41	95
District of Columbia	26	30	39	15	30	8	42
Virginia	133	225	361	69	60	52	96
West Virginia	74	103	127	39	23	23	56
North Carolina	146	269	453	84	68	59	104
South Carolina	66	123	211	86	72	26	102
Georgia	132	227	369	72	63	50	83
Florida	343	802	1,479	134	84	161	179

TABLE 3.3 (continued)

Region, Division, and State	Ages 75 and Over Population (in thousands) 1970	1985	2000	Percent Increase 1970–1985	1985–2000	Ages 85 and Over Population (in thousands), 1985	Percent Increase, 1970–1985
East South Central							
Kentucky	130	182	235	40	29	42	56
Tennessee	142	233	333	64	43	51	77
Alabama	118	194	272	64	40	42	71
Mississippi	81	128	171	58	34	28	64
West South Central							
Arkansas	91	140	187	54	34	30	61
Louisiana	107	173	236	62	36	39	75
Oklahoma	117	174	215	49	24	40	63
Texas	364	625	956	72	53	139	88
Mountain							
Montana	30	38	51	27	34	9	52
Idaho	28	43	61	54	42	10	74
Wyoming	12	17	20	40	18	4	84
Colorado	76	115	179	51	56	29	78
New Mexico	26	53	91	104	72	11	127
Arizona	54	144	298	167	107	28	195
Utah	29	51	79	76	55	11	82
Nevada	10	29	59	190	103	5	184
Pacific							
Washington	131	199	295	52	48	49	77
Oregon	91	142	193	56	36	34	84
California	696	1,098	1,789	58	63	260	83
Alaska	2	5	11	150	120	1	36
Hawaii	15	36	84	140	133	8	161

SOURCES: U.S. Bureau of the Census, *Current Population Reports*, series P-25, no. 1024 (May 1988), Tables 5 and 6, and no. 1017 (October 1988), Table 5; and 1970 Census of Population, *U.S. Summary: General Population Characteristics*, PC(1)-B1.

aFormerly the North Central region.

had 25 percent or more, and three counties had 30 percent or more (Charlotte, 34 percent; Pasco, 31 percent; and Sarasota, 30 percent). As is well known, Florida is the destination of large numbers of migrants from the North who have retired and have established new permanent year-round or seasonal residences in the retirement communities of the state.

The 100 counties in the United States with the largest percentages of persons aged 65 and over in 1980 (all with 22.0 percent or more) were distributed as follows:

State	Total	25.0 or More	23.0–24.9	Under 23.0
Total	100	25	37	38
Florida	14	8	3	3
Texas	32	7	14	11
Kansas	19	3	7	9
Missouri	12	1	5	6
Nebraska	8	1	3	4
Oklahoma	7	3	2	2
Arkansas	3	1	1	1
Other	5	1	2	2

Except for the counties in Florida, these counties tend to be small, like the older counties in general. The 86 counties outside Florida, most of which are in the West North Central and West South Central divisions, had an average population aged 65 and over of only 2,262, the 14 Florida counties had an average elderly population of 64,266, and counties in the United States overall had an average elderly population of 8,134.

From a simple numerical standpoint, the small rural counties of the West North Central and the West South Central divisions potentially have the most serious problems in providing services for the elderly. In addition to the relatively greater demand and the relatively low tax base, there are special problems of transportation, availability of facilities and resources, and delivery of services associated with the geographic dispersion and isolation of the population.

There is a close relationship between the current proportion of the population of a county that is aged 65 and over and the year the county reached its maximum population. In general, the earlier the maximum population was reached, the higher the current percentage of elderly persons. Some counties with large percentages of elderly not only are not gaining population but are experiencing a natural decrease (excess of deaths over births) in addition to net outmigration.

A four-way classification of the counties in the United States based on the 1970–1980 intercensal growth of the counties' elderly population has been developed by Rowles, Hanham, and Bohland.[4] Counties were subdivided into four types on the basis of whether or not the percent increase of the elderly population between the 1970 and 1980 censuses exceeded the national average percent increase (27 percent) and whether or not the increase in the percentage of elderly persons in the total population was above the national average (1.4 percentage points). Type I counties, those with percent increases of the elderly *and* with increases in the percentage of the elderly above the national figures, were heavily concentrated in the Southeast and the (Far) West. Type IV counties, those with percent increases of the elderly *and* with increases in the percentage of the elderly below the national figures, were concentrated in the middle and northern tier of states from East to West, but especially in the Midwest. Type II counties, those with a percent change in the elderly above the national figure *and* a change in the percentage elderly below the national figure, appeared mainly in the South from Virginia to Texas and the West. Type III counties, those with a percent change in the elderly below the national figure *and* a change in the percentage elderly above the national figure, appeared mainly in the tier of midwestern states from North Dakota to Texas.

McCarthy's analysis of geographic trends in aging since 1960, on the basis of data for counties, shows that elderly persons have become increasingly concentrated geographically.[5] These trends reflect a growing concentration of elderly persons in the Sunbelt states in general and in several specific retirement areas, including northern Michigan and a band of counties stretching from northwestern Arizona, the Ozarks in Arkansas, and central Texas to western North Carolina and eastern West Virginia.

Age Dependency Ratios

Age distributions of the population of states incorporate the effect of state differences in mortality and fertility, and the interchange of migrants and, in the form of elderly dependency ratios, have fairly direct implications for public programs in the states, particularly state variations in the demands made on those programs. The burden of supporting the elderly, as represented by the ratio of the elderly population to the working-age population, reaches a maximum in the West North Central Division (24 elderly per 100 workers in 1986), but it is also high in New England (22) and the Middle Atlantic Division (23). (See Table 3.4.) In

[4]G. D. Rowles, R. Q. Hanham, and J. R. Bohland, "Explaining Changes in the Regional Concentration of the Elderly in the USA," paper presented at the International Congress of Gerontology, New York, July 15, 1985.

[5]K. F. McCarthy, *The Elderly Population's Changing Spatial Distribution* (Santa Monica, CA: Rand, 1983).

TABLE 3.4

Elderly Dependency Ratios, by Geographic Division: 1950–2000

Division	Dependency Ratio[a]				Index to United States			
	1950	1970	1986	2000	1950	1970	1986	2000
United States	14.0	18.9	20.6	21.9	100	100	100	100
Northeast								
New England	16.4	20.5	22.3	22.5	117	108	108	103
Middle Atlantic	13.6	19.7	22.6	24.0	97	104	110	110
Midwest								
East North Central	14.5	18.3	20.7	21.9	104	97	100	100
West North Central	17.4	23.5	23.5	24.3	124	124	114	111
South								
South Atlantic	11.9	18.2	21.8	24.0	85	96	106	110
East South Central	13.6	19.5	21.3	22.3	97	103	103	102
West South Central	12.9	18.6	18.1	19.2	92	98	88	88
West								
Mountain	12.9	16.5	17.7	19.3	92	87	86	88
Pacific	13.9	16.8	17.9	18.9	99	89	87	86

SOURCES: Based on U.S. Bureau of the Census, 1970 Census of Population, U.S. Summary, Chapter B, Tables 61 and 62; 1950 Census of Population, U.S. Summary, series B, Table 62; and Current Population Reports, series P-25, no. 1017, (October 1988).

[a] $\dfrac{\text{Population aged 65 and over}}{\text{Population aged 20–64}} \times 100$.

every division the elderly dependency ratio increased four or more points between 1950 and 1986 but, for the Middle Atlantic, South Atlantic, and East South Central divisions, it increased much more than the national average (6.6 points).

Geographic variations in dependency are often diminished when child dependency is combined with elderly dependency because the two dependency measures tend to vary in opposite directions. If we assume that the public financial and social burden of providing for a child and an elderly person is the same, there is only a small difference in the public support burden from one part of the country to another, with the East South Central Division carrying the heaviest burden. If, however, we assume that the burden is greater for an elderly person, as may be maintained, then some geographic divisions (e.g., East South Central and West North Central) have a much heavier burden of support than others (e.g., West South Central, Mountain, and Pacific). (See Table 3.5.)

The Role of Internal Migration in State Population Changes

Estimates of net migration for states between 1970 and 1980 for the age group 65 and over (i.e., persons migrating at age 65 and over) help to identify the principal states of origin and destination of elderly migrants during the decade and to indicate the role of migration in the 1970–1980 change of the elderly population of states.[6] Estimates of net migration for states between 1950 and 1960 and between 1960 and 1970 for the cohorts aged *65 and over at mid decade* (e.g., 60 and over in 1960 and 70 and over in 1970) were compiled for comparison and combination with the estimates given for 1970–1980 for the age group 65 and over.[7] Estimates of net migration during a decade for cohorts aged 65

---

[6]Estimates of net migration for the *age group 65 and over* for this period were prepared on the assumption that they are as useful for many gerontological studies as estimates of net migration for the *cohort aged 65 and over* (age at the census or survey date) during the previous decade (e.g., a cohort aged 65 and over in 1980 and 55 in 1970) or quinquennium. Figures for cohorts over a five-year period are the type of figures normally secured in decennial censuses and figures for cohorts over a one-year period are commonly secured in the Current Population Survey.

[7]The estimates for 1970–1980 for the age group 65 and over were derived by subtracting estimates of "natural increase" for ages 65 and over during the decade (the number of persons reaching age 65 minus the number of deaths of persons 65 and over during the decade) from the net change in the number of persons 65 and over during the decade. The estimates for 1960–1970 of the cohorts aged 65 and over in 1965, and for 1950–1960 of the cohorts 65 and over in 1955, also employed a residual method. National census survival rates (rather than death statistics or life table survival rates) were used to allow for mortality.

TABLE 3.5
Total, Child, and Elderly Dependency Ratios, by Geographic Division: 1986

Division	Dependency Ratio			Index to United States		
	Total Ratio[a]	Child Ratio[b]	Elderly Ratio[c]	Total Ratio	Child Ratio	Elderly Ratio
United States	70.6	50.0	20.6	100	100	100
Northeast						
New England	67.4	45.1	22.3	95	90	108
Middle Atlantic	68.8	46.2	22.6	97	92	110
Midwest						
East North Central	71.8	51.1	20.7	102	102	100
West North Central	74.7	51.2	23.5	106	102	114
South						
South Atlantic	69.4	47.6	21.8	98	95	106
East South Central	74.7	53.5	21.3	106	107	103
West South Central	74.2	56.1	18.1	105	112	88
West						
Mountain	73.1	55.4	17.7	104	111	86
Pacific	66.6	48.6	17.9	94	97	87

SOURCE: Based on U.S. Bureau of the Census, *Current Population Reports*, series P-25, no. 1017 (October 1988).

[a] $\dfrac{\text{Population under age 20 + population aged 65 and over}}{\text{Population aged 20–64}} \times 100.$

[b] $\dfrac{\text{Population under age 20}}{\text{Population aged 20–64}} \times 100.$

[c] $\dfrac{\text{Population aged 65 and over}}{\text{Population aged 20–64}} \times 100.$

TABLE 3.6

Estimates of the Components of Change in the Population Aged 65 and Over, by State: 1970–1980 (numbers in thousands; Figures as of April 1 or the period April 1 to April 1)

Region, Division, and State	Population Aged 65 and Over		Increase, 1970–1980[a]	
	1980	1970[b]	Amount	Percent
United States	25,544	20,325	5,219	25.7
Regions				
Northeast	6,072	5,245	827	15.8
Midwest	6,691	5,790	901	15.6
South	8,484	6,149	2,335	38.0
West	4,298	3,141	1,157	36.8
Northeast				
New England	1,520	1,289	231	17.9
Middle Atlantic	4,551	3,955	596	15.1
Midwest				
East North Central	4,493	3,845	648	16.8
West North Central	2,199	1,945	254	13.0
South				
South Atlantic	4,363	2,996	1,367	45.6
East South Central	1,657	1,297	360	27.7
West South Central	2,463	1,856	607	32.7
West				
Mountain	1,060	714	346	48.6
Pacific	3,237	2,428	809	33.4
New England				
Maine	141	121	20	16.1
New Hampshire	103	82	21	25.5
Vermont	58	50	8	16.1
Massachusetts	727	641	86	13.3
Rhode Island	127	106	21	20.0
Connecticut	365	289	76	26.3
Middle Atlantic				
New York	2,161	1,975	186	9.4
New Jersey	860	697	163	23.3
Pennsylvania	1,531	1,283	248	19.3
East North Central				
Ohio	1,169	1,001	168	16.8
Indiana	585	495	90	18.2

TABLE 3.6 (*continued*)

| | | Net Migration[c] | |
Number Reaching Age 65	Deaths	Amount[d]	Percent[e]
17,547	12,405	+77	+0.3
4,339	3,188	−323	−5.7
4,620	3,537	−181	−2.9
5,700	3,804	+439	+6.0
2,889	1,877	+144	+3.9
1,028	775	−21	−1.6
3,311	2,413	−302	−7.1
3,197	2,395	−153	−3.7
1,422	1,142	−26	−1.3
2,872	1,851	+347	+9.4
1,150	813	+23	+1.6
1,678	1,139	+68	+3.2
702	432	+76	+8.5
2,186	1,446	+69	+2.4
93	74	—[f]	—[f]
67	51	+5	+5.3
38	31	+1	+1.1
490	382	−22	−3.3
87	63	−1	−1.8
253	175	−2	−0.9
1,588	1,158	−244	−11.8
620	436	−20	−2.7
1,103	819	−35	−2.6
836	640	−26	−2.5
408	315	−1	−0.4

TABLE 3.6 (*continued*)

Region, Division, and State	Population Aged 65 and Over		Increase, 1970–1980[a]	
	1980	1970[b]	Amount	Percent
Illinois	1,261	1,105	156	14.1
Michigan	912	766	146	19.1
Wisconsin	564	477	87	18.2
West North Central				
Minnesota	480	416	64	15.4
Iowa	387	356	31	8.9
Missouri	648	566	82	14.5
North Dakota	80	68	12	17.7
South Dakota	91	82	9	10.4
Nebraska	206	186	20	10.5
Kansas	306	270	36	13.2
South Atlantic				
Delaware	59	45	14	30.8
Maryland	396	301	95	31.6
District of Columbia	74	76	−2	−2.4
Virginia	505	375	130	34.7
West Virginia	238	200	38	19.0
North Carolina	602	420	182	43.4
South Carolina	287	197	90	46.2
Georgia	517	373	144	38.5
Florida	1,685	1,009	676	66.9
East South Central				
Kentucky	410	344	66	19.1
Tennessee	518	391	127	32.5
Alabama	440	333	107	32.1
Mississippi	289	229	60	26.1
West South Central				
Arkansas	312	241	71	29.6
Louisiana	404	311	93	30.1
Oklahoma	376	302	74	24.6
Texas	1,371	1,003	368	36.8
Mountain				
Montana	85	71	14	19.4
Idaho	94	70	24	34.8
Wyoming	37	31	6	18.6
Colorado	247	192	55	29.0
New Mexico	116	74	42	56.5
Arizona	307	166	141	85.1
Utah	109	79	30	38.1
Nevada	66	32	34	108.1

TABLE 3.6 (*continued*)

Components of Change, 1970–1980			
Number Reaching Age 65	Deaths	Net Migration[c]	
		Amount[d]	Percent[e]
917	681	−80	−6.8
664	474	−43	−5.2
373	286	—[f]	—[f]
306	237	−4	−1.1
246	208	−6	−1.8
434	347	−3	−0.7
54	39	−2	−3.8
57	46	−1	−2.9
129	107	−1	−1.1
196	157	−3	−1.4
42	30	+2	+3.9
289	194	—[f]	+0.1
60	41	−20	−28.4
361	237	+6	+1.4
171	128	−4	−2.4
426	265	+22	+4.3
208	125	+8	+3.2
371	237	+10	+2.3
944	593	+325	+24.1
281	218	+3	+0.7
359	244	+12	+2.6
310	208	+5	+1.3
200	144	+3	+1.3
204	145	+13	+4.8
289	200	+4	+1.2
247	183	+11	+3.2
938	610	+40	+3.4
59	43	−1	−2.8
64	41	+1	+1.7
27	19	−1	−6.8
164	114	+5	+2.2
80	44	+6	+6.0
188	102	+55	+23.3
74	46	+3	+2.9
46	23	+11	+22.1

TABLE 3.6 (*continued*)

Region, Division, and State	Population Aged 65 and Over		Increase, 1970–1980[a]	
	1980	1970[b]	Amount	Percent
Pacific				
Washington	431	327	104	32.1
Oregon	303	228	75	33.3
California	2,415	1,817	598	32.9
Alaska	12	8	4	52.8
Hawaii	76	49	27	56.2

SOURCES: U.S. Bureau of the Census, *Current Population Reports*, series P-23, no. 138 (August 1984). Based on U.S. Bureau of the Census, 1970 and 1980 Censuses of Population; U.S. National Center for Health Statistics, *Mortality*, various years, vol. 2, Part B, and mortality estimates by the U.S. Bureau of the Census.

[a] A minus sign denotes net decrease.
[b] 1970 census counts adjusted for net underenumeration.
[c] Plus sign denotes net inmigration and minus sign denotes net outmigration.
[d] Computed by the residual method from the population data and the other components shown.
[e] Net migration for 1970–1980 as a percentage of the population aged 65 and over in 1970.
[f] Dash denotes that figure rounds to zero or 0.0.

and over at mid decade approximate net migration for the age group 65 and over during the decade.

The estimates of net migration for 1970–1980 reflect a considerable movement during this decade of elderly persons out of the Middle Atlantic states and the East North Central states and into the South Atlantic states, the West South Central states, and the divisions of the West (Table 3.6). The Middle Atlantic Division lost 302,000 persons aged 65 and over through net outmigration (or 7 percent of its 1970 population) while the South Atlantic Division gained 347,000 (or 9 percent of its 1970 population). New York, Pennsylvania, Illinois, and Michigan were big losers, and Florida, Texas, Arizona, and California were big gainers. In percentage terms, New York, the District of Columbia, and Alaska were the leading losers, and Florida, Nevada, and Arizona were the leading gainers. To a large extent, but for different reasons, the elderly population moved in the same directions as the general population during the 1970–1980 decade. The general population showed higher rates of net migration into the West South Central states and the West, however.

TABLE 3.6 (*continued*)

| | Components of Change, 1970–1980 | | |
| | | Net Migration[c] | |
Number Reaching Age 65	Deaths	Amount[d]	Percent[e]
292	198	+11	+2.9
199	137	+14	+5.1
1,629	1,082	+50	+2.4
11	4	−2	−33.6
55	24	−2	−5.0

Net Interstate and Interregional Migration: 1950–1980

The interstate migration patterns of the elderly during the 1960s and 1950s were similar to those during the 1970s (Table 3.7). As in the 1970s, there were major losses through net outmigration from the states of the Middle Atlantic Division and the East North Central Division and major gains through net inmigration into the states of the South Atlantic Division, the West South Central Division, and the divisions of the West. The big gainers and big losers among the states during the 1950s, 1960s, and the 1970s are about the same. In sum, estimates of net interregional migration of the elderly for the years since 1950 reveal a rather consistent pattern of movement out of the North and into the South and West.

Estimates of net migration of the elderly population for the 1950–1980 period, by decades, for geographic divisions, with the corresponding average annual rates of net migration, are shown in Table 3.8. There was an estimated net migration out of the North of 1.2 million between 1950 and 1980 and an estimated net migration into the South and West of equal volume over the 30-year period. Over half of the net outmigration (650,000) left the Middle Atlantic Division and over half of the net inmigration entered the South Atlantic Division (656,000). The net losses from the Middle Atlantic Division doubled between 1950–1960 and 1970–1980 (from 153,000 to 302,000), while the net gains in the South Atlantic Division more than tripled over this period (from 110,000 to 347,000).

Rates of net migration tell a similar story, with variations. The Middle Atlantic Division remained the heaviest loser (7 per 1,000 population

TABLE 3.7

Estimates of the Net Migration of the Population Aged 65 and Over, by State: 1950–1980 (in thousands)

Region, Division and State	1950–1980		1970–1980	
	Amount	Average Annual Rate[a]	Amount	Rate[b]
United States	+5.3	—	+76.8	+0.3
New England				
Maine	−6.3	−0.04	+0.1	—
New Hampshire	+3.5	+0.04	+4.9	+5.3
Vermont	−2.0	−0.03	+0.6	+1.1
Massachusetts	−68.9	−0.11	−22.5	−3.3
Rhode Island	−7.8	−0.10	−2.1	−1.8
Connecticut	−6.2	−0.03	−0.9	−0.9
Middle Atlantic				
New York	−465.4	−0.45	−244.8	−11.8
New Jersey	−35.3	−0.22	−21.3	−2.7
Pennsylvania	−149.5	−0.46	−36.4	−2.6
East North Central				
Ohio	−93.4	−0.36	−27.4	−2.5
Indiana	−27.1	−0.21	−2.2	−0.4
Illinois	−197.5	−0.75	−80.9	−6.8
Michigan	−90.5	−0.52	−43.7	−5.2
Wisconsin	−8.1	−0.09	−2.5	—
West North Central				
Minnesota	−7.7	−0.08	−4.7	−1.1
Iowa	−18.6	−0.20	−6.9	−1.8
Missouri	−16.0	−0.11	−4.3	−0.7
North Dakota	−6.4	−0.36	−2.9	−3.8
South Dakota	−4.4	−0.22	−2.5	−2.9
Nebraska	−3.2	−0.05	−2.1	−1.1
Kansas	−2.8	−0.04	−3.9	−1.4
South Atlantic				
Delaware	+3.0	+0.27	+2.0	+3.9
Maryland	+4.2	+0.12	+0.3	+0.1
District of Columbia	−42.8	−1.82	−21.3	−28.4
Virginia	+7.0	+0.08	+6.0	+1.4
West Virginia	−18.2	−0.36	−5.3	−2.4
North Carolina	+23.8	+0.23	+22.1	+4.3
South Carolina	−3.2	−0.07	+7.8	+3.2
Georgia	+6.0	+0.07	+10.3	+2.3
Florida	+676.3	+6.20	+325.2	+24.1

TABLE 3.7 (*continued*)

1960–1970		1950–1960	
Amount	Rate[b]	Amount	Rate[b]
+25.4	+0.1	−97.1	−0.8
−3.5	−3.3	−2.9	−3.1
+0.3	+0.5	−1.8	−3.1
−0.8	−1.9	−1.7	−4.4
−18.9	−3.3	−27.4	−5.9
−2.0	−2.2	−3.7	−5.3
−0.4	−0.2	−2.9	−0.5
−130.6	−7.7	−90.0	−7.2
−6.1	−1.1	−7.8	−2.0
−57.5	−5.1	−55.5	−6.3
−37.8	−4.2	−28.1	−4.0
−15.3	−3.4	−9.6	−2.7
−61.3	−6.3	−55.3	−7.3
−25.2	−3.9	−21.6	−4.7
+2.7	+0.7	−10.5	−0.5
+4.8	+1.4	−7.7	−2.9
−2.9	−0.9	−8.8	−3.2
−7.7	−1.5	−4.0	−1.0
−0.1	−0.2	−3.4	−7.1
+0.6	+0.9	−2.6	−4.7
+2.7	+1.6	−3.7	−2.8
+1.5	+0.6	−0.3	−0.3
+0.3	+1.0	+0.6	+2.4
+4.1	+1.8	−0.2	−0.1
−13.3	−19.2	−8.2	−14.5
+1.1	+0.4	−0.2	−0.1
−7.8	−4.5	−5.1	−3.7
+5.1	+1.6	−3.4	−13.6
−3.5	−2.3	−7.5	−6.5
+0.3	+0.1	−4.6	−2.1
+212.2	+38.4	+138.9	+58.5

TABLE 3.7 (continued)

Region, Division and State	1950–1980		1970–1980	
	Amount	Average Annual Rate[a]	Amount	Rate[b]
East South Central				
Kentucky	−1.8	−0.02	+2.8	+0.7
Tennessee	+17.2	+0.17	+11.8	+2.6
Alabama	+4.9	+0.06	+5.0	+1.3
Mississippi	−7.0	−0.11	+3.5	+1.3
West South Central				
Arkansas	+18.7	+0.30	+13.2	+4.8
Louisiana	+1.0	+0.01	+4.2	+1.2
Oklahoma	+19.3	+0.49	+10.8	+3.2
Texas	+98.3	+0.42	+40.2	+3.4
Mountain				
Montana	−4.9	−0.26	−2.2	−2.8
Idaho	+2.5	+0.05	+1.4	+1.7
Wyoming	−3.5	−0.51	−2.3	−6.8
Colorado	+17.2	+0.35	+4.8	+2.2
New Mexico	+10.2	+0.61	+5.7	+6.0
Arizona	+97.0	+2.96	+55.0	+23.3
Utah	+5.8	+0.30	+2.8	+2.9
Nevada	+14.9	+1.85	+10.7	+22.1
Pacific				
Washington	+16.8	+0.19	+11.1	+2.9
Oregon	+25.5	+0.44	+13.6	+5.1
California	+243.4	+0.58	+50.3	+2.4
Alaska	−5.5	+4.82	−3.2	−33.6
Hawaii	−8.4	−2.12	−3.1	−5.0

SOURCES: 1970–1980: U.S. Bureau of the Census, *Current Population Reports*, series P-23, no. 138 by J. S. Siegel and M. Davidson (August 1984), Table 4.3. 1960–1970: "Net Migration of the Population, 1960–70, by Age, Sex, and Color," by G. K. Bowles and E. S. Lee, U.S. Dept. of Agriculture, University of Georgia, and National Science Foundation, *Population-Migration Report* (December 1975, parts 1–6. 1950–1960: U.S. Department of Agriculture, "Net Migration of the Population, 1950–60, by Age, Sex, and Color," by G. K. Bowles and J. D. Tarver (May 1965), parts 1–6. *Population-Migration Report*, vol. I.

NOTES: Estimates for 1970–1980 obtained by the vital statistics method; estimates for 1960–1970 and 1950–1960 obtained by the census survival rate method. Plus sign denotes net inmigration and minus sign denotes net outmigration. Dash denotes that figure rounds to zero or 0.0.

[a] Average of results from forward and reverse formulas for continuous compounding.
[b] Decennial rate per 100. Base is the population aged 65 and over in the state at the beginning of the decade.

TABLE 3.7 (*continued*)

1960–1970		1950–1960	
Amount	Rate[b]	Amount	Rate[b]
−1.7	−0.6	−2.9	−1.2
+3.7	+1.2	+1.7	+0.7
+2.3	+0.9	−2.4	−1.2
−4.3	−2.3	−6.2	−4.0
+8.7	+4.5	−3.1	−2.1
−3.4	−1.4	+0.2	+0.1
+5.6	+2.3	+3.0	+1.5
+34.3	+4.6	+23.8	+4.6
−0.7	−1.1	−2.0	−3.8
+1.1	+1.9	—	—
−0.7	−2.6	−0.5	−3.0
+5.5	+3.5	+6.9	+6.0
+2.4	+4.6	+2.2	+6.7
+27.0	+30.0	+15.0	+33.9
+2.1	+3.5	+0.9	+2.2
+2.8	+15.2	+1.4	+12.5
+3.2	+1.1	+2.5	+1.2
+9.9	+5.4	+2.0	+1.5
+89.6	+6.5	+103.4	+11.6
−1.4	−26.2	−0.9	−18.7
−2.4	−8.3	−2.9	−14.2

per year) and the South Atlantic Division remained the heaviest gainer (9 per 1,000 per year), but the Mountain Division was also a heavy gainer (8 per 1,000 per year).[8] As before, the East North Central Division and the Pacific Division were still important as loser and gainer, respectively.

[8]The average annual rate of net migration for each decade was calculated by adapting the formula used to determine the average annual rate of population growth by continuous compounding. A forward and reverse formula were both applied to derive two preliminary results. The forward formula is:

$$e^{r_1 t} = \frac{P^0_{65+} + M_{65+}}{P^0_{65+}} \tag{1}$$

TABLE 3.8

*Estimated Amounts and Rates of Net Migration of Persons Aged 65 and Over,
by Geographic Division: 1950–1980 (by decade)*

Division	Amount[a] (in thousands)			
	1950–1980	1950–1960	1960–1970	1970–1980
United States[c]	+4.3	−97.1	+24.7	+76.8
New England	−87.7	−40.5	−25.3	−21.9
Middle Atlantic	−650.2	−153.4	−194.3	−302.5
East North Central	−416.5	−125.2	−136.9	−154.4
West North Central	−59.0	−30.6	−1.0	−27.4
South Atlantic	+656.2	+110.4	+198.7	+347.1
East South Central	+13.2	−9.8	−0.1	+23.1
West South Central	+138.1	+23.9	+45.8	+68.4
Mountain	+139.2	+24.0	+39.5	+75.8
Pacific	+271.8	+104.2	+98.9	+68.7

SOURCES: 1970–1980: U.S. Bureau of the Census, "Demographic and Socioeconomic Aspects of Aging in the United States," by J. S. Siegel and M. Davidson, *Current Population Reports*, series P-23, no. 138 (August 1984), Table 4-4. 1960–1970: U.S. Department of Agriculture, University of Georgia, and National Science Foundation, "Net Migration of the Population, 1960–70, by Age, Sex, and Color," by G. K. Bowles and E. S. Lee, *Population-Migration Report* (December 1975), parts 1–6; 1950–1960: U.S. Department of Agriculture, "Net Migration of the Population, 1950–60, by Age, Sex, and Color," by G. K. Bowles and J. D. Tarver, *Population-Migration Report*, vol. 1 (May 1965), parts 1–6.

NOTES: Plus sign denotes net inmigration and minus sign denotes net outmigration. Dash denotes that figure rounds to 0.0.

[a] Amounts for 1970–1980 represent net migration between April 1, 1970, and April 1, 1980, at ages 65 and over computed by the vital statistics method. Amounts for 1960–1970 and 1950–1960 represent net migration in these decades for the cohorts aged 65 and over at mid decade, computed by the national census survival rate method.
[b] Calculated by averaging the forward the reverse average annual rates of net migration for each period, derived by the formula for continuous compounding.
[c] Figures shown are not independently valid as estimates of net immigration of persons aged 65 and over.

where P^0_{65+} represents the initial population aged 65 and over, M_{65+} net migration during the period, e the base of the system of natural logarithms, t the number of years in the period, and r_1 the forward annual average rate of net migration. The reverse formula is:

$$e^{r_2 t} = \frac{P^t_{65+}}{P^t_{65+} - M_{65+}} \tag{2}$$

where P^t_{65+} represents the terminal population aged 65 and over and r_2 the reverse average annual rate of net migration. Formulas (1) and (2) were solved for r_1 and r_2. The resulting values were then averaged to obtain the final value for the average annual rate of net migration. In effect, averaging allows for the interaction of migration with the other components of population change during the observation period.

TABLE 3.8 *(continued)*

	Average Annual Rate[b] (per 1,000)		
1950–1980	1950–1960	1960–1970	1970–1980
—	−0.7	+0.1	+0.3
−1.6	−4.1	−2.1	−1.6
−7.2	−5.3	−5.4	−7.2
−4.4	−4.3	−3.8	−3.8
−1.1	−2.0	−0.1	−1.3
+9.1	+6.5	+8.0	+9.7
+0.2	−1.1	—	+1.6
+3.0	+2.0	+2.8	+3.4
+7.8	+5.6	+6.5	+8.9
+4.7	+6.8	+4.7	+2.5

The role of net migration is somewhat different when the proportion of elderly in the population is considered. The effect of net migration on the change in the proportion of elderly in a state between two dates depends not only on the volume of inmigration and outmigration at the older ages in the intervening years, but also on the volume and direction of migration at the ages under 65 and the levels of fertility and mortality. Regional variations in mortality from state to state are small (Chapter 4) and have only a limited effect on state variations in the percentage elderly. On the other hand, geographic variations in fertility have a powerful effect. These factors work in combination. For example, the percentage elderly may rise as a result of both a decrease in the birth rate and a large outmigration of young people, or the percentage may remain essentially unchanged if the outmigration of older people offsets the outmigration of young people.

Aging-in-place is often an influential factor in the change in the proportion of elderly persons in an area. Aging-in-place means that the people are not moving out of their hometowns or their family homes as they grow older, but are living out their lives at their longtime residences. Aging-in-place has a perceptible effect when the nonmigrants reaching the older ages are relatively numerous compared with the younger cohorts that will replace them or with the older cohorts the nonmigrants are replacing. It becomes especially important as a factor, for example, when it is accompanied by other influences for aging, as outmigration of young persons, inmigration of older persons, or low fertility.

To ascertain the approximate role of internal migration in the shift in the proportions of elderly in the states in the last few decades, estimates of the net contribution of internal migration to the change in the proportion of persons aged 65 and over in each state between 1950 and 1980 were developed by a short-cut method. In brief, allowance was made for the change in the proportion aged 65 and over in each state for reasons other than internal migration by adjusting the 1950 proportion for each state, first, on the basis of the percentage change in the national proportion aged 65 and over between 1950 and 1980 and, second, on the basis of indexes of state variation in fertility for 1950–1980. The resulting expected proportions were then compared with the actual proportions in 1980 to determine the amount of change in the proportions due to internal migration. The estimates are subject to substantial error because the assumptions are major.

The estimates obtained suggest that internal migration had a significant influence on the change in the state proportions aged 65 and over between 1950 and 1980, contributing to the increase of the proportion in about half the states and the District of Columbia and inhibiting the potential increase in about half the states. As a result of internal migration between 1950 and 1980, 17 states and the District of Columbia added 1 point or more to the percentage of the population aged 65 and over and 18 states lost 1 point or more from the potential increase in the percentage aged 65 and over.

Change in Percent	Due to Migration	Due to All Factors
Total	51[a]	51[a]
Under −3.0	3	—
−3.0 to −1.0	15	—
−1.0 to +1.0	15	4
+1.0 to +3.0	13[a]	24
Over +3.0	5	23[a]

[a]Includes District of Columbia.

Internal migration accounted for one half or more of the increase between 1950 and 1980 in the proportion aged 65 and over in 15 states, offset the potential increase by one half or more in 5 states, and had a more limited effect in 30 states and the District of Columbia. Leading gainers were Hawaii, Florida, Arizona, Arkansas, New Mexico, North Dakota, South Dakota, Alabama, Louisiana, and Mississippi; and leading losers were New Hampshire, Massachusetts, Vermont, Indiana, and Washington. Note that the leading gainers are mostly in the South and

West and that the leading losers are mainly in the North, especially the Northeast.

Research carried out by Rowles, Hanham, and Bohland in 1985 was designed to determine the relative importance of four types of migration, defined by direction of movement (inmigration and outmigration) and age of migrant (elderly, nonelderly), in accounting for changes in the proportion of elderly among the states.[9] Migration data for states during the period 1975–1980 for the four categories, derived from the 1980 census, were correlated with the change in the proportion of elderly persons between 1970 and 1980. In all but nine states, the primary determinant of the change in the proportion of elderly persons among these four factors was the inmigration of nonelderly persons. The nine states in which inmigration of the elderly, outmigration of nonelderly, or outmigration of the elderly was more significant than inmigration of the nonelderly are Arizona, Florida, New Mexico, Arkansas, North Carolina, South Carolina, Washington, Wisconsin, and Kentucky. This list includes several Sunbelt retirement states in the South and West. In some of these states and others, aging-in-place and fertility are important explanatory factors in addition to migration, however.

Inmigration of nonelderly persons in some states is, of course, associated with outmigration of nonelderly persons in others. Outmigration of nonelderly persons has had an important effect on the concentration of the elderly population in several states, especially the band of midwestern states stretching from Minnesota in the north to Texas in the south and a cluster of states in the Southeast (except Florida and South Carolina). The outmigration of the young in these states is usually associated with the nonmigration of the elderly, or their aging in place.

Migration of the nonelderly and aging-in-place are the processes that have had the greatest influence on the age structure of states and counties. Compared with migration of the young and aging-in-place, migration of the elderly has played a generally secondary role. It did, however, play a relatively larger role in the concentration of the elderly between 1970 and 1980 than between 1960 and 1970 and between 1960 and 1980 than in the decades before 1960.[10] The role of direct migration of the elderly as a factor in the aging of state and local populations increased as the economic status of the elderly has improved and retirement centers have become more widely established.

[9]Rowles, Hanham, and Bohland (1985).

[10]McCarthy (1983). J. R. Bohland and G. D. Rowles, "The Significance of Elderly Migration to Changes in Elderly Population Concentration in the United States," *Journal of Gerontology* 43 (5) (September 1988):S145–152.

Patterns of Residential Mobility and Internal Migration

Age and Sex Variations

Although several states show relatively high net in- or outmigration rates for the elderly population, in general this age group moves relatively little. In the year 1985–1986, the (intercounty) migration rate for persons aged 65 and over was 2.1 percent, or about one third as great as the migration rate for the entire population aged 1 and over (6.7 percent).[11] (See Table 3.9.) Similar differences appeared for other classes of movers, such as interstate migrants, intracounty movers, male migrants, and female migrants. Of the less than 5 percent of elderly persons who moved in 1985–1986, about three fifths remained within the same county and only about two fifths moved to a different county.

From youth on, the older a person is, the less likely he or she is to move, except at the very old ages. Mobility rates and migration rates exhibit a generally downward progression with advancing age from age group 20–24 on. This has been the pattern for the last three decades at least, as may be seen from data for the years 1985–1986 and other paired years back to 1955–1956 (Table 3.9). The pattern of declining mobility and migration rates with increasing age corresponds to the typical succession of life course experiences, consisting of the departure of youth from the parental home to attend college, work, and/or marry, experimentation with jobs and home locations, the building of careers and families and the purchase of homes, and finally aging-in-place and retirement.

The broad age pattern of internal migration rates has been remarkably similar from country to country in the postwar years.[12] The heavy concentration of migrants among young adults is universally followed by a gradual decline except for a slight hump starting at the ages when people begin to retire in large numbers. The pattern of migration rates from the retirement ages on varies widely from country to country, however.

Since the 1950s, the elderly, like the nonelderly, have tended to move less, especially within the same county, but migration rates have

[11]Migration is defined here as a change of usual residence *between counties* as determined by comparing residences at the beginning and end of the specified period. Mobility encompasses all changes of usual residence as determined by comparing residences at the beginning and end of the period.

[12]A. Rogers, "Age Patterns of Elderly Migration: An International Comparison," *Demography* 25 (3) (August 1988):355–370.

also shown a general tendency to decline in this period. According to the Current Population Survey (CPS), in 1955–1956, 7.2 percent of the population aged 65 and over moved to a different house in the same county while in 1985–1986 only 2.8 percent did so (See Figure 3.2 and Table 3.9). Migration rates, already very low, dropped somewhat less, from 2.8 percent to 2.1 percent.

Data from the CPS of March 1985 suggest an acceleration of the general trend toward less mobility and migration of the elderly. The CPS reported a migration rate of only 6.9 percent for the elderly for 1980–1985 compared with 9.0 percent in 1975–1980 and a within-county mobility rate of only 9.2 percent compared with 13.5 percent in 1975–1980 (Table 3.10).[13]

Mobility Status	65 and Over	5 and Over	Ratio
Total	100.0	100.0	1.00
Same House	83.5	58.3	1.43
Total Movers	16.5	41.7	.40
Different house	16.2	39.9	.41
Same county	9.2	22.1	.42
Different county	6.9	17.8	.39
Same state	3.6	9.1	.40
Different state	3.3	8.7	.38
Movers from abroad	0.3	1.8	.17

These data also suggest that the mobility of the elderly relative to that of the general population has diminished slightly.

The migration of the working-age population and its dependents is mainly driven by economic and related motives—that is, to take a job, to look for a job, to accompany someone taking or looking for a job, or to secure housing appropriate to a new job. In contrast, the migration of the elderly is mainly driven by the attraction of the destination (e.g., its suitability for retirement), a variety of family reasons (e.g., to be closer to a relative), and an interest in a change of housing arrangements or neighborhood (e.g., lower rent, better accommodations).[14]

At the extreme upper end of the age distribution—age 80 and over—there is a rise in mobility rates. Tabulations of census data based on the 1970 and 1980 Public Use Microdata Samples, combined with the regular census tabulations, show that persons aged 85 and over are more

[13]Any implied changes are subject to question since they are affected by the comparability of the CPS and census data.

[14]Based on tabulations made at the Philadelphia Geriatric Center from the 1975 Annual Housing Survey, Public Use Microdata Sample.

TABLE 3.9

Mobility Rates and Migration Rates, by Age: 1955–1956 to 1985–1986
(Percentage of population in age group with different residences in paired years)

		1985–1986 Rates	
Initial Age	Terminal Age	Different House, Same County	Different County
All Ages	Total, 1 and Over	11.3	6.7
Under 4	1–4	17.8	9.1
4–12	5–13	12.3	6.1
13–16	14–17	8.9	5.0
17 and 18	18 and 19	12.6	8.4
19–23	20–24	22.2	13.1
24–33	25–34	17.5	10.3
34–43	35–44	9.7	6.0
44–63	45–64	8.8	3.8
64–73	65–74	2.3	2.0
74 and Over	75 and Over	3.2	2.3

SOURCE: U.S. Bureau of the Census, *Current Population Reports*, series P-20, various issues. Based on the Current Population Survey.

likely to have moved in the previous five years than persons aged 65–69.[15] In 1975–1980, 29 percent of the population aged 85 and over in 1980 moved to a new residence compared with 23 percent of those aged 65–69.[16]

	Terminal Ages	
Period	65–69	85 and Over
1955–1960	30.0	34.6
1965–1970	27.8	35.7
1975–1980	22.9	29.3

[15]These are terminal ages. The reader should be cautioned that mobility and migration rates for cohorts for a span of years, defined by the terminal ages, do not represent the mobility experience at *these* ages satisfactorily because mobility at younger ages is included. For example, migration rates for the terminal ages 65–69 over a five-year period, based on census or survey reports on residence five years earlier, encompass movements of persons who were aged 60–64 at the beginning of the period, thus often combining the movements of persons before and after retirement. Moreover, such census or survey data on migration tend to understate the gross volume of migration because they do not incorporate multiple moves and moves of migrants who died during the migration period. On the other hand, rates for one-year time periods exclude the migration of persons who died only in a one-year period, omit far fewer moves than rates for five-year periods and confound the age reference of the data relatively little. Rates for one-year time periods, partic-

TABLE 3.9 (*continued*)

1975–1976 Rates		1965–1966 Rates		1955–1956 Rates	
Different House, Same County	Different County	Different House, Same County	Different County	Different House, Same County	Different County
10.8	6.4	12.7	6.6	13.7	6.8
17.6	9.2	18.5	10.3	19.2	9.3
10.2	6.0	12.3	6.1	13.4	5.8
6.9	3.9	10.1	4.0	12.2	5.8
15.7	8.0	16.7	8.9	18.7	10.6
23.2	14.8	25.2	17.2	26.5	18.0
17.3	9.8	19.2	10.5	18.8	9.6
8.1	5.3	10.9	5.1	11.5	5.5
4.7	3.0	7.2	3.2	8.6	3.5
3.8	2.0	6.2	2.7 ⎫	7.2	2.8
3.1	2.1	6.8	2.2 ⎭		

The pattern of higher mobility at the latest ages of life has prevailed at least over the last few decades. In fact, there has been a secular rise in the relative level of mobility of the older group compared with the younger group, even while the absolute level of the mobility rates of both age groups, especially ages 65–69, declined.

Most of the older aged (85 and over) living in group quarters at the time of the 1970 and 1980 censuses (76 percent in 1970 and 60 percent in 1980) had moved in the previous five years to these residences, presumably nursing homes. Only a quarter and a fifth, respectively, of the older aged living in (private) households had moved during each of these periods.[17]

Period	In Group Quarters	In Households
1965–1970	75.9	26.1
1975–1980	59.7	20.1

ularly a series of one-year rates for several years, have several advantages, therefore, for analysis of migration for age groups. Their disadvantages are the instability associated with small numbers, large sampling error, and short-term historical effects.

[16]Unpublished tabulations by Ira Rosenwaike, University of Pennsylvania.

[17]Unpublished tabulations by Ira Rosenwaike, University of Pennsylvania.

FIGURE 3.2

Mobility Status of the Population Aged 65 and Over and 5 and Over in 1985 and 1960: 1980–1985 and 1955–1960

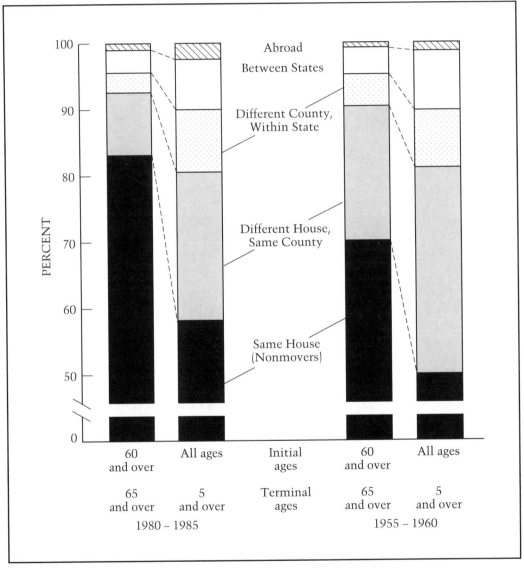

SOURCE: Table 3.10 for 1955–1960 data; and U.S. Bureau of the Census, *Current Population Reports,* series P-20, no. 420, for 1980–1985 data.

NOTE: Excludes institutional population and military population in barracks in 1985.

Between 1970 and 1980 there was a marked increase in the tendency on the part of very old people to continue living independently, that is, to remain in their homes and eschew institutional life.

To explore the mobility patterns of older persons in more detail, it is useful to examine the rates for intracounty movers and (intercounty) migrants, males and females, and detailed age groups, separately. Patterns of mobility at the older ages for male and female movers and migrants according to age are represented in Figure 3.3.

As at the younger ages, so at the older ages, mobility and migration patterns of men and women are determined by life course factors. There is a rise in the curves of migration at the starting ages of retirement—around age 60 for males and age 58 for females. Around age 78, the curves rise again. This turnaround reflects the move, first, to be near a primary caretaker, usually a close relative, when serious illness, disability, or death of a spouse first occurs, and, second, the move to institutional quarters, when independent living is no longer possible and the primary caregiver can no longer provide the necessary support.[18] The curves of intracounty mobility do not show the retirement peak characteristic of (longer-distance) migration, but make a single turnaround—about age 73 for men and 68 for women. This rise reflects the post-retirement types of moves noted above for migrants, but involves far shorter distances.

As may be seen in Figure 3.3, the curves for women and men cross over. The mobility curves cross over during the early retirement years and the migration curves cross over in the later retirement years. The (intracounty) mobility rate of women begins to exceed that of men around age 60, when women are retiring in great numbers, after remaining steadily below the rates for men from the peak mobility ages of 20–24. The crossover in the migration curve is delayed until ages 70–74. After the crossover, male and female rates tend to rise in parallel fashion, with the rates for women exceeding those for men to the end of life. The crossover results mainly from the difference in the age at marriage of husbands and wives and the difference in the ages of retirement of men and women. Women tend to take early retirement at reduced benefits more frequently than men. The gender crossover around the retirement ages also appears in the migration data of several More Developed Countries in various continents.[19]

For migrants, the first type of move—retirement migration—predominates in the migration from the Snowbelt to Sunbelt, and the second type—migration to be near a primary caregiver—predominates in

[18]See E. Litwak and C. F. Longino, Jr., "Migration Patterns among the Elderly: A Developmental Perspective," *Gerontologist* 27 (3) (June 1987):266–272.

[19]Rogers (1988).

TABLE 3.10

Distribution by Mobility Status of the Population Aged 65 and Over and 5 and Over in 1980 and 1960, by Sex and by Race: 1975–1980 and 1955–1960

Mobility Status and Period	All Classes			Male		
	Ages 65 and Over	Ages 5 and Over	Ratio[b]	Ages 65 and Over	Ages 5 and Over	Ratio[b]
1975–1980						
Total	100.0	100.0	1.00	100.0	100.0	1.00
Same House	77.0	53.6	1.44	78.3	52.5	1.49
Different House	22.5	44.5	0.51	21.3	45.4	0.47
Same county	13.5	25.1	0.54	12.2	25.1	0.49
Different county	9.0	19.5	0.46	9.0	20.3	0.45
Within state	4.6	9.8	0.47	4.5	10.0	0.45
Between states	4.4	9.7	0.46	4.6	10.3	0.44
Abroad	0.4	1.9	0.22	0.4	2.1	0.20
1955–1960[c]						
Total	100.0	100.0	1.00	100.0	100.0	1.00
Same House	70.1	49.9	1.40	70.7	49.1	1.44
Different House	29.7	48.8	0.61	29.1	49.4	0.59
Same county	20.5	30.8	0.67	19.9	30.6	0.65
Different county	9.3	18.1	0.51	9.2	18.8	0.49
Within state	5.0	8.9	0.57	4.9	9.0	0.55
Between states	4.2	9.2	0.46	4.2	9.8	0.43
Abroad	0.2	1.3	0.15	0.2	1.5	0.12

SOURCE: U.S. Bureau of the Census, 1980, Census of Population, *U.S. Summary: Detailed Characteristics*, vol. I, Chapter D, Table 259, and 1960, Census of Population, *U.S. Summary.* vol. I, series D, Table 164.

NOTE: Data for 1975–1980 relate to the movement of cohorts aged 60 and over in 1975 and 65 and over in 1980, and of cohorts of all ages in 1975 and 5 and over in 1980; that is, the period April 1, 1975, to April 1, 1980. Data for 1955–1960 relate to the movement of cohorts aged 60 and over in 1955 and 65 and over in 1960, and of cohorts of all ages in 1955 and 5 and over in 1960; that is, the period April 1, 1955, to April 1, 1960.)

[a]Black and other races for 1955–1960.
[b]Ratio of percentage aged 65 and over to percentage aged 5 and over.
[c]Persons who moved but whose place of residence in 1955 was not reported were distributed pro rata among movers whose place of residence was reported.

the counterstream. Relatively few areas are very important as destinations for retirement, and migration to these areas strongly influences the shape of the migration curve in later life. Interstate or long-distance migration of the young elderly is motivated by the quest for residential amenities and a recreational lifestyle, while migration of the old elderly is motivated by the need for physical assistance and support, first by

TABLE 3.10 (*continued*)

Female			Black[a]		
Ages 65 and Over	Ages 5 and Over	Ratio[b]	Ages 65 and Over	Ages 5 and Over	Ratio[b]
100.0	100.0	1.00	100.0	100.0	1.00
76.2	54.6	1.40	80.6	56.8	1.42
23.4	43.8	0.53	19.2	42.1	0.46
14.4	25.1	0.57	14.5	29.4	0.50
9.0	18.7	0.48	4.7	12.7	0.37
4.7	9.6	0.50	2.2	5.7	0.38
4.3	9.1	0.47	2.5	7.0	0.36
0.4	1.7	0.26	0.2	1.2	0.20
100.0	100.0	1.00	100.0	100.0	1.00
69.6	50.6	1.37	69.2	48.0	1.44
30.2	48.3	0.63	30.6	51.0	0.60
20.9	30.9	0.68	25.3	39.6	0.64
9.3	17.3	0.54	5.4	11.3	0.47
5.1	8.8	0.58	3.1	4.9	0.62
4.2	8.6	0.49	2.3	6.4	0.36
0.2	1.1	0.19	0.1	1.0	0.14

family caregivers and then by formal community care providers. Loss of spouse accounts in part for the increase in moves at the advanced ages, which, as we have seen, include relocation of both men and women to institutional residences.

Long-distance migration of the elderly tends to be selective with respect to sex, race, marital status, and socioeconomic status. Long-distance moves of the elderly are disproportionately made by married, white, young-elderly persons of substantial resources.[20] Short-distance moves favor persons of lower socioeconomic status; they are disproportionately made by unmarried, black, and old-elderly persons.

Migration in older age may largely be seen as accommodations to changes in health and income. At the early ages of retirement, those who can afford it and are sufficiently healthy move to new homes, often

[20]J. C. Biggar, "Who Moved Among the Elderly, 1965–1970: A Comparison of Types of Older Movers," *Research on Aging* 2 (1) (March 1980):73–92; Rogers (1988).

FIGURE 3.3

Age Patterns of Mobility for Men and Women Aged 50 Years and Over, by Type of Mobility: 1975–1980

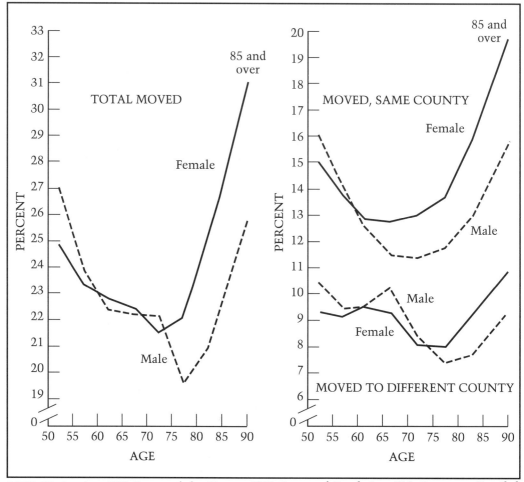

SOURCE: Based on U.S. Bureau of the Census, 1980 Census of Population: *U.S. Summary: Detailed Characteristics*, vol. I, Chapter D. Table 259.

in retirement communities in distant areas with attractive climates and amenities. When the migrants get older and health and income decline, they tend to return to the home communities first, to be near their relatives and then, when community care is required, to relocate to a nursing home. The less affluent forgo retirement migration and move short distances subsequent to the early retirement ages, first to be closer to their relatives when health and income begin to decline and then to relocate to a nursing home when their relatives can no longer care for them.

Interstate Migration in the Life Course

Elderly persons may not migrate much in their later years, but census data on state of birth and on state of prior residence of the population reflect considerable interstate movement of cohorts at earlier ages. In fact, the share of people still living in their state of birth is substantially diminished by the time the older ages are reached and, it may be inferred, only a minor share of the population at the older ages is still living in their county of birth. In 1980, only 59 or 60 percent of the native population of the United States in each five-year age group 55 and over was still living in their state of birth (Table 3.11).

Data for the birth cohorts aged 55–59 and over in 1950 (85–89 and over in 1980) confirm the pattern shown by the cross-sectional data. For example, the proportion of the cohort aged 55–59 in 1950 born outside its state of current residence already exceeded 35 percent in 1950; then it increased to only 41 percent by ages 75–79 in 1970, where it remained. The same pattern describes the older cohorts. Migration out of one's state of birth increased a little at the middle ages of life over the decades 1950–1980, but remained relatively stable at higher ages. As a result, the figures for 1960, 1970, and 1980 were nearly invariant at 39–41 percent from ages 55–59 on.[21]

Regional variations are pronounced. A very large share of the elderly people living in a state of the Northeast region or the Midwest region in 1980 was born in the same northeastern or midwestern state, but most elderly people living in a state of the West were born in another state, usually in a different region. In 1980, lifetime interstate migration for the five-year age groups 65 and over varied from 27–28 percent for the Northeast and 31–32 percent for the Midwest to 38 percent for the South and 74–79 percent for the West (Table 3.12). A comparison of data for younger and older cohorts for the 1960–1980 period for each of the regions shows that the vast portion of the interstate movement, especially of current residents of the West, occurred at rather young ages.[22] Only for the cohorts aged 45–49 to 55–59 in 1960 (65–69 to 75–79 in 1980) in the South were the proportions substantially higher in 1980 (38–39

[21]The proportions for 1950 are questionable since they seem unreasonably low. If valid, they imply a very rapid trend of interstate movement of the population after 1950.

[22]The 1980 census data for the Northeast and Midwest suggest an understatement of lifetime interstate migration since the proportions for cohorts do not monotonically accumulate. If we accept the data, we would have to assume substantial return migration and/or a negative relation between moving out of one's state of birth and the chance of survival, and there is no evidence for these assumptions.

TABLE 3.11

Percentage of the Native Population Aged 30 and Over Born Outside the State of Current Residence, by Age, for All Classes and Blacks: 1950–1980

Age	All Classes							Black		
	1950[b]	1955[a]	1960	1965[a]	1970	1975[a]	1980	1960	1970	1980
All Ages	26.5	27.8[c]	29.7	31.1[c]	32.0	32.1[c]	31.8	32.0	32.9	30.9
30–34	32.4	34.4	36.6	37.9	39.3	39.1	38.1	46.1	47.2	39.6
35–39	33.9	35.7	38.4	38.3	39.5	39.9	40.5	48.7	46.7	46.9
40–44	34.9	36.3	38.2	38.7	38.6	39.6	40.3	49.5	46.8	49.6
45–49	35.6	36.6	37.7	38.7	39.7	39.4	39.9	48.5	48.3	49.1
50–54	36.0	37.3	38.3	38.4	39.1	39.6	39.2	48.2	49.1	48.8
55–59	36.4	37.6	39.2	38.9	38.6	39.6	40.3	49.3	47.8	50.8
60–64	36.8	37.8	38.9	39.4	39.4	39.6	40.2	47.2	46.8	50.8
65–69	NA	NA	39.0	39.7	40.2	40.1	40.1	43.3	45.7	49.1
70–74			39.8	40.1	40.7	40.4	40.5	42.4	45.9	48.2
75–79	38.9	NA	40.3	40.8	41.0	40.6	40.4	40.9	44.1	47.7
80–84			41.7	42.0	42.1	41.0	40.3	40.8	43.5	46.7
85 and Over			43.8	43.8	43.9	42.2	40.6	39.7	44.0	43.5

SOURCE: Based on U.S. Bureau of the Census, 1950–1980, Censuses of Population, special reports on state of birth.

NOTES: Parallel lines delineate data for birth cohorts. NA = not available.

[a] Percentage for age groups estimated by averaging row and diagonal linear interpolations of percentages for census years.

[b] Five-year data obtained from 10-year data by interpolation.

[c] Figures for 1955, 1965, and 1975 estimated by cubic (1955, 1965) or parabolic (1975) polynomial interpolation of percentages for census years.

percent) than in 1960 (32 percent). The maximum proportion of inter-state migrants residing in the Northeast in 1980 (29 percent at ages 45–49) was reached in the West by ages 10–14.

The fact that the bulk of the moves of a cohort occurs when the cohort is less than middle-aged is reflected also in census data on gross interstate migration for the various census migration periods—that is, 1955–1960, 1965–1970, and 1975–1980, and in annual and quinquen-nial data on gross intercounty and interstate migration from the CPS. The demographic significance of such a pattern derives mainly from its effect on the geographic distribution of the elderly population and from its effect on the age structures of the areas of origin and destination. Because of their large size and their unconcentrated migration pattern, the baby-boom cohorts may considerably alter the pre-existing geo-graphic distribution of the elderly population and the share of elderly persons in the population of the various areas of the country as they move into the elderly ages after 2010.[23]

Census data on cohort migration indicate the share of the older pop-ulation that bears early life imprints imposed by rearing in a region dif-ferent from the region of current residence. The effects of such an envi-ronmental shift are unknown. We may speculate as to how spending one's childhood and youth in one region and one's adulthood in another may affect one's later health, socioeconomic status, and living condi-tions for better or worse. It is reasonable to surmise that marked changes over the life course in residential milieu influence the prospects for the quality of one's older years.

Gross Interstate and Interregional Migration: 1955–1960 to 1980–1985

Net amounts and net rates of migration give only a limited and potentially misleading indication of the actual volume of interstate and interregional movement of the elderly, since they describe only the bal-ance of movement into and out of an area or a net addition to popula-tion size.[24] We have to turn to data on gross inmigration and gross out-migration to secure more informative measures of the volume of migration of the elderly and of its social and economic impact.

[23]W. H. Frey, "Lifecourse Migration and Distribution of the Elderly Across U.S. Re-gions and Metropolitan Areas," *Economic Outlook USA* 13 (2) (1986):10–16.

[24]This point is evident from the fact that net migration rates for youth and middle-aged persons for particular states are often lower than those for the elderly, while national data on gross interstate migration typically decline monotonically between about ages 22 and 62 (Table 3.8). An increase in the rate of net inmigration of the elderly to a specific region over time may reflect an increase in the "efficiency" of the movement to the area rather than an increase in the actual volume of interregional movement to the area.

TABLE 3.12

Percentage of the Native Population Aged 45 and Over Born Outside the State of Current Residence, by Age, for Regions: 1960–1980

	Northeast			Midwest		
Age	1980	1970	1960	1980	1970	1960
All Ages	23.5	24.9	22.9	25.6	27.3	26.4
45–49	29.3	29.4	28.5	34.1	34.8	34.6
50–54	27.9	28.5	29.1	33.3	33.9	35.3
55–59	28.3	28.6	30.4	33.6	34.0	35.7
60–64	27.3	29.4	29.4	32.4	34.5	33.8
65–69	27.4	30.3	29.3	32.3	34.1	32.8
70–74	27.5	30.3	29.7	32.6	33.2	32.5
75–79	27.7	31.4	30.1	32.1	32.5	33.1
80–84	27.2	32.9	31.1	31.2	33.5	33.5
85 and Over	28.0	36.4	32.9	31.1	36.1	39.7

SOURCES: Based on U.S. Bureau of the Census, 1970 and 1960, Censuses of Population, special reports on state of birth; and unpublished Census Bureau tabulations for 1980, 1970, and 1960.

Interstate migration rates have tended to be rather stable, but the numbers of interstate migrants have increased sharply. According to decennial census data, the numbers nearly doubled (from 643,000 to 1,138,000) between 1955–1960 and 1975–1980 while the corresponding five-year rates remained nearly unchanged at about 4 percent (Tables 3.13 and 3.14). Consistent with the general decline in mobility and migration in the early 1980s, the interstate migration rate dropped to 3.3 percent in 1980–1985.

About 830,000 persons aged 65 and over in 1980 moved to one of the Sunbelt states (including migration between them) between 1975 and 1980 (Table 3.13).[25] Of all elderly *interstate* migrants during 1975–1980, about half moved to or in the South, where only one third of the elderly population lives. Nearly three quarters of the 550,000 interstate migrants living in the South in 1980 moved to the South from other regions, while only about one quarter came from another state in the South. During the same period, about 270,000 elderly migrants left a state in the South for another state, but most of them went to another state in the South.

The number of interstate migrants to and within the South and West has been growing steadily. Nearly twice as many elderly persons moved to and between the Sunbelt states during 1975–1980 as during 1955–1960 (Table 3.13). It is estimated that in the 30-year period 1950–1980

[25]The Sunbelt states consist of the states of the South and West.

TABLE 3.12 (*continued*)

	South			West	
1980	1970	1960	1980	1970	1960
32.5	30.7	26.4	49.3	51.8	52.9
37.0	35.9	31.5	67.3	69.6	71.7
37.2	35.1	31.6	67.4	72.1	74.4
38.4	33.7	32.5	70.1	72.4	77.2
38.9	34.6	33.7	72.8	74.9	78.3
38.3	35.8	34.4	73.6	77.2	78.6
38.4	37.6	35.2	75.6	78.3	81.4
37.8	38.2	35.0	78.2	78.0	83.1
38.6	38.0	36.5	78.7	80.3	83.5
37.9	38.8	38.0	79.2	80.1	85.0

the average annual number of older migrants to Arizona, North Carolina, and South Carolina more than tripled and the number of older migrants to each of the other Sunbelt states, except California and Louisiana, more than doubled.[26] The list of states receiving elderly migrants between 1975 and 1980 was headed by Florida, California, Arizona, and Texas, each of which received over 50,000 migrants.

Amounts and rates of gross *interregional* migration of the elderly reflect steadily increasing flows between the regions over the period 1955–1960 to 1975–1980, and an apparent drop in most interregional flows between 1975–1980 and 1980–1985 (Table 3.15). The largest declines in the gross rates between the last two quinquennial periods were shown by the outmigration rates from the Northeast and Midwest and the inmigration rates to the South and West. As a result, the West appeared to experience net outmigration of the elderly for the first time. Currently, nearly all the migration into the South originates in the Northeast and Midwest and nearly all the migration out of the latter two regions is destined for the South. The migration into and out of the West originates in and is destined for the other three regions with no particular directional concentration.[27]

The *states* of the Mountain Division and the South Atlantic Division experienced a large turnover of the elderly population as a result of

[26]J. C. Biggar, "The Graying of the Sunbelt: A Look at the Impact of Elderly Migration," *Population Trends and Policy Series* (Washington, D.C.: Population Reference Bureau, 1984).

[27]See also S. M. Golant, "Post-1980 Regional Migration Patterns of the U.S. Elderly Population," *Journal of Gerontology* 45 (4) (July 1990):SS135–140.

145

TABLE 3.13

Amount of Interstate Migration of the Cohorts Aged 65 and Over in 1980, 1970, and 1960, by Region and Division: 1975–1980, 1965–1970, and 1955–1960
(numbers in thousands)

Area	1975–1980 In- migration	Out- migration	Net Migration
United States	1,138	1,138	—
Regions			
Northeast	143	357	−213
Midwest	165	315	−150
South	551	271	+280
West	279	196	+ 83
Divisions			
New England	50	73	− 23
Middle Atlantic	94	284	−191
East North Central	103	232	−128
West North Central	62	84	− 22
South Atlantic	400	166	+234
East South Central	55	43	+ 12
West South Central	96	61	+ 35
Mountain	124	69	+ 55
Pacific	156	127	+ 29

SOURCES: U.S. Bureau of the Census, 1980 Census of Population, *Subject Reports*, "Geographic Mobility for States and the Nation," Table 25; 1970 Census of Population, *Subject Reports*, "Mobility for States and the Nation," Table 59; 1960 Census of Population, *Subject Reports*, "Mobility for States and State Economic Areas," Table 24.

NOTES: Plus sign denotes net inmigration and minus sign denotes net outmigration. Dash denotes zero.

migration, as measured by the gross interstate migration rate, or the sum of the interstate inmigration and outmigration rates:

Division	1975–1980	1965–1970	1955–1960
New England	8.1	7.0	6.9
Middle Atlantic	8.3	6.8	6.3
East North Central	7.5	7.1	6.9
West North Central	6.6	6.6	6.7
South Atlantic	13.0	13.0	13.8
East South Central	5.9	5.4	5.6
West South Central	6.4	5.4	5.3
Mountain	18.2	15.9	15.0
Pacific	8.7	8.1	9.1
Sum (unweighted)	82.7	75.3	75.6

SOURCE: Table 3.14.

TABLE 3.13 *(continued)*

	1965–1970			1955–1960	
In-migration	Out-migration	Net Migration	In-migration	Out-migration	Net Migration
802	802	—	643	643	—
118	239	−121	98	187	− 89
143	250	−107	120	221	−100
360	190	+170	268	147	+121
181	123	+ 58	157	89	+ 68
37	51	− 14	31	45	− 14
80	188	−108	67	142	− 75
90	178	− 89	76	151	− 75
54	72	− 19	44	70	− 25
269	113	+157	202	81	+121
34	35	− 1	27	31	− 4
57	42	+ 15	39	35	+ 4
67	44	+ 23	46	32	+ 14
115	79	+ 35	111	57	+ 54

Of the nine geographic divisions, six recorded increases in gross inter-state migration rates for the population aged 65 and over between 1955–1960 and 1975–1980. Comparison of the gross interstate migration rates for the nine divisions in these three periods indicates that there was little or no change in the gross volume of interstate migration between 1955–1960 and 1965–1970, but that there was a modest rise (11 percent) between 1965–1970 and 1975–1980.

In the 1975–1980 period the most sizable currents of interstate mi-gration consisted of migration out of the states of the Middle Atlantic Division (6 percent) and the East North Central Division (5 percent), into the states of the South Atlantic Division (9 percent), and into (12 percent) and out of (6 percent) the states of the Mountain Division (Ta-ble 3.14). Interstate migration in this period proved to be quite ineffi-cient since much of the inmigration was offset by outmigration, or the reverse.[28] For only one division—the Middle Atlantic Division—was the

[28]The efficiency of interstate migration was measured by the ratio of net interstate migration (disregarding signs) to gross interstate migration (the sum of inmigration and outmigration), that is, $|Mi - Mo|/|Mi + Mo|$.

TABLE 3.14

Interstate Migration Rates for the Cohorts Aged 65 and Over in 1980, 1970, and 1960, by Region and Division: 1975–1980, 1965–1970, and 1955–1960 (rates per 100 population at end of period)

Area	1975–1980		
	In-migration	Out-migration	Net Migration
United States	4.4	4.4	—
Regions			
Northeast	2.4	5.9	−3.5
Midwest	2.5	4.7	−2.3
South	6.5	3.2	+3.3
West	6.5	4.5	+2.0
Divisions			
New England	3.3	4.8	−1.5
Middle Atlantic	2.1	6.2	−4.2
East North Central	2.3	5.2	−2.9
West North Central	2.8	3.8	−1.0
South Atlantic	9.2	3.8	+5.4
East South Central	3.3	2.6	+0.7
West South Central	3.9	2.5	+1.4
Mountain	11.7	6.5	+5.1
Pacific	4.8	3.9	+0.9

SOURCES: Based on U.S. Bureau of the Census, 1980 Census of Population, *Subject Reports,* "Geographic Mobility for States and the Nation, Table 25; 1970 Census of Population, *Subject Reports,* "Mobility for States and the Nation," Table 59; 1960 Census of Population, *Subject Reports,* "Mobility for States and State Economic Areas," Table 24.

NOTES: Plus sign denotes net inmigration and minus sign denotes net outmigration. Dash denotes 0.0.

ratio of net to gross interstate migration as high as .50 and for only three out of the nine divisions was the ratio above .33.

New England	.185	South Atlantic	.415
Middle Atlantic	.506	East South Central	.119
East North Central	.386	West South Central	.219
West North Central	.152	Mountain	.280
		Pacific	.103

SOURCE: Table 3.14.

If we examine state data, we find that for only four states (New York, Illinois, Florida, Alaska) and the District of Columbia is the ratio of net to gross interstate migration as high as .50 and for only 12 states and the District of Columbia is it above .33 (Table 3.16). The two states experiencing the most efficient flow of elderly migrants were New York

TABLE 3.14 (*continued*)

1965–1970			1955–1960		
In-migration	Out-migration	Net Migration	In-migration	Out-migration	Net Migration
4.0	4.0	—	4.0	4.0	—
2.3	4.6	−2.3	2.2	4.2	−2.0
2.5	4.4	−1.9	2.4	4.4	−2.0
6.0	3.1	+2.8	6.0	3.3	+2.7
5.9	4.0	+1.9	6.7	3.8	+2.9
3.0	4.0	−1.1	2.8	4.1	−1.3
2.0	4.8	−2.7	2.0	4.3	−2.3
2.4	4.7	−2.3	2.3	4.6	−2.3
2.8	3.8	−1.0	2.6	4.1	−1.5
9.2	3.8	+5.3	9.8	4.0	+5.9
2.7	2.7	−0.1	2.6	3.0	−0.4
3.1	2.3	+0.8	2.8	2.5	+0.3
9.6	6.3	+3.3	8.9	6.1	+2.7
4.8	3.3	+1.5	6.0	3.1	+2.9

(.72) and Florida (.61), the former largely discharging migrants and the latter largely receiving them.

What this means generally is that there is far more movement of the elderly between the states than is reflected in estimates of population change and net migration data, and state governments have the task of planning and providing services for a considerably greater number of elderly residents than is shown by the net migration interchange. Furthermore, the interchange may involve more than mere numbers, but the characteristics of the migrants as well. We consider some of the characteristics of the migrants next.

Some Socioeconomic Variations

Variations by Education, Income, and Work Status

The extent to which older persons migrate varies according to their education, income, work status, and other characteristics. Furthermore,

TABLE 3.15

Immigration, Outmigration, and Net Migration Rates of the Cohorts Aged 65 and Over in 1985, 1980, 1970, and 1960, by Region: 1955–1960 to 1980–1985 (rates per 100 population at initial date of migration period unadjusted for deaths in the five-year period)

	1980–1985			1975–1980			1965–1970			1955–1960		
	In-	Out-	Net	In-	Out-	Net	In-	Out-	Net	In-	Out-	Net
Region												
Northeast	0.8	2.9	−2.1	0.8	4.2	−3.4	0.7	3.1	−2.3	0.7	2.7	−2.0
Midwest	1.3	2.2	−0.9	1.3	3.5	−2.2	1.2	3.1	−1.9	1.1	3.1	−2.0
South	3.4	1.2	+2.3	4.8	1.4	+3.4	4.3	1.4	+3.0	4.3	1.5	+2.8
West	1.7	2.1	−0.3	3.9	1.9	+2.0	3.8	1.8	+2.0	4.7	1.6	+3.1

SOURCES: Adapted from S. M. Golant, "Post-1980 Regional Migration Patterns of the U.S. Elderly Population, *Journal of Gerontology* 45 (4) (1990): S. 135–140. Based on U.S. Bureau of the Census, 1960–1980 decennial census reports; *Current Population Reports*, series P-20, no. 420. Copyright © The Gerontological Society of America. Reprinted by permission.

NOTES: The data for 1980–1985 are not completely comparable with the data for prior periods because of differences in population coverage, sample size and design, and collection systems. Plus sign denotes net inmigration and minus sign denotes net outmigration.

older migrants differ in educational level, income, and work status from older nonmigrants. Elderly interstate migrants tend to be of higher socioeconomic status, as measured by income and education, than other elderly persons.[29] The following 1980 census figures and 1985 survey figures illustrate the difference in terms of median income and percentage of high school graduates:

	Median Income		Percentage High School Graduates		
Migration Status	All Races 1980	Black 1980	All Races 1980	Black 1980	All Races 1985
Total, Aged 65 and Over	$4,665	$3,189	39	17	48
Interstate Migrants, 1975–1980 or 1980–1985	5,209	3,254	51	22	60
Difference	12%	2%	12	5	12

SOURCE: U.S. Bureau of the Census, 1980 Census of Population, "Geographic Mobility for States and the Nation," *Subject Reports*, PC80-2-2A, Tables 4 and 8; "Geographical Mobility: 1985," *Current Population Reports*, Series P-20, no. 420, Table 17.

The differences in both income and education are impressive. The figures for other mobility categories differ much less from the overall figures in income and education and are lower in some cases. Elderly black interstate migrants differ little, on the average, from other elderly blacks in median income and education.

According to the 1970 census data on migration for 1965–1970, the most recent published census data relating migration of the older population to their labor force status, older migrants are less likely to be working than older nonmigrants and older workers migrate much less than older nonworkers (Table 3.17). Many older persons are retired and since retired persons are not bound down by a job, they are more likely to migrate than older persons who continue to work. The migrant-nonmigrant difference is especially large among those aged 60–64 compared with those aged 50–59 or 65 and over. As noted earlier, at around age 60 retired persons tend to move to retirement residences in other states or to residences in the same state with greater amenities. This general pattern of differences continued to be evident in the CPS data on migration for 1980–1985.

Unemployed older workers, particularly men, distinguish themselves in migrating much more than employed older workers, migrating, in fact, at rates like those of persons not in the labor force. Alternatively

[29]See also Biggar (1980).

TABLE 3.16

Immigration, Outmigration, and Net Migration for the Cohorts Aged 65 and Over in 1980, for States, Divisions, and Regions: 1975–1980 (population size as of April 1, 1980, migration during 1975–80, ages 60 and over in 1975 and 65 and over in 1980)

Region, Division, and State	Amount (in thousands)			Rate[a]			Migration Efficiency Ratio[b]
	Immigration	Outmigration	Net Migration	Immigration	Outmigration	Net Migration	
United States	—	—	—	—	—	—	[c]
Northeast	**50.7**	**264.0**	**-213.3**	**0.8**	**4.3**	**-3.5**	**67.8**
New England	30.2	52.9	-22.7	2.0	3.5	-1.5	27.3
Maine	5.6	5.5	+0.1	4.0	3.9	+0.1	0.7
New Hampshire	8.6	7.1	+1.5	8.3	6.9	+1.4	9.4
Vermont	3.2	3.0	+0.3	5.6	5.1	+0.5	4.7
Massachusetts	15.6	31.3	-15.7	2.1	4.3	-2.2	33.4
Rhode Island	3.1	5.0	-1.9	2.5	4.0	-1.5	23.0
Connecticut	13.7	20.6	-6.9	3.7	5.6	-1.9	20.2
Middle Atlantic	44.3	235.0	-190.6	1.0	5.2	-4.2	68.2
New York	27.1	168.8	-141.7	1.3	7.8	-6.6	72.3
New Jersey	36.5	59.2	-22.6	4.2	6.9	-2.6	23.7
Pennsylvania	29.9	56.2	-26.3	1.9	3.7	-1.7	30.5
Midwest	**90.8**	**240.9**	**-150.4**	**1.4**	**3.6**	**-2.2**	**45.4**
East North Central	69.1	197.5	-128.4	1.5	4.4	-2.9	48.1
Ohio	26.3	56.4	-30.1	2.2	4.8	-2.6	36.4
Indiana	17.5	26.0	-8.5	3.0	4.4	-1.4	19.4
Illinois	26.4	80.5	-54.1	2.1	6.4	-4.3	50.6
Michigan	19.3	48.9	-29.7	2.1	5.4	-3.3	43.5
Wisconsin	13.9	19.9	-6.0	2.5	3.5	-1.1	17.8

TABLE 3.16 (continued)

Region, Division, and State	Amount (in thousands)			Rate[a]			Migration Efficiency Ratio[b]
	Inmigration	Outmigration	Net Migration	Inmigration	Outmigration	Net Migration	
West North Central	43.1	65.2	−22.1	2.0	3.0	−1.0	20.4
Minnesota	10.8	16.4	−5.6	2.2	3.4	−1.2	20.8
Iowa	8.0	15.2	−7.2	2.1	3.9	−1.9	30.9
Missouri	21.1	23.8	−2.7	3.3	3.7	−0.4	6.1
North Dakota	2.0	3.5	−1.5	2.5	4.4	−1.8	26.5
South Dakota	2.7	4.2	−1.5	3.0	4.6	−1.6	21.0
Nebraska	5.7	7.3	−1.7	2.8	3.6	−0.8	12.7
Kansas	11.3	13.2	−1.9	3.7	4.3	−0.6	7.9
South	**397.5**	**117.3**	**+280.2**	**4.7**	**1.4**	**+3.3**	**54.4**
South Atlantic	327.8	94.1	+233.7	7.5	2.2	+5.3	55.4
Delaware	4.4	3.1	+1.3	7.5	5.2	+2.2	17.6
Maryland	17.4	23.0	−5.5	4.4	5.8	−1.4	13.7
District of Columbia	2.8	9.0	−6.1	3.7	12.0	−8.3	52.8
Virginia	22.9	19.9	+2.9	4.5	3.9	+0.6	6.9
West Virginia	6.4	9.6	−3.2	2.7	4.0	−1.4	20.3
North Carolina	24.7	11.7	+13.0	4.1	1.9	+2.1	35.6
South Carolina	13.2	6.6	+6.7	4.6	2.3	+2.3	33.6
Georgia	21.4	13.4	+8.0	4.1	2.6	+1.5	22.9
Florida	286.7	70.4	+216.3	17.0	4.2	+12.8	60.6
East South Central	46.9	34.9	+12.1	2.8	2.1	+0.7	14.7
Kentucky	11.8	12.5	−0.8	2.9	3.1	−0.2	3.1
Tennessee	19.9	14.2	+5.7	3.8	2.7	+1.1	16.8
Alabama	13.5	9.0	+4.6	3.1	2.0	+1.0	20.3
Mississippi	9.7	7.2	+2.5	3.4	2.5	+0.9	14.8
West South Central	76.7	42.2	+34.5	3.1	1.7	+1.4	29.0
Arkansas	21.0	12.2	+8.8	6.7	3.9	+3.8	26.4

TABLE 3.16 (continued)

Region, Division, and State	Amount (in thousands)			Rate[a]			Migration Efficiency Ratio[b]
	Inmigration	Outmigration	Net Migration	Inmigration	Outmigration	Net Migration	
Louisiana	8.6	9.6	−1.0	2.1	2.4	−0.3	5.4
Oklahoma	15.6	12.9	+2.6	4.1	3.4	+0.7	9.2
Texas	50.7	26.6	+24.1	3.7	1.9	+1.8	31.2
West	**163.9**	**80.4**	**+83.5**	**3.9**	**1.9**	**+2.0**	**34.2**
Mountain	107.3	52.7	+54.5	10.1	5.0	+5.1	34.1
Montana	4.0	5.0	−1.1	4.7	5.9	−1.3	11.7
Idaho	6.9	5.7	+1.2	7.4	6.0	+1.3	9.9
Wyoming	1.9	3.2	−1.4	5.0	8.6	−3.7	26.9
Colorado	18.0	15.6	+2.4	7.3	6.3	+1.0	7.1
New Mexico	11.4	7.5	+3.8	9.8	6.5	+3.3	20.1
Arizona	61.4	21.3	+40.1	20.0	6.9	+13.1	48.5
Utah	6.3	4.1	+2.2	5.8	3.7	+2.0	21.4
Nevada	13.8	6.7	+7.1	21.0	10.2	+10.8	34.8
Pacific	116.6	87.6	+29.0	3.7	2.8	+0.9	14.2
Washington	24.4	15.2	+9.3	5.7	3.5	+2.1	23.4
Oregon	22.3	14.9	+7.4	7.4	4.9	+2.4	19.8
California	104.3	91.1	+13.2	4.3	3.8	+0.5	6.8
Alaska	0.8	2.9	−2.1	6.7	24.9	−18.2	57.8
Hawaii	3.7	2.5	+1.2	4.8	3.2	+1.6	19.7

SOURCE: Based on U.S. Bureau of the Census, 1980 Census of Population, *Subject Reports,* "Geographic Mobility for States and the Nation," PC80-2-2A.

NOTES: Plus sign denotes net inmigration and minus sign denotes net outmigration. Dash denotes zero or 0.0.

[a] Base is population aged 65 and over in the state in 1980.

[b] Calculated by the formula $\left| \dfrac{M_1 - M_0}{M_1 + M_0} \right| \times 100$, where M_1 represents inmigration, M_0 represents outmigration, and the ratio is taken without regard to sign. The possible range is from 0 to 100 percent.

[c] Not defined.

TABLE 3.17

Mobility and Migration Rates of Older Men and Women, by Labor Force Status: 1980–1985 and 1965–1970

Age and Type of Migration	Male			Female		
	In Labor Force		Not in Labor Force	In Labor Force		Not in Labor Force
	Total	Unemployed		Total	Unemployed	
1980–1985						
Ages 65 and Over						
Different house	13	a	16	14	a	17
Different county	5	a	8	4	a	7
Different state	3	a	4	2	a	3
1965–1970						
Ages 50–59						
Different house	26	37	35	26	34	26
Different county	9	13	13	8	12	10
Different state	4	7	6	3	6	5
Ages 60–64						
Different house	21	30	31	23	31	25
Different county	6	11	13	6	11	10
Different state	3	5	7	3	5	5
Ages 65 and Over						
Different house	20	29	25	24	29	25
Different county	6	10	10	7	9	9
Different state	3	5	5	3	5	4

SOURCE: U.S. Bureau of the Census, 1970 Census of Population, *Subject Reports*, "Employment Status and Work Experience," PC(2)-6A (1973), Table 10; *Current Population Reports*, series P-20, no. 420, Table 18.

NOTES: Rates based on reports of change of residence between 1965 and 1970 and 1970 census of population or between 1980 and 1985 CPS estimates of population. Rates per 100. Persons whose residence in 1965 was not reported are assumed to be distributed as those whose residence was reported.

a Omitted because of excessive sampling error.

viewed, older migrants have a higher unemployment rate than older nonmigrants. There is also a tendency for the difference in unemployment between older migrants and nonmigrants to increase with advancing age even while migration rates are falling. The unemployed worker is seeking work; those who lose a job are more motivated to migrate to find a job than those who are employed.

The Impact of Interstate Exchanges

Older interstate migrants also vary among themselves in economic status and educational level. The variations encompass age and health as well. Furthermore, there is an association between these characteristics and the states of origin and destination. This patterning of the migrants has program and policy implications. The exchange of elderly migrants between states works to the advantage of some states and to the disadvantage of others, considering the relative income level of the inmigrants and the outmigrants and their relative numbers. An index that measures the net gain or loss of median income through interstate migration of the elderly for a given state has been devised. It weights the median income of elderly inmigrants and elderly outmigrants by the corresponding inmigration rate and outmigration rate.[30]

According to this index, during the 1975–1980 period each of the Middle Atlantic states, East North Central states, and West North Central states were losers and most of the states of the South and West were gainers (Table 3.18). Florida, Arizona, Nevada, New Mexico, Arkansas, and Texas were the leading gainers, and the District of Columbia, New York, Illinois, Wyoming, Michigan, and New Jersey were the leading losers, in the order given (Figure 3.4). We may alternatively identify winners in the interstate migration exchange as the eight states for which the inmigrants had a substantially higher median income than the resident population, which in turn had a substantially higher median income than the outmigrants. In such an exchange, both inmigration and outmigration were, in effect, raising the income level of the residents. The corresponding losers were the 15 states that had the inverse experience; here both inmigration and outmigration tended to lower the income level of the residents.

Elderly migrants *to* Florida and Arizona tend to be "wealthier" (as measured by median income) than elderly migrants to all other states

---

[30]The formula for the index is $I_{mi}(M_i/P) - I_{mo}(M_o/P)$, where I_{mi} represents the median income of inmigrants, I_{mo} represents the median income of outmigrants, M_i/P the inmigration rate of persons aged 65 and over, and M_o/P the outmigration rate of persons aged 65 and over.

TABLE 3.18

Median Income of Interstate Migrants Aged 65 and Over and Index of Net Income Gain or Loss, by State: 1980

Region, Division, and State	Median Income (dollars)			Net Gain or Loss		Percent Difference in Median Income	
	Inmigrants	Outmigrants	Resident Population	Index[a] (dollars)	Rank	Inmigrants from Resident Population	Outmigrants from Resident Population
Northeast							
New England							
Maine	5,467	5,045	4,409	+19.45	24	+24.0	+14.4
New Hampshire	5,288	4,799	5,010	+108.79	12	+5.5	−4.2
Vermont	5,775	4,690	4,937	+84.23	15	+17.0	−5.0
Massachusetts	5,086	5,792	5,297	−140.31	43	−4.0	+9.3
Rhode Island	3,707	4,804	4,790	−98.78	37	−22.6	+0.3
Connecticut	5,413	6,287	5,774	−152.27	44	−6.3	+8.9
Middle Atlantic							
New York	4,461	6,097	5,339	−420.25	50	−16.4	+14.2
New Jersey	5,021	5,969	5,585	−197.50	46	−10.1	+6.9
Pennsylvania	4,705	5,318	5,204	−102.35	38	−9.6	+2.2
North Central							
East North Central							
Ohio	4,252	5,571	5,312	−173.25	45	−20.0	+4.9
Indiana	4,444	5,349	5,321	−104.37	39	−16.5	+0.5
Illinois	4,435	5,855	5,747	−280.76	49	−22.8	+1.9
Michigan	4,152	5,594	5,257	−212.31	47	−21.0	+6.4
Wisconsin	4,410	5,874	5,155	−98.40	36	−14.5	+13.9
West North Central							
Minnesota	4,835	5,337	4,998	−74.07	31	−3.3	+6.8
Iowa	4,572	4,912	5,420	−98.18	35	−15.6	−9.4
Missouri	4,519	4,570	4,838	−21.01	28	−6.6	−5.5
North Dakota	4,244	5,156	4,962	−117.77	41	−14.5	+3.9
South Dakota	3,963	4,420	4,437	−94.51	32	−10.7	−0.4
Nebraska	4,370	5,002	5,136	−57.67	30	−14.9	−2.6
Kansas	4,461	4,793	5,335	−42.38	29	−16.4	−10.2

TABLE 3.18 (continued)

Region, Division, and State	Median Income (dollars)			Net Gain or Loss		Percent Difference in Median Income	
	Immigrants	Outmigrants	Resident Population	Index[a] (dollars)	Rank	Inmigrants from Resident Population	Outmigrants from Resident Population
South							
South Atlantic							
Delaware	5,388	5,135	5,378	+133.62	10	+0.2	-4.5
Maryland	5,267	6,378	5,550	-138.01	42	-5.1	+14.9
District of Columbia	4,471	6,815	6,186	-650.51	51	-27.7	+10.2
Virginia	5,239	5,832	4,853	+7.03	25	+8.0	+20.2
West Virginia	4,154	4,902	4,820	-86.69	33	-13.8	+1.7
North Carolina	5,324	4,453	3,902	+131.25	11	+36.4	+14.1
South Carolina	5,064	3,973	3,851	+142.37	9	+31.5	+3.2
Georgia	4,579	4,197	3,855	+80.53	16	+18.8	+8.9
Florida	6,659	4,575	5,652	+940.46	1	+17.8	-19.1
East South Central							
Kentucky	4,277	4,256	4,206	-7.21	26	+1.7	-1.2
Tennessee	4,351	3,891	3,883	+60.82	18	+12.1	+0.2
Alabama	4,003	3,703	3,718	+47.60	21	+7.7	-0.4
Mississippi	4,000	3,434	3,347	+48.87	19	+19.5	+2.6
West South Central							
Arkansas	5,058	3,581	3,765	+199.88	5	+34.3	-4.9
Louisiana	4,240	4,325	3,911	-12.45	27	+8.4	+10.6
Oklahoma	4,272	4,258	4,471	+30.40	23	-4.5	-4.8
Texas	4,677	4,276	4,567	+173.69	6	+2.4	-6.4

TABLE 3.18 (continued)

Region, Division, and State	Median Income (dollars)			Net Gain or Loss		Percent Difference in Median Income	
	Inmigrants	Outmigrants	Resident Population	Index[a] (dollars)	Rank	Inmigrants from Resident Population	Outmigrants from Resident Population
West							
Mountain							
Montana	3,986	4,748	5,045	−95.15	34	−21.0	−5.9
Idaho	4,449	4,163	4,910	+76.61	17	−9.4	−15.2
Wyoming	4,385	5,655	5,392	−270.15	48	−18.7	+4.9
Colorado	5,019	5,024	5,403	+48.39	20	−7.1	−7.0
New Mexico	5,146	4,295	4,647	+224.41	4	+10.7	−7.6
Arizona	6,180	4,946	5,702	+891.25	2	+8.4	−13.3
Utah	4,980	5,424	5,617	+85.08	14	−11.3	−3.4
Nevada	5,509	5,132	5,934	+635.68	3	−7.2	−13.5
Pacific							
Washington	4,814	5,126	5,571	+92.30	13	−13.6	−8.0
Oregon	5,061	4,572	5,447	+147.38	7	−7.1	−16.1
California	5,159	5,033	6,034	+32.99	22	−14.5	−16.6
Alaska	4,610	5,591	6,291	−117.14	40	−26.7	−11.1
Hawaii	7,490	6,668	5,443	+146.07	8	+37.6	+22.5

SOURCE: Data on median income for inmigrants and outmigrants from U.S. Bureau of the Census, "Geographic Mobility for States and the Nation," PC 80-2-2A, Table 37.

NOTES: Median income in 1979, population size in 1980, migration during 1975–1980, ages 60 and over in 1975 and 65 and over in 1980. Excludes migration to and from abroad.

[a] Calculated by the formula $I_{Mi}(Mi/P) - I_{Mo}(Mo/P)$, where I_{Mi} represents the median income of inmigrants, I_{Mo} the median income of outmigrants, Mi/P the inmigration rate of persons aged 65 and over, and Mo/P the outmigrant rate of persons aged 65 and over.

159

FIGURE 3.4

Index of Net Median Income Gain or Loss Through Interstate Migration: 1979

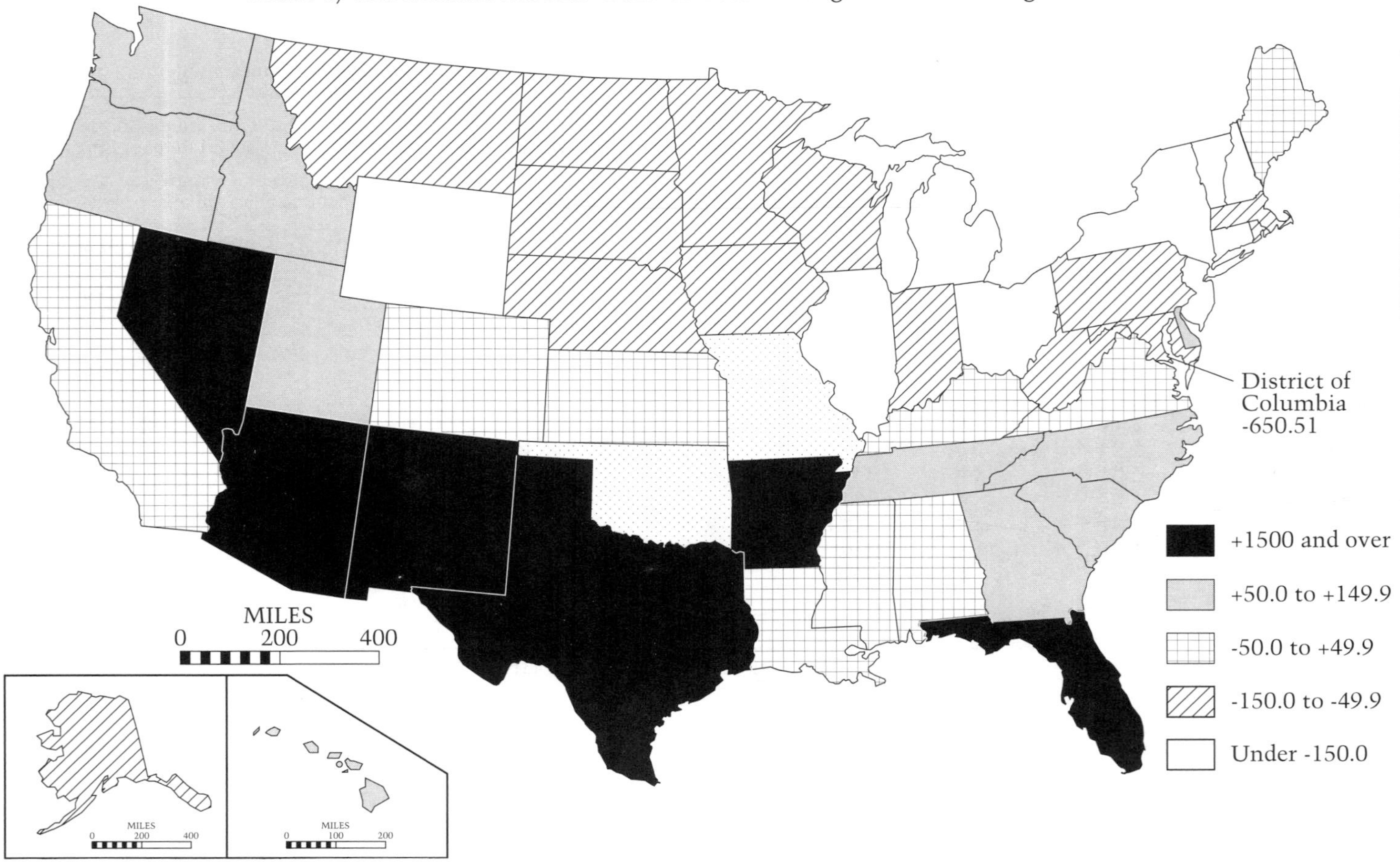

District of
Columbia
-650.51

+1500 and over

+50.0 to +149.9

-50.0 to +49.9

-150.0 to -49.9

Under -150.0

MILES

0   200   400

SOURCE: Based on Table 3.18.

NOTE: Difference between median income of inmigrants and outmigrants, each weighted by corresponding migration rate.

except Hawaii, the resident elderly population of the principal states of origin, and the resident elderly population of Florida and Arizona, the states of destination (Table 3.18).[31] At the same time, elderly migrants *from* Florida and Arizona tend to be less wealthy than the average oldster in these states, the elderly inmigrants to these states, and the elderly outmigrants from many other states. As a result, migration of elderly persons to Florida and Arizona raises the average economic level of the resident older population in these states and lowers it in the states of origin. Migration to and from them bolsters their economies and tends to depress those of the states of origin and destination paired with them, such as New York, Illinois, and Michigan.

Note particularly that the sizable exchange between New York and Florida favors Florida: New York loses its most affluent retirees commonly to Florida, and receives back elderly persons with relatively low incomes, albeit far fewer than it loses. The median income of retirees going to Florida was 46 percent higher than that of those leaving Florida and 18 percent higher than that of the state's resident elderly population. In New York, the figures were nearly reversed. Retirees moving out of New York had a median income 37 percent higher than those moving in and 14 percent higher than the resident elderly population. As a result of this exchange, New York is saddled with a growing burden of providing for an elderly population in need, while Florida is favored with wealthier retirees who can provide for themselves and pay their share of taxes. On one hand, this continual influx of economically advantaged retirees strengthens Florida's economy, helping it to offset the economic burden of the needy migrants. On the other, Florida's role as a retirement mecca imposes on it a major task of providing services for numerous dependent elderly.

In the West, special interest attaches to the economic impact of the large movement to California and Arizona and between them. Their economic ranks in the migration exchange, 22 and 2, differ sharply (Table 3.18). In the period 1975–1980 the elderly moving to California had a median income 14 percent less than the elderly residents of the state—a fact disadvantaging the state's economy—although the inmigrants had a higher median income than the migrants to most states of the South and West. The elderly leaving the state had a median income 17 percent less than the elderly residents, however—a fact favoring the state's economy. The migrants to California are, in general, more problem-laden than the migrants to Arizona. They are poorer and older and are more

---

[31]See also C. F. Longino, Jr., "Returning from the Sunbelt: Myths and Realities of Migratory Patterns Among the Elderly," in *Proceedings of Symposium on Returning from the Sunbelt*, March 15, 1985, Brookdale Institute, Columbia University, and International Exchange on Gerontology, University of South Florida, 1985; and Biggar (1984).

likely to be widowed and disabled.[32] They are also more likely to have come from a foreign country and to be unable to speak English well. In relative terms, the elderly new arrivals are an economic burden for California and an economic boon for Arizona.

Other implications of the interstate migration of older persons stem from the economic characteristics of the states of origin and destination. States with high worker earnings, and hence with high living costs, tended to have high rates of outmigration of older persons during 1975–1980, and states with high levels of unemployment and low living costs tended to have high levels of inmigration of older persons.[33] This is in sharp contrast to the pattern for migrants under age 55. Given the variations among the states in their economic characteristics, these tendencies suggest a spatial redistribution of the older and younger populations and of resources through different migration patterns. This spatial redistribution may temper economic differences among the states, bringing older, more affluent "dependents" to the poorer states and removing younger potential workers from them. On the other hand, it may result in an increased imbalance between taxpayers and revenues, and beneficiaries and benefits.

Residential Clustering

Variations by Type of Residential Area and Size of Place

About three quarters of the 25.5 million persons aged 65 and over in April 1980 lived in urban areas and nearly 6 in 10 lived in urbanized areas, large urban agglomerations consisting of a central city and an urban fringe (suburbs). Nearly one third of all elderly persons lived in central cities and over one quarter lived in the urban fringe.

The 1980 census shows a general inverse gradation in the proportion of persons aged 65 and over according to the size of the place of residence—with some exceptions, the larger the place, the lower the percentage of elderly people. The tiny town/open country population and the urban fringe were out of line with this rule. The highest proportion of elderly persons (15.4 percent) was found in small towns, that is, rural places of 1,000–2,500 inhabitants (Table 3.19). The next highest proportion was found in urban places outside urbanized areas, followed in order by the rural-farm population, central cities of urbanized areas,

---

[32]See Biggar (1984).

[33]W. J. Serow, "Determinants of Interstate Migration: Differences Between Elderly and Nonelderly Movers," *Journal of Gerontology* 42 (1) (January 1987):95–100.

other rural areas, and the urban fringe (9.9 percent). In the urban fringe, young families with children predominate.

The variation in the proportion of elderly persons among these residential categories was essentially the same in 1970, although the level of the proportions was consistently lower. Hence, the aging of the population was pervasive, affecting all types of residential areas—the open country, towns, and cities, large and small. Such widespread aging variously reflects the general decline of fertility, the general reduction of mortality, especially at the higher ages, and, depending on the type of residential area, the outmigration of youth, especially from high fertility areas, the inmigration of elderly persons, and aging-in-place of middle-aged residents.

The very high percentage of elderly persons in rural places of 1,000 to 2,500 inhabitants results largely from the outmigration of young people and aging-in-place of older people. We would expect these factors to apply with equal weight to the smaller rural places and the rural-farm population, but other factors appear to be offsetting them. A higher birth rate in the farm population may account for some of the difference between these residence categories. A factor of perhaps equal, if not greater, importance is the tendency of elderly farmers who can no longer operate their farms to take up residence in a town close to their farms.

Data on the distribution of the elderly population between metropolitan (SMSA) and nonmetropolitan areas for 1980, based on the CPS, show a similar inverse variation from high to low percentages of elderly persons according to the size of the area. We find a considerable range from nonmetropolitan counties with no place over 2,500 population (13.5 percent) to the parts of the larger metropolitan areas outside the central cities (8.9 percent). (See Table 3.20.) Elderly persons formed 12.3 percent of the total nonmetropolitan population compared with 10.9 percent of the total metropolitan population in 1980; thus, the nonmetropolitan and metropolitan elderly constituted about the same share of the U.S. elderly (37 percent and 63 percent) as the nonelderly. The most rapid aging between 1970 and 1980 occurred in the smaller metropolitan areas and nonmetropolitan areas with a large urban place.

The black population and the white population show the same general pattern of variation in the share of elderly by type of residential area and size of metropolitan area since the same factors have been influencing their age structures. The descending progression of the percentage of elderly according to the size and type of area is more regular and pronounced for blacks than for whites, however. For blacks the proportion for the nonmetropolitan areas without an urban place in 1980 (16 percent) was three times the proportion for the part of the larger metropolitan areas outside central cities (5 percent).

TABLE 3.19

Distribution of the Population Aged 65 and Over, by Urban and Rural Residence and Size of Place, and Percentage Aged 65 and Over of Total Population, for Whites, Blacks, and Hispanics: 1980 and 1970 (numbers in thousands)

Race/Hispanic Origin and Measure	All Areas	Urban Total	Urbanized Areas Total	Central Cities	Urban Fringe	Other Places 10,000 or More	2,500– 10,000
1980							
Total Number	25,498	19,001	15,158	7,992	7,166	1,734	2,109
White[a]	22,942	16,927	13,402	6,602	6,801	3,525	
Black[a]	2,067	1,666	1,407	1,151	256	259	
Hispanic[b]	673	598	516	336	180	82	
Percent of							
All Areas, Total	100.0	74.5	59.4	31.3	28.1	6.8	8.3
White[a]	100.0	73.8	58.4	28.8	29.6	15.4	
Black[a]	100.0	80.6	68.1	55.7	12.4	12.5	
Hispanic[b]	100.0	88.9	76.8	50.0	26.8	12.1	
Percent of							
All Ages, Total	11.3	11.4	10.9	11.9	9.9	12.9 [e]	14.7
White[a]	12.1	12.5	12.1	14.1	10.6	14.6	
Black[a]	7.8	7.4	7.0	7.6	5.2	10.4	
Hispanic[b]	4.6	4.6	4.5	4.7	4.1	5.2	
1970							
Percent of							
All Areas, Total	100.0	72.9	55.3	34.1	21.2	8.9	8.7
White[c]	100.0	72.6	54.8	33.5	22.4	9.0	8.8
Black	100.0	76.5	60.9	52.1	8.8	8.7	6.9
Hispanic[d]	100.0	86.3	70.9	50.8	20.2	7.6	7.9
Percent of							
All Ages, Total	9.9	9.8	9.4	10.7	7.8	10.8	12.2
White[c]	10.3	10.3	10.0	12.0	8.0	11.1	12.5
Black	6.9	6.5	6.0	6.2	5.4	8.7	9.7
Hispanic[d]	4.1	4.0	3.9	4.2	3.4	4.3	5.0

SOURCE: Based on U.S. Bureau of the Census, 1980 Census of Population, *U.S. Summary: General Social and Economic Characteristics,* vol. 1, Chapter C, Tables 98, 120, and 130; and 1970 Census of Population, *U.S. Summary,* vol. 1, Chapter B, Table 52, and Chapter C, Table 118.

NOTE: NA = not available.

[a] The data for whites (and for blacks to a relatively smaller extent) are affected by the fact that nearly 6 million Hispanic persons did not report a specific race in response to the "race" question in the 1980 census and hence were tabulated as "other race." According to the race/Hispanic origin cross-tabulation of the 1980 census, most Hispanics reporting on race report "white."
[b] Hispanics may be of any race.
[c] Excludes a small number of Hispanic persons who were tabulated as of "other race."
[d] For New York, New Jersey, and Pennsylvania, persons of Puerto Rican birth and parentage only; for five southwestern states, persons of Spanish language or Spanish surname; for the remaining states, persons of Spanish language. Hispanics may be of any race.
[e] Percentage for "other places" is 13.8.

TABLE 3.19 (*continued*)

| | Rural | | |
| | | Other Rural | |
Total	Places of 1,000–2,500	Total	Farm
6,498	1,085	5,413	712
6,014	NA	NA	691
401	NA	NA	17
75	NA	NA	4
25.5	4.3	21.2	2.8
26.2	NA	NA	3.0
19.4	NA	NA	0.8
11.1	NA	NA	0.7
10.9	15.4	10.3	12.7
11.1	NA	NA	12.7
10.3	NA	NA	14.9
5.1	NA	NA	5.6
27.1	4.5	22.6	NA
27.4	4.6	22.7	NA
23.5	2.8	20.7	NA
13.6	NA	NA	NA
10.1	13.6	9.6	NA
10.3	13.9	9.7	NA
8.7	10.4	8.5	NA
4.6	NA	NA	NA

The urban-rural distribution of elderly blacks differs from that for elderly whites principally in the former's much greater concentration in the central cities of urbanized areas. Of the 2.1 million blacks aged 65 and over in 1980, about two thirds lived in urbanized areas, and over four fifths of these, or well over half of all blacks aged 65 and over, lived in a central city.

The low proportion of elderly among the Hispanic population compared with whites and blacks is reflected in all residential categories. Even in rural areas, only 5 percent of Hispanics are aged 65 and over. The common view of elderly Hispanics as mostly congregated in the

TABLE 3.20

Distribution of the Population Aged 65 and Over, by Metropolitan Residence and Size of Metropolitan Area, and Percentage Aged 65 and Over of the Total Population, for Whites, Blacks, and Hispanics: 1980 and 1970
(numbers in thousands)

Race and Spanish Origin	Total	All Metropolitan Areas			Metropolitan Areas of 1 Million or More		Metropolitan Areas of Less Than 1 Million	
		Total	Central Cities	Outside Central Cities	In Central Cities	Outside Central Cities	In Central Cities	Outside Central Cities
1980								
Total Number	23,743	15,085	7,162	7,922	3,760	4,680	3,402	3,242
White	21,446	13,495	5,970	7,525	3,027	4,479	2,943	3,046
Black	2,019	1,377	1,055	321	643	170	413	151
Hispanic[b]	563	460	291	170	168	115	123	55
Percent of								
All Ages, Total	10.9	10.2	11.8	9.1	12.0	8.9	11.6	9.3
White	11.4	10.8	13.4	9.4	14.2	9.4	12.6	9.5
Black	7.9	7.0	7.4	5.9	7.1	4.9	7.8	7.9
Hispanic[b]	4.2	4.2	4.6	3.7	4.3	3.6	4.9	3.8
Percent of								
All Areas, Total	100.0	63.5	30.2	33.4	15.8	19.7	14.3	13.7
White	100.0	62.9	27.8	35.1	14.1	20.9	13.7	14.2
Black	100.0	68.2	52.3	15.9	31.8	8.4	20.5	7.5
Hispanic[b]	100.0	81.7	51.7	30.2	29.8	20.4	21.8	9.8
1970								
Total Number	19,235	12,344	6,640	5,704	3,816	3,484	2,825	2,220
White	17,532	11,207	5,751	5,457	3,251	3,348	2,500	2,108
Black	1,549	1,027	815	212	519	117	296	95
Hispanic[b]	405	317	216	101	134	64	82	37
Percent of								
All Ages, Total	9.6	9.0	10.6	7.7	11.1	7.7	9.9	7.7
White	10.0	9.4	11.8	7.8	13.0	7.8	10.5	7.7
Black	7.0	6.3	6.3	6.2	6.0	5.7	7.0	6.9
Hispanic[b]	4.5	4.3	4.6	3.7	4.5	3.6	4.8	3.8
Percent of								
All Areas, Total	100.0	64.2	34.5	29.7	19.8	18.1	14.7	11.5
White	100.0	63.9	32.8	31.1	18.5	19.1	14.3	12.0
Black	100.0	66.3	52.6	13.7	33.5	7.6	19.1	6.1
Hispanic[b]	100.0	78.3	53.3	24.9	33.1	15.8	20.2	9.1

SOURCES: U.S. Bureau of the Census, *Current Population Reports*, series P-23, no. 75, for 1970 data. Data for 1970 are based on 1-in-100 sample of the 1970 Census of Population. Data for 1980 are unpublished data based on the CPS; they have been adjusted to current independent estimates for age, sex, and race based on the 1970 census.

NOTES: Data exclude residents of institutions. Data pertain to the 1970 definition of metropolitan areas in 1970 and to the 1977 definition in 1980.

[a] Includes areas which gained metropolitan status between 1970 and 1977.
[b] Hispanics may be of any race.

TABLE 3.20 (*continued*)

| | Nonmetropolitan Areas[a] | | |
Total	In Counties with a Place of 25,000 or More	In Counties with a Place of 2,500– 24,999	In Counties with a Place of Less than 2,500
8,658	1,956	5,553	1,150
7,951	1,801	5,124	1,026
643	133	394	115
102	20	71	11
12.3	11.3	12.5	13.5
12.5	11.5	12.8	13.4
11.1	9.4	10.8	15.7
4.6	3.1	4.9	8.3
36.5	8.2	23.4	4.8
37.1	8.4	23.9	4.8
31.8	6.6	19.5	5.7
18.1	3.6	12.6	2.0
6,891	1,511	4,479	902
6,324	1,411	4,095	818
522	90	357	75
89	16	63	11
11.0	9.5	11.3	12.5
11.2	9.7	11.5	13.1
9.1	8.1	9.4	9.6
5.6	4.0	6.0	8.5
35.8	7.9	23.3	4.7
36.1	8.0	23.4	4.7
33.7	5.8	23.0	4.8
22.0	4.0	15.6	2.7

countryside, particularly on farms, is a fiction. The Hispanic population aged 65 and over is largely an urban population (89 percent in 1980), much more so than the white (74 percent) or black (81 percent) populations of these ages. Like the black population, the Hispanic population is heavily concentrated in the central cities of urbanized areas (50 percent in 1980), but a much greater share of the Hispanic population than of the black population lives in the urban fringe (27 percent vs. 12 percent). It is in the large cities and their suburbs, then, that the demand for housing, health care, and family services by elderly Hispanics will be largely felt.

Nonmetropolitan Areas

The share of the elderly population living in nonmetropolitan areas is now declining, but it is still a substantial segment of the total.[34] Only a little over one quarter of the elderly population lived in nonmetropolitan areas in 1986 compared with over one third in 1970.

In 1980 the nonmetropolitan elderly were concentrated in the South (43 percent of the total) and the Midwest (33 percent of the total). Less than one quarter of the nonmetropolitan elderly lived in the Northeast and West combined.

Numerous nonmetropolitan counties have high proportions of elderly. According to Glasgow, in over 500 nonmetropolitan counties one sixth or more of the population was aged 65 and over in 1980. These counties fall heavily in the mostly agricultural areas of the Midwest and in the retirement areas of Texas and the Ozarks (Figure 3.5). Glasgow estimates that nearly 500 nonmetropolitan counties experienced a large net inmigration of persons aged 60 and over between 1970 and 1980 and that about 700,000 persons aged 60 and over moved to nonmetropolitan counties in 1975–1980.

Type of Migration (in thousands)	Total, Ages 60 and Over	Ages 60–64	Ages 65–74	Ages 75 and Over
Metropolitan to Nonmetropolitan	698	234	317	147
Nonmetropolitan to Metropolitan	425	108	186	129
Net gain	275	126	131	18
Nonmetropolitan to Nonmetropolitan	1,589	392	683	514
Nonmetropolitan Nonmigrants	8,209	2,175	3,728	2,306

SOURCE: U.S. Department of Agriculture, "The Nonmetropolitan Elderly: Economic and Demographic Status," by N. Glasgow, *Rural Development Research Report*, no. 70 (June 1988), Table 7. Based on U.S. Bureau of the Census, 1980 Census of Population, Public Use Microdata Sample.

The nonmetropolitan elderly population has grown dramatically since 1950 and has been aging rapidly as a result of aging-in-place, outmigra-

[34]See U.S. Department of Agriculture, "The Nonmetropolitan Elderly: Economic and Demographic Status," by N. Glasgow, *Rural Development Research Report*, no. 70 (June 1988), for more details.

FIGURE 3.5

Nonmetropolitan Counties with One Sixth or More of the Total Population Aged 65 and Over: 1980

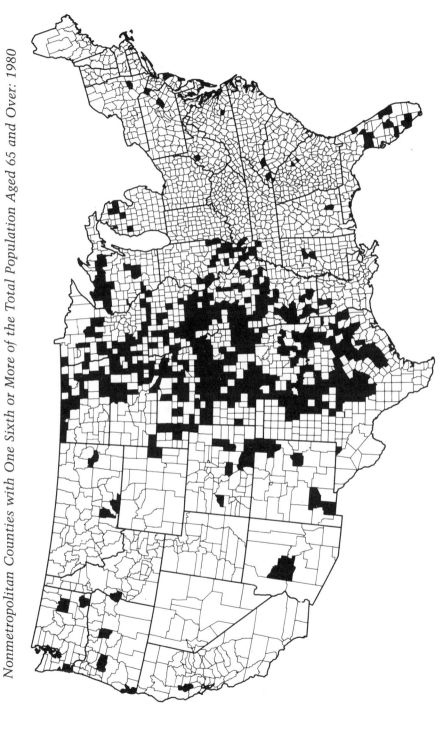

SOURCE: U.S. Department of Agriculture, "The Nonmetro Elderly: Economic and Demographic Status," by N. Glasgow, *Rural Development Research Report*, no. 70 (June 1988), Figure 2, p. 8.

NOTES: The nonmetropolitan county of Kalawao, Hawaii, which has a high percentage of persons aged 65 and over, was omitted from this map. U.S. figure = 12.0 percent.

tion of young persons from agricultural and mining areas, and inmigration of elderly persons from metropolitan areas. Although there are some areas in which retirees are concentrated, retirement counties are widely scattered in the United States (Figure 3.6).[35] Growth in nonmetropolitan retirement counties has continued at a rapid pace since 1980, much faster than in other nonmetropolitan counties (9.6 percent vs. 2.2 percent between 1980 and 1985). The inmigrants are mostly aged 65–74. After this age, declining health, reduced income, and widowhood lead to return migration to urban centers where the necessary health and social services are located or where the children of the migrants live.

Metropolitan and nonmetropolitan counties have different physical characteristics (e.g., population size, population density, geographic isolation, road systems, and economic base), which are associated with different needs (e.g., health care delivery, transportation, recreation, access to social services) as well as with different social and economic characteristics of the residents. Securing access to health care services presents a difficult problem for isolated, sparsely populated areas. Comprehensive, state-of-the-art medical care and facilities tend to be available only in large urban centers. Hence, traveling long distances to these centers may be required. This is usually possible only for the younger and more affluent segment of the elderly nonmetropolitan population. These are typically retirees who have recently migrated to the areas.

Another problem is the pressure on nonmetropolitan communities to serve the needs of the new arrivals from urban areas, who demand goods and services to a degree not usually available in nonmetropolitan areas. Some retirement communities may have to undergo vast changes to accommodate the new population growth. The problem is eased by the fact that the recent inmigrants are relatively more affluent than the resident elderly, so that the tax base is expanded, business activity is stimulated, and the economies of scale can be secured in various aspects of community life.

The problems are more serious for farming and farm-dependent communities that have high and increasing shares of elderly as a result of the outmigration of young persons and aging-in-place. Depression in the farm economy in the 1970s and 1980s has led to the decline and departure of businesses and services, the fall in farm incomes and farm land values, the erosion of the tax base, and, finally, reduced services for the elderly. Since the elderly in these areas tend to be older and poorer than in retirement communities, they are more dependent on local services.

[35]Nonmetropolitan retirement counties are those in which the population aged 60 and over grew by 15 percent from inmigration between 1970 and 1980.

FIGURE 3.6

Nonmetropolitan Retirement Counties: 1980

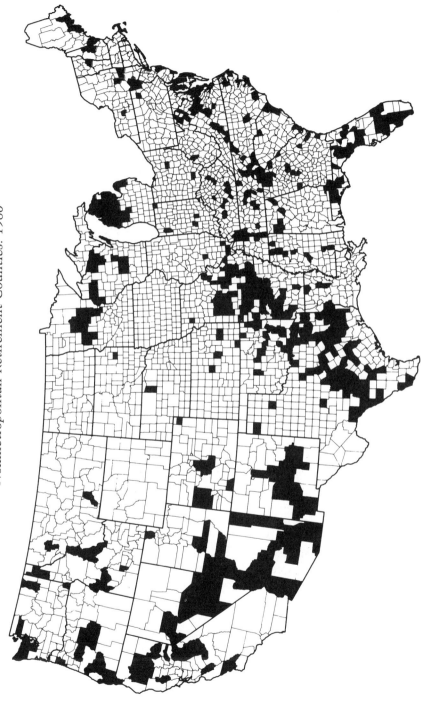

SOURCE: U.S. Department of Agriculture, "The Nonmetro Elderly: Economic and Demographic Status," by N. Glasgow, *Rural Development Research Report*, no. 70 (June 1988), Figure 3, p. 10.

NOTES: Nonmetropolitan retirement counties are those in which the population aged 60 and over grew by at least 15 percent from inmigration during 1970–1980. Nonmetropolitan retirement counties of Matanuska-Susitna, Alaska, and of Maui and Hawaii, Hawaii, were omitted from this map.

In sum, the elderly appear to have participated fully in the metro-politan-nonmetropolitan shifts and the deconcentration of the general population in the 1960s, 1970s, and even 1980s. Metropolitan-nonmet-ropolitan shifts of the elderly population give rise to particular problems relating to the service requirements of the elderly and the economic conditions of the nonmetropolitan areas where they settle.

Interregional-Metropolitan Migration

Recent interregional-metropolitan migration patterns of the elderly are described by rates of net migration for the metropolitan and non-metropolitan parts of regions for 1965–1970 and 1975–1980 developed by Frey (Table 3.21).[36] According to this analysis, the elderly tended to leave the large metropolitan areas of the North and, in lesser degree, the small metropolitan areas of the North and to head for the small metro-politan areas and nonmetropolitan areas of the South and West and, to a lesser degree, the nonmetropolitan areas of the North and the large metropolitan areas of the South and West. Elderly persons thus tended to follow the same migration paths as younger persons, often at higher (net) rates, but for different reasons. While the patterns of interregional-intermetropolitan net migration for the older population were the same in 1975–1980 and 1965–1970, the rates were generally higher in the more recent period.

Frey has examined the implications of the interregional-intermetro-politan migration streams of 1975–1980 for the future growth and dis-tribution of the elderly population in the nine regional-metropolitan res-idential areas identified in the study.[37] The results suggest great differences in the growth rates of the elderly in these areas between 1980 and 2030. The main result projected is a strong shift of the elderly from all three residential areas in the North to all three residential areas in the South and in the West (Table 3.22). Furthermore, according to the projections, the growth rates of the elderly population in all areas, especially the metropolitan areas (SMSAs) of the South and the three residential areas of the West, would far exceed the corresponding growth rates of the population under age 65. In large part, the maturing of the baby-boom cohorts in the first part of the next century will account for sharp dif-ferences in growth rates of the elderly and the nonelderly. The varia-tions in growth rates would also have a pronounced effect on the geo-

[36]Frey (1986). The Frey analysis considered nine areas—three regions (North, South, and West) and three metropolitan parts (large metropolitan areas, small metropolitan areas, and nonmetropolitan areas).

[37]Frey (1986) derived projections of the age-regional-metropolitan distribution of the U.S. population by use of the multiregional cohort-component method.

TABLE 3.21

Age-Specific Net Migration Rates of Persons Aged 55 and Over, by Age, for Metropolitan and Nonmetropolitan Parts of Regions: 1965–1970 and 1975–1980

Metropolitan Residence and Age at End of Period	North		South		West	
	1965–1970	1975–1980	1965–1970	1975–1980	1965–1970	1975–1980
Large Metropolitan Areas						
55–59	−2.1	−4.5	+3.7	+1.4	+1.1	−0.9
60–64	−4.0	−6.4	+6.0	+2.9	+1.0	−0.9
65–69	−5.7	−7.4	+9.3	+4.9	+1.7	—
70+	−2.8	−3.4	+6.1	+3.2	+2.1	+1.4
Small Metropolitan Areas						
55–59	−0.3	−1.7	+1.5	+3.4	+1.7	+4.7
60–64	−1.3	−2.4	+2.8	+5.0	+3.0	+5.7
65–69	−1.8	−2.5	+3.9	+5.9	+4.1	+5.9
70+	−0.4	−0.7	+2.8	+3.2	+3.5	+3.4
Nonmetropolitan Areas						
55–59	+0.2	+1.2	+0.6	+5.4	+0.5	+7.8
60–64	+1.6	+1.9	+2.1	+6.7	+1.4	+8.5
65–69	+1.8	+1.5	+2.4	+5.3	+2.3	+6.0
70+	−0.5	−0.5	−0.4	+1.1	−0.6	+1.2

SOURCE: Adapted from W. H. Frey, "Lifecourse Migration and Redistribution of the Elderly Across U.S. Regions and Metropolitan Areas," *Economic Outlook USA* 13 (2) (1986), Table 1 (based on U.S. decennial census data). Reprinted by permission, Survey Research Center, University of Michigan.

NOTES: Base of rates is population at beginning of period. Metropolitan areas are defined in terms of 1980 SMSAs, SCSAs, and, in New England, NECMA approximations of SCSAs. Where boundaries of census regions cross the boundaries of individual SMSAs, the territory for the entire SMSA is assigned to the region in which most of its population resides. Metropolitan areas with 1980 population greater than 1 million are classed as large metropolitan areas; all others are classed as small metropolitan areas. Plus sign denotes net inmigration and minus sign denotes net outmigration. Dash denotes 0.0.

graphic distribution of the elderly and on the share of the elderly in the total population of each area. According to the projections, for example, the share of the elderly in the total population would nearly double in the nonmetropolitan areas of the North and more than double in the small metropolitan areas of the West between 1980 and 2030.

Clustering Within Metropolitan Areas

In addition to the share of the elderly in metropolitan areas and other residential categories, just discussed, I consider two other measures of residential clustering of the elderly in metropolitan areas, the

TABLE 3.22

Projected Percent Changes in the Elderly Population of Metropolitan and Nonmetropolitan Parts of Regions Assuming 1965–1970 and 1975–1980 Rates for Age-Specific Migration Streams: 1980–2030

Area	Assuming 1975–1980 Rates			Assuming 1965–1970 Rates		
	Population 65 and Over	Total Population	Excess of 65 and Over	Population 65 and Over	Total Population	Excess of 65 and Over
Total, United States	+152.9	+24.5	+128.4	+152.9	+24.5	+128.4
North						
Large metropolitan areas	+71.9	−12.3	+84.2	+117.7	+17.5	+100.2
Small metropolitan areas	+116.9	+10.1	+106.8	+140.5	+23.6	+116.9
Nonmetropolitan areas	+100.2	+11.7	+88.5	+99.5	+6.3	+93.2
South						
Large metropolitan areas	+210.5	+44.1	+166.4	+238.6	+52.3	+186.3
Small metropolitan areas	+227.9	+48.8	+179.1	+185.5	+27.6	+157.9
Nonmetropolitan areas	+185.1	+46.9	+138.2	+123.8	+7.6	+116.2
West						
Large metropolitan areas	+205.2	+40.6	+164.6	+227.6	+51.3	+176.3
Small metropolitan areas	+286.3	+64.3	+222.0	+210.7	+27.8	+182.9
Nonmetropolitan areas	+268.1	+69.1	+199.0	+164.5	+12.0	+152.5

SOURCE: W. H. Frey, "Lifecourse Migration and Redistribution of the Elderly Across U.S. Regions and Metropolitan Areas," *Economic Outlook USA* 13 (2) (1986), Table 4. Reprinted by permission, Survey Research Center, University of Michigan.

NOTE: See Table 3.21 for definitions.

index of dissimilarity and the probability of intergroup contact. The first measures the difference in the percent distributions of the elderly and the nonelderly within metropolitan areas by small subdivisions (i.e., census tracts) and the second measures the probability of contact between the elderly and nonelderly within metropolitan areas.[38]

Some degree of residential clustering of the elderly population within metropolitan areas compared with the nonelderly population is common among the metropolitan areas of the United States. Using mainly the index of dissimilarity, various researchers have reported on the extent of residential clustering of the elderly within metropolitan areas in recent censuses.[39] Denton's study is the most recent and comprehensive, covering some 60 SMSAs in 1970 and 1980, and this discussion draws heavily on it.

Denton found that residential clustering of the elderly in the 60 SMSAs in 1980, as measured by the conventional index of dissimilarity, was substantial vis-à-vis adults under age 65 (index of 23), but it was even greater vis-à-vis children under age 15 (index of 30). (See Table 3.23.) Key elderly SMSAs (i.e., SMSAs with large proportions of elderly residents) show a more concentrated distribution of the elderly than most other SMSAs. Indexes of dissimilarity with respect to children under age

[38]D. S. Massey and N. S. Denton, "The Dimensions of Residential Segregation," unpublished paper, Population Studies Center, University of Pennsylvania, 1986. The index of dissimilarity is conventionally calculated as one half of the sum of the differences, taken without regard to sign, between the paired elements in two percent distributions. The formula is: $D = .5\Sigma[(X_i/X) - (Y_i/Y)]$, where X_i and Y_i are the populations in census tract i for the two age groups being compared, and X and Y are the (SMSA) totals for these age groups. D varies between zero and one. This index indicates that the percentages in the distribution of the population aged 65 and over would have to be shifted up by D percentage points for negative differences, and down by D percentage points for positive differences, to make the distribution of the population aged 65 and over agree with the distribution of the second population (e.g., population under 65). Since D is affected by the number of area units in the distribution, indexes of dissimilarity based on different numbers of area units (e.g., census tracts) are not strictly comparable (see footnote 43).

The probability of contact between two age groups is measured by $_xP_y = [(X_i/X)*(Y_i/t_i)]$, where t_i is the total population for tract i and the other symbols have the meanings defined above. The index varies between zero and one.

[39]D. S. Massey, "Residential Segregation and Spatial Distribution of a Non–Labor Force Population: The Needy Elderly and Disabled," *Economic Geography* 56 (3) (1980):190–200; J. P. Tierney, "A Comparative Examination of the Residential Segregation of Persons 65 to 75 and Persons 75 and Above in 18 United States Metropolitan Areas for 1970 and 1980," *Journal of Gerontology* 42 (1) (January 1987):101–106. Tierney reports that the aged (75 and over) have a more concentrated pattern than those aged 65–74 and this concentration increased significantly between 1970 and 1980. D. M. Cowgill, "Residential Segregation by Age in American Metropolitan Areas," *Journal of Gerontology* 33 (3) (May 1978):446–453. M. LaGory, R. A. Ward, and M. Mucatel, "Patterns of Age Segregation," *Sociological Focus* 14 (1) (January 1981):1–13. N. A. Denton, "Differences in Residential Segregation of the Elderly in the United States: Whites, Blacks, Hispanics, and Asians, 1970–1980," paper presented at the annual meeting of the Population Association of America, Chicago, April 29–May 2, 1987.

15 are very high for Miami (45), Fort Lauderdale (45), Tampa–St. Petersburg (37), and Phoenix (43), as well as Denver-Boulder (40), Minneapolis–St. Paul (40), Salt Lake–Ogden (39), and Washington, D.C. (39). Indexes of dissimilarity with respect to the population aged 15–64 are relatively high for these SMSAs as well. There was little or no change in residential clustering with respect to children or youths and adults under age 65 between 1970 and 1980.

A study by LaGory, Ward, and Mucatel of residential clustering of the elderly population in a sample of 70 metropolitan areas in 1970, employing data for the 612 census tracts within these metropolitan areas, showed a small degree of residential clustering for most areas, with marked residential clustering for some.[40] Conventional indexes of dissimilarity, comparing the distribution of the elderly with the distribution of the nonelderly, reflect considerable variation among the SMSAs. The indexes varied from 46 for the Washington, D.C., SMSA to 12 for the Wilkes-Barre–Hazleton SMSA, with an unweighted mean of 22 for the 70 areas. The most marked clustering occurred in the SMSAs of the South and West.

The probability of contact between the elderly and the working-age population in the 60 SMSAs examined by Denton (.66) was over three times higher than between the elderly and children (.20) in 1980.[41] (See Table 3.23.) The gap vis-à-vis children has been widening, and the gap vis-à-vis younger adults has been narrowing. The probability of contact with children declined by 6 points (from .26 to .20) during the 1970–1980 decade, while the probability of contact with working-age persons increased by 4 points (from .62 to .66). Every SMSA in the study experienced a rise in the probability of contact between the elderly and working-age persons between 1970 and 1980 and a decline in the probability of contact between the elderly and children. The 1980 SMSA child-elderly probabilities are typically low, and for various key elderly SMSAs they are strikingly low (e.g., Fort Lauderdale, .12, Tampa–St. Petersburg, .15, and Phoenix, .17). The probability of contact between the elderly and the working-age population exceeds .55 in all of the SMSAs, even in the four key elderly SMSAs.

These figures reflect the age-restricted environment in which many elderly live. Whether the low probability of contact with children or the moderate probability of contact with working-age persons improves or worsens the quality of life of the elderly depends on how quality of life is affected by living in an age-restricted environment. We need to consider also whether restricted contacts with children and younger adults

[40]LaGory et al. (1981).
[41]Denton (1987).

TABLE 3.23

Measures of Residential Clustering of the Population Aged 65 and Over Within 60 Major SMSAs Combined: 1980 and 1970

Measure	All Classes			Black 1980	Hispanic 1980
	1980	1970	Change		
Index of Dissimilarity					
Population aged 65 and over and under 15	29.8	31.0	−1.2	38.2	44.6
Population aged 65 and over and 15–64	23.2	23.3	−0.2	33.8	38.7
Probability of Contact Between a Person Aged 65 and Over and					
A child under age 15	.202	.257	−.056	.258	.255
A person aged 15–64	.655	.615	+.040	.623	.620
Another person aged 65 and over	.143	.127	+.016	.119	.124
Percentage of SMSA Population Aged 65 and Over in Central City	46.6	53.5	−6.9	77.1	55.9

SOURCE: N. A. Denton, "Differences in Residential Segregation of the Elderly in the United States: Whites, Blacks, Hispanics, and Asians, 1970–1980," paper presented at the annual meeting of the Population Association of America, Chicago, April 29–May 2, 1987.

adversely affect intergenerational relations. Denton asks whether restricted contacts of the elderly who live in SMSAs with few children affect the frequency and quality of their contacts with their own children and grandchildren. A key question is whether the elderly living in areas with few children will support school taxes in these areas. Another question relates to the influence of the dispersion or concentration of the elderly in an area on the effectiveness of the delivery of social services to the elderly in the area. Dispersion may mean difficulty in delivering services. On the other hand, it may mean increased contacts with other age groups, increased ties with family, improved intergenerational relations, and greater support for child-directed programs.

Central Cities

Analysis of data on the age of the residents in the census tracts of various large cities also shows that there is great variation in the proportion of elderly from one section of these cities to another, reflecting substantial residential clustering of the elderly.[42] For example, the proportion aged 65 and over in the census tracts of the District of Columbia

[42]J. M. Kennedy and G. F. DeJong, "Aged in Cities: Residential Segregation in 10 U.S.A. Central Cities," *Journal of Gerontology* 32 (1) (January 1977):197–202.

in 1980 varied from 0.3 percent to 60 percent compared with 12 percent for the entire city. In 17 of the 178 census tracts in the city (excluding two with populations under 100), 20 percent of the population was aged 65 and over in 1980. The conventional index of dissimilarity between the census tract distributions of persons under age 65 and persons 65 and over is 24. A similar picture of residential clustering of the elderly in certain sections of large cities emerges from an analysis of census tract data for other large cities. For example, in 20 of the 196 census tracts of Cleveland, 20 percent or more of the population was aged 65 and over in 1980; the citywide percentage was 13. The conventional index of dissimilarity is 19. An adjusted index for Cleveland that allows for the number of census tracts is 1.38.[43] For the District of Columbia the adjusted index is 1.82. Hence, the District of Columbia is 32 percent more age-segregated than Cleveland, even though the proportions of census tracts with large shares of elderly in the two cities is about the same.

The urban elderly do not concentrate in enclaves to the degree that urbanites of the major racial groups and Hispanics cluster in racial/ethnic enclaves. The data suggest only that there is a notable clustering of older people in some parts of large cities and a notable deficit of older people in other parts.

The major factor contributing to the residential clustering of the elderly in certain census tracts of cities is their tendency to remain behind in older neighborhoods. Many ancillary and supplementary elements are involved, however. They include limited means and inability to sell one's home advantageously, which prevent acting on the desire to move away; preference to stay in the same areas with friends and neighbors of the same social/ethnic background and age group; and movement from other parts of the city because of reduced space requirements following loss of a spouse or other family change and the desire for accessibility to public services. In sum, the elderly resist changing residences on social and psychological grounds and are prevented from moving on economic grounds. Suburbanization of young people leaving the central city adds further to the clustering. Many older persons move away only because severe economic setbacks and severe health problems prevent their maintaining independent living arrangements.[44]

[43]Since the index of dissimilarity (D) is affected by the number of area units in the distribution, the comparability of indexes of dissimilarity based on different numbers of area units (e.g., census tracts) would be improved by an adjustment for the number of areas. For this reason, an adjusted measure is computed here as the conventional index of dissimilarity divided by the square root of the number of census tracts. This measure varies over a much narrower range and is not subject to the same interpretation as the conventional index. It is more valid for comparisons between areas, however.

[44]S. M. Golant, "The Residential Location and Spatial Behavior of the Elderly," Department of Geography Research Paper no. 143, University of Chicago, 1972.

The characteristics of the metropolitan area that affect the supply of and demand for housing strongly influence the level of clustering. This effect is exercised through the cost of housing.[45] High housing costs serve as a disincentive for elderly persons to move. In large established cities particularly, housing markets are tight and housing prices are relatively high. At the same time, the housing owned by older persons tends to be older, is located in less desirable neighborhoods, and hence tends to have lesser market value. As a result, the elderly can sell their homes only at a great disadvantage, and they cannot easily afford to buy other homes.

In the Northeast and Midwest regions the elderly are disproportionately found in the lower income areas, particularly the inner city areas with older, rental, multi-unit housing, and many unattached individuals. In the South and West, they are less likely to be found in the inner city and lower income areas and are more likely to be found in areas with large numbers of retired persons.

Suburbs

The metropolitan elderly population is becoming increasingly suburban and the number of suburban elderly now exceed the number of central city elderly. According to the CPS of March 1986, 56 percent of the elderly metropolitan population live outside central cities.[46] The 1980 CPS and 1970 census 1-in-100 sample figures are 53 percent and 46 percent, respectively (Table 3.20). The prevailing view that the suburban elderly population is advantaged compared with the central city elderly population is sustained by a study of Logan and Spitze.[47] The suburban elderly have higher incomes and higher rates of homeownership, are less likely to live alone, rate their health higher, and have fewer functional limitations. The study showed, however, that average differences between suburban elderly and central city elderly tend to be small, that the differences within each type of area are much greater than the differences between them, and that they both have about the same level of needs. In fact, in the suburbs, as in central cities, there are large subgroups of elderly who are in need of social services and financial assistance. They tend to be renters, aged 75 and over, and single-person householders.[48]

[45]LaGory et al. (1981).

[46]U.S. Bureau of the Census, "Geographical Mobility: March 1985 to March 1986," *Current Population Reports,* series P-20, no. 425 (June 1988), Table 10.

[47]J. R. Logan and G. Spitze, "Suburbanization and Public Services for the Aging," *Gerontologist* 28 (5) (October 1988):644–647.

[48]M. Gutowski and T. Feild, *The Graying of Suburbia* (Washington, DC: Urban Institute, 1979).

In addition to reflecting growth of central city gerontic enclaves between 1950 and 1980, the census data also show the progress of these enclaves in suburban metropolitan America. Gerontic clustering in the suburbs is primarily due to aging-in-place of suburban residents and departure of young family members. The post–World War II young pioneer settlers of the suburbs are aging into their older years and, although some are returning to central cities and some are moving to retirement centers in nonmetropolitan areas, many are remaining behind in suburban areas to form clusters of elderly persons.[49] As the family grows older, the young members leave to work and attend school elsewhere, while the oldsters often remain in their old neighborhoods. Measurement of the natural concentrations of elderly may be confounded by the artificial concentrations in congregate housing, lifetime care communities, retirement villages, and nursing homes but, even after allowing for these special housing arrangements, evidence of gerontic clustering remains. These clusters tend to be geographically more dispersed and less distinctive than the gerontic enclaves often observed in central cities.

Clustering of the elderly in the suburbs is a typically postwar phenomenon, but it has not proceeded very rapidly in recent years. An analysis by Fitzpatrick and Logan of 800 places with over 10,000 population in 1980, located in the suburban portion of 54 of the 100 largest metropolitan areas, concludes that there was generally a slight tendency for clustering of the elderly in the suburbs to decline between 1960 and 1980.[50] The South and West show notably greater concentration of the elderly in their suburban areas than the Northeast and Midwest. Indexes of dissimilarity in age distribution for suburban areas in 1980 averaged 10 in the Northeast, 16 in the Midwest, 20 in the South, and 20 in the West. These values are lower than are found for entire metropolitan areas in the corresponding regions. That is to say, there is less clustering in suburbs than in central cities.

Summary

The aging of America's population is geographically pervasive. The patterns of internal migration have often intensified the roles of fertility and mortality in bringing about an aging of nearly all state populations

---

[49]S. M. Golant, ed., *Location and Environment of Elderly Population* (Washington, DC: Winston, 1979). Gutowski and Feild (1979).

[50]K. M. Fitzpatrick and J. R. Logan, "The Aging of the Suburbs, 1960–1980," *American Sociological Review* 50 (1) (February 1985):106–117.

and all type-of-residence areas between 1950 and 1980. Aging-in-place, the outmigration of youth, and declining fertility have been primarily responsible for the rapid aging of the population in many areas of the United States, but for some areas (e.g., Florida, Arizona) inmigration of the elderly has been the principal factor.

Mobility and migration rates of the elderly are relatively low both in an absolute sense and in comparison with the rates for younger age groups. With increasing age following youth, except at the advanced ages, people move less; at about age 75, mobility and migration rates appear to reverse.

If the elderly do migrate between states, they generally move first while still "young" to various retirement states, particularly Florida and Arizona, or various retirement areas in the nonmetropolitan parts of the South and West. Some also move to their country of origin, if foreign-born, or other areas abroad (e.g., Mexico). In seeking retirement residences, the interstate elderly migrants have followed the same general paths as interstate migrants in general—out of the Northeast and Midwest and into the South and West, especially out of the Middle Atlantic states and the East North Central states and into the South Atlantic and Mountain states. This movement is mainly in pursuit of retirement living, felicitous climate, and recreational amenities. More commonly, the less affluent elderly remain behind in rural hinterlands or large urban centers, particularly the deteriorated parts of these areas, where they have spent much or all of their adult lives. Some move off farms or out of hamlets and villages to nearby towns. Residential relocation of the older aged is commonly for reasons of ill health and dependency, first to live near or join members of the family and then to enter nursing homes.

Patterns of internal migration and of geographic redistribution of the elderly contribute to differences from area to area in the problems of the delivery of services, the size of the tax base and the volume of revenues, and the provision of formal and informal support to the elderly. Rural and nonmetropolitan areas present special problems because of the limited road and transportation system, geographic isolation, and fewer health facilities. Living conditions in retirement communities in nonmetropolitan areas tend to be more favorable than in other nonmetropolitan communities, where the elderly population is likely to be older, less affluent, and less healthy.

In the mid 1980s the elderly population was somewhat less likely to live in a metropolitan area than the general population, although the shares of the U.S. total approximated three quarters for both the elderly and the general population. At mid decade also well over half of the elderly metropolitan population lived in the suburbs. The older elderly tend to be no more or less concentrated in metropolitan areas than the younger elderly, and the metropolitan older elderly are not much more concentrated in central cities than the younger elderly.

There is a moderate clustering of the elderly in particular sections of central cities and the suburbs, especially the former. Several metropolitan areas, mostly in Florida and the West, are distinguished by their high indexes of concentration of elderly persons who tend to have low probabilities of contact with children. The intracity clustering of the elderly did not grow between 1970 and 1980, nor did clustering of the elderly within suburbs increase in this decade, even though we would expect such an increase to have occurred as the early postwar suburban youthful settlers moved into old age.

4

LONGEVITY

P ROGRESS in the control of the aging process from a demographic point of view has usually been measured in terms of the increase in longevity, as shown, for example, by increases in the proportion of the population surviving from birth to various ages or by gains in average years of remaining life. Progress is increasingly being measured, however, in terms of improvements in the health of the population, as shown, for example, by reductions in the incidence and prevalence of chronic illness or in the prevalence of disabling conditions and activity limitations.

Gerontologists agree that a principal thrust of health programs should be to add years of active healthy life, not merely to reduce the incidence of premature death. Assuming a human life span of about 100 years, Hayflick has suggested that it should be society's goal to "provide" to all persons healthy, active lives until their 100th birthday, when they would die peacefully.[1] This chapter will deal with the longevity dimension of the aging process, and the following one will deal with the health dimension. Neither has been an important subject of census investigation, although some direct and indirect materials are available from censuses. The discussion here will incorporate data from other sources, particularly the U.S. National Center for Health Statistics and the Office of the Actuary, U.S. Social Security Administration.

[1]L. Hayflick, "The Strategy of Senescence," *Gerontologist* 14 (1) (February 1974):37–45, esp. pp. 40 and 43.

TABLE 4.1

Life Expectancy at Various Ages, by Sex and Race: 1929–1931 to 1985

Age, Race, and Sex	Life Expectancy					Increase (years), 1968–1985
	1985	1968	1954	1939–1941	1929–1931	
All Classes						
At birth	74.7	70.2	69.6	63.6	59.3	4.5
55 years	24.2	21.5	21.3	19.3	18.5	2.7
65 years	16.7	14.6	14.4	12.8	12.3	2.1
75 years	10.8	9.1	9.0	7.6	7.3	1.7
80 years	8.1	6.8	6.9	5.7	5.4	1.3
White Male						
At birth	71.9	67.5	67.4	62.8	59.1	4.4
55 years	21.7	19.2	19.6	18.3	18.0	2.5
65 years	14.6	12.8	13.1	12.1	11.8	1.1
75 years	9.0	8.1	8.2	7.2	7.0	0.9
80 years	6.8	6.2	6.3	5.4	5.3	0.6
White Female						
At birth	78.7	74.9	73.6	67.3	62.7	3.8
55 years	26.7	24.3	23.5	20.7	19.6	2.4
65 years	18.7	16.4	15.7	13.6	12.8	2.3
75 years	11.7	9.8	9.4	7.9	7.6	1.9
80 years	8.7	7.0	7.0	5.9	5.6	1.7
Black Male[a]						
At birth	65.3	60.1	61.0	52.3	47.6	5.2
55 years	19.1	17.2	18.4	16.6	15.5	1.9
65 years	13.3	12.1	13.5	12.2	10.9	1.2
75 years	8.7	9.9	10.4	8.2	7.0	−1.2
80 years	6.7	8.7	9.1	6.6	5.4	−2.0
Black Female[a]						
At birth	73.5	67.5	65.8	55.6	49.5	6.0
55 years	24.0	21.2	21.3	18.4	16.3	2.8
65 years	17.0	15.1	15.7	13.9	12.2	2.2
75 years	11.1	11.5	12.0	9.8	8.6	−0.4
85 years	8.6	9.3	10.1	8.0	6.9	−0.7

SOURCE: Life tables published by the U.S. National Center for Health Statistics and the U.S. Bureau of the Census.

NOTE: Minus sign denotes a decrease.

[a] Black and "other races" for 1954 and 1968.

Trends in Life Expectancy

Progress in the reduction of mortality or the elimination of premature death is often summarized in terms of life expectancy at birth, which represents the average number of years of life remaining at birth according to the death rates prevailing in a given year. Life expectancy at birth has shown a tremendous increase in the last half century, having risen from 59.3 years in 1930 to 69.6 years in 1954 and further to 74.7 years in 1985 (Table 4.1 and Figure 4.1). That is, there was a gain of about 10 years in life expectancy in the 24 years from 1930 to 1954, and an additional gain of about 5 years in the 31 years from 1954 to 1985 (Table 4.2). The average annual gain was far greater in the earlier period: 0.4

FIGURE 4.1

Average Remaining Lifetime at Birth, Age 65, Age 75, and Age 80: 1929–1931, 1939–1941, 1954, 1968, and 1985

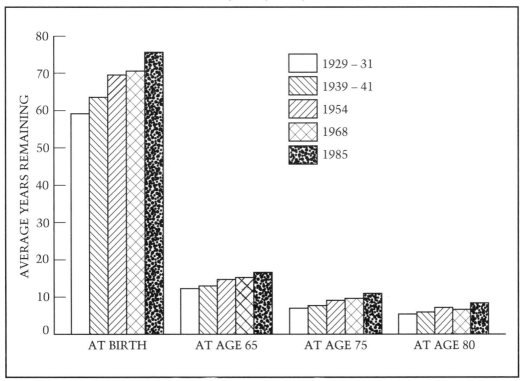

SOURCE: Table 4.1.

TABLE 4.2

Increase in Life Expectancy at Selected Ages, by Sex and Race: 1930–1954 and 1954–1985

Age, Race, and Sex	Amount (years)		As Percentage of Initial Value		As Percentage of Potential Increase[a]	
	1954–1985	1930–1954	1954–1985	1930–1954	1954–1985	1930–1954
All Classes						
At birth	5.1	10.3	7	17	17	25
65 years	2.3	2.1	16	17	11	9
75 years	1.8	1.7	20	23	11	10
White Male						
At birth	4.5	8.3	7	14	14	20
65 years	1.5	1.3	11	11	7	6
75 years	0.8	1.2	10	17	5	7
White Female						
At birth	5.1	10.9	7	17	19	29
65 years	3.0	2.9	19	23	16	13
75 years	2.3	1.8	24	24	15	10
Black Male						
At birth	4.3	13.4	7	28	11	26
65 years	−0.2	2.6	−1	24	b	11
75 years	−1.7	3.4	−16	49	b	19
Black Female						
At birth	7.7	16.3	12	33	23	32
65 years	1.3	3.5	8	29	7	15
75 years	−0.9	3.4	−9	40	b	21

SOURCE: Based on Table 4.1.

NOTES: Minus sign denotes a decrease. The 1930 life table is for 1929–1931 and the 1940 life table is for 1939–1941.

[a] Potential increase is the number of years required for total life expectancy at a particular age to reach 100.
[b] Not defined.

year versus 0.2 year. Two very different eras compose the 31-year period beginning in 1954, however, as almost all of the gain occurred after 1968. A plateau was reached about 1954, and little change occurred in the next 14 years. In the following 17 years (1968–1985), however, life expectancy at birth advanced steadily, and a gain of 4.5 years—that is, nearly all the gain in the entire 31 years from 1954 to 1985—was achieved.

Age Differences

Since life expectancy at birth depends on all the death rates from infancy to the oldest ages, changes in this measure do not identify the segments of the age scale in which the changes have occurred. It is useful to distinguish progress in life expectancy or survival at the ages under 65 from progress at ages 65 and over. We can measure changes in death rates in a specified age range in terms of a life table survival rate linking the initial and terminal ages of the age range and in terms of an age-bounded life expectancy value. According to the U.S. life table for 1929–1931, 54 percent of the newborn babies would reach age 65, while in 1985 the figure was 79 percent (Table 4.3). These figures imply a survival gain of 25 persons aged 65 per 100 babies in a little over half a century. The proportion of persons surviving from age 65 to age 80 was 35 percent in 1929–1931 and 57 percent in 1985; these figures imply a survival gain of 22 persons aged 80 per 100 persons aged 65. Accordingly, the chances of survival from birth to age 65 and from age 65 to age 80 are both much higher now than they were earlier. While the increases in the two age bands are about the same, the relative gain was much greater for the older age group (63 percent vs. 46 percent).

A different impression is obtained if the gain in survival is calculated as a share of the maximum possible gain.[2] For the age group under 65, 54 percent of the maximum possible gain in survival occurred between 1929–1931 and 1985, while for the age group 65 and over only 34 percent of the maximum possible gain occurred in this period. It is clear that the determination of which age group showed the greater progress depends on the measure of progress used.

A disproportionate share of the gains at the ages under 65 between 1929–1931 and 1985 occurred between 1929–1931 and 1954. The survival rate from birth to age 65 for 1954 (70 percent) was much closer to the rate for 1985 than to the rate for 1929–1931. A higher percentage of the maximum possible gain in survival at these ages also occurred between 1930 and 1954 than between 1954 and 1985. However, the survival rate from age 65 to age 80 for 1954 (46 percent) was more evenly distant from the rates in 1930 and 1985. In fact, survival at the older ages was relatively greater in the more recent period than in the earlier

---

[2]The gain in survival as a share of the maximum possible gain is computed as follows:

$$\frac{s_i^{t+a} - s_i^t}{1 - s_i^t}$$

where s_i^t represents the survival rate at some date and s_i^{t+a} represents the corresponding survival rate at a later date.

TABLE 4.3

Proportion Surviving from Birth to Age 65 and from Age 65 to Age 80, by Sex and Race: 1929–1931 to 1985

Age Interval, Race, and Sex	Proportion Surviving				
	1985	1968	1954	1939–1941	1929–1931
All Classes					
Birth to 65 years	.787	.711	.704	.604	.538
65–80 years	.571	.476	.460	.379	.350
White Male					
Birth to 65 years	.745	.654	.657	.583	.530
65–80 years	.472	.381	.395	.341	.325
White Female					
Birth to 65 years	.856	.811	.796	.687	.605
65–80 years	.662	.578	.530	.420	.381
Black Male[a]					
Birth to 65 years	.581	.475	.494	.354	.293
65–80 years	.403	.316	.381	.345	.281
Black Female					
Birth to 65 years	.749	.632	.584	.405	.309
65–80 years	.572	.467	.478	.421	.351

SOURCE: Based on life tables published by the U.S. National Center for Health Statistics and the U.S. Bureau of the Census.

[a]Black and "other races" for 1954 and 1968.

one on the basis of the percentage of the maximum possible gain. We observe, then, a shift over time in mortality progress from the young ages mainly to a more even gain among young and old ages.

Changes in "life expectancy" for ages under 65, represented here by the average years of life lived by a cohort between birth and age 65,[3]

[3]The value for average years of life lived (age-bounded life expectancy) between birth and age 65 is computed from the life table as:

$$\frac{T_0 - T_{65}}{l_0}$$

TABLE 4.3 *(continued)*

			Increase		
Amount		As Percentage of Initial Proportion		As Percentage of Potential Increase	
1954– 1985	1930– 1954	1954– 1985	1930– 1954	1954– 1985	1930– 1954
.083	.166	12	31	28	36
.111	.110	24	31	21	17
.088	.127	13	24	26	27
.077	.070	19	22	13	10
.060	.191	8	32	29	48
.132	.149	25	39	28	24
.087	.201	18	69	17	28
.022	.100	6	36	4	14
.165	.275	28	89	40	40
.094	.127	20	36	18	20

may be compared with changes in life expectancy at age 65, to illustrate further the comparative gains in these age ranges over the last half century. Average years of life lived under age 65 increased from 53 years in 1929–1931 to 59 years in 1954 and 62 years in 1985 (Table 4.4). Note that the peak possible value is 65 years. During the same period, average years of life remaining at age 65 moved ahead much more slowly in absolute terms, from 12 years in 1929–1931 to 14 years in 1954 and 17 years in 1985 (Tables 4.1 and 4.2). On a relative basis, however, progress in years added in this 55-year period was greater at ages 65 and over than ages under 65, especially in the 1954–1985 segment.

If the comparison of the gains in age-bounded life expectancy for the two age groups is considered in terms of the percentage of the maximum possible gain, assuming age 100 as the peak possible age for the

TABLE 4.4

Average Years Lived in Age Interval Under 65 Years and 65–80 Years, by Sex and Race: 1929–1931 to 1985

Age Interval, Race, and Sex	Average Years Lived				
	1985	1968	1954	1939–1941	1929–1931
All Classes					
Under 65 years	61.6	59.8	59.4	55.9	53.0
65–80 years	12.1	11.4	11.2	10.6	10.3
White Male					
Under 65 years	61.0	59.1	58.8	55.8	52.9
65–80 years	11.4	10.5	10.6	10.2	10.1
White Female					
Under 65 years	62.8	61.6	61.1	58.0	54.9
65–80 years	12.9	12.3	12.0	11.1	10.7
Black Male[a]					
Under 65 years	57.6	54.3	54.4	47.9	44.4
65 to 80 years	10.6	9.4	10.0	9.9	9.3
Black Female					
Under 65 years	60.8	58.0	56.6	49.9	45.7
65–80 years	12.1	10.8	10.9	10.6	9.8

SOURCE: Based on life tables published by the U.S. National Center for Health Statistics and the U.S. Bureau of the Census.

[a] Black and "other races" for 1954 and 1968.

range 65 and over,[4] the younger age group advanced a greater share of its maximum possible gain in the first period, 1929–1931 to 1954 (53 percent) than in the second period, 1954–1985 (39 percent), but for the older age group the gains were more nearly equal (9 percent vs. 11 per-

[4] The gain in age-bounded life expectancy between ages x and $x+z$ between time t and $t+a$ as a share of the maximum possible gain in life expectation between ages x and $x+z$ is computed as follows:

$$\frac{\dfrac{T_x^{t+a} - T_{x+z}^{t+a}}{l_x^{t+a}} - \dfrac{T_x^t - T_{x+z}^t}{l_x^t}}{Z - \dfrac{T_x^t - T_{x+z}^t}{l_x^t}}$$

TABLE 4.4 *(continued)*

		Increase			
Amount		As Percentage of Initial Value		As Percentage of Potential Value	
1954–1985	1930–1954	1954–1985	1930–1954	1954–1985	1930–1954
2.2	6.4	4	12	39	53
0.9	0.9	8	9	24	19
2.2	5.9	4	11	35	49
0.8	0.5	7	5	18	10
1.7	6.2	3	11	44	61
0.9	1.3	7	12	30	30
3.2	10.0	6	22	30	49
0.6	0.7	6	8	12	12
4.2	10.9	7	24	50	56
1.2	1.1	11	11	29	21

cent). These relations "hold up" even with adjustment for the number of years in each period.

A further comparison of average years lived between birth and age 65 and between age 65 and age 80 over the period 1930–1985 also gives support to the following generalizations. The gain in longevity was relatively greater at the younger ages, especially in the earlier period (1930–1954); in the later period (1954–1985) the relative gains fell off at the younger ages; and the relative gains at the older ages maintained a generally even pace.

where $\dfrac{T_x - T_{x+z}}{l_x}$ represents the basic formula for age-bounded life expectancy and Z is the number of years in the age range being analyzed.

TABLE 4.5

Death Rates for the Population Aged 55 and Over, by Age: 1940–1985

Measure and Year or Period	Ages 55–64	Ages 65–74	Ages 75–84	Ages 85 and Over	Ages 65 and Over	
					Observed	Adjusted[a]
Rates per 1,000						
1985	12.8	28.4	64.4	154.8	51.5	42.8
1968	17.0	37.2	82.9	195.8	61.4	55.3
1954[b]	17.4	37.9	86.0	181.6	58.6	56.0
1940[b]	22.2	48.4	112.0	235.7	72.2	72.2
Percent Change						
1968–1985	−24.7	−23.7	−22.3	−20.9	−16.1	−22.6
1954–1968	−2.3	−1.8	−3.6	+7.8	+4.8	−1.2
1940–1954	−21.6	−21.7	−23.2	−23.0	−18.8	−22.5
Average Annual Percent Change[c]						
1968–1985	−1.7	−1.6	−1.5	−1.4	−1.0	−1.5
1954–1968	−0.2	−0.1	−0.3	+0.5	+0.3	−0.1
1940–1954	−1.7	−1.7	−1.9	−1.9	−1.5	−1.8

SOURCES: Based on U.S. National Center for Health Statistics, *Vital Statistics of the United States,* various annual volumes; "Advance Report of Final Mortality Statistics, 1985," *Monthly Vital Statistics Report* 36 (5), Supplement (August 1987).

[a] Computed on the basis of the 1940 census population as standard.
[b] Excludes Alaska and Hawaii.
[c] Computed by the use of the formula for continuous compounding.

As suggested earlier, average years of life hardly increased between 1954 and 1968, both for ages under 65 and for ages 65 and over, but substantial progress was achieved before 1954 and after 1968. The sharp deceleration in the reduction in mortality at the older ages during the late 1950s and the early 1960s compared with prior and subsequent years is reflected also in the trend of age-specific death rates for the period 1940–1985 (Table 4.5 and Figure 4.2). For example, the death rates for ages 55–64, 65–74, 75–84, and 85 and over each dropped about 22 or 23 percent between 1940 and 1954 but remained nearly unchanged between 1954 and 1968. The annual data for the 1960s and 1970s show that a turning point in the trend of mortality at the older ages was reached about 1968 and that, in subsequent years, mortality at these ages resumed a strong downward trend, resembling that between 1940 and 1954.

The actual downward trend for ages 65 and over since 1940 is steeper than is suggested by the decline in the crude death rate for these ages.

FIGURE 4.2

Death Rates for the Population Aged 55 and Over, by Age: 1950–1985

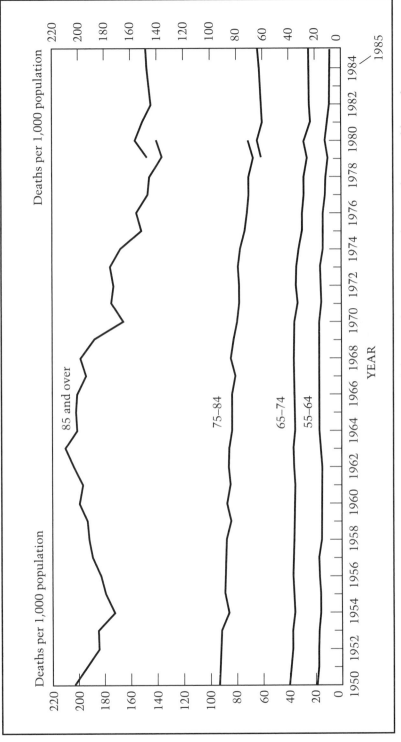

SOURCES: U.S. National Center for Health Statistics, *Vital Statistics of the United States, 1960 and 1970*, vol. 2; *Monthly Vital Statistics Report,* "Advance Report of Final Mortality Statistics," for 1985, 1984, 1983, 1982, and 1981; vols. on mortality statistics for earlier years.

NOTE: Points are plotted for each year. Death rates for 1979–1985 based on population estimates consistent with 1980 census. Death rates for 1970–1980 based on population estimates consistent with 1970 census. Disjuncture results from shift to 1980 census-consistent base.

The decline was retarded by the aging of the older population; the decline in the age-adjusted rate is greater.[5] The average annual rate of decline in the age-adjusted death rate for ages 65 and over between 1968 and 1985 was 1.5 percent compared with 0.1 percent between 1954 and 1968 and 1.8 percent between 1940 and 1954.

The reasons for the fluctuations in the trend of the age-specific death rates for the older population in the last several decades, and particularly for the lack of progress over an extended part of the period, are not well understood. The marked declines since 1968 may be a result principally of salutary changes in lifestyle and personal habits, and widespread health testing, especially for high blood pressure. The introduction of Medicare and Medicaid in 1965 and the expansion of private health insurance plans very likely also played a part. This general question is discussed further in this chapter in connection with the topics, causes of death and factors influencing mortality prospects.

The pace of the decline in age-specific death rates during the period 1968–1984 was itself slowing down (Table 4.6). This is mainly true for the death rates at the older ages, particularly ages 65–74 and 85 and over. At most younger ages the percent decline in death rates remained rather steady or showed increases for the period 1976–1984 compared with the period 1968–1976. The pattern of death rates was now more heavily weighted with the death rates at ages 65 and over.

Life Span and Rectangularization of the Survival Curve

The phenomenon of a limited life span is apparently general for animal life. For the human species, life span appears to be set between 95 and 105 years, or at about 100 years. At about this age, human life seems to expire even under optimum conditions and possibly even in the absence of specific major pathology. It is generally believed that the human life span has not changed at least since historic or late prehistoric times. Maximum life span, corresponding to the highest authenticated age to which a person has lived, is somewhat higher; it is currently 120 years.[6] Both life span and maximum life span may be inching upward as some have suggested, but the data are not precise enough to make a definitive determination. On the other hand, as we have seen, life ex-

[5]See also M. G. Kovar and L. A. Fingerhut, "Recent Trends in U.S. Mortality Among the Aged," in *Consequences of a Changing Population: Demographics of Aging,* Joint Hearings before the Select Committee on Population, U.S. House of Representatives, and the Select Committee on Aging, May 24, 1978.

[6]S. Izumi died in Japan in 1986 at 120 years, 237 days. K. White, the oldest living person, was 116 years old in 1990 and resides in Florida.

TABLE 4.6

Changes in Age-Specific Death Rates, Age-Specific Survival Rates, and the Age Pattern of Death Rates: 1968–1984

Age	Death Rate, 1984 [a]	Percent Change, Death Rates			Percent Change, Survival Rates, 1968–1984 [b]	Age Pattern of Death Rates	
		1968–1984	1968–1976	1976–1984		1968	1984
All Ages	862.3	−10.4	−8.1	−3.1	+0.11	100.0	100.0
Under 1	1,085.6	−52.1	−29.6	−31.9	+1.21	6.1	3.9
1–4	51.9	−42.1	−22.0	−25.8	+0.04	0.2	0.2
5–14	26.7	−37.9	−19.3	−23.1	+0.02	0.1	0.1
15–24	96.8	−21.7	−8.2	−14.7	+0.03	0.3	0.3
25–34	121.1	−23.0	−13.4	−11.1	+0.04	0.4	0.4
35–44	204.8	−36.0	−20.5	−19.4	+0.13	0.9	0.7
45–54	521.1	−30.6	−15.5	−17.9	+0.23	2.0	1.9
55–64	1,287.8	−24.4	−13.4	−12.7	+0.42	4.6	4.6
65–74	2,848.1	−23.5	−16.0	−8.9	+0.91	10.0	10.2
75–84	6,399.3	−22.8	−11.6	−12.7	+2.07	22.4	23.0
85 and Over	15,223.6	−22.3	−20.9	−1.7	+5.42	52.8	54.6
Age-Adjusted Rate [c]	545.9	−26.6	−15.6	−13.0	+0.20	X	X

SOURCES: Based on the U.S. National Center for Health Statistics, "Final Mortality Statistics, 1978," *Monthly Vital Statistics Report* 29 (6), Supplement 2 (September 1980), Table 2; "Advance Report of Final Mortality Statistics, 1985," *Monthly Vital Statistics Report* 36 (5), Supplement (August 1987).

NOTE: X = not applicable.

[a] Deaths per 100,000 population.
[b] Survival rates are complements of death rates in each year.
[c] Adjusted by the direct method on the basis of the age distribution of the population in 1940.

pectancy at birth—that is, the expected lifetime based on prevailing death rates—has been rising more or less steadily in the United States since records are available. The gap between life expectancy at birth and life span represents the difference between the level of longevity achieved and the level now theoretically possible.

The life table curve of survivors has been becoming increasingly rectangular in shape (Figure 4.3). The rectangularization of the survival curve may be measured by the trend of the share of the total area of the rectangle, formed by X at 100 on the X-axis and Y at 100 on the Y-axis, that is found under the survival curve. The percentages for white males and white females for selected years since 1890 are as follows:[7]

Year	White Males	White Females
1890 (Massachusetts)	42.5	44.5
1900–1902 (ODRS)[a]	48.2	51.1
1919–1921 (DRS of 1920)	56.3	58.5
1939–1941	62.8	67.3
1959–1961	67.6	74.2
1979–1981	70.8	78.2
1985	71.9	78.7
1988	72.3	78.9

[a] Original Death Registration States.

The curve of survivors almost resembled the hypotenuse of a right-angle triangle in the early part of this century, when mortality was high, but as death rates have fallen, it has become increasingly less steep and more level over most of the age span. The logical limit of the evolution of the present survival curve could be represented by a theoretical curve having a perfectly rectangular shape, that is, essentially flat over its entire width and then falling sharply just at the age corresponding to the life span. This type of theoretical construct implies the possible survival of all or nearly all newborn infants to age 100, the possible expiration of the entire cohort at about this age, and the existence of a fixed life span toward which life expectancy is gradually shifting.

One extension of the hypothesis maintains that life expectancy and life span have already essentially converged, that late-life morbidity has

[7] These figures are algebraically the same as life expectancy at birth. They assume that the human life span is fixed at 100 years and that few people live beyond age 100. If we assume, for example, that the range of ages represented by survivors is 105 years in 1988, then the percentages for this year drop to 68.9 for white males and 75.2 for white females.

The rectangularity of the survival curve may also be measured by the ratio of the average slope of the curve between age 5 and age 70 to the average slope of the curve after age 70.

FIGURE 4.3

Percentage of a Cohort of White Female Births Surviving to Each Later Age, According to Current Life Tables: 1890–2050

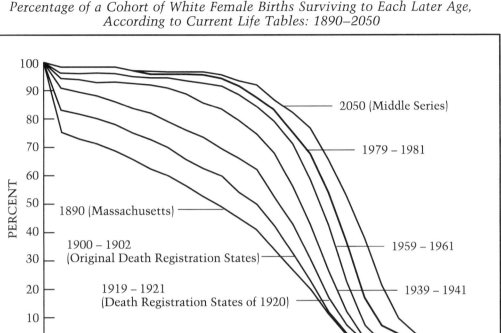

SOURCES: Based on life tables published by the U.S. National Center for Health Statistics or its predecessor agencies, and by the U.S. Social Security Administration, Office of the Actuary.

been compressed to a brief period of years, and that mortality will increasingly occur from natural causes.[8] The validity of this hypothesis is doubtful. The near-rectangularization of the survival curve will require decades to achieve since the gap between life expectancy and life span remains considerable (about 25 years). Many leading causes of death are far from conquered and new causes may emerge.[9] The evidence appears to contradict the generalization that the period of morbidity has been

[8]See J. F. Fries and L. M. Crapo, *Vitality and Aging: Implications of the Rectangular Curve* (San Francisco: Freeman, 1981), Chap. 11; J. F. Fries, "Aging, Natural Death, and the Compression of Morbidity," *New England Journal of Medicine* 303 (3) (July 17, 1980):130–135.

[9]E. L. Schneider and J. A. Brody, "Aging, Natural Death, and the Compression of Morbidity: Another View," *New England Journal of Medicine* 309 (14) (October 6, 1983):854–856.

sharply compressed. Furthermore, methods of extending human life span may be developed. Walford maintains that the modification of the human life span is possible and notes the effect of caloric restriction on the prolongation of life span in rats and mice.[10] There is already at hand statistical evidence to question the immobility of the human life span and, hence, the notion of the progressive rectangularization of the survival curve.

Sex Differences

Mortality of males is now well above that of females at every age of life. This fact is reflected in the much higher level of life expectancy for females than for males. In 1985, life expectancy at birth for females (78.2 years) exceeded that for males (71.2 years) by 7.0 years. A large part of the male-female difference in life expectancy at birth is accounted for by differences in the mortality of the sexes at ages over 65. In 1985, for example, life expectancy at age 65 for men (14.6 years) and women (18.6 years) differed by 4.0 years, while the difference between the sexes in average years of life lived under age 65 (60.6 years for males and 62.5 years for females) was only 1.9 years. Adjusting these figures for the indirect effects of mortality under age 65 on mortality at ages 65 and over brings them to 3.2 years and 3.8 years.[11] The relative contributions of ages 65 and over and ages under 65 to the difference between the sexes in life expectancy at birth are 45 percent and 55 percent, respectively; hence, the older ages account for nearly half of the difference.

Males and females have not shared equally in the reduction of mortality in the last half century, particularly at the older ages. In 1929–1931, white females had a moderate advantage over white males in life expectancy at birth (3.6 years). The gap widened in subsequent decades. (See Table 4.1.) Between 1929–1931 and 1979 about 4 years were added to the 1929–1931 difference. In the same period 3.4 years were added to the initial difference of one year in life expectancy at age 65.

Values for life expectancy at birth for males and females have shown a modest convergence since 1979, when the difference was at its peak of 7.8 years. The difference narrowed by 0.8 years by 1985. The convergence was due to a greater decline in death rates of males; the male increase in life expectancy at birth between 1979 and 1985 amounted to

---

[10]R. Walford, *Maximum Life Span* (New York: Norton 1983), and *The 120 Year Diet: How to Double Your Vital Years* (New York: Simon and Schuster, 1987).

[11]See United Nations, *Levels and Trends of Mortality Since 1950*, Population Studies, series A, no. 74 (New York: United Nations, 1982), p. 11.

1.2 years and the female increase to 0.4 years. The male-female difference in life expectancy at age 65 also fell—by 0.4 year.

In general, reductions in death rates for females at the older ages have outpaced those for males from the beginning of the century. In 1930, the death rate for males aged 65 and over was only slightly above that for females—10 percent (Table 4.7). With progressive divergence of the rates, the relative difference reached nearly 40 percent in 1985.

Genetic and nongenetic (environmental) factors play complexly interrelated roles in influencing the relative longevity of males and females.[12] The relative importance of genetic and environmental factors cannot be easily established and is a matter of debate. On the one hand, there is strong evidence supporting a biological basis for the difference in the mortality levels of the sexes. For example, male late fetal and infant mortality, particularly the latter, is greater than female late fetal and infant mortality in the industrialized countries. It is general among mammals in captivity for the males of the species to have a lesser longevity and probably a lesser life span than females.[13] A study of the mortality of men and women in Catholic teaching orders, based on the premise that the living conditions of the sexes are essentially equal, tends to support the biological hypothesis.[14] Physiological differences, especially in responses to stress, appear to favor women.[15] Research by Frankenhaueser shows that women under stress secrete less of the stress hormones. Thus, the bodily changes that result from stress would be less pronounced for women; this difference appears to be a health advantage.[16]

According to an alternative hypothesis, the tendency for women to live longer than men results largely from differences in the environment, roles, and lifestyles of men and women.[17] Social factors appear to account for an important part of the male-female difference in longevity,

---

[12]I. Waldron, "Sex Differences in Human Mortality: The Role of Genetic Factors," *Social Science Medicine* 17 (6) (1983):321–333.

[13]K. Ralls, R. L. Brownell, Jr., and J. Ballou, "Differential Mortality by Sex and Age in Mammals, with Specific Reference to the Sperm Whale," in *Sperm Whales: Special Issue*, Reports of the International Whaling Commission, Cambridge, 1980.

[14]F. C. Madigan, "Are Sex Mortality Differentials Biologically Caused?" *Milbank Memorial Fund Quarterly* 35 (2) (1957):202–203.

[15]E. R. Ramey, "The Natural Capacity for Health in Women," in P. W. Berman and E. R. Ramey, eds., *Women: A Developmental Perspective*, Washington, DC: National Institutes of Health (April 1982).

[16]M. Frankenhaueser, "Psychoneuroendocrine Sex Difference in Adaptation to the Psychosocial Environment," paper presented at the Sereno Symposium, Siena, Italy, 1976. See also M. Frankenhaueser, M. Von Wright, A. Collins, J. Von Wright, G. Sedvall, and C. Swahn, "Sex Differences in Psychoneuroendocrine Reactions to Examination Stress," *Psychosomatic Medicine* 40 (1978):334–343.

[17]I. Waldron, "Why Do Women Live Longer Than Men?" Part 1, *Journal of Human Stress* 2 (1) (March 1976):2–13; I. Waldron and S. Johnston, "Why Do Women Live Longer Than Men?" Part 2, *Journal of Human Stress* 2 (2) (June 1976):19–29.

TABLE 4.7

Ratios of Male to Female Death Rates for the Population Aged 55 and Over, by Age and Race: 1930–1985

Race and Year	Ages 55–64	Ages 65–74	Ages 75–84	Ages 85 and Over	Ages 65 and Over
All Races					
1985	1.85	1.83	1.64	1.28	1.36
1968	2.08	1.88	1.46	1.18	1.44
1954[a]	1.82	1.57	1.29	1.06	1.30
1940[a]	1.45	1.29	1.17	1.08	1.17
1930[b]	1.25	1.19	1.12	1.07	1.10
White					
1985	1.88	1.86	1.66	1.29	1.35
1968	2.19	1.94	1.47	1.19	1.45
1954[a]	1.91	1.59	1.29	1.04	1.31
1940[a]	1.50	1.30	1.16	1.07	1.17
1930[b]	1.28	1.20	1.11	1.06	1.10
Black					
1985	1.75	1.68	1.49	1.24	1.41
1968	1.58	1.49	1.36	1.20	1.37
1954[a,c]	1.33	1.35	1.29	1.30	1.24
1940[a,c]	1.11	1.22	1.29	1.25	1.18
1930[b]	0.98	1.12	1.29	1.22	1.13

SOURCES: Based on U.S. Bureau of the Census, *U.S. Life Tables,* 1930 (1936); U.S. National Center for Health Statistics, *Vital Statistics of the United States,* annual volumes for 1940, 1954, and 1968; "Advance Report of Final Mortality Statistics, 1985," *Monthly Vital Statistics Report* 36 (5), Supplement (August 1987).

[a] Excludes Alaska and Hawaii.
[b] Texas, Alaska, and Hawaii excluded from Death Registration States.
[c] Black and "other races" for 1954 and 1940.

either directly or indirectly by their interaction with genetic or biological factors. Generally, males are engaged in the more stressful, physically demanding, and hazardous occupations. Cigarette smoking, one of many factors that have distinguished the typical lifestyle and personal habits of men and women in past years, has been identified as a major contributor to the difference.[18] Women are more likely to secure earlier

[18] I. Waldron, "The Contribution of Smoking to Sex Differences in Mortality," paper presented at the annual meeting of the Population Association of America, Boston, March 1985; R. D. Retherford, "Tobacco Smoking and the Sex Mortality Differential," *Demography* 9 (2) (1972):203–216; R. D. Retherford, *The Changing Sex Differential in Mortality* (Westport, CT, Greenwood Press, 1975); S. H. Preston, "Older Male Mortality and Cigarette Smoking: A Demographic Analysis," *Population Monograph Series*, no. 7, University of California, Berkeley, 1970.

diagnosis and appropriate treatment for health conditions, including particularly the serious illnesses. Women are less likely to be self-destructive (suicide, alcoholism), to engage in acts of violence (homicide), or to be aggressive and excessive risk takers (auto accidents).

Most of the divergence of male and female mortality occurred during the post–World War II period, when differences in the lifestyles and roles of men and women have been sharply diminishing. Women have been leaving the home and entering the labor force in large numbers since World War II. These longtime changes appear to have had little effect in reducing the male-female difference in mortality, and may in fact have contributed to increasing it. For many women, work outside the home has the effect of reducing stress and improving health.[19] An exception may be women employed in low-skilled jobs with husbands having traditional views of women's roles and with several children. Only since 1979 has there appeared any indication that the increasing labor force participation of women (including participation in traditionally male occupations), the decreasing labor force participation of men, and other approximations of the lifestyles of men and women (e.g., smoking habits) might have brought male and female longevity closer.

We may have a better basis at a future date for arriving at an answer to the question as to why women outlive men if the present tendencies toward the diminution of the differences in the environment, roles, and lifestyles of men and women continue. In the USSR, where there is less differentiation in the occupational roles of men and women than in the United States, there is an even greater gap in life expectancy at birth in favor of females (10 years in 1984–1985).[20]

One tentative hypothesis regarding the basis of the difference in life expectancy of the sexes may be offered. It has genetic (physiological), environmental, and psychological elements, but we omit further comment on the environmental factors. A substantial part of the difference reflects the biological superiority of women. With the virtual elimination of the infective and parasitic diseases, which took a particularly heavy toll of women during childbearing prior to World War II, and the subsequent emergence of the "chronic degenerative" or endogenous diseases (e.g., diseases of the heart, malignant neoplasms, and cerebrovascular diseases) as the leading causes, this biological superiority has been increasingly evidenced. For reasons that are not well understood, males succumb more frequently and more readily to most of the endogenous

---

[19]L. M. Verbrugge and J. H. Madans, "Social Roles and Health Trends of American Women," *Milbank Memorial Fund Quarterly* 63 (4) (Fall 1985):691–735, esp. p. 724.

[20]A. Blum and R. Pressat, "Une nouvelle table de mortalité pour l'URSS (1984–85)," *Population* 42 (6) (November–December 1987):843–862. Much of the gap between males and females in life expectancy has been attributed to excessive use of alcohol by men.

diseases. A genetic or physiological basis for the difference in mortality may lie partly in the more favorable status of females with respect to hormonal balance, cholesterol metabolism, the clotting factor, the elasticity and proneness to injury of the vascular lining, the immune function, and the response to stress.

A psychological basis for the difference in mortality may lie in the difference in personality structures of men and women, arising from the very different ways in which young boys and girls have been socialized in our society. Until recently, boys have been typically trained from earliest childhood to be aggressive, competitive, and career-oriented—that is, imbued with the necessity of pursuing an occupation, supporting a family, and dealing competitively at work and play ("win-or-perish" ethic)—while girls have been trained to be more passive, nurturing, and cooperative. This variation in rearing practices and personality structure may contribute to the greater male risks of exposure to stress, which is physiologically more compromising for men than for women. New rearing practices are emerging, but they take effect slowly.

Race Differences

Although the mortality gap between the races has been decreasing at a fast and steady pace, life expectancy at birth for whites (75.3 years) was still well above that for blacks (69.5 years) in 1985.[21] Most of the difference of 5.8 years is accounted for by the lower mortality of whites at ages under 65. The difference between the races in average years of life lived from birth to age 65 was about 2.6 years, but the indirect effects of mortality under age 65 on mortality at ages 65 and over raise the contribution of these ages to 4.7 years. The difference in life expectancy at age 65 (16.8 years for whites and 15.3 years for blacks) was 1.5 years, but the adjusted contribution to the total race difference was only 1.1 years. Hence, four fifths of the difference in the life expectancy at birth of whites and blacks results from the lower mortality of whites at ages below 65 and one fifth from the lower mortality of whites at ages 65 and over.

According to the official statistics for 1985, the death rate of blacks exceeds that of whites at each five-year age group up to 80–84, and then

---

[21]None of these measures has been adjusted to take account of the difference in coverage of whites and blacks in the censuses, which have counted the white population more completely than the black population. Inasmuch as such an adjustment would generally reduce black death rates more than white death rates, the mortality differences between the races are, in fact, usually smaller than indicated here. See Appendix 2A.

at ages 85 and over falls below it. The reported death rate for blacks was 33 percent higher than the reported death rate for whites at ages 70–74, 17 percent higher at ages 75–79, 18 percent higher at ages 80–84, and 17 percent lower at ages 85 and over (Table 4.8). In 1940 the estimated age of the crossover was 73 (for both males and females); in 1980 it was 84 (males) and 85 (females). (See Table 4.9.)

The direction and magnitude of the differences between the death rates of the races at the older ages are subject to uncertainty because of probable errors in the rates. The basic data for blacks have been shown to be subject to substantial error; the rates for blacks are much more affected than those for whites by coverage errors and age misreporting

TABLE 4.8

Ratios of Black to White Death Rates for the Population Aged 55 and Over, by Age and Sex: 1930–1985

Sex and Year	Ages 55–64	Ages 65–74	Ages 75–84	Ages 85 and Over	Ages 65 and Over
Both Sexes					
1985	1.66	1.36	1.18	.83	1.09
1968	1.64	1.32	0.94	.70	1.00
1954 [a,b]	1.70	1.33	0.82	.53	0.98
1940 [a,b]	1.79	1.08	0.85	.73	1.01
1930 [c]	1.79	1.26	0.92	.89	1.15
Male					
1985	1.64	1.32	1.11	.80	1.11
1968	1.45	1.17	0.89	.69	0.96
1954 [a,b]	1.49	1.08	0.80	.56	0.95
1940 [a,b]	1.47	1.16	0.89	.79	1.02
1930 [c]	1.58	1.22	0.99	.96	1.16
Female					
1985	1.75	1.45	1.23	.83	1.07
1968	2.01	1.52	0.97	.69	1.02
1954 [a,b]	2.13	1.27	0.81	.60	1.00
1940 [a,b]	1.97	1.26	0.80	.68	1.00
1930 [c]	2.08	1.30	0.85	.83	1.14

SOURCES: Based on U.S. Bureau of the Census, *U.S. Life Tables, 1930* (1936); U.S. National Center for Health Statistics, *Vital Statistics of the United States,* annual volumes for 1940, 1954, and 1968; "Advance Report of Final Mortality Statistics, 1985," *Monthly Vital Statistics Report* 36 (5), Supplement (August 1987).

[a] Excludes Alaska and Hawaii.
[b] Black and "other races" for 1954 and 1940.
[c] Texas, Alaska, and Hawaii excluded from Death Registration States.

TABLE 4.9

Estimated Age of Crossover of Death Rates for Whites and Blacks:
1929–1931 to 1985

Period or Year	Both Sexes	Male	Female
1929–1931	77	80	75
1939–1941	73[a]	73	73
1949–1951[b]	75	74	76
1959–1961[b]	76	75	77
1969–1971	79[a]	78	80
1979–1981	85	84	85
1985	(85+)	(85+)	(85+)

NOTE: Based on unabridged U.S. life tables except in 1985.

[a]Use of data for all races other than white, instead of data for blacks only, gives the same results.
[b]Data for all races other than white are used to represent black.

in the census and by age misreporting on death certificates. (See Appendix Table 2A.1.) The crossover may be a statistical artifact, therefore. The evidence for this view is not mainly empirical but analogical, however;[22] Scandinavian countries, with data of good quality, do not show the crossover.

Both empirical and theoretical considerations support the crossover. Death rates based wholly on Social Security (Medicare) data also indicate a crossover of the rates for the two races at a very high age. One community longitudinal study which carefully checked ages of decedents confirmed the crossover.[23] Numerous paired comparisons of population groups within and between countries having data of good quality show the crossover phenomenon.[24]

[22]N. G. Bennett, "The Roots of Crossover Mortality: Imperfect Data vs. Heterogeneity of Frailty," paper presented at the Workshop on the Methodologies of Forecasting Life Expectancy and Active Life Expectancy, National Institutes of Health, Bethesda, MD, June 1985; A. J. Coale and E. Kisker, "Mortality Crossovers: Reality or Bad Data?" *Population Studies* 40 (3) (November 1986):389–401.
[23]S. Wing, K. G. Manton, E. Stallard, C. G. Haines, and H. A. Tyroler, "The Black/White Mortality Crossover: Investigation in a Community-based Study," *Journal of Gerontology* 40 (1) (January 1985):78–84.
[24]C. B. Nam and K. A. Ockay, "Factors Contributing to the Mortality Crossover Pattern: Effects of Development Level, Overall Mortality Level, and Causes of Death," *Proceedings of the 18th General Conference of the International Union for the Scientific Study of Population*, Mexico City, August 8–13, 1977; and C. B. Nam, N. L. Weatherby, and K. A. Ockay, "Causes of Death Which Contribute to the Mortality Crossover Effect," *Social Biology* 25 (4) (Winter 1978):306–314; M. M. MacMillen and C. Nam, "Mortality Crossovers by Cause of Death and Race in the U.S. in the 1970's," paper presented at a meeting of the International Union for the Scientific Study of Population, Florence, 1985.

I am inclined to conclude that the crossover phenomenon is real. There is an acceptable body of theory that can be adduced to explain it. This theory incorporates the concepts of the survival of the fit, population heterogeneity with respect to health risks, and race differences in physiological risk factors. Those blacks who have survived the excessive environmental stresses of their younger years may be destined to live an especially long life. A refined version of this hypothesis offered by Manton and his associates attributes the crossover phenomenon to the effect of differential mortality selection on a heterogeneous population.[25] They reason that if populations are heterogeneous with respect to their members' endowment for longevity, a crossover, or at least a convergence, of the age-specific mortality rates of two populations can occur if one population has markedly higher earlier mortality. The more robust make up a larger proportion of the survivors for blacks at the older ages than for whites and, hence, blacks have lower death rates at these ages.

Socioeconomic Differences

The chances of reaching age 65 are clearly better for the more affluent and better educated. There is strong evidence of differences in death rates according to socioeconomic status at the ages under 65. An analysis of death rates in the four-month period, May–August 1960, based on a match of death certificates and census records conducted by Kitagawa and Hauser, indicates that, in general, death rates vary inversely with educational attainment, income, and occupational level.[26] This pattern is clearly shown for whites aged 25–64, but applies somewhat less forcefully to blacks aged 25–64 and to persons aged 65 and over. More recent studies confirm the persistence of class differences in mortality, but they are much more limited in scope.[27]

[25]K. G. Manton, S. S. Poss, and S. Wing, "The Black/White Mortality Crossover: Investigation from the Perspective of the Components of Aging," *Gerontologist* 19 (3) (June 1979):291–300; K. G. Manton and E. Stallard, "Methods for Evaluating the Heterogeneity of Aging Processes Using Vital Statistics Data: Explaining the Black/White Mortality Crossover by a Model of Mortality Selection," *Human Biology* 53 (1981):47–67.

[26]E. M. Kitagawa and P. M. Hauser, *Differential Mortality in the United States: A Study in Socioeconomic Epidemiology* (Cambridge, MA: Harvard University Press, 1973), esp. pp. 11, 14, and 157.

[27]M. M. MacMillen and H. M. Rosenberg, "New Research Directions on Socio-Economic Differential Mortality in the United States of America," *Socio-Economic Differential Mortality in Industrialized Societies*, vol. 3, United Nations Population Division, World Health Organization, and Committee for International Cooperation in National Research in Demography, 1984.

According to the Kitagawa-Hauser study, in 1960 the average years of life remaining at age 25 and at age 65 for white males and white females varied according to years of school completed as follows:[28]

Sex and Years of School Completed	Average Years of Life Remaining at	
	Age 25	Age 65
Males		
Elementary, 5–7 years	43.6	12.9
Elementary, 8 years	44.8	13.0
High school, 1–3 years	45.6	13.5
High school, 4 years	46.0	12.9
College, 1 year or more	47.1	13.1
Females		
Elementary, 5–7 years	50.5	16.0
Elementary, 8 years	51.1	16.2
High school, 1–3 years	53.4	18.0
High school, 4 years	52.2	16.3
College, 1 year or more	56.4	20.8

Some of the difference between the death rates of whites and blacks at ages 25 and over may be accounted for by differences in the socioeconomic status of the race groups. For example, if the life expectancy figures of whites at age 25 for educational attainment categories in 1960 are weighted by the educational attainment distribution of blacks, about one fifth of the white-black gap in overall life expectancy would be erased. Hence, there is still a large difference between the races when socioeconomic status is held constant. In addition to socioeconomic status, other social, economic, and cultural factors may contribute to the difference between the death rates for the races. Genetic factors may also play a part; investigations have revealed that specific gene-linked diseases have an affinity for certain ethnic and racial groups.[29]

Causes of Death

Diseases of the heart far outrank any other cause of death among persons aged 65 and over (Table 4.10). Malignant neoplasms (cancer) hold

[28]Kitagawa and Hauser (1973), p. 17.
[29]A. Shiloh and I. C. Selavan, eds., *The Jews*, Ethnic Groups of America: Their Morbidity, Mortality, and Behavior Disorders, vol. 1, esp. pp. xv and xvi; and *The Blacks*, vol. 2 (Springfield, IL: Thomas, 1974 and 1975). See also H. Rothschild, (ed.), *Biocultural Aspects of Disease* (New York: Academic Press, 1981).

TABLE 4.10

Death Rates for the 10 Leading Causes of Death for the Population Aged 55 and Over, by Age: 1985 (rates per 100,000 population)

Cause of Death by Rank[a]	Ages 55–64	Ages 65–74	Ages 75–84	Ages 85 and Over	Ages 65 and Over
All Causes	1,282.7	2,838.6	6,445.1	15,480.3	5,153.3
1. Diseases of the Heart (390–398, 402, 404–429)	439.1	1,080.6	2,712.6	7,275.0	2,173.0
2. Malignant Neoplasms (140–208)	450.5	838.3	1,281.0	1,591.5	1,046.7
3. Cerebrovascular Diseases (430–438)	54.3	171.3	605.8	1,837.5	463.8
4. Chronic Obstructive Pulmonary Diseases and Allied Conditions (490–496)	47.5	147.9	291.6	360.0	212.5
5. Pneumonia and Influenza (480–487)	18.5	57.8	241.3	1,023.5	206.2
6. Diabetes Mellitus (250)	26.1	59.7	128.1	214.9	95.6
7. Accidents and Adverse Effects (E800–E949)	36.6	50.5	107.7	254.3	87.5
Motor vehicle (E810–E825)	15.5	17.7	27.6	26.1	21.6
All other (E800–E807, E826–E949)	21.1	32.8	80.1	228.3	65.9
8. Atherosclerosis (440)	4.0	17.6	82.3	465.8	79.8
9. Nephritis, Nephrotic Syndrome, and Nephrosis (580–589)	9.7	27.7	78.1	213.7	61.0
10. Septicemia (038)	8.8	21.5	61.5	159.6	47.0
All Other Causes	187.7	366.3	855.1	2,084.5	680.5

SOURCES: Based on the U.S. National Center for Health Statistics, "Advance Report of Final Mortality Statistics, 1985," *Monthly Vital Statistics Report* 36 (5), Supplement (August 1987); population data from U.S. Bureau of the Census, *Current Population Reports,* series P-25, no. 965 (March 1985).

NOTE: The 10 leading causes were identified on the basis of rates for the population aged 65 and over as a group.

[a]Ninth Revision, International Classification of Diseases, 1975. Figures in parentheses represent codes in the International Classification.

second place. Heart diseases accounted for 42 percent and cancer accounted for 20 percent of elderly deaths in 1985; taken together, these two causes accounted for over 3 in 5 deaths at ages 65 and over. Other leading causes, in rank order, are cerebrovascular diseases (mainly stroke); chronic obstructive pulmonary diseases (COPD) and other allied conditions; influenza and pneumonia; diabetes; accidents and adverse effects; atherosclerosis; nephritis, nephrotic syndrome, and nephrosis; and septicemia. Each of these is far less frequent than diseases of the heart and cancer, however.

The rank order and relative frequency of the causes vary with age. Most striking are the reduced role of cancer with rising age (from 30 percent at ages 65–74 to 10 percent at ages 85 and over) and the increased role of major cardiovascular diseases (from 45 percent to 62 percent). Pneumonia and influenza and nephritis rise in importance and COPD and diabetes fall.

Heart diseases were the major cause of death of the elderly in 1950 and remain so today, even though in recent years, particularly since 1968, there has been a spectacular decline in the death rate from this cause. For example, there was a 35 percent decline between 1968 and 1985 at ages 65–74. Mortality among the elderly has plunged since 1968 because of a marked reduction of death rates from several major chronic causes, particularly the major cardiovascular diseases.

Goldman and Cook have analyzed the basis of the decline in elderly mortality between 1968 and 1976, the period of most rapid decline.[30] In this period the death rate from heart diseases for the elderly fell 29 percent. Goldman and Cook estimate that more than half the decline resulted from reductions in cigarette smoking and in levels of serum cholesterol and 40 percent resulted from medical intervention. More than half of the 22 percent overall decline in mortality of the elderly between 1968 and 1976 was due to the decline in heart diseases and another third was due to the decrease in stroke. Death rates from cancer, however, and especially lung cancer, increased in this period. They have been increasing for several decades and they continue to rise.

Because of the low level of death rates at ages under 65 and the relative agedness of the population, the average age of persons dying from most of the leading causes is now over age 65. In 1979, the median age at death was 76 for persons dying from heart disease, 69 for malignant neoplasms, 80 for cerebrovascular diseases, 73 for COPD, 80 for influenza and pneumonia, and 73 for diabetes. For all causes combined, the median age of persons dying in 1979 was about 72. In 1900, when infectious and parasitic illnesses were much more common and the population was much younger, the median age of death was only about 36. The doubling of the median age at death reflects the joint effect of the

---

[30]L. Goldman and E. F. Cook, "The Decline of Ischemic Heart Disease Mortality Rates: An Analysis of the Comparative Effects of Medical Intervention and Changes in Lifestyle," *Annals of Internal Medicine* 101 (6) (December 1984):825–836.

shift in the age pattern of mortality rates and the shift in the age distribution of the population. The median age at death in 1979 of the leading causes of death at ages 65 and over, according to rank, are as follows:

Cause of Death[a]	Median Age
Accidents and Adverse Effects	34.6
Chronic Liver Disease and Cirrhosis	58.2
Malignant Neoplasms	68.8
Chronic Obstructive Pulmonary Diseases and Allied Conditions	72.6
Diabetes Mellitus	73.0
Diseases of the Heart	75.7
Nephritis, Nephrotic Syndrome, and Nephrosis	75.9
Cerebrovascular Diseases	79.6
Pneumonia and Influenza	80.5
Atherosclerosis	84.9

SOURCE: Based on U.S. National Center for Health Statistics, *Vital Statistics of the United States, 1979*, vol. 2, Part A, Table 1-25.

[a]Ninth Revision, International Classification of Diseases, 1975.

Sex and Race Variations

Death rates for older men are much greater than those for older women for several leading causes of death, as shown by ratios of male death rates to female death rates for the 10 leading causes at ages 65 and over in 1988 (Table 4.11). There is a considerable excess of male mortality for diseases of the heart, malignant neoplasms, accidents and adverse effects, and especially COPD, and a moderate excess for pneumonia and influenza and nephritis. On the other hand, the rates for cerebrovascular diseases, atherosclerosis, septicemia, and diabetes either show little preference for one sex or the other or are somewhat higher for women. At ages 65–74 and at ages 75–84 the rates for men for all 10 leading causes except diabetes are well above those for women; and at ages 85 and over, only the ratios for cerebrovascular diseases and atherosclerosis do not show an excess for men, although the ratios for diabetes and septicemia are very low.

Between 1978 and 1988 there were decreases in the death rates at ages 65 and over for nearly all leading causes of death for both men and women. For some leading causes (e.g., diseases of the heart, cerebrovascular diseases, atherosclerosis, and diabetes), death rates fell by roughly

TABLE 4.11

Ratios of Male to Female Death Rates for the 10 Leading Causes of Death for the Population Aged 65 and Over, by Age: 1988 and 1978

Causes of Death by Rank[a]	1988[b]				1978[c]			
	Ages 65 and Over	Ages 65–74	Ages 75–84	Ages 85 and Over	Ages 65 and Over	Ages 65–74	Ages 75–84	Ages 85 and Over
All Causes	1.30	1.74	1.59	1.27	1.45	1.96	1.60	1.28
1. Diseases of Heart	1.84	1.98	1.53	1.15	1.40	2.14	1.52	1.20
2. Malignant Neoplasms	1.66	1.63	1.89	1.96	1.79	1.83	1.93	1.88
3. Cerebrovascular Diseases	0.88	1.29	1.15	0.94	0.97	1.39	1.14	0.98
4. Chronic Obstructive Pulmonary Diseases and Allied Conditions	2.15	1.89	2.56	3.16	3.84	3.59	4.77	3.80
5. Pneumonia and Influenza	1.21	1.97	1.77	1.42	1.49	2.26	1.89	1.52
6. Diabetes Mellitus	0.91	1.00	1.03	1.04	0.88	1.00	0.92	0.92
7. Accidents and Adverse Effects	1.50	1.94	1.11	1.66	1.62	2.14	1.74	1.48
Motor vehicle accidents	1.93	1.81	1.97	3.51	2.36	2.14	2.51	4.22
All other	1.37	2.00	1.62	1.51	1.43	2.14	1.55	1.34
8. Atherosclerosis	0.83	1.70	1.30	0.96	0.92	1.61	1.22	1.04
9. Nephritis, Nephrotic Syndrome, and Nephrosis	1.29	1.40	1.61	1.71	1.68	1.65	2.02	1.97
10. Septicemia	1.01	1.40	1.27	1.07	1.40	1.55	1.63	1.49

SOURCES: U.S. National Center for Health Statistics, *Vital Statistics of the United States, 1988*, vol. 2, Part A (1990); "Advance Report of Final Mortality Statistics, 1978," *Monthly Vital Statistics Report*" 29 (6), Supplement 2 (September 1980), Tables 1–10; and *Vital Statistics of the United States, 1978*, vol. 2, Part A (1980).

[a]Based on U.S. National Center for Health Statistics, "Advance Report of Final Mortality Statistics, 1988," *Monthly Vital Statistics Report* 39 (7), Supplement (November 1990), p. 21. The ten leading causes of death were defined on the basis of rates for the population 65 and over for both sexes combined in 1988.

[b]Based on Ninth Revision, International Classification of Diseases.

[c]Based on Eighth Revision, International Classification of Diseases.

equal percentages for men and women.[31] For COPD and some other leading causes, death rates fell more rapidly for men or rose less for men. For malignant neoplasms death rates increased for both men and women between 1978 and 1988, with the relative increases being greater for women. As a result, the relative differences between the death rates of males and females aged 65 and over widened for some leading causes between 1978 and 1988 and narrowed for others.

The net effect of these changes in age-sex-cause-specific death rates has been to decrease slightly the excess of the death rate of males over the death rate of females for ages 65 and over between 1978 and 1988. Death rates for age groups 55 and over for the 10 leading causes, for men and women in 1988, and the percent changes, 1978–1988, 1968–1978, and 1954–1968 are shown in Appendix Table 4B.1.

Comparison of cause-specific death rates of elderly blacks and whites presents a picture somewhat analogous to that for males and females. Death rates for diseases of the heart are rather similar for blacks and whites. The rates for blacks are substantially or considerably higher, however, for cerebrovascular diseases, malignant neoplasms, septicemia, accidents and adverse effects, diabetes, and nephritis (Table 4.12). Rates for blacks are considerably lower for COPD, atherosclerosis, and pneumonia and influenza. As in the male-female comparison, the black-white difference depends, however, on the age detail examined.

The striking differences apparent between the relative levels of mortality for whites and blacks at ages 65–74, 75–84, and 85 and over described earlier are reflected in the rates for the 10 leading causes of death. The rates at ages 65–74 for all major causes of death except COPD are substantially or considerably higher for blacks than for whites. At ages 75–84, the relative levels often go in different directions, but most causes show an excess of black mortality. The death rates of blacks for cerebrovascular diseases, diabetes, septicemia, and nephritis are substantially or considerably higher than those of whites; the rate for COPD is considerably lower, and the rates for the other leading causes (e.g., heart diseases, cancer) differ little or moderately. For ages 85 and over, the rates for most of the 10 leading causes (except nephritis and septicemia especially) are much lower for blacks than for whites. As suggested earlier, the real shift from ages 65–74 to ages 85 and over may be less pronounced than is indicated by the figures in Table 4.12, which are affected by errors of reporting both in the census and in the death registration.

---

[31]See also C. H. Patrick, Y. Y. Palesch, M. Feinleib, and J. A. Brody, "Sex Differences in Declining Cohort Death Rates from Heart Diseases," *American Journal of Public Health* 72 (2) (February 1982):161–166.

TABLE 4.12

Ratios of Black to White Death Rates for the 10 Leading Causes of Death for the Population Aged 65 and Over, by Age: 1988 and 1978

Cause of Death by Rank[a]	1988[b]				1978[c]			
	Ages 65 and Over	Ages 65–74	Ages 75–84	Ages 85 and Over	Ages 65 and Over	Ages 65–74	Ages 75–84	Ages 85 and Over
All Causes	1.11	1.37	1.18	0.85	0.97	1.22	1.06	0.60
1. Diseases of Heart	1.05	1.34	1.16	0.80	0.86	1.10	0.95	0.55
2. Malignant Neoplasms	1.19	1.23	1.18	1.05	1.02	1.12	1.06	0.69
3. Cerebrovascular Diseases	1.24	2.04	1.36	0.83	1.10	1.84	1.19	0.60
4. Chronic Obstructive Pulmonary Diseases and Allied Conditions	0.60	0.71	0.58	0.48	0.46	0.48	0.47	0.41
5. Pneumonia and Influenza	0.80	1.46	0.95	0.58	0.84	1.41	0.98	0.49
6. Diabetes Mellitus	1.93	2.34	1.98	1.40	1.53	1.99	1.57	0.78
7. Accidents and Adverse Effects	1.19	1.53	1.22	0.88	1.05	1.42	1.09	0.56
Motor vehicle accidents	0.99	1.13	0.85	0.94	1.08	1.16	1.13	0.68
All other	1.27	1.79	1.38	0.87	1.04	1.57	1.08	0.54
8. Atherosclerosis	0.77	1.34	1.19	0.66	0.72	1.34	0.93	0.47
9. Nephritis, Nephrotic Syndrome, and Nephrosis	1.68	2.71	2.19	1.56	2.52	3.23	2.73	1.44
10. Septicemia	1.92	2.52	2.06	1.58	2.04	2.54	2.29	1.28

SOURCES: U.S. National Center for Health Statistics, *Vital Statistics of the United States, 1988*, vol. 2, Part A (1990); "Advance Report of Final Mortality Statistics, 1978," *Monthly Vital Statistics Report* 29 (6), Supplement 2 (September 1980), Tables 1–10; and *Vital Statistics of the United States, 1978*, vol. 2, Part A (1980).

[a] Based on U.S. National Center for Health Statistics, "Advance Report of Final Mortality Statistics, 1988," *Monthly Vital Statistics Report* 39 (7), Supplement (November 1990), p. 21. The ten leading causes of death were defined on the basis of rates for the population 65 and over for all races combined in 1988.

[b] Based on Ninth Revision, International Classification of Diseases.

[c] Based on Eighth Revision, International Classification of Diseases. "Black and other races" data used for "black."

Analysis by Life Tables

Some diseases have been virtually eliminated, statistically speaking, since they contribute little to the total death rate. Their complete elimination in fact would add very little to life expectancy. For instance, according to life tables for 1979–1981 eliminating various causes of death,[32] completely eliminating influenza and pneumonia would add a mere 0.3 year to life expectancy at birth (Table 4.13). On the other hand, if diseases of the heart were completely eliminated, there would be a 5.8-year gain in life expectancy at birth and a 5.1-year gain in life expectancy at age 65. These estimates are based on the assumption that the risks from different causes are independent even though this assumption is patently contrary to fact.[33] Malignant neoplasms rank second with respect to the gain to be realized—3.0 years at birth and 1.8 years at age 65. Since this cause affects a wide span of ages, the gain at age 65 is much less than at birth. The gain at birth from eliminating any other major category, even cerebrovascular diseases, amounts to less than one year.

According to life tables for 1979–1981 disaggregating deaths according to major causes, a newborn infant has a 41 percent chance of eventually dying from a heart disease, a 20 percent chance of eventually dying from cancer, and a 10 percent chance of eventually dying from a cerebrovascular disease (Table 4.14). The chance is 55 percent for major cardiovascular diseases taken as a group. The probability at birth of eventually dying from any other major cause is less than 5 percent. Death rates at ages below 65, except infancy, have fallen so low that the chances of eventually dying from most major causes at age 65 are not grossly different from the chances of eventually dying from them at birth and are usually about the same (exceptions being accidents and cancer).

A comparison of the life tables eliminating cancer for 1979–1981 and 1969–1971 implies a small increase over this period in the gain in life expectancy that would result from eliminating cancer and a moderate increase in the probability of eventually dying from cancer.[34] These increases are consistent with the rise in cancer mortality in this period.

[32]U.S. National Center for Health Statistics, "U.S. Life Tables Eliminating Certain Causes of Death," by R. Armstrong and L. Curtin, *U.S. Decennial Life Tables, 1979–81,* vol. I, no. 2 (1986).

[33]The sum of the gains in life expectancy at birth calculated for all cause categories is less than 20 years, even though the obvious result of eliminating all causes is to increase life expectancy without limit.

[34]U.S. National Center for Health Statistics, "U.S. Life Tables by Causes of Death; 1969–71," by T. N. E. Greville, F. Bayo, and R. S. Foster, *U.S. Life Tables, 1969–71,* vol. 1, no. 5 (May 1975). See also "U.S. Life Tables by Causes of Death, 1959–61," by T. N. E. Greville, *U.S. Life Tables, 1959–61,* vol. 1, no. 6 (1968); and S. Preston, N. Keyfitz, and R. Schoen, *Causes of Death: Life Tables for National Populations* (New York: Seminar Press, 1972), pp. 768–771.

TABLE 4.13

Gain in Life Expectancy at Birth and at Age 65, in Years, Due to Elimination of Various Causes of Death, by Race and Sex: 1979–1981 and 1969–1971

Period and Cause of Death	Total		White Male	
	At Birth	At Age 65	At Birth	At Age 65
1979–1981				
Major cardiovascular diseases	9.8	9.4	8.5	7.7
Diseases of the heart	5.8	5.1	5.8	4.8
Cerebrovascular diseases	0.9	0.9	0.6	0.6
Atherosclerosis	0.1	0.2	0.1	0.1
Malignant neoplasms[b]	3.0	1.8	2.9	1.9
Influenza and pneumonia	0.3	0.2	0.2	0.2
Diabetes mellitus	0.2	0.2	0.2	0.1
Motor vehicle accidents	0.6	—	0.9	—
All accidents excluding motor vehicle	0.5	0.1	0.6	0.1
Chronic obstructive pulmonary diseases and allied conditions	0.3	0.1	0.4	0.4
Chronic liver disease and cirrhosis	0.3	0.1	0.3	0.1
Nephritis, nephrotic syndrome, and nephrosis	0.1	0.1	0.1	0.1
Infective and parasitic diseases	0.1	0.1	0.1	—
Tuberculosis, all forms	—	—	—	—
1969–1971				
Major cardiovascular diseases[c]	11.8	11.4	10.5	9.5
Diseases of the heart	5.9	5.1	6.1	4.9
Cerebrovascular diseases	1.2	1.2	0.9	0.9
Arteriosclerosis	0.1	0.2	0.1	0.1
Malignant neoplasms[c]	2.5	1.4	2.3	1.4
Influenza and pneumonia	0.5	0.2	0.4	0.2
Diabetes mellitus	0.2	0.2	0.2	0.1
Motor vehicle accidents	0.7	0.1	0.9	0.1
All accidents excluding motor vehicle	0.6	0.1	0.8	0.1
Infective and parasitic diseases	0.2	0.1	0.1	—
Tuberculosis, all forms	—	—	—	—

SOURCES: U.S. National Center for Health Statistics, "U.S. Life Tables Eliminating Certain Causes of Death," by R. Armstrong and L. R. Curtin, *U.S. Decennial Life Tables, 1979–81*, vol. 1, no. 2 (1986); "United States Life Tables by Causes of Death, 1969–71," by T. N. E. Greville, F. Bayo, and R. S. Foster, *U. S. Decennial Life Tables, 1969–71*, vol. 1, no. 5 (May 1975).

NOTES: Data for 1979–1981 based on the Ninth Revision of the International Classification of Diseases; data for 1969–1971 based on the Eighth Revision of the International Classification of Diseases, Injuries, and Causes of Death. Dash denotes that figure rounds to 0.0.

[a] Black and other races for 1969–1971.
[b] Malignant neoplasms including lymphatic and hematopoietic tissues.
[c] Major cardiovascular-renal diseases for 1969–1971.

TABLE 4.13 *(continued)*

White Female		Black Male[a]		Black Female[a]	
At Birth	At Age 65	At Birth	At Age 65	At Birth	At Age 65
10.2	10.3	8.0	7.3	11.6	11.3
5.3	5.1	5.2	4.3	6.2	5.6
1.1	1.0	1.0	0.9	1.5	1.4
0.2	0.2	0.1	0.1	0.1	0.2
3.0	1.6	3.2	2.3	3.0	1.6
0.3	0.2	0.4	0.2	0.3	0.2
0.2	0.2	0.2	0.2	0.5	0.4
0.4	—	0.6	0.1	0.2	—
0.3	0.1	0.9	0.2	0.4	0.1
0.2	0.2	0.2	0.2	0.1	0.1
0.2	—	0.5	0.1	0.3	—
0.1	0.1	0.2	0.1	0.2	0.2
0.1	—	0.2	0.1	0.2	0.1
—	—	0.1	—	—	—
12.0	12.2	10.4	10.4	15.3	15.1
5.2	5.0	5.3	4.8	6.3	5.8
1.4	1.3	1.4	1.3	2.2	1.9
0.2	0.2	0.1	0.2	0.2	0.2
2.6	1.2	2.3	1.7	2.4	1.2
0.4	0.2	0.8	0.3	0.7	0.3
0.3	0.2	0.2	0.2	0.6	0.4
0.4	0.1	1.0	0.1	0.4	—
0.4	0.1	1.2	0.2	0.5	0.1
0.1	—	0.4	0.1	0.3	0.1
—	—	0.1	0.1	0.1	—

There was virtually no difference in the gains in life expectancy at birth or at age 65 from eliminating diseases of the heart from the two tables.

Persons who escape death from one cause must eventually die from some other cause. If death rates from a particular cause are sharply reduced, age-specific death rates for some other causes tend to rise because of the effect of multiple-cause mortality, the competing risks of death, and the limited human life span.[35] Age-specific death rates must

[35] J. Cohen, "Competing Risks, Without Independence," paper presented at the annual meeting of the Population Association of America, Boston, March 28–30, 1985.

TABLE 4.14

Probability at Birth and at Age 65 of Eventually Dying from Various Causes, by Race and Sex: 1979–1981 and 1969–1971

Cause of Death and Year	Total		White Male	
	At Birth	At Age 65	At Birth	At Age 65
1979–1981				
Major cardiovascular diseases	.545	.609	.516	.571
Diseases of the heart	.412	.452	.412	.444
Cerebrovascular diseases	.098	.116	.073	.089
Atherosclerosis	.020	.025	.014	.019
Malignant neoplasms[b]	.196	.176	.210	.203
Influenza and pneumonia	.031	.036	.029	.035
Diabetes mellitus	.017	.018	.013	.014
Motor vehicle accidents	.016	.004	.024	.005
All accidents excluding motor vehicle	.021	.014	.025	.014
Chronic obstructive pulmonary diseases and allied conditions	.027	.029	.040	.047
Chronic liver disease and cirrhosis	.012	.006	.015	.008
Nephritis, nephrotic syndrome, and nephrosis	.009	.010	.008	.010
Infective and parasitic diseases	.008	.008	.007	.007
Tuberculosis, all forms	.001	.001	.001	.001
1969–1971				
Major cardiovascular diseases[c]	.588	.672	.565	.640
Diseases of the heart	.412	.460	.422	.460
Cerebrovascular diseases	.122	.149	.095	.122
Arteriosclerosis	.022	.030	.016	.023
Malignant neoplasms[b]	.163	.145	.169	.164
Influenza and pneumonia	.034	.037	.032	.037
Diabetes mellitus	.020	.021	.015	.016
Motor vehicle accidents	.020	.006	.028	.007
All accidents excluding motor vehicle	.026	.018	.030	.016
Infective and parasitic diseases	.007	.005	.007	.006
Tuberculosis, all forms	.002	.002	.003	.003

SOURCE: U.S. National Center for Health Statistics, "U.S. Life Tables Eliminating Certain Causes of Death," by R. Armstrong and L. R. Curtin, *U.S. Decennial Life Tables, 1979–81*, vol. 1, no. 2 (1986); "U.S. Life Tables by Causes of Death, 1969–71," by T. N. E., Greville, F. Bayo, and R. S. Foster, *U.S. Decennial Life Tables, 1969–71*, vol. 1, no. 5 (May 1975).

NOTE: Data for 1979–1981 based on the Ninth Revision of the International Classification of Diseases; data for 1969–1971 based on the Eighth Revision of the International Classification of Diseases, Injuries, and Causes of Death. Dash denotes zero.

[a] Black and other races for 1969–1971.
[b] Malignant neoplasms including lymphatic and hematopoietic tissues.
[c] Major cardiovascular-renal diseases for 1969–1971.

TABLE 4.14 (*continued*)

White Female		Black Male[a]		Black Female[a]	
At Birth	At Age 65	At Birth	At Age 65	At Birth	At Age 65
.589	.647	.431	.523	.550	.625
.427	.467	.326	.385	.390	.438
.123	.136	.082	.107	.126	.146
.027	.031	.010	.016	.019	.024
.183	.152	.215	.230	.172	.145
.034	.038	.027	.031	.023	.026
.020	.020	.016	.018	.034	.035
.010	.003	.022	.006	.006	.002
.016	.014	.035	.018	.019	.015
.018	.017	.020	.025	.008	.007
.008	.004	.021	.006	.012	.003
.008	.009	.014	.018	.017	.018
.008	.007	.015	.015	.015	.014
—	—	.004	.003	.002	.002
.632	.706	.472	.606	.593	.694
.421	.468	.317	.401	.372	.436
.151	.171	.106	.146	.160	.190
.030	.037	.011	.021	.020	.029
.159	.128	.154	.168	.135	.112
.035	.037	.040	.041	.035	.034
.024	.025	.017	.018	.037	.035
.012	.004	.032	.008	.011	.003
.021	.019	.043	.018	.022	.017
.006	.004	.017	.013	.012	.008
.001	.001	.008	.007	.004	.003

rise in late life and approximate 1.0 (i.e., certainty of death) at the ages just preceding the limits of life. Until life expectancy approximates the human life span more closely, it is likely, however, that general age-specific death rates at most or all ages will continue to decline as a result of the reduction of death rates from one or more causes. Moreover, since more persons will survive to the older ages, more persons will tend to die of some of the existing causes in spite of the lower death rates. We may have the seeming paradox that general age-specific death rates and age-specific death rates for particular causes may continue to decline while the chances of eventually dying from these causes may increase.

If a particular cause of death was eliminated, given the fact that the risks from the various causes are not independent, more persons would tend to die from other causes as a result of the increase both in the population at risk and in the death rates from these other causes. The extent to which a particular cause of death would be affected by the elimination of some other cause depends on the rank order and proximity of the median ages of the various causes, the relative magnitudes of the rates, and their tendency to occur jointly. Since multiple causes are often involved in the event of death, the elimination of one cause may account for death from another cause with only a short lag.[36] With the elimination of cancer, for example, few additional lives would probably be saved in the short run.[37] There is, however, considerable uncertainty as to the effect of an assumed reduction in the death rate from a particular cause on the death rates from other causes.[38] The elimination of the cardiovascular diseases would very probably result in major additions to population size, since survivorship at the older ages particularly would improve. Under such conditions and conditions of continuing low fertility, both the number and proportion of persons at the older ages would increase greatly.[39]

The tables eliminating various causes of death provide guides as to where it may be most effective to apply resources in reducing death rates. To be realistic, the estimates of years gained need to be adjusted for the effects of competing risks, however. Although greater gains in life expectancy can be made by eliminating one cause rather than another, other considerations, such as the relative economic costs of losing lives to the different diseases and of maintaining lives impaired by different diseases, should also be taken into account in developing a policy on allocation of research resources.[40]

[36]K. G. Manton, H. D. Tolley, and S. S. Poss, "Life Table Techniques for Multiple Cause Mortality," *Demography* 13 (4) (November 1976):541–564; and K. G. Manton and S. S. Poss, "Effects of Dependency Among Causes of Death for Cause Elimination of Life Table Strategies," *Demography* 16 (2) (May 1979):313–327.

[37]N. Keyfitz, "What Difference Would It Make If Cancer Were Eradicated? An Examination of the Taeuber Paradox," *Demography* 14 (4) (November 1977): 411–418.

[38]Cohen (1985).

[39]For an extended discussion of the demographic and social consequences of the elimination of various causes of death, see S. Preston, *Mortality Patterns in National Populations, with Special Reference to Recorded Causes of Death* (New York: Academic Press, 1976), esp. chap. 7.

[40]See, for example, U.S. National Center for Health Statistics, "Social and Economic Implications of Cancer in the United States," by D. P. Rice and T. A. Hodgson, *Vital and*

Geographic Variations

Death rates for states show a steady, rapid convergence from at least 1929–1931 (when the first complete set of life tables for states was prepared) to 1959–1961. By 1959–1961, the variation in life expectancy at birth and at age 65 among the states had become rather small and, since that date, the variation has changed little, particularly if each sex-race group is considered separately. This variation has been measured by the average (mean) deviation of the values for the states around the unweighted average (mean) of all the values using sets of state life tables for 1979–1981, 1969–1971, and 1959–1961. The mean deviation for life expectancy at birth was 1.0 year in 1979–1981, 1.2 years in 1969–1971, and 1.1 years in 1959–1961 (Table 4.15). The values for life expectancy at birth for the "best" state and the "worst" state (excluding the District of Columbia) in 1979–1981 differed by 5.3 years. Part of the state variation is the result of the large difference in life expectancy among the races, in combination with a large difference in race composition from state to state.

The West North Central Division appears to have the most favorable position with respect to life expectancy at birth and the South Atlantic Division the least favorable one, even though the geographic differences are small. The six leading states in 1979–1981 were Hawaii, Minnesota, Iowa, Utah, North Dakota, and Nebraska, and the six trailing states were Louisiana, South Carolina, Mississippi, Georgia, Alaska, and Alabama. Most states in the West, Midwest, and New England exceeded the national figure, while most states in the Middle Atlantic Division and the South fell below the national average.

By 1979–1981, life expectancy at birth for white females and white males in the lead state (Hawaii) had reached 80.1 years and 73.0 years, respectively (Table 4.15). The corresponding figures for blacks were much lower: 75.7 years for females and 67.5 years for males (Massachusetts). At age 65, the best state showed only modest differences between the races in life expectancy. The figures for 1979–1981 indicate about the same modest variation for blacks as for whites among the states in death rates below age 65; state variation in death rates at ages 65 and over for each race was even smaller. Depending on sex and race, expectancy values at birth were 3.4 years to 4.8 years lower for the worst state (excluding DC) than for the best state, and expectancy values at age 65 were 2 to 2.5 years lower (Table 4.15).

Health Statistics, series 3, no. 20 (March 1981); and J. M. Poterba and L. H. Summers, "Public Policy Implications of Declining Old-Age Mortality," paper prepared for the Brookings Conference on Retirement and Aging, Washington, DC, May 2, 1985.

TABLE 4.15

Variation in Life Expectancy at Birth and at Age 65, by Race and Sex, for States:
1979–1981 and 1959–1961

Period, Age, and Area	Total	White		
		Male	Female	Difference[b]
1979–1981				
At Birth				
High state[c]	77.0	73.0	80.1	7.0
United States	73.9	70.8	78.2	7.4
Low state[c]	71.7	69.0	76.7	7.7
Mean Deviation[e]	1.05	0.75	0.57	−0.18
At Age 65				
High state[c]	18.0	15.9	19.7	3.8
United States	16.5	14.3	18.5	4.3
Low state[c]	15.7	13.5	17.8	4.3
Mean Deviation[e]	0.45	0.47	0.39	−0.08
1959–1961				
At Birth				
High state[c]	72.0	69.2[f]	75.7[f]	6.5
United States	69.9	67.6	74.2	6.6
Low state[c]	66.4	64.6[f]	72.7[f]	8.1
Mean Deviation[h]	1.06	0.68	0.62	−0.06
At Age 65				
High state[c]	15.7	14.3	17.4	3.1
United States	14.4	13.0	15.9	2.9
Low state[c]	13.6	12.1	15.0	2.9
Mean Deviation[h]	0.41	0.44	0.47	0.03

SOURCE: Based on U.S. National Center for Health Statistics, *U.S. Decennial Life Tables, 1979–1981*, vol. 2; *State Life Tables* (1985); *State Life Tables, 1959–61* (1966).

[a] Black only in 1979–1981. Black and "other races" in 1959–1961.
[b] Excess of female over male value or white over black value. A minus sign denotes an excess of male over female or an excess of black over white.
[c] Excluding the District of Columbia.
[d] Thirty states only.
[e] Mean deviation around U.S. unweighted average. For "black," 30 states and District of Columbia.
[f] Forty-eight states (excluding Alaska, Hawaii, and the District of Columbia).
[g] Twenty-one states (excluding California, Hawaii, Oklahoma, 26 other states, and the District of Columbia).
[h] Mean deviation around U.S. unweighted average. For "black," 21 states (excluding California, Hawaii, and Oklahoma, and 26 other states) and the District of Columbia.

TABLE 4.15 (*continued*)

Black[a]			Race Difference[b]	
Male	Female	Difference[b]	Male	Female
67.5[d]	75.7[d]	8.2	5.5	4.3
64.1	72.9	8.8	6.7	5.3
62.7[d]	71.8[d]	9.1	6.3	4.9
0.99	0.66	−0.33	−0.24	−0.09
14.5[d]	18.7[d]	4.2	1.4	1.0
13.3	17.1	3.8	1.0	1.4
12.6[d]	16.6[d]	4.1	0.9	1.2
0.36	0.33	−0.03	0.11	0.06
64.3[g]	67.9[g]	3.6	4.9	7.8
61.5	66.5	5.0	6.1	7.7
57.3[g]	63.4[g]	6.1	7.3	9.3
1.13	0.90	−0.23	−0.45	−0.28
13.7[g]	16.3[g]	2.6	0.6	1.1
12.8	15.1	2.3	0.2	0.8
11.7[g]	13.9[g]	2.2	0.4	1.1
0.47	0.53	0.06	−0.03	−0.06

Prospects for Mortality Reduction

Factors Influencing Mortality Prospects

The future trend of death rates in part determines prospective changes in the number of elderly persons as well as prospective trends in the shape of the age distribution. Mortality prospects also directly affect requirements for health care and other social services.

We may identify the factors that influence the prospects for reducing mortality as biomedical developments and socioeconomic developments, including changes in personal habits and lifestyle and community action. First, there is the possibility of developing new diagnostic and therapeutic procedures for some conditions as well as the possibility of devising techniques for slowing the aging process. The considerable gap between current life expectancy and life span suggests that knowledge of the causes, prevention, and treatment of most chronic diseases is quite limited and that much remains to be done in the way of medical research. There have been many developments in medical technology in recent decades, and they may be the most important factor making it possible for people who have survived to old age to live to extreme old age and even reach the life span mark.[41] Major reductions in death rates at the older ages may also result from current and prospective research in molecular biology designed to delay the aging process.

Some reductions in mortality could be achieved by extending the application of present medical knowledge relating to the prevention, diagnosis, and treatment of the major illnesses through health education and public information campaigns (with respect, for example, to personal habits and lifestyle, blood pressure testing, use of prescribed medication, breast self-examination); changes in the health care system, including the financing and delivery of health services (e.g., extension of public and private health insurance programs; relocation of health personnel and facilities to areas with shortages; expansion of programs to improve the competence of health personnel); and intensification of community efforts to create or maintain a healthful environment. Iatrogenic illness and the adverse effects of ill-prescribed multiple medications are serious problems. Focusing the attention of the public on the concept of personal responsibility for one's health and on the practice of good personal hygiene, healthful lifestyle, and safety at work and at home would be a useful component of the nonmedical efforts to reduce mortality.

Various elements in personal hygiene and lifestyle have been identified as associated with longevity.[42] A study by Belloc and Breslow and a follow-up study by Wiley and Camacho reported that 45-year-old men who practice seven healthful habits (i.e., exercising regularly, maintaining moderate weight, not eating snacks, eating breakfast, not smoking, not drinking excessively, sleeping at least seven hours a day) would gain several years of life over those practicing three or fewer of these habits.[43]

[41]J. L. Avorn, "Medicine, Health, and the Geriatric Transformation," *Daedalus* 115 (1) (Winter 1986):211–225.

[42]See M. Susser, "Industrialization, Urbanization, and Health: An Epidemiological View," and E. Nightingale, "Prospects for Reducing Mortality in Developed Countries by Changes in Day-to-Day Behavior," in *International Population Conference, Manila, 1981* (Liège: International Union for the Scientific Study of Population, 1981).

[43]N. B. Belloc and L. Breslow, "Relationship of Physical Health Status and Health Practices," *Preventive Medicine* 1 (1972):409–421; and J. A. Wiley and T. C. Camacho, "Life Style and Future Health: Evidence from the Alameda County Study," *Preventive Medicine* 9 (1980):1–21.

The U.S. Public Health Service has estimated that deficiencies in lifestyle, the environment, and the health care delivery system account for approximately three quarters of the mortality in the United States from heart disease, cancer, cerebrovascular disease, and arteriosclerosis, and that lifestyle alone accounts for 54 percent, 37 percent, 50 percent, and 49 percent of the mortality from these diseases, respectively.[44]

Smoking, improper dietary habits, excessive alcohol consumption, stress, and lack of exercise have a proven effect on the incidence of endogenous diseases. Prospects for increased life expectancy are improved by the evidence that the personal habits and lifestyle of Americans are changing in a small way for the better (Chapter 5). It seems reasonable to believe that the changes that have begun will continue and become more widespread. We may ask, then, to what extent life expectancy would increase if the portion of mortality caused by adverse lifestyles was eliminated. It is estimated that under these circumstances about 7.0 years would be added to the life expectancy of females at birth and nearly as many at age 65. This is a substantial gain and suggests a specific avenue for progress.

Comparative Analysis

One procedure for trying to anticipate mortality levels is to postulate that the United States as a whole will attain the level of the most advanced areas, either a state of the United States or foreign country, or the level of the most advanced socioeconomic group within the United States, at some specified future date. For example, we can postulate that the U.S. population can achieve the level of, say, U.S. white males and females who have completed at least one year of college. We can also consider composite mortality patterns combining the record of the best state or foreign country at each age.

According to state life tables for 1979–1981, life expectancy at birth for the best state (Hawaii) exceeded the figure for the United States as a whole by 3.1 years. (See Table 4.15.) The best expectancy figure at age 65 (also for Hawaii) exceeded the U.S. figure by merely 1.5 years. These differences suggest little room for improvement before the United States does as well as the best state. The United States surpassed the best state of 1969–1971 around 1980. A similar comparison for the sex-race groups indicates that the difference between life expectancy at birth for males in the United States, 70.1 years, and males in the best state, 74.6 years (non-Caucasian males in Hawaii) is 4.5 years and that the difference

[44]U.S. Centers for Disease Control, *Ten Leading Causes of Death in the United States* (Washington, DC: U.S. Government Printing Office, 1978).

between females in the United States, 77.6 years, and females in the best state, 80.7 years (non-Caucasian females in Hawaii) is 3.1 years. At age 65, the corresponding differences for males and females are small and about equal for the sexes (1.3 years). Comparisons are made here between all races in the United States and specific race categories in the states on the assumption that approximate convergence of mortality for the races is a reasonable prospect.

Even less improvement for the United States is suggested by the experience of the countries with the lowest mortality, in particular certain countries of northwestern Europe, Japan, Australia, and New Zealand. Japan may be selected as the single country with the best current overall record. Japan's advantage over the United States in life expectancy at birth for females in 1982 was only 1.6 years. On the other hand, at age 65 the United States figure for females exceeded the corresponding figure for Japan by 0.4 year. Generally, death rates for females in the United States are higher than those for females in Japan at ages under 65 and lower at ages 65 and over. A few Nordic countries have slightly higher life expectancies at age 65 for females than Japan. The U.S. disadvantage in life expectancy at birth for males vis-à-vis Japan is greater than for females but still small. In 1982 Japan's figure for males exceeded the U.S. figure for males by 3.3 years. At age 65 the Japanese advantage for males was only 0.8 year.

If we combine the lowest death rates at each age, for the countries with reliable data, into a single hypothetical life table, the possibility of additional increases in life expectancy in the United States is suggested. I have combined data for years mostly around 1981. The resulting deficits in the life expectancy of the United States compared with the best-country composite are only modest, however. The values for life expectancy for females in the composite table, 81.2 years at birth and 19.7 years at age 65, imply advantages of 3.4 years and 1.1 years over the corresponding U.S. values. Advantages for males are a little larger. The best-country composite figures for males, 75.4 years at birth and 16.0 years at age 65, imply differences of 5.0 years and 1.4 years over the corresponding U.S. values.

As an approach to the measurement of the biological limit of the decline in mortality, Bourgeois-Pichat examined the levels of endogenous mortality in Norway, a country which has very low mortality and, until recently, had the lowest recorded age-specific death rates in many ages.[45] Such calculations provide some indication of the prospects implicit in the present cause-structure of deaths. In Bourgeois-Pichat's

---

[45]J. Bourgeois-Pichat, "Essai sur la mortalité 'biologique' de l'homme," *Population* (Paris) 7 (3) (July–September 1952):381–394; "Future Outlook for Mortality Decline in the World," in *Prospects of Population: Methodology and Assumptions* (Papers of the Ad Hoc

scheme endogenous mortality encompasses all mortality except that due to infectious and parasitic diseases, respiratory diseases, and accidents, poisonings, and violence.[46] "Limits" to life expectancy were calculated for Norway in 1977: namely, 80.7 years for females and 75.0 years for males at birth, and 19.4 years for females and 15.7 years for males at age 65. These are offered as provisional figures which could change with future advances in medicine, socioeconomic developments, or shifts in lifestyle. The "limits" of life expectancy at birth for both females and males agree approximately with the best-country composite (81.2 years and 75.4 years, respectively), as do the "limits" of life expectancy at age 65. At the same time, the gap between life expectancy at birth in the United States and the 1977 limit for Norway is only modest, averaging 3.8 years. At age 65, the difference for both males and females is small, averaging only 1.0 year.

In view of the positive relation between longevity and educational level, expected gains in the educational attainment of the population should contribute to the prospects for increased longevity. Kitagawa has estimated that if all males and females aged 25 and over had the death rates of white males and white females who had completed one year of college or more, life expectancy at age 25 in 1960 would increase by about 3.9 years.[47] Assuming the same differences in longevity between the educational classes in 1980 as in 1960, the rise in the educational attainment of the population since 1960 suggests the current possibility of an increase of 2.1 years in life expectancy at age 25 if class differences were eradicated.

Taken by itself, this brief comparative analysis of mortality data suggests that a major increase in life expectancy in the United States should not be expected in the next few decades. Other indicators suggest a different outlook, however. For example, the elimination of the life-style factor as a cause of death produced a substantial gain, although such a risk-factor model is only theoretical. The experience of the years

---

Group of Experts on Demographic Projections), Population Studies, series A, no. 67 (New York: United Nations, 1979); and "La transition démographique: Vieillissement de la population," in *Population Science in the Service of Mankind,* Conference on Science in the Service of Life, sponsored by the Institute of Life and the International Union for the Scientific Study of Population, Vichy, France, 1979.

[46]Endogenous causes of death are those which, presumably, have an essentially genetic or biological basis and are less amenable to control; they differ from the exogenous causes, which have an essentially environmental or social basis. Calculations of the "limits" of life expectancy based on endogenous mortality are subject to question: It is impossible to make an exact separation between endogenous and exogenous mortality since the classification is partially arbitrary; some exogenous causes of mortality (e.g., accidents) cannot be assumed to decline to extinction; and changes in lifestyle, improvements in the delivery of health care, and medical progress may contribute to a substantial reduction, if not control, of some endogenous causes.

[47]E. Kitagawa, "On Mortality," *Demography* 14 (4) (November 1977):381–389.

since 1968 has demonstrated that death rates at the older ages can be sharply reduced. For the first time, we have seen marked declines in the leading endogenous causes of death. We can now be sanguine about the possibilities of further substantial reductions in old-age mortality. The pace of the reductions may still vary widely. Note that the rate of decline in death rates at the older ages slackened in the second part of the 1968–1984 period (i.e., 1976–1984). This deceleration may continue. The fluctuations in the trend of death rates in the last half century suggest a greater degree of uncertainty in projections of mortality than heretofore assumed.

Official Projections

The set of projections of mortality issued by the Social Security Administration (SSA) in 1985 consists of three series of figures. Series I and III cover a wide range and may serve as an uncertainty interval for Series II. The projections of life expectancy at birth and at age 65 assumed in the three series are shown in Table 4.16. The three projections of life expectancy at birth in 2050 are 85 years (III), 81 years (II), and 78 years (I). In Series III, life expectancy at birth would rise from 71 to 80 years for males and from 78 to 89 years for females between 1983 and 2050. Total life expectancy at age 65 (including the 65 years lived) would rise from 79 to 86 years for males and from 84 to 92 years for females. Series III, the lowest mortality series, implies a nearly 50 percent decline in age-specific death rates between 1983 and 2050.

In the light of the sharp fluctuations in the rate of decline of death rates in the last several decades, the marked drop in death rates at the older ages in the last few decades, and the special purpose of the SSA projections, especially Series III (i.e., to represent the maximum likely life expectancy and to yield the maximum likely proportion of the elderly), such high target values are reasonable. These targets far exceed the biological limits determined on the basis of data for Norway in 1977 or the levels of the best state, the best country, or the best-country composite. Past projections of the SSA have consistently tended to understate the prospects for decline in mortality (Appendix Table 4A.1).

The Census Bureau projections of mortality issued in 1984 correspond to those of the SSA to a large extent. The high and middle series essentially agree with Series I and II; the low series represents a moderation of the trend of Series III and hence a further attenuation of the rapid downward trend of the 1968–1984 period. The values for life expectancy in this series are shown in Table 4.17.

TABLE 4.16

Social Security Administration Projections of Life Expectancy at Birth and at Age 65 for Males and Females: 1983–2050

| Year and Series | Average Years Remaining | | | | Total Years Expected at Age 65 | | Life Endurancies[a] | | | |
| | At Birth | | At Age 65 | | | | .01 | | .001 | |
	Male	Female	Male	Female	Male	Female	Male	Female	Male	Female
1983	71.1	78.3	14.5	18.8	79.5	83.8	98	102	104	108
2000										
I	72.4	79.7	14.9	19.6	79.9	84.6	NA	NA	NA	NA
II	73.9	81.2	15.8	20.7	80.8	85.7	101	105	107	111
III	75.4	82.7	16.7	21.8	81.7	86.8	NA	NA	NA	NA
2030										
I	73.3	80.6	15.5	20.4	80.5	85.4	NA	NA	NA	NA
II	75.5	82.9	16.8	22.0	81.8	87.0	103	108	109	113
III	78.7	86.3	19.1	24.6	84.1	89.6	NA	NA	NA	NA
2050										
I	73.9	81.2	15.9	20.9	80.9	85.9	NA	NA	NA	NA
II	76.4	84.0	17.6	23.0	82.6	88.0	104	109	111	115
III	80.5	88.6	20.8	26.5	85.8	91.5	NA	NA	NA	NA

SOURCES: U.S. Social Security Administration, Office of the Actuary, "Social Security Area Population Projections, 1985," by A. H. Wade, *Actuarial Study*, no. 95 (October 1985), Tables 8a, 8b; "Life Tables for the United States, 1900–2050," by J. F. Faber and A. H. Wade, *Actuarial Study* no. 89 (December 1983), Table 6.

NOTE: NA = not available.

[a] Age to which the indicated proportion of newborn children survives. The data refer to Series II.

TABLE 4.17

Census Bureau Projections of Life Expectancy at Birth and at Age 65 for Males and Females: 1982–2050

| Year and Series | Average Years Remaining | | | | Total Years Expected at Age 65 | |
| | At Birth | | At Age 65 | | | |
	Male	Female	Male	Female	Male	Female
1982	70.6	78.1	14.5	18.8	79.5	83.8
2000						
High mortality	71.7	79.2	15.0	19.6	80.0	84.6
Middle mortality	72.9	80.5	15.7	20.5	80.7	85.5
Low mortality	74.3	82.0	16.4	21.7	81.4	86.7
2030						
High mortality	72.5	80.1	15.5	20.3	80.5	85.3
Middle mortality	74.6	82.5	16.8	22.1	81.8	87.1
Low mortality	77.1	85.7	18.3	24.7	83.3	89.7
2050						
High mortality	72.9	80.5	15.8	20.6	80.8	85.6
Middle mortality	75.5	83.6	17.4	23.1	82.4	88.1
Low mortality	78.6	87.8	19.6	26.6	84.6	91.6

SOURCE: U.S. Bureau of the Census, "Projections of the Population of the United States, by Age, Sex, and Race: 1983 to 2080," by G. Spencer, *Current Population Reports*, series P-25, no. 952 (May 1984), Table B-5.

Conclusion

In general, life expectancy is expected to continue upward, though at a somewhat attenuated pace compared with the experience of the recent past. If the average annual rates of decrease in age-specific death rates for females recorded in the 1968–1976 period continue to prevail in the next 65 years—that is, to the year 2050—life expectancy at birth for females would approximate 100 in that year. This is a highly unlikely possibility. None of the official projections of life expectancy at birth even roughly approximate the 100-year mark, although the SSA high projection series for 2050 implies a 0.1 percent probability of survival to age 115 and a total life expectancy for females at age 65 of 92 years. The steadily increasing share of the actual population over 100 does suggest that measured life span is creeping slowly upward.

We can expect to see an increasing rectangularization of the survival curve. Under less favorable circumstances, there will be a steady, slow decline in age-specific death rates combined with a slowly increasing rectangularization of the survival curve; and under more favorable circumstances, there will be a rapid decline in age-specific death rates and a slight rise in the measured life span, resulting in a rapidly increasing rectangularization of the survival curve. Derectangularization would require increases in death rates or a substantial rise in the measured life span, trends that are possible but less likely to occur. The prospects for reducing death rates at the older ages, reshaping the survival curve, and extending the human life span remain a matter of debate.

We can hypothesize that, with present knowledge or a modest extension of it, a life expectancy at birth of 82 years for females and 76 years for males, and a life expectancy at age 65 of 21 years for females and 17 years for males will be attained in the next quarter century. Reaching the target cited for the life expectancy of males at birth may be quite difficult, however.

As noted earlier, a substantial excess of female over male life expectancy at birth appears in the countries with low mortality. Male-female differences for countries with low mortality vary from 3.6 years (Israel) to 9.9 years (USSR). Differences for states in the United States in 1979–1981 are consistently high, varying little around the national average of 7.5 years (from 6.2 years for Hawaii to 8.2 years for Wyoming).

An examination of trends in the sex differences in life expectancy at birth in several northern European countries reveals that, except for minor fluctuations, the differences had never been higher than at present and that the differences had never diminished after the modern period of increase. This finding suggests that there is no model for the United States to follow in reversing its course. The biological limits to life expectancy for males and females in Norway as of 1977 based on endogenous mortality imply only a slight convergence of male and female mortality (5.7 years) compared with the actual difference for Norway in 1977 (6.5 years). More generally, historical and comparative analysis in itself suggests no great convergence of male and female life expectancy in the United States in the near future.

The male-female difference in life expectancy in the United States has just modestly receded from its all-time maximum. Although it may continue to decline by a moderate amount over the next few decades, a substantial gap will remain. Complete or near-complete convergence of male and female death rates in the foreseeable future is now considered highly unlikely.

Summary

There has been rapid progress since 1968 in reducing death rates, especially among the elderly. These improvements appear to be more a result of lifestyle changes, availability of public and private health insurance programs, and widespread health testing than medical developments. For reasons unknown, there was almost no progress in reducing mortality from 1954 to 1968 following decades of rapid improvement.

Life expectancy at birth increased five years between 1954 and 1985, from about 70 years to 75 years. Life expectancy at age 65 increased from 14.4 years in 1954 to 16.7 years in 1985, and most of that gain occurred since 1968. Nearly four fifths of those born in 1985 are expected to reach age 65 compared with seven tenths of those born in 1954, according to current life tables. Survival from age 65 to age 80 also showed striking gains in the 1954–1985 period, but again most of the gain occurred since 1968. Mortality measures typically show greater progress below age 65 than at ages 65 and over before 1954 or 1968, but in the period since 1954 or 1968, progress has been greater at ages 65 and over or at least more similar to that below age 65.

There remains a gap of about 25 years between current life expectancy at birth and life span, the age that humans can reach under optimum conditions (about 100 years). This difference suggests how much progress is required in modifying lifestyles and personal habits, finding treatments for major diseases, and making the environment more safe.

Death rates of males are well above those of females at every age. The current gap in life expectancy at birth (7.0 years in 1985) is only moderately above that in 1954 but nearly twice that in 1930. Recent more rapid declines in the mortality of males than females has reduced the gender gap from the peak in 1979 (7.8 years). Much of the difference in life expectancy between males and females (about 45 percent) occurs at ages 65 and over.

A large difference in the longevity of the races still remains even though the massive gap of the pre–World War II years has been sharply reduced. In 1985 life expectancy at birth for whites (over 75 years) exceeded that for blacks (nearly 70 years) by nearly 6 years. In 1930 the gap was over 13 years. Life expectancy at age 65 for the races is not now and has not been very different, the white-black gap being 1.5 years currently. In the face of conflicting evidence, the crossover of death rates is believed to be real, even though the data for blacks are affected by serious reporting errors.

In 1985, heart disease accounted for over two fifths of all deaths to persons aged 65 and over and cancer accounted for one fifth. Death rates for heart disease, cerebrovascular disease, and some other leading causes have plunged since 1968, but death rates for cancer, especially lung cancer, have increased.

With advancing age in later life, death rates from cardiovascular diseases rise much more steeply than the cancer death rate. As a result, the median age at death from heart disease is several years higher than that for cancer deaths. For all causes combined, the median age at death has more than doubled to nearly 75 years since 1900.

Death rates at ages 65 and over for men for most of the 10 leading causes of death are well above those for women. Only the death rates for cerebrovascular diseases, atherosclerosis, and diabetes are higher for women, and this is actually the case only at ages 85 and over. At ages 65–74 death rates for most of the 10 leading causes of death are higher for blacks than whites, but the opposite is found at ages 85 and over.

According to cause-elimination life tables for 1979–1981, assuming independence of the causes of death, if diseases of the heart were eliminated, there would be a 5.8-year gain in life expectancy at birth and a 5.1-year gain at age 65. For cancer, the gains would be 3.0 years at birth and 1.8 years at age 65. The gains at birth from eliminating any other major cause of death would be less than one year. If some causes were sharply reduced or eliminated, the combinations of morbid conditions and the interdependence of risks would tend to bring about a rise in other causes. Potential gains in life expectancy from the elimination of these other causes as well as the chances of ever dying from them would then rise.

The difference in life expectancy at birth among the states is relatively small, with a mean variation around the U.S. average of only 1.1 years and a gap of only about 5 years between the highest and the lowest states. The range is from 77 years for Hawaii to 72 years for Louisiana. The West North Central states tend to appear at the top of the list and the South Atlantic states at the bottom.

A notable increase in life expectancy in the United States may occur in the next several decades, as a result of new medical developments, the wider adoption by the public of more healthful lifestyles and personal habits, and environmental improvements. The experience of recent decades has demonstrated that many of the endogenous diseases of later life, long considered intractable, are responsive to control measures, but this experience has also demonstrated that new causes may arise, some old causes may reappear, and others may continue to resist all efforts at control.

Historical and comparative analysis as well as an evaluation of the contribution of genetic and nongenetic factors suggests no great conver-

TABLE 4A.1

Comparison of Actual Values for Average Remaining Lifetime and Average Years in Age Interval with Values Projected by the Social Security Administration: 1982–1983

Age, Sex, and Mortality Assumption	Actual, 1982–1983	Average Years of Life Remaining or in Interval		
		Projected, 1982–1983[b]		
		Actuarial Study, no. 46 (1957)	Actuarial Study, no. 62 (1966)	Actuarial Study, no. 72 (1974)
At birth				
Male				
Low	71.0	72.3	69.4	68.2
High		68.6	68.0	
Female				
Low	78.2	77.9	75.6	75.9
High		75.0	74.4	
Under Age 65				
Male				
Low	60.5	60.8	59.7	59.4
High		59.4	59.1	
Female				
Low	62.4	62.5	61.7	61.7
High		61.6	61.3	
At Age 65				
Male				
Low	14.5	15.2	13.9	13.3
High		13.6	13.4	
Female				
Low	18.7	17.9	16.8	17.5
High		16.5	16.3	

SOURCES: Extracted from or estimated from U.S. National Center for Health Statistics, *Monthly Vital Statistics Report* 33 (9), Supplement (December 1984); and 34 (6), Supplement 2 (September 1985). U.S. Social Security Administration, Office of the Actuary, *Actuarial Study*, no. 46, by T. N. E. Greville (May 1957); *Actuarial Study*, no. 62, by F. Bayo (December 1966); and *Actuarial Study*, no. 72, by F. Bayo and S. F. McKay (July 1974).

[a] Projected value minus actual value.
[b] Base dates of projections of mortality are 1953, 1959–1961, and 1972 for the three sets.

gence of the life expectancy of males and females in the near future. The evidence is that mere approximation of the roles and lifestyles of men and women does not greatly reduce the difference. The difference appears to have a substantial biological component as well as environmental and psychosocial components.

TABLE 4A.1 *(continued)*

		Difference[a]		
Actuarial Study, no. 46 (1957)		Actuarial Study, no. 62 (1966)		Actuarial Study, no. 72 (1974)
{	+1.3 −2.4	−1.6 −3.0	}	−2.7
{	−0.3 −3.2	−2.6 −3.8	}	−2.3
{	+0.3 −1.1	−0.8 −1.4	}	−1.1
{	+0.1 −0.8	−0.7 −1.1	}	−0.7
{	+0.7 −0.9	−0.6 −1.1	}	−1.2
{	−0.8 −2.2	−1.9 −2.4	}	−1.2

Appendix 4A. Evaluations of Past Official Projections of Mortality

The Office of the Actuary, U.S. Social Security Administration (SSA), has been preparing projections of mortality and of population with some regularity since the 1940s in connection with the funding of the Social Security system. The earliest of these sets of projections was published in 1946 and the latest have appeared annually during the 1980s. This appendix presents a general assessment of the SSA projections of mortality in terms of a comparison of the life expectancy values corresponding to several sets of projections with the actual values. The basic method used by the SSA in deriving its mortality projections has been to analyze the past trend of age, sex, and cause-of-death-specific death rates (10 major groups) and then to impute prospective percent decreases to the rates for a specified future period. Future changes in overall age-specific death rates were obtained as weighted averages of the changes in the cause-specific rates. Either one, two, or three series of projections, representing medium, high and low, or medium, high, and low alternatives, were prepared. The evaluation made here is limited to the sets of projections published in 1957, 1966, and 1974. The actual base years of these sets of projections are 1953, 1959–1961, and 1972, respectively. The projections of life expectancy in these three sets, shown or implied for January 1, 1983 (or 1980–1985), are compared with actual values for this date.

The SSA projections of death rates made in 1957 (Actuarial Study no. 46) prove to be rather consistent with actual developments to date. Indeed, the high and low projections of life expectancy generally encompass the actual figures for 1982–1983, as shown in Table 4A.1. There was, however, a tendency to understate life expectancy (i.e., overstate mortality), as suggested by the fact that the projected high mortality figure consistently deviated more from the actual figure than the low mortality figure and that both the high and low projected figures for life expectancy of females at birth and at age 65 fell below the actual 1982–1983 figures.

The SSA projections for life expectancy at birth and at age 65 made in 1966 and 1974 (Actuarial Studies nos. 62 and 72), consistently fell below the actual figures in 1982–1983. In fact, the overstatement of mortality in the low series in Actuarial Study no. 62 nearly equaled the overstatement in the high series of 1957. There was a tendency, also, to overstate female mortality by more than male mortality. Even though the target year was 8 years closer, the projections of life expectancy published in 1974 for males were as far below the target values as the projections of 1966. The understatement in life expectancy at birth was 2.7 years for males and 2.3 years for females.

The sharp slowdown in the rate of mortality improvement experienced during the late 1950s and early 1960s was followed by a marked downward trend in the late 1960s, the 1970s, and the 1980s. SSA appears to have had an essentially conservative view of the prospects for reducing mortality in the 1950s, 1960s, and 1970s. In addition, in formulating assumptions in the 1960s and 1970s, it appears to have relied heavily on current and recent trends in mortality. It did not recognize the sharp changes in the trends that were in progress in the late 1960s and the 1970s and did not anticipate the extent of the declines that were to come in the 1970s and the 1980s. SSA's recent mortality projections, the ones employed in this monograph, are more "radical."

Appendix 4B. Supplementary Note on Changes in Longevity: 1985–1988

This note, which briefly summarizes changes in longevity and survival for the period 1985–1988, supplements the more detailed information already presented for the years up to 1985. In sum, overall changes in longevity were slight, but the leading causes of death at the older ages showed rather marked shifts in opposing directions.

Life expectancy at birth rose a bit between 1985 and 1988, but the increase was confined to the white population. As has occurred a few times earlier in the last few decades, life expectancy at birth receded slightly for the black population, particularly for black males.

Year	All Groups	White Male	White Female	Black Male	Black Female
1988	74.9	72.3	78.9	64.9	73.4
1985	74.7	71.9	78.7	65.3	73.5

As a result, the long-term trend of convergence of black and white life expectancy went into abeyance. The male-female difference in life expectancy at birth for whites narrowed slightly while the corresponding difference for blacks widened slightly.

Life expectancy at age 65 and the probability of survival between age 65 and age 80, as well as the corresponding measures for the ages under 65, moved up a bit or remained unchanged.

| Year | Average Years Lived in Interval | | Probability of Survival | |
	Ages 65 and Over	Birth to Age 65	Age 65 to Age 80	Birth to Age 65
1988	16.9	61.6	.582	.791
1985	16.7	61.6	.571	.787

The male-female difference in life expectancy at age 65 remained at about 4 years while the white-black difference remained at about 1.5 years.

TABLE 4B.1

Death Rates for the 10 Leading Causes of Death for Males and Females Aged 55 and Over, by Age, 1988, and Percent Changes, 1978–1988, 1968–1978, and 1954–1968 (rates per 100,000 population)

Cause of Death and Sex[a]	Ages 55–64				Ages 65–74			
		Percent Change				Percent Change		
	1988	1978–1988	1968–1978	1954–1968	1988	1978–1988	1968–1978	1954–1968
All Causes	1,235.6	−12.8	−17.8	−1.9	2,729.8	−9.9	−21.3	−1.6
Male	1,606.9	−15.7	−19.5	+4.0	3,573.8	−14.6	−19.2	+8.0
Female	904.7	−7.3	−14.3	−8.9	2,056.1	−3.8	−23.2	−10.0
Diseases of the Heart (390–398, 402, 404–429)[b]								
Male	584.7	−26.1	−24.4	+2.6	1,358.1	−22.9	−24.0	+6.9
Female	237.0	−15.2	−25.8	−12.6	685.6	−16.7	−30.5	−9.6
Malignant Neoplasms (140–208)[c]								
Male	526.7	+0.9	+3.7	+15.0	1,072.7	−0.4	+5.1	+18.9
Female	376.6	+1.8	+8.4	−3.4	659.2	−12.0	+2.5	−6.2
Cerebrovascular Diseases (430–438)								
Male	59.5	−30.2	−41.5	−22.4	176.5	−39.2	−41.5	−12.3
Female	44.0	−31.4	−37.5	−36.1	137.3	−34.0	−43.0	−23.8
Pneumonia and Influenza (480–487)[d]								
Male	25.1	−24.2	−43.8	+51.8	82.5	−14.2	−38.5	+64.9
Female	13.3	−15.8	−42.5	+57.6	41.8	−1.6	−41.1	+35.4
Atherosclerosis (440)[e]								
Male	4.9	−24.6	−27.8	−31.0	19.5	−36.9	−40.7	−28.3
Female	2.5	−24.2	−34.0	−35.9	11.5	−40.1	−43.7	−32.5
Diabetes Mellitus (250)								
Male	28.6	+5.1	−28.4	+27.6	61.8	−4.0	−28.9	+26.1
Female	27.5	+3.4	−34.0	−15.1	62.1	−3.7	−39.5	−8.7
Motor Vehicle Accidents (E810–E825)[f]								
Male	21.5	−20.4	−35.7	+8.6	25.6	−16.9	−40.0	−0.6
Female	10.5	−7.9	−32.9	+14.3	14.1	−2.1	−40.2	+19.6

TABLE 4B.1 (*continued*)

	Ages 75–84				Ages 85 and Over		
	Percent Change					Percent Change		
1988	1978–1988	1968–1978	1954–1968	1988	1978–1988	1968–1978	1954–1968
6,231.3	−13.3	−11.0	−3.6	15,394.0	+6.0	−25.0	+7.8
8,223.2	−12.4	−5.0	+4.2	18,370.8	+6.4	−15.3	+16.0
5,173.3	−11.8	−14.1	−8.5	14,508.1	+7.1	−29.3	+3.9
3,239.1	−20.3	−9.7	+5.6	7,830.9	−2.0	−15.5	+21.4
2,122.4	−20.4	−16.4	−5.8	6,810.1	+2.0	−27.5	+9.4
1,861.0	+0.6	+25.8	+10.8	2,527.9	+18.3	+17.7	+14.6
982.6	+2.5	+12.7	−10.6	1,292.8	+13.5	−10.5	−4.1
603.2	−38.7	−28.2	−6.4	1,625.6	−27.6	−33.4	+24.4
523.7	−39.5	−29.2	−11.7	1,738.4	−24.4	−38.9	+13.8
352.4	−5.1	−11.1	+66.7	1,428.2	+30.0	−14.8	+77.7
199.6	+1.6	−23.3	+38.3	1,005.9	+39.2	−34.2	+57.6
81.8	−49.5	−31.5	−33.6	385.2	−58.9	−39.4	−16.4
63.1	−52.6	−33.5	−31.6	400.1	−36.7	−45.2	−21.0
127.3	−7.5	−14.3	+26.6	229.2	+14.9	−15.8	+76.5
123.7	−17.8	−24.5	+18.0	219.3	+0.8	−19.9	+59.2
43.5	−0.1	−31.4	−3.2	60.0	+18.6	−27.2	+4.2
22.1	+11.1	−27.9	+13.7	17.1	+42.5	−44.7	−11.1

TABLE 4B.1 *(continued)*

Cause of Death and Sex[a]	Ages 55–64				Ages 65–74			
		Percent Change				Percent Change		
	1988	1978–1988	1968–1978	1954–1968	1988	1978–1988	1968–1978	1954–1968
All Other Accidents and Adverse Effects (E800–E807, E826–E949)[g]								
Male	29.7	−28.8	−26.5	+0.4	43.1	−23.3	−29.8	−9.5
Female	10.2	−32.5	−18.4	+5.2	21.3	−18.7	−31.8	−26.3
Bronchitis, Emphysema, and Asthma (490–493)[h]								
Male	18.5	−32.2	−60.6	NA	57.3	−33.8	−53.7	NA
Female	13.9	+7.8	−19.4	NA	33.3	+38.2	−8.4	NA
Chronic Liver Disease and Cirrhosis (571)[i]								
Male	45.7	−25.8	−8.2	+57.7	48.7	−23.5	+1.6	+18.6
Female	19.8	−27.7	−2.5	+68.5	24.1	−2.0	+0.8	+13.8

SOURCE: U.S. National Center for Health Statistics, *Vital Statistics of the United States*, annual volumes for 1954, 1968, 1978, and 1988.

NOTE: NA = not available.

[a] Data for 1988 are based on the Ninth Revision, International Classification of Diseases; data for 1978 and 1968 are based on the Eighth Revision, International Classification of Diseases, Injuries, and Causes of Death; data for 1954 are based on the Sixth Revision. Codes following cause of death correspond to the Ninth Revision.
[b] Codes 390–398, 402, 404, 410–429 in 1978.
[c] Codes 140–209 in 1978.
[d] Codes 470–474, 480–486 in 1978.
[e] Arteriosclerosis in 1978.
[f] E810–E823 in 1978.
[g] E800–E807, E825–E949 in 1978.
[h] In 1988 these causes are a subcategory of chronic obstructive pulmonary diseases and allied conditions, identified as a leading cause (codes 490–496 in 1978).
[i] Cirrhosis of liver in 1978.

Death rates at the older ages, except for ages 85 and over, continued to fall. The impressive declines recorded for ages 85 and over before 1976 have been replaced by small increases.

Year	Deaths per 1,000 Population			
	55–64	65–74	75–84	85 and Over
1988	12.4	27.3	63.2	155.9
1985	12.8	28.4	64.5	154.8

TABLE 4B.1 (*continued*)

	Ages 75–84				Ages 85 and Over			
		Percent Change					Percent Change	
1988	1978–1988	1968–1978	1954–1968	1988	1978–1988	1968–1978	1954–1968
100.2	−20.7	−16.6	−23.9	314.5	+2.7	−29.0	−25.5
62.0	−23.9	−36.5	−42.7	208.4	−9.0	−54.4	−41.3
127.9	−28.6	−34.1	NA	175.1	−3.5	−35.2	NA
51.0	+35.6	−8.1	NA	65.8	+37.7	−39.1	NA
43.8	−8.0	+11.0	−6.7	33.8	+13.8	+2.4	−34.8
25.5	+23.2	+8.4	−25.3	14.6	+15.0	−33.2	−39.8

The identity and rank order of the 10 leading causes of death at ages 65 and over remained unchanged, but shifts in the rates for these causes were notable. Death rates for the major cardiovascular diseases, especially atherosclerosis, continued their dramatic declines while death rates for cancer and the other leading causes moved upward.

More detailed data for 1988 on sex, race, and leading causes of death at the older ages are given in Appendix Table 4B.1.

5

HEALTH

THIS CHAPTER is concerned with the health status of the elderly as measured by the extent of acute and chronic conditions and disability and the extent to which health services are utilized. The data presented are drawn principally from the National Health Interview Survey (NHIS), which is conducted by the National Center for Health Statistics (NCHS).[1] This survey covers the civilian noninstitutional population, that is, the total resident population excluding the population in institutions and the military population. About 5 percent of the population aged 65 and over currently resides in institutions and less than 0.1 percent is in the armed forces. Some information on the health status of the older population is also available from the decennial censuses, surveys conducted by the Census Bureau (CPS, SIPP), records of the Social Security Administration and the Health Care Financing Administration, and other surveys conducted by the U.S. Public Health Service.

[1]Data on the health of the U.S. population are presented mainly in U.S. National Center for Health Statistics, *Vital and Health Statistics,* series 10 (various numbers); and *Health, United States* (annual).

Acute Conditions

According to data for 1982, the population aged 65 and over suffered from only about half as many acute conditions per person as the general population. The elderly population experienced 92 acute conditions per 100 persons, while the population as a whole experienced 167 such conditions per 100 persons. (See Table 5.1.) Because the average number of days of restricted activity per acute condition for the population aged 65 and over was more than twice (8.0 days) that for the population under age 65 (3.8 days), the elderly population had a disproportionate number of restricted activity days as a result of acute conditions: 737 days per 100 persons aged 65 and over compared with 644 days per 100 persons of all ages.

The same relationship appears in more pronounced degree with respect to injuries. Although the older population had only three quarters as many injuries per person in 1982 as the younger population, older persons experienced about two thirds more days of restricted activity from injuries per person. This reversal is again explained by the far lower average number of days of restricted activity per episode for the general population (9.1 days) than for those aged 65 and over (18.9 days).

Respiratory conditions accounted for two fifths of all acute conditions (acute illnesses plus injuries) among those aged 65 and over (Table 5.2).[2] Injuries accounted for another one fifth. The incidence rate for respiratory conditions for this age group was much lower than for the total population, however, as was the incidence rate for injuries.

Chronic Conditions

Two thirds of elderly persons describe their own health as good, very good, or excellent compared with that of others at their age (Table 5.1). At the same time, clinical measures and survey data clearly indicate that a very large portion of the elderly in the community suffer from chronic conditions, many from multiple chronic conditions. Some 85 percent of the noninstitutional population aged 65 and over reported a chronic disease in the NHIS of 1975–1976.[3] This figure undoubtedly

---

[2]See also U.S. National Center for Health Statistics, "Acute Conditions: Incidence and Associated Disability, United States, July 1977–June 1978," by P. W. Ries, *Vital and Health Statistics*, series 10, no. 132 (September 1979).

[3]U.S. National Center for Health Statistics and National Center for Health Services Research, "Elderly People: The Population 65 Years and Over," by M. G. Kovar, in *Health, United States, 1976–77*, Part A, Chapter 1 (1978).

TABLE 5.1

Selected Health Indicators for the Population in Broad Age Groups, by Sex and by Race: 1982

	Both Sexes				Male			
		45 and Over				45 and Over		
Health Indicator	All Ages	Total	45–64	65 and Over	All Ages	Total	45–64	65 and Over
Percent Assessing Health as Fair or Poor	11.5	26.3	21.4	34.9	10.5	25.6	20.7	35.4
Number of Acute Conditions per 100 Persons per Year[a]	167	101	107	92	156	80	NA	NA
Days of restricted activity associated with acute conditions per 100 persons per year	644	644	590	737	581	531	NA	NA
Days of bed disability associated with acute conditions per 100 persons per year	296	282	253	332	260	247	NA	NA
Days of work loss associated with acute conditions per 100 currently employed persons[b]	275	261	272	NA	233	219	NA	NA
Number of Episodes of Persons Injured per 100 Persons per Year	26.4	20.3	20.1	20.6	29.6	18.5	NA	NA
Days of restricted activity associated with episodes of persons injured per 100 persons per year	239	354	335	389	243	265	NA	NA
Days of bed disability associated with injuries per 100 persons per year	80	120	105	146	80	88	NA	NA
Days of Restricted Activity per Person per Year Due to Acute and Chronic Conditions	14.3	24.4	20.2	31.6	12.5	21.3	18.4	27.3
Days of bed disability	6.4	10.7	8.4	14.7	5.4	9.6	7.8	13.1
Days of work loss or school loss[b]	4.6	5.6	5.6	5.3	4.1	5.1	5.2	4.7
Percent with Chronic Conditions[c]								
With limitations of activity	14.2	NA	10.5[d]	45.0	14.3	NA	10.9[d]	48.2
With limitations in major activity	10.6	NA	7.3[d]	38.3	10.8	NA	7.6[d]	43.2

SOURCE: U.S. National Center for Health Statistics, *Vital and Health Statistics*, series 10, no. 150 (September 1985); and series 10, no. 130 (November 1979). Based on the National Health Interview Survey.

NOTES: Data are based on household interviews of the civilian noninstitutional population. Conditions involving neither restricted activity nor medical attention are excluded. NA = not available.

[a] Includes both acute illnesses and injuries. [d] Data are for ages under 65.
[b] Restricted to ages 18 and over. [e] Comparable figures are not available.
[c] Data are for 1978. [f] Estimate has relative standard error greater than 30 percent.

TABLE 5.1 (*continued*)

	Female				Black		
		45 and Over				45 and Over	
All Ages	Total	45–64	65 and Over	All Ages	Total	45–64	65 and Over
12.4	26.9	22.0	34.5	21.0	43.9	38.2	55.1
178	119	NA	NA	131	85	NA	NA
703	736	NA	NA	604	754	NA	NA
329	310	NA	NA	316	385	NA	NA
330	320	NA	NA	312	320	NA	NA
23.4	21.8	NA	NA	19.4	15.0	NA	NA
236	439	NA	NA	276	507	NA	NA
81	147	NA	NA	99	143	NA	NA
16.0	26.8	21.8	34.6	16.3	35.4	31.6	42.9
7.3	11.7	9.0	15.8	8.4	17.6	15.4	22.0
5.2	6.2	6.2	6.1	4.8	6.6	7.2	1.3[f]
14.1	NA	10.1[d]	42.7				
10.3	NA	6.9[d]	34.9		([e])		

TABLE 5.2

Annual Average Incidence Rate for Acute Conditions for Persons Aged 55 and Over, by Type of Condition, Sex, Age, and Race: 1982–1984
(number per 100 persons)

Age, Race, and Sex	All Acute Conditions	Respiratory	Digestive	Other Acute Illnesses	Injuries
All Classes[a]					
55–64	104	51	4	30	19
65 and over	97	39	6	31	21
65–74	99	42	6	33	18
75–84	90	33	6	28	22
85 and over	113	33	9	31	40
White Male					
55–64	85	44	2[b]	23	16
65 and over	81	38	5	23	16
65–74	84	41	5	24	14
75 and over	75	32	3[b]	22	19
White Female					
55–64	124	60	4	36	23
65 and over	110	40	8	36	26
65–74	113	46	7	38	22
75 and over	107	33	8	33	32
Black Male					
55–64	83	34	7[b]	29[b]	13[b]
65 and over	78	17[b]	10[b]	44	7[b]
Black Female					
55–64	99	39	5[b]	37	18[b]
65 and over	92	41	2[b]	33	16[b]

SOURCE: U.S. National Center for Health Statistics, *Vital and Health Statistics*, series 3, no. 25 (June 1987), Table 15.

NOTES: Data are based on household interviews of the civilian noninstitutional population obtained in the National Health Interview Survey. Acute conditions comprise acute illnesses and injuries.

[a] Includes races other than white or black.
[b] Numerator of estimate has relative standard error greater than 30 percent.

understates the extent of chronic diseases because some persons have conditions they do not know about or deliberately fail to report.

Common chronic conditions reported by the elderly living in the community are, in rank order, arthritis, hypertension, and heart conditions (Table 5.3). Common impairments reported by the elderly are hearing impairments, orthopedic impairments, cataracts, and other visual impairments.[4] Each of these were reported for 10 percent or more of the elderly population in the NHIS for 1982–1984 (Table 5.4).

The elderly are much more likely than younger people to have a chronic condition *and* to be limited in their activity as a result of that condition. In 1978, 45 percent of persons aged 65 and over were limited in their activity as a result of a chronic condition, while only 10 percent of those under age 65 were so limited (Table 5.1). Most of these—38 percent of the older age group and 7 percent of the younger age group— were limited in their major activity. If the NHIS results are comparable, by 1983–1984 these ratios had fallen sharply. In these years, only 40 percent of the population aged 65 and over were limited in their activity and only 25 percent were limited in their major activity (Table 5.5). The proportion of the noninstitutional population limited in their major activity because of chronic illness did not approach half until ages 85 and over.

As a group, the elderly experience more than twice as many days of restricted activity due to acute and chronic conditions as the general population (in 1982, 32 days vs. 14 days). Those elderly who work, however, do not experience a marked difference in the number of lost work days compared with the younger working population—about five days a year, on the average, for both groups (Table 5.1).

The leading chronic conditions (including impairments) causing limitation of activity among noninstitutional persons aged 65 and over in 1979 were arthritis and rheumatism (46 percent of the noninstitutional population with a chronic condition), heart conditions (24 percent), hypertension without heart involvement (12 percent), impairments of the lower extremities and hips, and impairments of the back or spine.[5] Other conditions causing limitation of activity were hearing impairments, visual impairments, and emphysema.

---

[4]Poor oral health is also a common health problem among the elderly. About half of all persons aged 65 and over are completely edentulous; that is, they lack all their natural teeth. The lack of teeth or poor fit of dentures typically affects the ability to chew, limits the choice of food, and lowers nutritional levels. A substantial reduction in complete edentulousness has occurred in the postwar years, however, as a result of a change in attitudes of dentists and the public toward retention of the natural dentition, increased ability of patients to purchase expensive treatment whether out of pocket or through dental insurance, and fluoridation of the water supply and toothpaste. See B. A. Burt, "The Oral Health of Older Americans," *American Journal of Public Health* 76 (1986):1133–1134.

[5]U.S. National Center for Health Statistics, "Current Estimates from the National Health Interview Survey, United States, 1979," by S. S. Jack, *Vital and Health Statistics,* series 10, no. 136 (April 1981); see also "Limitation of Activity Due to Chronic Conditions, United States, 1974," by C. S. Wilder, *Vital and Health Statistics,* series 10, no. 111, (June 1977).

TABLE 5.3

Annual Average Prevalence Ratio for Selected Chronic Conditions for Persons Aged 55 and Over, by Type of Condition, Sex, Age, and Race: 1982–1984 (number per 1,000 persons)

Sex, Age, and Race	Arthritis	Hypertension	Ischemic Heart Disease	Diabetes	Chronic Bronchitis	Emphysema
All Classes[a]						
55–64	351	307	93	72	51	32
65 and over	486	395	136	90	58	40
65–74	476	394	137	94	63	43
75–84	498	398	135	86	51	41
85 and over	520	393	122	81	43[b]	17[b]
White Male						
55–64	280	286	142	64	42	25
65 and over	392	317	178	80	53	63
65–74	391	335	192	74	52	53
75 and over	395	281	152	91	53	82
White Female						
55–64	413	310	60	63	56	16
65 and over	540	429	119	85	66	20
65–74	527	414	110	90	75	24
75 and over	559	450	132	78	54	15[b]
Black Male						
55–64	283	365	60[b]	153	46[b]	23[b]
65 and over	468	371	61[b]	121	16[b]	41[b]
Black Female						
55–64	471	504	38[b]	149	79	27[b]
65 and over	640	643	77[b]	211	36[b]	12[b]

SOURCE: U.S. National Center for Health Statistics, *Vital and Health Statistics*, vol. 3, no. 25 (June 1987), Table 17.

NOTE: Data are based on household interviews of the civilian noninstitutional population obtained in the National Health Interview Survey.

[a] Includes races other than white or black.

[b] Numerator of estimate has relative standard error greater than 30 percent.

The joint prevalence of chronic conditions among the older population is common. Recent information on the occurrence of multiple conditions in the noninstitutionalized population aged 60 and over is available from the 1984 Supplement on Aging of the NHIS.[6] Nearly four fifths of the population had at least one of the nine most common chronic conditions among the older population[7] and nearly one half had two or more of these conditions:

Number of Conditions	Percent
Total	100
0	21
1	30
2	26
3	15
4	6
5 or More	2

The percentage with two or more conditions rose with increasing age and, for each age group, was higher for women than for men. For example, for those aged 80 and over, 70 percent of the women and 53 percent of the men had two or more of the nine conditions.

Trends in Morbidity

Since the turn of the century, there has been a pronounced shift in the pattern of the causes of morbidity, as with the causes of mortality, from the predominance of infectious and parasitic diseases to the predominance of endogenous, accident-caused, and "self-imposed" conditions. These three categories of causes of morbidity rose markedly relative to others. The first—chronic endogenous diseases—includes diseases of the heart, cancer, cerebrovascular diseases, diabetes, kidney diseases,

[6]U.S. National Center for Health Statistics, "Aging in the Eighties: The Prevalence of Comorbidity and its Association with Disability," by J. M. Guralnik, A. Z. LaCroix, D. F. Everett, and M. G. Kovar, *Vital and Health Statistics*, Advance Data, no. 170 (May 1989). See also D. P. Rice and M. La Plante, "The Burden of Multiple Chronic Conditions," a paper presented at the annual meeting of the American Public Health Association, November 1984; and "Chronic Illness, Disability, and Increasing Longevity," in S. Sullivan and M. E. Lewis, eds., *The Economics and Ethics of Long-Term Care and Disability* (Washington, DC: American Enterprise Institute, 1988).
[7]The conditions and the percentage of the population with these conditions are arthritis (49), hypertension (42), cataracts (20), heart disease (14), varicose veins (10), diabetes (10), cancer (7), osteoporosis or hip fracture (6), and stroke (5).

TABLE 5.4

Annual Average Prevalence Ratio for Selected Impairments for Persons Aged 55 and Over, by Type of Impairment, Sex, Age, and Race: 1982–1984
(number per 1,000 persons)

Race, Sex, and Age	Hearing Impairment	Deformity or Orthopedic Impairment	Cataract	Other Visual Impairments
All Classes				
55–64	181	150	31	56
65 and over	309	168	149	98
65–74	261	165	94	73
75–84	361	162	218	120
85 and over	496	211	327	219
White Male				
55–64	255	151	27	72
65 and over	368	144	105	106
White Female				
55–64	129	145	33	36
65 and over	276	180	186	89
Black Male				
55–64	75[b]	186	21[b]	80[b]
65 and over	262	171	80[b]	148
Black Female				
55–64	152	168	34[b]	98
65 and over	261	208	136	113

SOURCE: U.S. National Center for Health Statistics, *Vital and Health Statistics,* series 3, no. 25 (June 1987), Table 16.

NOTE: Data based on household interviews of the civilian noninstitutional population obtained in the National Health Interview Survey.

[a] Includes races other than white and black.
[b] Numerator of estimate has relative standard error greater than 30 percent.

arthritis and rheumatism, and emphysema. The second—accidents—includes especially motor vehicle accidents, and the third includes conditions either largely caused by or greatly aggravated by stress, such as drug dependency, mental illness, peptic ulcers, attempted suicide, and hypertension. Although morbidity and mortality have both declined sharply since 1900, the improvement in morbidity has been much less than that in mortality.[8]

[8] A. R. Omran, "Epidemiologic Transition in the United States: The Health Factor in Population Change," *Population Bulletin* 32 (2) (May 1977), Population Reference Bureau, Washington, DC.

TABLE 5.5

Annual Average Percent Distribution of the Population Aged 55 and Over by Degree of Activity Limitation Due to Chronic Conditions, According to Age, Sex, and Race: 1983–1984

| Age, Race, and Sex | No Activity Limitation | Limited | | |
		Not in Major Activity	In Amount or Kind of Major Activity	Unable to Carry on Major Activity
All Classes				
55–64	70	7	12	11
65 and over	60	15	14	11
65–74	63	13	13	11
75–84	61	17	14	8
85 and over	40	12	27	20
White Male				
55–64	72	5	9	14
65 and over	61	16	10	13
65–74	62	13	10	15
75–84	63	20	10	7
85 and over	44	18	21	17
White Female				
55–64	72	8	13	7
65 and over	61	14	16	8
65–74	65	14	15	7
75–84	60	16	16	8
85 and over	39	10	30	21
Black Male				
55–64	62	4	8	26
65 and over	54	15	13	18
65–74	54	13	11	22
75 and over	53	19	17	11
Black Female				
55–64	56	10	19	15
65 and over	47	14	24	14
65–74	50	16	22	12
75 and over	44	12	28	17

SOURCE: U.S. National Center for Health Statistics, *Vital and Health Statistics*, series 3, no. 25 (June 1987), Table 14.

NOTE: Data are based on household interviews of the civilian noninstitutional population obtained in the National Health Interview Survey.

The measures suggest that little or no improvement occurred in the health status of the elderly population during the period 1961–1982.[9] The proportion of persons aged 65 and over with limitations of activity rose between 1969–1970 and 1978 (from 42 percent to 45 percent). The proportion with limitations in a major activity, in particular, remained at about the same level in this period (37 percent vs. 38 percent). On the other hand, "restricted activity days per person per year" for the population aged 65 and over fell from 38 in 1965 to 32 in 1982. "Bed-disability days per person per year" was about the same in 1982 as in 1965 (15 vs. 14). An apparent exception may support the generalization that measures of morbidity did not generally decline: The number of "work days lost per employed person" aged 65 and over decreased from 8 days in 1965 to 5 days in 1982, but this decline may be a result of improvements in retirement benefits permitting those in poor health to retire earlier and causing a selective retention of healthier employees.[10] Paradoxically, the apparent stability or retrogression in the health status of the elderly occurred while the population aged 65 and over experienced a sharp reduction in death rates.[11] The marked decline in mortality since the late 1960s contrasts sharply with the halting progress or stalled state of morbidity in this period.

Seven health indicators compiled by Palmore from the NHIS for the period from 1961–1965 to 1976–1981 also present a mixed picture of the progress in the health status of the elderly population in recent decades.[12] Injuries per 100 persons, percentage of persons with visual impairments, and percentage of persons with hearing impairments increased; days of bed disability per person, acute conditions per 100 persons, and percentage of persons with severe visual impairments decreased; and days of restricted activity per person showed little or no change. The pattern of changes is somewhat different if we confine ourselves to the period from 1966–1970 to 1976–1981. There is particular interest in considering the shorter time span, because in the several years prior to 1968 mortality showed little improvement. In this more limited period,

[9]The year 1961 is the earliest year for which morbidity and disability information is available for the elderly from the NHIS.

[10]U.S. Public Health Service, (1978). See footnote 3.

[11]A. Colvez and M. Blanchet, "Disability Trends in the United States Population, 1966–76: Analysis of Reported Causes," *American Journal of Public Health* 71 (5) (May 1981):464–471. J. J. Feldman, "Work Ability of the Aged Under Conditions of Improving Mortality," *Milbank Memorial Fund Quarterly* 61 (3) (Summer 1983):430–444. L. M. Verbrugge, "Longer Life But Worsening Health? Trends in Health and Mortality of Middle-Aged and Older Persons," *Milbank Memorial Fund Quarterly* 62 (3) (Fall 1984):475–519. E. M. Crimmins, "Evidence on the Compression of Morbidity," *Gerontological Perspecta* 1 (1987):45–49.

[12]E. B. Palmore, "Trends in the Health of the Aged," *Gerontologist* 26 (3) (June 1986):298–302.

days of restricted activity per person increased and injuries per 100 persons showed a more marked increase than in the longer period, while days of bed disability per person, acute conditions per 100 persons, and percentage of persons with severe visual impairments showed smaller decreases.

A much more favorable picture of change in the health conditions of the elderly emerges when Palmore considers the change in each measure for this age group in the form of a ratio relating the value for the age group to the value over all ages. In this form, the changes in all seven measures are notably downward for the period from 1961–1965 to 1976–1981. Similarly, the four measures for which change can be computed for 1966–1970 to 1976–1981 in this form show consistent modest decreases over this period. The relative improvement of the health of the elderly may correspond to a lesser improvement or greater deterioration of the health of the general population. Although, according to these data, the health of elderly people has been improving relative to that of the rest of the population, the deteriorating health of the elderly population, as well as of the rest of the population, should be a cause for public concern.

Group Differences

Sex Differences

Various morbidity and disability measures based on self-reports of health conditions obtained in the NHIS in 1982 or 1982–1984 indicate poorer health among elderly women than elderly men. (See Tables 5.1–5.4.) Elderly females have higher annual incidence rates per 100 persons per year for acute conditions (e.g., 110 for white females vs. 81 for white males). Elderly females experience a larger number of days of restricted activity per person per year due to acute and chronic conditions (35) than elderly males (27), associated with a larger number of days of bed disability per person (16 vs. 13) and, for employed persons, a larger number of days of work loss per worker (6.1 vs. 4.7). For some leading chronic conditions (e.g., arthritis, hypertension, chronic bronchitis) and for some leading impairments (e.g., deformity or orthopedic impairment, cataract), the prevalence ratios are higher for elderly females than for elderly males.

The relation of other measures for men and women was similar at ages 45 and over to those listed for ages 65 and over (e.g., number of acute conditions per 100 persons per year and the associated days of restricted activity, days of bed disability, and days of work loss; number of episodes of persons injured per 100 persons per year and the associated days of restricted activity and days of bed disability). (See Table 5.1.)

On the other hand, in 1978 the percentage of females aged 65 and over with chronic conditions involving limitations of activity, especially limitations of major activity, was 8 points lower than that of males (35 percent vs. 43 percent).[13]

As indicated earlier, males have higher death rates than females at all older ages, and for most leading causes of death at these ages. This seeming paradox—that the "unhealthier" female sex is the one less likely to die—has several possible underlying explanations. First, diseases for which males show an excess are chronic diseases that predominate as causes of death (e.g., heart disease and emphysema), while those for which females show an excess predominate as causes of nonlethal illness (e.g., arthritis, osteoporosis). The greatest female excess occurs for acute conditions, which are the most common causes of illness but are rarely causes of death. Second, the demographic characteristics of the older population may also contribute to the apparent excess of female morbidity. Since elderly women are more likely to be living alone and therefore not to be sharing their household with another member who would care for them in case of illness, they are more likely to have to resort to professional help when a need arises. Moreover, women are more concentrated at the very oldest ages than men. Here the relative frequency of illness is greater than at the younger ages, where men are concentrated.[14]

In addition, a large part of the sex reversal in morbidity and mortality may be due to the interview situation and patterns of behavior during illness. Proxy respondents tend to underreport the morbidity of others; a majority of proxy interviews are given by females reporting on the health status of males who are absent. This practice would result in an understatement of male morbidity in the health reports. Females are also more likely to seek health care when ill. Being ill is more socially acceptable among women and they generally have fewer constraints on scheduling their time. As a result of their experience with pregnancy, childbirth, and menstrual problems, they are more accustomed to medical checkups and have less psychological resistance to admitting illness

---

[13]See also M. G. Kovar, "Health of the Elderly and Use of Health Services," *Public Health Reports* 42 (1) (January–February 1977):9–19.

[14]This factor is not generally relevant for age-specific rates of self-reported illness.

and to seeking help when ill. However, in spite of the evidence given for a sex reversal in morbidity and mortality, the reversal does not appear in clinical data in the limited instances when NHIS data and clinical data can be compared.[15]

The excess female morbidity may reflect acquired risks, representing the net result of differences in lifestyle, health habits, exposure to psychological stress, and the risk of injury at work and play. The sexes differ in their degree of satisfaction with their major roles and activities (i.e., home management, participation in work force), the level of stress they experience, and the degree of exposure to hazards on the job and at home. The sexes differ also in their health histories in earlier life. Finally, physiological and genetic influences may play a part.

From her studies, Verbrugge concludes that women's more frequent health care is largely due to their greater morbidity, and not merely to their greater proclivity to recognize and report their illnesses.[16] However, if men and women were exposed to similar social risks, the female excesses in morbidity would narrow and male excesses would emerge. She further concludes that biological factors are at work in men's poorer long-run health and higher mortality.

While disability prevalence ratios are generally higher for elderly females than for elderly males, they can be misleading indicators of the risks of certain health events occurring to individuals. Manton examined the risks of moving into and out of various functionally impaired states with longitudinal data from the 1982 and 1984 Long-Term Care Surveys.[17] These data show that over this two-year period the risks of becoming disabled were roughly the same for males and females and were in fact lower up to age 85 for females. The greater prevalence of impairments among females resulted from the longer life expectancy of females and the longer time spent by females in their impaired states.

Differences between the sexes in the incidence, prevalence, and duration of disability have major implications for the level and types of long-term-care services required by older persons of each sex.

[15]L. M. Verbrugge, "Sex Differentials in Morbidity and Mortality in the United States," *Social Biology* 23 (4) (Winter 1976):275–296; and "Women and Men: Mortality and Health of Older People," in M. W. Riley, B. B. Hess, and K. Bond, eds., *Aging in Society: Selected Reviews of Recent Research* (Hillsdale, NJ: Lawrence Erlbaum, 1983).

[16]L. M. Verbrugge, "Sex Differences in Health Behavior, Morbidity, and Mortality," paper presented at the NIH Conference on Gender and Longevity, Bethesda, MD, September 17–18, 1987.

[17]K. G. Manton, "A Longitudinal Study of Functional Change and Mortality in the United States," *Journal of Gerontology* 43 (5) (1988):S153–161.

Race Differences

The very limited data on the health of the older black population suggest that, overall, the health situation of elderly blacks is poorer than that of elderly whites. Some indicators are indirect or subjective. Data from the 1980 National Medical Care Utilization and Expenditure Survey show that a higher proportion of the black elderly than of the white elderly have no regular source of care (14 and 9 percent, respectively). Community clinics are a more likely source of care for the black elderly (16 percent) than for the white elderly (9 percent).[18]

According to data from the 1982 NHIS, 55 percent of elderly blacks assessed their health as fair or poor, while only 35 percent of the general elderly population gave this unfavorable assessment. Blacks aged 65 and over had over one third more days of restricted activity per person per year due to acute and chronic conditions (43 days) than the general elderly population (32 days). (See Table 5.1.) The proportions of blacks aged 65 and over with arthritis, hypertension, and diabetes in 1982–1984 far exceeded the proportions of whites (Table 5.3). Much higher proportions of elderly blacks than whites were limited in a major activity or unable to carry on a major activity due to a chronic condition in this period (Table 5.5). On the other hand, elderly blacks showed a lower incidence rate of acute conditions than elderly whites (Table 5.2).

Much more data on the health situation of blacks can be compiled for ages 45 and over and ages 45–64. Five measures of the health conditions of blacks and whites at ages 45–64 for 1969 and 1981 have been examined by Gibson for evidence suggesting differences in the level and trend of the health conditions of the two races at the older ages (Table 5.6).[19] These data show not only that blacks have a greater degree of disability and illness in midlife than whites, but that the gap between the races has been widening. Of the five measure in 1981, three were substantially higher for blacks than whites and two were about the same. The difference was especially great for the number of bed disability days per person—nearly twice as great—and for the number of restricted activity days per person—nearly 160 percent as great. Although all five health indicators worsened or did not improve for whites between 1969 and 1981, compared with four indicators for blacks, the retrogression tended to be larger for blacks. Whether or not the health of whites and blacks worsened in the last few decades, and whether or not the health

---

[18]U.S. Health Care Financing Administration, "Access to Health Care Among Aged Medicare Beneficiaries," series B, Descriptive Report no. 3, HHS Publication no. 84-20203 (1984).

[19]These data were derived from unpublished NCHS data by Rose C. Gibson of the Institute for Survey Research, University of Michigan.

TABLE 5.6

Selected Measures of Disability for Blacks and Whites Aged 45–64: 1969 and 1981

Measure and Race	1969	1981	1969–1981 Changes
Percent Unable to Carry on Major Activity			
Blacks	8.0	6.0	−2.0
Whites	4.0	6.0	+2.0
Percent Limited in Amount or Kind of Major Activity			
Blacks	12.9	16.7	+3.8
Whites	11.4	11.9	+0.5
Percent Not Limited in Major Activity but Otherwise Limited			
Blacks	3.1	4.2	+1.1
Whites	3.2	4.8	+1.6
Number of Restricted Activity Days per Person			
Blacks	27.4	41.1	+13.7
Whites	19.3	26.0	+6.7
Number of Bed Disability Days per Person			
Blacks	11.8	15.3	+3.5
Whites	7.1	8.3	+1.2

SOURCE: Derived by R. C. Gibson from U.S. National Center for Health Statistics unpublished data and published in R. C. Gibson, *Blacks in an Aging Society*, report of a conference sponsored by the Aging Society Project, Carnegie Corporation of New York (July 1986). Reprinted by permission, Carnegie Corporation of New York.

of blacks lost ground to whites in this period, blacks remain greatly disadvantaged compared with whites, as shown by a broad range of health measures.

The differences in the health status of whites and blacks are generally related to the poorer economic status of blacks.[20] More specifically, the differences stem, first, from such physical risk factors and lifestyle behaviors as heavy smoking, excessive use of alcohol, deficiencies in diet and nutrition, hypertension, and obesity. Other factors are less health knowledge, failure of public health education programs to reach blacks, and black attitudes toward prevention, treatment, and help-seeking behavior. Next are economic barriers to access to health care and greater

[20]K. G. Manton, C. H. Patrick, and K. W. Johnson, "Health Differentials Between Blacks and Whites: Recent Trends in Mortality and Morbidity," *Milbank Memorial Fund Quarterly* 65 (supplement 1) (1987):129–199.

lack of private health insurance. Blacks are more likely to turn to public sources of health care (e.g., clinics, Medicaid) and are, therefore, more likely to receive poorer health services. Even if Medicare is available, the health problems of many blacks started at a younger age. In addition, blacks are often engaged in more hazardous occupations. Genetic factors may also play a part, perhaps, in producing a greater risk of hypertension and obesity in later life. The factors enumerated combine and interact in unknown degree.

Data on "work disability" of whites and blacks aged 55 and over are available from the 1970 census, the March 1982 Current Population Survey (CPS), and the 1984–1985 Survey of Income and Program Participation (SIPP). Data on "public transportation disability" are available from the 1980 census for persons aged 65 and over of various races. This material is discussed later in the chapter.

Geographic Variations

The elderly living in nonmetropolitan areas are more likely to have a chronic health condition that limits their activities than the elderly living in metropolitan areas. According to the NHIS for 1982, 44 percent of the nonmetropolitan population aged 65 and over reported an activity limitation due to a chronic health condition compared with 39 percent of the metropolitan population. The nonmetropolitan elderly are also more likely to need hospitalization than the metropolitan elderly. In 1982 the former had an average of 34 hospital stays per 100 persons while the latter had 28 stays. On the other hand, the nonmetropolitan population experienced about the same number of days of restricted activity per person per year as the metropolitan population, had about the same incidence of acute conditions, and had about the same length of hospital stay.

The nonmetropolitan-metropolitan difference in the prevalence of chronic conditions with activity limitation was about the same in 1973–1974 as in 1982, but the prevalence figures were higher than in 1982. In those years the figures on days of restricted activity favored the metropolitan elderly and were also higher than in 1982. This suggests that both the absolute and the relative health situation of the nonmetropolitan population was improving in some respects in this period.

Because of the greater prevalence of chronic conditions among nonmetropolitan elderly, they require more medical assistance than the metropolitan elderly. Yet many rural counties with rapidly growing elderly populations are poor and lack sufficient services for the elderly. The greater frequency of hospitalization and need for in-patient care in nonmetropolitan areas may result in part from the lack of out-patient facilities and the limited availability of physicians. A serious issue relating to the distribution of health care resources is evident.[21]

Disability

Public Transportation Disability

The 1980 census included a question concerning health conditions that limit or prevent a person from using public transportation. Although there are serious concerns about the accuracy of the data obtained for the elderly,[22] some of the principal results are presented. As expected, the proportion of persons with a public transportation disability is much higher for the elderly (15 percent) than for the population aged 16–64 (1.8 percent). Some 3.6 million noninstitutional persons aged 65 and over reported a transportation disability.

State variations in the extent of public transportation disability, depicted in Figure 5.1, suggest differences from state to state in the need to provide special services for the disabled. States in the South have the heaviest burden, and states in the West North Central Division and the northern part of the Mountain Division have the least burden.

Public transportation disability showed little variation according to residence category (urban-rural, city size), except for the comparatively small proportion disabled in the rural-farm population. This exception is fortunate, since management of the problem of public transportation disability is especially difficult in the open country.

Substantial variation appears among the elderly of various races and the Hispanic population:

Race/Spanish Origin	Percentage of Group Disabled	Percentage of Total Disabled
Total	14.9	100.0
White	14.1	85.5
Black	22.2	12.4
American Indian	21.0	0.4
Asian and Pacific Islander	12.5	0.4
Spanish Origin	17.6	3.2

[21]See U.S. Department of Agriculture, "Rural Elderly in Demographic Perspective," by N. Glasgow and C. Beale, *Rural Development Perspectives* 2 (October 1985):22–26.

[22]These concerns are based on field experience at the time of the census and an examination of the completed 1980 census questionnaires. Pretests of the question on disability had shown that the responses were subject to a high degree of inconsistency and that a large proportion of the cases were not reported and had to be assigned.

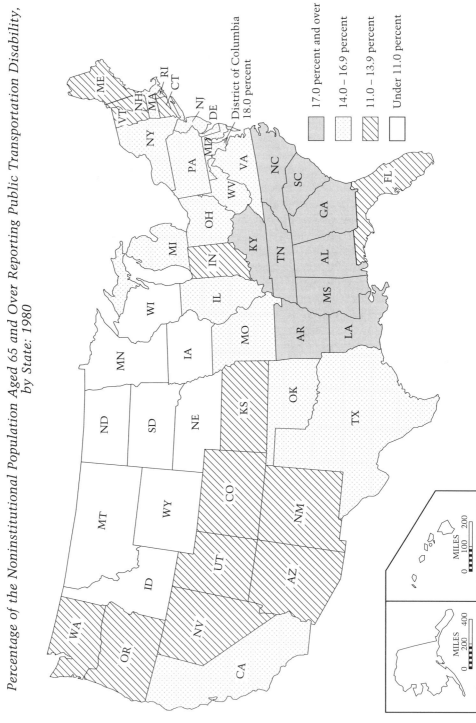

FIGURE 5.1

Percentage of the Noninstitutional Population Aged 65 and Over Reporting Public Transportation Disability, by State: 1980

17.0 percent and over

14.0 – 16.9 percent

11.0 – 13.9 percent

Under 11.0 percent

District of Columbia
18.0 percent

SOURCE: U.S. Bureau of the Census, 1980 Census of Population, *General Social and Economic Characteristics*, PC 80-1-C, Table 70, state reports.

Blacks, American Indians, and Hispanics have relatively high levels of transportation disability. None of the groups except blacks and whites, however, have sizable numbers of older disabled members, mainly because few members of these groups are elderly.

Work Disability

The 1984–1985 SIPP, the March 1982 CPS, the 1980 census, and the 1970 census included a question on health conditions which limit the kind or amount of work a person can do at a job or prevent the person from working at a job. Cross-sectional data on work disability show that the older a person is, the more likely he or she is to have a work disability. Data from the March 1982 CPS reveal, for example, that the prevalence of work disability increased steadily from 3 percent among youths aged 16–24 to around 30 percent among persons aged 65–74. The percentages for men and women aged 45–74 are:

Age	Men	Women
45–54	12.8	11.7
55–64	26.2	22.3
65–74	31.4	28.4

Work disability appears to increase at an accelerated pace before and around the normal ages of retirement and then to level off. In 1982 the share of the population reporting a work disability climbed from 24 percent at ages 55–64 to 29 percent at ages 65–69 and then rose merely to 30 percent at ages 70–74 (Table 5.7). The generalization is also loosely supported by the figures for 1970, when the proportion with a work disability jumped from 20 percent at ages 55–59 to 24 percent at ages 60–61 and 27 percent at ages 62–64.

Do the changes in the prevalence of work disability indicate improvement or retrogression in the health of the population in the last few decades? The census and survey data, as shown in Table 5.7, suggest some retrogression, or at least no improvement. Work disability was about the same at ages 55–64 in 1970 and 1982 and was apparently much higher in 1984–1985 than in 1982 at ages 65–72. Serious problems of comparability from survey to survey affect interpretation of trends, however. Feldman interprets the NHIS data on work disability as providing evidence of an increase in the prevalence of work disability among men.[23] Data from the NHIS of 1970, 1975, and 1980 show steady increases in work disability ratios for men in the older age categories.

[23]Feldman (1983).

TABLE 5.7

Percentage of the Older Population Reporting a Work Disability,
by Sex: 1970, 1982 and, 1984–1985

Year and Age	Both Sexes	Male	Female
1984–1985			
18–64	12.1	11.7	12.4
65–72	37.8	40.8	38.0
1982			
16–64	8.9	9.3	8.5
55–64	24.1	26.2	22.3
65–74	29.7	31.4	28.4
65–69	29.1	32.0	26.8
70–74	30.1	30.5	30.3
1970			
18–64	10.8	11.7	9.9
55–64	22.8	24.2	21.5
55–59	20.0	20.9	19.1
60–64	26.0	28.1	24.2
60–61	24.3	25.7	23.0
62–64	27.3	29.9	25.0

SOURCES: U.S. Bureau of the Census, *Current Population Reports*, series P-70, no. 8 (December 1986), Table D; series P-23, no. 127 (July 1983), Tables A and I; and 1970 Census of Population, *Subject Reports*, PC(2)-6C (January 1973).

NOTES: Omitted 5-year and 10-year detail for ages 55–64 and 65–74 is not available. Because of changes in question wording and survey design, it is risky to draw inferences regarding trends in disability from these data.

Feldman also cites evidence of a lower level of work disability among men aged 55–64 in 1949 than during the 1970s, and an even lower level in 1935. Ycas, on the other hand, concluded that the prevalence of work disability has merely fluctuated.[24]

The proportion of older persons with a work disability is much greater for those not in the labor force than for those in the labor force, especially for males (Table 5.8). This finding is not surprising, since at these ages withdrawal from the labor force is often the consequence of a work disability. In addition, a higher percentage of males than females, both in and out of the labor force, report a work disability. A striking 64 percent of males aged 55–64 not in the labor force in 1982 had a work disability. Furthermore, a higher percentage of blacks than whites report

[24]M. A. Ycas, "Recent Trends in Health Near the Age of Retirement: New Findings from the Health Interview Survey," *Social Security Bulletin* 50 (2) (February 1978):9–12.

TABLE 5.8

Percentage of the Older Population Reporting a Work Disability, by Race, Sex, and Work Status: 1970, 1982, and 1984–1985

Age and Work Status	White		Black	
	Male	Female	Male	Female
1984–1985				
16–64	11.5	11.9	15.0	16.4
With a job	7.1[a]	6.4[a]	NA	NA
Other than with a job	31.4[a]	21.3[a]	NA	NA
65–72	39.6	35.8	57.8	58.0
With a job	25.2[a]	17.2[a]	NA	NA
Other than with a job	45.3[a]	40.9[a]	NA	NA
1982				
16–64	9.3[a]	8.5[a]	NA	NA
In labor force	4.6[a]	3.3[a]	NA	NA
Not in labor force	35.2[a]	16.5[a]	NA	NA
55–64	26.2[a]	22.3[a]	NA	NA
In labor force	10.3[a]	6.6[a]	NA	NA
Not in labor force	64.4[a]	33.6[a]	NA	NA
65–74	30.8	26.9	39.1	43.8
Employed	11.6	12.5	17.6	15.0
Other than employed	36.4	28.6	42.9	75.3
1970				
18–64	11.5	9.3	14.2	14.7
In labor force	8.6	5.5	8.8	7.8
Not in labor force	36.0	12.9	41.1	23.4
55–64	23.7	20.4	30.4	32.6
In labor force	15.1	9.3	15.8	14.6
Not in labor force	63.7	28.3	71.5	48.1
55–59	20.4	18.1	27.0	29.3
In labor force	14.0	9.1	14.7	13.4
Not in labor force	69.9	26.3	73.7	46.1
60–64	27.6	23.0	34.6	36.6
In labor force	16.6	10.6	17.3	16.4
Not in labor force	60.4	30.1	69.8	49.9

SOURCES: U.S. Bureau of the Census, 1970 Census of Population, *Subject Reports*, "Persons with Work Disability," PC(2)-6C (January 1973), Table 4; *Current Population Reports*, series P-23, no. 127 (July 1983), Tables 2 and 7; series P-70, no. 8, (December 1986), Tables D and 3.

NOTE: NA = not available.

[a] All races.

a work disability for each sex/work status category. This is consistent with other findings suggesting poorer health and the adoption of the disability role among older blacks.[25]

ADL Limitations

An indication of the more severe effects of chronic conditions is given by measures of limitation of mobility. In 1984, 30 percent of those aged 65 and over were limited in their mobility (i.e., had difficulty walking one quarter of a mile) as a result of a chronic condition (Table 5.9). About 19 percent of the elderly had difficulty walking, and 10 percent were confined to the house.

There were steep gradations in the share of the population having mobility difficulties with increasing age for every level of difficulty. For example, well over one half of those aged 85 and over had difficulty walking one quarter of a mile compared with nearly one quarter of those aged 65–74. Similarly, the percentage of older aged persons having difficulty walking at all was three times the percentage for the young elderly. In addition, the share of women at every level of mobility difficulty was substantially above that for men for every age over 64. For example, at ages 75–84 the percentage of women with a mobility difficulty was 5–10 points above that for men, depending on the level of difficulty.

Pronounced changes in the ability to carry out daily activities also occur over the older age range. In 1982 only 4.5 percent of the noninstitutional population aged 65–74 said they needed help with one or more home management activities, so-called instrumental activities of daily living (IADL) such as shopping, doing routine household chores, preparing meals, or handling money, whereas 10 percent of persons aged 85 and over reported needing such help (Table 5.10). In addition, 4 percent and 18 percent of these two age groups, respectively, reported needing help with at least one self-care activity of daily living (ADL) such as eating, dressing, bathing, and toileting (Table 5.10).[26] Again, there is a rather consistent pattern of larger shares of women having IADL and ADL limitations than men—taking age and degree of limitation into

[25]R. C. Gibson, "Reconceptualizing Retirement for Black Americans," *Gerontologist* 27 (6) (December 1987):691–698.
[26]See also U.S. National Center for Health Statistics, "Americans Needing Help to Function at Home," by B. Feller, *Vital and Health Statistics*, Advance Data, series 10, no. 92 (September 1983), Tables 1, 2, and 3.

TABLE 5.9

*Percentage of the Noninstitutional Population Aged 65 and Over with Difficulties
of Mobility, by Type of Difficulty, Sex, and Age: 1984*

Sex and Age	Difficulty Walking Quarter Mile	Difficulty Walking Up 10 Steps	Difficulty Walking	Difficulty Getting Outside	Difficulty Getting Into or Out of Bed or Chair
Male					
65 and over	25.4	19.1	15.5	6.3	5.6
65–74	21.9	16.2	12.9	4.5	4.8
75–84	29.1	22.4	18.3	7.5	5.9
85 and over	48.3	36.5	32.2	21.8	12.7
Female					
65 and over	32.5	28.5	20.9	11.8	9.7
65–74	24.5	22.6	15.1	6.5	7.0
75–84	39.4	33.3	25.7	15.3	11.2
85 and over	61.5	51.2	43.3	35.4	22.2

SOURCE: U.S. National Center for Health Statistics, "Health Statistics on Older Persons, United States, 1986," *Vital and Health Statistics*, series 3, no. 25 (June 1987).

NOTES: Data based on the National Health Interview Survey, 1984 Supplement on Aging. Percent for "does not do or unknown" was not prorated and was assumed not to have the difficulties cited.

account. Figures 5.2 and 5.3 are graphic representations of the extent of specific IADL and ADL limitations, respectively, by age, for 1984.

According to the data from the 1984 Supplement on Aging to the NHIS, the proportion of the older population who have difficulties with ADL or who receive help with one or more activities of daily living increases directly with the number of chronic conditions, from none of the chronic conditions identified earlier to five or more of them (Table 5.11).[27] Moreover, within each age group there is a systematic increase in the proportion with ADL disability as the number of conditions increases, and for a particular number of conditions there is a gradual increase in the proportion with ADL disability as age increases. The percentages for women consistently exceed those for men. Hence, the number of conditions appears to be a useful indicator of the likelihood of severe disability in older men and women.

Conservative projections of the elderly population living in the community with ADL limitations, prepared by Manton and Liu on the

[27]U.S. National Center for Health Statistics (May 1989).

TABLE 5.10

Percentage of the Noninstitutional Population Aged 65 and Over with ADL Limitations, by Sex and Age: 1982

			ADL[a] Score		
Age and Sex	Total	IADL[b] Only	Mildly Disabled[c]	Disabled[d]	Severely Disabled[e]
65 and Over					
Both sexes	18.9	6.0	6.6	2.8	3.5
Male	16.0	5.4	5.1	2.3	3.3
Female	20.9	6.4	7.7	3.2	3.6
65–74					
Both sexes	12.6	4.5	4.2	1.8	2.1
Male	11.7	4.2	3.4	1.7	2.4
Female	13.3	4.8	4.7	1.9	1.9
75–84					
Both sexes	25.0	7.9	9.0	3.6	4.5
Male	20.9	7.1	6.5	2.5	4.6
Female	27.6	8.5	10.3	4.3	4.4
85 and Over					
Both sexes	45.8	10.2	17.4	7.8	10.4
Male	40.8	9.9	15.7	7.7	7.5
Female	48.2	10.3	18.2	7.9	11.8

SOURCE: Preliminary data from the 1982 National Long-Term Care Survey. Cited in K. Manton and K. Liu, "The Future Growth of the Long-Term Care Population: Projections Based on the 1977 National Nursing Home Survey and the 1982 Long-Term Care Survey," presented at the Third National Leadership Conference on Long-Term Care Issues, Washington, DC, March 7–9, 1984; and in U.S. Senate, Special Committee on Aging, *America in Transition: An Aging Society* (June 1985), p. 65.

[a] Activities of daily living: eating, dressing, bathing, toileting.
[b] Instrumental activities of daily living: preparing meals, shopping, managing money, using the telephone, and doing housework.
[c] Limited, but not in a self-care ADL activity.
[d] Limited in amount or kind of ADL activity.
[e] Unable to carry on ADL activities.

basis of data from the 1982 Long-Term Care Survey, indicate a near doubling of this population between 1985 and 2020, from 5.2 million to 10.1 million (Table 5.12). As a percentage of the population, its growth is expected to be small, from 18.2 to 19.2 percent. The severely disabled population is expected to grow at nearly the same rate as the total population with ADL limitations between 1985 and 2020—from 1.0 million to 1.9 million. The projected increases in the total number of persons with ADL limitations and the number severely disabled reflect mainly

FIGURE 5.2

Percentage of the Noninstitutional Population Aged 65 and Over Who Have Difficulty with Instrumental Activities of Daily Living, by Type of Activity and Age: 1984

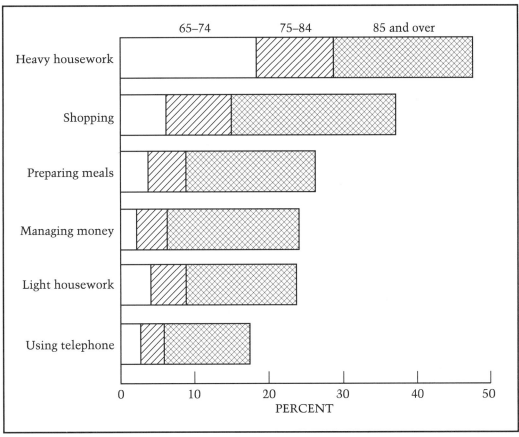

SOURCE: U.S. National Center for Health Statistics; data from the National Health Interview Survey, 1984 Supplement on Aging.

the projected changes in the total population aged 65 and over and its age structure between now and 2020.

The Duration of Active Life

The sharp advance in the reduction of mortality at the older ages in the last two decades has raised questions regarding the meaning of this

FIGURE 5.3

Percentage of the Noninstitutional Population Aged 65 and Over Who Have
Difficulty with Personal-Care Activities of Daily Living, by Type of Activity
and Age: 1984

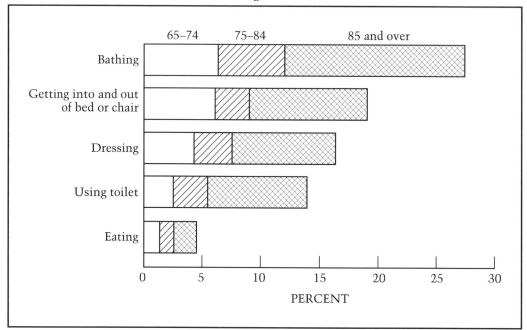

SOURCE: U.S. National Center for Health Statistics; data from the National Health Interview Survey, 1984 Supplement on Aging.

NOTE: Rank order follows percent for ages 65 and over.

rollback of the age at death for the duration of chronic illness and dependency in the later years.[28] Some fear that it has extended the period
of poor health and incapacitation.[29] Others believe that life expectancy
at birth will soon level off and that the period in later life beset by
chronic illness will be reduced or eliminated.[30] A third view sees mortality and morbidity changing in parallel fashion.[31]

[28]K. G. Manton, "Changing Concepts of Mortality and Morbidity in the Elderly Population," *Milbank Memorial Fund Quarterly* 60 (2) (Spring 1982):183–244; L. Verbrugge
(1984).
[29]E. M. Gruenberg, "The Failure of Success," *Milbank Memorial Fund Quarterly* 55
(1) (1977):3–24.
[30]J. F. Fries, "Aging, Natural Health, and the Compression of Morbidity," *New England Journal of Medicine* 303 (3) (1980):130–135; "The Compression of Morbidity," *Milbank Memorial Fund Quarterly* 61 (3) (1983):397–419.
[31]E. L. Schneider and J. A. Brody, "Aging, Natural Death, and the Compression of
Morbidity: Another View," *New England Journal of Medicine* 309 (14) (1983):854–856;
Manton (1982).

TABLE 5.11

Percentage of the Population Aged 60–69 and 80 and Over with a Specified Number of Chronic Conditions That Is Receiving Help or Having Difficulty with One Activity or More of Daily Living, by Sex and Age: 1984

	Number of Conditions					
Sex and Age	0	1	2	3	4	5 or More
Percentage of Population Receiving Help						
Male						
60–69	1	3	6	11	19	23
80 and over	3	16	20	17	31	50
Female						
60–69	1	4	4	10	12	21
80 and over	6	14	17	22	38	58
Percentage of Population Having Difficulty						
Male						
60–69	4	9	17	30	50	45
80 and over	13	29	37	33	52	57
Female						
60–69	3	10	17	27	34	61
80 and over	14	24	39	52	67	79

SOURCE: U.S. National Center For Health Statistics, *Vital and Health Statistics,* Advance Data, no. 170 (May 1989), Table 2.

Not enough data are available to permit a full debate on the subject, let alone a resolution of the question, but appropriate morbidity rates and life table measures are being developed. Just as measures from a conventional life table have been used to chart progress in the control of mortality, so tables of active or independent life are being designed to chart progress in the control of morbidity. A series of such tables could tell us whether the mean duration of healthy (i.e., active, independent) life was increasing or not and whether the share of total remaining life to be lived in good health was rising, staying the same, or falling (representing the three theoretical positions outlined above).

Using data from the 1986 Longitudinal Study of Aging (LSOA), Rogers and associates prepared tables of active or independent life for the population of the United States following the multistate life table model.[32]

[32] A. Rogers, R. G. Rogers, and A. Belanger, "Active Life Among the Elderly in the United States: Multistate Life Table Estimates and Population Projections," *Milbank Memorial Fund Quarterly* 67 (3-4) (1989):370–411.

TABLE 5.12

Estimates and Projections of the Noninstitutional Population Aged 65 and Over with ADL Limitations: 1980–2040

Year	Number (in thousands)		Percentage of Population[a]		Percent Increase Over 1985	
	Total	Severely Disabled	Total	Severely Disabled	Total	Severely Disabled
1980	4,627	848	18.0	3.3	X	X
1985	5,234	987	18.2	3.4	—	—
1990	6,029	1,123	18.8	3.5	15.2	13.8
1995	6,712	1,265	19.3	3.6	28.2	28.2
2000	7,262	1,384	20.0	3.8	38.7	38.7
2020	10,118	1,927	19.2	3.7	93.3	95.2
2040	14,416	2,806	21.4	4.2	175.4	184.3

SOURCE: Calculated on the basis of projections of the U.S. population prepared by the U.S. Social Security Administration and preliminary data from the 1982 National Long-Term Care Survey. See K. Manton and K. Liu, "The Future Growth of the Long-Term Care Population: Projections Based on the 1977 National Nursing Home Survey and the 1982 Long-Term Care Survey," presented at the Third National Leadership Conference on Long-Term Care Issues, Washington, DC, March 7–9, 1984.

NOTES: X = not applicable. Dash denotes zero.

[a] Base includes the institutional population. Hence, the percentages shown here differ from those shown for the same categories in Table 5.10.

Active or independent life is defined narrowly in terms of ADL limitations (i.e., not dependent on others for carrying out the activities of daily life). The tables distinguish years of dependent life and years of independent life for the dependent population and the independent population at age 70. Illustrative results are as follows:

Life Expectancy	Population Independent at Age 70	Population Dependent at Age 70
Age 70		
Total Years	13.4	12.5
Independent	10.1	6.4
Dependent	3.4	6.1
Percent dependent	25	49
Age 84		
Total Years	6.6	5.9
Independent	3.9	1.4
Dependent	2.7	4.5
Percent dependent	41	76

NOTE: The official NCHS figures for 1986 for ages 70 and 84 are 13.6 years and 6.4 years, respectively.

We note that the initially independent population has a higher total life expectancy at age 70, and is expected to spend a much smaller share of its remaining life in a dependent state, than the initially dependent population. For those independent at age 70, one quarter of their remaining life is expected to be dependent, but for those dependent at age 70, about one half of their remaining life is expected to be dependent. By age 84 those shares have risen markedly, as dependent life expectancy declines more slowly than independent life expectancy.

Comparable tables of active or independent life are not available for the United States or a major subdivision of the United States to describe the direction and extent of change in active or independent life for the older population over any lengthy period, such as the post–World War II era. An attempt to develop comparable measures of disability-free life expectancy in the United States for 1970 and 1980 was made by Crimmins and associates, employing the prevalence ratio method of life table construction and data from the 1970 and 1980 population censuses and the NHIS.[33] Some principal results are:

[33]E. M. Crimmins, Y. Saito, and D. Ingegneri, "Changes in Life Expectancy and Disability-Free Life Expectancy in the United States," *Population and Development Review* 15 (2) (June 1989):235–267.

Life Expectancy at Age 65	Male			Female		
	1970	1980	Change	1970	1980	Change
Total Years	13.0	14.2	+1.2	16.8	18.4	+1.6
Without Disability	6.4	6.6	+0.2	8.7	8.9	+0.2
With Disability	6.6	7.6	+1.0	8.1	9.5	+1.4
Long-term[a]	6.4	7.4	+1.0	7.7	9.1	+1.4

[a] Including institutional years.

Most of the increase in life expectancy at age 65 between 1970 and 1980, for both males and females, was concentrated in the disabled state. The increase was in fact almost entirely in long-term disability, with both men and women showing about a one-year increase in long-term disability. At birth also, most of the increase in life expectancy was in years with a disability, particularly with a long-term disability. Crimmins and associates also present expectancy figures for life expectancy with bed disability for 1965, 1970, and 1980, which show essentially opposite results from those just described above for the trend of disability.

We cannot obtain consistent answers from existing tables of active life to the question of whether health has been improving or worsening since World War II while longevity has been increasing. The answer depends on the definition of health employed as well as our assessment of such factors as the quality of self-reports of activity-limitation, improvements in diagnostic methods, shifting public participation in and utilization of health care programs, changing tendencies to report disability, and the increase in the public's knowledge about health and health standards. I propose the hypothesis that the health of the elderly population (e.g., percentage with chronic and acute illness and with activity limitation) is worsening as the population ages, but that progress in the management of health conditions may be delaying the onset of severe disability and/or dependence, and may be reducing the severity of some conditions, if not effecting an increase in their recovery rate.

Rogers and associates have carried out a sensitivity analysis to show the effect of a delay of four years in the onset of disability, and of an increase of 50 percent in the rate of recovery from dependency, on years of active life and the percentage of remaining life that is active.[34] In combination, these hypothetical changes add 1.3 to 2.1 years to remaining active life at age 70 (depending on whether life expectancy gains are being measured for the initially dependent or initially independent population).

[34] A. Rogers, R. G. Rogers, and A. Belanger, "Longer Life But Worse Health? Measurement and Dynamics," *Gerontologist* 30 (5) (October 1990):640–649.

It is of special interest to consider whether men and women differ in the share of remaining life to be lived as disabled or dependent in older age. There are national data for 1984 and 1986 and for 1970 and 1980, and data for Massachusetts for 1974. Rogers and associates have shown, by use of data from the 1986 LSOA and multistate life table methods, that much of the excess of the life expectancy of females over males is likely to be spent in the dependent state:

Life Expectancy at Age 70	Population Independent at Age 70	Population Dependent at Age 70
Male		
Total Years	11.3	9.9
Independent	9.3	5.9
Dependent	2.0	4.0
Percent dependent	18	40
Female		
Total Years	15.4	14.5
Independent	10.9	6.8
Dependent	4.5	7.7
Percent dependent	29	53

We note that the numbers of independent years remaining for males and females are somewhat closer to one another than the numbers of dependent years remaining and that the percentage of the remaining years to be lived in a dependent condition for women substantially exceeds the percentage for men. This pattern of differences in male-female life expectancy prevails also at the higher ages. From these data, it appears, therefore, that much of the excess longevity of women in later life will be spent in a dependent condition.

In their study of disability-free life expectancy for 1970 and 1980, Crimmins and associates found that while more than one half of the additional years women have to live at age 65 are years free of disability, one third (1970) and two fifths (1980) of these additional years are years of long-term disability or institutionalization:

Additional Years	1980	1970
Total Years	4.2	3.8
Without Disability	2.3	2.3
With Disability	1.9	1.5
Long-term[a]	1.7	1.3

[a] Including institutional years.

Similarly, Katz and his associates estimated that, according to the mortality and (ADL) dependency rates of Massachusetts in 1974, elderly men and women at age 65 would live roughly the same number of years of active life (9.3 years and 10.6 years), but that women would live a far larger share of their total remaining years in a dependent condition than men (46 percent vs. 29 percent).[35] At age 85 these shares are very large: 49 percent for males and 64 percent for females.

A summary compilation by Colvez, Robine et al. of the available tables of active life, or life expectancy "without incapacity," published since 1970 for various Western countries, sustains the findings of Katz et al. that active life expectancy for women is much closer to active life expectancy for men than is total life expectancy for women to that for men, especially at age 65.[36]

These figures have tremendous implications. The longevity advantage of women may not be an unmixed blessing, even if we disregard the fact that the additional years are typically years of widowhood and solitary living. They are also mostly years of activity limitation, and possibly ADL dependent years.

Utilization of Health Care Services

Measures of the extent of the use of health care services may be interpreted as indicators of health status, but they are more confidently interpreted only as showing the extent to which health services are used. The extent of use may not reflect the extent of need, and there may be variation in the relation of use to need among segments of the population. I consider next physician and dentist care, hospital care, and nursing home care.

Physician and Dentist Visits

After early childhood, the average number of physician visits increases directly with age, with the rise accelerating at the older ages.

---

[35]S. Katz, L. G. Branch, et al., "Active Life Expectancy," *New England Journal of Medicine* 309 (20) (November 17, 1983):218–224. Rogers et al. (1990) maintain that measures of active life expectancy computed by the double decrement life table model, such as those of Katz et al., are biased downward and that measures derived by the multistate life table model are preferable.

[36]A. Colvez, J. M. Robine, et al., "Life Expectancy Without Incapacity in France in 1982," *Population* (Paris) 4 (6) (November–December 1986):1025–1042.

Persons aged 65 and over make, on the average, 2.6 visits per person per year more than those of all ages (Table 5.13). Physician visits per person per year numbered 7.8 at ages 65 and over and 5.2 for the general population in 1982. The average number of visits of elderly persons to physicians appears to have been much lower in the 1970s; the yearly figure ranged only from 6.3 to 6.9 visits. The marked rise in the early 1980s may have resulted from questionnaire changes rather than a shift in actual practice, however.

At all ages after childhood, males have fewer physician contacts per person per year than females. In 1982 the figures for the elderly were 7.2 and 8.1, respectively (Table 5.14). To what extent this gender gap represents a higher sickness rate for women and to what extent it represents merely a more complete reporting of physician visits of women or a greater tendency of women to check up on their health is not known. Even when the two sexes made the same assessment of their health, elderly women had more physician contacts on the average than elderly men (Table 5.15). This pattern appears to persist, when health assessment is held constant, only for white persons since for blacks there is little difference between the sexes or the difference goes in the other direction.

In general, we see little difference after childhood between the races in average number of physician contacts. Family income does affect the frequency of physician contacts, however. Depending on the age group, the averages are highest at the extremes of income. At ages 65 and over the affluent make more visits than other income groups, including the poor. In 1982 there were 8.8 visits for persons in families with incomes $35,000 and over and 7.9 visits for persons in families with incomes under $10,000 (Table 5.14).

There are data on the proportion of elderly persons who have not seen a physician for two or more years, but they are difficult to interpret (Table 5.16). Do we have a measure of health status or a measure of the tendency to seek out or avoid health care? Among the elderly, notably greater shares of men than women, of whites than blacks, and of persons in lower-income families than persons in higher-income families have not contacted a physician in a two-year period. Do the men, whites, and lower-income persons suffer less illness or do they visit physicians less when ill? Different situations may apply to different groups. Whites may be less ill, men may be less ill and/or concern themselves less with health care, and poorer persons may have fewer funds to spend on health care. Overall, some 12 percent of elderly persons in 1982 had had their last physician contact two or more years earlier. This figure compares with nearly 14 percent for the general population, and is consistent with the thesis that the younger population suffers less illness.

TABLE 5.13

Average Number of Physician and Dentist Contacts per Person per Year, by Broad Age Group: 1964–1982

Age of Patient	Physician Contacts					Dentist Contacts			
	1964	1970	1976	1981	1982[a]	1964	1970	1976	1981
Total[b]	4.6	4.6	4.9	4.6	5.2	1.6	1.5	1.6	1.7
Under 45	4.2	4.3	4.4	4.2	4.5	1.7	1.8	1.6	1.7
45–64	5.0	5.2	5.7	5.1	6.1	1.7	1.5	1.8	1.8
65 and Over	6.7	6.3	6.9	6.3	7.8	0.8	1.1	1.2	1.5

SOURCES: U.S. National Center for Health Statistics, *Vital and Health Statistics*, series 10, no. 150 (September 1985); and no. 139 (December 1981); and *Health, United States, 1984*, Tables 42 and 46. Based on the National Health Interview Survey.

NOTES: Data are based on household interviews of a sample of the civilian noninstitutional population; do not include physician contacts while an overnight patient in a hospital.

[a] May not be comparable with earlier figures because of questionnaire changes.
[b] Age-adjusted by the direct method on the basis of the 1970 civilian noninstitutionalized population, using four age groups.

TABLE 5.14

Average Number of Physician Contacts per Person per Year for Broad Age Groups, by Sex, by Race, and by Family Income: 1982

Age	Total	Sex		Race		Family Income			
		Male	Female	White	Black	Under $10,000	$10,000–$19,000	$20,000–$34,999	$35,000 and Over
All Ages	5.2	4.5	5.8	5.3	4.6	6.2	4.9	5.0	5.0
Under 18	4.2	4.2	4.1	4.4	2.9	4.2	3.6	4.5	5.0
18–44	4.7	3.5	5.8	4.7	4.6	6.1	4.3	4.8	4.5
45–64	6.1	5.7	6.5	6.1	6.6	7.6	6.7	5.7	5.6
65 and Over	7.7[a]	7.2	8.1	7.8	7.4	7.9	7.6	7.7	8.8

SOURCE: U.S. National Center for Health Statistics, *Vital and Health Statistics*, series 10, no. 150 (September 1985), Table 69. Based on the National Health Interview Survey.

NOTES: Data are based on household interviews of the civilian noninstitutionalized population; do not include physician contacts while an overnight patient in a hospital.

[a] Percentages for ages 65–74 and ages 75 and over are 7.4 and 8.4, respectively.

TABLE 5.15

Average Number of Physician Contacts per Person, by Sex, Age, Race, and Respondent-Assessed Health Status: 1982–1984

	All Races		Blacks	
Sex and Age	Good or Excellent Health	Fair or Poor Health	Good or Excellent Health	Fair or Poor Health
Male				
65 and over	5.1	11.1	4.5	10.0
75 and over	5.6	12.7	4.7[a]	12.3
Female				
65 and over	5.8	12.4	4.4	10.7
75 and over	6.1	12.2	4.3	10.6

SOURCE: U.S. National Center for Health Statistics, *Vital and Health Statistics*, series 3, no. 25 (June 1987), Table 46. Based on the National Health Interview Survey.

[a] Relative standard error greater than 30 percent.

TABLE 5.16

Percentage of Persons Aged 65 and Over with Last Physician Contact Two or More Years Earlier, by Sex, by Race, and by Family Income: 1982

Characteristic	Ages 65 and Over	Ages 45–64	All Ages
Total	12.0	16.2	13.6
Male	14.1	20.0	17.4
Female	10.7	12.7	10.1
White	12.2	16.5	13.6
Black	9.9	13.0	12.9
Family Income			
Under $10,000	12.2	15.0	13.2
$10,000–$19,999	12.6	17.8	14.8
$20,000–$34,999	9.7	16.3	13.2
$35,000 and Over	9.8	13.7	11.8

SOURCE: U.S. National Center for Health Statistics, *Vital and Health Statistics*, series 10, no. 150 (September 1985), Table 70. Based on the National Health Interview Survey.

NOTE: Includes physician contacts while an overnight patient in a hospital.

Most elderly persons do not visit a dentist and, in spite of greater need to do so, are less likely to visit a dentist than persons under age 65. Over two thirds of the elderly did not visit a dentist in 1975.[37] Persons aged 65 and over visited a dentist 1.5 times on the average in 1981, while those under age 65 visited a dentist 1.7 times (Table 5.13). Lack of dental care is a serious problem among the elderly. Over two fifths of the edentulous elderly fail to secure dental care, needed in order to have properly fitting, useful dentures. Lack of financial resources appears to be a significant factor in the falling off of visits to the dentist in older age and the resulting inadequacy of dental care among older persons.

Hospital Care

As expected, the elderly utilize hospitals far more than the rest of the population. Discharge rates, average hospital stay, and the days-of-hospital-care ratio generally increase steadily with increasing age after childhood (Table 5.17). For the population aged 65 and over the discharge rate from short-term hospitals was 2.5 times as great as for the population as a whole in 1982 (399 vs. 158 discharges per 1,000 population). The Medicare Amendments to the Social Security Act which went into effect in 1966 greatly influenced the trend of hospital admissions of elderly persons. After increasing slowly between 1960 and 1965, the rate of admissions of elderly persons to short-term hospitals climbed rapidly during the late 1960s and early 1970s, and then nearly stabilized in the late 1970s. The influence of Medicare is seen also in the fact that admission rates for older persons increased more rapidly than for younger persons in the 1970s.

The average length of hospital stay of persons aged 65 and over also substantially exceeds that for the population as a whole. For 1982 the comparative figures were 10.1 days and 7.1 days. The figures have been converging. During the 1970s, the average length of stay decreased for both elderly persons and persons under age 65, especially the former. As a result, the difference between the age classes dropped from 4 days to 3 days during this decade.

"Days of hospital care per 1,000 persons" was over 3.5 times as great for elderly persons as for the general population in 1982. The difference between the age classes for days of hospital care was much greater than the corresponding difference for the hospital discharge rate (2.5 times) because the average stay per patient was much longer for elderly persons (1.5 times).

[37]U.S. Public Health Service (1978), p. 16. See footnote 3.

TABLE 5.17

Hospital Utilization Rates for Broad Age Groups, by Sex: 1982

Age and Sex	Discharges per 1,000 Population	Days of Care per 1,000 Population	Average Length of Stay (days)
Both Sexes			
All ages	158.5	1,101.7	7.1
Under 45	121.9[a]	611.5[a]	5.0
45–64	195.5	1,536.7	7.9
65 and over	398.8	4,026.2	10.1
Male			
All ages	140.5	1,047.6	7.5
Under 45	85.8[a]	494.5[a]	5.8
45–64	196.3	1,521.5	7.8
65 and over	428.1	4,188.0	9.8
Female			
All ages	176.5	1,157.7	6.8
Under 45	157.5[a]	726.9[a]	4.6
45–64	194.8	1,550.4	8.0
65 and over	379.1	3,917.6	10.3

SOURCE: U.S. National Center for Health Statistics, *Health, United States, 1984*, Tables 48 and 49.

NOTES: Relates to the civilian noninstitutional population and inpatients in nonfederal, short-stay hospitals; excludes persons who died in the hospital and persons with stays of less than one day. Data are based on a sample of hospital records.

[a] Obtained as weighted average of rates for ages under 15 and 15–44 given in source.

Elderly males utilize hospitals more than elderly females. The number of days of care per 1,000 persons was 7 percent greater for elderly males (4,188) than for elderly females (3,918) in 1982. Although the average length-of-stay figure was slightly lower for males than for females, the discharge rate was much higher (13 percent).

There was little variation by sex, race, or family income in the shares of elderly persons experiencing various numbers of hospital episodes in 1982 (Table 5.18). Yet the chances of a hospital episode were slightly greater for elderly men and elderly persons of low income. Overall, about 80 percent of those aged 65 and over had no hospital episodes, about 15 percent had one episode, and 5 percent had two or more. There is a marked variation by age, however. A much greater share of the general population than of the elderly population had no hospital episodes, and a much smaller share had one or more episodes. Specifically, for the population as a whole, about 9 in 10 persons had no hospital episodes.

At ages below 65, increasing family income substantially reduced the risk of a hospital episode.

A study of the use of Medicare benefits made by Davis provides additional information on the trend of hospital use and the socioeconomic characteristics of hospital users.[38] She too found a difference in the rate of utilization of hospital care before and after the advent of Medicare. After the Medicare program went into effect, the rate of hospitalization increased for the population aged 65 and over and decreased for the population under age 65. Davis's analysis showed also that, after the introduction of Medicare and Medicaid, there was a decrease in the disparity of the hospitalization rates of blacks and whites. The reduction of the financial barrier to care changed the pattern of use by blacks, who previously had lower levels of utilization. The advent of Medicare and Medicaid also had a great impact on the use of nursing home care, which is considered next.

Nursing Home Care

About 5 percent of the population aged 65 and over reside in nursing homes, and a small additional percentage reside in chronic disease hospitals, psychiatric hospitals, Veterans Administration hospitals, and other long-term-care facilities.[39] The share rises sharply with increasing age from a negligible level below age 75. Only 1.3 percent of persons aged 65–74 are nursing home residents, but the figure for persons aged 85 and over is 22 percent. Only the older aged in nursing homes make up any substantial portion of the general population at the same age.

The nursing home population is concentrated among the aged. Nine in 10 of the 1.5 million residents of nursing homes in 1985 were aged 65 and over (Table 5.19). Three in 4 were aged 75 and over, and 4 in 10 were aged 85 and over. The share of aged residents has been steadily climbing, while the share of young elderly has been diminishing. In 1963, when the number of nursing home residents (505,000) was far smaller than in the mid 1980s, a much lower proportion of the residents (29

---

[38]K. Davis, "Equal Treatment and Unequal Benefits: The Medicare Program," *Milbank Memorial Fund Quarterly* 53 (4) (1975).

[39]The first surveys of nursing homes conducted on a regular basis were those in 1963, 1964, and 1969. These three surveys included data not only on nursing homes but also on personal-care homes. Nursing homes provide skilled nursing care, while personal-care homes do not. Later surveys, starting with the 1973–1974 survey and including those of 1976, 1977, and 1985, collected data only on nursing homes. Valid comparisons can be made with the earlier surveys, however, since only about 5 percent of the population covered in the earlier surveys were in personal-care homes.

TABLE 5.18

Percent Distribution of the Population Aged 65 and Over by Number of Short-Stay Hospital Episodes, by Sex, by Race, and by Family Income: 1982

Characteristic	Ages 65 and Over				
	Total	No Episodes	1 Episode	2 Episodes	3 or More Episodes
Total	100.0	80.0	14.6	3.8	1.5
Male	100.0	78.5	15.7	4.0	1.8
Female	100.0	81.1	13.9	3.7	1.3
White	100.0	80.0	14.6	3.8	1.5
Black	100.0	80.1	15.4	3.1	1.4[b]
Family Income					
Less than $10,000	100.0	78.9	15.5	4.1	1.6
$10,000–$19,999	100.0	80.7	14.3	3.5	1.5
$20,000–$34,999	100.0	80.9	14.0	3.5	1.6
$35,000 and over	100.0	81.9	12.9	4.0	1.3[b]

SOURCE: U.S. National Center for Health Statistics, *Vital and Health Statistics*, series 10, no. 150 (September 1985), Table 71. Based on the National Health Interview Survey.

[a] Excluding deliveries.
[b] Numerator has relative standard error greater than 30 percent.

percent) was aged 85 and over. Then, nursing home residents made up only 2.7 percent of the population aged 65 and over and 15 percent of the population aged 85 and over.

Between 1963 and 1969, a period during which the Medicare and Medicaid programs went into effect and were even accumulating a few years of experience, the number of residents of nursing homes and their share of the older population increased greatly, particularly the number and share of very old residents. The number of elderly residents increased at an average annual rate of 8.0 percent. By 1969, elderly nursing home residents made up 3.7 percent of the population aged 65 and over and 20 percent of the population aged 85 and over. The age distribution of residents in nursing homes also showed a substantial rise in the proportion of residents aged 85 and over between 1963 and 1969.

The more recent surveys—for example, those of 1977 and 1985—imply somewhat smaller rates of increase in the number of nursing home residents than the survey of 1969. An average annual increase of 5.5 percent occurred between 1969 and 1977 and of 1.9 percent between

TABLE 5.18 *(continued)*

Total	No Episodes	1 Episode	2 Episodes	3 or More Episodes
100.0	91.0	7.1	1.3	0.6
100.0	91.6	6.7	1.2	0.6
100.0	90.5	7.6	1.4	0.6
100.0	90.9	7.2	1.3	0.6
100.0	91.2	6.9	1.4	0.5
100.0	87.7	9.1	2.2	1.0
100.0	90.8	7.1	1.4	0.6
100.0	92.3	6.4	0.9	0.4
100.0	93.0	6.0	0.8	0.3

1977 and 1985.[40] Unlike the increases in the number of elderly persons in nursing homes prior to 1969, the increases between 1969 and 1985, especially those between 1977 and 1985, resulted mainly from growth of the elderly population and only secondarily from increases in the rate of nursing home utilization.

The great majority of elderly residents of nursing homes are women. In 1985 three fourths of the residents in nursing homes aged 65 and over and four fifths of those aged 85 and over were female. The proportion of females among elderly residents has been generally rising and is much higher now than it was in the 1960s, especially at ages 85 and over:

Age Group	1985	1977	1969	1963
All Ages	72	71	69	66
Under 65	49	54	52	47
65 and Over	74	74	71	68
65–74	62	62	63	61
75–84	72	74	72	69
85 and Over	81	80	76	72

SOURCE: Table 5.19.

[40]In addition to the sources of Table 5.19, see U.S. Bureau of the Census, "1976 Survey of Institutionalized Persons: A Study of Persons Receiving Long-Term Care," *Current Population Reports*, series P-23, no. 69 (1978).

TABLE 5.19

Distribution of Residents in Nursing Homes and Personal-Care Homes by Broad Age Group, by Sex and by Race: 1969, 1977, and 1985

Sex, Race, and Age	Number of Residents (in thousands)		
	1969	1977[b]	1985
Total All Classes	815	1,303	1,475
Male	252	375	411[c]
Female	563	928	1,055[c]
White	779	1,201	1,346
Black and other races	37	102	120[c]
Total	815	1,303	1,475
Under 65	93	177	159[d]
65 and over	722	1,126	1,316
65–74	139	211	212
75–84	322	465	509
85 and over	262	450	595
Male	252	375	411[c]
Under 65	45	81	81[d]
65 and over	207	294	330
65–74	52	80	80
75–84	91	122	139
85 and over	64	92	111
Female	563	928	1,055[c]
Under 65	48	96	78[d]
65 and over	515	832	977
65–74	86	131	131
75–84	231	343	365
85 and over	198	358	482
White	779	1,201	1,346
Under 65	84	141	121[d]
65 and over	695	1,060	1,225
Black and Other Races	37	102	120[c]
Under 65	10	36	38[d]
65 and over	27	66	82

SOURCES: U.S. National Center for Health Statistics, *Vital and Health Statistics*, series 13, no. 43 (1979); and *Health, United States, 1985* (December 1985), Tables 56 and 57.

NOTE: Data are based on a sample of nursing homes. Dash denotes that figure rounds to 0.0.

[a] Based on U.S. Bureau of the Census estimates of the resident population.
[b] Includes residents in domiciliary care homes.
[c] Excludes races other than white and black.
[d] Estimated.

TABLE 5.19 *(continued)*

Percentage of Total for All Age Categories			Percentage of Total Population in Specified Categories[a]		
1969	1977[b]	1985	1969	1977[b]	1985
100.0	100.0	100.0	0.4	0.6	0.6
30.9	28.8	28.0	0.3	0.4	0.4
69.1	71.2	72.0	0.5	0.8	0.9
95.6	92.2	91.8	0.4	0.6	0.7
4.5	7.8	8.2	0.1	0.3	0.4
100.0	100.0	100.0	0.4	0.6	0.6
11.4	13.6	10.8[d]	0.1	0.1	0.1
88.6	86.4	89.2	3.7	4.8	4.6
16.8	16.2	14.4	1.2	1.5	1.3
39.6	35.7	34.5	5.2	6.8	5.7
32.1	34.5	40.3	20.3	21.6	22.1
100.0	100.0	100.0	0.3	0.4	0.4
17.9	21.6	19.7[d]	0.1	0.1	0.1
82.1	78.4	80.3	2.5	3.1	3.0
20.2	21.3	19.5	1.0	1.3	1.1
36.1	32.5	33.8	3.6	4.7	4.1
25.4	24.5	27.0	13.1	14.0	14.5
100.0	100.0	100.0	0.5	0.8	0.9
8.5	10.3	7.4[d]	0.1	0.1	0.1
91.5	89.7	92.6	4.6	6.0	5.7
15.3	14.1	12.4	1.3	1.6	1.4
41.2	37.0	34.6	6.2	8.1	6.4
35.2	38.6	45.7	24.8	25.2	25.0
100.0	100.0	100.0	0.4	0.6	0.5
10.8	11.7	9.0[d]	0.1	0.1	0.1
89.2	88.3	91.0	3.9	5.0	4.5
100.0	100.0	100.0	0.1	0.3	0.5
27.0	35.3	31.7[d]	—	0.2	0.1
73.0	64.7	68.3	1.6	3.0	3.4

A comparison between the elderly nursing home population and its noninstitutional counterpart reveals several major differences in basic demographic characteristics—that is, sex, age, race, and marital composition. Although females exceed males in both population groups, the excess is far more pronounced in the nursing home population. In 1985 the noninstitutional elderly population consisted of 60 percent women and 40 percent men, whereas the elderly population in nursing homes consisted of 74 percent women and 26 percent men. Women enter nursing homes at a greater rate than men and stay longer on the average. Blacks and other nonwhite races constitute a disproportionately small segment of the nursing home population. Only 6 percent of the elderly nursing home population is black or other nonwhite race, while 8 percent of the general population aged 65 and over is black or other nonwhite race.

Another difference between the noninstitutional population and the nursing home population relates to marital distribution. The nursing home population is less likely to be married and more likely to be widowed. In 1977, 54 percent of the elderly noninstitutional population was married compared with only 12 percent of the elderly nursing home population. A little over 36 percent of the elderly noninstitutional population was widowed compared with 62 percent of the elderly nursing home population. Another pronounced difference between the two populations, already intimated, is the older age distribution of the nursing home population. Less than two fifths of the elderly noninstitutional population aged 65 and over was aged 75 and over in 1985 compared with over four fifths of the elderly nursing home population (Table 5.19).[41] It is evident that persons are more likely to spend time in a nursing home if they experience greater longevity and if they are not currently living with a spouse. These conditions describe elderly women more accurately than elderly men.

All or nearly all the residents of long-term-care facilities suffer from multiple chronic conditions and functional impairments. The most common primary health conditions in the institutional population are atherosclerosis (hardening of the arteries), senility, cerebrovascular disease (stroke), and mental disorders, and these are all likely to be associated with functional impairments.[42] For most of the residents of nursing homes the functional impairments are severe. In 1985, of nursing home residents aged 75–84, 76 percent required assistance in dressing, 60 percent required assistance in toilet matters, and 70 percent required assistance in mobility or were not mobile (Table 5.20). Incontinence and need for assistance in eating were other common problems. The degree of dysfunctionality was strongly associated with age, so that the shares of residents having these impairments were much greater for those aged 85 and over. Larger proportions of residents required assistance for these impairments in 1985 than in 1977. To what extent this was due to de-

41U.S. National Center for Health Statistics, "The National Nursing Home Survey: 1977 Summary for the United States," *Vital and Health Statistics*, series 13, no. 43 (July 1979); and U.S. Bureau of the Census, "Marital Status and Living Arrangements: March 1977," *Current Population Reports*, series P-20, no. 323 (April 1978).
42U.S. Public Health Service (1978).

TABLE 5.20

Percentage of Nursing Home Residents Aged 65 and Over Having Various Dysfunctions, by Age Group: 1985 and 1977

Functional Status	1985			1977		
	Ages 65–74	Ages 75–84	Ages 85 and Over	Ages 65–74	Ages 75–84	Ages 85 and Over
Dressing: Requires Assistance	70.2	75.9	81.9	61.2	72.5	75.8
Toilet Room: Requires Assistance or Does Not Use	56.6	60.3	68.2	46.9	54.3	59.0
Mobility: Requires Assistance or Not Mobile	60.5	69.6	81.9	56.9	66.8	77.6
Continence: Difficulties in Control	42.9	55.1	58.1	37.6	47.1	52.2
Eating: Requires Assistance	33.5	39.1	44.0	27.1	33.8	36.5
Vision: Severely Impaired or Lost	6.7	8.0	12.8	5.9	8.7	14.2
Hearing: Severely Impaired or Lost	2.2	2.6	8.8	2.6	3.6	9.1

SOURCES: Based on U.S. National Center for Health Statistics, Health, United States, 1984, Table 54; Vital and Health Statistics, vol. 3, no. 25 (June 1987), Tables 59 and 57; unpublished data from the National Nursing Home Survey for 1977 and 1985.

NOTES: Data are based on a sample of nursing homes; exclude residents of domiciliary care homes.

teriorating health of the older population, a greater tendency to use nursing homes for the more severely impaired persons, or administrative or legal pressures is not clear.

Even without substantial changes in the share of the general population in each older age segment residing in nursing homes, the nursing home population is expected to grow rapidly in the next several decades as a result of the growth and aging of the elderly population: the higher the age group, the higher the growth rate. Under the assumption stated, the number of nursing home residents aged 65 and over is expected to double between 1985 and 2015, and the number aged 85 and over is expected to double between 1985 and 2005 (Table 5.21). The share of the population aged 65 and over in nursing homes will generally rise under these assumptions, with expected peaks of 6.1 percent in 2010 and 6.8 percent in 2040. Vast increases in public and private expenditures will be required to accommodate to these developments, barring a radical change in the way long-term care is managed and financed.

The Cost of Health Care

In 1984, personal health care expenditures for the elderly amounted to $120.4 billion, or 34 percent of the total personal health care bill.[43] Since persons aged 65 and over made up only 11 percent of the total population, they accounted for a disproportionately large share of total personal health care expenditures. Hospital care, nursing home care, and physicians' services constituted the major health care expenses of the elderly, in that order. Of the total per capita health care expenditures for the elderly in 1984 ($4202), nearly one half went for hospital services and about one fifth each went to nursing homes and physicians.

	Per Capita	Percent	Private	Government
Total	$4,202	100.0	$1,379	$2,823
Hospital	1,900	45.2	216	1,684
Physician	868	20.7	344	524
Nursing Home	880	20.9	457	423
Other	554	13.2	362	192

SOURCE: U.S. National Center for Health Statistics, *Vital and Health Statistics*, series 3, no. 25 (June 1987), Table 60.

[43]D. Waldo and H. C. Lazenby, "Demographic Characteristics and Health Care Use and Expenditures by the Aged in the United States, 1977–1984," *Health Care Financing Review* 6 (1) (Fall 1984):1–29.

TABLE 5.21

Projections of Nursing Home Residents Aged 65 and Over, by Broad Age Group: 1985–2040

Year	Number (in thousands)				Percent Increase Over 1985				Percentage of Population:
	Total, 65 and Over	65–74	75–84	85 and Over	Total, 65 and Over	65–74	75–84	85 and Over	Total, 65 and Over
1985	1,316	212	509	595	—	—	—	—	4.6
1990	1,541	226	581	733	17	7	14	23	4.9
1995	1,770	232	635	903	34	9	25	52	5.2
2000	2,005	221	691	1,093	52	4	36	84	5.7
2010	2,398	254	690	1,454	82	20	36	144	6.1
2020	2,750	373	807	1,570	109	76	58	164	5.3
2030	3,519	430	1,190	1,898	168	103	134	219	5.4
2040	4,560	365	1,379	2,816	246	72	171	374	6.8

SOURCES: Projections prepared by author. Projections based on age-sex specific nursing home ratios for 1985 from the National Nursing Home Survey, conducted by the National Center for Health Statistics, and on population projections published by the U.S. Bureau of the Census. See U.S. National Center for Health Statistics, *Vital and Health Statistics*, series 3, no. 25 (June 1987), Table 57; and U.S. Bureau of the Census, *Current Population Reports*, series P-25, no. 952 (May 1984), Table 6, middle series.

NOTE: Dash denotes zero.

About one quarter was paid out of pocket and two thirds was covered by government programs, principally Medicare for hospitals and physicians and Medicaid for nursing homes.

Per capita expenditures for health care services generally increase with age (after early childhood), as does the use of health care services.[44] In 1978, for example, the health care expenditure per capita for ages 65 and over, $2026, was well over three times the figure of $597 for ages under 65. The relative difference between the age groups was somewhat over 3 to 1 for hospital care and somewhat less than 3 to 1 for physicians' services. A small proportion of persons account for the lion's share of the health care expenditures of the group aged 65 and over. The group who died or were institutionalized during 1980 (about 5 percent of the elderly living in the community) accounted for 22 percent of the total health care expenses of elderly persons in the community in that year.[45]

There has been a dramatic increase in the costs of health care services since 1965. Health care expenditures for elderly persons have been rising much faster than the overall cost of living. Per capita costs for personal health care for the elderly showed a continuous marked rise between 1965 and 1984, from $472 in 1965 to $2,026 in 1978 and $4,202 in 1984. In the first quinquennium of this period—1965–1970—per capita costs of health care nearly doubled. The cost for physicians' services increased over 60 percent, the cost for hospital care doubled, and the cost for nursing home care more than tripled. These increases were largely due to more extensive utilization of services and much less to price inflation.

In the period 1970–1978, per capita personal health care expenditures for elderly persons increased about 11 percent per year, or nearly 2.3 times, with relatively little variation in the percentage increase for the principal categories of health care. In these years, inflation was the major factor in the increase of the cost of health care. The general inflation rate based on the consumer price index averaged 6.4 percent per year. The difference between the general inflation rate and the change in per capita expenditures for health care can be accounted for mainly by the cost of technological improvements and excessive inflation in the health care industry.

In 1977–1984 health care costs per capita rose less rapidly than the general consumer price index. Yet, in this period health care expenditures for the elderly more than doubled.[46] The major factor contributing

---

[44]C. F. Fisher, "Differences by Age Groups in Health Care Spending," *Health Care Financing Review* 1 (4) (Spring 1980):65–90.

[45]U.S. National Center for Health Statistics, *Vital and Health Statistics*, series 3, no. 25 (June 1987), p. 76.

[46]Waldo and Lazenby (1984).

to this increase was price inflation, but changes in equipment and services (including technological developments), increased per capita demand, and population growth also contributed. The U.S. Health Care Financing Administration has estimated that from 1977 to 1984 population growth accounted for only 15 percent of the overall increase in health care expenditures for the elderly population, price inflation accounted for 63 percent, and other factors, including increased per capita demand and new equipment and services, accounted for 22 percent.[47] (Population growth allows for both the rise in the number of elderly persons and the aging of the elderly population.) The per capita demand for health services increased as the proportion of the population with chronic health conditions rose and as the coverage of the population by public and private health insurance programs was extended.

As we see, population changes have not been an important factor in the increased costs of health care services for the elderly. The future relative contribution of population changes will depend largely on the extent of inflation of health care costs. The population share is expected to rise sharply, in any case, when the baby-boom cohorts become elderly.

According to data obtained in the Survey of Income and Education conducted by the U.S. Bureau of the Census in 1976, nearly all persons aged 65 and over have some type of health insurance, commonly both public and private insurance. A much smaller percentage of younger persons have health insurance.

Age Group	Total	Without Coverage	With Coverage			
			Total	Private Only	Public Only	Public and Private
All Ages	100.0	10.2	89.8	63.4	12.7	13.6
25–44	100.0	9.3	90.7	72.0	8.3	10.3
45–64	100.0	7.6	92.4	70.0	8.8	13.5
65 and Over	100.0	1.0	99.0	1.5	37.7	59.8

SOURCE: U.S. Congress, Congressional Budget Office, *Profile of Health Care Coverage: The Haves and the Have-Nots* (1979).

These findings for the elderly were essentially confirmed by recent data from SIPP, which found that 99 percent of persons aged 65 and over had health insurance for the entire period between February 1985 and May 1987 through Medicare.[48] In addition, many of the elderly had private insurance for this period as well.

[47]Unpublished data.

[48]U.S. Bureau of the Census, "Health Insurance Coverage: 1986–1988," *Current Population Reports*, series P-70, no. 17 (September 1990).

Health in Relation to Education and Income
Educational Level and Health

Recent evidence of the relation between educational level and health at the older ages is provided by data on work disability for 1982 from the CPS.[49] The data reflect a strong inverse relation between work disability and educational level. At ages 65–74, 20 percent of college graduates report a work disability compared with 43 percent of those who did not complete elementary school. The extent of work disability at ages 55–64 for persons not completing elementary school (44 percent) is also strikingly high compared with the figure for persons of these ages who are college graduates (15 percent). Lower educational attainment is associated with a higher level of work disability at all the younger ages as well, although the shares of the population with work disability are lower at these ages.

This association may be explained in part by the difference in the educational and physical requirements of various jobs, leading to different respondent definitions of work disability. Jobs requiring a college education do not commonly make the same physical demands on a worker as jobs requiring only an elementary school education. Moreover, many jobs requiring little education are hazardous and expose the workers to special physical risks, including environmental risks. The rest of the association is explained by real differences in health, evaluated without regard to the type of work.

Income and Health

As shown by several health indicators, the health status of older persons deteriorates as income falls. For example, the percentage of persons aged 65 and over limited in activity because of chronic conditions increases as family income decreases. Over one half of the elderly persons in families with incomes of less than $5,000 per year in 1979–1980 were limited in activity compared with less than two fifths of those in families with incomes of $25,000 or more (Table 5.22). Persons aged 65 and over in lower-income families were twice as likely to assess their health as poor or fair as persons in higher-income families (40 percent vs. 21 percent). The number of bed disability days per person per year

[49]U.S. Bureau of the Census, "Labor Force Status and Other Characteristics of Persons with a Work Disability: 1982," by J. McNeil, *Current Population Reports*, series P-23, no. 127 (July 1983), Tables I and 1.

TABLE 5.22

Health Indicators for Low-Income Group (Less Than $5,000) and High-Income Group ($25,000 and Over) Aged 65 and Over and 45–64: 1979–1980

Health Indicator	Ages 65 and Over				Ages 45–64			
	Family Income		Difference[a]		Family Income		Difference[a]	
	Less Than $5,000	$25,000 and Over	Amount	Ratio	Less Than $5,000	$25,000 and Over	Amount	Ratio
Percent Limited in Activity Due to Chronic Conditions	55.3	37.8	17.5	1.5	54.9	14.2	40.7	3.9
Percent Assessing Own Health as Fair or Poor	39.6	21.3	18.3	1.9	52.0	10.0	42.0	5.2
Number of Acute Conditions per 100 Persons per Year	132	99	33	1.3	162	138	24	1.2
Number of Bed Disability Days per Person per Year	18.6	12.0	6.6	1.6	22.7	4.8	17.9	4.7
Number of Doctor Visits per Person per Year	6.4	6.8	−0.4	0.9	8.1	4.8	3.3	1.7
For persons assessing their health as fair or poor	9.2	10.2	−1.0	0.9	11.6	11.6	—	1.0
Number of Dental Visits per Person per Year	1.0	2.8	−1.8	0.4	1.1	2.5	−1.4	0.4
Number of Short-Stay Hospital Days per 100 Persons per Year	326	278	49	1.2	312	98	214	3.2
For persons assessing their health as fair or poor	521	688	−167	0.8	472	374	99	1.3

SOURCE: U.S. National Center for Health Statistics, *Vital and Health Statistics*, series 10, no. 147 (January 1985).

NOTE: Dash denotes that figure rounds to zero.

[a] Excess of low-income group over high-income group. Minus sign denotes an excess of high-income group over low-income group.

was substantially higher (1.6 times) for persons in lower-income families than for persons in higher-income families.

In considering the association between income and use of health services, it is important to take self-assessed health status into account. Persons in lower-income families make nearly the same number of doctor visits as persons in higher-income families and spend more days in hospitals per person per year than persons in higher-income families. In 1979–1980 persons in families with incomes of less than $5,000 per year spent 1.2 times as many days per year in short-stay hospitals as did persons in families with annual incomes of $25,000 and over. However, the higher-income group makes more doctor visits and spends more days in hospitals when self-assessed health status is reported as poor or fair.[50] For persons assessing their health as fair or poor, on the average, 0.8 day was spent in the hospital by the lower-income group for each day spent in the hospital by the higher-income group.

The relative frequency of dental visits is particularly sensitive to income. Elderly persons in families with annual incomes of $25,000 and over made almost three times as many dental visits per person per year as elderly persons in families earning less than $5,000 per year.

The pattern of differences in health status according to income is similar—and even more pronounced—for persons aged 45–64.

Personal Factors in Health

As suggested earlier, the health status of the population could be improved greatly without major new developments in diagnostic and therapeutic modalities or the discovery of techniques of slowing the aging process. Improvement could be effected through the extension of existing methods of health care and treatment to geographic and socioeconomic segments of the population not now fully serviced, the modification of personal behavior, greater community action relating to health, changes in the financing and delivery of health care services, and more widespread implementation of programs for the retraining of health care personnel. Problems exist now in the form of maldistribution of health care resources, socioeconomic differences in health risks, the adverse effect of certain types of personal behavior and environmental conditions on health, and the failure of many health care practitioners to em-

[50]See J. C. Kleinman, M. Gold, and D. Makiec, "Use of Ambulatory Medical Care by the Poor: Another Look at Equity," *Medical Care* 19 (10) (October 1981):1011–1029.

ploy the latest knowledge and techniques. Community action concerned, for example, with public health education, environmental protection, mass testing for high blood pressure, and industrial safety could be intensified. Implementation of these steps would bring many benefits to the individual and to society, including reduced health expenditures and increased worker productivity.

Certain personal habits and aspects of lifestyle have been linked to various health conditions, particularly such conditions as cancer, cardiovascular diseases, and emphysema.[51] They include cigarette smoking, excessive alcohol consumption, persistent stress at work and home, inadequate sleep (less than seven hours), not eating breakfast, lack of regular exercise, poor dietary habits, and snacking. Certain physical conditions that can be controlled—such as obesity, elevated serum cholesterol, and elevated blood pressure—have also been linked to various health conditions.

There is also evidence that regular mental and social activity is a positive factor in maintaining health and effective functioning in later years. Continuing meaningful social roles and having a large number of satisfying and appropriate interpersonal "transactions" may be as important in maintaining health in later years as the personal habits enumerated.

The evidence for the indirect effects of pronounced obesity on conditions like diabetes, hypertension, and heart disease is strong.[52] There is also strong evidence for the adverse effects of diets with excessive fat on the health of middle-aged and older persons. Fat has been indicted for its role in malignant neoplasms and cardiovascular diseases. Excessive salt has been shown to be a contributing agent in cardiovascular diseases. The evidence on the relation of smoking to health (e.g., chronic obstructive lung disease) is also quite strong.[53]

According to the NHIS of 1983, large segments of the elderly population as well as of the middle-aged population have personal habits that subject them to excessive health risks (Table 5.23). For example, 34 percent of the population aged 55–64 eat snacks every day and 19 percent

[51]M. Susser, "Industrialization, Urbanization, and Health: An Epidemiological View," in *International Population Conference, Manila, 1981* (Liège: International Union for the Scientific Study of Population, 1981); E. Nightingale, "Prospects for Reducing Mortality in Developed Countries by Changes in Day-to-Day Behavior," in *International Population Conference, Manila, 1981* (Liège: International Union for the Scientific Study of Population, 1981).

[52]T. Dwyer and B. S. Hetzel, "A Comparison of Trends of Coronary Heart Disease Mortality in Australia, England and Wales, and U.S.A. with Reference to Three Major Risk Factors—Hypertension, Cigarette Smoking and Diet," *International Journal of Epidemiology* 9 (1980):65–71.

[53]S. W. Burney, "Morbidity and Mortality in a Healthy Aging Male Population: 10-Year Survey," *Gerontologist* 12 (1) (February 1972):49–54.

TABLE 5.23

Percentage of the Population Aged 45 and Over Reporting Selected Health Practices, by Age Group, 1983; and Relative Changes in the Percentages: 1977–1983

Age	Sleeps Less Than 7 Hours	Never Eats Breakfast	Snacks Every Day	Less Physically Active Than Contemporaries	Had 5 or More Drinks on Any One Day[a]	Current Smoker	30 Percent or More Above Desirable Weight[b]
Percent, 1983							
45–54	27.5	27.2	37.8	13.3	30.2	36.5	21.9
55–64	28.0	19.1	34.4	17.1	21.2	30.2	21.3
65–74	26.5	10.5	32.8	16.1	13.2	21.5	21.5
75 and over	26.4	4.4	26.6	16.0	5.0	8.5	11.6
Ratio, Percent in 1983 to Percent in 1977							
45–54	1.20	1.12	1.03	1.11	1.13	0.92	1.25
55–64	1.23	1.10	0.99	1.00	1.15	0.88	1.09
65–74	1.16	1.13	1.12	1.10	1.42	1.00	1.14
75 and over	1.18	0.77	1.00	1.00	1.39	0.85	0.97

SOURCE: U.S. National Center for Health Statistics, *Vital and Health Statistics*, Advance Data, no. 118 (June 30, 1986).

NOTE: Based on household interviews of a sample of the civilian noninstitutional population.

[a] The 1977 question asked about 5 or more drinks on any one occasion in the past year, while the 1983 question asked about 5 or more drinks on any one day in the past year.
[b] Desirable weight based on 1960 Metropolitan Life Insurance Company standards. NHIS data are self-reported, and estimates may vary from those that would be obtained if physical measurements were taken.

TABLE 5.24

Percentage of Men and Women Aged 45 and Over Smoking Cigarettes, by Sex and Race: 1965–1983

Sex and Age	Total				Black[a]		
	1965	1976	1980[b]	1983[c]	1965	1976	1980[b]
Male							
45–64	51.9	41.3	40.8	35.6	57.9	49.7	48.8
65 and over	28.5	23.0	17.9	20.8	36.4	26.4	27.9
Female							
45–64	32.0	34.8	30.8	30.5	25.7	38.1	34.3
65 and over	9.6	12.8	16.8	13.5	7.1	9.2	9.4

SOURCE: U.S. National Center for Health Statistics, *Health, United States, 1984*, Table 33.

NOTES: A smoker is a person who has smoked at least 100 cigarettes and who now smokes. Data are based on household interviews of a sample of the civilian noninstitutional population. Base of percentages excludes persons with unknown smoking status.

[a] In 1965 and 1976 the racial classification of persons in the National Health Interview Survey was determined by interview and observation. In 1980 and 1983 race was determined by asking the household respondent.
[b] Final estimates; based on data for the last six months of 1980.
[c] Provisional estimates; based on data for the first six months of 1983.

TABLE 5.25

Percentage Overweight, with Elevated Blood Pressure, and with Elevated Serum Cholesterol, for the Population Aged 45–74, by Broad Age Group, Sex, and Race: 1976–1980

Physical Characteristic and Age	Total		Black	
	Male	Female	Male	Female
Overweight[a]				
45–54	29.7	31.5	41.4	59.6
55–64	26.6	35.9	25.5	60.0
65–74	23.7	33.5	25.1	56.0
Elevated Blood Pressure[b]				
45–54	20.9	14.9	23.0	37.3
55–64	23.7	20.0	39.2	36.4
65–74	24.9	27.9	27.5	43.4
Elevated Cholesterol[c]				
45–54	21.1	23.9	25.3	25.8
55–64	22.5	35.5	24.2	32.0
65–74	18.9	35.0	18.7	30.3

SOURCE: U.S. National Center for Health Statistics, *Health, United States, 1984*, Tables 37, 38, and 39.

NOTE: Data are based on physical examination of a sample of the civilian noninstitutional population.

[a]Overweight is defined for men as body mass index greater than or equal to 28 kilograms/meter^2 and for women as body mass greater than or equal to 35 kilograms/meter$^{1.5}$.
[b]Elevated blood pressure is defined as either systolic pressure of at least 160 mm Hg or diastolic pressure of at least 95 mm Hg or both, based on the average of three readings.
[c]Elevated serum cholesterol is defined as cholesterol levels of at least 250 mg/100 ml.

never eat breakfast. About 28 percent of the population aged 55–64 sleep less than seven hours each day and about 17 percent are less physically active than their contemporaries. About 30 percent of the population at these ages are smokers and 21 percent are excessive drinkers. At higher ages the percentages fall off, but not especially so until age 75. For most of these health practices, there was little improvement since 1977; smoking was the main exception. (See Table 5.24.)

Substantial proportions of the population aged 55 and over have physical conditions contributing to the onset and persistence of various chronic conditions. Thirty percent are overweight, 24 percent have elevated blood pressure, and 29 percent have elevated serum cholesterol (Table 5.25).

Identifying areas of responsibility of the individual should not cloud the fact that much remains to be done in the form of medical research and development. Knowledge of the causes and prevention of most chronic diseases is limited so that intense effort is needed here too.[54]

Summary

Since the turn of the century, the nature of illness among the older population has changed dramatically with respect to both the causal pattern and the average duration of illness. Acute conditions from infectious and parasitic diseases were predominant in the early part of this century; chronic diseases, accidents, and stress-related conditions are now the most prevalent health problems of elderly persons. The latter conditions tend to last much longer and even to persist indefinitely.

As a group, the population aged 65 and over is healthier than is assumed by the general public. Moreover, two thirds of elderly persons describe their own health as good or excellent compared with the health of others of their own age.

Many assume that because there have been dramatic improvements in longevity, the older population is healthier than ever before. Others conclude, from the indicators available, that there is more chronic illness and associated limitation of activity among the elderly. At best, the health status of the elderly has been relatively stable over the two decades since 1965, and measures based on the NHIS generally show no major improvements.

With increasing age, particularly at the older ages, health tends to worsen. Older persons are more likely than younger persons to suffer from chronic illnesses that cause limited or total disability. As a group, the elderly experience twice as many days of restricted activity because of illness as the general population. The extension of longevity means that people who used to die from, say, a heart attack now often survive, but with a chronic illness that limits their activities. It also has resulted in an increase in the number and share of persons with nonlethal disabling chronic conditions.

The leading chronic conditions that cause limitations of activity for the elderly are arthritis and rheumatism, hypertension without heart involvement, heart conditions, impairments of the lower extremities and

[54]J. A. Brody, "Length of Life and the Health of Older People," *National Forum* (Fall 1982):5. Schneider and Brody (1983).

hips, and impairments of the back and spine. Arthritis and rheumatism and heart conditions account for half of the conditions that cause limitations of the activities of the elderly. Major impairments of the elderly also include hearing and vision impairments.

Many of the most serious health conditions and hence the great need for assistance do not occur until age 80 and over. Multiple chronic illnesses become more common with increasing age. Of those aged 85 and over, nearly two thirds are either institutionalized or seriously limited in their ability to take care of some of their basic needs without help. On the other hand, those aged 65–74 are in relatively good health, and only 6 to 7 percent are either institutionalized or in need of help for the basic activities of life.

While elderly men have higher death rates than elderly women, elderly women have higher rates of both chronic illnesses and acute conditions. The diseases that commonly affect elderly men (e.g., heart disease and cancer) tend to be lethal, while the diseases that commonly affect elderly women (e.g., arthritis and osteoporosis) are chronic nonlethal diseases. On the other hand, men are more likely than women to report that their health prevents them from carrying out at least one major activity.

There is much variation also in the health of different racial, economic, and geographic residence groups among the elderly population. The health situation of elderly blacks is generally poorer than that of elderly whites. A higher proportion of elderly blacks than elderly whites have no regular source of care, and clinics are a more common source of care for blacks than whites.

More generally, good health is associated with higher economic status. The elderly with higher incomes tend to have better health than those with lower incomes. Their health needs receive more attention. The elderly poor who report their health as fair or poor make fewer visits to physicians than the highest income groups among the elderly who report their health as fair or poor.

A somewhat larger proportion of the elderly living in nonmetropolitan areas report chronic health problems than do the metropolitan elderly. The average duration of illness is also higher for the nonmetropolitan elderly. Given the greater prevalence and duration of chronic conditions, the nonmetropolitan elderly are more likely to require health services than the elderly in metropolitan areas, even though such services are less available to them.

The rapidly increasing number of older aged persons suggests that health expenditures, under current health policy and programs, will continue to climb, even apart from technological developments, price inflation, and other factors. In 1984 an estimated $120 billion was spent on health services for the elderly, constituting about 3 percent of the gross national product. About two thirds of this expenditure was covered by government programs, principally Medicare and Medicaid.

The following four areas for advancing public policy relating to the health of the elderly are suggested: (1) expansion of public education programs to encourage preventive health care and modification of personal behavior relating to smoking, sleep, alcohol consumption, stress, exercise, and diet; (2) increase in community action in the areas of public safety, environmental protection, and mass testing for high blood pressure, excessive cholesterol levels, cancer, and visual impairments; (3) concentration of research on the diseases that disproportionately kill men and the diseases that disproportionately cause chronic debilitating conditions among women; and (4) an increase in research into the interrelationships of social support, lifestyle, and health.

MARITAL STATUS, LIVING ARRANGEMENTS, AND INSTITUTIONALIZATION

T HIS CHAPTER and the following ones are concerned with the principal social and economic characteristics of the older population, the variation in these characteristics over time and over the life cycle, and some implications of the changes and variations. In this chapter I consider the marital characteristics, living arrangements, and family support system of the elderly population. In the following chapters I consider their education, labor force participation, and retirement; their income and economic status; and, finally, their housing.

Marital Status and Marriage

Age and Sex Variations

With advancing age, shifts in the marital status of men and women follow the same general course, but they are much more dramatic for women. The proportions of men and women who are currently married increase sharply between ages 25 and 30, reach a peak and plateau at about age 35, and then fall steadily through the rest of the life cycle. After about age 45, the proportion of married men tends increasingly to exceed the proportion of married women (Table 6.1). The proportions of divorced men and women follow a somewhat similar course, lagging a

TABLE 6.1

Marital Distribution of the Population Aged 15 and Over, by Broad Age Group and Sex: 1985 and 1950

Sex and Marital Status	Total, Ages 15 and Over	Ages 15–24	Ages 25–44	Ages 45–54	Ages 55–64	Ages 65–74	Ages 75 and Over
1985							
Male	100.0	100.0	100.0	100.0	100.0	100.0	100.0
Single	30.0	86.7	21.1	6.3	6.1	5.2	5.3
Married	61.5	12.7	69.7	83.9	84.0	81.2	69.4
Spouse present	58.7	11.6	66.2	79.7	81.2	78.9	67.4
Widowed	2.4	—	0.2	1.2	3.7	9.3	22.7
Divorced	6.0	0.7	8.8	8.7	6.2	4.2	2.7
Female	100.0	100.0	100.0	100.0	100.0	100.0	100.0
Single	22.7	74.8	14.4	4.6	3.7	4.4	6.2
Married	57.1	22.9	72.5	76.3	70.0	51.1	23.8
Spouse present	53.6	20.7	67.5	72.3	67.0	49.1	22.8
Widowed	11.9	—	1.3	7.0	17.4	38.9	67.7
Divorced	8.2	2.0	11.8	12.1	8.9	5.6	2.4
1950							
Male	100.0	100.0	100.0	100.0	100.0	100.0	100.0
Single	24.9	77.4	14.3	8.5	8.4	8.6	7.8
Married	68.9	21.9	82.9	85.7	81.4	71.4	52.4
Spouse present	65.4	20.1	78.9	81.3	77.4	67.7	49.0
Widowed	4.2	0.1	0.6	2.8	7.6	17.9	38.5
Divorced	2.0	0.5	2.2	3.0	2.6	2.1	1.3
Female	100.0	100.0	100.0	100.0	100.0	100.0	100.0
Single	18.5	56.4	9.9	7.8	7.9	8.7	9.5
Married	67.0	42.4	84.5	77.6	65.0	43.9	18.7
Spouse present	63.4	39.5	80.4	73.5	61.6	41.2	16.7
Widowed	12.0	0.3	2.4	11.1	24.7	46.1	71.2
Divorced	2.4	1.0	3.1	3.5	2.4	1.4	0.6

SOURCES: U.S. Bureau of the Census, *Current Population Reports*, series P-20, no. 410 (November 1986), Table 1; 1950 Census of Population, *U.S. Summary: Detailed Characteristics*, series PC-D, Table 104.

NOTE: Dash denotes that figure rounds to 0.0.

few years behind the proportions of married men and women. Divorce rises sharply through the 30s, reaches a peak at about age 40, and then drops off gradually. The proportion of widows is relatively low up to the mid 40s and then increases rapidly through the rest of the life cycle. The proportion of widowers becomes substantial only after age 65, but remains below the proportion of widows throughout the older ages.

Three in 4 men aged 65 and over were married and lived with their wives in 1985; only 1 in 7 was widowed. On the other hand, only 2 in 5 women aged 65 and over were married and living with a husband and about 1 in 2 was widowed. In addition, 1.5 percent of the men and 1.0 percent of the women were living together as members of unmarried couples. (See also Figure 6.1)

The marital distribution of the population shifts notably with advancing age in the older age range, particularly for women (Table 6.2). The decrease after age 55 in the proportion of married women living with their husbands is abrupt compared with the gentle decline in the proportion of married men living with their wives. In 1980, only 1 in 16 women aged 85 and over was married and living with her husband, while nearly 1 in 2 women aged 65–74 was currently married. On the other hand, about 4 in 10 men aged 85 and over were married and living with their wives, while at ages 65–74 the proportion was 8 in 10. The rise in the proportions of men and women who are widowed at ages 65 and over complements the decline in the proportions married. At ages 85 and over, four fifths of the women are widowed compared with less than one half of the men.

This general pattern applies to whites and blacks alike. A comparison of the figures shows, however, that much higher proportions of elderly whites are married and much higher proportions of elderly blacks are widowed. This pattern of black-white variation applies in marked degree at ages 65–74. About 64 percent of whites at these ages were married and living with their spouses in 1985 compared with 44 percent of blacks. The complementary figures on widowhood are 25 percent for whites and 58 percent for blacks.

The marital composition of elderly men underwent substantial changes between 1950 and 1984. There was a marked increase in the proportion married and a marked decline in the proportion widowed, in spite of the aging of the elderly male population. The proportion widowed dropped from 24 percent to 14 percent while the proportion married rose from 66 percent to 78 percent. Most of the change in the marital distribution of elderly men occurred in the 1950–1960 decade and in the 1970–1985 period. The changes in the marital distribution of elderly women between 1950 and 1985 were small in comparison. They consisted of slight rises in the proportions married and divorced and slight declines in the proportions widowed and single.

FIGURE 6.1

Distribution of the Male and Female Populations Aged 65 and Over, by Marital Status: 1988 and 1950

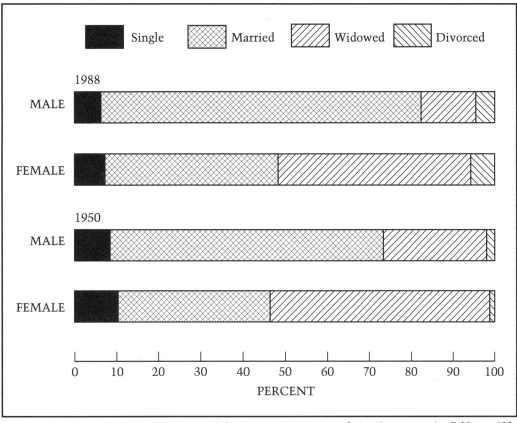

SOURCE: Table 6.1 for 1950; U.S. Bureau of the Census, *Current Population Reports*, series P-20, no. 433, for 1988.

NOTE: Excludes institutional population in 1988.

These shifts resulted partly from the increase in the tendency to marry in the early decades of this century prior to World War II and partly from the increase in the chances of joint survival of married partners in later decades. For example, the proportion of males married at ages 25–29 rose from 56 percent to 63 percent between 1910 and 1940 and the proportions never married in these same cohorts at ages 45–49 fell from 11 percent to 7 percent between 1930 and 1960. The chances for joint survival of marriage partners, say for 10 years at ages 60 (males) and 57 (females), rose from 58 percent in 1950 to 66 percent in 1980.

TABLE 6.2

Marital Distribution of the Population Aged 65 and Over, by Age and Sex: 1950–1980

Marital Status	Male				Female			
	Ages 65 and Over	Ages 65–74	Ages 75–84	Ages 85 and Over	Ages 65 and Over	Ages 65–74	Ages 75–84	Ages 85 and Over
1950								
Total	100.0	100.0	100.0	100.0	100.0	100.0	100.0	100.0
Single	8.4	8.6	7.9	7.7	8.9	8.7	9.4	9.7
Married	65.7	71.4	55.4	33.6	35.7	43.9	21.0	7.0
Spouse present	62.1	67.7	51.9	30.4	33.2	41.2	18.9	5.3
Widowed	24.1	17.9	35.4	57.9	54.3	46.1	68.9	82.9
Divorced	1.9	2.1	1.4	0.8	1.1	1.4	0.7	0.4
1960								
Total	100.0	100.0	100.0	100.0	100.0	100.0	100.0	100.0
Single	7.7	7.7	7.8	7.1	8.5	8.1	9.0	9.6
Married	70.8	76.7	61.1	38.7	37.4	46.2	23.5	8.2
Spouse present	67.0	73.0	57.1	34.2	34.7	43.3	21.1	6.3
Widowed	19.1	13.0	29.2	52.8	52.1	43.3	66.0	81.4
Divorced	2.3	2.5	2.0	1.4	2.0	2.4	1.4	0.8
1970								
Total	100.0	100.0	100.0	100.0[a]	100.0	100.0	100.0	100.0[a]
Single	7.5	7.2	7.4	8.3	8.1	7.6	8.5	9.5
Married	72.4	78.6	65.0	42.4	36.5	46.6	23.8	9.9
Spouse present	68.3	74.9	60.4	36.7	33.9	43.9	21.4	7.7
Widowed	17.1	10.9	25.0	47.0	52.2	42.0	65.2	79.0
Divorced	3.0	3.3	2.6	2.3	3.2	3.8	2.5	1.6

TABLE 6.2 (continued)

Marital Status	Male				Female			
	Ages 65 and Over	Ages 65–74	Ages 75–84	Ages 85 and Over	Ages 65 and Over	Ages 65–74	Ages 75–84	Ages 85 and Over
1980								
Total	100.0	100.0	100.0	100.0	100.0	100.0	100.0	100.0
Single	5.5	5.4	5.7	5.6	6.7	6.2	7.1	7.9
Married	76.3	81.6	70.3	48.4	37.5	49.4	24.9	8.4
Spouse present	72.5	78.4	65.9	41.1	35.0	46.9	22.5	6.1
Widowed	14.6	8.9	21.0	43.8	51.7	39.3	64.8	81.8
Divorced	3.6	4.1	3.0	2.1	4.2	5.1	3.3	2.0

SOURCES: U.S. Bureau of the Census, 1950–1980 Censuses of Population, U.S. Summary, series PC-D, Tables 264, 203, 176, and 102 in 1980, 1970, 1960, and 1950, respectively.

[a] Based on Public Use Microdata Sample for ages 85–99 only, provided by I. Rosenwaike, University of Pennsylvania.

Part of the actual increase in joint survival resulted from a small narrowing of the age gap between marriage partners. This effect was partially offset by a decrease in the tendency to marry or remarry in middle and older age and by an increase in the tendency to divorce. This is suggested by the drop of 32 percent in the marriage rate of unmarried women aged 45 and over between 1950 and 1982 and by the rise of 35 percent in the divorce rate of married women aged 45–49 between 1970 and 1982.[1]

Age Cycle of Proportions Married and Widowed

Users of census data commonly make inferences regarding the age cycle for marital status or other demographic phenomena on the basis of the variation of the proportions or rates for the phenomenon by age in a particular calendar year. Yet, as a description of the age cycle of the demographic characteristic or event, such period, or cross-sectional, analysis is likely to be misleading. The age cycle for a real cohort may differ substantially. Moreover, the apparent age cycle based on cross-sectional data is likely to vary from year to year.

The age cycles for real cohorts also differ from one birth cohort to another since, in addition to age effects, they are each subject to cohort effects (i.e., variations from birth cohort to birth cohort resulting from differences in the characteristics and experiences of specific cohorts) and period effects (i.e., variations in the age cycle from year to year resulting from common historical influences in particular years). The average of the age-to-age percent changes in the proportions married for each pair of adjacent ages, for a series of birth cohorts—in this case spanning the four 10-year periods from 1940 to 1980—is presumed to be essentially free of cohort effects and period effects. The averages represent a generalization of the age-to-age percent changes for birth cohorts in the proportion married in recent decades. The basic figures are shown in Appendix Table 6A.1, the derived figures are shown in Appendix Table 6A.2, and Appendix 6A describes the procedure in more detail.

These generalized age-to-age percent changes in the proportion married over the age cycle have been converted to generalized percentages married at each age in the age cycle, first, by establishing average figures

---

[1]To reflect the joint effect of marriage formation and dissolution in the older age range, we should employ a net marriage rate, such as the number of marriages of persons aged 45 and over per 1,000 unmarried population 45 and over, minus the number of divorces and "widowings" of persons aged 45 and over per 1,000 married persons 45 and over. The data necessary for computing this type of measure are not available, however.

for the proportions married at certain younger ages as starting values and, then, by applying the generalized age-to-age percent changes sequentially to these averages and the resulting figures for the proportions married at each age. The average of the proportions married at ages 25–29 and the average for ages 30–34, for the five census years, 1940–1980, were adopted as starting values. The generalized cohort age cycle derived in this way is presented in Table 6.3 in juxtaposition to the corresponding generalized period "age cycle," which uses the same starting values for ages 25–29 and 30–34 as the cohort age cycle.[2]

The comparison between the generalized cohort and period age cycles suggests that, over this 40-year period, the cohort age cycle for the proportion married shows less diminution of the proportion with increasing age after ages 50–54 than would be inferred from the period age cycle. The relatively low proportions of men and women married in later life shown by the period cycle reflect, in part, the lower marriage rates of cohorts born early in this century and, in part, the greater mortality of marriage partners in those cohorts.

A similar analysis of the proportions widowed indicates that the cross-sectional data on widowhood, while describing the variation of widowhood by age within single calendar years, grossly misrepresents the age-to-age shifts of widowhood for real cohorts in the post-1940 era (Table 6.4). The cohort proportions exhibit a much smaller rise at the older ages than the period proportions. The more rapid rise in the period data reflects the mixture of the experience of younger and older cohorts, the former of which experienced lower mortality levels as they moved through the age cycle than the latter. This suggests that the rise in widowhood with advancing age has become more and more attenuated and that younger cohorts of today may show even lower proportions of widowhood when they reach the older ages than today's older cohorts.

Factors Contributing to Differences Between the Sexes

Of the several factors responsible for the higher proportion of married men than married women in the older population and the higher proportion of widows than widowers, the major factor is the much higher mortality of married men than married women. The effect of this difference is sharpened by the fact that husbands are typically a few years

[2]Alternatively, data for 10-year age groups at 10-year intervals from 1940 to 1980 from the census or data for 5-year age groups at 5-year time periods from 1950 to 1985 from the Current Population Survey could have been used to develop generalized cohort and period age cycles for the postwar period.

TABLE 6.3
Period and Cohort Generalized Age Cycles for Percentages Married, by Sex: 1940–1980

Age	Male Period	Male Cohort	Female Period	Female Cohort
25–29 [a]	70.5	70.5	79.0	79.0
30–34 [a]	81.8	81.8	84.7	83.7
35–39	86.0	85.9	83.7	82.7
40–44	86.5	84.2	83.3	82.3
45–49	87.1	85.4	81.2	78.9
50–54	85.5	85.3	76.5	75.8
55–59	84.7	83.0	70.7	69.3
60–64	81.8	83.7	61.8	62.4
65–69	78.3	75.9	51.0	51.6
70–74	72.2	79.4	38.5	40.7
75–79	64.7	60.4	26.6	28.4
80–84	53.8	68.9	15.7	17.7
85 and Over	39.2	45.0	8.0	9.2

SOURCES: Based on Tables 6A.1 and 6A.2.

NOTE: Based on decennial census data.

[a] Anchor ages. Percentages married are averages for 1940–1980.

TABLE 6.4

Period and Cohort Generalized Age Cycles for Percentages Widowed, by Sex:
1940–1980

Age	Male				Female			
	Period		Cohort		Period		Cohort	
45–49[a]	1.8		1.8		7.4		7.4	
50–54[a]		3.0		3.0		11.9		11.9
55–59	4.7		3.6		18.8		16.2	
60–64		7.6		6.1		27.8		24.9
65–69	12.1		7.6		40.2		31.8	
70–74		18.4		12.2		52.4		43.8
75–79	27.6		14.6		66.1		49.9	
80–84		39.7		22.5		76.4		61.7
85 and Over	57.4		26.8		86.0		63.5	

SOURCES: Based on Tables 6A.1 and 6A.2.

NOTE: Based on decennial census data.

[a]Anchor ages. Percentages widowed are averages for 1940–1980.

older than their wives. The median difference between the ages of husbands and wives for husbands aged 55–74 in 1984 was 3.0 to 3.5 years.[3] (See Table 6.5.) The median ages at marriage, for women aged 40 and over marrying in 1965, differed by about 3.5 to 4.0 years from those of their male marriage partners.[4]

An indication of the current differences in the death rates of older married men and their wives may be secured by comparing the death rates for married men in various older age groups with those for married women 2.5 years younger, for 1979–1981. The comparison is shown in Table 6.6. Death rates for husbands run over two times greater than those for wives at the older ages. A similar comparison for 1949–1951 implies that the mortality gap between husbands and wives widened in the three decades from 1950 to 1980, as the mortality gap between men and women generally widened. This factor largely accounts for the divergent trends in the widowhood of men and women during this period.

Another factor accounting for the higher proportion of widows than widowers and the higher proportion of married men than married women is the higher remarriage rate of widowers. In 1982, the reported remarriage rate (remarriages per 1,000 widowed and divorced persons) at ages

[3]U.S. Bureau of the Census, *Current Population Reports,* series P-20, no. 398 (April 1985), Table 17.
[4]U.S. National Center for Health Statistics, *Vital Statistics of the United States, 1976,* vol. 3: *Marriage and Divorce,* 1980, Table 1-7.

TABLE 6.5

Percent Distribution of Husbands Aged 55 and Over, by Age of Wife, and of Wives Aged 55 and Over, by Age of Husband: 1984

Age	All Ages	Ages Under 55	Ages 55–64	Ages 65–74	Ages 75 and Over	Median
		Percentage of Husbands by Age of Wife				
Age of husband						
55–64	100.0	35.7	59.8	4.3	0.2	56.9
65–74	100.0	4.5	38.4	53.9	3.2	66.0
75 and over	100.0	0.8	6.8	41.7	50.7	74.6[a]
		Percentage of Wives by Age of Husband				
Age of Wife						
55–64	100.0	4.9	65.1	27.8	2.2	62.4
65–74	100.0	0.6	8.3	68.0	23.1	71.4
75 and over	100.0	0.3	1.0	12.6	86.1	80.0[a]

SOURCE: Based on U.S. Bureau of the Census, *Current Population Reports*, series P-20, no. 398 (April 1985), Table 17.

[a] Calculated from 1980 census data.

65 and over was 18 for widowers and 2 for widows.[5] The reported remarriage rate at ages 45–64 was 59 for widowers and 12 for widows. These figures indicate not only the wide gap in the remarriage rates of older men and women (9 to 1 and 5 to 1, respectively) but also the relative infrequency of marriage among elderly persons, particularly women.[6] About four fifths of the marriages of women and nearly three quarters of those of men aged 65 and over are marriages of widowed persons; few single and divorced persons marry after age 55.

The higher remarriage rates of elderly widowers than of elderly widows is a result of social norms that encourage elderly men to marry younger women, particularly women under age 65 (and discourage the opposite), a stronger motivation for men to remarry, and the relatively large pool of unmarried older women from which a partner can be selected compared with the relatively small pool of unmarried older men. The demographic advantage of older men in the marriage market is considerable.[7] In 1984 the proportion of unmarried women aged 65 and over

[5] U.S. National Center for Health Statistics, "Advance Report of Final Marriage Statistics, 1982," *Monthly Vital Statistics Report* 34 (3), Supplement (June 28, 1985).

[6] See also J. Treas and A. Van Hilst, "Marriage and Remarriage Rates Among Older Americans," *Gerontologist* 16 (2) (1976):132–136.

[7] For specific measures of mate availability at various ages from 20 to 64, see N. Goldman, C. F. Westoff, and C. Hammerslough, "Demography of the Marriage Market in

was more than 2.5 times as great as the proportion of unmarried men at these ages (Table 6.1), and unmarried women outnumbered unmarried men by 4 to 1, or nearly 7 million (Table 6.7).

As a result of the differences in the death rates of married men and married women, and in spite of the higher death rates of widows than wives (Table 6.8), most married women outlive their husbands by many years. At current death rates, married women who become widowed at age 65 outlive their husbands, on the average, by about 16 years, and married men who become widowed at age 68 outlive their wives by about 10 years.[8] Married women at age 65 are likely to outlive their husbands at age 68 by about 6 years on the average (without specification of a particular age at death of the husband or wife or the sex of the first decedent).[9] The surviving partner, if female, is highly likely to remain a widow until death because of the very low remarriage rate of widows at the higher ages.[10]

Living Arrangements

Various changes in living arrangements have accompanied the marital changes of the postwar decades described. Most outstanding has been the sharp increase in the proportion of elderly women living alone and the concomitant sharp decline in the proportion of elderly women living with other family members. There has been relatively little notable change in the living arrangements of elderly men, except possibly for the rise in the proportion of men living with spouses, associated with the decline in death rates, and the offsetting drop in the proportion living with other family members.

the United States," *Population Index* 50 (1) (Spring 1984):5–25. These authors point out that the age difference in marriage increases for older men while it remains the same for women as they age. Accordingly, older men draw on the large pool of younger women also.

[8]The figure for females was approximated by the life expectancy of females at age 65, adjusted for the difference between the mortality level of widowed women and all women, and the figure for males was approximated by the life expectancy of males at age 68, adjusted for the difference between the mortality level of widowed men and all men. This procedure allows for the fact that the men and women were married at the time of the death.

[9]Approximated by the difference between the life expectancy of married females who are widowed at age 65 and the life expectancy of married males who are widowed at age 68.

[10]The average duration of widowhood will be slightly lower than these figures indicate, particularly for males, because of remarriage. See the discussion of family life cycle.

TABLE 6.6

Comparative Mortality of Older Married Men and Women, by Age: 1979–1981, 1959–1961, and 1949–1951

Male		Female		Ratio, Male/Female		
Age[a]	Rate, 1979–1981[b]	Age[a]	Rate 1979–1981[b]	1979–1981	1959–1961	1949–1951
60.0–65.0	1925.6	57.5–62.5	793.4	2.43	2.34	1.99
65.0–70.0	2976.1	62.5–67.5	1170.7	2.54	2.21	1.87
70.0–75.0	4469.5	67.5–72.5	1765.5	2.53	1.99	1.74
75.0 and Over	8940.2	72.5 and Over	4043.6	2.21	1.75	1.56

SOURCES: 1979–1981: based on unpublished tabulations of the U.S. National Center for Health Statistics; 1959–1961 and 1949–1951: based on *Vital and Health Statistics*, series 20, nos. 8a and 8b (December 1970), and *Vital Statistics—Special Reports*, vol. 39, no. 7 (May 1956), Table 2.

[a]Exact ages.
[b]Per 100,000 population.

TABLE 6.7

Excess of Unmarried Women Aged 65 and Over, Over Unmarried Men Aged 65 and Over: 1950–2020

Year	Amount (in thousands)	As Percentage of Unmarried Female Population
Census or Estimates[a]		
1950	2,228	53.1
1960	3,433	61.7
1970	5,077	68.5
1980	7,096	74.5
1984[b]	6,982	74.6
Projections[c]		
1990	8,585	75.0
2000	9,639	74.6
2020	12,304	69.4

[a] Census figures except for 1984.
[b] CPS estimates.
[c] Based on figures of the U.S. Social Security Administration, Office of the Actuary, adjusted for consistency with the 1984 CPS data on marital distribution and the middle series of population projections of the U.S. Bureau of the Census.

Family Status

The living arrangements of older men and older women are quite different in several ways. A far larger share of elderly men than of elderly women live in families, that is, with one or more relatives. About 79 percent of men aged 65 and over and 53 percent of women aged 65 and over lived with one relative or more in 1985 (Table 6.9). Most elderly men (71 percent) are husbands in married-couple families; that is, they live in households maintained by themselves and their wives as co-householders. A very small proportion (3 percent) are "other male" family householders; that is, they live in households maintained by themselves only, without a spouse but with other relatives. In sharp contrast, only 35 percent of the women aged 65 and over are wives in married-couple families. Some are "other female" householders living with family members (9 percent), but the largest share consists of non-family householders (39 percent), who live alone or with one nonrelative or more.

The family status of elderly men and women was much more similar just after World War II and even in 1960. Between 1960 and 1985, however, the proportion of women living in families tended to fall (from

TABLE 6.8

Comparative Mortality of Older Persons According to Marital Status, by Age and Sex: 1979–1981 and 1949–1951

Age	Male					Female				
	All Classes	Single	Married	Widowed	Divorced	All Classes	Single	Married	Widowed	Divorced
1979–1981										
55–64	1.00	1.63	0.86	1.88	1.98	1.00	1.33	0.84	1.42	1.31
65–74	1.00	1.35	0.89	1.49	1.62	1.00	1.11	0.82	1.19	1.14
75 and over	1.00	1.23	0.87	1.40	2.15	1.00	1.08	0.63	1.11	0.90
1949–1951										
55–64	1.00	1.46	0.89	1.44	1.75	1.00	0.98	0.90	1.24	1.21
65–74	1.00	1.32	0.89	1.18	1.56	1.00	0.97	0.90	1.06	1.31
75 and over	1.00	1.15	0.84	1.16	1.45	1.00	1.02	0.75	1.05	1.27

SOURCES: 1979–1981: based on unpublished tabulations of the U.S. National Center for Health Statistics; 1949–1951: based on *Vital Statistics—Special Reports*, vol. 39, no. 7 (May 8, 1956), Table 2.

NOTE: Deaths rates are shown as index numbers based on the death rates of the total male or female population at each age.

TABLE 6.9

Percent Distribution by Family Status of the Population Aged 65 and Over, by Sex: 1960 and 1985

Family Status	Both Sexes 1985	Both Sexes 1960	Male 1985	Male 1960	Female 1985	Female 1960
Total	100.0	100.0	100.0	100.0	100.0	100.0
In Families	63.7	73.0	79.4	80.2	52.9	67.0
Householder	34.5	37.6	70.7	70.0	10.2	10.9
Married, spouse present	28.4	29.4	68.1	65.1	1.6	—
Other family householder	6.2	8.2	2.6	4.9	8.6	10.9
Spouse of householder	21.5	18.4	3.2	—	33.8	33.6
Other relative	7.5	16.9	5.4	10.1	8.9	22.5
Nonrelative of householder	0.1	0.1	0.1	0.1	—	—
Not in Families	36.4	27.0	20.6	19.8	47.1	32.9
Nonfamily householder	29.4	19.7	14.8	12.7	39.3	25.4
Other unrelated persons in household	1.1	2.5	1.6	2.6	0.7	2.4
Group quarters, total	5.9	4.8	4.2	4.5	7.1	5.1
Institutions	5.5	3.8	3.7	3.4	6.8	4.1
Other	0.4	1.0	0.5	1.0	0.3	1.0

SOURCES: 1985: U.S. Census Bureau, *Current Population Reports*, series P-20, no. 410 (November 1986), Table 2; 1960: 1960 Census of Population, *Special Reports*, PC (2)-4D, Table 2.

NOTES: 1985 data are based on the CPS; 1960 data are census data. Dash denotes that figure rounds to 0.0.

67 to 53 percent), while the proportion of men living in families remained essentially unchanged (80 percent in 1960). (See Table 6.9.) The decrease of women in families during this period resulted largely from the decrease in "other relatives," that is, women in families other than as co-householders in married-couple households or as householders (from 23 percent to 9 percent). The proportion of women who were co-householders hardly changed and the proportion of women who were "other family householders" showed a small decline. For men, small decreases in "other family householders" and "other relatives" were largely offset by a rise in co-householders (from 65 percent to 71 percent).

Persons Living Alone or with Nonrelatives

With advancing age above 55, there is a marked decline in the proportion of the population living in married-couple families and a concomitant increase in the proportion living alone and in the proportion living with other relatives. In 1980 at ages 60–64 the proportion of persons living alone was only 12 percent but, by ages 75 and over, it had grown to 34 percent. If nonrelatives in households are included, the proportion at ages 60–64 rises to 17 percent and that at ages 75 and over rises to 36 percent. A larger share of the population aged 65 and over lives alone (28 percent), or lives alone or with nonrelatives (30 percent), than any younger age group.

The proportion of elderly women living alone rises with advancing age far above the proportion for elderly men. Nearly 1 in 2 women aged 85 and over lived alone in 1980 compared with 1 in 3 aged 65–74. One in 4 men aged 85 and over lived alone compared with 1 in 7 aged 65–74. Living alone in later life is often viewed as problematic, but interpreting these and related figures in a positive light, we should be comforted by the remarkably large proportion of older-aged men and women who are able to maintain themselves independently. Most of the older-aged men and women not living alone, who are living in the community, are living with spouses or other relatives in households.

As the National Health Interview Survey (NHIS) 1984 Supplement on Aging and the 1985 Current Population Survey (CPS) show, the demographic characteristics of the elderly who live alone are sharply different from those of the elderly who live with others.[11] Four fifths of

[11]U.S. Bureau of the Census, "Marital Status and Living Arrangements: March 1985," *Current Population Reports*, series P-20, no. 410 (November 1986); and U.S. National Center for Health Statistics, "Aging in the Eighties, Age 65 Years and Over and Living Alone, Contacts with Family, Friends, and Neighbors, Preliminary Data from the Supplement on Aging to the National Health Interview Survey: United States, January–June 1984," by M. G. Kovar, *Vital and Health Statistics*, Advance Data, no. 116 (May 1986).

the elderly who live alone are women; only half of the elderly who live with others are women (Table 6.10). In addition, the elderly who live alone are older than other elderly. Their average age is 75.2 years compared with 73.4 years for other elderly. One half of the elderly solitary householders are aged 75 and over and more than one tenth are aged 85 and over compared with one third and one sixteenth, respectively, of those who live with others. More than three quarters of the elderly living alone are widows, while only one fifth of the elderly who live with others consist of widowed, divorced, and never-married women.

The elderly who live alone are more likely to be female, older, and widowed than the elderly who live with others for several interrelated reasons: A married person who has lost a mate is more likely to have been a wife than a husband before the event since death rates of wives are much lower than death rates of husbands; widowers are much more likely to remarry, and widows have a greater tendency than widowers to live alone or with relatives other than a spouse; persons who have lost their spouses are likely to be older than persons whose spouses are still living; and the households of the elderly living with others often include a spouse (77 percent), that is, these elderly are not likely to be widowed.

Since 1950, and especially since 1960, the proportion of elderly individuals, particularly women, who maintain their own households, living either alone or with nonrelatives, has increased sharply. Such "primary" individuals, or nonfamily householders, made up only 13 percent of the men and 25 percent of the women aged 65 and over in 1960, but by 1985 the shares had grown to 15 percent and 39 percent, respectively (Table 6.9). Over the last several decades, both older women and older men have been much less inclined to live with other people, whether relatives or nonrelatives, if they no longer had a spouse. This change is most marked for aged women and for the years since 1960. Specifically, about 26 percent of the women aged 75 and over lived alone in 1960 compared with about 50 percent in 1985 (Table 6.10). At the same time the share living with persons other than a spouse (principally other relatives) fell precipitously from 54 percent to 27 percent.

Some of the increase in the number of elderly women living alone results from the increase in the number of elderly persons and shifts in marital composition, but the bulk of it is accounted for by a rise in the proportion of solitary householders.[12] There has been an increased tendency for older persons who do not have spouses to live separately—that is, to live apart from children, other relatives, and nonrelatives (Figure 6.2). The trend toward independent living could have resulted partly

---

[12]F. E. Kobrin, "The Fall of Household Size and the Rise of the Primary Individual in the United States," *Demography* 13 (1) (February 1976):127–138.

TABLE 6.10

Living Arrangements of the Population Aged 65 and Over, by Age and Sex: 1960 and 1985
(noninstitutional population; numbers in thousands)

Age and Living Arrangements	Population, 1985			Percent Distribution					
				1985			1960		
	Both Sexes	Male	Female	Both Sexes	Male	Female	Both Sexes	Male	Female
65 and Over	26,818	11,014	15,804	100.0	100.0	100.0	100.0	100.0	100.0
Living									
Alone	8,112	1,614	6,498	30.2	14.7	41.1	18.6	12.1	24.1
With spouse	14,317	8,260	6,057	53.4	75.0	38.3	51.1	69.2	36.2
With other relatives	3,738	823	2,913	13.9	7.5	18.4	24.8	13.9	33.9
With nonrelatives only	651	317	336	2.4	2.9	2.1	5.5	4.8	5.7
65–74	16,576	7,259	9,317	100.0	100.0	100.0	100.0	100.0	100.0
Living									
Alone	4,130	868	3,262	24.9	12.0	35.0	17.3	10.7	23.0
With spouse	10,306	5,729	4,577	62.2	78.9	49.1	58.2	74.6	44.2
With other relatives	1,757	452	1,303	10.6	6.2	14.0	19.6	10.3	27.8
With nonrelatives only	383	210	175	2.3	2.9	1.9	4.9	4.4	5.0
75 and Over	10,242	3,755	6,487	100.0	100.0	100.0	100.0	100.0	100.0
Living									
Alone	3,982	746	3,236	38.9	19.9	49.9	21.4	15.1	26.2
With spouse	4,011	2,531	1,480	39.2	67.4	22.8	36.1	56.9	20.1
With other relatives	1,981	371	1,610	19.3	9.9	24.8	35.8	22.1	46.3
With nonrelatives only	268	107	161	2.6	2.8	2.5	6.7	5.9	7.3

SOURCES: 1985: U.S. Bureau of the Census, *Current Population Reports*, series P-20, no. 410 (November 1986), Table A-12; 1960: 1960 Census of Population, *Subject Reports*, PC (2)-4B, Tables 2 and 15.

NOTE: 1985 data are based on the CPS; 1960 data are census data.

FIGURE 6.2

Living Arrangements of the Population Aged 65–74 and 75 Years and Over:
1960–1985

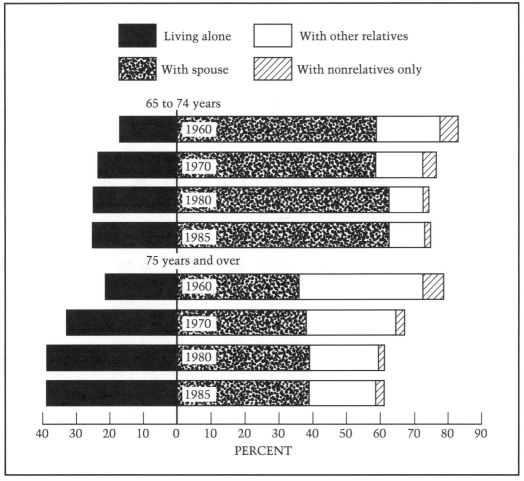

SOURCE: U.S. Bureau of the Census, *Current Population Reports*, series P-20, no. 410 (November 1986), Table A-12.

NOTE: Excludes institutional population.

from demographic shifts, partly from improvements in economic and health status, and partly from a desire for privacy and freedom from dependence on others. Since the influence of demographic and economic factors has been modest, it may be inferred that cultural influences—

that is, an increase in the desire or taste for privacy and independence in itself—have been the principal factor in the transition.[13]

The pattern and trend described are more characteristic of whites than blacks. Aged white women are much more likely to live alone than aged black women (51 percent versus 39 percent). The latter are much more likely than the former to live with other family members if they have no husband (49 percent versus 29 percent). We can only speculate as to whether this difference is a sign of family solidarity or, alternatively, a sign of greater economic need and physical dependency.

Trends in Number of Older Households

In 1985, 18.2 million households were maintained by a person aged 65 and over. Because of the decreasing size of households, the number of elderly households has been growing more rapidly than the number of elderly persons. Like the population, among elderly households the older households are growing more rapidly than the younger households. Between 1975 and 1985, for example, households headed by persons aged 75 and over increased by 37 percent while households headed by persons aged 65–74 increased by only 22 percent.

The rate of growth of elderly households steadily diminished between 1950 and 1970 but has fluctuated since 1970. According to projections prepared by the Census Bureau, household growth will be somewhat smaller in the 1990s than in the 1980s (11 percent compared with 23 percent) and far smaller than in the 1950s, when the number of elderly households increased by 46 percent. A series of estimates and projections of older households for age groups, 1950–2000, are given in Table 6.11.[14]

Family and Nonfamily Households

In 1985, only 54 percent of the households maintained by persons aged 65 and over were family households[15] (Table 6.12). Over 80 percent

---

[13] L. L. Santi, "Household Headship Among Unmarried Persons in the United States, 1970–1985," *Demography* 27 (2) (May 1990):219–232.

[14] In developing the projections of households, the Census Bureau utilized CPS data from 1959 to 1985 for various marital and household categories (130 age-sex-marital-household status groups). Projections of the 130 series were derived by a combination of statistical time series modeling and demographic analysis. Series A, B, and C assume different rates of change in each set of 130 series. The marital-household proportions were applied to middle population projections of the Census Bureau.

[15] Family and nonfamily households are distinguished by whether or not the householder has a relative in the household. The variations and trends described are affected to a small extent by the change in the way householders were identified in the census of

of the family households and 45 percent of all households consisted of married-couple households. The other leading household type among the elderly was nonfamily households maintained by women, which made up 37 percent of all households and 80 percent of nonfamily households. Considerably smaller proportions of households were maintained by female family householders with no husband present and by male non-family householders.

Following a gradual drop in the young adult years, there is a steady rise in the percentage of households maintained by women (not in married couples) as the age of the householder moves above ages 35–39. According to the 1980 census, the proportion exceeded 25 percent by ages 60–64 and 50 percent by ages 75–79. The rise with advancing age in the proportion of households maintained by women was evident in 1950, but it has become steeper in recent decades. In 1950 the proportion did not cross 25 percent until ages 65–69 and remained below 50 percent at all higher ages. As a result, actual birth cohorts show a much more rapid rise, with advancing age, in the proportion of households maintained by women than the current cross-sectional data. For example, the proportion of female householders increased from ages 35–44 to ages 65–74 in 1980 by 21 percentage points, but the birth cohort aged 35–44 in 1950 showed an increase of 34 points up to ages 65–74 in 1980. Assuming the same age-to-age cohort progression as in the recent past, we can expect the percentage of households maintained by women at the older ages to continue to rise rapidly.

Households with elderly householders tend to be small, especially those headed by a man or woman without spouse present. In 1984 the number of persons per household with householders aged 65 and over was only three fifths as great as the number of persons per household with householders aged 18–64.

Age of Householder	All Households	Married-Couple Householders	Male Householders	Female Householders
All Ages	2.71	3.32	1.61	1.96
65 and Over	1.76	2.28	1.36	1.34
18–64	3.02	3.56	1.64	2.30
Ratio (per 100)	58.3	64.0	82.9	58.3

SOURCE: U.S. Bureau of Census, *Current Population Reports*, series P-20, no. 398 (April 1985); Table 22.

1980 and in the CPS beginning in 1980. From that year a male or female member of a married couple could be designated the householder; previously, the male member of the couple was routinely designated head of the household. Households headed by married couples are now classified as married-couple households. I have referred to the members of these married couples as co-householders. Tabulations of the family status of persons show the members of the married couple as householder and spouse of householder.

TABLE 6.11

Estimates and Projections of Households Maintained by Persons Aged 55 and Over, by Age: 1950–2000 (numbers in thousands)

	Ages 55–64			Ages 65–74			Ages 75 and Over		
		Change in Preceding Period			Change in Preceding Period			Change in Preceding Period	
Year	Number	Amount	Percent	Number	Amount	Percent	Number	Amount	Percent
1950	7,492	X	X	NA	X	X	NA	X	X
1955	7,919	+427	+5.7	NA	NA	NA	NA	NA	NA
1960	8,599	+680	+8.6	6,380	NA	NA	3,045	NA	NA
1965	9,600	+1,001	+11.6	7,173	+793	+12.4	3,790	+745	+24.5
1970	10,824	+1,224	+12.8	7,744	+571	+8.0	4,756	+966	+25.5
1975	11,301	+477	+4.4	8,910	+1,166	+15.1	5,350	+594	+12.5
1980	12,525	+1,224	+10.8	10,112	+1,202	+13.5	6,432	+1,082	+20.2
1985	13,073	+548	+4.4	10,851	+739	+7.3	7,305	+873	+13.6
Series B[a]									
1990[b]	12,311	−714	−5.5	11,672	+770	+7.1	8,724	+1,330	+18.2
1995	12,233	−78	−0.6	12,006	+334	+2.9	9,876	+1,152	+13.2
2000	13,903	+1,670	+13.7	11,516	−490	−4.1	11,126	+1,250	+12.7
Series A									
1990[b]	12,345	−683	−5.2	11,746	+852	+7.8	8,793	+1,417	+19.2
1995	12,279	−66	−0.5	12,120	+374	+3.2	10,014	+1,221	+13.9
2000	13,947	+1,668	+13.6	11,627	−493	−4.1	11,326	+1,312	+13.1
Series C									
1990[b]	12,272	−751	−5.7	11,588	+691	+6.4	8,649	+1,260	+17.2
1995	12,166	−106	−0.9	11,849	+261	+2.3	9,715	+1,066	+12.3
2000	13,805	+1,639	+13.5	11,311	−538	−4.5	10,867	+1,152	+11.9

SOURCES: 1950–1985, U.S. Bureau of the Census, *Current Population Reports,* series P-20, various numbers; 1990–2000, U.S. Bureau of the Census, *Current Population Reports,* series P-25, no. 986 (May 1986).

NOTES: Reference date is March 1 for estimates and July 1 for projections. Estimates based on the CPS.

X = not applicable. NA = not available.

[a] Series B is the middle series.
[b] Change has been adjusted to a five-year period.

Moreover, the size of older households declines gradually with increasing age of the householder. According to 1980 census data, the decline was from 2.4 persons for households with male householders (including those reported in married-couple households) aged 55–59 to 1.8 persons for households with male householders aged 85 and over, and from 1.5 to 1.1 persons for households with female householders (including those

TABLE 6.11 *(continued)*

| | Ages 65 and Over | | | All Ages | | |
| | Change in Preceding Period | | | Change in Preceding Period | |
Number	Amount	Percent	Number	Amount	Percent
6,456	X	X	43,554	X	X
7,898	+1,442	+22.3	47,874	+4,320	+9.9
9,425	+1,527	+19.3	52,799	+4,925	+10.3
10,963	+1,538	+16.3	57,436	+4,637	+8.8
12,500	+1,537	+14.0	63,401	+5,965	+10.4
14,260	+1,760	+14.1	71,120	+7,719	+12.2
16,544	+2,284	+16.0	80,776	+9,656	+13.6
18,156	+1,612	+9.7	86,789	+6,013	+7.4
20,396	+2,100	+11.6	94,227	+6,973	+8.0
21,882	+1,486	+7.3	100,308	+6,081	+6.5
22,642	+760	+3.5	105,933	+5,625	+5.6
20,539	+2,234	+12.3	95,243	+7,926	+9.1
22,134	+1,595	+7.8	102,785	+7,542	+7.9
22,953	+819	+3.7	110,217	+7,432	+7.2
20,237	+1,951	+10.7	93,297	+6,101	+7.0
21,564	+1,327	+6.6	98,180	+4,883	+5.2
22,178	+614	+2.8	102,440	+4,260	+4.3

reported in married-couple households) of the corresponding ages. These figures reflect a substantial drop in size of household with advancing age for male-headed households, but only a moderate drop for female-headed households. The much greater size of male-headed elderly households than female-headed elderly households is a result of the fact that the former include mainly married-couple households (in which men were nearly always reported as the householder), while the latter consist mainly of women living alone.

The average size of elderly households has been falling sharply as the share of householders living alone has grown and the share of householders living with relatives or nonrelatives has fallen. The small and declining size of households maintained by older persons has particular

TABLE 6.12

Percent Distribution of Households, by Type, for Households Maintained by Persons Aged 55 and Over, by Age Group: 1960, 1985, and 2000

Year and Age	All Households	Family Households		Other Family Households		Nonfamily Households		
		Total	Married Couple	Male Householder	Female Householder	Total	Male Householder	Female Householder
1960 (April Census)								
55–64	100.0	79.5	68.5	2.7	8.4	20.5	6.5	14.0
65 and over	100.0	65.6	51.4	3.9	10.4	34.4	10.0	24.4
65–74	100.0	68.7	56.0	3.2	9.5	31.3	8.9	22.4
75 and over	100.0	58.9	41.1	5.3	12.4	41.1	12.4	28.8
1985 (March CPS)								
55–64	100.0	74.9	63.9	2.4	8.7	25.1	8.2	16.9
65 and over	100.0	54.1	44.5	1.6	8.0	45.9	9.3	36.6
65–74	100.0	60.6	51.8	1.6	7.3	39.4	8.4	30.9
75 and over	100.0	44.2	33.4	1.6	9.1	55.8	10.5	45.3
2000 (July 1)[a]								
55–64	100.0	74.0	63.3	2.6	8.1	26.0	10.2	15.8
65 and over	100.0	50.9	42.7	1.4	6.9	49.1	10.6	38.4
65–74	100.0	59.1	51.4	1.4	6.2	40.9	9.8	31.1
75 and over	100.0	42.5	33.6	1.3	7.6	57.5	11.4	46.0

SOURCES: Based on unpublished tabulations of the U.S. Bureau of the Census, consistent with *Current Population Reports*, series P-25, no. 986 (May 1986); *Current Population Reports*, series P-20, no. 411 (September 1986), Table D; 1960 Census of Population, *U.S. Summary: Detailed Characteristics*, PC(1)-1D, Table 181.

[a] Series B projections.

implications for their housing needs and hence for the development of housing plans and policies. A household consisting of one or two persons clearly needs less space than a married couple with children. Consumption patterns in general are different for smaller households, especially one-person households. There are implications for health, social support, and other areas as well, including particularly the availability and demand for formal health and other social services.

Prospects Relating to Marital Composition and Living Arrangements

Whether the trends described with respect to marital composition, living arrangements, and household composition will continue in the future will depend on several factors: the evolution of attitudes regarding marriage, divorce, and living together; future changes in the economic and social status of women; shifting attitudes with regard to living alone or with others; the prospects for the reduction of mortality, especially in later life; and, quite important, the prospects for the convergence of male and female death rates.

According to projections prepared by the Social Security Administration, the marital composition of the elderly population will show little change between 1984 and 2000, except for moderate rises in the shares of divorced men and women.[16] As a result, the numbers of married and widowed men and women will grow at about the same rates. Between 2000 and 2020, however, with the arrival of the first baby-boom cohorts, the scene is expected to be quite different. The shares of single and divorced persons, especially single men and divorced women, will rise sharply while the shares of widowed men and women will fall sharply.

According to the projections prepared by the Census Bureau, the proportion of all elderly households that are maintained by married couples is expected to decline slightly between 1985 (45 percent) and 2000 (43 percent). (See Table 6.12.) During the same period the proportion of elderly households in which the householder is an elderly male living alone or with nonrelatives is expected to increase slightly (from 9 percent to 11 percent). The proportion of elderly households in which the householder is an elderly female living alone or with nonrelatives is also projected to change little from now (37 percent) until the end of the century (38 percent). All types of households with householders aged 75 and over are expected to show only modest or negligible shifts.

---

[16]U.S. Social Security Administration, Office of the Actuary, "*Social Security Area Population Projections, 1984*," by A. Wade, *Actuarial Study* no. 92 (May 1984).

The author's view is that these projections greatly understate the probable future increase in the share of elderly households headed by women living alone. It seems likely that at least 40 percent of the households maintained by persons aged 65 and over will be headed by women living alone or with nonrelatives in 2000. By 2000, over 50 percent of the households with householders aged 75 and over will be headed by women living alone or with nonrelatives. Over 60 percent of the women aged 75 and over may be living alone or with nonrelatives. Marginal living arrangements such as cohabitation of unmarried couples, which now characterize only a very small proportion of the elderly population, are expected to increase, but only slowly.

Elderly Households and Aging of Households

We can examine societal aging through aggregate changes in the number and characteristics of families and households as units as well as through aggregate changes in the number and characteristics of individuals. For this purpose, we track the trend of societal aging by changes in the proportion of elderly households—that is, households with a householder aged 65 or older.

The relative frequency of elderly households has increased sharply in the last several decades. The proportion of elderly households among all households increased from 15 percent in 1950 to 21 percent in 1985 (Table 6.13). Increases were actually limited to married-couple households and nonfamily households maintained by women; the proportions for other types of households dropped sharply in this period (Table 6.14). The basis for these changes is, in the case of married-couple households, the continuing reduction in mortality, which has helped to extend the period of joint married life and the greater tendency of couples to live apart; and where a marriage partner has died, the greater desire of elderly persons, especially women, to live independently.

The aged and even the older aged have tended more and more to run their own households. Households maintained by persons aged 75 and over and 85 and over constituted only 4 percent and 0.5 percent of all households, respectively, in 1950, but the percentages have been rising steadily since that time and by 1980 stood at 8 percent and 1.4 percent. At mid decade 8.4 percent of all households were headed by persons aged 75 and over.

Changes in the median age of householders and changes in the proportion of households with at least one elderly member tell a different story about the trend in the aging of households (Table 6.13). These trends

TABLE 6.13

Percentage of All Households Maintained by Persons Aged 55 and Over, by Age: 1950–2000

Year	Ages 55 and Over	Ages 65 and Over	Ages 75 and Over	Median Age
1950	32.0	14.8	NA	46.0
1955	33.0	16.5	5.0	46.5
1960	34.1	17.9	5.8	47.3
1965	35.8	19.1	6.6	47.9
1970	36.8	19.7	7.5	48.1
1975	35.9	20.1	7.5	47.3
1980	36.0	20.5	8.0	46.1
1985	36.0	20.9	8.4	45.4
Series B				
1990	34.7	21.6	9.3	45.0
1995	34.0	21.8	9.8	46.1
2000	34.5	21.4	10.5	47.4
Series A				
2000	33.5	20.8	10.3	47.0
Series C				
2000	35.1	21.6	10.6	47.6

SOURCES: Based on U.S. Bureau of the Census, *Current Population Reports*, series P-20, various numbers; series P-25, no. 986.

NOTES: Data from the CPS. Projections are based on the population excluding armed forces overseas and in barracks in the United States.

have not paralleled the trend in the proportion of elderly households closely. The median age of householders has fluctuated; it was 45 years in 1985, 48 years in 1970, and 46 years in 1950. Only the median age of householders in married-couple households and the median age of female nonfamily householders rose steadily in this period, as occurred with the proportion of elderly households. The proportion of households with at least one elderly member has been rising, but more slowly than the proportion of elderly households. An estimated 23 percent of households had a member aged 65 or older in 1985 compared with an estimated 21 percent in 1950 (Table 6.15).

About 20.1 million households included an elderly member in 1985. In addition to the 18.2 million households maintained by elderly persons, about 2.0 million other households (2 percent of the total) included an elderly member (Table 6.15). Just after World War II, when a much smaller proportion of households were headed by elderly persons

TABLE 6.14

Percentage of All Households with Householders Aged 65 and Over, by Age and Type of Household: 1985, 1980, and 1960

| | | Family Households | | | | Nonfamily Households | | |
| | | | | | Other Family Households | | | | |
Age and Year	Total Households	Total	Married Couple	Male Householder	Female Householder	Total	Male Householder	Female Householder
1985 CPS								
65 and over	20.9	15.6	16.0	13.2	14.4	34.7	16.7	47.7
75 and over	8.4	5.1	4.8	5.3	6.6	16.9	7.6	23.7
1980 Census								
65 and over	20.0	14.9	14.9	15.6	15.0	34.3	17.1	46.9
75 and over	7.6	4.6	4.2	6.7	6.5	16.1	7.6	22.2
85 and over	1.4	0.7	0.5	1.8	1.5	3.2	1.7	4.3
1960 Census								
65 and over	17.5	13.5	12.1	28.2	23.2	39.9	31.1	45.3
75 and over	5.4	3.7	3.0	12.0	8.6	14.8	11.9	16.5
85 and over	0.7	0.4	0.3	2.4	1.4	1.9	1.7	2.1

SOURCES: Based on U.S. Bureau of the Census, *Current Population Reports*, series P-20, no. 411 (September 1986), Table D; 1980 Census of Population, *U.S. Summary: Detailed Characteristics*, PC80-1-D1-A, Table 265; 1960 Census of Population, *U.S. Summary: Detailed Characteristics*, PC(1)-1D, Table 181.

TABLE 6.15

Estimates of Households with Members Aged 65 and Over, by Number of Elderly Members: 1985, 1980, and 1950
(numbers in thousands)

Type of Household	1985 Number	1985 Percentage of Total	1980 Number	1980 Percentage of Total	1950 Number	1950 Percentage of Total
Total Households	86,789	100.0	80,467	100.0	42,251	100.0
Households with One or More Members Aged 65 and over	20,128	23.2	18,275	22.7	8,957	21.2
One member 65 and over	13,435	15.5	12,537	15.6	6,349	15.0
Two or more members 65 and over	6,693	7.7	5,738	7.1	2,608	6.2
Householder aged 65 and over	18,156	20.9	16,131	20.0	6,428	15.2
Other member aged 65 and over	1,972	2.3	2,141	2.7	2,529	6.0
Households with Two Generations of Persons Aged 65 and over	NA	NA	193	0.24	148	0.35

SOURCES: Estimates prepared by the author; U.S. Bureau of the Census, reports of 1950 and 1980 Censuses of Population; and *Current Population Reports*, series P-20, no. 411, Table 20.

NOTE: NA = not available.

than they are today, a much larger share of the households (6 percent) included an elderly member in households other than those with elderly householders. The number of the latter households has fallen by over one fifth. As we saw, however, the likelihood that a household includes an elderly member has not changed much since 1950. In 1985 the elderly member other than the householder is more likely to be a wife or husband of the householder and less likely to be a parent or other relative, and a much larger share of households have elderly householders who live alone.

About one third of all households with an elderly member have two or more elderly members, mostly members of married couples. In a very small percentage of households, persons of two older generations live together. In 1980 0.24 percent of all households (1.2 percent of the households maintained by the elderly), or 193.000 households, contained parents and children who were both aged 65 and over.[17] Although this situation is rather uncommon, it is relatively less common now than it was a generation ago, when 0.35 percent of the households contained members of two older generations. These special households may present more than the average share of problems for elderly householders.

Family Life Cycle

I consider next the family life cycle or marital life cycle, the sequence of critical stages or transitions through which a family passes in the years following its formation. The concept is used as a framework for the study of changes over time in the composition and characteristics of the family. Life cycle stages are usually measured in terms of the mean or median ages at which the critical events occur. These events include age at first marriage, age at birth of first child, age at birth of last child, age at which last child leaves home, age at dissolution of marriage through divorce or the death of the husband or wife, and age at death. Other related measures are the duration of first marriage, duration of widowhood, and duration of divorce. The specific parameters of the family life cycle vary from one birth cohort to another. Analysis of the family life cycle is important in gerontological studies because of its

[17]These estimates were derived from census data by combining appropriate proportions of the households with a parent aged 80 and over and households with a child 65 and over. Note that these figures greatly understate the proportion of all aged persons who have living elderly children since many of the children may be living separately in their own households.

TABLE 6.16

Mean Age at Which Selected Critical Life Events Occurred for Ever-Married Mothers Born 1900–1949, by Birth Cohort: June 1980

	Birth Cohort				
Life Cycle Event	1940–1949	1930–1939	1920–1929	1910–1919	1900–1909
Age at First Marriage	20.8	20.7	21.6	22.4	22.2
Age at Birth of First Child	22.5	22.5	23.6	24.6	24.4
Age at Birth of Last Child	27.4[a]	29.7	31.3	31.7	31.4
Mean Number of Children	2.59[a]	3.41	3.33	3.03	2.99

SOURCE: G. B. Spanier, P. A. Roos, and J. Shockey, "Marital Trajectories of American Women: Variations in the Life Course," *Journal of Marriage and the Family* 47 (November 1985): 993–1003.

Copyrighted 1985 by the National Council on Family Relations, 3989 Central Ave., N.E., Suite #550, Minneapolis, MN 55421. Reprinted by permission.

NOTE: Based on the June 1980 CPS.

[a]Incomplete fertility.

focus on the changing social, economic, and demographic experiences of the family and its members as they age and the impact of the experiences in earlier life on experiences in later life.

Drawing on a study by Spanier and associates, Table 6.16 illustrates the early segments of the family life cycle with ages for selected life cycle events experienced by several groups of birth cohorts of ever-married mothers.[18] The table shows changes up to 1980 in the timing of several critical events for five groups of cohorts born from 1900–1909 to 1940–1949. The first and last groups of cohorts were aged 75–84 and 35–44, respectively, in 1985. The youngest cohorts married at substantially younger ages than the oldest cohorts. The mean age at first marriage of the 1940–1949 cohorts was 20.8 years and that of the 1900–1909 cohorts was 22.2 years, implying a difference of 1.4 years. The intervals between the mean ages at marriage and motherhood, and between the mean ages at the first and last births, also declined. The interval between marriage and motherhood dropped by one half year, from 2.2 years for the oldest cohorts to 1.7 years for the youngest cohorts, and the interval between the first and last births dropped by 2.1 years.[19]

[18]G. B. Spanier, P. A. Roos, and J. Shockey, "Marital Trajectories of American Women: Variations in the Life Course," *Journal of Marriage and the Family* 47 (November 1985):993–1003.
[19]The last figure may be biased upward because of incomplete data for the 1940–1949 cohorts.

TABLE 6.17

Measures of the Marital Life Cycle of Men and Women, for Selected Birth Cohorts: 1898–1902 to 1948–1950

	Male					
	Cohort Born in					1980 (period data)
Item (in years)	1898–1902	1908–1912	1918–1922	1938–1942[a]	1948–1950[a]	
Percentage Ever Marrying of Those Surviving to Age 15	88.8	92.6	94.1	96.2	93.9	89.2
Average Age at First Marriage	26.3	26.2	25.0	23.3	23.7	26.3
Average Duration of First Marriage	28.4	29.1	29.6	27.1	24.4	23.8
Percentage of First Marriages Ending in						
Divorce	21.4	25.4	30.2	40.8	45.7	44.4
Widowhood	25.8	23.8	22.1	18.3	16.7	17.1
Death	52.7	50.8	47.7	40.9	37.6	38.5
Average Age at						
Widowhood	62.0	65.5	67.8	70.2	70.7	71.1
Divorce	40.7	40.8	39.9	38.8	36.7	37.1
Average Duration of						
Widowhood	6.8	7.0	7.4	7.6	7.7	7.7
Divorce	4.8	4.6	4.8	5.8	5.9	6.0

SOURCE: R. Schoen, W. Urton, K. Woodward, and J. Baj, "Marriage and Divorce in Twentieth Century American Cohorts," *Demography* 22 (1) (February 1985): 101–114. Copyright © 1985, Population Association of America. Reprinted by permission.

NOTE: Based on current census data and vital statistics, and estimates as required.

[a] Projected in part.

As a result of the change from the oldest to the youngest cohorts in mean age at first marriage, and in the intervals between marriage, first birth, and last birth, the average age of completing childbearing fell markedly, from 31.4 years for the 1900–1909 cohorts to 27.4 years for the 1940–1949 cohorts. These groups of cohorts completed their childbearing not only at very different ages but also in very different historical periods, the oldest in the Depression years and the youngest in the 1970s. If the mean age of departure from home by the last child did not appreciably change between the 1950s and the 1980s, the ages of the women when the last child left home differed also by about 4.0 years. The mean age of departure of the last child from home has probably changed little on balance in this period because of apparent declines in

TABLE 6.17 (*continued*)

		Female			
		Cohort Born in			
1898–1902	1908–1912	1918–1922	1938–1942	1948–1950	1980 (period data)
91.7	93.1	95.9	97.3	95.4	90.8
22.7	23.2	22.3	21.1	21.8	24.1
29.0	29.9	30.5	29.0	26.0	24.4
20.5	23.8	28.6	36.9	42.1	42.9
53.6	52.4	49.4	44.2	40.6	40.0
25.9	23.8	22.0	18.9	17.3	17.1
62.9	65.0	66.3	67.2	67.6	67.9
37.1	37.4	36.2	36.0	33.8	33.1
15.2	15.1	15.0	15.0	15.0	15.0
9.5	9.1	9.3	12.1	11.5	10.8

the early part of the period and apparent rises in the later part.[20] Members of the youngest cohorts would be only about age 47 on the average when the last child left home compared with age 51 for the oldest cohorts, if the mean age of departure is 20 years.

Measures of the later segments of the family life cycles of men and women as well as the earlier segments, for cohorts born from 1898–1902 to 1948–1950, have been developed by Schoen and his associates (Table 6.17).[21] Again, the experience of later and earlier birth cohorts is

[20]Direct survey information or other satisfactory estimates of the age of departure of the last child from home are lacking. Census or CPS data do not permit an accurate estimate of change in this important life cycle event. One indicator, the mean age of young persons over 17 living with their parents, has been rising in the last four decades.

[21]R. Schoen, W. Urton, K. Woodrow, and J. Baj, "Marriage and Divorce in Twentieth Century American Cohorts," *Demography* 22 (1) (February 1985):110–114. These measures recognize the fact that many marriages terminate through divorce as well as death of a partner, that some wives predecease their husbands, and that the period of widowhood and "divorcehood" may be shortened by remarriage.

seen to be rather different in many respects. Men and women in their 70s and 80s around 1980 were somewhat less likely to have married in their lifetime and tended to marry later than is true of persons in their 30s and 40s around 1980.

According to the Schoen et al. figures, the proportion of first marriages ending in widowhood or death for both men and women steadily declined for these cohorts over time. For example, the proportion of marriages of women ending in widowhood dropped from 52 percent for the 1908–1912 cohorts to a projected 41 percent for the 1948–1950 cohorts; these figures roughly resemble the proportions of marriages of men ending in death (51 percent and 38 percent). Women born at or before the turn of the century experienced widowhood at younger ages (63) than will be true for women born in the 1930s and 1940s (68), but were more likely to remarry (14 percent vs. 8 percent). Women in their 30s and 40s around 1980 can expect, on the average, to live 15 years as widows, about the same as for the cohorts in their 70s and 80s around 1980.

The rate of marital dissolution has also sharply increased. Some 42 percent and 46 percent of marriages of women and men, respectively, in their 30s and 40s around 1980 are expected to end in divorce, while only about 1 in 4 or 5 marriages of persons in their 70s and 80s around 1980 had ended in divorce. The mean age at which women became divorced declined by three years and the average duration of divorced life before death or remarriage increased by two years or so. The patterns of marriage dissolution have changed in similar ways for men. The small proportion of husbands in the 1908–1912 birth cohorts who outlived their wives became widowed at age 66 while men in the 1948–1950 birth cohorts can expect to become widowed at age 71. These figures generally run a few years higher than those for women. Men in both groups of cohorts experienced or can expect to experience, on the average, 7–8 years of widowhood, about half as many years of widowhood as women.

In more recent years the parameters of the family life cycle have been reversing their direction. The 1948–1950 birth cohorts had already begun to show a turnaround in certain marriage parameters, specifically the lower proportions marrying and the higher age at first marriage than the cohorts of 1938–1942. Period calculations for 1980 resemble the pattern of the cohorts of 1948–1950 for both men and women with respect to the marriage parameters and suggest a continuation of the most recent cohort trends. In general, the most recent cohorts have shown a tendency to marry less, to marry later, to have a first child later, to have fewer children, and to divorce more and earlier than the cohorts of 1938–1942. These trends in combination with the greatly reduced mortality will mean that young women of today will spend a larger proportion of their lives as unmarried women before and after married life and a smaller proportion of their lives as married women and as parents.[22]

Family Support
Familial Dependency Ratios

In considering the question of support for the elderly, two dimensions of the topic are distinguished: support by the family network, particularly adult children, and support by the society or community. From a demographic view, support by the family is analyzed principally in terms of the relative numbers of elderly persons and their children, and societal support is analyzed in terms of the relative numbers of elderly persons and persons of working age. These measures reflect the effects of age composition and changes in it on the support problem and do not measure actual economic, social, physical, or psychological support. Currently, the family network functions mainly in the sphere of informal social and psychological support of the elderly and the community functions mainly in the sphere of formal economic support, although a substantial amount of income is transferred between family members of different generations[23] and some social support is provided to the elderly by the community.

A common economic assumption made in the use of these measures, especially societal dependency ratios, is that the older segment of the population is an economic burden on the younger segment and hence must be financially supported by it. A common ethical inference is that each generation has an obligation to support the previous generation when the time comes. Accordingly, questions as to the extent and nature of the support, the feasibility and propriety of providing support, and the role of intergenerational equity arise in interpreting the various measures of intergenerational support, but these issues are barely touched on in this monograph. Measures of family support are considered in this chapter and measures of societal support are considered in Chapters 1, 2, and 7—both from a circumscribed demographic viewpoint.

Ratios relating persons aged 65–79 to those aged 45–49, characteristic ages linking elderly parents and their adult children, and ratios relating persons aged 85 and over to those aged 65–69, wherein two older generations are linked as parent and child, are the two types of familial

---

[22]S. C. Watkins, J. A. Menken, and J. Bongaarts, "Demographic Foundations of Family Change," *American Sociological Review* 52 (June 1987):346–358, esp. p. 354.

[23]U.S. Bureau of the Census, "Who's Helping Out?" *Current Population Reports,* series P-70, no. 13 (October 1988).

aged-dependency ratios employed here. Fluctuations in these measures mainly reflect changes in age distribution at the older ages, resulting from generational shifts in fertility levels over half a century earlier, as modified by mortality and immigration in subsequent years. Patently, such measures do not allow for the distribution of children among the parents.

Familial aged-dependency ratios have been increasing steadily in recent decades, but they will show wide fluctuations in the next several decades because of the fluctuations in the number of births in the last half century. The ratio of persons aged 65–79 to those aged 45–49 has been climbing steadily since at least 1950, showing a rapid rise in the 1970s and early 1980s and reaching a peak of 193 (per 100) in 1985. It is then expected to fall steeply and to reach a trough of 114 around 2005, as the large birth cohorts of the postwar period attain ages 45–49 (Table 6.18). In 2005, elderly women will have relatively far more children to provide support to them than elderly women of the mid 1980s. The decline in birth rates and in numbers of births which occurred in the years after 1965 and the entry of the baby-boom cohorts into the ranks of the elderly will produce a sharp rise in the ratio after 2010, when ages 45–49 and 65–79 begin to be affected by these two antithetical trends. A peak of about 253 persons aged 65–79 per 100 persons aged 45–49 will probably be reached in the mid 2020s. The pattern of high elderly-parent/adult-child ratios will continue throughout several subsequent decades if fertility remains low and especially if the population becomes stationary or declines.[24]

Changes in death rates up to middle age (e.g., birth to ages 45–49) have become of small importance in determining the trend in the ratio of elderly parents to their adult children. Before 1950, and especially before World War II, infant and child mortality played an important role—albeit secondary to the role of fertility—in determining the number of surviving middle-aged children, but fertility changes now almost wholly determine this number (Table 6.19). The survival rate of mothers to old age (e.g., 17.5–32.5 years to 65.0–80.0 years in exact ages) has a strong depressive effect on the ratio, however. For example, this survival rate is still only 76 percent according to the generation life table for birth year 1935, although it has been steadily and rapidly rising according to recent current life tables.

According to the generation life tables for birth years 1925 (daughters) and 1900 (mothers), the relative survival of mothers to old age and

---

[24]A stationary population is a population with zero population growth and an unchanging age distribution. A stationary population with twenty-first century mortality would have a familial dependency ratio of 224 per 100.

TABLE 6.18

Familial Aged-Dependency Ratios, by Race and Number of Older Generations:
1930–2030

Year (July 1)	All Races		Black	
	One Elderly Generation[a]	Two Elderly Generations[b]	One Elderly Generation[a]	Two Elderly Generations[b]
1930	95	10	50[c]	14[c]
1940	95	10	79[c]	13[c]
1950	116	12	88	11
1960	129	15	101	14
1970	135	20	116	16
1980	185	26	152	21
1985	193	29	152	25
Projections[d]				
1990	174	33	139	31
2000	126	54	94	48
2010	126	56	86	49
2020	220	43	155	35
2030	242	47	182	35
High series[e]	240	58	185	43
Low series[e]	241	38	178	28

SOURCE: Based on U.S. Census Bureau, *Current Population Reports*, series P-25, various numbers.

[a] $\dfrac{\text{Population aged 65--79}}{\text{Population aged 45--49}} \times 100$.

[b] $\dfrac{\text{Population aged 85 and over}}{\text{Population aged 65--69}} \times 100$.

[c] Includes other nonwhite races.
[d] Middle series, except as indicated.
[e] Based on highest population series or lowest population series.

of their daughters to middle age was 0.73. The improvement in the survival of mothers has been relatively greater than that of children, but even according to the generation life tables for birth years 1975 (daughters) and 1950 (mothers), the relative survival of mothers to old age and of their children to middle age is only 0.81. The reduction in the premature death of parents contributes to a rise in the parental support burden, while the increased survival of children contributes to a fall in it. The sharp decline in the mortality of the elderly since the late 1960s has been intensifying the effect of declines in the number of births between the two world wars, especially during the 1930s, in raising the ratio of elderly parents to their adult children during the 1970s and early 1980s.

TABLE 6.19

Relative Survival of Women from Parenthood to Old Age and of Newborn Girls to Middle Age, According to Generation Life Tables for Birth Years 1900–1950 (Mothers) and 1925–1975 (Daughters)

Year of Birth of Mothers	Approximate Exposure Period		Survival Rate, Birth to Middle Age[a]	Survival Rate, Parenthood to Old Age[b]	Relative Survival of Mothers and Daughters
	Initial Year	Terminal Year			
1900	1925	1970	.8568	.6262	.731
1905	1930	1975	.8757	.6613	.755
1915	1940	1985	.9079	.7027	.774
1925	1950	1995	.9366	.7337	.783
1935	1960	2005	.9459	.7559	.799
1945	1970	2015	.9549	.7741	.811
1950	1975	2020	.9594	.7810	.814

SOURCE: Based on unpublished generation life tables provided by the U.S. Social Security Administration, Office of the Actuary. See *Actuarial Study*, no. 89, by J. F. Faber and A. H. Wade (December 1983).

[a] Survival rates from birth to ages 45.0 ↔ 50.0 (exact ages) for females.
[b] Survival rates from ages 17.5 ↔ 32.5 years (exact ages) to 65.0 ↔ 80.0 years (exact ages) for females.

The fluctuations in familial aged-dependency ratios for the black population are similar to those for the white population, but the ratios are much lower (152 in 1985). (See Table 6.18.) This suggests that, so far as mere numbers of persons are concerned, the family support problem should be less severe for blacks. Other factors influence the situation, however, such as the greater lack of resources and the greater proportion of single-parent households among blacks. Differences in dependency ratios for various groups reflect historical differences in the fertility, mortality, and immigration of the groups. Immigration has had an important effect on the age distribution of some groups, such as Hispanics, who have experienced a large volume of immigration in recent years. Dependency ratios for Hispanics remain low (96 for 1985) for this reason and because of high fertility.

Many middle-aged persons have the joint tasks of contributing to the support of both aged parents and children of college age. This problem occurred in especially acute form in the early 1980s, as shown by the series of ratios of persons aged 17.5–22.5 *and* 72.5–77.5 to persons aged 45.0–50.0 (in exact ages) for the period 1950–2030 presented in Table 6.20.[25] The ratio was at a peak in the 1980s because of the rela-

[25]The ages of aged parents and of children of college age were selected to correspond approximately to a median age of childbearing of 27.5 years. The figures in Table 6.20 reflect merely the effect of age composition, and significance should be attached only to fluctuations over time, not the absolute level of individual figures.

TABLE 6.20

Familial Dependency Ratios with Three Generations: 1950–2030

Year	Youth[a]	Aged[b]	Total[c]
1950	122	30	152
1960	111	36	147
1970	151	38	190
1980	197	53	250
1984	178	56	234
1990	130	51	181
2000	92	41	133
2010	91	35	126
2020	103	62	165
2030	97	75	172

SOURCE: Based on U.S. Bureau of the Census, *Current Population Reports*, series P-25, nos. 311, 519, 917, 965, and 952 (middle series).

[a] $\dfrac{\text{Population aged 17.5–22.5}}{\text{Population aged 45.0–50.0}} \times 100.$

[b] $\dfrac{\text{Population aged 72.5–77.5}}{\text{Population aged 45.0–50.0}} \times 100.$

[c] $\dfrac{\text{Population aged 17.5–22.5 + population aged 72.5–77.5}}{\text{Population aged 45.0–50.0}} \times 100.$

tively large number of aged persons *and* college-age persons, and the relatively small number of middle-aged persons. The level of 1980–1985 may never be reached again. The issue will be a continuing one, but the burden will gradually diminish up to about 2000–2010, as the baby-boom cohorts join the band of middle-aged children. By 2015 the baby-boom cohorts will have begun to move into the elderly age classes and the "baby-bust" cohorts in turn will have replaced the baby-boom cohorts at ages 45–49; so the tri-generational dependency ratio will rise rapidly again.

Many persons of extreme old age depend upon adult children who are themselves elderly. A series of ratios of persons aged 85 and over to those aged 65–69 may be used to represent the past and prospective shifts in the burden on young-elderly children of supporting their older-aged parents. The past trend in this ratio has been roughly similar to that of the ratio of elderly parents (aged 65–79) to their middle-aged children (aged 45–49), with an appropriate (20-year) time lag (Table 6.18). The burden of the older aged on young-elderly children has increased greatly in recent decades. There were 12 persons aged 85 and over for every 100 persons aged 65–69 in 1950, but by 1985 the ratio had grown nearly two and a half times to 29. The series is expected to move steadily upward in the next few decades, reaching a first peak of 61 in 2005, as the increasingly larger birth cohorts of 1900–1920 attain age 85. The decline in the number of births during the 1920s will contribute to a steady decline in the ratios during the 2010s. After 2030 we may expect a great leap forward as the baby-boom cohorts begin to arrive at age 85. Fluctuations of births during the Depression and later years, affecting the provider population aged 65–69, will at times intensify or moderate the effect of the earlier birth trends.

A generation ago, parents were not as likely to reach old age as they are today. The phenomenon of large numbers of people, mostly women, reaching very old ages is touching more and more families. In fact, it is new to human experience for a large majority of middle-aged women to have living mothers. Menken has estimated by computer simulation on the basis of the rates of fertility, mortality, and marriage for 1940 and 1980 that the proportion of 50-year-old women with living mothers jumped from 37 percent to 65 percent in this period.[26]

Relatives Inside and Outside the Household

Familial support of elderly persons comes first from spouses, children, and other close relatives living in the household. In 1985, 67 percent of persons aged 65 and over (82 percent of men and 57 percent of women) lived with one or more relatives in a family household.[27] A generation earlier persons aged 65 and over were much more likely to live with a relative. In 1950, 76 percent of the elderly population lived with one or more relatives in a family household. The decline occurred in spite of an increase in the proportion of elderly persons living with spouses.

As described earlier, the great majority of elderly men live with wives. For elderly women, husbands are the most common relative with whom they live, but most elderly women live with someone other than a husband or they live alone. In 1985, three quarters of the men aged 65 and over and nearly two fifths of the women aged 65 and over were living with a spouse. The proportions have risen sharply since 1950. Then, only three fifths of the men and one third of the women aged 65 and over were living with a spouse.

The likelihood of having a spouse drops sharply with age, but the figure is still strikingly high for men at the oldest ages. In 1980 83 per-

[26]J. L. Menken, "Age and Fertility: How Late Can You Wait?" *Demography* 22 (4) (November 1985):469–484.

[27]U.S. Bureau of the Census, *Current Population Reports*, Series P-20, no. 410 (November 1986), Table A-12.

cent of men aged 65–69 had wives and the proportion fell to 48 percent for men aged 85 and over. Approximately 55 percent of the women aged 65–69 had husbands, but at ages 85 and over only 17 percent did. The very large share of older aged men who live with spouses and the very small share of older aged women who do show that the support problem in old age has a strong sex-selective feature and a strong relationship-selective feature. This is further illustrated by the prominent role of women in accepting responsibility for support of parents or parents-in-law, as noted below.

Few elderly persons live in the same household as their children. An estimated 6.8 percent did so in 1980.[28] The proportion rises steadily with advancing age among the elderly, but it never gets very high. It is 10 percent at ages 75 and over and 17 percent at ages 85 and over. Obviously, the proportion of elderly whose children live with them represents a massive understatement of the proportion of elderly persons who have living children; the vast majority of elderly persons live in their own households apart from their children. The author estimates, on the basis of demographic analysis of 1980 census data, that 73 percent of all women aged 65 and over had at least one living child in that year.[29]

Race	1980	1970
All Races	73.4	72.6
White	74.0	72.8
Black	64.9	65.7

The level of potential support implied by such figures was about the same in 1970 as in 1980.[30]

The NHIS 1984 Supplement on Aging provides us with a more current figure for the proportion of elderly persons with living children. It

[28]This figure was approximated from 1980 census data as the proportion that parents aged 65 and over and selected shares of children aged 40 and over, taken together, constitute of all persons aged 65 and over.

[29]Tabulations of the National Sample Survey of the Aged of 1975 show much higher percentages than the estimates for 1970 or 1980 given here: 78.5 percent for all women, 79 percent for white women, and 71 percent for black women. The survey figures are patently too high since they greatly exceed the maxima tenable on the basis of the two censuses. Unpublished tabulations of the original survey data were provided to the author by Beth Soldo and Emily Agree of Georgetown University.

[30]The 1980 figures would be expected to show a decline, reflecting the arrival of the very-low-fertility cohorts of 1905–1914 (those with the "Depression babies") into the elderly fold and the associated shift in the parity distribution. Other factors appear to have had an opposite influence, however. The increased survival of children, the higher survival of mothers than nonmothers, and differential accuracy of reporting in the two censuses may explain the general constancy of the proportion.

relates to persons aged 65 and over living alone. This figure, 71 percent, is close to our estimate for women aged 65 and over for 1980.

Living Children	Total	No Living Siblings	Living Siblings
Total	100.0	27.7	72.3
None	28.8	10.7	18.2
1	19.1	5.4	13.7
2–4	42.2	9.9	32.3
5 or more	9.8	1.8	8.1

SOURCE: U.S. National Center for Health Statistics, *NCHS Advance Data*, no. 116 (May 1986), Table B.

About one fifth of the elderly living alone had only one living child and over one half had two or more children. Over one quarter had no living sibling and about one tenth had neither a child nor a sibling.

A much larger proportion of the elderly population is expected to have a living child in the year 2005 (when the parents of the baby-boom babies are elderly) than in 1980 or 1984, but in 2025 (when the parents of the baby-bust babies are elderly), the contrary situation will prevail. It is anticipated that in the next several decades the pace of improvement in survival at the older ages will exceed that at the younger ages, as in the recent past, that fertility will remain low, and that a larger share of women will choose to be childless.[31] Hence, in the long run, apart from the effects of the baby boom, the proportion of elderly women having a living child is expected to fall and to remain relatively low.

Generational Size and Structure of Families

Generational analysis of families provides further insight into their dependency and support problems and the extent and nature of familial intergenerational relationships. Old persons now commonly have grandchildren and occasionally have great-grandchildren, living inside and outside the household, who provide some psychological, social, and

[31]See discussion in Chapter 1. See also J. Treas, "The Great American Fertility Debate: Generational Balance and Support of the Aged," *Gerontologist* 21 (1) (February 1981):98–103; C. F. Westoff, "Fertility Decline in the West: Causes and Prospects," *Population and Development Review* 9 (1) (March 1983):99–105; C. F. Westoff, "Some Speculations on the Future of Marriage and Fertility," *Family Planning Perspectives* 10 (2) (March–April 1978):79–83; D. Wulf, "Low Fertility in Europe: A Report from the 1981 IUSSP Meeting," *International Family Planning Perspectives* 8 (2) (June 1982):63–69; and D. J. van de Kaa, "Europe's Second Demographic Transition," *Population Bulletin* 42 (1) (March 1987). Population Reference Bureau, Washington, DC.

physical support. The average number of living "generations" in a "family" has been undergoing a gradual increase in the past several decades, mainly as a result of increasing longevity. The number of relationships among the different generations in a direct line has grown at the expense of those among siblings, uncles, aunts, and cousins. In this regard, family members include persons occupying different housing units and the number of generations is based on the number of tiers in a parent-child line of ascendancy or descendancy (e.g., three generations for a grandparent-parent-child line).

Recent censuses provide little useful information regarding the changing generational size of families. They do not give information on the relationship of family members not living in the same housing unit, and they do not commonly classify census families according to the relationship of their members to the householder. The 1960 and 1970 censuses, unlike the 1950 and 1980 censuses, did provide a classification of census families by relationship. They show that only 4.4 percent and 5.5 percent, respectively, of all families were three- or four-generation families. Since family members residing outside the particular household of reference are not included in these figures and since family members are in fact usually dispersed among a number of census households, these figures grossly understate the proportion of multigenerational families.

Some information has been obtained from special surveys. A survey of a national probability sample of persons aged 65 and over interviewed in 1962 indicated that a substantial share—40 percent—of the elderly population had great-grandchildren.[32] Shanas reported in 1980, on the basis of a national sample survey taken in 1975, that 75 percent of the elderly were grandparents, that nearly half of the grandparents were or would become great-grandparents, and that, accordingly, about 38 percent of the elderly belonged to four-generation families.[33] A conference held at the National Institute on Aging in 1981 reported a much higher figure—namely, 50 percent. These figures suggest a high relative frequency of four-generation families in the years indicated. They are, however, necessarily overstatements of the proportion of all families that are four-generation families since only elderly persons were included in the reporting universe and they presumably reported the maximum number of generations to which they belonged. This type of anchoring tends to overstate the proportion of four-generation families because it

[32]P. Townsend, "The Emergence of the Four-Generation Family in Industrial Society," in B. L. Neugarten, ed., *Middle Age and Aging* (Chicago: University of Chicago Press, 1968).

[33]Reported in G. O. Hagestad, "The Aging Society as a Context for Family Life," *Daedalus* 115 (1) (Winter 1985):77–117.

omits families without living elders and other household units that might give lower alternative responses of generational size.

I surmise that, if reports regarding family size were compiled for each individual, families would now contain, on the average, a little over three generations, compared with families about 1950, when they contained between two and three generations. This trend is expected to continue, but by 2025 the average family is still expected to have between three and four generations. In fact, a crude application of demographic analysis results in a low estimate of the mean number of generations per family of about 3.0 currently, compared with 2.5 in 1950, and a low projection of 3.3 by about 2025. Corresponding high estimates and projections for 1950, 1988, and 2025 are 2.9, 3.4, and 3.7. The mean number of generations per family increased by one half generation between 1950 and 1988, and it is expected to increase by an additional three tenths generation between 1988 and 2025, assuming that the Census Bureau's middle mortality projections prevail. The slower growth of the generational size of families anticipated results from the assumption of a slower rise in longevity in the future than in the last several decades and stability in the other demographic factors.

The mean number of generations per family depends mainly on survival rates throughout life, particularly survival rates from birth to the childbearing ages, and the mean age at birth of first child, but it is secondarily dependent on the percentage of women who marry, the mean age at first marriage, the extent of infertility among married women, the divorce rate, and other similar factors. During the first several decades of this century we generally saw a rise in life expectancy, a rise in marriage rates, a decline in the proportion of married women who are infertile, and a decline in the mean age of women at childbearing. We are continuing to experience an increase in longevity, but the other trends have undergone reversals. For example, the mean age of women at childbearing fell from 27.0 years for the birth cohorts of 1900–1909 to 24.9 years for the birth cohorts of 1940–1949, then rose again to 26.2 years for calendar year 1985.

Although none of the factors affecting the mean number of generations in a family is easily predictable, I expect the mean to continue to rise, but more slowly than in the past. The only factor whose trend tends to be essentially monotonic (i.e., noncyclical) is longevity. Changes in the other factors are affected largely by changes in attitudes, fashions, and economic conditions. Even though marriage rates, fertility rates, and the timing of births may fluctuate, mortality is likely to show a more or less steady decline and to have a dominant effect on the average number of generations.

The structure of the family network has also been changing. Its "length" has been expanding and its "width" has been contracting. There may be three or four grandparents and perhaps a great-grandparent or two, but the number of collateral kin (i.e., brothers and sisters) and affinal kin (i.e., kin by marriage), as contrasted with ascendant and descendant kin, is decreasing and is expected to continue decreasing. The general decline in fertility has tended to reduce the size of the total familial support system,[34] and a continuation of low fertility should contribute further to reducing it. It is expected that, in spite of increasing longevity, elderly persons of the future will have fewer living lineal descendants than elderly persons did in the past. It is also likely that elderly persons will have a smaller total number of living relatives, counting brothers and sisters and their descendants as well as their own children, grandchildren, and great-grandchildren. Remarriage along the way may have extended the number of relatives somewhat in the form of stepchildren, step-grandchildren, and half brothers and sisters, or merely replaced some affinal kin with others. Old persons may fall along a wide continuum from the spinster or widow who has no children or other close relatives to the grand matriarch who presides over a family of four generations with numerous grandchildren and great-grandchildren.

To describe the probable frequencies of kin under a prospective stationary regime, I draw on the research of Pullum.[35] It involved a series of computer simulations, assuming no mortality and the expected lifetime fertility distribution of women aged 25–29 in the June 1978 CPS. Substantial portions of the population would have no or very few siblings, aunts, uncles, or cousins. The chance of having a grandchild in one's lifetime is 87 percent, and the chance of not having 2, 3, 4, or 5 grandchildren is 64 percent. The chance of having a brother or sister is 93 percent, and the chance of having only 1 or 2 brothers or sisters is 74 percent. The average person would have 1.00 daughter, 2.06 sons or daughters, 4.24 grandchildren, and 1.72 brothers or sisters.

Finally, we note that the mere paucity of relatives does not prove that there will not be enough of them to provide the necessary support. The support system will be influenced by factors other than the numbers and types of living kin. Among these are the numerical distribution of family members among the elderly, the geographical dispersion of family members, their socioeconomic characteristics, attitudes on the part of the elderly toward receiving support from relatives, attitudes on

[34]J. Treas, "Family Support Systems for the Aged: Some Social and Demographic Considerations," *Gerontologist* 17 (6) (1977):486–491. See also J. D. Bartlema, *Developments in Kinship Networks for the Aged in the Netherlands*, Reeks Sociale Zekerheids Wetenschap, Katholieke Universiteit Brabant (Tilburg, 1987).

[35]T. W. Pullum, "The Eventual Frequencies of Kin in a Stable Population," *Demography* 19 (2) (November 1982):549–565.

the part of relatives toward providing support, and the community support system.

Extent of Family Contacts and Care

Adequacy of family contacts and care would seem most problematic for those elderly living alone. Two questions in particular relating to the life situation of the elderly living alone should concern us beyond the formal demographic characteristics of this group. First, are they lonely to the extent that the quality of their lives is adversely affected? Second, does the increase in the share of solitary persons among the elderly imply less family support? My response to the first question is mixed but essentially positive, while my response to the second question is a qualified negative. Later I consider whether the elderly who live alone are at an especially high risk of needing formal support (e.g., long-term care under institutional auspices).

Living alone is generally viewed negatively, not only compared with living with a spouse but also compared with living with another relative or even a nonrelative. It is reasonable to hypothesize that those living alone are isolated and lonely. They may be neither one nor the other, or both, however.

To live alone is not necessarily to be isolated, and most elderly who live alone are not isolated. The great majority have one or more living children and/or one or more living siblings, have frequent contact with their children, siblings, and friends, have lived for a long time in the same house or neighborhood or live in retirement communities, and have telephones that are used for contacts. According to the NHIS 1984 Supplement on Aging, few of the elderly living alone failed to be in contact with an immediate family member or friend in the previous two weeks.[36] Eighty-four percent of all elderly persons living alone had talked with someone or socialized with someone within the two weeks. Only 5 percent reported no contact with family members or friends in person or by telephone within the two-week period.

On the other hand, the elderly who live alone have fewer contacts and fewer individuals on whom they can call during a health or financial crisis than the elderly who live with family members. Some types of solitary elderly are more likely to suffer from isolation than others. As shown by the Aging Supplement, they include the 29 percent who have no living children, the 28 percent who have no living siblings—particularly the 11 percent who have no living siblings and no living

[36]U.S. National Center for Health Statistics (May 1986).

children, the 3 percent who had a child but reported that they never or nearly never saw the child, the 24 percent who moved into their current home in the last five years, and the 6 percent who had no telephone.[37]

While the elderly who live with relatives or nonrelatives and most of the elderly who live alone are not isolated, the latter may still be lonely or have a difficult time living alone. The NCHS survey on aging does not try to get at the essential feelings of the unattached elderly. It is the author's hypothesis that loneliness is a pervasive characteristic of the elderly who do not live with adult partners, even allowing for the occasional need for solitude. A Swedish study concluded that loneliness in the postretirement years is a rather common problem and that the important factors related to the feeling of loneliness are the loss of a spouse, lack of contacts with children and old friends, and "depression of mood."[38] Another Swedish study found that 20 percent of the people aged 60–64 felt lonely; the proportion was more than twice as great for those aged 80 and over.[39] Men seem to have a more difficult time living alone than women because many do not know how to manage a house and, in particular, do not know how to cook. As a result, men living alone are more likely to engage in poor eating behavior.[40]

The increased proportion of elderly persons living alone should not be taken as an indication that family members are less likely to care for their elderly parents now than they did a generation ago. In fact, the opposite appears to be the case. The amount of nonmonetary assistance to the elderly is considerable. Laurie reports that for every disabled person living in a nursing home, two or more equally impaired elderly live with and are cared for by their families.[41] On the basis of data from the 1982 Long-Term Care Survey, Stone, Cafferata, and Sangl estimated that 2.2 million persons were providing unpaid assistance to 1.6 million elderly persons.[42] Brody conservatively estimates that over 5 million adult

[37]U.S. National Center for Health Statistics (May 1986). Since some of these groups overlap, they are not additive.

[38]S. Berg, D. Mellstrom, G. Perrson, and A. Svanborg, "Loneliness in Swedish Aged," *Journal of Gerontology* 36 (3) (May 1981):342–349.

[39]Government of Sweden, SOU, Pensionnar, *The Pensioneer Survey, 1977*, 75, Norstedts (Stockholm, 1977).

[40]M. A. Davis, S. P. Murphy, and J. M. Neuhaus, "Living Arrangements and Eating Behaviors of Older Adults in the United States, *Journal of Gerontology* 43 (3) (May 1988):S96–98.

[41]W. F. Laurie, "Employing the Duke OARS Methodology in Cost Comparisons: Home Services and Institutionalization," Duke University, Center for the Study of Aging and Human Development, *Advances in Research* 2 (2) (1978).

[42]R. Stone, G. L. Cafferata, and J. Sangl, "Caregivers of the Frail Elderly: A National Profile," *Gerontologist* 27 (5) (October 1987):616–626. See also B. J. Soldo and J. Myllyluoma, "Caregivers Who Live with Dependent Elderly," *Gerontologist* 23 (6) (December 1983):605–611.

children are involved in parent care at any given time.[43] Families provide 80 to 90 percent of personal care and help with household tasks, transportation, and shopping for the elderly. Coresidence of the elderly and their children has by no means disappeared, especially if the elderly parent is chronically ill. One seventh of the elderly and one fifth of the aged live with relatives other than a spouse (mostly adult children).[44] (See Table 6.10.)

Usually the adult daughters are the caregivers, and often they must leave the work force or work only part time to provide care at the very time in their lives when they need to plan for their own old age. Many of these adult women caregivers must deal with widowhood and reduced incomes themselves even while they try to care for their parents and parents-in-law. Moreover, with the recent trend toward postponement of childbearing, these women may still be involved in rearing and supporting children, who, together with a job, may absorb all their time and energy. The possible emotional, physical, and financial burden on the individual families may be tremendous, especially when there are two generations of elderly people, one or both of whom require special care. In fact, this burden may be so great that the children/grandchildren of the elderly generations may be incapable of carrying it, and the burden may have to be shifted wholly or largely to the community. Institutionalization may be required.

Group Quarters and Institutional Population

The Share of Elderly Residing in Group Quarters and Institutions

A small share of the elderly do not live in households, but in so-called group quarters, units occupied jointly by several unrelated persons. The vast majority of these are residents of institutions, mostly homes for the aged or nursing homes, while a very small minority live in the community, that is, in noninstitutional group quarters. In 1980 the total group quarters population accounted for some 5.8 percent of

---

[43]E. M. Brody, "Parent Care as a Normative Family Stress," *Gerontologist* 25 (1) (February 1985):19–29.

[44]Nevertheless, according to Bumpass, there is evidence of weakening in intergenerational ties. The proportion of the elderly seeing a child at least once a week declined by 25 percent between 1962 and 1984 and the proportions reporting help with household repairs by men and help with housework by women declined markedly between 1962 and 1987. L. L. Bumpass, "What's Happening to the Family? Interactions Between Demographic and Institutional Change," *Demography* 27 (4) (November 1990):483–498.

the population aged 65 and over, and the segment living in the community accounted for only 0.5 percent. The percentages of the population in group quarters at various older ages in 1980 are:

Age	Total	In Institutions	Others
60–64	1.2	0.9	0.3
65 and Over	5.8	5.3	0.5
65–74	2.2	1.8	0.4
75 and Over	11.4	10.6	0.8

SOURCE: U.S. Bureau of the Census, 1980 Census of Population, *Subject Reports*, PC80-2-4D.

At any one time, only a small share of the elderly population is institutionalized. In 1985, an estimated 5.5 percent of the elderly population resided in institutions. The figure has been gliding upward since at least 1950 (Table 6.21). Half of the 1950–1980 increase from 3.1 percent to 5.2 percent resulted from an increase in the age-specific proportions of the elderly who are institutionalized, while the other half resulted from the aging of the older population. If the age distribution had not changed since 1950, the overall proportion aged 65 and over in institutions in 1980 would be only 4.2 percent.

The increase between 1950 and 1980 in the overall proportion of the population aged 65 and over institutionalized also depends on the rise, with increasing age, in the proportion of elderly persons resident in institutions in each of these years. According to 1980 census data, the proportion of adult institutional residents is at a minimum at about ages 45–54 for males (0.7 percent) and at ages 20–44 for females (0.3 percent), and then rises steadily with increasing age.[45] Only 1.4 percent of the population aged 65–69 and 5.0 percent of the population aged 75–79 are institutionalized, but the figure rises steeply to 18 percent at ages 85–89 and 32 percent at ages 95 and over.

Because of differences in the trend of the proportion of the population resident in institutions between 1950 and 1980 at different older ages, the proportion rose far more sharply with advancing age from 55–59 to 85–89 in 1980 than in 1950 (24 points vs. 9 points for females and 14 points vs. 6 points for males). (See Table 6.21.) As a further consequence, the amount of the rise in the proportion from ages 55–59 to 85–89 in 1950 shown by the cross-sectional data greatly understates the rise for the actual cohort that was aged 55–59 in 1950 and 85–89 in 1980.

[45]U.S. Bureau of the Census, 1980 Census of Population, "Persons in Institutions and Other Group Quarters," *Subject Reports*, PC80-2-4D, October 1984.

TABLE 6.21

Percentage of the Population Aged 55 and Over in Institutions, by Age and Sex: 1950–1980

Age	Both Sexes				Male				Female			
	1980	1970	1960	1950	1980	1970	1960	1950	1980	1970	1960	1950
Total 55 and Over	3.2	3.0	2.6	2.3	2.3	2.5	2.5	2.4	3.9	3.4	2.6	2.2
55–59	0.7	0.9	1.3	1.4	0.8	1.1	1.6	1.8	0.6	0.7	1.0	1.1
60–64	0.9	1.2	1.5	1.6	1.0	1.4	1.9	2.0	0.8	1.0	1.2	1.3
65–69	1.4	1.7	1.8	1.8	1.4	1.8	2.0	2.0	1.3	1.6	1.6	1.6
70–74	2.5	2.7	2.7	2.6	2.2	2.5	2.6	2.6	2.6	2.9	2.7	2.5
75–79	5.0	5.2	4.4	3.9	3.9	4.2	3.8	3.8	5.7	5.9	4.8	4.3
80–84	10.4	10.2	7.8	6.2	7.3	7.5	6.3	5.7	12.0	11.9	8.9	6.6
85 and over	22.7	18.0	12.8	9.4	15.8	13.0	10.3	8.3	25.7	20.8	14.4	10.2
65 and over	5.2	4.8	3.7	3.1	4.0	3.7	3.3	3.0	6.3	5.6	4.1	3.2
75 and over	10.6	9.2	6.8	5.4	9.6	6.8	5.5	4.8	12.4	10.8	7.7	5.9

SOURCE: U.S. Bureau of the Census, 1950–1980 Censuses of Population, *Special Reports* on the institutional population.

Characteristics of the Institutional Population

Residents of institutions are concentrated at the higher ages. In 1980 nearly 80 percent of residents aged 65 and over were aged 75 and over (Table 6.22). The median age of the institutional population aged 65 and over was about 82. Moreover, institutionalization has come at increasingly older ages over the last several decades. In 1950 the group aged 65–74 made up 46 percent of institutional residents aged 65 and over and the group aged 85 and over made up 14 percent. Now, out of every 100 residents aged 65 and over, 21 are aged 65–74 and 38 are 85 and over.

The proportion of females in the institutionalized elderly population greatly exceeds their proportion in the general elderly population. Most elderly residents of institutions are women, and the female share has been rising—even more rapidly than the female share in the general population aged 65 and over (Table 6.22). In 1980, over 7 in 10 residents aged 65 and over were women and about 4 in 5 residents aged 85 and over were women; in 1950 the ratios were less than 3 in 5 and less than 2 in 3, respectively. Similarly, the proportion of the female population aged 65 and over that is institutionalized (6.3 percent) is nearly two thirds greater than the corresponding proportion for the male population (4.0 percent). Underlying the excess proportion of women is the far greater pool of elderly women from which to draw. The gender difference is also associated with the greater tendency of women to live alone or with relatives other than spouses (usually as widows), their poorer economic status, and their higher average age, which is, in part, a consequence of their greater longevity and "cause" of greater illness and disability.

The institutional population aged 65 and over is much more likely than the general population at these ages to be single, widowed, or divorced, and much less likely to be married (Table 6.23). Nearly 3 in 4 female residents aged 65 and over and 4 in 5 residents aged 75 and over are widowed. Yet nearly all elderly residents—9 in 10—have living relatives, if not spouses.[46]

In recent decades there has been a pronounced change in the types of facilities in which the older institutional population resides. Nearly all—92 percent—of the over 1.34 million persons aged 65 and over residing in institutions in 1980 lived in nursing homes and homes for the

---

[46]U.S. Bureau of the Census, "1976 Survey of Institutionalized Persons: A Study of Persons Receiving Long-Term Care," *Current Population Reports*, P-23, no. 69 (August 1978).

TABLE 6.22

Population Aged 65 Years and Over in Institutions, by Age, Sex, and Race/Hispanic Origin: 1950–1980

Age, Race, and Hispanic Origin	Population, 1980 (in thousands)			Percent Female		Percent Increase		
	Total	Male	Female	1980	1950	1970–1980	1960–1970	1950–1960
All Classes								
65 and over	1,340	374	967	72	55	39	57	60
75 and over	1,052	254	798	76	60	49	87	80
85 and over	509	108	401	79	64	87	129	119
Black[a]								
65 and over	78	29	49	63	46	60	56	86
75 and over	50	16	34	68	50	90	96	111
85 and over	20	5	15	75	56	125	157	141
Hispanic Origin								
65 and over	18	7	10	59	NA	111	NA	NA
75 and over	12	5	8	63	NA	130	NA	NA
85 and over	5	2	3	66	NA	150	NA	NA

SOURCE: U.S. Bureau of the Census, 1950–1980 Censuses of Population, *Special Reports* on the institutional population.

NOTE: NA = not available.

[a] Black and "other races" for 1950 and 1960.

TABLE 6.23

Marital Distribution of Men and Women Aged 65 and Over and 75 and Over in Institutions: 1980

| | Male | | | | Female | | | |
| | Ages 65 and Over | | Ages 75 and Over | | Ages 65 and Over | | Ages 75 and Over | |
Marital Status	In Institutions	Total Population	In Institutions	Total Population	In Institutions	Total Population	In Institutions	Total Population
Total	100.0	100.0	100.0	100.0	100.0	100.0	100.0	100.0
Single	23.6	5.5	17.8	5.7	13.7	6.7	12.0	7.3
Married[a]	27.5	76.3	27.8	66.2	9.0	37.5	7.5	20.9
Widowed	40.8	14.6	49.2	25.3	73.8	51.7	78.0	68.8
Divorced	8.1	3.6	5.3	2.8	3.5	4.2	2.5	3.0

SOURCE: U.S. Bureau of the Census, 1980 Census of Population, *Subject Reports,* PC80-40, and *U.S. Summary: Detailed Characteristics,* PC80-1-D1-A.

[a]Including married, spouse absent.

TABLE 6.24

Population Aged 65 and Over in Institutions, by Type of Institution and Age of Resident: 1950–1980

		Ages 65 and Over				
			Percent Increase		Percentage of Total	
Type of Institution	Number, 1980 (in thousands)	1970– 1980	1960– 1970	1950– 1960	1980	1950
Total Population in Institutions	1,340	38.5	57.3	59.6	100.0	100.0
Homes for the Aged	1,233	54.9	105.1	78.3	92.0	56.4
Mental Hospitals and Schools for the Mentally Handicapped[a]	51	−58.5	−32.2	25.5	3.8	37.8
Other	56	−16.5	7.9	99.1	4.2	5.8
Total Noninstitutional Population	24,209	26.8	22.5	31.2	X	X

SOURCES: U.S. Bureau of the Census, 1950–1980 Censuses of Population, special reports on the institutional population.

NOTES: Minus sign denotes a decrease. X = not applicable.

[a]The small number of residents of schools for the mentally handicapped aged 65 and over in 1950 and 1960 were distributed by age groups on the basis of the distribution of the population in mental hospitals.

aged without skilled nursing care.[47] The 1980 figure of 1.23 million persons in homes for the aged exceeded the 1970 figure by 55 percent (Table 6.24). During the same period the number of elderly persons in mental hospitals declined by 58 percent. This trend continues a pattern of change from the 1950s. In 1980, only 4 percent of institutionalized persons aged 65 and over resided in mental hospitals compared with 38 percent in 1950. The decrease in the use of mental hospitals is partly a result of the introduction of Medicare and Medicaid, with patients shifting to facilities eligible for federal and state repayment of costs, partly a result of the increased availability of residential board-and-care facilities, and partly a result of the development of psychotropic drugs, permitting management of many mental patients outside mental hospitals and the implementation of a new policy of deinstitutionalization.

The proportion of elderly persons in institutions is likely to grow in the next few decades because of the rapid increase anticipated for this

[47]The Census Bureau category "homes for the aged" consists almost wholly of nursing homes, that is, homes for the aged that provide skilled nursing care.

TABLE 6.24 (*continued*)

	Ages 75 and Over						Ages 85 and Over				
	Percent Increase			Percentage of Total			Percent Increase			Percentage of Total	
Number, 1980 (in thousands)	1970– 1980	1960– 1970	1950– 1960	1980	1950	Number, 1980 (in thousands)	1970– 1980	1960– 1970	1950– 1960	1980	1950
1,052	49.4	87.0	79.7	100.0	100.0	509	87.3	128.5	119.0	100.0	100.0
994	60.4	119.3	94.7	94.5	69.3	488	95.9	153.2	132.3	95.8	77.9
24	−56.4	−25.1	32.3	2.3	26.9	7	44.3	17.6	50.5	1.4	18.9
34	17.5	47.1	142.0	3.2	3.8	14	39.9	93.3	196.5	2.8	3.2
7,917	14.3	39.0	36.7	X	X	1,731	39.7	66.4	44.5	X	X

period in the size of the aged population and in its share of the older population. This trend is significant because disability and functional limitations, and hence the risk of institutionalization, increase with advancing age. The effects of the shift in age distribution will be intensified by the previously noted changes in the childbearing patterns and work roles of the middle-aged daughters of aged parents. Although they have been the major source of social support for their parents, their growing involvement in the labor force and/or in rearing and supporting children make them less readily available for this task than earlier. Institutionalization of the parents may be increasingly necessary as more families experience the severe stresses associated with maintaining an aged dependent person at home while trying to cope with other duties.

On the other hand, medical advances could obviate the need to institutionalize many of those currently in institutions. Nearly one fourth of those in nursing homes are there because of the debilitating effects of stroke;[48] but ways of preventing the severe brain damage that accompanies stroke in many victims are being devised,[49] and changes in living

[48]U.S. National Center for Health Statistics, "1977 National Nursing Home Survey," *Vital and Health Statistics Reports*, series 13, no. 43 (July 1979).
[49]J. H. Wood et al., "Augmentation of Cerebral Blood Flow Induced by Hemodilution in Stroke Patients After Superficial Temporal-Middle Cerebral Arterial Bypass Operation," *Neurosurgery* 5 (4) (1984):535–539.

habits hold promise for the further reduction in the incidence of stroke. A large proportion of the institutionalized elderly are victims of Alzheimer's disease, which, as some believe, may be caused by a virus, toxic metal deposits, or an enzyme shortage, and thus may be preventable.[50] Increased survival of spouses, as well as increased survival of siblings and friends, should help reduce the need to institutionalize family members who cannot function independently. Given these developments, it may be unwise to commit substantial public funds to the building of long-term care facilities. Moreover, home care, with help from the private sector or social agencies, should be preferable to institutionalization.

Movement into and out of Institutions

The percentage of elderly persons in institutions is not a good measure of the utilization of institutions by the elderly both because of the great variation in the proportion from age group to age group and because of the considerable gross movement of the elderly into and out of institutions.[51] That is, the stock figure, or the count of residents at a given date, does not provide a measure of the flow, or the gross movement, during a period. Much more than 5 percent of the elderly population will spend some part of their lifetime, or even some part of a given year, in an institution. Several studies show that there is considerable gross movement of the elderly into and out of institutions in the course of a year. The principal studies are noted below.

I begin with an illustration. An estimated 1,117,500 persons were discharged from nursing homes in 1976 compared with an estimated nursing home population of 1,303,000 in 1977 and 1,076,000 in 1973–1974.[52] To measure the movement into and out of institutions, it is useful to compare the relation between total change in the size of the

[50]U.S. National Institutes of Health, National Institute of Neurological and Communicative Disorders and Stroke, *The Dementias: Hope Through Research*, Publication no. 83-2252, June 1983, pp. 15–20.

[51]See R. Kastenbaum and S. Candy, "The 4-Percent Fallacy: A Methodological and Empirical Critique of Extended Care Facility Population Statistics," *International Journal of Aging and Human Development* 4 (1973):15–21.

[52]U.S. National Center for Health Statistics, "A Comparison of Nursing Home Residents and Discharges from the 1977 National Nursing Home Survey: United States," *Vital and Health Statistics*, Advance Data, no. 28 (1978).

U.S. National Center for Health Statistics, "Nursing Home Utilization in California, Illinois, Massachusetts, New York and Texas: 1977 National Nursing Home Survey," *Vital and Health Statistics*, series 13, no. 48 (1980).

U.S. National Center for Health Statistics, (1979).

institutional population over a year and the components of change in this population during the year:

$$R_1 - R_0 = A - D$$

where R_0 and R_1 represent residents at the initial and terminal dates during a period, respectively, and A and D represent admissions and discharges (including deaths), respectively, during the period. This equation can be roughly evaluated for nursing home admissions in 1976 by inserting the values given above and an estimate of the nursing home population in 1976 obtained by interpolation:

$$1,303,000 - 1,238,000 = A - 1,117,000$$
$$A = 1,182,000$$

The maximal level of demand on nursing homes in any one year may be represented by the sum of the resident population and total admissions during the year. For 1976, this figure was approximately 2,420,000 ($= 1,238,000 + 1,182,000$), or nearly twice the number of residents. This number represents 10 percent of the population aged 65 and over.[53] Given the large number of admissions each year in relation to the number of residents, the number of different persons spending some time in long-term-care facilities during the year is sizeable.

Most persons admitted to nursing homes stay for short periods (i.e., less than three months). Medicaid patients who were discharged in 1976 spent an average (median) of 24 days in a nursing home.[54] An actuarial analysis by Manton, Woodbury, and Liu, based on the National Nursing Home Survey of 1977, showed that one third of admissions are for less than 30 days and three quarters are for less than a year.[55] The median stay is only 79 days, but the average (mean) length of stay is far greater, 456 days, because a small proportion (2 percent) remain over 10 years. About 17 percent of the residents die within the first year and another 19 percent die shortly after discharge.[56] Clearly, many stays are not long

---

[53]Liu and Palesch's estimate of 9 percent for use of nursing homes by the elderly at some time in any given calendar year (including repeat admissions) approaches this maximum. See K. Liu and Y. Palesch, "The Nursing Home Population: Different Perspectives and Implications for Policy," *Health Care Financing Review* 3 (2) (December 1981):15–23.

[54]U.S. National Center for Health Statistics (1980).

[55]K. G. Manton, M. A. Woodbury, and K. Liu, "Life Table Methods for Assessing the Dynamics of U.S. Nursing Home Utilization: 1976–77," *Journal of Gerontology* 39 (1) (1984):79–87. Alternative, more recent estimates of length of stay in nursing homes were published in D. A. Spence and J. Wiener, "Nursing Home Length of Stay Patterns: Results from the 1985 National Nursing Home Survey," *Gerontologist* 30 (1) (February 1990):16–20.

[56]K. Liu and K. G. Manton, "The Characteristics and Utilization Patterns of Admission Cohorts of Nursing Home Patients," *Gerontologist* 19 (1) (1979):53–55.

term and nursing homes are much used for recuperative and terminal care.

Life table analysis of 1980 census data on the institutional population suggests that a person aged 65 may expect to spend about 1 year on the average (1.13 years, both sexes; .59 year, males; 1.49 years, females) in an institution during his or her remaining lifetime. For a person aged 65 who is already residing in an institution, the figure is much higher.

Various estimates have been made by life table methods of an elderly individual's lifetime risk of institutionalization.[57] McConnel has estimated that this risk approaches and may exceed 50 percent, while Liang and Tu estimate the risk at 36 percent. Although these figures may seem high, they are not unreasonable in the light of the fact that most admissions are short term, as noted earlier. The contrast between the proportion of the elderly in institutions at any time—1 in 20—and the proportion who will spend some time in an institution in their lifetime—more than 1 in 3—is a striking difference having important human, programmatic, and policy implications.

Factors Associated with Institutionalization

To a large extent the factors associated with institutionalization are similar to those associated with a shift from independent living to living with others on the occasion of disabling ill health. Disabling ill health is a general prerequisite for institutionalization, but the actual risk of institutionalization will be influenced by a host of other factors, among which are the availability of kin, family size, prior living arrangements, and the demographic and socioeconomic characteristics of the dysfunctional person and his/her kin. The age and sex of the person are strong indicators. Aged women, for example, have a higher risk than other age-sex groups because they are more likely to be living alone, to be unmarried, and to have an activity-limiting disability. The risk of institution-

---

[57]For a nonactuarial method, see D. K. Ingram and J. R. Barry, "National Statistics on Deaths in Nursing Homes: Interpretations and Implications," *Gerontologist* 17 (3) (June 1977):303–308. This study uses deaths in nursing homes to measure the lifetime chance of institutionalization. Measures based on deaths in institutions tend to give minimal estimates of lifetime utilization.

C. E. McConnel, "A Note on the Lifetime Risk of Nursing Home Residency," *Gerontologist* 24 (2) (April 1984):193–198. See also L. Vicente, J. Wiley, and R. A. Carrington, "The Risk of Institutionalization Before Death, *Gerontologist* 19 (1) (February 1979):52–55.

J. Liang and E. Jow-Ching Tu, "Estimating Lifetime Risk of Nursing Home Residency: A Further Note," *Gerontologist* 26 (5) (October 1986):560–563.

alization is much greater for those who live alone[58] and for those who are unmarried. The effect of the marital status of the dysfunctional person on his/her institutionalization is suggested also by the greater length of stay of unmarried persons (539 days vs. 278 days).[59]

This risk is greatly influenced by family size and the availability of kin, which delineate the possibilities of living with others in a family setting.[60] These possibilities are influenced not only by the identification of kin members (children, siblings) but also by their sex, age, and marital, labor force, and income statuses. The number of children ever born reported in decennial censuses, a rough measure of the availability of kin, is, for example, directly associated with shared living arrangements and indirectly associated with institutionalization.[61] The socioeconomic elements (marital, work, and income statuses) principally identify the competing demands on the adult child. Married children are less available than unmarried children, especially if the married child is a son. The risk of institutionalization appears to be greater for an unmarried woman with only a married son than for one who has only a married daughter. Higher income makes possible the purchase of services to keep dysfunctional family members at home.

Formal measurement of the contribution of different combinations of characteristics to the risk of institutionalization of elderly persons within the short term (2.5 years) and within the long term (7 years) was made by Shapiro and Tate, using a multiple logistic regression model with data for Manitoba.[62] Here are some selected results. On the basis of age alone, a person aged 85 and over has a 16 percent probability of entering a nursing home in the short term. Absence of a spouse (e.g., unmarried, living alone) raises the probability to 19 percent. A recent hospital admission, living in retirement housing, having at least one problem with the activities of daily living, and having a mental impairment raise the probability to 62 percent. On the other hand, a person aged 85 and over with a spouse at home has a 7 percent chance of institutionalization, which decreases to 4 percent if no other risk factors are

[58]Brody (1985); L. G. Branch and A. M. Jette, "A Prospective Study of Long-term Care Institutionalization Among the Aged," *American Journal of Public Health* 72 (1982):1373–1379.

[59]Liu and Manton (1979).

[60]E. Brody, W. Poulshock, and C. F. Masciocchi, "The Family Care Unit: A Major Consideration in the Long-term Support System," *Gerontologist* 18 (5) (October 1978):556–561.

[61]D. Wolf and B. J. Soldo, "Household Composition Choices of Older Unmarried Women," *Demography* 25 (3) (August 1988):387–403.

[62]E. Shapiro and R. Tate, "Who Is Really at Risk of Institutionalization?" *Gerontologist* 28 (2) (April 1988):237–245.

present. The probabilities of institutionalization in the long term for age groups 85 and over and 75–84 are very high when certain additional risk characteristics (poor self-rated health, sex female, problem remembering names) are present (86 percent and 73 percent, respectively). On the other hand, when all risk factors except age are absent, the probabilities, even in the long term, are low (12 percent and 6 percent, respectively).

Summary

Elderly men are much more likely than elderly women to be married and living in a family setting. The gap grows with advancing age, and at ages 85 and over only 1 in 16 women is married and living with a husband compared with 4 in 10 men. This difference is accounted for by greater mortality of married men than married women, augmented by the three–four year age gap between marital partners, and by the vastly higher remarriage rates of elderly men, resulting mainly from the far less favorable marriage market for older women.

At mid decade nearly all elderly males and elderly females maintained their own households either alone or as members of husband-wife households. Two in 5 elderly women live alone compared with 1 in 7 elderly men. The proportions increase sharply with advancing age, and at ages 75 and over about 1 in 2 women and 1 in 5 men live alone. The proportion for women has increased greatly since 1960, as widows and other unmarried women have chosen increasingly to live independently, that is, apart from other family members and nonrelatives, particularly if their health and resources permit. The share of men living alone has increased only modestly since 1960, but there has been a substantial rise in the share of men living with a wife, offset by a substantial drop in the share living with family members other than a wife. By 2000, 1 in 4 men aged 65 and over and 3 in 5 women aged 65 and over will be living alone.

Well over two fifths of all elderly households are maintained by women not in married-couple households. The only type of household that has increased since 1960 is female-headed nonfamily households, which are mostly solitary women (from 24 to 37 percent).

One fifth of all households are now headed by elderly persons, and an even greater share of households include an elderly person. Just after World War II only 1 in 7 households was headed by an elderly person. The share of households including an elderly person has hardly grown, however, as elderly persons, their children, and other relatives have less and less commonly remained as members of the same household and have established their own households. Dysfunctional parents often return to live with their adult children at the advanced ages, however, when they no longer can maintain an independent household.

Very few households have two generations of elderly persons, and this share has been falling. In general, the number of generations within households has been declining as a result of the departure of young persons from their parental households and the greater tendency of unmarried persons to live independently. Furthermore, male widowers tend to remarry and continue to maintain their own households. Middle-aged married couples hardly ever live with their parents and elderly couples hardly ever live with their children. On the other hand, the average number of generations in a "family," including persons lineally related in different households, has been growing steadily and is expected to continue to grow, mainly as a result of the increase in longevity. Families so defined are becoming more vertical and less horizontal in structure as the effect of low fertility is added to that of low mortality.

Today's older aged women have had very different family life cycle experiences from today's late middle-aged and young elderly women, the parents of the baby-boom generation. The younger cohorts married and divorced in greater proportions, married younger, had their first child sooner after marriage, spaced their births more closely together, and completed childbearing at an earlier age. In spite of having many children, they were much younger when their last child left home. A smaller share of the marriages of the younger cohorts will end in widowhood and, if widowed, they will be older when they become widowed. Both groups of cohorts can expect to spend about 15 years as widows. The children of the younger cohorts, the baby-boom generation, are reversing the marriage and fertility behavior of their parents but continuing their divorce behavior on its past trajectory.

The family support situation, as reflected in familial aged-dependency ratios relating persons aged 65–79 to those aged 45–49, is now at a peak level, as is the situation with respect to the relative number of elderly persons and college-age children, on the one hand, and middle-aged persons, on the other. The situation will ease as the baby-boom parents reach old age, but it will be strained once again when, after 2010, the baby-boom children begin to reach old age. Reduction in premature deaths of parents and the decrease in fertility since 1965 are the chief demographic factors in the prospective increase in the potential support burden of the elderly on their children. For the first time a large majority of middle-aged women have living mothers.

Contacts of elderly persons with children, siblings, and friends are frequent, and few elderly persons are isolated. Only 11 percent of elderly persons living alone do not have a living child or sibling; these individuals may present special needs among the elderly living alone. Most of the nonmonetary support obtained by elderly dependents is provided by family members—by a spouse if one is available, otherwise a daughter or daughter-in-law. Most older women who share a home with a child live with a daughter, particularly an unmarried daughter.

Only a small proportion of elderly persons now reside in institutional settings at any time—about 5.5 percent—but a far larger proportion of the elderly population, perhaps as much as 50 percent, will spend some part of their lives in an institution, commonly a few to several months. The proportion of the population residing in institutions rises so slowly with advancing age that it does not exceed 15 percent until ages 85–89—an indication of the considerable degree of informal support provided by relatives and friends. In comparison with the elderly population in the community, the institutionalized population is older and consists largely of women and unmarried persons (mostly widows). Population changes alone suggest that the institutional population will grow very rapidly in the next several decades.

The probability of admission to an institution in later life, assuming similar health conditions, depends on the characteristics of the person, the availability, number, and characteristics of kin, and the scope and effectiveness of support programs in the community. The risk of institutionalization in later life is greatest for aged women, especially if they are living alone and/or are unmarried, and have a disabling mental health condition.

Appendix 6A. Method of Deriving Generalized Age Cycles for the Proportions Married and Other Characteristics

This appendix describes the procedure that was used to develop generalized cohort age cycles and generalized period "age cycles" for various socioeconomic characteristics, such as marital status, labor force participation, median income, and home ownership. A comparison of generalized age cycles based on cross-sectional (or period) data and generalized age cycles based on cohort data aids in determining how closely the age variation in the characteristic in a particular calendar year, especially the shifts at the older ages, represents the age variation for the characteristic as shown by actual birth cohorts in a recent period. The generalized cohort age cycles developed for various socioeconomic characteristics are intended as estimates of the underlying age cycles for these characteristics in the post–World War II era.

362

The age cycles for the individual birth cohorts employed in the calculations may be interpreted as deviations around the generalized cohort age cycle. The age cycle for an individual birth cohort varies from the generalized cohort age cycle both because of the unique demographic and social characteristics of the particular birth cohort (cohort effect) and also because of its unique exposure to particular historical events at particular ages (period effect). The generalized cohort age cycle in effect averages the numerical impact of the different characteristics and postwar experiences of the individual cohorts and of the different historical experiences to which the various cohorts were exposed.

The steps in the derivation of generalized age cycles are described in terms of data for the proportions married for 5-year age groups and 5-year time intervals, as with CPS data. The procedure described is one variation among several possibilities. When the procedure is applied to decennial census data, the data are for 5-year age groups at 10-year intervals and some modifications are required.

First, proportions of persons married in 5-year age groups at 5-year time intervals were calculated from ages 25–29 to 75 and over for the period 1950–1985. Second, ratios of these proportions, linking the figures for the *adjacent* 5-year dates and the *adjacent* 5-year groups, were derived:

$$r_i = \frac{{}_5P_{a+5}^{y+5}}{{}_5P_a^y}$$

where ${}_5P_a^y$ equals the proportion married in a 5-year age group in a given year and ${}_5P_{a+5}^{y+5}$ equals the proportion married in the following 5-year age group five years later. Third, the seven ratios in step two linking the same pairs of ages for the seven quinquennial periods were averaged arithmetically:

$$\bar{r}_i = \frac{\sum_{i=1}^{n-1} r_i}{n-1}$$

where n equals eight. We now have a single set of ratios linking *adjacent* age groups over the entire age cycle for *adjacent* years from ages 25–29 on. These are denominated generalized age-to-age cohort relative changes.

Fourth, ratios of proportions married in *adjacent* 5-year age groups for the *same* year were computed for the whole matrix of proportions:

$$r_j = \frac{{}_5P_{a+5}^y}{{}_5P_a^y}$$

TABLE 6A.1

Percentages Married and Widowed of the Population Aged 25 and Over, by Age and Sex: 1940–1980

Marital Status and Age	Male				
	1940	1950	1960	1970	1980
Married					
25–29	62.7	74.2	77.2	77.1	61.1
30–34	77.2	84.3	85.6	85.7	76.3
35–39	81.6	86.8	88.3	87.9	82.4
40–44	83.2	87.1	89.1	87.9	84.7
45–49	83.6	86.2	88.5	88.3	85.6
50–54	81.9	85.0	86.9	87.9	85.4
55–59	79.9	83.1	84.7	86.6	85.8
60–64	76.7	79.3	82.9	84.5	85.3
65–69	71.9	74.0	79.4	80.6	83.0
70–74	64.9	67.5	73.1	75.8	79.6
75–79	56.1	59.0	64.7	68.8	73.6
80–84	45.8	48.2	53.7	58.0	64.4
85 and over	33.0	33.6	38.7	42.4[a]	48.4
Widowed					
25–29	0.4	0.3	0.2	0.3	0.1
30–34	0.7	0.4	0.3	0.3	0.2
35–39	1.3	0.7	0.5	0.5	0.3
40–44	2.1	1.2	0.8	0.8	0.5
45–49	3.2	2.1	1.4	1.3	1.0
50–54	5.1	3.7	2.3	2.1	1.8
55–59	7.4	5.9	3.8	3.2	2.8
60–64	11.1	9.6	6.5	5.2	4.6
65–69	16.2	15.0	10.2	8.8	7.3
70–74	23.8	22.2	16.8	13.8	11.2
75–79	33.3	31.4	25.3	21.2	17.6
80–84	44.7	43.3	37.2	32.0	27.3
85 and over	58.5	57.9	52.8	47.0[a]	43.8

SOURCES: U.S. Bureau of the Census, 1950–1980 Censuses of Population, *U.S. Summary*, series PC-D, Tables 102, 176, 203, and 264 for 1940 and 1950, 1960, 1970, and 1980, respectively.

[a]Based on 1970 Census Public Use Microdata Sample for ages 85–99 only; provided by I. Rosenwaike, University of Pennsylvania.

Fifth, the ratios in step four linking the same pairs of ages in the various years were averaged arithmetically:

$$\bar{r}_j = \frac{\sum_{j=1}^{n} r_j}{n}$$

TABLE 6A.1 (*continued*)

Female				
1940	1950	1960	1970	1980
74.1	83.3	86.2	82.5	68.8
80.4	86.2	88.7	86.1	77.3
81.5	85.5	88.2	86.6	80.1
80.6	83.1	85.9	85.3	80.8
78.3	79.8	82.5	83.2	80.2
73.3	75.0	77.0	78.7	77.7
67.2	69.1	69.9	72.2	73.4
58.0	60.1	61.4	63.1	65.7
46.5	48.9	51.6	52.0	54.8
34.3	36.6	39.1	40.0	42.7
23.0	24.7	27.4	27.9	29.5
13.5	14.2	16.2	17.2	17.7
6.7	7.0	8.2	9.9[a]	8.4
1.3	0.9	0.7	1.1	0.5
2.5	1.6	1.2	1.5	0.9
4.6	2.7	2.2	2.2	1.6
7.3	5.0	4.0	3.7	2.8
10.7	8.6	6.7	5.9	5.0
15.9	13.9	11.1	10.0	8.7
22.4	20.5	17.9	16.1	14.2
31.3	29.7	27.6	24.9	22.6
43.1	41.1	37.9	36.5	33.8
55.5	53.3	50.4	49.0	46.2
67.3	65.1	62.2	61.1	60.0
77.1	75.9	73.1	71.9	72.3
85.1	82.9	81.4	79.0[a]	81.8

where *n* equals eight. We now have a single set of ratios linking adjacent age groups. These are denominated generalized age-to-age period relative changes.

Sixth, the arithmetic mean of the proportions married for 1950–1985 at ages 25–29 was calculated:

$$P''_{25-29} = \frac{\sum\limits_{y=1}^{n} P^y_{25-29}}{n}$$

TABLE 6A.2

Average Period and Cohort Age-to-Age Relative Changes for Proportions Married and Widowed, by Sex: 1940–1980

Age		Male		Female	
Initial	Terminal	Period Average	Cohort Average	Period Average	Cohort Average
Married					
25–29	35–39	1.2207	1.1954	1.0727	1.0471
30–34	40–44	1.0575	1.0501	0.9942	0.9826
35–39	45–49	1.0126	1.0124	0.9583	0.9534
40–44	50–54	0.9888	0.9944	0.9185	0.9210
45–49	55–59	0.9720	0.9817	0.8709	0.8790
50–54	60–64	0.9567	0.9716	0.8075	0.8232
55–59	65–69	0.9252	0.9479	0.7209	0.7443
60–64	70–74	0.8819	0.9146	0.6242	0.6524
65–69	75–79	0.8266	0.8686	0.5211	0.5499
70–74	80–84	0.7457	0.7953	0.4081	0.4348
75–79	85–89[a]	0.6059	0.6534	0.3027	0.3247
Widowed					
45–49	55–59	2.6196	2.0232	2.5435	2.2018
50–54	60–64	2.5258	2.0226	2.3359	2.0892
55–59	65–69	2.5546	2.0882	2.1387	1.9555
60–64	70–74	2.4260	2.0067	1.8812	1.7577
65–69	75–79	2.2899	1.9258	1.6471	1.5699
70–74	80–84	2.1598	1.8445	1.4592	1.4103
75–79	85–89[a]	2.0787	1.8360	1.3006	1.2728

SOURCE: See text and Table 6A.1.

[a] 85 and over.

This is a single value. Seventh, the ratios in step three were applied to the single value in step six in a sequential fashion to obtain the generalized cohort proportions married. The formula used to derive the cohort generalized proportion (P') for ages 30–34, for example, was

$$P'_{30-34} = P'_{25-29} \times \bar{r}_i, \, {}^{30-34}_{25-29}$$

Then, this product was multiplied by the ratio (r_i) linking ages 30–34 and 35–39, to obtain the cohort generalized proportion married for ages 35–39, and so forth. Such sequential multiplication covering the whole age range above ages 25–29 produces the cohort generalized age cycle. Finally, the ratios (r_j) in step five were applied to the single value in step six in a sequential fashion to derive the period generalized age cycle.

The formula used to derive the generalized period proportion married (P'') for ages 30–34, for example, was

$$P''_{30-34} = P''_{25-29} \; \bar{r}_{j, \; {25-29 \atop 30-34}}}$$

The initial or anchor ages used in this monograph in developing the generalized age cycles vary from characteristic to characteristic. The calculations for the age cycles do not commonly begin with the lowest tabulated ages. For the proportions married shown by the census, the initial ages selected were 25–29 and 30–34; for the proportions widowed, the initial ages selected were 45–49 and 50–54; for the proportions in the labor force shown by the CPS, the initial ages are 25–29; for median income, the initial ages are 25–34, and for home ownership, the initial ages are 15–24. Note that the level of the generalized age cycles will vary on the basis of the choice of anchor ages, but not their pattern.

7

EDUCATION, WORK, AND RETIREMENT

T HIS CHAPTER deals with the education-work-retirement dimension of the life course and the demographic, social, and economic aspects of these activities in later life. Social trends of the past several decades suggest that the linear model for experiencing and representing education, work, and leisure in the life course needs substantial revision. In fact, pursuit of these activities in compact consecutive blocks of experience in the order named, corresponding to childhood and youth, adulthood, and old age, may no longer be the modal pattern. Changing individual needs as well as the demands of society are bringing about a reordering of the stages of this progression on the part of many persons and a repetition of the stages in later life by some. Specifically, we observe a weakening of the exclusive association of education and youth, the extension of education into the later years in the form of recapacitation of displaced homemakers and worker retraining, the interweaving of leisure into the work years, and the intermittent voluntary exit from and reentry into the work force. A formal quantitative analysis of the education-work-retirement dimension of the life cycle and its trend is needed, but has not been attempted here.

Education

Educational Level

Age, sex, and race variations. Measured in terms of the percentage of high school graduates, educational attainment is much lower for older persons than for the total adult population. As of 1985, the percentage of the population aged 65 and over who had graduated from high school was more than one third less than the percentage of those aged 25 and over. The median years of school completed, a far less sensitive measure, was only one tenth less.

According to the Current Population Survey (CPS) for 1985, about 1 in 6 elderly men and women had discontinued their formal schooling at the eighth grade, 2 in 3 had completed one or more years of high school, 1 in 2 were high school graduates, and 1 in 5 had completed one or more years of college. This is in sharp contrast to the record of the general adult population, a very small proportion of whom (1 in 16) had only an elementary-school education and a very large proportion of whom (3 in 4) had completed high school.

While educational attainment declines with increasing age in any calendar year, such an inverse relationship cannot normally apply to an actual birth cohort.[1] The inverse relationship observed between age and educational attainment in cross-sectional data reflects the cumulative experience up to different ages of many different cohorts. This experience has included an increase in educational opportunities available to each younger cohort and increasing pursuit of the additional schooling afforded by these opportunities. These factors have been associated with the rise in the socioeconomic status of the population and related intergenerational influences. Another, albeit secondary, factor has been the distinctive history of immigration to the United States. The large influx of immigrants in the late years of the nineteenth century and the early years of the twentieth century and the sharp curtailment of immigration following World War I have resulted in a larger concentration of foreign-born persons among the elderly population (19 percent in 1960 and 12 percent in 1980) than among the middle-aged population (10 and 6 percent). This fact is significant in the present context because the elderly foreign-born population has a somewhat lower educational level than the elderly native population. While the immigrant waves brought many

---

[1]A decline might occur at the older ages through the effects of immigration or an inverse correlation between educational level and survival probabilities. The former factor would contribute to only a small or minor decline, and the evidence contradicts an inverse relation between educational level and chances of survival.

people to the United States who had little education, they also infused new impetus into the spirit of striving for educational advancement, which they pursued through their children, many of whom are young-elderly today.

There is a marked disparity between the educational attainment of elderly whites and elderly blacks. As of 1985, 1 in 3 elderly white men compared with 2 in 3 elderly black men had discontinued their schooling at or before the eighth grade. On the other hand, about 4 in 5 elderly white men had completed one or more years of high school compared with 1 in 3 elderly black men. The proportion of high school graduates was 22 percent among blacks and 57 percent among whites. Differences between white and black women were similar. The principal factors underlying the lower educational level of blacks at the higher ages are their relatively depressed economic status at younger ages, past social and economic discrimination, unstable family structure, and residential

TABLE 7.1

Percentage of High School Graduates for Birth Cohorts, by Sex: 1950–1980

Birth Years	1950	1960	1970	1980	Age in 1980	Average Difference, 1950–1980[a]
Male						
1945–1955				84.4	25–34	X
1935–1945			71.5	77.1	35–44	+5.6
1925–1935		56.4	60.9	65.6	45–54	+4.6
1915–1925	47.3	50.0	52.6	56.2	55–64	+3.0
1905–1915	35.2	35.9	38.4	41.2	65–74	+2.0
Before 1905	25.6	24.5	26.3	29.6	75 and over	+1.3
Before 1895	20.0	17.9	21.0		85 and over	+0.5
Before 1885	15.9	15.2			95 and over	−0.7
Female						
1945–1955				84.0	25–34	X
1935–1945			71.2	76.3	35–44	+5.1
1925–1935		59.8	62.7	66.6	45–54	+3.4
1915–1925	51.1	53.3	55.1	57.5	55–64	+2.1
1905–1915	39.2	39.9	42.2	44.0	65–74	+1.6
Before 1905	29.7	28.7	31.3	34.3	75 and over	+1.5
Before 1895	22.7	21.5	26.0		85 and over	+1.6
Before 1885	19.0	19.6			95 and over	+0.6

SOURCES: Based on U.S. decennial censuses, 1950–1980.

NOTE: X = not applicable.

[a] Average absolute change per decade in percentages of high school graduates for birth cohorts.

clustering in racial and low-income enclaves. Under such circumstances the typical consequences appear to be reduced motivation in academic success, a poor quality of teachers and education, and, particularly, the lack of family values supportive of higher educational and occupational goals.

Trends and prospects. In the postwar years, the educational level of the older population has been rising rapidly, as more recent, better-educated cohorts have moved into the older ages (Table 7.1). The proportion of persons aged 65 and over who completed high school rose from 17 percent in 1950 to 27 percent in 1970, 39 percent in 1980, and 48 percent in 1985. It is expected to pass 50 percent before 1990 and 60 percent in the late 1990s and to reach 75 percent about 2010 (Table 7.2). The projections of high-school graduates were developed by a cohort methodology, described in Appendix 7A.

Because of the slower improvement in the educational attainment of persons below age 65, the relative gap between the educational level of the population aged 65 and over and the population aged 25 and over has been narrowing. This gap will continue to narrow and by 2000 the proportion of high school graduates aged 65 and over (63 percent) is expected to be only one fifth below the proportion for the entire adult population (80 percent). The relative deficit in educational attainment is slightly smaller for elderly women than elderly men and is expected to remain so at least until the end of this century. The gap in educa-

TABLE 7.2

Projections of the Percentage of Male and Female High School Graduates, Aged 55 and Over, by Age: 1980–2020

Sex and Age	1980	1990	2000	2010	2020
Male					
55–64	56.2	67.5	80.6	89.6	NA
65 and over	37.2	51.0	63.4	76.8	88.4
65–74	41.2	57.8	69.5	82.9	92.2
75 and over	29.6	39.8	55.5	68.1	81.7
Female					
55–64	57.5	67.7	78.1	86.5	NA
65 and over	39.9	51.4	62.6	74.0	84.5
65–74	44.0	58.4	68.8	79.3	87.9
75 and over	34.3	43.4	57.2	69.1	80.4

SOURCE: See Appendix 7A and Table 7.1.

NOTES: Consistent with decennial census data to 1980. NA = not available.

tional level of elderly whites and blacks was massive in 1950 but had narrowed greatly by 1985. Cohort analysis of the data suggests that the gap will continue to narrow briskly in future years.

The passing from the scene of the pre–World War I immigrants and the current and prospective arrival at the older ages of their children—beneficiaries of the post–World War II movement toward general equality in educational opportunity—is hastening the rise in the average educational level of the older population. It is rapidly becoming a moderately well-educated group that can articulate its interests and participate effectively in debate on public issues. It is, in fact, becoming a self-conscious political interest group, and it may begin voting as a bloc on various public issues. The older population's record on voting participation is already among the highest of any age group.

Literacy

Illiteracy poses special difficulties for the elderly in securing necessary services. Although, as noted, there has been a relatively large increase in the educational level of elderly persons in the last several decades, a small proportion of elderly persons still cannot read or write. Illiteracy appears to be greater among the elderly than among younger persons, even though illiteracy is quite low at all ages. In 1979, nearly 2 percent of the elderly reported an inability to read or write while only about 0.5 percent of all persons aged 14 and over reported an inability to read or write.

The extent of illiteracy varies particularly among the elderly of different nativity-parentage groups, with the foreign-born reporting a small amount of illiteracy (4.1 percent) and natives of foreign or mixed parentage reporting a negligible amount (0.6 percent). Illiteracy among elderly blacks is rather marked (6.8 percent) compared with elderly whites (1.1 percent). Literacy among elderly blacks is destined to improve rapidly, however, as the younger, more literate cohorts move into the older age brackets.

Illiteracy among the elderly does not appear to be a serious problem in terms of numbers currently involved or prospective numbers, except for a few special groups, but the problem has a wider dimension. To take full advantage of available services and to function effectively in our society require far more than mere literacy. We need also to consider the extent of functional illiteracy among older persons. This denotes so limited an ability to read and write that one's ability to conduct everyday business is restricted. High functional illiteracy may be measured

TABLE 7.3

Percentage of the Population Aged 60 and Over With High Functional Illiteracy, by Age, Sex, and Race/Spanish Origin: 1980 and 1950

Year, Sex, Race/Spanish Origin	Ages 60–64	Ages 65–69	Ages 70–74	Ages 75 and Over	Ages 65 and Over	Ages 85 and Over
1980						
Total both sexes	4.7	6.1	7.6	11.6	8.7	14.8
Male	5.4	7.2	9.0	13.9	10.0	19.1
Female	4.0	5.2	6.5	10.4	7.7	12.9
Total black	16.1	21.4	26.1	34.0	27.2	37.9
Male	20.7	28.2	33.7	42.0	34.3	47.5
Female	12.5	16.4	20.8	29.3	22.4	33.1
Total Spanish origin	26.8	31.9	37.4	43.8	37.6	NA
Male	25.8	31.4	37.5	44.9	37.7	NA
Female	27.7	32.4	37.3	43.0	37.5	NA
1950[a]						
Total both sexes	19.1	22.3	22.4	24.1	22.9	NA
Male	20.2	24.5	25.5	27.6	25.7	NA
Female	17.4	20.3	19.7	21.3	20.4	NA
Total black	50.0	58.3	61.7	68.9	62.1	NA
Male	52.8	61.1	64.0	70.4	64.4	NA
Female	47.1	55.7	59.5	67.5	59.9	NA

SOURCES: U.S. Bureau of the Census, 1950 Census of Population, *U.S. Summary: Detailed Characteristics*, Table 115; 1980 Census of Population, *U.S. Summary: Detailed Characteristics*, Table 262. Data for ages 85 and over in 1980 were provided by Ira Rosenwaike, University of Pennsylvania, on the basis of the 1980 census Public Use Microdata Sample, or estimated by the author.

NOTES: Percentage completing less than five years of elementary school as proxy for high functional illiteracy. NA = not available.

[a] Percentages are based on persons reporting on years of school completed. About 4 percent of the population aged 65 and over did not report on years of school completed. Data for persons of Spanish origin are not available. Data for "black" include other nonwhite races.

indirectly as the failure to complete more than four years of elementary school.[2]

While high functional illiteracy defined in this way has declined markedly since World War II in nearly all population groups, a substantial proportion of older persons, especially persons aged 75 and over, are still handicapped in this way. One fifteenth of the population aged 65 and over was functionally illiterate by this minimal standard in 1985 compared with over one fifth in 1950 (Table 7.3). Functional illiteracy

[2] A more adequate measure of high functional illiteracy would be the completion of less than eight years of elementary school, and a more realistic, even if rather stringent, measure of functional illiteracy would be the completion of less than four years of high school.

so defined remains quite high among elderly blacks and Hispanics. The proportion for blacks dropped over half since 1950; yet, nearly one quarter of blacks aged 65 and over were functionally illiterate in 1985. More than one third of elderly Hispanics are currently limited in this way.

The presence of a functionally literate spouse could mitigate the effects of functional illiteracy among the elderly, but this advantage does not often come to them. About one third of the elderly men and nearly three quarters of the elderly women who completed less than five years of schooling are not living with spouses at all.[3] About three fifths of wives who are functionally illiterate by this minimal standard have functionally illiterate husbands and over one third of the husbands who are functionally illiterate have functionally illiterate wives. Over two thirds of the husbands who did not finish elementary school have wives who did not finish elementary school. In view of the fact that many older persons have difficulties in securing appropriate services because of their inability to read and write at an adult level, it is unfortunate that literate spouses are often unavailable or unable to provide the necessary assistance to their partners to offset this deficiency.

An increase in functional illiteracy among older persons occurs with advancing age, as shown by data for 1980 (Table 7.3). As with other data on educational level and as explained earlier, the rise is a result of cohort succession—that is, the fact that the more recent cohorts reaching the older ages have tended to progress farther in school than earlier ones. On this basis we can reasonably expect further declines in functional illiteracy among the older population, especially in the light of the current public campaign to provide literacy training among adults.

Work

Trends in Labor Force Participation

Variations by age and sex. Important public policy issues are linked to changes in labor force participation among the older population as well as among younger persons. The labor force participation ratios (LFPR) of middle-aged and elderly men and women changed dramatically in the postwar period.[4] Those for men declined sharply in every five-year age

---

[3]U.S. Bureau of the Census, "Educational Attainment in the United States: March 1982 to 1985," *Current Population Reports*, series P-20, no. 415 (November 1987), Tables 3 and 5.

[4]This analysis of changes in LFPR makes use of both census data and CPS data. The former provides age detail for ages 75 and over and the latter provides time detail at quinquennial intervals to 1985.

category from age 55, with the rate of decline tending to rise as age increased (Tables 7.4 and 7.5). Those for women increased sharply at all ages under 65. These changes tended to bring the level and pattern of male and female LFPR into a new proximity (Figure 7.1). Consideration of these and related trends will provide a factual basis for analyzing various policy issues relating to the economic status of the elderly, particularly those relating to retirement and Social Security funding.

The largest percent declines in LFPR since 1950 occurred among men in the age groups 65 and over (Figure 7.2). Between 1950 and 1980, the LFPR at ages 65–69 fell by more than half (from 64 percent to 29 percent). The LFPR of men aged 70–74 was also more than halved by 1980 (from 43 percent to 18 percent). The same sharp percentage decline occurred for the LFPR of men aged 75 and over at a still lower level (from 21 percent to 9 percent).

TABLE 7.4

Percentage of the Civilian Noninstitutional Population Aged 45 and Over in the Labor Force, by Age and Sex: 1950–1985

Sex and Year	Ages 45–49	Ages 50–54	Ages 55–59	Ages 60–64	Ages 65–69	Ages 70–74	Ages 75 and Over
Male							
1950	96.5	95.0	89.9	83.4	63.9	43.2	21.3
1955	97.1	95.7	92.5	82.6	57.0	37.1	19.4
1960	96.9	94.7	91.6	81.1	46.8	31.6	17.5
1965	96.1	95.0	90.2	78.0	43.0	24.8	14.1
1970	95.3	93.0	89.5	75.0	41.6	25.2	12.0
1975	94.1	90.1	84.4	65.5	31.7	21.1	10.1
1980	93.2	89.2	81.7	60.8	28.5	17.9	8.8
1985	93.3	88.6	79.6	55.6	24.5	14.9	7.0
Mean	95.3	92.7	87.4	72.8	42.1	26.9	13.8
Female							
1950	39.9	35.7	29.7	23.8	15.5	7.9	3.2
1955	45.8	41.5	35.6	29.0	17.8	9.2	4.0
1960	50.7	48.7	42.2	31.4	17.6	9.5	4.4
1965	51.7	50.1	47.1	34.0	17.4	9.1	3.7
1970	55.0	53.8	49.0	36.1	17.3	9.1	3.4
1975	55.9	53.3	47.9	33.3	14.5	7.6	3.0
1980	62.1	57.8	48.5	33.2	15.1	7.5	2.5
1985	67.8	60.8	50.3	33.4	13.5	7.6	2.2
Mean	53.6	50.2	43.8	31.8	15.9	8.4	3.3

SOURCES: U.S. Bureau of Labor Statistics, *Special Labor Force Reports*, nos. 4, 69, 129, and 185; *Employment and Earnings* (January 1981 and January 1986); unpublished data for 1955; and estimates for 1950.

NOTE: Based on the CPS.

TABLE 7.5

Percent Change in Labor Force Participation Ratios of the Population Aged 45 and Over, by Age and Sex: 1950–1985

Sex and Period	Ages 45–49	Ages 50–54	Ages 55–59	Ages 60–64	Ages 65–69	Ages 70 and Over
Male						
1950–1985	−3.3	−6.7	−11.5	−33.3	−61.7	−67.2
1950–1960	+0.4	−0.3	+1.9	−2.8	−26.8	−23.7
1960–1970	−1.7	−1.8	−2.3	−7.5	−11.1	−27.9
1970–1980	−2.2	−4.1	−8.7	−18.9	−31.5	−26.1
1980–1985[a]	+0.1	−0.7	−2.6	−8.6	−14.0	−19.2
Female						
1950–1985	+69.9	+70.3	+69.4	+40.3	−12.9	−24.6
1950–1960	+27.1	+36.4	+42.1	+31.9	+13.5	+22.8
1960–1970	+8.5	+10.5	+16.1	+15.0	−1.7	−18.6
1970–1980	+12.9	+7.4	−1.0	−8.0	−12.7	−19.3
1980–1985[a]	+9.2	+5.2	+3.7	+0.6	−10.6	−6.5

SOURCE: Table 7.4.

NOTE: Based on the CPS.

[a]Note that this is a five-year period while the other component periods are decades.

In the next five years, the ratio for age group 65–69 fell another 4 percentage points. Thus, by 1985 only 1 in 4 men in their late 60s was in the labor force. The LFPR of men in the age group 70 and over also continued to fall after 1980, and by 1985 only 1 in 10 men at these ages was in the labor force. The LFPR of men aged 65 and over as a whole declined by a massive two thirds between 1950 and 1985 to 16 percent. The Bureau of Labor Statistics has projected a continuation of the decline to 11 percent in 1995, implying a drop of about one third in these 10 years.[5]

Relative declines at the ages below 65 were notably smaller. Among men aged 55–64 considered as a group, there was a decline of about one fifth between 1950 and 1985 to a LFPR of 70 percent, with about half of the decline taking place during the 1970s. The decline at these ages is expected to continue to 1995, when the projected worker ratio for the age group would be 10 percent lower than in 1985—that is, 63.

The data suggest that since around 1970 there has been a substantial increase in the proclivity of men to leave the labor force between

[5]H. N. Fullerton, Jr., "The 1995 Labor Force: BLS' Latest Projections," *Monthly Labor Review* 108 (11) (November 1985):17–25.

FIGURE 7.1

Percentage of the Male and Female Populations in the Civilian Labor Force, by Age: 1985

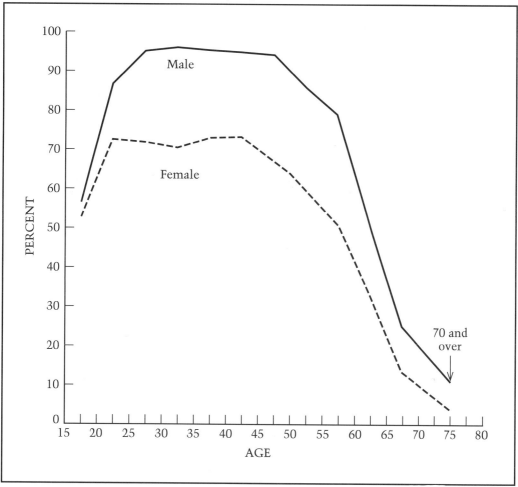

SOURCE: U.S. Bureau of Labor Statistics, *Employment and Earnings* (January 1986), Table 3.

NOTE: Points are plotted at center of age groups; point for age group 70 and over plotted at 75.0.

ages 55 and 65 compared with earlier decades. Although the pace of the labor force decline for men aged 55–59 and 60–64 was much slower than among men aged 65 and over, there is a clear suggestion of a growing tendency for men to retire well below the normal retirement age of 65. Additional suggestions of this tendency are given by the labor force

FIGURE 7.2

*Percentage of the Male Population Aged 55 and Over in the Civilian Labor Force,
by Age: 1950–1985*

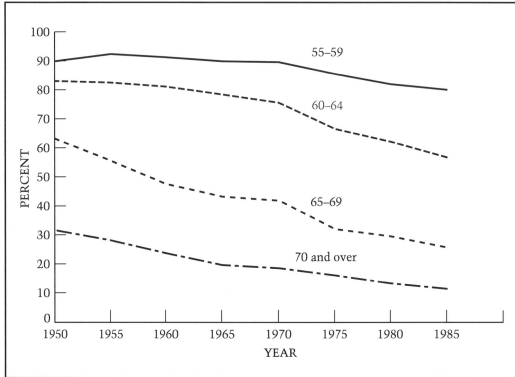

SOURCE: U.S. Bureau of Labor Statistics, *Handbook of Labor Statistics, Bulletin no. 2217* (June 1985),
Table 5; *Employment and Earnings* (January 1986), Table 3.

declines, albeit small, at ages 50–54 and 45–59.[6] Further analysis of these
data is required, however, before they can be used to describe retirement
trends. (See the section on retirement trends below.)

The pattern of change in the LFPR of women has been quite different. There were massive increases between 1950 and 1985 in the LFPR
of women at most ages (Tables 7.4 and 7.5), reaching about 70 percent
at ages 45–49 to 55–59 and then diminishing to 40 percent at ages 60–

---

[6]It is possible that some of the newly "retired" are shifting to the underground economy, particularly those retiring at the younger age groups. At these ages, probably more
retirees are claiming disability or are laid off than are retiring voluntarily. See later discussion.

378

64. There were declines of 13 percent at ages 65–69 and 25 percent at ages 70 and over. The pattern of changes in LFPR at the older ages shifted sharply from decade to decade (Figure 7.3). The rapid gains that the women aged 55–59 experienced during the 1950–1985 period occurred mainly during the 1950s, with increases sharply decelerating in the 1950s and 1960s and coming to a virtual halt during the 1970s. Women aged 60–64 had a similar experience. Even at ages 65 and over, where declines predominated, there were moderate increases in the 1950s before the decreases became really substantial in the 1970s. The Bureau of Labor Statistics anticipates a further decline at ages 65 and over from a LFPR of 7 percent in 1985 to 5 percent in 1995.

FIGURE 7.3

Percentage of the Female Population Aged 55 and Over in the Civilian Labor Force, by Age: 1950–1985

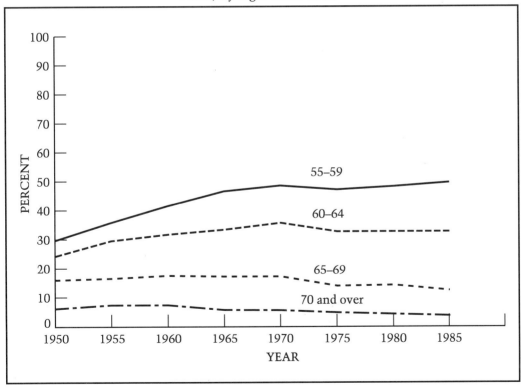

SOURCE: U.S. Bureau of Labor Statistics, *Handbook of Labor Statistics,* Bulletin no. 2217 (June 1985), Table 5; *Employment and Earnings* (January 1986), Table 3.

To measure the net effect of the opposing trends in male-female labor force participation, we examine the changes in the general economic activity ratio (GEAR), the percentage of the potential worker population (currently defined as the population aged 16 and over) that is economically active. In 1950 (when the potential worker population was defined as the population aged 14 and over) the female GEAR was 29 percent and the male GEAR was 79 percent. By 1980 the GEAR for women had reached 50 percent while that for men had dropped to 75 percent. The net effect of these opposing trends was a substantial increase in the total GEAR from 53 percent to 62 percent and a decline in the ratio of the male GEAR to the female GEAR from 2.7 to 1.5. This trend continued during the first half of the 1980s, but more slowly.

The massive increases in women's LFPR have far more than compensated for the decline in men's LFPR in the postwar period. The 80 percent rise between 1950 and 1985 in the GEAR of women was great enough not only to offset the small percent decline in the GEAR of men but also to bring about a marked increase (about 25 percent) in the GEAR of both sexes combined. According to the most recent projections of the U.S. Bureau of Labor Statistics, this supercompensatory trend is expected to continue into the future.[7] By 1995 the GEAR of both sexes combined is expected to reach 66 percent, approximately 13 percentage points greater than it was in 1950.

Cross-sectional versus cohort changes. The pattern of continuous decline in the labor force participation of men with increasing age after ages 30–34 or 35–39, shown by the decennial censuses for 1940–1980 and by the CPS for 1950–1985, is evident from cohort or longitudinal analysis of the data as well as period or cross-sectional analysis. Viewed broadly, the CPS data show little difference between the cross-sectional pattern and the cohort pattern for men from ages 45–49 on. Male worker ratios dropped by 74 percent between ages 45–49 and ages 65–69 in 1985 (i.e., measured on a cross-sectional basis) and by 75 percent when measured for the cohort aged 45–49 in 1965 and 65–69 in 1985. (See Table 7.4.)

A greater decline of the cohort data than of the cross-sectional data is shown when worker ratios in a cohort generalized age cycle are compared with those in a period generalized age cycle, particularly at the older ages.[8] In the generalized age cycle based on cross-sectional data for 1950–1985 and anchored to the average LFPR for ages 45–49 for this

---

[7]Fullerton (1985).

[8]Generalized age cycles of worker ratios for the post–World War II era were calculated to measure the difference between period changes and cohort changes over the age cycle in this period. They were derived from the CPS data by averaging the relative changes in worker ratios from one five-year age group to the next over the 1950–1985 period and then applying the average age-to-age relative changes sequentially to the average worker

TABLE 7.6

Period and Cohort Generalized Age Cycles for Labor Force
Participation Ratios of the Population Aged 45 and Over,
by Sex: 1950–1985

	Male		Female	
Age	Period	Cohort	Period	Cohort
45–49	95.3	95.3	53.6	53.6
50–54	92.6	92.0	50.2	54.5
55–59	87.4	85.9	43.7	51.6
60–64	72.4	68.9	32.0	40.5
65–69	41.0	35.2	16.4	21.3
70–74	26.1	19.4	8.6	11.0
75 and Over	13.2	8.5	3.3	4.3

SOURCE: See Table 7.4 and Appendix 6A.

NOTES: Ratios are anchored to average ratios, 1950–1985, at ages 45–49. Based on the CPS.

period, 41 percent of men are still in the labor force at ages 65–69, but cohort data anchored to the same average ratio for ages 45–49 show only 35 percent at ages 65–69 (Table 7.6). The reduction between these ages is 57 percent and 63 percent, respectively. In other words, cross-sectional data on labor force participation give a conservative indication of the reduction in worker ratios with increasing age at the older ages compared with cohort data. The more conservative decline in the cross-sectional data is a result of the fact that, to a greater or lesser extent, worker ratios have fallen at all ages in midlife and beyond between 1950 and 1985. The general findings noted here based on CPS data for 1950–1985 are supported also by the census data for 1940–1980, although the census results are more moderate. (See Appendix Tables 7B.1 and 7B.2.)

Any program designed to influence the trend of worker ratios for men at the older ages should recognize the robustness of the secular decline and the steepness of the fall in later life. The fall as shown by generalized cross-sectional data reflects the general postwar pattern of age changes in the same year, linking the experience of numerous cohorts, while the cohort age cycle reflects the general age pattern for a real cohort. To the extent that the two age distributions of LFPR are different, the cohort distribution provides a more realistic account of the age pattern as it was experienced, on the average, in the postwar era.

ratios for ages 45–49 over the same period. See Appendix 6A for a fuller explanation of this type of calculation.

Analysis of LFPR for females in the last several decades indicates a rather different relation of the cohort and cross-sectional age cycles from that shown for males. Generally, women are tending increasingly to enter and remain in the labor force until old age, as more and more of them try to supplement their husbands' incomes, establish or maintain independent households, pursue careers, and achieve economic security in old age in their own right. As a result, the cohort LFPR of women decline much less with increasing age than the period LFPR. Women's LFPR dropped by 80 percent between ages 45–49 and ages 65–69 in 1985, and by 74 percent when measured for the cohort aged 45–49 in 1965 and 65–69 in 1985.

Generalized period and cohort cycles for female worker ratios based on CPS data for 1950–1985 show similar declines. The period cycle shows a midlife peak in the female LFPR of 54 percent at ages 45–49, after which the LFPR fall steadily (Table 7.6). Period age-to-age changes of LFPR for women exceed the corresponding cohort age-to-age changes by large amounts over most of the age range, especially at the middle ages. Accordingly, worker ratios in the generalized age cycle based on cohort shifts substantially exceed worker ratios in the generalized age cycle based on period shifts. In the latter, for example, there is a 69 percent drop in the worker ratio from ages 45–49 to ages 65–69, but in the former the drop is only 60 percent. These results are confirmed by the generalized age cycles based on census data, with the census results being more pronounced.

Thus, unlike the situation with men, the period data exaggerate the real drop in the labor force participation of women at the older ages. Any policy to sustain labor force participation of women in later life would be aided by the more moderate drop in LFPR as women age, reflected by actual cohorts. The drop is still considerable, however, and it will be difficult to reduce it even if public policy is directed toward that goal.

International variations. The secular declines in the LFPR of older men and elderly women observed in the United States are not at all unusual in the industrialized countries. Country and regional estimates of LFPR published by the International Labor Office in 1986 show quite similar trends for men aged 65 and over in the More Developed Countries (MDC), particularly the countries of western and northern Europe.[9] (See Table 7.7.) Declines among older men under age 65 such as seen in the United States have also been observed in the MDC. For example, the declines in the LFPR of men aged 60–64 between 1950 and 1980 in

---

[9]International Labor Office, *World Summary*, 3rd. ed. Economically Active Population, Estimates and Projections, 1950–2025, vol. 5 (Geneva, 1986).

TABLE 7.7

Labor Force Participation Ratios for Older Men and Women in Selected More Developed Countries, by Age: 1950, 1980, and 2000

Country and Age	Male			Female		
	1950	1980	2000	1950	1980	2000
United States						
55–59	91.5	82.1	81.7	30.2	49.0	47.2
60–64	81.6	60.1	58.8	23.9	33.3	30.3
65 and over	45.0	19.1	16.2	9.9	8.1	4.3
United Kingdom						
55–59	97.4	91.8	91.4	24.6	55.9	54.4
60–64	93.6	75.0	73.8	15.0	24.7	23.0
65 and over	34.4	11.0	9.7	6.1	4.2	2.2
France						
55–59	84.8	73.3	72.5	40.3	42.0	39.2
60–64	81.8	33.8	32.4	38.2	19.1	16.2
65 and over	37.2	6.0	4.6	14.3	2.5	1.3
Federal Republic of Germany						
55–59	88.0	81.6	81.2	29.9	36.6	35.3
60–64	73.9	40.1	39.3	21.3	14.5	13.2
65 and over	27.5	4.9	4.2	9.6	3.6	1.9
Sweden						
55–59	93.3	87.9	87.1	26.2	66.4	62.8
60–64	82.7	70.4	68.1	19.0	41.4	36.2
65 and over	36.4	10.3	8.2	8.3	2.6	1.4
USSR						
55–59	89.5	78.8	73.9	50.9	25.0	21.5
60–64	86.5	30.6	26.7	42.6	9.7	7.1
65 and over	49.0	10.0	6.3	35.0	3.0	1.4
Japan						
55–59	89.5	94.0	93.0	44.1	50.7	47.3
60–64	80.9	81.8	78.4	37.4	38.8	33.0
65 and over	54.5	45.8	35.1	21.6	16.2	8.5
Australia						
55–59	92.2	82.6	81.9	16.8	34.1	32.1
60–64	81.4	57.7	55.6	11.3	16.6	14.3
65 and over	32.7	13.5	10.6	4.8	5.0	2.6

SOURCE: International Labor Office, *Economically Active Population, Estimates and Projections, 1950–2025*, vol. 4, *Northern America, Europe, Oceania, and USSR*, 3rd ed.(Geneva, 1986).

France and the USSR were more than twice as great as in the United States. On the other hand, Japan was exceptional and little change in LFPR among men under age 65 occurred there in this period.

The decline between 1950 and 1980 in the LFPR of women aged 65 and over was greater in most other MDC than in the United States. The decline was precipitous in the USSR, where the worker ratio fell from 35 percent to 3 percent. At ages below 65 the trends differed, with rises in some MDC and declines in others. For example, the LFPR of women aged 60–64 increased between 1950 and 1980 in the United States, northern Europe, and Australia, and declined in the USSR and eastern, western, and southern Europe. There was virtually no change in Japan, where the LFPR remained high (about 38 percent). The trend among women aged 55–59 was upward between 1950 and 1980 in the MDC, except in eastern Europe and the USSR. The magnitude of the changes varied greatly, from a huge 40-point rise in Sweden to a large 26-point decline in the USSR and a moderate 19-point rise in the United States.

In connection with a comparative analysis of retirement-age policy in the United States and five other MDC (Denmark, France, Sweden, West Germany, the United Kingdom) conducted in 1981, Rix and Fischer concluded that the trend toward reduced labor force participation at the older ages in these countries would continue.[10] In fact, the projections of LFPR prepared by the International Labor Office show similar downward trends for men at the older ages in these countries, continuing those of the past, and a substantial acceleration of the trend in Japan. For women, the projections to 2000 show small declines in all MDC.

Variations in Patterns of Work

Part-time/full-time work. Part-time work (during the work week) is very common among the elderly population, as it is among the very young. In 1985, among persons aged 65 and over employed in nonagricultural industries, 48 percent worked at voluntary part-time jobs.[11] This figure is close to the corresponding figure for persons aged 16–19 (51 percent). The figure for all part-time elderly workers, including those who worked part time for economic reasons as well as those who did so voluntarily, is 53 percent.

Even as the share of the elderly population in the labor force declined in the postwar period, those who remained have increasingly

---

[10]S. Rix and P. Fischer, *Retirement-Age Policy: An International Perspective* (Washington, DC: American Institutes for Research, 1981).

[11]U.S. Bureau of Labor Statistics, *Employment and Earnings* (January 1986), p. 191.

worked only part time. Of men aged 65 and over in the labor force, 47 percent worked part time in 1985 compared with only 30 percent in 1960. On the other hand, for men aged 45–64 in the labor force, the percentage working part time remained around a mere 6 percent during this period. The trends just noted for men were similar for women but apply to women with less relative force since women typically work part time to a greater extent than men. Of women aged 65 and over in the labor force, 62 percent worked part time in 1985 compared with 43 percent in 1960. Among working women aged 45–64, the percentage working part time varied little from about 25 percent between 1960 and 1985.[12] While the prevalence of part-time work has been increasing in recent decades among the elderly, there does not seem to have been any clear trend with regard to the number of weeks worked by the elderly during the year.

Most workers, old and young alike, believe that paid part-time work after retirement would be preferable to regular full-time work. A Louis Harris survey taken in 1981 found that 57–75 percent of the workers aged 55 and over would like to work part time under various options after retirement.[13] These respondents felt that a flexible work schedule (e.g., sharing a job, working less than five days a week, or working 70 hours every two weeks) would be preferable to the standard work week. Older workers want to work part time after retirement because they want to enjoy the additional hours of leisure as a reward after a long work career while continuing to earn money up to the Social Security ceilings, or because a health condition limits their ability to work full time.

It is not clear why the percentages actually working part time are far less than the percentages reporting a preference for part-time work in the survey. One possible explanation is that the supply of such jobs is not sufficient to meet the demand—a situation due in part to the concern of employers regarding the feasibility of flexible work schedules. The increase in the percentage of the work force working part time may indicate that the gap between supply and demand is narrowing.

The combination of a large decline in the LFPR of elderly men in recent decades and a substantial decline in the prevalence of full-time employment implies a massive reduction in total hours worked by elderly men. The decline in total hours worked by elderly women, however, has been small—much smaller than for elderly men—inasmuch as

---

[12]U.S. Bureau of Labor Statistics (1986), p. 191. See also U.S. Senate, Special Committee on Aging, *Developments in Aging: 1985*, vol. 3 (Washington, DC: U.S. Government Printing Office, 1985):60–61.

[13]L. Harris and Associates, *Aging in the Eighties: America in Transition*, a Survey Conducted for the National Council on Aging, 1981, cited in U.S. Senate (1985), p. 60.

TABLE 7.8

Percentage Unemployed in the Civilian Labor Force, by Sex and Age: 1950–1985

	Percent			Index		
Sex and Year	Ages 25–54	Ages 55–64	Ages 65 and Over	Ages 25–54	Ages 55–64	Ages 65 and Over
Male						
1950	4.0	4.9	4.8	100	122	120
1955	3.2	4.3	4.0	100	134	125
1960	4.2	4.6	4.2	100	110	100
1965	2.6	3.3	3.5	100	127	135
1970	2.8	2.8	3.3	100	100	118
1975	5.7	4.3	5.4	100	75	95
1980	5.1	3.4	3.1	100	67	61
1985	5.6	4.3	3.1	100	77	55
Female						
1950	4.9	4.5	3.4	100	92	69
1955	4.3	. 3.8	2.3	100	88	53
1960	5.0	3.4	2.9	100	68	58
1965	4.3	2.8	2.9	100	65	67
1970	4.5	2.7	3.1	100	60	69
1975	7.4	5.1	5.0	100	69	68
1980	5.9	3.3	3.1	100	56	53
1985	6.2	4.3	3.3	100	69	53

SOURCES: U.S. Bureau of Labor Statistics, *Handbook of Labor Statistics* (June 1985), Table 27; and *Employment and Earnings* (January 1986), p. 154.

the decrease in the prevalence of full-time employment of elderly women has been accompanied by only a modest decline in their labor force participation in recent years.

The number of weeks worked during the year, as well as the number of hours worked during the week, is negatively related to age. In 1979, for example, according to 1980 census data, 80 percent of men aged 50–54, 71 percent of men aged 60–64, and 50 percent of men aged 65–69 worked 50–52 weeks.[14] Among women, the relationship was not as strong and the proportions working year round were consistently lower. The corresponding figures are 63 percent, 60 percent, and 47 percent.

Unemployment. Elderly workers do not commonly experience a higher level of unemployment than workers in the prime working ages

[14]U.S. Bureau of the Census, 1980 Census of Population, *U.S. Summary: Detailed Characteristics* (1981), Table 273.

(i.e., ages 25–54), even though they commonly experience more weeks of unemployment during a year (combining all spells of unemployment). Their level of unemployment, as well as that of workers aged 55–64, relative to the level of unemployment for the prime working ages, has, in fact, been falling (Table 7.8). From 1950 to about 1970, men in the labor force aged 55–64 and 65 and over had higher percentages unemployed than men in the prime working ages. By 1980, however, the percentage unemployed for men in the older ages had dropped to well below that for men aged 25–54. The percentages unemployed for women aged 55 and over were consistently below the percentages unemployed for women aged 25–54 in this entire period. By the early 1980s, the unemployment ratios for women aged 55 and over were only a little over half the unemployment ratio for those aged 25–54.

The lower unemployment ratio of older male workers and, possibly, the secular decline of their unemployment ratio reflect, in part, voluntary choices and, in part, forced decisions to withdraw from the labor force. Older workers are far less likely to be employed in cyclically sensitive industries; they are more likely to be protected from layoffs by virtue of their seniority; they are more likely to have alternative sources of income, such as pensions or Social Security, permitting them to retire when their job is at risk; and they are more likely to receive financial inducements from their employers to retire during periods of high unemployment.[15] In addition, older workers are more likely than younger workers to become discouraged and leave the labor force when they become unemployed and cannot find a job.

The annual average probability of men aged 60 and over leaving unemployment by withdrawing from the labor force (.275) during the 14-year period 1968–1981 was three times as great as that for men aged 25–44 (.089).[16] At the same time, the probability of becoming unemployed was much greater for the younger men (.194 vs. .327). The differences among women were much smaller, but in the same directions as for men.

In spite of the apparent readiness of many elderly persons to withdraw from the labor force, many elderly want to work and they experience more weeks of unemployment in a year than younger workers. Male workers aged 65 and over with unemployment experience in 1984 were unemployed 2.2 weeks longer, on the average, than male workers aged 25–54. The median weeks of unemployment for workers of various

[15]P. L. Rones, "The Labor Market Problems of Older Workers," *Monthly Labor Review* 106 (5) (May 1983):3–12, esp. pp. 3–4.
[16]Rones (1983), p. 6.

ages *with unemployment experience* in selected years from 1973 to 1984 are:

	1973	1975	1978	1981	1984
Male					
25–54	8.9	14.2	11.6	13.7	15.4
55–64	11.3	17.1	13.7	13.6	17.3
65 and over	14.9	19.1	18.3	16.2	17.6
Female					
25–54	6.9	11.3	9.1	11.3	12.5
55–64	10.8	16.6	11.7	11.2	14.1
65 and over	8.6	19.1	14.3	13.3	14.9

SOURCES: P. Rones "The Labor Market Problem of Older Workers," *Monthly Labor Review* (May 1983); 3–12, esp. p. 7; and unpublished tabulations of the U.S. Bureau of Labor Statistics.

On the basis of a different set of data, unemployed male workers aged 65 and over were unemployed less time in 1985, on the average, in their *current spell of unemployment* (9.7 weeks) compared with unemployed workers aged 25–54 (10.2 weeks).[17] Female workers showed the same pattern. The difference in the direction of the two measures of duration of unemployment suggests that elderly people may experience more spells of unemployment than those aged 25–54. In summary, older workers do not have especially high levels of unemployment but, when they become unemployed, they are less likely to find a job, likely to remain unemployed longer, and more likely to quit the labor force in discouragement than workers in the prime working ages.

Older unemployed workers tend to get less help from government agencies in their quest for employment. Fewer of them are tested, counseled, given training, referred for job interviews, or placed in jobs. In general, most employers do not consider it worthwhile or cost-effective to train older persons, because older workers have shorter work-life expectancy, they have lower levels of education, and their learning abilities and productivity are assumed to decline with age.[18]

Gross movement into and out of the labor force. The simplest model of labor force mobility is one in which a person enters the labor force, remains in it for an extended and continuous period, and then withdraws permanently. Such a model fits reality poorly, however. According to tables of working life based on work experience in 1979–1980, for

---

[17]U.S. Bureau of Labor Statistics, *Employment and Earnings* (January 1986), p. 168.

[18]J. H. Schulz, *The Economics of Aging*, 3rd ed. (New York, NY: Van Nostrand Reinhold, 1985).

example, men averaged 3.9 entries and 3.6 voluntary exits (i.e., exits other than as a result of death) per lifetime and women averaged 5.5 entries and 5.4 voluntary exits per lifetime.[19] Even if we exclude the ages under 25, the average number of entries and exits still substantially exceeds one. At the older ages, data on net exits from the labor force mask a small turnover in labor force participation, since there are still numerous accessions at these ages. Data on net change in LFPR provide only a partial and potentially misleading view of labor force mobility, therefore.

Three different sources have been used to provide information on gross labor force mobility. They are the decennial censuses of 1960, 1970, and 1980; tables of working life based on data from various CPSs conducted in 1979 and 1980; and the 1969–1975 Retirement History Survey of the Social Security Administration.

The decennial censuses of 1960, 1970, and 1980 provide data on whether or not a person worked at any time during the year preceding the census and whether or not he/she was in the labor force during the census reference week. Thus, we can identify persons who were economically active during both periods, neither period, or only one of the two periods. On this basis we can develop an approximate measure of the extent to which the activity status of individuals changed between one year and the next.[20]

Activity status during the preceding year proved to be an excellent predictor of activity status during the census reference week. Over 90 percent of persons aged 55–64 had an apparently stable status around the censuses of 1960, 1970, and 1980 (Table 7.9). The great majority of men at these ages (about 70–80 percent) were economically active during both periods, while most women (about 50–60 percent) were consistently inactive. These types of worker behavior have been declining and other patterns have been increasing, particularly inactive status at both periods for men. Most men and women aged 65 and over were consistently inactive.

The percentage consistently inactive for men aged 65 and over showed a considerable increase between 1959–1960 and 1979–1980. The 1979–

---

[19]U.S. Bureau of Labor Statistics, *Worklife Estimates: Effects of Race and Education,* by S. Smith, Bulletin no. 2254 (February 1986), Table 4, p. 5.

[20]The time intervals over which the change of status is measured can vary from a few months (from December of the preceding year to April of the census year) up to 15 months (from January of the preceding year to April of the census year). The measure of mobility obtained from these data is approximate because an individual's work experience during the preceding year is not equivalent to his/her labor force status. Work experience during the preceding year is limited to those who were employed, whereas the labor force concept includes the unemployed. Another problem is that changes in one's status during the period from January 1 of the census year to the census reference week are ignored.

TABLE 7.9

Comparison of Economic Activity Status During the Year Preceding the Decennial Census and During the Census Labor Force Reference Week, for Men and Women Aged 55–64 and 65 and Over: 1960, 1970, and 1980 (percentage of total)

Sex and Activity Status[a]	Ages 55–64			Ages 65 and Over		
	1980	1970	1960	1980	1970	1960
Total Male	100.0	100.0	100.0	100.0	100.0	100.0
A1	69.2	79.4	82.2	17.6	23.8	29.7
2	7.0	6.6	5.0	8.2	11.4	11.2
B1	2.1	1.2	1.1	1.6	1.2	0.9
2	21.7	12.8	11.7	72.5	63.6	58.2
Total Female	100.0	100.0	100.0	100.0	100.0	100.0
A1	39.3	40.7	33.7	7.1	9.0	9.8
2	6.5	7.1	6.3	3.8	5.0	4.1
B1	2.4	1.6	1.3	1.1	1.0	0.6
2	51.9	50.5	58.7	88.1	84.9	85.5

SOURCES: U.S. Bureau of the Census, 1960 Census of Population, *Subject Reports*, PC(2)-6A, Table 16; 1970 Census of Population, *Subject Reports*, PC(2)-6A, Tables 520 and 521, and *Subject Reports*, PC(2)-8B, Table 1; and 1980 Census of Population, *U.S. Summary: Detailed Characteristics*, PC(1)-D1, Tables 215 and 218, and *Subject Reports*, PC(2)-8B, Table 1.

[a] A. Worked at some time during the year preceding the decennial census.
    1. Was in the labor force during the census reference week.
    2. Was *not* in the labor force during the census reference week.
B. Did *not* work at any time during the year preceding the decennial census.
    1. Was in the labor force during the census reference week.
    2. Was *not* in the labor force during the census reference week.

1980 figure was 73 percent and the 1959–1960 figure was 58 percent. Among elderly women the comparable figure remained fairly stable during this 20-year period at 85–88 percent.

The probability of remaining active appears to be directly associated with the number of weeks worked. Of men aged 60–64 who worked 50–52 weeks in 1969, for instance, 97 percent were in the labor force during the 1970 census reference week; of those who worked 14–26 weeks, 53 percent were still in the labor force; and of those who worked less than 14 weeks, only 36 percent remained in the labor force. The pattern was similar for women in this age group.[21]

These data indicate a very large measure of stability in the activity status of the elderly during a period of about 3–15 months, and the changes in status that did occur preponderantly fit the expected pattern

[21] U.S. Bureau of the Census, 1970 Census of Population, *Subject Reports*, PC(2)-6A, Table 22.

of the elderly dropping out of the labor force. The other type of change, from inactive to active status, occurred very infrequently although its frequency tended to rise between 1960 and 1980.

CPS-based working-life-table data provide a more refined measure of gross changes in labor force status over a year than the census data discussed above. Comparing the labor force status of the same individuals at two dates 12 months apart in 1979 and 1980 furnishes data on the consistency of labor force status at the two survey dates. With these data, tables of working life were constructed by the Bureau of Labor Statistics following the "increment-decrement model." Such tables measure gross movement into and out of the labor force as well as net movement.[22]

Among the older population the probability during a 12-month period of remaining in the same status, either active or inactive, is very high, whereas the likelihood of a change in status, either an entry or an exit, is relatively low, as we have seen with the decennial census data. The transition probabilities (i.e., the probability of being in the same or different labor force status) for each sex at age 60 and at age 65 are:

Transition	Age 60		Age 65	
	Male	Female	Male	Female
Inactive to Inactive	.899	.935	.904	.946
Active to Active	.841	.814	.731	.735
Inactive to Active	.082	.056	.068	.040
Active to Inactive	.140	.177	.241	.251

SOURCE: Based on U.S. Bureau of Labor Statistics (February 1986), Tables A-1 and A-4.

At these ages, as with the census data, the probability of an exit from active status is much greater than the probability of an entry into that status. Yet, there is an 8 percent probability for men and 6 percent probability for women at age 60 of abandoning retirement status.

According to the 1979–1980 tables of working life, the voluntary separation rate (based on total population) begins to exceed the accession rate (based on total population) around age 40 for both men and women. The excess (i.e., the net separation or net mobility rate) rises to a peak at ages 60–64 and then declines until ages 70–74 (Table 7.10). (The very high net separation rate at ages 75 and over reflects the few entries at these ages.) The age patterns of net separations at the older ages are quite similar for men and women, unlike the component patterns of accessions and separations.

[22]U.S. Bureau of Labor Statistics (February 1986), Tables A-1 and A-4.

TABLE 7.10

Net and Gross Labor Force Mobility Rates, for Men and Women Aged 45 and Over, by Age: 1979–1980 (annual rate per 1,000 population)

Sex and Age	Accession Rate	Total Separation Rate[a]	Voluntary Separation Rate	Net Mobility Rate[b]	Gross Mobility Rate[c]	Ratio, Net Rate/ Gross Rate[d]
Male						
45–49	21.2	32.9	27.6	−6.4	48.8	(−)13.1
50–54	23.5	43.1	34.9	−11.4	58.4	(−)19.5
55–59	29.2	75.0	64.1	−34.9	93.3	(−)37.4
60–64	44.5	115.8	104.9	−60.4	149.4	(−)40.4
65–69	54.8	91.8	82.8	−28.0	137.6	(−)20.3
70–74	42.9	66.9	58.1	−15.2	101.0	(−)15.0
75 and over	3.6	78.8	72.5	−68.9	76.1	(−)90.5
Female						
45–49	58.4	70.6	68.6	−10.2	127.0	(−)8.0
50–54	50.8	67.2	64.3	−13.5	115.1	(−)11.7
55–59	41.7	73.6	70.1	−28.4	111.8	(−)25.4
60–64	38.8	79.0	75.5	−36.7	114.3	(−)32.1
65–69	34.7	57.3	54.5	−19.8	89.2	(−)22.2
70–74	29.8	40.1	37.4	−7.6	67.2	(−)11.3
75 and over	3.0	41.3	39.7	−36.7	42.7	(−)85.9

SOURCE: Based on U.S. Bureau of Labor Statistics, *Worklife Estimates: Effects of Race and Education,* by S. Smith, Bulletin no. 2254 (February 1986), Tables B1, 2, and 3.

[a] Voluntary separations plus deaths of economically active persons. Also referred to as gross separations.
[b] Accession rate minus voluntary separation rate.
[c] Accession rate plus voluntary separation rate.
[d] Ratio per 100; minus sign may be disregarded.

Perhaps the most notable fact about the pattern of labor mobility at the older ages is that substantial entries still occur at these ages and that the accession rates for men at these ages are higher than the accession rates at most younger ages.[23] For example, the accession rate of men aged 65–69, 5.5 percent, is higher than that at any age after ages 25–29. This suggests the desirability of distinguishing primary and secondary retirements or thinking in terms of stages of retirement.

Data on accessions and separations permit a measure of the efficiency of the movement into and out of the labor force as well as a

---

[23] For evidence of the increase in the volume of both exits and reentries into the labor force between 1972 and 1980 on the basis of tables of working life, see M. D. Hayward, W. R. Grady, and S. D. McLaughlin, "Changes in the Retirement Process Among Older Men in the United States: 1972–1980," *Demography* 25 (3) (August 1988):331–378.

measure of the relative contribution of accessions and separations. The efficiency of labor force mobility varies greatly at the older ages. At its maximum (for men aged 55–59 and 60–64), the ratio (per 100) of the net mobility rate (i.e., the net separation rate) to the gross mobility rate (i.e., the sum of the accession rate and the separation rate) is about 40 percent (Table 7.10). Otherwise, the net separation rate amounts to no more than one third of the gross mobility rate (for women aged 60–64) and generally much less. (Since nearly all movements at the terminal age category, 75 and over, are separations, the ratio of the net separation rate to the gross mobility rate for this age group is viewed as exceptional.)

Another view of the age pattern of labor mobility is obtained from rates of accession and separation for 1979–1980 calculated in relation to the specific population exposed to risk. Such probabilities of accession and separation have complementary age patterns; with increasing age there is a steady and rapid decline in accession rates and a steady and rapid rise in separation rates.

Age	Male	Female
Accession Rate[a]		
55–59	120.9	81.1
60–64	88.6	56.4
65–69	75.3	41.8
70–74	52.0	33.3
75 and over	3.9	3.1
Separation Rate[b]		
55–59	98.9	151.5
60–64	232.5	253.5
65–69	337.9	339.4
70–74	381.8	384.5
75 and over	1000.0	1000.0

SOURCE: U.S. Bureau of Labor Statistics (February 1986), Tables B-7 and B-8.

[a] Labor force accessions per 1,000 inactive males or females.
[b] Total labor force separations per 1,000 active males or females.

The chance of a man entering the labor force at the older ages is greater than that of a woman and the chance of a man leaving it is generally less. For example, at ages 60–64 there is a 9 percent chance of a man entering the labor force and a 6 percent chance of a woman doing so. The chances of leaving the labor force at these ages are 23 percent and 25 percent for men and women, respectively.

The Retirement History Survey provides information on labor mobility of white men, aged 58–63 in 1969, for 1969–1975, derived by comparing the retirement status of individuals at two-year intervals.[24] Although this measure of mobility differs in a number of ways from those described earlier, the results support the finding previously noted— namely, that while the main tendency over a short period is for an elderly person's activity status to remain unchanged, there are significant, though modest, changes in activity status within the periods. The two-year transition rates show full retirement to be a highly stable state, nonretirement to be a considerably less stable state, and partial retirement to be a relatively unstable state. Ninety-three percent of those fully retired at the beginning of the two-year intervals were fully retired at the end of them, 61 percent of those not retired at all at the beginning were in that state at the end, and only 49 percent of those who were partially retired at the outset had that status at the end. The average duration of partial retirement appears to have been only a few years.

As we would expect, the most frequent type of change was from nonretirement or partial retirement to full retirement. Twenty-seven percent of nonretired persons and 43 percent of partially retired persons were fully retired two years later. Much less common were changes from more retirement to less. Six percent of those fully retired shifted to partial retirement, and 8 percent of the partially retired changed to nonretirement. Virtually no one went from full retirement to nonretirement.

Within the narrow age range 58–67, there was almost no age variation in the two-year continuation rate of full retirement around the very high level of 93 percent. Partial retirement varied somewhat more by age. In the age range 59–64 the continuation rates were 45–48 percent, at age 65 the rate was 51 percent, and for those aged 66 or 67, it was 60 percent. As expected, the continuation rate for those in nonretirement status varied greatly by age, dropping sharply from 87 percent at age 58 to 27 percent at age 64.[25] There was a particularly large difference between ages 62 and 63 (63 percent vs. 33 percent) that may be accounted for by the availability of Social Security retirement benefits beginning at age 62.

---

[24]The Retirement History Survey is a 10-year longitudinal survey of a national sample of 11,153 persons aged 58–63 in 1969. The analysis reported here was limited to white men who had not been self-employed before retirement, for the years 1969, 1971, 1973, and 1975. Retirement status rather than labor force status was considered in this study. The responses to the question "Do you consider yourself to be completely retired, partially retired, or not retired at all?" served as the basis for classifying respondents into three retirement categories. The status of each individual at the beginning and end of each of three two-year intervals—1969–1971, 1971–1973, and 1973–1975—was compared to determine retirement transitions. A. L. Gustman and T. L. Steinmeier, "Modeling the Retirement Process for Policy Evaluation and Research," *Monthly Labor Review* 107 (7) (July 1984):26–33.
[25]Gustman and Steinmeier (1984), Table 3, p. 29.

In sum, a considerable minority of elderly white men who retired during the period 1969–1975 continued to remain economically active enough to regard themselves as only partially retired, although most men who retired did so fully. A small number of men went back to work after a period of complete retirement or shifted from partial retirement to nonretirement. Most partially retired men soon went on to full retirement, however.

Factors Affecting Trends in Labor Force Participation

Factors depressing labor force participation of men. A number of factors may be enumerated to account for the steady decline in the labor force participation ratios (LFPR) of older men since 1950, but the essential basis is the increasing financial ability of older workers to retire, supported by a willingness to exchange a portion of current consumption for additional leisure.[26] Retirement has become increasingly acceptable—indeed, regarded as an entitlement, if not a reward.

We can consider the factors depressing labor force participation of men in more detail under the headings of financial ability, health, and other factors. The growth in financial independence of older workers is a combined effect of the rise in real earnings and assets of older workers, the more widespread eligibility of workers for benefits under Social Security and especially private pension plans, the advent of Medicare and private health insurance programs, and various other supporting and subsidiary economic factors.

A major factor in the decline of LFPR has been the long-term growth in real wages that has increased the lifetime wealth of successive cohorts.[27] Real median income of family householders aged 45–54, for example, increased 43 percent during the 1950s and again during the 1960s. Although there was a drastic deceleration to 6 percent during the 1970s, real income for this group more than doubled between 1950 and 1980.[28]

---

[26]P. L. Rones, "Older Men—The Choice Between Work and Retirement," *Monthly Labor Review* 101 (11) (November 1978):3–10; C. Rosenfeld and S. Brown, "The Labor Force Status of Older Workers," *Monthly Labor Review* 102 (11) (November 1979):12–18; and J. R. Storey, "Financial Disincentives for Continued Work by Older Americans," paper presented at the annual meeting of the Gerontological Society of America, San Diego, November 23, 1980.

[27]R. L. Clark and D. T. Barker, *Reversing the Trend Toward Early Retirement* (Washington, DC: American Enterprise Institute for Public Policy Research, 1981).

[28]R. L. Clark and D. A. Sumner, "Inflation and the Real Income of the Elderly: Recent Evidence and Expectations for the Future," *Gerontologist* 25 (2) (April 1985), esp. p. 150.

An indication of the long-term growth in assets is given by data on median net worth for newly retired workers in 1941–1942 and 1982. The median net worth (in 1982 dollars) of married couples jumped from $11,230 in 1941–1942 to $68,000 in 1982.[29] (Inflation in the value of homes probably accounts for an important part of the rise in the net worth of older persons during this period in spite of the adjustment for the value of the dollar.)

Social Security coverage has greatly expanded and benefits have greatly grown since the inception of the program in 1935. Benefits under Social Security have been adjusted for cost-of-living increases since 1975; in addition, they have been increased in constant dollars. After adjustment for inflation, real benefits were 2.3 times greater in mid 1983 than in 1950.[30] The ages of eligibility have been expanded too. Older workers first become eligible for reduced Social Security benefits at age 62 (for men beginning in 1961 and for women beginning in 1956), although the initial age for full Social Security benefits remains 65 (beginning in 1935).

The marked increase in job-specific public and private pension systems and in the size of benefits has also enhanced the financial ability of many older workers to retire.[31] In 1984 two thirds of American workers were covered by a pension plan provided by their employers; that is, they were working for a covered company.[32] The percentage of newly retired workers with pensions other than Social Security increased between 1941–1942 and 1982 from 17 percent to 56 percent for married persons and from 13 percent to 42 percent for nonmarried persons.[33] In recent decades, the benefits from employer pension plans have been rising at the same rate as earnings, despite the trend toward earlier retirement.

Relatively few workers who are not self-employed wish to continue working full time beyond age 65 if they can receive an employer-provided or union-provided pension or if they lose their primary job by termination without such a pension. Many quit by age 62 under such conditions. The increasing availability and size of job-specific pensions will continue to militate against a delay in retirement. Social Security alone would not commonly lead to a decision to retire. Several researchers

[29]M. A. Ycas and S. Grad, "Income of Retirement Aged Persons in the United States," *Social Security Bulletin* 50 (7) (July 1987):Tables 14 and 15.

[30]G. S. Fields and O. S. Mitchell, *Retirement, Pensions, and Social Security* (Cambridge, MA: MIT Press, 1984), p. 10.

[31]U.S. General Accounting Office, *Retirement Before Age 65: Trends, Costs, and National Issues*, Report to the Chairman, Select Committee on Aging, House of Representatives (July 1986), Figure 2.1 and Table 2.1.

[32]U.S. Bureau of the Census, "Pensions: Worker Coverage and Retirement Income, 1984," *Current Population Reports*, series P-70, no. 12 (September 1987).

[33]Ycas and Grad (1987), Table 14.

maintain that Social Security has been responsible for only a very small part of the decrease in retirement age, but it has caused a significant bunching around the ages of 62 and 65.[34]

Ill health or disability has been an important reason for early retirement of older men. The available evidence suggests that the proportion of men aged 50–64 who are unable to work because of a disability has been increasing in the last several decades.

According to the March 1984 CPS, among males who did not work in 1983, health or disability was cited as the primary reason by about two thirds of those aged 50–54, over one half of those aged 55–61, and nearly one third of those aged 62–64.[35] According to the 1984 Aging Supplement to the NHIS, 51 percent of men aged 55–59 and 39 percent of men aged 60–64 who had retired did so for reasons of health.[36]

Older persons are less likely to be in the labor force than younger persons partly because more older persons suffer from a work disability and those with a work disability are much less likely to be in the labor force than those without one. In fact, having a work disability has a considerable impact on the LFPR of older men and women, as the following data from the March 1982 CPS indicate:

	Percent in Labor Force	
Sex and Age	With a Work Disability	Without a Work Disability
Male		
45–54	44.2	97.4
55–64	27.8	85.8
65–74[a]	8.3	28.2
Female		
45–54	21.6	67.0
55–64	12.4	50.5
65–74[a]	4.9	13.4

SOURCE: U.S. Bureau of the Census, *Current Population Reports*, series P-23, no. 127 (July 1983), Tables 6 and 7.

[a]Percent employed.

It is notable that many persons with a work disability manage to be economically active. For example, over one quarter of the men aged 55–

[34]C. J. Ruhm, "Why Older Americans Stop Working," *Gerontologist* 29 (3) (1989):294–299, esp. p. 296.
[35]Cited in U.S. General Accounting Office (1986), Table 3.7.
[36]U.S. National Center for Health Statistics, *Vital and Health Statistics*, Advance Data, no. 136 (May 1987).

64 and one twelfth of the men aged 65–74 reporting a work disability were in the labor force in 1982. In trying to interpret these data, we observe that a much larger percentage of persons in the labor force reporting a work disability are self-employed than of those not reporting a work disability: For example, among men aged 65–74 the figures were 44 percent and 28 percent, respectively.[37]

The relationship between labor force participation and work disability leads us to ask whether the striking decline in the LFPR of older men in the postwar period was caused to an important degree by an increase in the prevalence of work disability or by a deterioration in the health of workers. The evidence is unclear and mixed. Feldman noted the increase in the prevalence of work disability of men at ages 50–69 between 1970 and 1980, and possibly since earlier years, and concluded that the increase in work disability could account for some of the decrease in LFPR.[38] On reviewing these and other data, Ycas concluded that since the decline in LFPR had not closely paralleled changes in the prevalence of work disability, these changes were not responsible for the decline in LFPR.[39]

Data from the Social Security Administration on the share of eligible workers aged 62–64 who are receiving disability benefits show a marked general rise between 1965 and 1985. (See Table 7.20 below.) The proportion for men more than doubled between 1965 and 1980 and then fell off to 13 percent in 1985. The proportion for women increased from 4 to 8 percent in these years following the same pattern. While the rise in the proportion of eligible workers drawing disabled worker benefits may have resulted mainly from a rise in the prevalence of work disability, increasing familiarity with the disability-entitlement program, an increasing predisposition toward retirement, and increasing abuse of the program may also have been involved.

A contrary position is taken in a recent General Accounting Office study citing CPS data for March 1974, 1979, and 1984 on the percentage of older men who did no work during the preceding year and who gave health or disability as the reason.[40] Poor health was reported by older persons with declining frequency between 1974 and 1984.

---

[37]U.S. Bureau of the Census, "Labor Force Status and Other Characteristics of Persons with a Work Disability: 1982," by J. McNeil, *Current Population Reports,* series P-23, no. 127 (July 1983), Tables C and 7.

[38]J. J. Feldman, "Work Ability of the Aged Under Conditions of Improving Mortality," *Milbank Memorial Fund Quarterly* 61, no. 3 (Summer 1983):430–444.

[39]M. A. Ycas, "Recent Trends in Health Near the Age of Retirement: New Findings from the Health Interview Survey," *Social Security Bulletin* 50 (2) (February 1987):9–12.

[40]U.S. General Accounting Office (1986), Table 3.8, p. 43.

| | Percent | | |
Age	1973	1978	1983
55–61	68.3	64.4	51.6
62–64	51.8	39.6	30.0
65 and Over	21.6	17.1	13.9

The Social Security Administration's 1982 New Beneficiary Survey also found that of those men who had left wage and salary jobs and become entitled to benefits at ages 62–64, a declining percentage reported that they had left their last job for health reasons between 1968 and 1982.[41] The respective figures were 54 percent and 29 percent.

Many other factors have been influencing the tendency to leave the labor force. These include pressures exerted by employers on older workers to retire, withdrawal of discouraged older workers from the labor force in the face of continuing inability to find work or age discrimination in hiring, the decline in self-employment (a class of work which tends to discourage early retirement), and the decline in jobs for which little education and skill are required. Other factors include continuing, if not growing, job dissatisfaction, the general decline in the number of family dependents, and the sharp rise in the proportion of married-couple families with female members who work. Of special importance, in the light of the fact that the selfhood and self-esteem of males in our society are largely defined in terms of work and occupation, is the growing public acceptability of retirement as a right after a "lifetime of hard work."

Occupations for which the educational qualifications are very low, such as factory worker and farm and nonfarm laborer, have been declining in importance. Some employers may increase educational requirements needed to perform a particular job because an ample supply of unemployed persons who can satisfy the original educational requirements is available. Since unemployed older men tend to have less education than younger workers, they are at a disadvantage when seeking jobs. This disadvantage is reflected in their longer average duration of unemployment.[42] Moreover, there are probably fewer jobs for older workers now than formerly, and there may be greater institutional barriers to part-time employment.

Although older workers are often protected by seniority against job loss, they are as vulnerable as younger workers to plant shutdowns or

---

[41]S. R. Sherman, "Reported Reasons Retired Workers Left Their Last Job: Findings from the New Beneficiary Survey," *Social Security Bulletin* 48 (3) (March 1985):25–26.

[42]Rones (1978). See also Schulz (1985); and U.S. Bureau of Labor Statistics, *Employment and Earnings* (January 1986), Table A-17.

business closings. Confronted by a job change, older workers face many problems. One is discrimination by employers in being hired. This practice is rationalized by assumptions regarding the poor health prospects, limited trainability, and low adaptability of older workers. The higher cost of pensions and fringe benefits borne by employers contributes to the reluctance of employers to hire older workers. Because of age discrimination in hiring, older workers are often discouraged from seeking employment and withdraw from the labor force.

Factors affecting labor force participation of women. The LFPR of middle-aged women increased considerably during the period 1950–1985, as was described. It may be recalled also that the rise of the LFPR of women aged 65 and over during the 1950s was reversed during the following decades and that the decline accelerated in the 1960s and 1970s.

The gains in women's LFPR in the postwar period resulted in part from an increase in the willingness of women, especially wives and mothers, to enter and remain in the labor force and in part from an increase in the demand for labor as men became less available. In addition, major changes in the industrial and occupational structure of the labor force, specifically the decline in farming and the shift out of blue collar occupations into white collar occupations, favored the employment of women. The increase in the educational level of women aged 45 and over permitted them to compete more successfully with men in the labor market and to enter professional, technical, and managerial positions in large numbers. The rise in their educational attainment contributed to a rise in their wage rates, and in turn rising wages attracted women into the job market.

The women's movement and related influences contributed to changes in attitudes toward women's employment. This movement supported changing views as to the roles, needs, and aspirations of women which reflected a desire by them to be independent and to pursue their own careers. It became increasingly acceptable for wives and mothers to have jobs and careers. Legislation prohibiting sex discrimination in employment also contributed to support the entry of women into the workplace and to protect their position in it. Furthermore, high inflation and rising standards of living have served as economic incentives for wives to increase family income through employment.[43] The high inflation and interest rates of the 1970s and early 1980s forced many women into the labor force to supplement their husbands' incomes.[44] The tendency

[43]L. J. Waite, "U.S. Women at Work," *Population Bulletin* 36 (2) (May 1981), Population Reference Bureau, Washington, DC.

[44]The causal path between inflation and the trend toward two-worker families (resulting in an increase in consumer spending) flows both ways. The labor force trend is itself a factor in inflation, albeit a secondary one. See N. J. Semler and A. Tella, "Inflation

of children to leave home at an early age reduced the parents' burden of household management. The rise in the divorce rate and in the proportion of women maintaining their own households drew more women into the labor force for reasons of economic necessity, self-fulfillment, or the desire to structure leisure time.[45]

Factors tending to sustain labor force participation. There are some influences working to reverse the trend toward falling worker ratios of older men and elderly women. These include the introduction of flexible work programs, the recent history of very high inflation rates and anticipation of their return, the decline in the proportion of younger workers and the resulting improvement in the competitive earnings position of older workers, and the outlawing of mandatory retirement at age 65. Efforts to reduce the abuse of disability as a basis for retirement, advances in the treatment and management of chronic conditions, and changes in personal habits and lifestyles consonant with improved health should give additional support to the prospect of a rise in worker ratios. Government programs aimed at improving health and safety conditions and prohibiting use of toxic and carcinogenic substances in the workplace may also decrease the proportion of workers retiring because of ill health.

Private pensions have not kept pace with inflation. Between 1973 and 1981, the annual inflation rate fluctuated between 6 percent (1973, 1976) and 14 percent (1980). The rate was sharply reduced in the early 1980s, however. If inflation rates had continued at, or even close to, the very high levels of the late 1970s, the purchasing power of most private pensions would have eroded rapidly. As it was, workers continued to leave the work force in large numbers at an early age. Some workers eligible for early retirement may be holding their jobs in fear of a return to the extremely high rates of inflation experienced earlier. Many may be forced to delay retirement if heavy inflationary pressures reappear.

Because of the increasing availability and use of early retirement provisions under private pension plans and the high and increasing levels of life expectancy at the older ages, many retirees who receive private pension incomes will have long periods of retirement. For example, according to the death rates of 1986, one half of the men surviving to age 62 are expected to live another 16.5 years and one quarter are expected to live another 23 years. At age 62 one half and one quarter of the women are expected to live another 21.5 and 28 years, respectively.

and Labor Force Participation," in *Stagflation: The Causes, Effects, and Solutions,* vol. 4, studies prepared for the use of the Special Study on Economic Change of the Joint Economic Committee, Congress of the United States (December 17, 1980).

[45]The causal path flows both ways. The rise in the labor force participation of spouses is a factor in rising divorce rates, albeit a secondary one.

We cannot say whether this prospect will encourage or discourage continuing at work.

The proportion of younger workers will diminish as a result of the decline in birth rates in the 1960s and 1970s, and this trend may relax the pressure on older workers to retire. There may even be a shortage of workers in various lines of work, especially unskilled work. The demand for labor may encourage some older persons to remain in the labor force for a longer period so as to augment their retirement benefits. They will "retire" and return to the work force in less skilled occupations or as part-time workers.

Government actions may also induce or at least permit some workers to remain in the labor force who would not otherwise continue working. Until 1978, the age at which compulsory retirement was permitted was, in effect, 65. This age was implied in the Age Discrimination in Employment Act (ADEA) of 1967, which prohibited age discrimination in hiring, discharge, compensation, and other terms of employment of persons up through age 64. The law was amended in 1978 to include workers in private industry up through age 69 and in 1986 to prohibit mandatory age retirement altogether. It is unlikely, however, that the change in coverage under the 1978 and 1986 amendments to ADEA has had or will have a sizable impact on employment of older workers.

The 1983 amendments to the Social Security Act were designed to remove the disincentives to work, but they are not likely to do so, at least not in the short term.[46] The amendments mainly stipulate a gradual increase in the age of entitlement to full benefits from age 65 in 2002 to age 66 in 2009 and age 67 in 2027.[47] As a result of the changes mandated by the new law, some workers will choose to delay retirement or be forced to do so, but the new law is expected to have little effect on actual retirement age.[48] A significant effect may be achieved only by elimination of early retirement under Social Security and a rise in the retirement age under private pension plans.[49]

---

[46]R. F. Boaz, "The 1983 Amendments to the Social Security Act: Will They Delay Retirement? A Summary of the Evidence," *Gerontologist* 27 (2) (April 1987):151–156.

[47]They also gradually increase the benefits for delayed retirement over an 18-year period beginning in 1990, from 3 percent to 8 percent per year, for persons born after 1924, for each year that prospective retirees continue to work past age 65; reduce the share of full benefits awarded at age 62 from the current 80 percent to 75 percent by 2005 and to 70 percent by 2022; and, beginning in 1990, lower, from 50 cents to 33 cents for each dollar of earnings above the exempt amount, the benefits of persons with earnings above the exempt amount who are entitled to full benefits.

[48]U.S. National Commission on Employment Policy, *Restructuring Social Security: How Will Retirement Ages Respond?* by G. S. Fields and O. S. Mitchell (Washington, DC: U.S. Government Printing Office, 1983).

[49]Ruhm (1989), p. 298.

Official Projections of Labor Force Participation

This discussion of factors affecting the labor force participation of older persons in past years provides a basis for considering the outlook for the short-term future. The task of projecting labor force trends of the older population is rendered difficult because some factors support an increase in the proportions of older workers in the labor force, while others support a decrease. As we have seen, there has been a persistent downward trend in labor force participation ratios (LFPR) in spite of the many factors that could contribute to an increase. The projections of the labor force prepared by the U.S. Bureau of Labor Statistics in 1985 extend only to 1995 and postulate a continuation of the trends of the previous two decades in the labor force participation of older men and women.[50] Three series of projections (middle, high, and low) were developed, each based on a different assumption regarding the rate of change in LFPR after 1984. Each of the three series of ratios was combined with the middle population projections of the Census Bureau published in 1984 (base year 1982).

Under the middle assumption, there is an implied drop in the worker ratio for men aged 55–64 between 1985 and 1995 of approximately 5

[50]Fullerton (1985). The Bureau of Labor Statistics has revised its projections of the labor force since releasing those of November 1985 and since the tables in this monograph were prepared. Revised projections were published in U.S. Bureau of Labor Statistics, "Labor Force Projections: 1986 to 2000," by H. N. Fullerton, Jr., *Monthly Labor Review* 110(9) (September 1987). Again, three alternative series of civilian labor force projections were generated by combining the Census Bureau's middle population projections and three series of LFPR projections. These extend from 1986 to 2000. The principal results for the middle growth series are as follows:

Age and Sex	LFPR			Labor Force (in millions)		Percent Change
	1986	2000	Change	1986	2000	
Male						
16 and over	76.3	74.7	−1.6	65.4	73.1	+12
55–64	67.3	63.2	−4.1	7.0	7.2	+4
65 and over	16.0	9.9	−6.1	1.8	1.4	−25
Female						
16 and over	55.3	61.5	+6.2	52.4	65.6	+25
55–64	42.3	45.8	+3.5	4.9	5.7	+16
65 and over	7.4	5.4	−2.0	1.2	1.0	−14

TABLE 7.11

Civilian Male and Female Labor Force and Participation Ratios for Selected Ages, Actual and Projected: 1975, 1985 and 1995

Participation Ratio

Sex and Age	1975	1985	1995 High	1995 Middle	1995 Low	Absolute Change 1975–1985	Absolute Change 1985–1995[a]
Male,							
16 and over	77.9	76.3	77.8	75.3	71.9	−1.6	−1.0
55–64	75.6	67.9	} 37.3	62.6	} 29.7	−7.7	−5.3
65 and over	21.6	15.8		11.0		−5.8	−4.8
Female,							
16 and over	46.3	54.5	61.4	58.9	57.2	+8.2	+4.4
55–64	40.9	42.0	} 20.2	42.7	} 18.5	+1.1	+0.7
65 and over	8.2	7.3		5.5		−0.9	−1.8

(The braced High and Low values apply jointly to the 55–64 and 65-and-over rows.)

Labor Force (thousands)

Sex and Age	1975	1985	1995 High	1995 Middle	1995 Low	Percent Change 1975–1985	Percent Change 1985–1995[a]
Male,							
16 and over	56,299	64,411	71,621	69,282	66,219	+14.4	+7.6
55–64	7,023	7,060	} 8,612	6,119	} 6,750	+0.5	−13.3
65 and over	1,914	1,750		1,423		−8.6	−18.7
Female,							
16 and over	37,475	51,050	62,464	59,888	58,192	+36.2	+17.3
55–64	4,323	4,932	} 6,060	4,695	} 5,565	+14.1	−4.8
65 and over	1,042	1,156		1,049		+10.9	−9.3

(The braced High and Low values apply jointly to the 55–64 and 65-and-over rows.)

SOURCES: H. N. Fullerton, Jr. "The 1995 Labor Force: BLS' Latest Projections," *Monthly Labor Review* 108(11) (November 1985): 17–25, Tables 4 and 5; and U.S. Bureau of Labor Statistics, *Employment and Earnings* (January 1986), Table 3.

NOTE: Base year of projections is 1984.

[a] Middle series.

percentage points, and the projected male work force aged 55–64 decreases by 13 percent (Table 7.11). Under the high assumption, the projected male worker ratio for this age group increases by a few percentage points and, under the low assumption, there is a pronounced decline, amounting to 14 percentage points.

Worker ratios for men aged 65 and over are assumed to remain unchanged or to decline between 1985 and 1995. The middle series shows a projected drop of 5 percentage points in the worker ratio and 19 percent in the number of male workers. The high series assumes near constancy of the worker ratio and the low series assumes a drop of 9 percentage points.

The projected LFPR for women aged 55–64 increases slightly between 1985 and 1995 under the medium assumption. There is a somewhat greater increase under the high assumption and a slight decrease under the low assumption. The projected LFPR for women aged 65 and over show a continuous decline between 1985 and 1995 under the various assumptions. The medium series shows a decline of 2 percentage points in the LFPR and a 9 percent decline in the number in the labor force.

The pattern of future changes for whites and blacks is assumed to be similar. However, the projected LFPR are lower for older black men than for older white men and, conversely, the projected ratios are higher for black women than for white women. These relations resemble those in the past.

If these projections are realized, especially the low growth series, but also the middle growth series, we can anticipate a continuation of the rise in the ratio of older nonworkers to workers. As will be discussed further, such a development would contribute to the possibility of serious problems for the solvency of the Social Security Trust Funds, especially the Social Security Retirement System, and would add to the financial burden on taxpayers, workers, and employers in maintaining the solvency of the system.

Characteristics of Workers and Nonworkers

In addition to variations by gender and age, the levels and trends of LFPR at the older ages vary according to such demographic and socioeconomic characteristics as type of residence (e.g., farm, nonfarm), race and Hispanic origin, marital and household status, educational level, occupation and class of worker (e.g., employed, self-employed), and income. I briefly consider some of these variations next.

TABLE 7.12

Percentage Rural-Farm of the Total Labor Force and of the General Population Aged 65–69, by Sex and Race: 1940–1980

| Race and Year | Labor Force | | Population | | Ratio, | LFPR RF [a] / LFPR Total |
	Male	Female	Male	Female	Male	Female
All Classes						
1940	34.2	14.7	26.4	19.2	1.3	0.8
1950	22.5	7.6	17.4	12.5	1.3	0.6
1960	13.7	4.4	9.7	7.1	1.4	0.6
1970	9.0	2.7	6.2	4.2	1.5	0.6
1980[b]	7.2	2.5	3.6	2.3	2.0	1.1
Nonwhite						
1940	52.0	30.8	40.3	31.5	1.3	1.0
1950	34.7	13.9	25.2	18.8	1.4	0.7
1960	14.0	3.8	9.7	7.0	1.4	0.5
1970[c]	5.1	1.4	3.4	2.3	1.5	0.6
1980[b,c]	2.0	0.8	1.0	0.6	2.0	1.3

SOURCES: U.S. Bureau of the Census, various decennial census reports, 1940–1980.

[a] Ratio of rural-farm labor force participation ratio to total labor force participation ratio.
[b] Ages 65 and over.
[c] Black only.

Variations by residence. According to decennial census data, the LFPR of elderly men residing on farms have been substantially higher, and the LFPR of elderly women residing on farms have been lower, than the LFPR of elderly men and women, respectively, in the nonfarm sector (Table 7.12). Like self-employed workers in the nonfarm sector, farmers tend to continue working beyond the normal retirement ages. Their wives, on the other hand, commonly work at nonfarm jobs, from which they withdraw at an early age.

The LFPR of elderly rural-farm men declined less rapidly than the LFPR of elderly nonfarm men in the period 1950–1980. The LFPR of elderly women in the nonfarm sector declined only from the 1960s while the LFPR of women on the farm continued their steady rise. The LFPR of black women aged 65 and over in the rural-farm sector have been declining steadily, however.

As a result of these changes and the drop in the farm population, the percentage of the elderly labor force residing on farms has been declining very rapidly. The farm share of the elderly labor force has in fact been declining for all sex and race categories. For example, 52 percent of economically active black males aged 65–69 were in the rural-farm sector in 1940, but only a few percent remained on farms by 1980 (Table 7.12). The massive movement out of agriculture and off farms on the part of elderly workers intensified the national labor force trends observed for elderly workers, particularly the declines for men.

The decline in the worker ratios of elderly men in the rural-farm sector and the decline in the farm share of the elderly labor force are related in part to a decline in the demand for farm products, an increase in agricultural productivity, a displacement of the family farm by large industrialized farms, and a general slump in the farm economy. Since a large share of farm residents do not earn their living principally from farm operations, the poor state of the farm economy can account for only a part of the drop in older farm workers. Many older farm families have been favored by the same social insurance and pension programs as the general population; this has also led older farm workers to quit work in large numbers.

Variations by race and Spanish origin. The proportions of black and Hispanic men working have tended to be lower than, or about the same as, those of white men at ages 55 and over (Table 7.13). On the other hand, the LFPR of older black women have tended to be higher than

TABLE 7.13

Labor Force Participation Ratios of Whites and Other Races Aged 45 and Over, by Sex and Age: 1955 and 1985

Age and Year	Male		Female		Ratio, Females to Males	
	White	Other Races	White	Other Races	White	Other Races
45–54						
1955	96.7	94.4	42.7	54.7	.44	.58
1985	92.0	84.0	64.2	65.3	.70	.78
Percent change	−4.9	−11.0	+50.4	+19.4	X	X
55–64						
1955	88.4	83.3	31.8	40.7	.36	.49
1985	68.8	60.6	41.5	45.2	.60	.75
Percent change	−22.2	−27.3	+30.5	+11.1	X	X
65 and over						
1955	39.6	40.0	10.5	12.3	.27	.31
1985	15.9	14.5	7.0	9.3	.44	.64
Percent change	−59.8	−63.8	−33.3	−24.4	X	X

SOURCES: Based on U.S. Bureau of Labor Statistics, *Handbook of Labor Statistics* (June 1985), Tables 3, 4, and 5; *Employment and Earnings* (January 1986), pp. 154, 155, and 157.

NOTES: "Other races" are almost entirely black. Based on the CPS. X = not applicable.

those of white women. Older black women work in greater proportions because they must do so; they are less likely to be living with a spouse and be eligible for private pensions or Social Security benefits. The LFPR of older Hispanic women are strikingly low compared with the LFPR of older black and white women, in spite of economic need, presumably because of cultural pressures.

As a result, the gap between the LFPR of men and women is greater for older Hispanics than for the older population as a whole.

	Hispanic Population			Total Population
	LFPR			
Age and Year	Male	Female	Ratio, Females/ Males	Ratio, Females/ Males
45–54				
1970	90.0	43.4	.48	.58
1980	88.3	53.0	.60	.66
55–64				
1970	77.9	30.1	.39	.52
1980	72.2	37.4	.52	.57
65 and Over				
1970	24.8	7.9	.32	.36
1980	20.6	7.9	.38	.43

SOURCE: Based on U.S. Bureau of the Census, Census of Population, *U.S. Summary: Detailed Characteristics*, 1970, Table 215; and 1980, Table 272; App. Table 7B.1.

The postwar trends of labor force participation of older black and Hispanic men and women have been essentially similar to those of older white men and women. The LFPR of the race/Hispanic groups have responded to the same general influences. Yet the responses were different in degree. The decline for black men at the middle ages has been more marked than for white men, so that the LFPR for the two races were farther apart in 1985 than in 1955. At ages 65 and over the sharp declines for both blacks and whites kept the LFPR close to one another. A more rapid improvement in their pension situation and greatly increased use of disability as a path to retirement may be an important part of the explanation for the especially rapid drop in the LFPR of older black men. The disabled worker role has seemed particularly attractive to blacks because of their history of, and expectation of, low future earnings.[51]

[51]R. C. Gibson, "Reconceptualizing Retirement for Black Americans," *Gerontologist* 27 (6) (December 1987):691–698, esp. p. 692.

Variations by marital and household status. There is a historical tendency for the labor force participation of older women who are married to be relatively low if their husbands are in the labor force, and for the labor force participation of older men who are married to be relatively high if their wives are in the labor force. Simply stated, the wife is less likely to be working if the husband is working, as is usually the case, and the husband is very likely to be working if the wife is working. For example, the worker ratio in 1980 of men aged 65 and over whose wives worked during the preceding year was twice as great as that of their counterparts whose wives did not work (50 percent vs. 25 percent).[52]

The LFPR of older men living with their wives have been greater in the postwar period than those of older men in other marital classes, particularly previously married men (Table 7.14), but the worker ratios have been converging. LFPR have been sharply declining since 1955 for older married men as well as for those in other marital categories. For example, worker ratios declined by well over half for elderly married men and for elderly widowed and divorced men between 1955 and 1983.

Labor force participation of older single women has been high compared with that of other older women. In 1983 the LFPR of single women aged 65 and over were about two thirds greater than those of women in other marital classes. Single women, especially, continue to work in the older ages in order to maintain social contacts, preserve a productive structure in their lives, and support themselves.

By the early 1980s the differences between the female marital classes had sharply diminished because of a rise in the LFPR of older wives and the near-stability or decline in the labor force participation of other older women. Between 1955 and 1983, for example, the LFPR of wives living with their husbands increased by 60 percent for those aged 45–64 and 11 percent for those aged 65 and over, while the LFPR of widowed and divorced women in these ages increased by only 7 percent or declined by 30 percent, respectively.

As expected, the LFPR of older male householders (including men in married couples) are much greater than those of older men who are not householders. In 1970, for instance, the difference was more than 30 percentage points for men aged 45–64 and 16 percentage points for men aged 65 years and over.[53] There are at least two possible but intersecting explanations for this difference. One is that these men have greater responsibility for supporting family members. The fact that the LFPR of

---

[52]U.S. Bureau of the Census, 1980 Census of Population, *U.S. Summary: Detailed Characteristics,* PC 80-1-D1-A, Table 275.

[53]More recent data are not available. U.S. Bureau of the Census, 1970 Census of Population, *Subject Reports,* PC2-6A, Table 4.

TABLE 7.14

Labor Force Participation Ratios of the Population Aged 45 and Over, by Sex, Age, and Marital Status: 1955–1983

	Male		Female	
Marital Status and Year	Ages 45–64	Ages 65 and Over	Ages 45–64	Ages 65 and Over
Never Married				
1955	85.3	33.0	74.8	24.5
1965	78.1	23.2	76.1	22.4
1975	69.9	21.0	68.3	15.8
1983	66.5	19.2	64.2	12.5
Ratio, 1983/1955[a]	78.0	58.2	85.8	51.0
Married, Spouse Present				
1955	94.2	44.6	29.9	6.6
1965	92.6	31.0	39.5	6.7
1975	86.8	23.3	43.8	7.0
1983	82.4	18.6	47.9	7.3
Ratio, 1983/1955[a]	87.5	41.7	160.2	110.6
Other Marital Statuses[b]				
1955	85.1	28.0	55.9	11.2
1965	80.8	18.7	61.6	10.5
1975	73.4	15.4	59.0	8.3
1983	73.3	12.7	60.0	7.8
Ratio, 1983/1955[a]	86.1	45.4	107.3	69.6
Ratio to Married, Spouse Present, 1983[a]				
Never married	80.7	103.2	134.0	171.2
Other marital status	89.0	68.3	125.3	106.8

SOURCE: U.S. Bureau of Labor Statistics, *Handbook of Labor Statistics* (June 1985), Table 6.

[a] Ratios per 100.
[b] Includes married with spouse absent, widowed, and divorced.

older female householders (not including women in married couples) are greater than those of other older women as well as other (nonhouseholder) older men provides some support for this explanation. A second reason for the higher LFPR of older male householders is that they are better educated. The positive association of labor force participation with education is discussed further below.

Variations by educational level. Relating the labor force patterns of the elderly to their educational level will help us understand better the past trends of LFPR. A positive relationship between the highest grade completed and LFPR may be observed in each census from 1940 to 1980.[54] (See Table 7.15.) Even though the educational level of the elderly increased considerably during this period, the increase apparently had little effect on the changes in the overall LFPR of the older ages.

Almost without exception, higher education levels are associated with higher LFPR. Detailed education data show rather clearly how sensitive LFPR have been to variations in educational attainment. Among women aged 55–64 in 1970, for example, the LFPR rose steadily from 25 percent for those with no years of school completed to 62 percent for college graduates. Because of the greater normative pressure for men to be in the labor force, the LFPR of men in these ages were substantially higher and not as strongly related to education as the LFPR for women. Nevertheless, the relationship was pronounced.

	Percent	
Years of School Completed	Male	Female
No Schooling	56.9	24.6
Eighth Grade	78.7	36.8
High School Graduate	86.0	47.3
College Graduate or Higher	89.4	61.8

SOURCE: U.S. Bureau of the Census, 1970 Census of Population, *Subject Reports,* PC(2)-5B.

There has been a major shift in the educational level of the older population since 1940. Seventy-five percent of the men aged 55–64 in 1940, for example, had completed no more than the eighth grade and only 4 percent of them had graduated from college. By 1980, only 25 percent of the men in this age group had completed no more than the

[54]The requisite data are readily available in considerable detail in published reports of the 1950, 1960, and 1970 Censuses of Population. The published data for 1940, however, are limited to the age categories 45–54 and 55–64 and are reported only for the native white and Negro populations. Estimates were made for the remaining population, almost all of whom were foreign-born whites; the results were combined with the published data to produce the requisite data for the population irrespective of race or nativity. Census data on education cross-classified by labor force status were not tabulated in 1980 in the age detail that was needed. Estimates were made by using the distributions of the numbers in the labor force and the numbers not in the labor force (by age and sex) by educational level in 1970 and sequentially adjusting them pro rata to the reported 1980 totals for each educational level (not by labor force status) and labor force status (not by educational level).

The 1980 estimates were prepared for only half of the number of educational levels shown for the earlier census dates. There are, then, two sets of data, one presenting LFPR in eight educational categories (1940–1970) and the other presenting LFPR in four educational categories (1940–1980). The 1980 data are not completely comparable to the more detailed earlier data.

TABLE 7.15

Index of Variation in Labor Force Participation Ratios, by Years of School Completed at the Older Ages: 1950 and 1980

Age and Years of School Completed	Male		Female	
	1950	1980	1950	1980
55–64	100	100	100	100
0–7	96	76	77	70
8–11	102	95	96	89
12–15	104	107	129	107
16 and over	107	114	208	142
65–74	100	100	100	100
0–7	90	70	74	61
8–11	105	91	100	85
12–15	113	115	144	119
16 and over	127	151	224	171
75 and Over	100	100	100	100
0–7	84	60	73	65
8–11	105	92	96	84
12–15	129	140	162	142
16 and over	178	193	246	181

SOURCES: Based on U.S. Bureau of the Census, 1950 and 1980 Censuses of Population; 1950: *Special Reports*, Part 5, Chapter B, Table 9; 1980: estimated by the author from Chapter D, Tables 262 and 272, and 1970 census data. See footnote 54.

NOTE: Ratio of labor force participation ratio at a particular educational level to average for that age group per 100.

eighth grade and 14 percent had graduated from college. Since the positive relationship between LFPR and education at these ages became stronger from one decade to the next as 1980 was approached, we would expect the increase in educational attainment to have "caused" an increase in LFPR of men aged 55–64. If we calculate the LFPR in 1940 on the assumption that the distribution of these men by educational attainment in 1940 was the same as it was in 1980, we obtain a LFPR in 1940 of 85.5 percent. The actual ratio in 1940 was 83.7 percent. The structural change (i.e., the change in educational distribution) slightly countered the decline in the proclivity to remain in the labor force. The size of the decline would have been about 14 percentage points, rather than 12 points, if the structural change had not taken place.

In 1980, 46 percent of the men aged 65 and over had completed no more than the eighth grade, while about 10 percent had graduated from college. Calculating the LFPR of men aged 65 and over in 1950 on the same type of assumption as before regarding the educational distribution of these men in 1950 (i.e., that it is the same as in 1980) resulted in a LFPR of 44.7 percent compared with the actual 41.4 percent.[55] By 1980 the LFPR of men aged 65 and over had fallen to 19.3 percent. Hence, the increase in education among men of these ages between 1950 and 1980 offset only about 3 percentage points of the potential drop of about 25 points produced by their growing inclination to leave the labor force. Thus, the preponderance of the change in LFPR was determined not by changes in the educational distribution of the elderly but by changes in education-specific LFPR.

Among men aged 65 and over, there were declines in LFPR at all educational levels from at least the 1950s. The timing of the start of the decline in the LFPR of men under age 65 between 1950 and 1980 was related to their level of education. There was little or no decline until the 1970s for those who had graduated from high school, no decline until the 1960s for those who had completed only 8–11 years of school, and for those with less education, the decline appears to have begun as early as the 1940s. As a result of the differences in the timing and magnitude of the declines, the cross-sectional relationship between education and LFPR for older men became stronger from decade to decade between 1940 and 1980.

The LFPR of women under age 65 increased greatly at all educational levels until the 1970s, when some declines occurred. Education-specific LFPR of women aged 65 and over were quite low throughout the period 1950–1980, fluctuating slightly for most groups with little net change.

Analysis of percent declines in LFPR during each decade for each 10-year age-sex-education category from a cohort perspective is also possible (Table 7.16). Except among women who were aged 45–54 in 1940 and 1950, all the cohorts, male and female, at each educational level shown in the table experienced declines in their LFPR as they aged. A positive association between age and the rate of decline in LFPR is observed at every *level of education*. Among men, *at each age* there was a uniformly negative association between the rate of decline in LFPR and education—that is, the less the workers' education, the greater the likelihood of their quitting the labor force. Among women this association was generally but not uniformly negative and was weaker than among men.

Aside from the increases in LFPR of women who were aged 45–54 in 1940 and 1950, the rate of cohort decline in LFPR of men and women increased from one decade to the next between 1950 and 1980 at every

---

[55]Since the age category 55–64 was the highest for which education-specific LFPR were provided in 1940, it was not possible to approximate the effect of the increase in education on the LFPR between 1940 and 1980 for those aged 65 years and over.

TABLE 7.16

Percent Decline in Labor Force Participation Ratios for 10-Year Birth Cohorts, by Age, Sex, and Years of School Completed: 1940–1950 to 1970–1980

Sex, Initial Ages, and Years of School Completed	1940–1950	1950–1960	1960–1970	1970–1980
Male				
45–54	9.3	9.5	13.6	23.0
0–7	11.1	13.6	20.3	34.5
8–11	8.7	8.2	14.2	26.0
12–15	7.8	6.6	10.4	20.2
16 and over	6.1	4.4	8.4	16.6
55–64	38.7	55.0	61.5	69.5
0–7	43.3	61.3	67.2	75.4
8–11	36.4	53.9	62.7	72.2
12–15	32.7	44.8	55.5	67.1
16 and over	26.2	35.4	46.2	58.4
65–74	NA	69.6	67.7	71.7
0–7	NA	74.8	73.5	78.2
8–11	NA	69.0	68.5	73.6
12–15	NA	59.5	61.8	67.4
16 and over	NA	49.6	57.1	64.2
Female				
45–54	−6.3	−6.4	9.2	21.4
0–7	8.5	2.6	19.7	28.9
8–11	−14.1	−11.3	10.2	25.3
12–15	−9.4	−8.7	6.9	20.2
16 and over	−5.6	−10.2	8.6	12.5
55–64	37.2	42.6	61.1	72.2
0–7	46.9	48.4	65.3	76.5
8–11	31.8	39.8	62.2	74.7
12–15	31.2	38.0	58.3	70.3
16 and over	39.8	38.0	59.5	67.3
65–74	NA	58.3	65.2	77.2
0–7	NA	59.2	67.0	78.3
8–11	NA	58.3	68.4	79.5
12–15	NA	58.1	62.8	75.1
16 and over	NA	54.1	70.3	77.5

SOURCES: Based on U.S. Bureau of the Census, 1940–1980 Censuses of Population; 1940: estimated by the author from *Special Report on Education,* Tables 17 and 18; 1950: *Special Reports,* Part 5, Chapter B, Table 9; 1960: *Subject Reports,* PC(2)-5B, Tables 2 and 4; 1970: *Subject Reports,* PC(2)-5B, Tables 2, 5, and 6; 1980: estimated by the author from Chapter D, Tables 262 and 272, and 1970 census data.

NOTES: NA = not available. Minus sign denotes an increase.

educational level. In addition, the LFPR of women declined at roughly the same rate at each educational level during each decade in the period as the LFPR for men.

Occupational groups and class of worker. The percentage elderly in each occupational class, except farming and services, varies little from the percentage elderly in the labor force as a whole. The percentage elderly in the entire labor force was only 3.3 percent for men and 2.8 percent for women in 1980. In the exceptional cases about 10 percent of male farmers and 5.5 percent of male service workers were elderly.

The elderly labor force became increasingly white collar in the post-war period (Table 7.17). In general, we see a shift out of farming and blue collar occupations into white collar occupations. Among women, there were large movements out of private household work and factory employment ("operatives"), and into clerical, sales, and service work. Among men, farming and "laborers" lost heavily, while sales, professional, and service occupations experienced large gains. (For a discussion of the comparability of the data for 1970 and 1980, see Appendix 7C.)

There appears also to have been a large decline in self-employment and a large rise in wage and salary workers between 1950 and 1980 among those aged 65 and over, even though complete data on class of worker for age groups are not available in the decennial census reports for these years.[56] Between 1950 and 1970 the percentage of wage and salary workers among the elderly showed a marked increase.

	1950	1960	1970
Male	60.5	64.5	72.7
Female	79.3	80.1	87.0

[56]This inference is based partly on the fact that between 1950 and 1980 the percentage of all employed persons (all ages) who were self-employed declined considerably (from 21 percent to 9 percent for men and from 6 percent to 4 percent for women). (See U.S. Bureau of the Census, 1980 Census of Population, PC 80-1-C1, Table 91.) The inference is based also on changes in the number of elderly wage and salary workers. From the censuses of 1950, 1960, and 1970, one can obtain the percentage of wage and salary workers in the elderly experienced civilian labor force. The remainder of the experienced civilian labor force comprises the self-employed and unpaid family workers. Unpaid family workers, however, accounted for a very small percentage of the total labor force in 1950 and an even smaller percentage in later years. Among women, for example, 3 percent of employed persons aged 14 and over in 1950 were unpaid family workers. By 1980, the comparable figure was only 0.8 percent. The figures for men are about half of those for women. (See U.S. Bureau of the Census, PC80-1-C1, Table 91.) Unpaid family workers constituted a negligible proportion of the labor force among the elderly also. CPS data for 1980 show that 0.4 percent of elderly men and 1.5 percent of elderly women in nonagricultural industries were unpaid family workers. (See U.S. Bureau of Labor Statistics, *Employment and Earnings,* January 1981, p. 182.) Thus, the percentage of elderly self-employed workers may be approximated by subtracting the percentage of elderly wage and salary workers from 100.

Note that most elderly workers, especially elderly female workers, were wage and salary workers in 1970 as in 1950. Given the minute share of unpaid family workers, there can be little doubt that there was a marked percent decline in self-employment among elderly workers between 1950 and 1970.

	1950	1960	1970
Male	39.5	35.5	27.3
Female	20.7	19.9	13.0

Given the further decline in self-employment of all employed persons between 1970 and 1980, it is likely that self-employment among the elderly also continued to decline between 1970 and 1980.

TABLE 7.17

Occupational Distribution of the Population Aged 65 and Over, by Sex: 1950 and 1980

	Male			Female		
Occupational Class	1950	1980	Change, 1950–1980	1950	1980	Change, 1950–1980
Total	100.0	100.0	—	100.0	100.0	—
Professionals, Technicians, and Kindred Workers	6.0	14.5	+8.5	12.4	13.5	+1.1
Managers, Officials, and Proprietors, Excluding Farmers	12.2	14.9	+2.7	8.0	6.9	−1.1
Clerical and Kindred Workers	4.6	7.3	+2.7	9.4	26.2	+16.8
Sales Workers	5.7	10.5	+4.8	7.4	10.4	+3.0
Craftsmen, Foremen, and Kindred Workers	15.3	13.5	−1.8	1.5	1.8	+0.3
Operatives and Kindred Workers	10.2	10.6	+0.4	15.2	8.7	−6.5
Service Workers, Excluding Private-Household Workers	10.2	15.0	+4.8	17.8	22.7	+4.9
Private-Household Workers	0.4	0.2	−0.2	20.6	7.6	−13.0
Laborers, Excluding Farm and Mine Workers	7.8	3.7	−4.1	0.8	0.6	−0.2
Farmers and Farm Managers	22.6 } 9.8		−17.8	3.8 } 1.6		−5.3
Farm Laborers and Foremen	5.0 }			3.1 }		

SOURCES: U.S. Bureau of the Census, 1950 Census of Population, *Special Reports,* "Occupational Characteristics"; 1980 Census of Population, *U.S. Summary: Detailed Characteristics,* PC80-1-D1-A, Table 280, adjusted to be comparable to 1950.

NOTE: Experienced civilian labor force in 1950; employed labor force in 1980. Dash represents zero.

The significant question in connection with the decline in self-employment is whether it has contributed to the decline in the LFPR of the elderly. The common-sense inference is that it has, because self-employed persons tend to remain in the work force until very late ages.[57] Sheldon carefully examined the limited evidence that was available a generation ago and came to the conclusion that the evidence did not support the inference.[58] There is no doubt about an association between the two trends, but it would be difficult to prove a cause-effect relationship.

Labor reserve at older ages. Many of the elderly who are not currently in the labor force but who were in the labor force previously have skills which could be put to use in volunteer work or during public emergencies. The shorter the interval since these nonworking elderly were last in the labor force, the more likely they are to be available for work and the more adequate their work skills are likely to be. It would be useful, therefore, to ascertain the potential numbers in the elderly labor reserve and the potential skills they have. (The labor reserve is only a rough guide since it includes disabled persons and many persons not disposed to work even though they had recent work experience.)

The percentages of men and women aged 60 and over who were in the labor reserve in 1960 and 1980 (defined as persons not currently in the labor force who had been in the labor force at some time in the last five years) are as follows:[59]

	Census Data: 1960	CPS Data: 1980
Male		
Total	100.0	100.0
Labor Force	45.5	32.3
Labor Reserve	23.5	20.3
All Others	31.0	47.4
Female		
Total	100.0	100.0
Labor Force	16.0	14.9
Labor Reserve	10.5	11.2
All Others	73.5	73.9

[57]The percentage of elderly persons, for example, was two to four times as great among the self-employed as among wage and salary workers in 1980 and 1985. See U.S. Bureau of Labor Statistics, *Employment and Earnings* (January 1981), p. 82; and (January 1986), Table 23, p. 180.

[58]H. D. Sheldon, *The Older Population of the United States* (New York: Wiley, 1958), pp. 59 and 81.

[59]Data on the labor reserve were presented in the 1960 and 1970 censuses and the 1980 CPS. The censuses defined the labor reserve as persons not currently in the labor

TABLE 7.18

Occupational Distribution of the Labor Reserve Aged 65 and Over, by Sex: 1970

Occupation	Percent, 1970		Change, 1960–1970	
	Male	Female	Male	Female
Total	100.0	100.0	—	—
Professionals, Technicians, and Kindred Workers	7.0	14.1	+2.4	+3.2
Farmers and Farm Managers	7.4	0.7	−2.4	−1.0
Managers, Officials, and Proprietors, Excluding Farmers	10.9	5.3	+1.0	+0.6
Clerical and Kindred Workers	7.0	21.6	+0.7	+7.4
Sales Workers	5.6	9.4	+0.7	+0.3
Craftsmen, Foremen, and Kindred Workers	23.3	2.0	+0.1	+0.5
Operatives and Kindred Workers	16.2	15.8	−0.9	−2.4
Private-Household Workers	0.2	10.8	—	−4.9
Service Workers, Excluding Private-Household Workers	11.1	17.6	+0.7	−1.6
Farm Laborers and Foremen	3.8	1.9	−0.2	−2.2
Laborers, Excluding Farm and Mine Workers	7.6	0.9	−2.1	+0.3

SOURCES: U.S. Bureau of the Census, 1970 Census of Population, *Subject Reports*, "Persons Not Employed," PC(2)-6B, Tables 12 and 13; and 1960 Census of Population, *Subject Reports*, "Labor Reserve," PC(2)-6C, Tables 10 and 11.

NOTES: "Occupation not reported" was distributed pro rata. "Labor reserve" refers to persons not in the labor force during the reference week who had some work experience within the 10 years preceding the census year. Persons working in the period January–March of the census year were also included. Dash denotes that figure rounds to 0.0 or represents zero.

There was little change in the work distribution of women between 1960 and 1980. In each year, 1 in 6 or 7 of the women aged 60 and over was in the labor force, about 1 in 9 was in the labor reserve, and nearly 3 in 4 were neither in the labor force nor in the labor reserve. Among older men, however, a large redistribution occurred, involving a large drop in the percentage in the labor force, a moderate decrease in the

force who had been in the labor force at some time during the preceding 10 years. Data from the 1980 CPS identify people not currently in the labor force who had been in the labor force at some time during the preceding 5 years (but not the preceding 10 years). Since data on the preceding 5 years are also available from the 1960 census, the preceding 5 years was taken as the period defining the size of the labor reserve for the present purpose, and change was measured between 1960 and 1980 on this basis.

percentage in the labor reserve, and a massive increase in the percentage who were neither in the labor force nor in the labor reserve. Over the course of two decades a large share of the retirees moved into and then out of the labor reserve, as defined above.

Data on the occupational distribution of persons in the labor reserve are available only for persons aged 65 and over in 1960 and 1970. (They refer to persons not currently in the labor force who had work experience during the preceding 10 years.) In 1970, among elderly men in the labor reserve, 23 percent were craftsmen, foremen, and related workers; 16 percent "operatives;" and 11 percent (each) service workers, farm laborers/farm managers/farmers, and nonfarm managers/officials/proprietors. The principal occupations of elderly women in the labor reserve were clerical work (22 percent), factory work (i.e., operatives) (16 percent), service work (18 percent), and professional and technical work (14 percent). (See Table 7.18.)

Between 1960 and 1970 the occupational distribution of the elderly labor reserve tended to shift as the elderly labor force had shifted a decade earlier. Farming and blue collar occupations declined, while white collar occupations grew. The most notable changes were the drop (5 percentage points) in the percentage of elderly women formerly engaged as private household workers and the rise (7 points) in the percentage of elderly women formerly engaged as clerical workers. To a substantial degree, the labor reserve, especially the male labor reserve, has occupational skills that are less and less needed as the economy shifts from an essentially manufacturing profile to an essentially information and service profile.

Retirement Trends and Some Implications

Trends in Retirement Age

The conventional or "normal" retirement age is generally considered to be 65. This age is identified in numerous pieces of legislation and is in fact a common age of retirement. Workers retire at many different ages, however. The trends in labor force participation suggest that the average age of retirement is falling and that greater proportions of workers are retiring at earlier ages.

Measurement of retirement age is complicated by the fact that there are different ways of defining, and therefore measuring, retirement. There are two basic concepts. The first concept defines retirement as a shift in the principal source of income from earnings to a pension on leaving the work force in older age. A variation of this concept considers those persons retired who leave a long-term job (or career) in older age, usually with a pension, even if they continue to work full or part time. According to this concept, retirement does not necessarily involve nonemployment although the majority of retired persons are not employed.

The second concept defines retirement as complete withdrawal from the labor force in older age for reasons other than death. According to this concept, at the time of observation the older individual is not working or pursuing a job. He or she may or may not be receiving a pension. This concept recognizes the possibility of a return to the labor force and, in fact, many voluntary exits (i.e., exits excluding deaths) from the labor force are not permanent. Net voluntary exits would therefore be a more useful and also a more accurate, measure of retirement of the population than gross voluntary exits. Among persons aged 65 and over, however, relatively few change their status from fully inactive to fully active and the average duration of active life after an exit is short. Hence, gross voluntary exits can serve as an approximate measure of permanent withdrawal from the labor force for persons aged 65 and over.

Still other concepts mix the elements of each of the concepts described or build in other components. Elements involved include the receipt of earned income, receipt of a pension, amount of earned income, number of hours worked per week, number of weeks worked per year, and the range of ages selected. Other dimensions of the measurement of retirement include whether the measure refers to a birth cohort or to the population in a particular year and whether the data are derived from a census, sample survey, or administrative records. The various concepts of retirement and ways of measuring it give somewhat different indications as to the level and trend of the average age of retirement.

There are many suggestive indications of a decline in the retirement age of men in recent decades. One indication is given by the trend of worker ratios at the older ages over the postwar period. As was described earlier, the labor force participation ratio (LFPR) of men aged 55–64 declined steadily from 87 percent in 1950 to 68 percent in 1985. The data show an even larger decline in the LFPR of men aged 65 and over in this period, from 46 percent in 1950 to 16 percent in 1985. Use of LFPR to measure the trend in retirement age is consistent with the definition of retirement as complete withdrawal from the labor force at the older ages for reasons other than death.

A decline in average age of retirement, however, cannot be inferred directly from declines in LFPR. In fact, LFPR can decline without a change in the average age of retirement, especially if there are large declines in the ratios at the higher ages (e.g., ages 65 and over). Time-series changes in LFPR as indicators of changes in age of retirement are confounded by the effect of mortality and net immigration as well as the inappropriate design of the measurement procedure. Ideally, the age distributions of persons withdrawing from the labor force during a series of periods should be analyzed, but these are not available.

In order to measure the extent and pace of the decline in retirement age, we consider here trends in retirement age on the basis of a variety of sources of data and methods, in particular data from the Bureau of Labor Statistics and the Social Security Administration. The change in the age of retirement has been estimated over the period 1940–1985 or 1950–1985 on the basis of data in tables of working life and labor force participation ratios derived from the CPS. These estimates are compared with estimates of retirement trends derived mainly from Social Security data on persons receiving retirement benefits.[60]

Changes in the age of retirement were first measured by computing the median age of the net and gross numbers of persons voluntarily exiting from the labor force at each age in the age range 50–75 given in, or calculated from, the series of tables of working life published by the Bureau of Labor Statistics for 1940 to 1979–1980.[61] The computation on the basis of numbers exiting given in tables of working life yields results

---

[60]The direct measurement of retirement is not possible from decennial census or CPS data. The census and CPS lack a concept of retirement. They have not provided separate information on pension income and have not attempted to identify persons who have permanently withdrawn from the labor force. Recent U.S. censuses combine "pensions" in the same question with "unemployment compensation, veterans' payments, alimony or child support, and any other sort of income received regularly." The problem is mitigated by the fact that Social Security or Railroad Retirement income is asked for separately and over 90 percent of the people aged 65 and over receive Social Security income. The problem is much greater for persons under age 65. In the 1990 census, a separate question on "retirement, survivor, or disability pensions" will be included, however. A tabulation of older persons according to their previous and current labor force status, receipt of pension income, hours worked last week, weeks worked last year, and amount of income by type would provide a basis for developing information on retirement as both a polytomous and a dichotomous variable, and even an interval variable, according to different definitions.

[61]U.S. Bureau of Labor Statistics, *Worklife Estimates: Effects of Race and Education*, by S. Smith, Bulletin no. 2254 (February 1986); U.S. Bureau of Labor Statistics, *Tables of Working Life: The Increment-Decrement Model*, by S. Smith, Bulletin no. 2135 (November 1982). H. N. Fullerton, Jr., and J. J. Byrne, "Length of Working Life for Men and Women, 1970," *Monthly Labor Review* 99 (2) (February 1976); reprinted as Special Labor Force Report no. 187. S. H. Garfinkle, "The Length of Working Life for Males, 1900–60," in C. B. Nam, ed., *Population and Society* (Boston: Houghton Mifflin, 1968); also published as U.S. Manpower Administration, Manpower Report no. 8 (1963).

independent of the effect of the age distribution of the actual population.[62] The median ages of the gross and net exits of males, based on single-year-of-age data in the range 50–75, are as follows:[63]

Year	Gross Exits	Net Exits
Increment-Decrement Tables		
1979–1980	62.6	61.7
1977	63.2	62.4
1970	64.6	64.8
Decrement Tables		
1968	NA	65.3
1960	NA	65.0
1950	NA	65.8
1940	NA	65.8

NOTES: Based on single-year-of-age data; NA = not available.

The series of median ages of the net exits reflects a negligible or modest decrease over the period 1940–1968, amounting to 0.5 year, and then a marked decline in the 1970s, amounting to 3.1 years. The decrease for the whole period 1940–1980 fell between 3.6 years and 4.1 years. Most of the decline between 1940 and 1980 occurred in the 1970s according to these estimates.

Another indication of the trend in the average age of retirement over the period 1940–1980 may be obtained from estimates of actual retirees in the appropriate years. For this purpose rates of net exits from the labor force, given in or derived from tables of working life, were applied to the actual labor force in ages 50–74 at decennial intervals, 1940–1980. The estimates of the median ages of retirement for men obtained by this method, shown along with median ages of the net exits in the life table, are as follows:

[62]The tables of working life for 1940–1968 do not contain separate rates of labor force entry and labor force exit. Hence, only net exits, that is, the balance of gross exits (excluding deaths) and gross entries, can be calculated and used in the derivation of the median ages. A change in the methodology of constructing the tables after 1968 permitted the inclusion in the tables of data on gross labor force exits and gross labor force entries. These increment-decrement tables employed separate transition probabilities for entries, exits, and deaths.

[63]Extension of the age range over which net exits are calculated has little effect on the median age, raising it by only a fraction of a year in each calendar year when the age range 50–79 is covered rather than 50–75. The largest difference occurs in 1950, when the median age would be raised by 0.5 year.

	Actual Labor Force		Life Table Labor Force	
Year	Median	Change	Median	Change
1980	61.7	−2.3	61.8	−2.9
1970	64.0	−0.7[a]	64.7	−0.3[a]
1960	64.7	−0.6	65.0	−0.9
1950	65.3	−0.1	66.0	+0.1
1940	65.4	X	65.9	X

NOTES: Based on grouped data. Pertains to net exits, excluding deaths. X = not applicable.

[a] Affected by change in methodology of life tables.

On this basis, the median age of retirement declined 3.7 years between 1940 and 1980 and most of the decline occurred in the 1970s as before. The medians based on the actual labor force and the medians based on the life table labor force (both series being based on the same set of life table rates of net exits) show rather similar overall amounts and decennial patterns of decline.

Historical data on net exit rates from tables of working life for women are less complete. They are mainly limited to the 1970–1980 period. Women retired, on the average, 0.5 to one year younger than men in this decade. Average retirement age declined by about three years between 1970 and 1980, a shift somewhat greater than that for men.

An alternative form of analysis designed to measure changes in age of retirement is based on labor force participation ratios (LFPR) and labor force data. This method employs the shifts in LFPR on a *cohort* basis to derive estimates of retirements and the median age of retirement. The cohort percent change (decline) in LFPR is given by:

$$1 - (r_2 \div r_1)$$

where r_1 represents the LFPR at the initial date for a given five-year age group and r_2 represents the LFPR at the terminal date for the same birth cohort five years later.[64] Cohort percent changes in LFPR, adjusted for mortality, approximate net separation rates, from which net separations can be derived.

A preliminary analysis of cohort shifts in LFPR from the CPS for 1950–1985 suggests a strong trend toward earlier retirement of both men and women in this period. Except for women aged 45–49 (initial ages) in several periods and women aged 50–54 in 1955–1960, LFPR declined

[64] This formula reduces to (separations-accessions)/(survivors at mid period of the labor force) under certain simplified assumptions of mortality.

on a cohort basis at all ages in all periods (Table 7.19). Furthermore, with few exceptions, the higher the age and the more recent the period, the greater was the pace of the decline. Larger declines at the older ages in themselves suggest a high age at retirement. We look rather for a relative diminution or slowing over time of the withdrawal rates at the older ages and a relative rise in the withdrawal rates at the younger ages. In fact, the changes have followed this pattern. Withdrawal rates accelerated less and less over time with increasing age.

In order to derive estimates of the median age at retirement, the cohort percent declines in LFPR have to be transformed into the numbers of net separations. This was accomplished by the following formula:

$$W = \sqrt{s} \left(1 - \frac{r_2}{r_1}\right) L_1$$

where $1 - \frac{r_2}{r_1}$ = proportionate cohort decline in LFPR in five-year period

s = five-year life table survival rate

L_1 = labor force at initial date

W = net voluntary separations for the cohort over five-year period

The formula, in effect, converts cohort percent declines in LFPR into net separation rates by making a special allowance for deaths and then derives absolute numbers by multiplying the net separation rates against the initial labor force. Next the absolute numbers of net voluntary separations for five-year cohorts were interpolated to centered figures for five-year age groups.[65] The median age at retirement was then calculated for each quinquennial time period from the absolute numbers of net voluntary separations for five-year age groups.

Estimates of the median ages at retirement for five-year periods were based on cohort changes in LFPR from ages 45–49 to 75–79 derived from the CPS for 1950–1985:

Period	Male	Female
1950–1955	66.9	67.7
1955–1960	65.8	66.2
1960–1965	65.2	64.6
1965–1970	64.2	64.2
1970–1975	63.4	63.0
1975–1980	63.0	63.2
1980–1985	62.8	62.7

[65]The Karup-King Third-Difference Osculatory Formula was used for the interpolation.

TABLE 7.19

Cohort Percent Declines in LFPR, for Men and Women Aged 45 and Over, by Age: 1950–1985

Sex and Period	Terminal Ages/Initial Ages					
	50–54 45–49	55–59 50–54	60–64 55–59	65–69 60–64	70–74 65–69	75+ 70–74
Male						
1950–1955	0.8	2.6	8.1	31.7	41.9	55.1
1955–1960	2.5	4.3	12.3	43.3	44.6	52.8
1960–1965	2.0	4.8	14.8	47.0	47.0	55.4
1965–1970	3.2	5.8	16.9	46.7	41.4	51.6
1970–1975	5.5	9.2	26.8	57.7	49.3	59.9
1975–1980	5.2	9.3	28.0	56.5	43.5	58.3
1980–1985	4.9	10.8	32.0	59.7	47.7	60.9
Ratio 1980–85 / 1950–55	6.1	4.2	4.0	1.9	1.1	1.1
Female						
1950–1955	−4.0	0.3	2.4	25.2	40.6	49.4
1955–1960	−6.3	−1.7	11.8	39.3	46.6	52.2
1960–1965	1.2	3.3	19.4	44.6	48.3	61.1
1965–1970	−4.1	2.2	23.4	49.1	47.7	62.6
1970–1975	3.1	11.0	32.0	59.8	56.1	67.0
1975–1980	−3.4	9.0	30.7	54.7	48.3	67.1
1980–1985	2.1	13.0	31.1	59.3	49.7	70.7
Ratio 1980–85 / 1950–55	x	43.3	13.0	2.4	1.2	1.4

NOTES: Rates per 100. Minus sign denotes net accessions. Based on labor force participation ratios from the CPS in Table 7.4 and the following formula:

$$1 - \left({}_5r_{a+5}^{t+5} \div {}_5r_a^t\right)$$

where ${}_5r_a^t$ represents a LFPR in a five-year age group at the initial date.

x = not applicable.

The estimates show a decline of 4.1 years in median retirement age for men, from 66.9 years in 1950–1955 to 62.8 years in 1980–1985. The more rapid decline occurred in the earlier part of the 30-year period 1953–1983, that is, from "1953" to "1973," when the average quinquennial decline was 0.9 year compared with the average quinquennial decline of 0.3 year from "1973" to "1983." The results show a decline of 5.0 years in median retirement age for women, from 67.7 years in 1950–1955 to 62.7 years in 1980–1985. For women also, a disproportionate share of the decline occurred in the earlier part of the 30-year period. While the results do not particularly reflect the introduction of the early retirement option in Social Security in 1956 (for women) and in 1961 (for men), they do reflect the general expansion of coverage and benefits in Social Security and other pension programs. This expansion was rapid at first and then slowed as the systems matured. The apparent diminution of the pace of the decline in retirement age suggests that the decline may be coming to an end and that retirement age may be approaching a lower limit.

Cumulative data for birth cohorts from the Continuous Work History Sample of the Social Security Administration have been used by Kastenbaum to show a strong trend toward more frequent early retirement among men.[66] On the basis of an analysis of LFPR, Reimers reached a different conclusion for the earlier birth cohorts.[67]

If retirement is defined as leaving a long-term job and subsequently receiving a pension, we can consider data of a different sort. We can examine the shift in the proportions of persons eligible for retired-worker benefits actually receiving retirement benefits under the Social Security program. The changes in these proportions over time at the same ages, like changes in LFPR used in this way, are inappropriate for measuring changes in retirement age, particularly without further mathematical treatment. The figures appear to indicate, however, that larger shares of workers are retiring both at an early age and at a late age and, further, that the average age of retirement is declining. In the early 1970s, there was a rapid increase in the proportion of male workers who retired with full benefits and an even more rapid increase in the proportion of workers who retired with reduced benefits. The proportion of eligible men receiving full benefits at ages 65–71 rose from 73 percent in 1960 to 79 percent in 1970 and further to 90 percent in 1985 (Table 7.20). The proportion of eligible men who retired at ages 62–64 (with reduced benefits) increased from 25 percent in 1965 to 33 percent in 1975 and further to 43 percent in 1985. For the younger women there was a roughly parallel increase; 42 percent of eligible women received benefits in 1960, 40 per-

---

[66]B. Kastenbaum, "The Measurement of Early Retirement," *Journal of the American Statistical Association* 80 (389) (March 1985):38–45. Retirement is defined as cessation of economic activity for causes other than death and emigration. He found that the rate of retirement for men between ages 54 and 64 increased substantially, and in a fairly regular fashion, from .301 for the cohort born in 1903 to .422 for the cohort born in 1910.

[67]C. Reimers, "Is the Average Age at Retirement Changing?" *Journal of the American Statistical Association* 71 (355) (September 1976):552–558. She found that the mean age of retirement for men who retired between ages 52.5 and 72.5 was relatively stable over the cohorts born between 1866 and 1900 (reaching the terminal age 72.5 from about 1938 to 1972), while the variation around the mean decreased. She attributes the stability in the mean retirement age to the effects of improved health on the ability to work until an advanced age.

TABLE 7.20

Percentage of Workers Aged 62 and Over Eligible for Retired-Worker Benefits with Benefits in Current-Payment Status, by Age Group and Sex: 1960–1985

Year (January 1)	Ages 62–64			Ages 65 and Over[a]		
	Total	Retired	Disabled	Total	65–71	72 and Over
Both Sexes						
1985	57	46	11	94	88	99
1980	55	42	13	94	89	99
1975	50	39	11	93	85	99
1970	39	31	8	90	80	100
1965	38	32	6	89	80	100
1960	b	b	b	85	76	97
Male						
1985	56	43	13	95	90	100
1980	52	36	15	95	90	100
1975	46	33	13	93	87	100
1970	34	24	10	90	79	100
1965	32	25	7	89	79	100
1960	b	b	b	84	73	97
Female						
1985	58	50	8	92	85	99
1980	59	49	10	93	87	99
1975	56	48	8	93	83	99
1970	46	40	6	90	81	99
1965	47	44	4	89	80	100
1960	44	42	2	87	82	96

SOURCE: U.S. Social Security Administration, *Social Security Bulletin,* Annual Statistical Supplement (1984–1985), Table 33.

NOTE: Insured workers represent those with sufficient "quarters of coverage" to meet the eligibility requirements for retired-worker or disabled-worker benefits.

[a] At age 65, disabled worker benefits are converted to retired-worker benefits.
[b] Retired-worker benefits, actuarially reduced, were first payable at ages 62–64 to women in 1956 and to men in 1961.

cent in 1970, and 50 percent in 1985. For the older women, there was little change. The relative rise in the share of recipients was much greater among persons under age 65 than among persons aged 65 and over.

A marked increase in the proportion of men and women aged 62–64 who drew disabled-worker benefits contributed to the sharp rise in the total proportion retired at these ages. The proportion of men aged 62–64 who drew disabled-worker benefits rose from 7 percent in 1960 to 15 percent in 1980 and then fell back to 13 percent in 1985. The proportion of women of this age group drawing disabled-worker benefits increased from 2 percent to 10 percent between 1960 and 1980 and then fell back to 8 percent in 1985. The rise in the proportion of workers drawing such benefits up to 1980 resulted not only from a possible rise in disability rates and an increased proclivity toward retirement, but also from a generally greater familiarity with the disability-entitlement program and an apparent increase in abuse of the program.

The Social Security Administration also publishes data on the mean age of men and women who receive a Social Security retirement benefit award in each year.[68] The mean age of men who received SSA retirement benefit awards dropped by 5.1 years between 1940 and 1985, according to these data:

Year	Male	Female
1940	68.8	68.1
1945	69.6	73.3
1950	68.7	68.0
1955	68.4	67.8
1960	66.8	65.2[a]
1965	65.8[a]	66.2
1970	64.4	63.9
1975	64.0	63.7
1980	63.9	63.5
1985[b]	63.7	63.4

SOURCE: U.S. Social Security Administration, *Social Security Bulletin,* Annual Statistical Supplement (1989), Table 6B-5, p. 256.

[a]Retirement at reduced benefits at age 62 was initiated for men in 1961 and women in 1956.
[b]Based on 1 percent sample.

Nearly all of the decline (4.3 years) occurred between 1950 and 1970. The mean age of women declined by a similar amount—4.7 years—and again nearly all of the decline (4.1 years) occurred between 1950 and 1970.

In sum, the various cross-sectional estimates agree as to the general direction and magnitude of the changes in average age of retirement for men over the 1940–1985 and 1950–1985 periods. They reflect a decline

---

[68]These figures have an upward bias because persons receiving benefits under the disability insurance program are transferred to the retirement program on reaching age 65. Moreover, only persons receiving partial or full Social Security benefits are included; hence, the lower age limit is 62. From our earlier estimates, from one eighth (1950) to one third (1985) of retirees are under age 62. The figures may also be biased (in an unknown direction) as a result of the rapid expansion in the coverage of the Social Security program between 1940 and 1970.

of 3.7 to 5.1 years. They disagree as to the distribution of the decline by decades, however. I prefer to give principal weight to the awards data from the Social Security Administration on the ground that these data represent relatively direct measures of retirement, even if biased, and to the estimates based on the CPS labor force data, which were especially crafted for this purpose. Accordingly, it can be concluded that a disproportionate share of the decline occurred in the 1950s and 1960s. The pace of the decline has slowed greatly since 1970, with virtual cessation of change by 1980. The pattern of change in average retirement age for women was nearly the same as for men, with levels being merely a bit lower.

Like labor force participation, retirement age varies not only with gender but with various other demographic and socioeconomic characteristics. Using data from the CPS, the census, and other sources, estimates of retirement age could be derived for some of these characteristics. For example, measurement of the variation in the median age of retirement of men in 1980 according to educational level indicates an irregular relation between retirement age and level of education. The expected relation between median age of retirement and a particular characteristic (e.g., educational level) may be confounded by the fact that the age distribution of persons with the characteristic may offset the effect of the pattern of the retirement rates on the age pattern of retired persons. If, in the present example, the medians are computed on the basis of separation rates rather than separations, we find a pronounced direct relation between age of retirement and educational level.

International Variations in Retirement Age

Information on the trend in the age at retirement in 10 industrialized countries since 1960 was secured in a survey conducted by the International Social Security Association in 1978.[69] It found a trend toward awarding pensions at earlier ages in many of the countries. This trend apparently continued after the late 1970s, when the survey terminated, as is indicated by a reference to the "current trend toward a lower retirement age" made in the first *World Labor Report*, published in 1984.[70] The largest drop in retirement age of men occurred in the most developed of the countries surveyed, but the variation in retirement age in

[69]M. B. Tracy, "Trends in Retirement," *International Social Security Review* 31 (2) (1979):131–159. The countries studied were Austria, Denmark, Finland, France, the Federal Republic of Germany, Hungary, Norway, Sweden, the United Kingdom, and the United States.
[70]International Labor Office, *World Labor Report* 1 (Geneva, 1984), p. 160.

the developed countries is small. The main supporting reason for the trend appeared to be legislation which gave workers greater opportunities to retire before the normal retirement age. Other factors, however, must have been influential, for even in countries where few options for receiving an early pension were available, workers seemed to be retiring earlier. It is also notable that provisions seeking to defer retirement, usually via a formula for increasing benefit payments, appeared to have had very little success.

Pampel and Weiss identify two factors in developed countries leading to earlier retirement.[71] First, economic growth and the need for a younger, more educated labor force with the latest skills give young workers a competitive advantage, forcing older workers out of the labor force at mandatory retirement ages. Second, government policies make retirement more attractive financially and induce older workers to leave the labor force voluntarily. On the basis of a regression analysis of pooled time-series data for every fifth year between 1950 and 1975, for 18 developed countries, the authors conclude surprisingly that the first factor is more important than the second. Hence, they reason, the ability of governments to reverse the trends in labor force participation appears to be limited. Although drastic cuts in benefits would raise labor force participation, modest changes in benefits, coverage, or age of eligibility would have little effect without concomitant changes in the labor demands of the economy.

Both cross-sectional and longitudinal data support the generalization that age of retirement is inversely related to the level of economic development.[72] Furthermore, as economic development proceeds, early retirement becomes increasingly prevalent.[73] Pampel and Weiss maintain that changes in economic demand for workers are important in explaining the decline in labor force participation of older men in the less developed countries as well as the more developed ones, and perhaps more so in the former, since there is less experience with public pension programs.

[71]F. C. Pampel and J. A. Weiss, "Economic Development, Pension Policies, and the Labor Force Participation of Aged Males: A Cross-National, Longitudinal Approach," *American Journal of Sociology* 89 (2) (September 1983):350–372.

[72]J. D. Durand, *The Labor Force in Economic Development* (Princeton, NJ: Princeton University Press, 1975), p. 149.

[73]United Nations, *World Population Trends: 1983 Monitoring Report*, Population and Development Interrelations and Population Policies, vol. 2 (New York: United Nations, 1985), p. 73.

Some Implications of the Trends in Work and Retirement

Changes in labor force participation and retirement practices, in combination with changes in population age-sex structure and death rates, have been modifying the share of total life devoted to work, the age-sex structure of the labor force, and the balance of older nonworkers to workers. These changes have numerous implications for the economy and the economic status of the population. The large and continuing decline in the LFPR of men aged 55 and over and the steady rise in the share of retirements at the ages below 65, accompanying the extension of life expectancy, have increased the duration of the retirement period. These changes have contributed to an unfavorable shift in the balance of retired persons to workers, tending to make more difficult the provision of services and benefits to the former while augmenting the financial and other burdens of the latter. These demographic and economic changes have an important bearing on the funding and solvency of the Social Security system of old-age and survivors' benefits and the Medicare program of old-age hospital and medical insurance. I next explore the implications of the trends in labor force participation and retirement more fully.

The duration of worklife. Postwar declines in the labor force participation and death rates of men are reflected in reductions in the average years of worklife and in the share of total life devoted to work. Table 7.21 summarizes the data for 1940–1980 with measures for ages 20 and 50.

Over this period, worklife expectancy of men at age 20 declined by nearly three years while nonworklife expectancy rose by about eight years. All the years of life expectancy gained between 1940 and 1980 (five years) were applied to "leisure" or nonworklife and, in addition, some of the years of worklife were converted to nonworklife.[74] This pattern of changes was even more pronounced at the older ages, especially during the 1970s. At age 50, for example, between 1940 and 1980 worklife expectancy fell by three years and nonworklife expectancy rose by over six years. In the 1970–1980 decade alone, average nonworklife increased and average worklife declined by more than half the 40-year total changes.

In sum, men at the older ages are experiencing many more years of leisure and fewer years of work. Delayed entry into the labor force and

---

[74]The estimates given by the conventional life table model for 1940–1970 become increasingly unrealistic over this period so that comparisons are made only between the conventional model for 1940 and the increment-decrement model for 1970 and 1979–1980.

TABLE 7.21

Total Life Expectancy, Worklife Expectancy, and Nonworklife Expectancy at Age 20 and Age 50, by Sex: 1940 to 1979–1980

Sex and Year	At Age 20				At Age 50			
	Total Life Expectancy	Worklife Expectancy[a]	Nonworklife Expectancy[a]	Percent, Worklife of Total Life	Total Life Expectancy	Worklife Expectancy[a]	Nonworklife Expectancy[a]	Percent, Worklife of Total Life
Male								
Conventional Model								
1940	46.8	39.7	7.1	84.8	21.8	14.6	7.2	67.0
1950	48.9	41.4	7.5	84.7	22.6	15.7	6.9	69.5
1960	49.6	40.9	8.7	82.5	22.8	14.8	8.0	64.9
1970	49.6	39.4	10.2	79.4	23.2	13.8	9.4	59.5
Increment-Decrement Model								
1970	49.6	37.3	12.3	75.2	23.2	13.4	9.8	57.8
1979–1980	51.8	36.8	15.0	71.0	25.0	11.6	13.4	46.4
Change								
1940–1980[b]	+5.0	−2.9	+7.9	−13.8	+3.2	−3.0	+6.2	−20.6
1940–1970[b]	+2.8	−2.4	+5.2	−9.6	+1.4	−1.2	+2.6	−9.2
1970–1980	+2.2	−0.5	+2.7	−4.2	+1.8	−1.8	+3.6	−11.4
Female								
Conventional Model								
1940	50.4	11.9	38.5	23.6	24.4	3.1	21.3	12.7
1950	53.7	14.5	39.2	27.0	26.4	4.5	21.9	17.0
1960	55.7	18.6	37.1	33.4	27.6	NA	NA	NA
1970	56.7	22.0	34.7	38.8	28.9	NA	NA	NA

TABLE 7.21 (continued)

Sex and Year	At Age 20				At Age 50			
	Total Life Expectancy	Worklife Expectancy[a]	Nonworklife Expectancy[a]	Percent, Worklife of Total Life	Total Life Expectancy	Worklife Expectancy[a]	Nonworklife Expectancy[a]	Percent, Worklife of Total Life
Increment-Decrement Model								
1970	56.7	21.3	35.4	37.6	28.9	7.5	21.4	26.0
1979–1980	59.1	27.2	31.9	46.0	30.8	8.0	22.8	26.0
Change								
1940–1980[b]	+8.7	+15.3	−6.6	+22.4	+6.4	+4.9	+1.5	+13.3
1940–1970[b]	+6.3	+9.4	−3.1	+14.0	+4.5	+4.4	+0.1	+13.3
1970–1980	+2.4	+5.9	−3.5	+8.4	+1.9	+0.5	+1.4	—

SOURCES: Based on U.S. Bureau of Labor Statistics, *Tables of Working Life: The Increment-Decrement Model*, by S. Smith, Bulletin no. 2135 (November 1982), esp. text table 3; *Worklife Estimates: Effects of Race and Education*, by S. Smith, Bulletin 2254 (February 1986), esp. text table 3; *Length of Working Life for Men and Women, 1970*, by H. N. Fullerton, Jr., and J. J. Bryne, Special Labor Force Report no. 187, reprinted from *Monthly Labor Review* (February 1976); *Tables of Working Life for Women, 1950*, by S. H. Garfinkle, Bulletin no. 1204, reprinted from *Monthly Labor Review* (June, August, and October 1956); S. H. Garfinkle, "The Length of Working Life for Males, 1900–60," in C. B. Nam, ed., *Population and Society* (Boston: Houghton Mifflin, 1968), pp. 626–640; and estimates by the author.

NOTE: NA = not available. Dash = rounds to 0.0.

[a] For the total population, not the labor force only.
[b] Based on conventional-model estimates for 1940 and increment-decrement-model estimates for 1970 and 1979–1980.

earlier retirement are narrowing the age span of worklife and, in combination with rising life expectancy, are greatly widening the age span
of leisure life. These changes in average worklife and average nonworklife are reflected in a sharp drop in the proportion of average total life
devoted to worklife between 1940 and 1980. At age 20 this proportion
fell 14 points (from 85 percent in 1940 to 71 percent in 1980), and at age
50 the proportion fell 21 points (from 67 percent to 46 percent).

Given the different pattern of changes for the labor force participation of women in the postwar decades, we should expect to find a very
different shift in the relationship between average years of worklife and
average years of nonworklife for women, and we do. Among women,
average worklife has increased far faster than average total life, so that
the share of total life devoted to work has risen sharply. At age 20 the
proportion increased from 24 percent in 1940 to 38 percent in 1970 and
46 percent in 1980. Nonworklife expectancy declined by seven years.
The pattern of change was different for women at the older ages, especially in the 1970s. In general, over the 1940–1980 period, women at the
older ages, unlike younger women, have used their added years of life to
extend both their years of work and their years of leisure. Overall, there
appears to have been a small increase in nonworklife (1.5 years) and a
substantial rise in worklife (5 years). During the 1970s, however, there
was very little gain in worklife at age 50 (0.5 years), even though life
expectancy rose almost two years. Most of the gain in life expectancy
during the 1970s was allocated to nonworklife and virtually all of the
increase in nonworklife between 1940 and 1980 took place during the
1970s.

The positive relation between educational level and labor force participation translates itself into a strong positive relation between educational level and length of working life. Tables of working life for 1979–
1980 show a worklife expectancy at age 20 seven years greater for men
who completed 15 years of school or more (40 years) than for men who
did not finish high school (33 years).[75] (See Table 7.22.) This variation is
maintained at higher ages. At age 60, for example, men with three or
more years of college have a worklife expectancy (six years) twice as
great as men who did not finish high school (three years). The variation
is even more pronounced for women although worklife expectancies are
much lower. Women aged 20 who did not finish high school have a
worklife expectancy 11 years less than women who completed 15 years
of school or more. Presumably most of the former women have "careers" as homemakers and most of the latter have careers in the workplace.

[75]These figures probably understate the variation of worklife with educational level
because the survival probabilities used in the derivation of the tables of working life do
not reflect the variation for educational level.

TABLE 7.22

Worklife Expectancy and Percentage of Life Economically Active for the Population at Selected Ages, by Sex and Years of School Completed: 1979–1980

Sex and Years of Schooling Completed	Worklife Expectancy			Percentage of Life Economically Active		
	20 Years	40 Years	60 Years	20 Years	40 Years	60 Years
Total Male	36.8	20.0	4.4	71	60	25
Less than high school	32.6	17.3	3.3	63	51	19
High school to 14 years	37.6	20.6	4.7	73	61	27
15 years or more	39.5	22.8	6.3	76	68	36
Total Female	27.2	14.3	3.0	46	36	13
Less than high school	20.2	10.9	2.3	34	27	10
High school to 14 years	27.7	14.9	3.3	47	37	15
15 years or more	31.6	17.1	3.5	53	43	16

SOURCE: Based on U.S. Bureau of Labor Statistics, *Worklife Estimates: Effects of Race and Education*, by S. Smith, Bulletin no. 2254 (February 1986), esp. text table 4.

Both men and women pursue longer and more continuous careers if they have a higher education. Not only is higher education associated with later retirement but, among the men who retire, the more educated are most prone to return to the work force. Higher education is also associated with career commitment, especially among self-employed professionals, such as physicians, lawyers, and consulting statisticians. Since the requirements for many occupations are defined in terms of educational levels, the general relations described imply that persons in the professions and senior managerial occupations tend to continue in the work force longer than other workers, often past age 65. Health problems may play a greater role in the shorter duration of worklife of persons who do not finish high school and in their lesser likelihood to return to work after they retire.

The aging of the labor force. It is of great interest to ascertain whether the aging of the general population is reflected in the aging of the labor force, as is commonly assumed. The age structure of the labor force has implications for worker productivity and production, labor costs, and worker mobility (i.e., geographic relocation, promotion and reassignment). We may measure change in the age structure of the labor force in terms of the median age of workers or the share of workers aged 50 or 55 and over.

According to CPS data, the median age of the civilian labor force reached a peak around 1960 at 40.5 years.[76]

[76]H. N. Fullerton, Jr. (1985); and H. N. Fullerton, Jr., and J. Tschetter, "The 1995 Labor Force: A Second Look," *Monthly Labor Review* 106 (11) (November 1983):3–10.

Year	Median Age	Year	Median Age
1955	40.0	1995	37.6
1960	40.5	2000	39.0
1965	40.2	2010	40.1
1970	39.0	2020	39.7
1975	35.8	2030	39.7
1980	35.5		
1984	35.2		

After a modest drop between 1960 and 1970, the median age fell precipitously to 35.8 years in 1975 and then more gradually to 35.2 years in 1984. The labor force was younger in 1984 than it had been for at least 35 years, mainly because of the baby boom.

Census data and CPS data are generally consistent in their indications of the age shifts in the labor force between 1950 and 1980. Male and female labor force data from the censuses (including armed forces resident in the United States) reflect modest fluctuations in the median age between 1950 and 1970 (except for females 1950–1960) and a marked fall in the 1970s.

Year	Both Sexes	Male	Female
1950	38.2	39.0	36.3
1960	40.1	39.9	40.4
1970	39.3	39.3	39.2
1980	34.8	35.2	34.2

Change in the census proportions of the labor force aged 50 and 55 and over also reflect a "younging" of the labor force in recent decades. Only 13 percent of the labor force was aged 55 and over in 1985 compared with 18 percent in 1970 and 1960.

Year	Ages 55 and Over			Ages 50 and Over		
	Both Sexes	Male	Female	Both Sexes	Male	Female
1950	16.7	18.3	12.5	24.9	26.9	20.3
1960	17.8	18.1	17.0	27.4	27.5	27.1
1970	17.7	17.9	17.4	27.3	27.3	27.1
1980	14.4	15.1	13.6	22.3	23.1	21.3
1985	12.7	13.4	11.9	19.6	20.4	18.6

SOURCES: Various decennial census reports, Part D or Chapter D, except 1985 (CPS).

In sum, it appears that while the general population has been aging rapidly, the labor force has been getting younger.

The age structure of the labor force is greatly affected by the movement of the baby-boom cohorts through the working ages. These cohorts began entering the working ages in large numbers after about 1965, and nearly all members of these cohorts were still in the younger working ages in 1985. The baby-boom cohorts will be moving into the older working ages in the near future, however. As the early members move into ages 40–49 in the 1985–1995 decade, the median age of workers will shift gradually upward. According to the middle projections of the Bureau of Labor Statistics, the median age of the labor force will increase between 1984 and 1995 from 35.2 to 37.6.[77] In 1995 the median age will still be well below the peak in 1960, however. Assuming no pronounced changes in worker ratios after 1995, the trend should continue upward for another decade or so as the remaining baby-boom cohorts move into the older working ages. Thereafter, we may expect no change or a modest decline in the median age of the labor force as the baby-boom workers gradually retire. The median age should be about 40 over the period 2010–2030.[78] This is nearly the same level as the previous peak in the 1960s.

In 1995, after a decade in which the median age of the work force will have been rising (and the proportion aged 55 and over falling), the work force will still be heavily concentrated (three-quarters) in the typically most productive ages, 25–54. If recent trends continue, older workers will tend to drop out of the labor force in great numbers just after the most productive ages. Accordingly, the aging of the labor force anticipated for most of the remaining years of this century (1985–2000) should not be viewed with concern because of any adverse effect on its productivity or on the opportunities for promotion of younger workers.

The trend toward early retirement may reverse itself, however, particularly after the first decades of the next century, so that the possibility of these adverse effects should not be disregarded. Admittedly, with the rapid advances in the technological requirements of various jobs, skills can become obsolete much faster than they did in the past. Therefore, there might be some reason to be concerned about the aging of the work force, even in this century, if adequate retraining programs are not instituted. The greater concern now, however, should be for the loss of

[77]The rise in the median age after 1985 will occur in spite of the projected decline in labor force participation of older workers and a continuation of the decline in the share of workers aged 55 and over. The projections show a drop from 13.1 percent of the labor force aged 55 and over in 1984 to 10.3 percent in 1995.

[78]Under conditions of population stationarity, reflecting a time when the baby-boom cohorts will have passed entirely or largely out of the working ages, and at 1979–1980 levels of labor force participation and survivorship, the median age of the labor force would rise to only 39.3 years (39.5 years for males and 39.1 years for females), a level still below that experienced from 1955 to 1965.

the skilled manpower and the productive capacity of older workers, and for the restrictions on the opportunity for work and income experienced by them.

Economic dependency. Another consequence of the sharp shifts in the labor force participation of men and women and in population age-sex structure in recent decades is a shift in the balance of older non-workers to workers. This shift in turn affects the relation between aggregate financial and other support requirements of older persons and society's ability to secure the funds necessary for this support. Examining the dependency situation with actual data on the economically active population provides a more realistic perspective on the capacity of the population to support its elderly members than do age dependency measures.[79] One measure of economic dependency, the elderly economic dependency ratio (elderly EDR), represents the ratio of economically inactive, noninstitutionalized persons aged 65 and over to the total civilian economically active population aged 16 and over. Another is the child economic dependency ratio (child EDR), which relates all noninstitutionalized children under age 16 to the total civilian economically active population.

Since 1950 more and more elderly persons have had to be supported by fewer and fewer workers. The elderly EDR increased rather steadily between 1950 and 1985, from 13 in 1950 to 21 in 1985, or by 8 elderly nonworkers per 100 workers (Table 7.23). About three fourths of the increase in this period occurred by 1965 and half of the small remaining gain occurred between 1980 and 1985. These fluctuations reflect the joint, and to some extent offsetting, effect of the aging of the population, the rise in labor force participation of women under age 65, and the decline in the labor force participation of older men. The increase in the elderly EDR would have been much more rapid if it had not been for the huge increase in the female labor force, which kept pace on the whole with the increase in the number of economically inactive men and women aged 65 and over.

The dependency ratio for older females far exceeds the dependency ratio for older males although the ratios have been converging.[80] The

---

[79] Economic dependency ratios measure the combined effect of economic and demographic structural factors in the economic support situation. Age dependency ratios measure the contribution of only the factor of age structure in economic dependency (although they are useful also for estimating the relative needs for various services). On the other hand, economic dependency ratios fail to allow for such factors in the calculus as unemployment, part-time work, and productivity, as well as the economic contribution of homemakers and volunteer work.

[80] Economic dependency ratios for males (or females) relate economically inactive males (or females) to the labor force of both sexes combined in a given year. No logical significance is attached to dependency ratios based on the labor force of a particular sex in a given year.

TABLE 7.23

Adult and Elderly Economic Dependency Ratios, by Sex: 1950–2030

Sex and Year	Not in LF 65+ Total LF		Not in LF 55+ Total LF		Not in LF 16+ Total LF		Not in LF 65+ Not in LF 16+	
Both Sexes								
1950	13.4		22.8		68.8		19.5	
1955	16.0		25.0		68.7		23.3	
1960	17.4		26.1		68.4		25.5	
1965	19.2		27.8		69.9		27.5	
1970	19.1		27.5		65.6		29.1	
1975	19.8		28.9		63.3		31.3	
1980	19.9		28.8		56.9		35.0	
1985	20.9		29.7		54.3		38.4	
1995[a]	22.9		30.6		50.0		45.7	
	A	B	A	B	A	B	A	B
2010[b]	24.1	23.2	35.4	NA	55.2	43.9	43.7	52.9
2030[b]	40.1	39.0	51.5	NA	70.4	57.8	56.9	67.4
Male								
1950	4.7		6.1		11.1		42.1	
1955	5.9		7.2		11.7		50.5	
1960	6.6		8.0		13.3		49.8	
1965	7.4		9.1		15.5		47.9	
1970	7.2		8.9		15.8		45.3	
1975	7.4		9.8		17.1		43.4	
1980	7.6		10.2		16.8		45.1	
1985	8.1		11.0		17.4		46.5	
1995[a]	8.9		11.7		17.6		50.7	
	A	B	A	B	A	B	A	B
2010[b]	9.4	9.3	13.8	NA	19.8	17.4	47.7	53.5
2030[b]	16.4	16.4	20.8	NA	26.6	24.3	61.7	67.6
Female								
1950	8.7		16.7		57.7		15.1	
1955	10.1		17.7		56.9		17.7	
1960	10.8		18.1		55.1		19.6	

SOURCES: For 1950–1980, based on data in U.S. Bureau of Labor Statistics, *Handbook of Labor Statistics* (June 1985), Tables 4 and 13; for 1985, based on data in U.S. Bureau of Labor Statistics, *Employment and Earnings* (January 1986), p. 154. For projections, see text and notes below.

NOTES: Armed forces are excluded from the labor force and the institutional population is excluded from the "not in labor force" category. Base of dependency ratios for males and females is the labor force aged 16 and over for both sexes. Measures expressed per 100. NA = not available.

[a]Based on data in H. N. Fullerton, Jr., "The 1995 Labor Force: BLS' Latest Projections," *Monthly Labor Review* 108 (11) (November 1985):17–25. Middle series of labor force projections.
[b]Series A assumes no change in sex-age specific labor force participation ratios after 1995, as projected to that date by the U.S. Bureau of Labor Statistics. Series B assumes a continuation of the 1985–1995 trend of general labor force participation ratios, but at a declining pace. Both series assume the middle population projections of the U.S. Bureau of the Census.

TABLE 7.23 (*continued*)

Sex and Year	Not in LF 65+ Total LF		Not in LF 55+ Total LF		Not in LF 16+ Total LF		Not in LF 65+ Not in LF 16+	
1965	11.8		18.7		54.4		21.7	
1970	11.9		18.6		49.8		23.9	
1975	12.4		19.1		46.3		26.8	
1980	12.4		18.7		40.1		30.8	
1985	12.8		18.7		37.0		34.6	
1995[a]	14.0		18.8		32.4		43.0	
	A	B	A	B	A	B	A	B
2010[b]	14.7	13.9	21.6	NA	35.4	26.5	41.4	52.5
2030[b]	23.6	22.5	30.7	NA	43.7	32.4	54.0	67.3

elderly EDR for women rose between 1950 and 1985, but at a much slower pace than the elderly EDR for men (Table 7.23). The dependency ratios of males and females aged 55 and over show a pattern similar to those aged 65 and over. The comparison tells us that many more women in older age than men are dependents, but the more rapid withdrawal of older men from the labor force and the strong movement of women into the labor force are causing the relative difference to diminish.

The EDR for those aged 65 and over may be seen as a function of the share of all economically inactive persons aged 16 and over who are aged 65 and over and the EDR for the population aged 16 and over (adult EDR). That is,

$$\frac{\text{Not in LF } 65+}{\text{Total LF}} = \frac{\text{Not in LF } 16+}{\text{Total LF}} \times \frac{\text{Not in LF } 65+}{\text{Not in LF } 16+}$$

It is of interest, therefore, to examine the trend of these two factors. The proportion of the inactive population that is elderly doubled between 1950 and 1985. There was a gradual increase from 19 percent to 38 percent in this 35-year period (Table 7.23). This trend was heavily influenced by the rapid upward trends in the proportion of elderly women and in the proportion of working women. The proportion of the inactive female population that is elderly increased sharply between 1950 and 1985 from 15 percent to 35 percent. There was only a small rise in the proportion of the inactive male population that is elderly in this period. The male proportion in 1985—46 percent—was not unlike the share for much of the period since 1950.

The EDR for persons aged 16 and over showed a substantial drop between 1950 and 1985, from 69 to 54. This decline was the net effect of opposing male and female trends, with the figure for women dropping sharply and the figure for men rising sharply. This difference is explained by the difference in the trends of labor force participation of the two sexes.

The projections of the labor force made by the Bureau of Labor Statistics for 1995 have been extended by the author to 2030 for purposes of carrying the projections of EDR forward to 2030. Two alternative series of EDR were developed for the period 1995–2030. Series A is based on the assumption that the LFPR for men and women aged 16–64 and 65 and over in 1995 would remain unchanged. Series B is based on the assumption that the 1985–1995 trends in general male and female LFPR for these (four) sex-age groups would continue, but at a generally declining pace.[81] Series A EDR reflect only the impact of the projected population changes after 1995, whereas series B EDR reflect the impact of projected changes in the general LFPR as well as projected population changes (i.e., the distribution by sex and two broad age groups).

There is relatively little difference between the two series of elderly EDR (Table 7.23). This fact suggests that projected population changes account for much more of the projected changes in the EDR than the projected changes in the general LFPR. Both Series A and Series B show

---

[81] More specifically, in Series B the mean annual percentage-point changes in the general LFPR for males and females aged 16–64 and 65 and over for 1985–1995 were assumed to remain constant to the year 2000 and then decline linearly to zero by the decade 2020–2030. In Series A, age-specific LFPR in the age range 16–64 and the general LFPR for ages 65 and over were assumed to remain unchanged.

The resulting projections of the general LFPR for men and women aged 16–64 and 65 and over are as follows:

| Year | Assumption A | | Assumption B | | | |
| | Ages 16–64 | | Ages 16–64 | | Ages 65+ | |
	Male	Female	Male	Female	Male	Female
1985	85.4	64.1	85.4	64.1	15.8	7.3
1995	85.8	71.1	85.8	71.1	11.0	5.5
2000	85.2	70.0	86.0	74.6	8.6	4.6
2010	83.7	68.4	86.3	79.3	5.4	3.4
2020	83.1	67.8	86.4	81.6	3.8	2.8
2030	83.7	68.7	86.4	81.6	3.8	2.8

NOTE: Assumption A for males and females 65+: LFPR of 1995 (11.0 percent and 5.5 percent) apply in all later years.

The number in the labor force in each category was obtained as the product of the age-specific LFPR or general LFPR, and population projections for the corresponding categories. The Census Bureau's middle series, adjusted to a civilian noninstitutional basis, was used for this purpose. Subtracting the labor force from the population produced the number not in the labor force. These calculations yielded the data needed for projecting the two series of economic dependency ratios shown in Table 7.23.

large rises in the elderly EDR between 2010 and 2030 after rather modest rises or even declines between 1985 and 2010. The shifts in age distribution associated with the movement of the baby-boom cohorts into the age band 65 and over will be determinative in these changes.

Alternatively stated, the key element in the shifts in elderly EDR may be identified as the aging of the adult population. The projected percentages aged 65 and over of the civilian noninstitutional population aged 16 and over, for 1985–2030, are as follows:

Year	Both Sexes	Male	Female
1985	15.1	13.1	17.0
1995	16.5	14.1	18.7
2010	16.8	14.3	19.9
2020	21.0	18.5	23.3
2030	25.5	22.7	28.0

Like these percentages, the elderly EDR will rise sharply after 2010.

Public policy must balance the needs of all age segments of the dependent population. From a broader point of view, therefore, the economic dependency of elderly persons must be considered in association with the economic dependency of persons at other ages, since a rise in the number and economic costs of elderly dependents may be offset or augmented by changes in the number and economic costs of dependents at these other ages. In addition to the many persons aged 16–64 who are economically inactive—including the large number of "house-spouses"—all persons under age 16 are considered to be economically inactive.

Economic dependency ratios for ages 16–64 and ages under 16 showed marked declines between 1965 and 1985 because of the entry of the baby-boom cohorts into the working ages, the rise in the share of women who work, and the falling off of fertility. As a result, the total economic dependency ratio fell sharply in these two decades, in spite of the rise in elderly dependency (Table 7.24 and Figure 7.4). Economic dependency for these younger age groups is expected to continue falling to 1995 or 2000, as is economic dependency for all ages combined. Although the elderly dependency ratio rises almost steadily, even in 2010, of the three age categories, the elderly still account for the smallest share of the dependent population. Then, a dramatic rise in overall dependency occurs as elderly dependency leaps upward and child dependency stops declining.

In 1965 100 workers supported 154 nonworkers, in 1985 100 workers supported 103 nonworkers, and in 2010 100 workers will have to support only about 96 nonworkers. In 2030 100 workers will have to

TABLE 7.24

Economic Dependency Ratios, by Broad Age Group: 1955–2030

Year	Total All Ages	Under Age 16	Ages 16–64	Ages 65 and Over
1955	147.3	78.6	52.7	16.0
1965	154.0	84.1	50.7	19.2
1975	125.7	62.4	43.5	19.8
1985	102.5	48.2	33.4	20.9
1995	96.7	46.7	27.1	22.9
2000	95.5	44.5	28.3	22.7
2010	95.5	40.3	31.1	24.1
2020	105.1	41.6	31.8	31.7
2030	111.8	41.4	30.3	40.1

SOURCE: See text and Table 7.23.

NOTES: Armed forces are excluded from the labor force and the institutional population is excluded from the economically inactive population. Figures for years after 2000 are Series A projections. Measures expressed per 100.

support 112 nonworkers, however. This is about where we were in 1980, but the mix of elderly dependents, other adult dependents, and children will have shifted dramatically, as the following data show:

Year	Total	Age		
		Under 16	16–64	65 and Over
1955	100	53	36	11
1985	100	47	33	20
2010	100	42	33	25
2030	100	37	27	36

In 1955, the midpoint of the baby-boom period, the EDR for the population under age 16 was almost five times greater than that for the population aged 65 and over (Table 7.24). By 1985 this ratio had been reduced by about half. According to the projections, by 2030, it will be about 1:1. The significance of this shift can be enormous.

Slower growth of the child population in the next few decades will permit the conversion of some funds and facilities from use by children to the service of the elderly. However, the support costs for older persons tend to be public responsibilities compared with the support costs for children, which tend to be private family responsibilities (even though the cost of educating children is largely a public expense).

FIGURE 7.4

Economic Dependency Ratios, by Age: 1950–2030

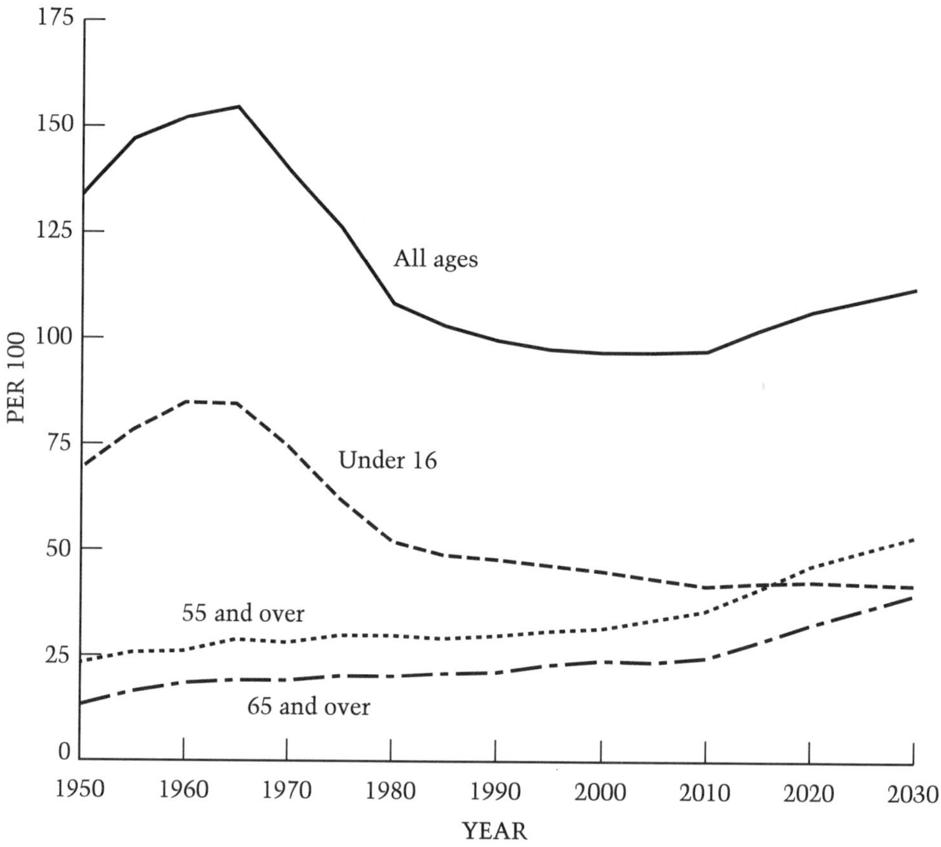

SOURCES: Tables 7.23 and 7.24.

The public support cost for an elderly person is also greater than that for a child. Clark and Spengler have estimated, in fact, that during the 1970s the annual public support cost for an elderly person was three times as much as that for a child.[82] When public support costs per per-

[82] R. L. Clark and J. J. Spengler, "Dependency Ratios: Their Use in Economic Analysis," in J. L. Simon and J. DaVanzo, eds., *Research in Population Economics*, vol. 2 (Greenwich, CT: JAI Press, 1980), p. 72. See also J. H. Schulz (1985); and R. L. Clark and J. J. Spengler, "Changing Demography and Dependency Costs: The Implications of Future Dependency Ratios and Their Composition," in B. R. Herzog, ed., *Aging and Income: Programs and Prospects for the Elderly* (New York: Human Sciences Press, 1978).

son for the three age segments—children, working-age adults, and the elderly—are taken into account and applied to the numbers of persons in these age segments, the elderly account for the largest share of the total public dependency burden, both at present and in the years to 2030. However, Wander estimated from German data that the cost of raising a child from birth to age 20 was about one fourth to one third greater than the cost of supporting a person aged 60 or older over his or her remaining lifetime.[83] Some of the difference between Wander's estimates and Clark and Spengler's is due to the differences in their data and methods, but much of the difference may be conceptual. Clark and Spengler evaluated public costs only, while Wander measured total costs.

In sum, unless the future trends in the age-sex structure of the population and in labor force participation vary markedly from those assumed here, by the end of this century nearly one quarter of the inactive population will be elderly; and by the end of the third decade of the next century, over one third will be elderly. The small declines in the economic dependency of both children and working-age adults that may occur during the 2010–2030 period are not expected to offset much of the sharp rise in elderly economic dependency in this period, so that the total economic dependency ratio is almost certain to show a large increase. The aggregate public support costs for elderly dependents may now already be greater than those for working-age dependents and children combined and will almost certainly be far greater by 2030.

Demographic and Related Factors in Funding Social Security

The demographic trends described in this chapter and in earlier chapters, particularly the trend of economic dependency, have important implications for the financing of the Social Security retirement program. In order to understand the relation of these demographic trends and the funding of the Social Security retirement program, it is useful first to set forth some general concepts relating to retirement plans. The analysis applies, with some modifications, to company-specific plans as well as to the Social Security program.

When workers participate in any retirement plan, they pay a defined payroll tax and postpone current satisfaction of some goods and services

---

[83] H. Wander, "Zero Population Growth Now: The Lessons from Europe," in T. J. Espenshade and W. J. Serow, eds., *The Economic Consequences of Slowing Population Growth* (New York: Academic Press, 1978), pp. 57–58.

so as to have a claim on goods and services when they retire. This claim may be gradually augmented by an adjustment for inflation (i.e., change in value of money) and for interest (i.e., payment for use of money) on the basis of the current rates. If the system is sound actuarially and is managed as an insurance program, benefits will be determined actuarially in relation to premiums on the basis of the risk experience of the particular population group (as defined by age, sex, and other characteristics) and the need for an adequate reserve. The typically long time-lag between payment of contributions and receipt of benefits, with the likelihood of severe price fluctuations in the interim, complicates the task of managing the retirement plan trust fund.

The aggregate annual contributions to a retirement trust fund will reflect in part the changing size of the cohorts of workers who contribute to the fund. Large elderly cohorts of workers will have made larger total contributions to the fund than small elderly cohorts, other factors being equal; and hence, a larger fund should be available to provide benefits to the larger cohorts. The contributions to the fund of each cohort of workers and of each worker will also reflect differences in the earnings record of workers, permitting variable benefits to individuals according to contributions.

The Social Security retirement program is not a typical insurance program, however; it has many elements of a welfare program. The need to provide adequate benefits in the face of brief participation by many charter and newly covered workers, periodically high levels of unemployment and underemployment, and a long period of inflation have prevented it from operating as an insurance scheme. The current crop of workers and employers has typically contributed the funds needed to pay benefits to persons who are now retired. Since the program is a combination of an insurance system and a welfare system and since it is financed essentially on a pay-as-you-go basis, a principal demographic factor affecting Social Security funding is the fluctuations in the relative sizes of the population of contributing ages and the population of beneficiary ages. A rise in the beneficiary/contributor ratio can place a heavy burden on the system unless the levels of contributions, benefits, and reserves have been structured to allow for the shifts or unless there are modifications in the contributor and/or beneficiary universe.

Changes in the beneficiary/contributor ratio can be measured approximately by shifts in elderly economic dependency ratios. These changes can be closely measured only for the next few decades inasmuch as future fertility changes begin to affect the balance of the elderly population and the working-age population after this period and fertility cannot be predicted with great accuracy. Questions of the feasibility of providing the necessary economic support arise when the older population is very large in relation to the working-age population, as it is expected to be, for example, in the years 2010–2030. This now appears likely to happen even if future fertility is higher than at present.

In addition to the changing size of birth cohorts and their relative numbers, other demographic changes which affect the trend of economic dependency ratios include shifts in life expectancy, changes in the length of working life, and the trend in labor force participation ratios. The actual course of economic dependency is also affected by shifts in employment and unemployment ratios and in the balance of full- and part-time work. These factors affect the number of equivalent full-time workers who are actually at work and the number of equivalent full-time retired persons who are actually retired.

In recent decades we have experienced increases in life expectancy, a rising age of entry into the labor force, and a falling age of withdrawal from the labor force. As we have seen, the increased years of life have gone into additional years of leisure rather than increased years of work, especially for men. These changes have extended the period of life during which beneficiaries draw money from the Social Security Trust Fund and reduced the period of life during which workers contribute to it. The extension of total life expectancy and the reduction in worklife expectancy for men between 1950–1955 and 1980–1985 reduced the period of life for making contributions by about four years and lengthened the period of life for receiving benefits by about four to five years. In combination with the rising numbers of births before World War I and relatively low fertility in the ensuing period, these changes have brought about a gradual increase in the economic dependency ratio and in the ratio of beneficiaries to contributors.

The decline in the age of retirement and the increase in longevity have had a marked effect on the cost of the Social Security retirement program through their effect on the periods for paying out benefits and receiving contributions. To illustrate the impact of the decline in the age of retirement on Social Security expenditures, some simple model calculations have been carried out. These show the change in direct lifetime expenditures, made by Social Security for the retirement of men, resulting from the change in retirement age between 1953 and 1983. The calculations have also been designed to show the relative influence of changes in life expectancy, retirement age, and the annual benefits per se.

As described above, the mean age of men who received a Social Security retirement benefit award declined by 4.9 years (from 68.6 to 63.7) between 1953 and 1983 and the median age of retirement estimated from CPS data on the labor force declined by 4.1 years (from 66.9 to 62.8) between 1950–1955 and 1980–1985. Our model calculations evaluate the effect of both of these estimates on retirement expenditures. The estimates of costs relate only to retirement benefits for the retirees themselves.[84]

The decline of 4.9 years in the average age of retirement between 1953 and 1983 corresponds to an increase of 4.3 years in life expectancy at the average age of retirement in this period (from 11.1 years in 1953 to 15.4 years in 1983). Almost two thirds of the increase in life expectancy resulted from the downward shift in the age of retirement (2.8 years out of 4.3 years) and about one third resulted from the improvement in mortality. The estimated direct lifetime Social Security retirement benefit per retiree to be collected by the awardee cohort of 1983 is $21,482 (adjusted for inflation). Thus, there was an increase of 1.6 times in the real dollar value of the direct lifetime retirement benefit in this 30-year period. A little over one half of the increase resulted from the increase in the annual benefit itself and less than one third resulted from the decrease in the average age of retirement. If there had been no increase in annual benefits per se, benefits would have increased by $5,700, or 69 percent, nearly two thirds of the total increase being a result of the increase in longevity.

The results using two alternative estimates of age of retirement are summarized, in terms of the percentage of the increase contributed by each factor and mean lifetime benefits, as follows:

	A[a]	B[b]
Increase in Real Lifetime Benefits (percent)	100	100
Increase from real benefits per se	55	59
Increase from longevity	16	17
Decrease in retirement age	29	24
Mean Lifetime Benefits, total[c]		
1953	$ 8,214	$ 8,880
1983	21,482	22,179
Percent increase	162	150
Mean Lifetime Benefits, 1983		
Assuming no change in average retirement age	$15,484	$16,739
Assuming no change in real benefits per se	13,914	15,007

[a]Estimates correspond to the decline between 1953 and 1983 in the mean age of those awarded a Social Security retirement benefit.
[b]Estimates correspond to the decline between 1950–1955 and 1980–1985 in the median age of the net voluntary withdrawals from the labor force at ages 45 and over.
[c]Adjusted for inflation.

[84]The direct lifetime cost per retiree can be calculated by multiplying the annual benefit by the number of years it was received. It was assumed, for simplicity's sake, that

The high levels of unemployment, underemployment, and inflation characterizing the economy of the late 1970s and early 1980s exacerbated the problem of maintaining the solvency of the Social Security Trust Fund. Soaring inflation, in fact, precipitated downward adjustments of benefits for cost-of-living increases when it was seen that the program was becoming financially pressed. On the other hand, the explosive effect of inflation on benefits was offset in part by the increase in the contributions of workers to the fund as a result of inflation in their pay. The sharp rise in labor force participation of women also tended temporarily to mitigate the problem. The effect of the latter factor will diminish and may even reverse itself as the female labor reserve contracts and as working women reach retirement age in large numbers and begin to draw benefits in their own right.

Prospective demands on the Social Security Trust Fund can be met by raising the normal age of retirement (i.e., the age for receipt of full benefits), eliminating or reducing benefits for early retirement, providing tax or other inducements for continuing to work or returning to work after retirement, raising general taxes, taxing benefits, eliminating minimum benefits, expanding the universe of potential contributors (e.g., requiring the participation of federal, state, and local government workers), imposing a higher contribution rate on worker earnings, and levying the contribution rate on a broader income base. The most painless solution would be a voluntary rise in the typical age at retirement, aided by a relaxation of all mandatory age requirements and an expansion of the opportunities for productive work by the elderly, including flexible work programs and retraining to upgrade work skills. This solution cannot be depended upon, however.

A mandatory rise in the normal age of retirement would appear to be a more dependable solution. This may have some adverse side effects, such as slowing down the rate of advancement through work organizations and discouraging the employment of youth. It may be justified, however, on the ground of a broad public policy directed at maintaining the viability of the Social Security retirement program. On the other

the average annual benefit per retiree remains the same throughout the remaining lifetime of each annual cohort of retirees and that longevity is fixed for the cohort as of the year of retirement. These assumptions have obvious limitations. The average number of years during which benefits are received was obtained from the appropriate life table as the average number of years of life remaining at the average age at retirement.

To estimate the effect of the change in average age at retirement, we subtract the effect due to mortality improvement from the difference in the two life expectancy values at the average age of retirement in 1953 and 1983. To estimate the effect of the change in mortality, we calculate the change in life expectancy between 1953 and 1983 at a fixed age chosen as the age midway between the retirement ages. The direct annual cost is obtained by multiplying by 12 the monthly benefit amounts received by the awardee cohorts as reported in the Annual Statistical Supplements of the *Social Security Bulletin*. The Consumer Price Index has been used to adjust for inflation.

hand, support of the elderly by the current crop of workers, without penalizing the elderly in the ways noted, can be justified by an ethical judgment that each generation has an obligation to support the previous generation, on grounds of intergenerational equity, that is, to reciprocate for the support the older generation gave to the younger generation as children.

In the reexamination of the financing of the Social Security program in the early 1980s conducted by the National Commission on Social Security Reform, all of the approaches listed above were considered and several were adopted in the amendments of the Social Security Act passed in 1983. According to these amendments, the normal age of retirement with full benefits will be raised gradually from 65 to 67 between 2002 and 2027; benefits for persons with gross incomes of $25,000 and over are taxable effective at once; and the Social Security tax rate on worker earnings and the earnings base on which the tax rate is levied are being gradually raised. During the mid 1980s the Social Security Trust Fund has been accumulating a surplus because of the new tax regulations, reduced inflation, and decreased unemployment.

A periodic review of the condition of the fund will be necessary, especially in order to plan for the crunch expected in the early part of the next century, when the baby-boom cohorts reach the ages of retirement. Because of the difficulties of anticipating the levels of longevity, fertility, economic growth, inflation, and employment, and because of the prospective sharp rise in the aged-dependency ratio, further subsidies from the current crop of workers (i.e., intergenerational transfers) through an increase in payroll contributions and/or general taxation may be necessary. In addition, the elderly themselves may have to make further concessions, as enumerated earlier.

The concepts of age dependency and economic dependency of the elderly may become less and less relevant in the long run as more and more workers participate in effective public and private job-specific plans and the share of retirement income from Social Security declines for most workers. Participation in these plans and part-time employment would provide the extra measure of security needed to supplement the rather meager allowances under the Social Security program and reduce the pressure on the Social Security program to replace former earnings.

Changes in the age distribution of the population may become the dominant factor affecting the condition of the Social Security Trust Fund when the baby-boom cohorts come of age, but in the nearer future the slow increase in the relative size of the older population and the working-age population will not in itself greatly strain the fund. During this earlier period, other factors, such as the levels of unemployment, economic growth, and inflation, are expected to have a more dominant effect on the solvency of the fund. This period provides an opportunity to prepare for and avert a crisis in politico-economic planning and intergenerational relationships.

Because of the high financial costs of early retirement for many persons and society, careful consideration should be given to the factors conducive to early retirement and to the ways by which this practice could be reversed.[85] It is ironic, however, that a major social goal pursued for most of this century and now finally nearing achievement, the entitlement to retirement on the part of workers at an early age after long years of work, must now be viewed as a social problem. Alternatively, low fertility in the years since 1965 can be seen as *the* problem and an increase in fertility as the cure. A rise in fertility must come soon, however, if the effects of the baby boom, increased longevity, and low labor force participation of the older population are to be offset by a larger youthful labor force.

Summary

The pattern of linear progression in the life course, from education to work to retirement, fairly universal in the past, is in flux. The stages are being reordered to some degree in many different ways in individual lives; and in particular, the postcareer years are often not exclusively years of leisure.

Elderly persons have considerably lower educational attainment than the adult population in general, but the educational level of the elderly population has been rising steadily and sharply as more recent cohorts with more years of schooling have moved into the older ages. This pattern of change will continue in the future. Cohort analysis reflects the obvious fact that educational attainment remains rather stable with increasing age and does not really decline as the cross-sectional data suggest.

The educational level of the elderly has great influence on their current income. Since most elderly do not work, their educational level does not directly determine their current earnings but was important in past years. Moreover, it affects their ability to take advantage of the programs designed to benefit them. Without sufficient education they cannot learn about the programs and handle the red tape necessary to

---

[85]H. L. Sheppard and S. E. Rix, *The Graying of Working America: The Coming Crisis of Retirement-Age Policy* (New York: Free Press, 1977), chaps. 9 and 10; Clark and Barker (1981).

secure the benefits. A small percentage of the elderly, considered as being of high functional illiteracy, are particularly disadvantaged. In some segments of the population, however, the percentage is considerable. Over one quarter of the black elderly and more than one third of the Hispanic elderly fit this conservative definition of functional illiteracy.

Labor force participation ratios (LFPR) have been falling at nearly all ages among men, with declines from one third to two thirds at the older ages between 1950 and 1985. The process intensified with the passage of time, as Medicare was initiated, private pension plans and Social Security participation were expanded, and legislation designed to protect the job security of older people, such as ADEA and ERISA, was enacted. LFPR for elderly women have also been dropping but more moderately than for men, while LFPR at the younger years from ages 60–64 down have been rising. Increasing feminization of the older labor force is one consequence of these changes.

Retirement has become increasingly acceptable as a type of social behavior, and workers choose to retire when they think they can afford it—usually when they receive pensions from a private pension plan, with or without benefits from Social Security. Early (pre–age 62) retirement is usually motivated by health reasons or layoff. Patterns in other industrialized countries have been similar.

Changes in retirement age can be approximated by data on the age of new Social Security retirement beneficiaries, by analysis of LFPR linked in cohort form, and by use of tables of working life. The preferred measures of retirement age indicate a decline in median age of retirement of men and women from ages 67–68 to 63–64 between 1950 and 1985, or by four to five years. These measures show that most of the decline in retirement age occurred between 1950 and 1970 and that the more moderate decline in the 1970s was followed by a further slowing down in the 1980s as the median age fell close to age 62, the age of reduced benefits under Social Security.

Race, marital status, household composition, and type of residence affect the extent of labor force participation of the older population. Attachment of the working elderly to the labor force is often partial. About half the working elderly do so part time, and part-time work has been increasing. While the elderly do not have higher unemployment ratios than younger workers, when they are unemployed they are likely to remain unemployed for longer periods. Moreover, they are more likely to withdraw from the labor force as discouraged workers when they experience prolonged unemployment.

Data on exits from and entries into the labor force for 1979–1980 suggest a far greater probability of remaining in the same labor force status over any year than of changing status. For those who change status, exit from the labor force is far more likely than entry, although even at age 60 there is an 8 percent (male) and 6 percent (female) probability of entering the labor force. Such reentries were more common in 1980 than in 1972, probably because of more uncertainty regarding the state of the economy.

The shifts in LFPR, in the volume and age of retirements, and in survival rates have important economic implications, among which are the changes in the duration of worklife, the aging of the labor force, the rise in elderly economic dependency, and the impact on the Social Security program of old-age insurance and the Federal programs of health insurance.

A direct consequence of the trends in labor force participation, retirement, and longevity between 1940 and 1980 has been a large increase in the length of nonworking life for older men, associated with a sharp decline in the share of total life devoted to work, and a moderate increase in working life for older women, associated with a substantial increase in the share of total life devoted to work.

The other three consequences of the trends in labor force participation, retirement, and longevity are all directly affected by the movement of the baby-boom cohorts up the age scale and their eventual attainment of old age. This movement accounts in part for the fall of the median age of the labor force to the mid 1980s and its projected rise through the 1990s to a plateau in the 2000s. The median age of the labor force will not reattain the peak level of 1960 even by 2005, when all the members of the baby-boom cohorts will be over age 40. There are no necessarily negative consequences of the aging of the labor force. However, labor mobility within organizations and between geographic areas may be slowed and affect the rate of promotion and the accommodation of the labor force to the local demand for labor.

The movement of the baby-boom cohorts accounts in large part for the anticipated modest rise in the elderly economic dependency ratio until 2010 and its subsequent sharp leap upward. If the analysis of economic dependency is broadened to allow for the economic dependency of persons of working age and children, a different trend emerges. The trend of total economic dependency has been declining since 1965, and not until after about 2010, when the elderly dependency ratio begins its steep rise, will total dependency show a rise. The increasing need for public responsibility of financial support of children as well as the elderly gives the level of total dependency added significance for policy-making.

Finally, the movement of the baby-boom cohorts and its effect on the elderly economic dependency ratio will put considerable stress on the Social Security system after 2010. The trend of this measure is influenced by past and prospective increases in longevity and declines in the age of retirement. The latter factor taxes the system doubly because newly retired workers not only stop contributing to the system but become beneficiaries of the system. The viability of the system has possibly been enhanced by a mandated rise in the normal age of retirement after 2002 and other changes limiting benefits and raising contributions, but transitory factors like excessive inflation and unemployment levels can be more determinative.

Appendix 7A. *Projections of Educational Level*

Because educational level is essentially a stable social characteristic for individuals (i.e., neither reversible nor accumulative) after about age 35, the present record for persons aged 35 and over and, even more confidently, the present and past records foreshadow closely the educational level of the older population for several decades to come. The future distribution of the population by educational level at any age over 35 is largely determined by the educational distribution of the population at the corresponding younger age and earlier date. In fact, current data on the proportion of high school graduates for ages 25 and over directly foreshadow the proportion of high school graduates y years older y years later since nearly all persons graduating high school have done so by age 25.

An examination of the proportion of persons completing high school between 1950 and 1980 for birth cohorts reveals a remarkable consistency in the reporting of educational level over these decades, with only a gradual rise in the proportion. Table 7.1 arrays the proportions of high school graduates for 1950–1980 by birth cohorts and indicates the average (absolute) decennial cohort change. Changes in the educational distribution of birth cohorts between one date and another come about from (1) the addition to the cohort of net immigrants with a different distribution by educational level than the initial population, (2) differences in survival rates for persons with different levels of education, and (3) changes from census to census in the accuracy of reporting and coverage of groups with different levels of education. Increasing overstatement of educational level in successive censuses, differences in survival rates favoring high school graduates, and a higher educational level of more recent immigrants could all theoretically have played some part in the tendency for the percentage of high school graduates in a particular cohort to rise, but the one factor for which there is direct evidence of a consistent augmentative role is differential survival.

A first approximation of the proportion of high school graduates at some future date is secured by assuming no change in the educational

TABLE 7A.1

Calculation of Projections of the Percentage of High School Graduates Aged 55 and Over, by Age and Sex: 1980–2020

Sex and Age	Adjustment Factor[a]	Percentage High School Graduates				
		1980	1990	2000	2010	2020
Male						
25–34	1.016[b]	84.4	NA	X	X	X
35–44	1.016[b]	77.1	85.8	NA	X	X
45–54	1.029[b]	65.6	78.3	87.1	NA	X
55–64	1.029[b]	56.2	67.5	80.6	89.6	NA
65–74	1.022	41.2	57.8	69.5	82.9	92.2
75–84	1.022[c]	NA	42.1	59.1	71.0	84.8
85 and over	1.022[c]	NA	30.3	43.0	60.4	72.6
75 and over	1.022[c]	29.6	39.8[d]	55.5[d]	68.1[d]	81.7[d]
65 and over[e]	X	37.2	51.0	63.4	76.8	88.4
Female						
25–34	1.007[b]	84.0	NA	X	X	X
35–44	1.007[b]	76.3	84.6	NA	X	X
45–54	1.016[b]	66.6	76.8	85.2	NA	X
55–64	1.016[b]	57.5	67.7	78.1	86.5	NA
65–74	1.049	44.0	58.4	68.8	79.3	87.9
75–84	1.049[c]	NA	46.2	61.3	72.1	83.2
85 and over	1.049[c]	NA	36.0	48.4	64.3	75.7
75 and over	1.049[c]	34.3	43.4[d]	57.2[d]	69.1[d]	80.4[d]
65 and over[e]	X	39.9	51.4	62.6	74.0	84.5

SOURCE: See text of Appendix 7A.

NOTES: NA = not available; X = not applicable. Based on decennial census data for 1980.

[a] Derived from E. M. Kitagawa and P. M. Hauser, *Differential Mortality in the United States: A Study in Socioeconomic Epidemiology* (Cambridge, MA: Harvard University Press, 1973), Chap. 2.
[b] Factor for 20-year age group is assumed to apply to component 10-year age groups.
[c] Assumed to be the same as for age group 65–74.
[d] Computed by weighting percentages for age groups 75–84 and 85 and over.
[e] Computed by weighting percentages for age groups 65–74 and 75 and over.

distribution for cohorts aged 25 and over in 1980, for all years following 1980. On this basis, from the proportion of high school graduates aged 45–54 in 1980, we can immediately determine the proportion of high school graduates aged 55–64 in 1990, aged 65–74 in 2000, and aged 75–84 in 2010. Improved projections can be derived by incorporating some allowance for the higher survival of high school graduates than of non-graduates and for other factors. A simple device for doing this is to adjust the preliminary projection of the proportion of high school graduates for any birth cohort upward by its average increase from one age to the next between censuses over the last two, three, or four census decades. As we can see in Table 7.1, this average increase varies from near zero to several percentage points, depending on the cohort.

A more conservative device for making an allowance for the greater survival of high school graduates is to adjust the preliminary projections on the basis of findings from research on differential mortality in the United States. I employed the results of the study carried out by Kitagawa and Hauser in 1960.[1] From their data, we are able to infer the difference between high school graduates and nongraduates in survival rates from age 25 to age 75 in three age bands for males and females. The ratios of the survival rates for high school graduates to survival rates for all persons in the specified groups are as follows:

Age	Male	Female
25–44	1.016	1.007
45–64	1.029	1.016
65–74	1.022	1.049

These factors were adapted for use in adjusting the preliminary proportions of high school graduates for differences between educational categories in survival rates.

The calculations are shown in Table 7A.1. To derive the projections of the proportions of high school graduates for age groups 55 and over shown in Tables 7A.1 and 7.2, the proportions for each age group were multiplied sequentially by the factors displayed above as they were carried forward to higher ages. The proportions for broad age groups (e.g., 65 and over) were obtained by weighting the component proportions according to population projections for the component age groups in the appropriate years.

Appendix 7B. *Supplementary Tables on Labor Force Participation*

[1]E. M. Kitagawa and P. M. Hauser, *Differential Mortality in the United States: A Study in Socioeconomic Epidemiology* (Cambridge, MA: Harvard University Press, 1973).

TABLE 7B.1

Percentage of the Population Aged 45 and Over in the Labor Force, by Age and Sex: 1950–1980

Age	Both Sexes				Male				Female			
	1980	1970	1960	1950	1980	1970	1960	1950	1980	1970	1960	1950
45–49	76.3	72.5	70.6	63.6	92.0	93.5	94.4	93.2	61.5	53.0	47.4	34.8
50–54	71.7	71.0	68.6	60.4	88.5	91.4	92.2	90.6	56.3	52.0	45.8	30.8
55–59	63.6	66.2	63.1	56.1	80.6	86.8	87.7	86.7	48.4	47.4	39.7	25.9
60–64	46.2	53.4	52.4	49.7	60.4	73.0	77.6	79.4	34.0	36.1	29.5	20.5
65–69	21.3	26.9	29.3	35.4	29.2	39.0	43.8	59.8	15.0	17.2	16.6	12.8
70–74	12.2	14.8	18.3	21.9	18.3	22.4	28.7	38.7	7.8	9.1	9.6	6.6
75–79	} 6.2ᵃ	9.0	11.7	13.1	} 10.3ᵃ	14.2	19.5	24.2	} 3.7ᵃ	5.5	5.6	3.5
80–84		5.6	6.6	6.8		9.1	11.5	13.2		3.5	3.0	1.7
85 and Over	2.4ᵇ	4.6ᵇ	3.9	3.5	4.2ᵇ	6.8ᵇ	7.0	6.9	1.6ᵇ	3.4ᵇ	2.0	1.2
75 and Over	5.3	7.6	9.0	9.8	9.1	12.0	15.5	18.6	3.2	4.7	4.2	2.6

SOURCES: U.S. Bureau of the Census, 1950 Census of Population, U.S. Summary: Detailed Characteristics, Table 118; 1960 Census of Population, U.S. Summary: Detailed Characteristics, Table 194; 1970 Census of Population, U.S. Summary: Detailed Characteristics, Table 215; 1980 Census of Population, U.S. Summary: Detailed Characteristics, Table 272.

NOTES: Total labor force as percentage of total resident population. Decennial census data.

ᵃ Derived by author from estimates for 85 and over and census figures for 75 and over.
ᵇ Based on 1980 census Public Use Microdata Sample tabulations or 1970 census Public Use Microdata Sample tabulations (for ages 85–99 only) provided by Ira Rosenwaike, University of Pennsylvania.

TABLE 7B.2

Period and Cohort Generalized Age Cycles for Labor Force Participation Ratios, by Sex: 1940–1980

Age	Male				Female			
	Period		Cohort		Period		Cohort	
20–24	83.9		84.3		52.4		45.3	
25–29		92.8		92.8		43.0		43.0
30–34	94.8		94.8		41.0		41.0	
35–39		95.1		94.8		43.1		53.5
40–44	94.5		94.4		45.0		57.1	
45–49		93.3		93.0		44.0		68.6
50–54	90.7		90.3		40.9		66.7	
55–59		85.9		84.9		35.6		71.1
60–64	73.9		72.0		27.0		56.2	
65–69		46.0		41.8		15.0		37.1
70–74	28.8		25.0		7.9		20.0	
75 and Over		14.7		11.3		3.6		10.0

SOURCES: See Tables 7B.1 and Appendix 6A.

NOTES: Ratios are anchored to average ratios, 1940–1980, at ages 25–29 and 30–34. Based on decennial census data.

Appendix 7C. *Comparability of Census Data on Occupations*

In assembling the data on the trend in the occupational distribution of the elderly in the labor force, a major problem is that the occupational data in the 1980 census are based on a substantially revised classification compared with the data for 1970 and earlier years. The only published information available on a comparable basis is given in a table in a 1980 census report showing the occupational distribution of employed persons aged 16 and over in 1970 and 1980 following the 1980 classification. The comparable data for ages 16 and over show very little change between 1970 and 1980. By far the largest changes were an increase of 2.5 percentage points for men and 3.6 percentage points for women in executive, administrative, and managerial occupations.

Lacking a tested alternative, we assume here that the occupational data for ages 65 and over in 1980 are affected by reclassification in the same way as the occupational data for ages 16 and over in 1980. With this assumption, the occupational data for the elderly in 1980 were reclassified to the categories of 1970. The figures on the occupational distribution of elderly workers in 1980 which are presented in Table 7.17

458

TABLE 7C.1

Comparability Ratios for Major Occupational Groups: 1980/1970

1970 Classification	1980 Classification	Comparability Ratio	
		Men	Women
Total, all categories	Total, all categories	1.000	1.000
Professional, technical, and related workers	Professional specialty	1.136	1.025
Managers and administrators	Executive, administrative, and managerial occupations	1.106	.979
Clerical and related workers	Administrative support occupations (including clerical)	1.056	1.081
Sales workers	Sales occupations	.716	.679
Craft and related workers	Precision production, craft and repair occupations	1.005	.681
Operatives	Machine operators, assemblers and inspectors, and transportation and material moving occupations	1.067	1.223
Service workers, excluding private household	Service, excluding private household occupations	.988	1.025
Private household workers	Private household occupations	.857	1.000
Laborers, except farm	Handlers, equipment cleaners, helpers and laborers	.916	.398
Farmers, farm managers, farm laborers, farm supervisors	Farming, forestry, and fishing occupations	.808	.882

were obtained by equating the categories paired in Table 7C.1 and applying the comparability ratios shown to the 1980 reported occupational data for the population aged 65 and over. The occupational distribution for 1980 shown in Table 7.17 should be interpreted with great caution, inasmuch as the data were based on very crude adjustments and comparability ratios for the actual population aged 65 and over are not available.

8

ECONOMIC STATUS

Money Income of Individuals and Families

Age Variations in Individual Income

ALTHOUGH we are concerned primarily with the income of elderly individuals and elderly families (i.e., those with householders aged 65 and over), we also need to examine the income of younger individuals and families (i.e., those with householders at the preretirement and younger ages).[1] This will serve two purposes: first, to compare income in later life with income in earlier years and, second, to measure the evolution of income over the life course.

---

[1]To the extent possible, I consider also the income of the elderly in component age groups, since an analysis of the income data on the elderly in which all the elderly are lumped together in a single age group may be misleading. The very old tend to have different financial resources from the new-old, because of the diminution with time and age of incompletely replaced resources, the difference in each group's earnings and pension programs prior to retirement, and differences in marital composition. For example, the income of those who retired in the 1980s is much higher than the income of those who retired in the 1960s. The needs and expenditure patterns of persons who are just 65 years old and persons who are 80 or 85 years old—some of whom retired 15 or 20 years earlier—are often quite different. For example, the very old have larger expenditures for health and housing as a result of chronic illnesses and sizable home repair bills.

The level of median income shows a characteristic pattern of variation with age in any year. Incomes are typically at a peak in the middle working years (Tables 8.1 and 8.2). The incomes of young workers and the elderly are considerably lower. After the peak ages median income drops, at first slowly and then sharply at the retirement ages.

The ages of peak income for men have tended to rise over time. In 1950 the peak for men occurred in the age band 35–44; in 1985 the peak age band was 40–49. These shifts resulted mainly from shifts in levels of labor force participation, supply and demand for labor, and occupational composition.

Data on relative median income (i.e., the median income in an age group in a particular year relative to the median income of all persons reporting some income in the particular year) serve to reflect the shifts in the peak age of median income. They also demonstrate that the more recent the data, the higher the relative income at most ages, especially

TABLE 8.1

Median Income for Age Groups as a Ratio of the Median for All Ages Combined, for Males: 1950–1980

Age[a]	Birth Cohorts[b] (diagonal)	Year 1980	Year 1970	Year 1960	Year 1950	Birth Cohorts[c] (diagonal)
14–19	1960–1966	.163[d]	.140	.175	.179	1930–1936
20–24	1955–1960	.616	.567	.626	.686	1925–1930
25–29	1950–1955	1.034	1.156	1.173	1.124	1920–1925
30–34	1945–1950	1.309	1.326	1.173	1.124	1915–1920
35–39	1940–1945	1.496	1.394	1.329	1.263	1910–1915
40–44	1935–1940	1.544	1.419	1.329	1.263	1905–1910
45–49	1930–1935	1.566	1.397	1.240	1.224	1900–1905
50–54	1925–1930	1.496	1.322	1.240	1.224	1895–1900
55–59	1920–1925	1.377	1.207	1.065	1.048	1890–1895
60–64	1915–1920	1.106	1.032	1.065	1.048	1885–1890
65–69	1910–1915	.704	.561	.492	.463	1880–1885
70–74	1905–1910	.575	.431	.492	.463	1875–1880
75 and Over	Before 1905	.464	.332	.299	.463	Before 1875

SOURCE: Based on U.S. Bureau of the Census, 1950–1980 Censuses of Population, *U.S. Summary: Detailed Characteristics.*

NOTE: Base of ratios is median income for ages 15 and over in 1980 and ages 14 and over in 1970, 1960, and 1950. Income for preceding year.

[a] Age in all calendar years.
[b] Years of birth for age groups in 1980.
[c] Years of birth for age groups in 1950.
[d] Ages 15–19.

TABLE 8.2

Median Income for Age Groups as a Ratio of the Median for All Ages Combined, for Females: 1950–1980

Age[a]	Birth Cohorts[b] (diagonal)	Year				Birth Cohorts[c] (diagonal)
		1980	1970	1960	1950	
14–19	1960–1966	.312[d]	.346	.492	.407	1930–1936
20–24	1955–1960	.978	1.158	1.182	1.240	1925–1930
25–29	1950–1955	1.420	1.474	1.306	1.272	1920–1925
30–34	1945–1950	1.417	1.357			1915–1920
35–39	1940–1945	1.371	1.403	1.441	1.320	1910–1915
40–44	1935–1940	1.396	1.496			1905–1910
45–49	1930–1935	1.403	1.562	1.544	1.279	1900–1905
50–54	1925–1930	1.378	1.551			1895–1900
55–59	1920–1925	1.297	1.475	1.138	.978	1890–1895
60–64	1915–1920	.940	1.019			1885–1890
65–69	1910–1915	.726	.669	.575	.585	1880–1885
70–74	1905–1910	.733	.640			1875–1880
75 and Over	Before 1905	.703	.573	.517		Before 1875

SOURCE: Based on U.S. Bureau of the Census, 1950–1980 Censuses of Population, *U.S. Summary, Detailed Characteristics.*

NOTE: Base of ratios is median income for ages 15 and over in 1980 and ages 14 and over in 1970, 1960, and 1950. Income for preceding year.

[a] Age in all calendar years.
[b] Years of birth for age groups in 1980.
[c] Years of birth for age groups in 1950.
[d] Ages 15–19.

the older ages. Relative income of men in 1980 was higher than it was in previous census years for all age groups 55 and over—from about 60 percent (at ages 65 and over) to 124 percent (at ages 55–64) of the general average in 1980 compared with 46 percent to 105 percent in 1950. This may be explained in great part by the large increases in Social Security benefits and private pensions in the 1970s. Relative income was also higher for all age groups from 35 to 54 in 1980—some 50–53 percent above the general average compared with only 22–26 percent for the corresponding age groups in 1950.

For birth cohorts of men, a fall in the age of peak median income from 1950 to 1980 (in constant 1979 dollars) is suggested by the data. These ages have consistently been 45–54 or 55–64. Peak income has been rising with each later cohort, however. The ages of peak median income, and the peak median income, for several cohorts of men and calendar years are as follows:

	Cohort Data			Cross-sectional Data		
Ages in 1980	Peak Income	Ages at Peak Income	Years of Peak Income[a]	Peak Income	Ages at Peak Income	Year[a]
45–54[b]	$18,654	45–54	1980	$18,654	45–54	1980
55–64	17,361	45–54	1970	17,948	35–44	1970
65–74	14,381	55–64	1970	13,608	35–44	1960
75+	10,906	55–64	1960	9,394	35–44	1950

SOURCE: Based on decennial census data.

NOTE: Data for 1950–1970 adjusted for changes in cost of living.

[a] Year reported; data for preceding year.
[b] Truncated cohort.

Cross-sectional comparison tends to exaggerate the falloff in income experienced by actual cohorts of men as the members move from the terminal working ages (55–64) to the initial retirement ages (65–74). The decline in the income of actual cohorts of men at the older ages tends to be more moderate.

Percent Decline: Ages 55–64 to 65–74			
Cross-sectional Data		Cohort Data[a]	
Year[b]	Percent	Period[b]	Percent
1950	NA	1950–1960	35.7
1960	53.8	1960–1970	40.8
1970	55.1	1970–1980	44.9
1980	48.6		

SOURCE: Based on decennial census data.

[a] Adjusted for changes in cost of living.
[b] Year reported; data for preceding year.

For example, median income fell by 55 percent between ages 55–64 and 65–74 in 1970 and by 49 percent in 1980 on a cross-sectional basis, but by only 45 percent on a cohort basis between 1970 and 1980. The difference appears to be diminishing, however. As shown by cross-sectional data, postretirement incomes for men appear to have replaced a larger share of preretirement incomes in 1980 than in 1970. More specifically, the replacement ratio based on a comparison of incomes at ages 55–64 and 65–74 rose between 1970 and 1980 from 45 percent to 51 percent.[2] As shown by cohort data, however, the replacement ratio fell between

[2] The replacement ratio is calculated here as the complement of the percent decline in median income between the preretirement ages and the postretirement ages.

1960–1970 and 1970–1980 from 59 percent to 55 percent. If we accept the latter figures as representing the actual share of income replaced, men retiring between 1970 and 1980 replaced only 55 percent of their preretirement income.

In general, cross-sectional income data for men exaggerate the drop-off in income as an indication of the experience of real cohorts that are aging. The income of older persons largely reflects earnings at an earlier time, when incomes tended to be lower than they are today for various reasons, including lower pay scales, more limited education, skill, and productivity of the work force, and fewer pension programs.[3]

Median incomes for the ages 25 and over for women were consistently greater in 1980 than in 1950, as for men, but the patterns of the sexes are different. In 1950, peak income for women came at ages 35–44. In 1980, peak income came at ages 25–29 and 45–49; in fact, the ages with the highest incomes spanned 25–54. The ages of peak median income in the cross-sectional data appear to have risen (in constant dollars), except for the alternative peak at ages 25–29 in 1980. (On the other hand, newer cohorts of women were earning their peak incomes at earlier ages than prior cohorts.) Peak incomes rose about three quarters between 1950 and 1980.

	Cohort Data			Cross-sectional Data		
Age in 1980	Peak Income	Ages at Peak Income	Year of Peak Income[a]	Peak Income	Ages at Peak Income	Year[a]
45–54[b]	$7,317	45–54	1980	$7,468	25–34	1980[c]
				7,317	45–54	
55–64	7,175	45–54	1970	7,175	45–54	1970
65–74	5,751	55–64	1970	5,441	45–54	1960
75 and Over	4,011	55–64	1960	4,153	35–44	1950

SOURCE: Based on decennial census data.

NOTE: Data for 1950–1970 adjusted for changes in cost of living.

[a] Year reported; data for preceding year.
[b] Truncated cohort.
[c] There were two broad peaks in 1980.

Cohort data for females, as for males, have shown less drop-off in income around the retirement ages than cross-sectional data, and the differences appear to be diminishing:

[3] See "Age and Economic Activities: Life Cycle Patterns," Chapter 5 in R. L. Clark and J. J. Spengler, *The Economics of Individual and Population Aging* (Cambridge: Cambridge University Press, 1980).

Percent Decline: Ages 55–64 to 65–74			
Cross-sectional Data		Cohort Data[a]	
Year[b]	Percent	Period	Percent
1950	NA	1950–1960	34.0
1960	49.5	1960–1970	24.6
1970	47.4	1970–1980	33.4
1980	34.6		

SOURCE: Based on decennial census data.

NOTE: NA = not available.

[a] Adjusted for changes in cost of living.
[b] Year reported; data for preceding year.

In sum, for both men and women, income declines around retirement age are more moderate in the real life course than are represented in cross-sectional data on income. Furthermore, whether measured in cohort or cross-sectional terms, the replacement ratios for median income between the ages before retirement (i.e., 55–64) and the ages after retirement (i.e., 65–74), the complements of the numbers just displayed, are much higher for women than for men, even though the actual amounts of income are much lower for women. Future cohorts of working-age women are destined to reach old age with much work experience and, hence, with their own entitlements to Social Security and private pensions. This will contribute greatly to enhancing their economic status in the older years.

We may reasonably expect that a cohort aged 15–34 in a particular year just after World War II will have a much higher level of income at the older ages in the appropriate later years than prevails at these same ages in the starting years. This inference is based on a comparison of appropriate cohort and period distributions of median incomes for persons taken from decennial censuses. A more general indication is obtained from a comparison of generalized period age cycles and generalized cohort age cycles of median incomes. They were derived, as described in Appendix 6A, by averaging the age-to-age relative shifts in median income for every census year from 1950 to 1980 and anchoring these average ratios to the average median income at ages 25–34. The generalized cohort age cycle represents approximately the age pattern of individual incomes in the postwar era without specific cohort or period influences. The generalized period age cycle has similar attributes but is a synthetic cohort.

All age groups over 25–34 show a much higher income in the generalized cohort cycle than in the generalized period cycle (Table 8.3).

TABLE 8.3

Period and Cohort Generalized Age Cycles for the Median Income of Persons, by Sex: 1950–1980

Age	Male		Female	
	Period	Cohort	Period	Cohort
15–24	$ 4,588	$ 3,855	$3,480	$3,038
25–34	12,564	12,564	5,652	5,652
35–44	14,782	18,025	5,853	7,235
45–54	14,317	22,029	6,037	9,203
55–64	12,094	23,670	4,673	8,783
65–74	5,742	14,081	2,654	6,090
75 and Over	3,786	12,089	2,424	7,703

NOTES: See Appendix 6A for explanation of method. Based on decennial census data. Income is for year preceding the census year.

The cohort-period difference reflects the fact that each new later cohort has tended to out-earn its period counterpart of a given initial date, and has displayed a smaller income drop-off rate as the cohort aged than the period data with which it has a common terminal age group. In another sense, the period-cohort difference reflects an increase in real income in the postwar period—an increase that resulted from an increase in worker productivity and an expanding economy.

Although the income of the elderly tends to be lower than that of persons in midlife, the former group has been, on the whole, better protected from inflation. Legislation has been in effect since 1975 that calls for automatic indexing of Social Security benefits, that is, adjusting benefits each year to compensate for the reduction in purchasing power resulting from inflation. The pension income for federal government employees is also indexed. As a result, Social Security benefits and federal employee pensions kept pace with inflation, at least until the early 1980s. (Since 1982, when inflation slowed considerably, the automatic increments have been sharply reduced or delayed because of budgetary pressures.) For the most part, therefore, the notion that the elderly have been living on fixed incomes is a fiction.[4] Grimaldi maintains further that, largely because of the rapid growth in home ownership costs after

[4]See R. L. Clark, G. L. Maddox, R. P. Schrimper, and D. A. Sumner, *Inflation and the Economic Well-Being of the Elderly* (Baltimore, MD: Johns Hopkins University Press, 1986); and R. L. Clark and D. A. Sumner, "Inflation and the Real Income of the Elderly: Recent Evidence and Expectations for the Future," *Gerontologist* 25 (2) (April 1985):146–152.

1977, the method used to index Social Security benefits resulted in an overcompensation of the elderly for inflation.[5]

The elderly who were in the middle-income category prior to retirement are more likely to be adversely affected by inflation after retirement than those who were in the low- or high-income categories. While Social Security income is essentially protected against inflation, private pension income, received by many middle-income persons, is not commonly so protected. However, many persons in the middle-income category have savings to supplement their benefits under Social Security and private pension plans.

Variations in Family Income by Type of Family

We can reasonably infer from the above that the age of the householder makes a great difference in household income. Families with householders aged 65 and over have considerably lower incomes than families overall. In 1985, the median income of families with householders aged 65 and over ($19,162) was only two thirds the median income of all families ($27,735). (See Table 8.4.) The balance has been shifting and, in the decade and a half from 1970 to 1985, there was a notable convergence of the median incomes of elderly families and all families. The ratio of the medians rose from 0.51 in 1970 to 0.69 in 1985. In prior decades the ratio registered divergence or stability; in 1950 it was 0.57. (See Figure 8.1.)

The median income of elderly families in 1985 was 6.6 times greater than in 1960 and 3.8 times greater than in 1970. Even with adjustment for the declining value of the dollar, the median income of elderly families showed large increases in recent decades. In constant dollars, their income increased about 82 percent over the 1960–1985 period and 37 percent over the 1970–1985 period. The notable increase since 1960, especially in relation to the increase of all families, reflects in part the comparatively favorable economic policies affecting the elderly in this period.

Whether the householder is living with relatives or not makes a considerable difference in household income. Elderly unrelated individuals (i.e., those not living with any relatives) have much lower incomes than families with elderly householders. In 1985, unrelated individuals aged 65 and over had a median income only two fifths as great ($7,568) as families with householders aged 65 and over ($19,162). (See Table

---

[5]P. L. Grimaldi, "Measured Inflation and the Elderly, 1973 to 1981," *Gerontologist* 22 (4) (August 1982):347–353.

TABLE 8.4

Median Income of Families with Householders Aged 65 and Over, by Type of Family, and of Unrelated Individuals Aged 65 and Over, by Sex: 1950–1985

Year and Measure	Families				Unrelated Individuals		
	Total	Married-Couple Families	Other Families		Total	Male	Female
			Male Householder[a]	Female Householder[a]			
Householder or Unrelated Individual Aged 65 and Over							
1985	$19,162	$19,423	$19,671	$17,218	$7,568	$9,075	$7,268
1980	12,882	12,951	13,342	12,285	5,096	5,746	4,957
1970	5,053	4,966	6,722	5,370	1,951	2,250	1,888
1960	2,897	2,813	4,063	3,139	1,053	1,313	960
1950	1,903	NA	NA	NA	646	NA	NA
Ratio, Householders Aged 65 and Over to Householders Aged 15 and Over[b,c]							
1985	69.1	62.5	87.0	126.0	64.1	60.9	73.7
1980	61.3	56.0	76.2	118.0	61.4	52.5	74.3
1970	51.2	47.2	74.6	105.4	62.2	49.6	76.0
1960	51.5	48.0	83.6	105.8	61.2	52.9	69.7
1950	57.3	NA	NA	NA	61.8	NA	NA

TABLE 8.4 (continued)

Year and Measure	Families		Other Families		Unrelated Individuals		
	Total	Married-Couple Families	Male Householder[a]	Female Householder[a]	Total	Male	Female
Ratio, Type of Family or Unrelated Individual to Total Families[c,d]							
1985	100.0	101.4	102.7	89.0	39.5	47.4	37.9
1980	100.0	100.5	103.6	95.4	39.6	44.6	38.5
1970	100.0	98.3	133.0	106.3	38.6	44.5	37.4
1960	100.0	97.1	140.2	140.2	36.3	45.3	33.1
1950	100.0	NA	NA	NA	33.9	NA	NA

SOURCES: Based on U.S. Bureau of the Census, *Current Population Reports*, series P-60, nos. 9, 37, 97, 132, and 154; and unpublished tabulations.

NOTE: Based on the current population survey. NA = not available.

[a] No spouse present.
[b] Alternatively, the ratio of unrelated individuals aged 65 and over to unrelated individuals aged 15 and over.
[c] Ratios per 100.
[d] Householder aged 65 and over.

FIGURE 8.1

Ratio of Median Income for Families with Householders Aged 65 and Over to Median Income for All Families: 1960–1985

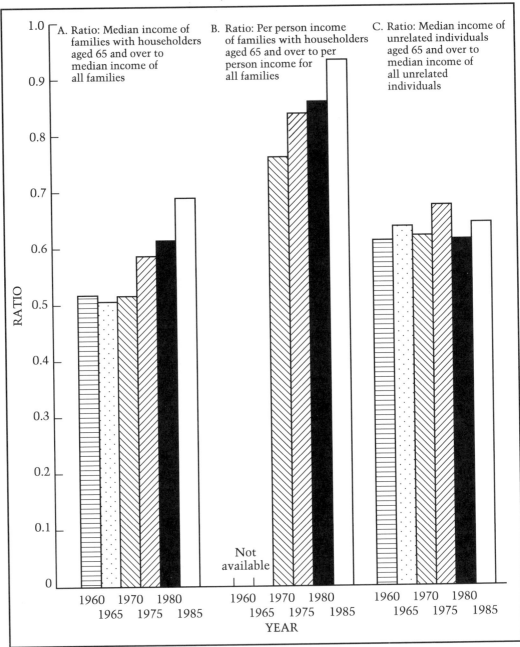

SOURCES: Tables 8.4 and 8.17; U.S. Bureau of the Census, various *Current Population Reports*, series P-60 and P-20.

8.4.) The incomes of the two types of households rose at about the same pace between 1970 and 1985 (3.8 times), so that their relative levels have not been changing.

For families maintained by women, with no husband present, the incomes of older families were well above those of younger families. This was the reverse of the relation for families maintained by men, with no wife present, as well as for married-couple families and unrelated individuals. In 1985 families maintained by men aged 65 and over had a median income 13 percent below that of all families maintained by men, while the median income of families maintained by women aged 65 and over was 26 percent above that of all families maintained by women. However, elderly families headed by women, with no husband present, were faring relatively worse than elderly families headed by men, with no wife present.

In any year both family incomes and incomes of unrelated individuals fall off rapidly in older age, especially at the point of retirement. The median income of families with householders aged 65 and over in 1985 was only three fifths as great as that of families with householders aged 55–64. The drop-off was far less pronounced for family households without a spouse present than for married-couple households, apparently because a larger share of the unmarried householders chose to continue working. The median income of families maintained by either men or women aged 65 and over was about nine tenths as large as that of families maintained by men or women aged 55–64. The age difference in general reflects not only the higher proportion of retired householders in the older age group but also a shift, both voluntary and involuntary, to less remunerative part-time and less skilled jobs. It reflects, too, the difference in the lifetime earning histories of different birth cohorts, with earlier birth cohorts tending to have poorer earning histories.

Income Distribution

Even with large reductions in the share of low-income elderly family households and large increases in the share of high-income elderly family households between 1970 and 1985, the proportions in 1985 remain, respectively, well above and well below the corresponding figures for all family households. The proportion of family households with householders aged 65 and over, with an income under $10,000, decreased from 55 percent in 1970 to 17 percent in 1985, and the proportion with an income $35,000 and over increased from 4 percent to 20 percent (Table 8.5).

TABLE 8.5

Percentages of Low-Income and High-Income Households with
Householders Aged 65 and Over, by Race: 1985

	All Races		Black	
Type of Household	Under $10,000	$35,000 and Over	Under $10,000	$35,000 and Over
Family Households	17	20	38	7
Married couples	15	17	34	8
Male	22	24	47	5
Female	26	18	44	6
Nonfamily households	64	3	85	1
Male	54	5	76	—
Female	67	3	88	1

SOURCE: U.S. Bureau of the Census, *Current Population Reports*, series P-70, no. 156, Tables 17 and 18.

NOTE: Dash denotes that figure rounds to zero.

The incomes of elderly nonfamily households were concentrated near the lower end of the income range in both 1985 and 1970, with much larger percentages receiving incomes below $10,000 than elderly family households. The concentration at the lower end of the income scale is diminishing, however. For example, 64 percent of the nonfamily households received less than $10,000 in income in 1985 compared with 89 percent in 1970. In constant dollars, the percentages for 1970 and 1985 would be closer, but they would still reflect the need for much additional improvement for nonfamily households. Even with adjusted dollars, the proportion for nonfamily households in 1985 would exceed the corresponding figure for family households in 1985 to the same extent as the nominal figures (64 percent vs. 17 percent).

Sex and Race Variations

There are sizable gender and racial (white-black) gaps in income and, as a consequence, a gigantic gender-racial gap (i.e., white males vs. black females). Considering the four sex-race groups purely in terms of race or gender differences, the greatest difference is between white women and white men and the least difference is between black women and white women. In general, the gender gap substantially exceeds the racial gap.

Direct evidence of a huge gap in the incomes of men and women throughout worklife is provided by a comparison of the median incomes of men and women over the adult years for 1985 reported in the Current Population Survey (CPS) for 1986. Ratios of female to male incomes (per 100) are:

Age	Ratio (per 100)	Age	Ratio (per 100)
20–24	71	55–64	35
25–34	53	65–69	52
35–44	40	70 and Over	62
45–54	37		

Female incomes amounted to about one half or less of male incomes at the prime working ages of 25–54. The ratio rises in the older ages from about one third at ages 55–64 to three fifths at ages 70 and over, as male incomes fall more steeply than female incomes.

Historically more general evidence of the gender gap over the life course is given by ratios of the median incomes of women to men based on the cohort generalized age cycle for the postwar years developed in this monograph.[6] These ratios (per 100) also provide a striking indication of the deficits of women's incomes.

Age	Ratio (per 100)	Age	Ratio (per 100)
15–24	79	55–64	37
25–34	45	65–74	43
35–44	40	75 and Over	64
45–54	42		

In these data, which average the cohort experience since World War II, the median income of women never exceeds 45 percent of the median income of men between ages 25 and 74. The rise from 37 percent at ages 55–64 to 64 percent at ages 75 and over is again the result of the steeper fall of men's incomes than women's at the older ages.

Evidence of the gender gap in family incomes is limited to a comparison of the incomes of male and female family householders and the incomes of male and female unrelated individuals. According to the CPS, in 1985 the median income of female family householders aged 65 and

[6]Essentially the same ratios were obtained by use of the period generalized age cycle for the postwar years.

over was 12 percent below that of male family householders aged 65 and over, and the income of elderly unrelated women was 20 percent below that of elderly unrelated men (Table 8.4).[7]

Direct evidence for the huge racial and ethnic gap in incomes throughout worklife is given by ratios of median incomes for broad age groups for 1985, calculated from the CPS of 1986. Ratios (per 100) of incomes of blacks to whites and Hispanics to whites are:

Age	Ratio (per 100)	
	Black/White	Hispanic/White
18–24	60	93
20–24	59	NA
25–64	74	71
25–34	72	
35–44	78	NA
45–54	77	
55–64	61	
65 and Over	60	66
65–69	56	NA
70 and over	62	NA

NOTE: NA = not available.

In the prime working ages both blacks and Hispanics received only about three quarters or less of the income of whites, and in the retirement ages they received only two thirds or less of the income of whites.

A sizable gap has existed between the family incomes of blacks and whites since at least 1970 (Table 8.6). In 1985 the median income of families with an elderly black householder was only 60 percent of that of families with an elderly white householder. The ratio varied little by type of household, whether a married-couple household or a female-headed family household. The corresponding Hispanic ratio was a little less favorable (57 percent). Black unrelated individuals show a similar gap in relation to white unrelated individuals (64 percent).

A comparison of income distributions at particular ages for blacks and "all races," according to type of household, provides more detail on the variations in the racial gap (Table 8.5). For example, 44 percent of black female-headed family households received less than $10,000, while 26 percent of female-headed family households of "all races" fell in this category. The figures are reversed for incomes of $35,000 and over (6

[7]These figures exclude married-couple families since the income of the married partners is combined. Partners in married couples typically receive very different amounts of income.

percent vs. 18 percent). The vast majority of black nonfamily householders (85 percent) received less than $10,000 compared with less than two
thirds of "all races" nonfamily householders.

Since the gender gap in income is sizable for each race and Hispanics and the racial and Hispanic gap in income is sizable for each sex, we
should expect the combined effect of sex and race/Hispanic ethnicity on
income to be extreme. This is shown by ratios (per 100) of median income for each sex-race/Hispanic group to the income of white males at
the older ages in 1985.

| | Ratio to White Male | | | | |
Age	White Female	Black Male	Black Female	Hispanic Male	Hispanic Female
55–59	32	52	29	NA	NA
60–64	37	50	29	NA	NA
65–69	51	54	34 ⎱	62	41
70 and Over	62	58	42 ⎰		

NOTE: NA = not available.

All groups fare poorly, particularly black females and Hispanic females.
These two groups are affected jointly in an unfavorable direction by both
gender and race/ethnic income differences. Data on incomes of elderly
families and unrelated individuals with white and black householders
of each sex are provided in Table 8.6.

Poverty Status

Age, Sex, and Race Variations

The vast majority of elderly persons are not poor, as is often believed, and in fact elderly persons are less likely to be poor than younger
persons.[8] The poverty ratio for those aged 65 and over in 1985 was 13
percent compared with 14 percent for all persons. If, however, the comparison is restricted to adults aged 18–64, because of the marked poverty ratio of children (21 percent), elderly persons are more likely to be
poor (Table 8.7).

---

[8]Poverty is determined on the basis of reported total money income. Poverty thresh-
olds are as defined by the U.S. Office of Management and Budget and currently differ on
the basis of family size, number of family members under age 18, and age of householder
(under age 65 and age 65 and over). The total money income of each family and each
unrelated individual in the sample is compared with the appropriate poverty threshold to
determine the poverty status of each family, family member, or unrelated individual.

TABLE 8.6

Median Income of Families with White and Black Householders Aged 65 and Over, by Type of Family, and of White and Black Unrelated Individuals Aged 65 and Over, by Sex: 1970–1985

| Race and Year | Families | | Other Families | | Unrelated Individuals | | |
	Total	Married-Couple Families	Male Householder[a]	Female Householder[a]	Total	Male	Female
Householder or Unrelated Individual Aged 65 and Over							
White							
1985	$19,815	$19,877	$23,846	$18,854	$7,922	$9,692	$7,607
1980	13,382	13,306	14,279	13,744	5,354	6,166	5,186
1970	5,263	5,107	7,320	5,909	2,005	2,365	1,937
Black							
1985	$11,937	$12,375	b	$11,013	$5,027	$5,736	$4,880
1980	8,383	8,510	$ 9,039	7,966	3,718	4,848	3,558
1970	3,282	3,359	b	2,878	1,443	1,708	1,357

TABLE 8.6 (continued)

| | Families | | | | Unrelated Individuals | | |
| Race and Year | Total | Married-Couple Families | Other Families | | Total | Male | Female |
			Male Householder[a]	Female Householder[a]			
Ratio, Householders Aged 65 and Over to Householders Aged 15 and Over[c,d]							
White							
1985	68.0	63.0	98.6	119.1	64.7	61.4	74.4
1980	61.1	57.5	76.2	115.4	61.1	52.8	74.8
1970	51.4	47.6	76.9	102.7	61.1	48.6	74.1
Black							
1985	71.1	50.4	NA	118.4	64.6	55.5	73.6
1980	66.1	45.8	72.0	107.3	68.9	67.4	88.7
1970	52.3	43.0	NA	80.5	68.2	51.4	82.5
Ratio, Black to White[c]							
1985	60.2	62.3	NA	58.4	63.5	59.2	64.2
1980	62.7	64.0	63.3	58.0	69.4	78.6	68.6
1970	62.4	65.8	NA	48.7	72.0	72.2	70.1

SOURCES: Based on U.S. Bureau of the Census, *Current Population Reports*, series P-60, nos. 97, 132, and 154; and unpublished tabulations.

NOTE: Based on Current Population Survey. NA = not available.

[a] No spouse present.
[b] Base less than 75,000.
[c] Alternatively, ratio of unrelated individuals aged 65 and over to unrelated individuals aged 15 and over.
[d] Ratios per 100.

Poverty among the elderly population was still considerable even a few decades ago. Between 1959 and 1985 the percentage of the elderly in poverty declined sharply—more sharply than poverty in the general population.

Year	Ages 65 and Over	All Persons	Ratio per 100
1959	35.2	22.4	157
1966	28.5	14.7	204
1970	24.6	12.6	195
1975	15.3	12.3	124
1980	15.7	13.0	121
1985	12.6	14.0	90

SOURCE: U.S. Bureau of the Census, *Current Population Reports*, series P-60, no. 154 (August 1986), Table 16.

In 1959, 35 percent of the elderly had incomes below the poverty level and the poverty ratio of the elderly was half again above that of the general population. By 1985 the proportion of the elderly with incomes below the poverty level was only 90 percent of that for the general population. Progress among the elderly was nearly continuous for the quarter century after 1959, but the rest of the population showed little progress after the late 1960s. The positive effects of the new programs benefiting the elderly (e.g., SSI, Medicare, Medicaid, ERISA, ADEA), as well as the growth of the established programs (i.e., federal Social Security and employer retirement programs), are evident, as are the negative effects of the retrenchment of programs benefiting children during the 1980s.

The higher level of poverty of older blacks compared with older whites is well known, but the relatively greater poverty of older women compared with older men is less widely recognized (Table 8.7). The gender difference has been dubbed the "feminization of poverty." The phrase is particularly applicable at the older ages because a large share of the elderly population is female. In 1985 there were nearly three times as many poor elderly women (2.6 million) as poor elderly men (0.9 million); nearly one-sixth of the elderly women were poor compared with one-twelfth of the elderly men. The feminization of poverty in later life is a result of factors similar to those contributing to the lower income of women in later life: high widowhood rates and low remarriage rates for women, retirement without a pension, gender inequalities at earlier ages in occupational options and in pay levels, and employment in low-skilled jobs and low-paying jobs in earlier years. The excess poverty of women in old age reflects the greater concentration of working women in peripheral industries in their working years. Men tend to be concentrated in the core industries, which offer more steady work, higher pay, and a greater range of fringe benefits. The earnings gap between the sexes is marked and, as explained later, is not fully accounted for by differences in education, work experience, or work interruptions. Gender discrimination is presumably responsible in part, among other factors, and is believed to remain widespread.

Economically, the black elderly are still trailing well behind the white elderly, even though both groups shared in the progress of the last few decades. Nearly one third of all elderly blacks are poor and an even larger share of elderly black women are poor (Table 8.7). The factors noted above accounting for the high poverty ratio of the general elderly female population apply with even more force to the black elderly female population.[9]

Household Status and Living Arrangements

Because of these sex-race differences in the extent of poverty among individuals, the sex and race of the householder are important factors related to the poverty status of family members. Poverty is more likely to occur, therefore, in households headed by women and by blacks. The

[9]The Survey of Income and Program Participation (SIPP) data indicate consistently lower levels of poverty for age, sex, and race groups in 1985 and may be more accurate than the corresponding CPS figures.

Age, Sex, and Race/Ethnicity	CPS	SIPP	Percentage Point Difference
Total	14.0	10.4	3.6
Under 18	20.7	17.1	3.6
18–64	11.3	7.9	3.4
65 and Over	12.6	8.9	3.7
Male	12.3	9.0	3.3
Female	15.6	11.7	3.9
White	11.4	7.7	3.7
Black	31.3	27.9	3.4
Hispanic	29.0	23.5	5.5

SOURCE: U.S. Bureau of the Census, *Current Population Reports*, Series P-70, no. 18 (June 1990), Table I.

The SIPP data are secured as of the month of reference and therefore represent family composition more accurately at the reference date and minimize the recall period.

TABLE 8.7

Percentage of Persons Below the Poverty Level, by Broad Age Group, Sex, and Race/Spanish Origin: 1985

Sex and Age	Total	White	Black	Spanish Origin
Total, Both Sexes	14.0	11.4	31.3	29.0
Under 18	20.7	16.2	43.6	40.3
18–64	11.3	9.5	24.3	22.6
55–64	10.5	8.9	25.8	19.0
65 and Over	12.6	11.0	31.5	23.9
Total, Male	12.3	10.1	27.4	27.4
Under 18	20.3	15.9	43.2	41.0
18–64	9.3	8.1	17.5	19.6
55–64	9.0	7.7	21.9	16.5
65 and Over	8.5	6.9	26.6	19.1
Total, Female	15.6	12.6	34.8	30.6
Under 18	21.1	16.5	44.0	39.5
18–64	13.3	10.8	30.0	25.5
55–64	11.9	10.1	29.0	21.2
65 and Over	15.6	13.8	34.8	27.4

SOURCE: U.S. Bureau of the Census, *Current Population Reports*, series P-60, no. 154 (August 1986), Table 18.

NOTE: Based on Current Population Survey.

percentage of persons aged 65 and over in households headed by women (no husband present), with incomes below the poverty level in 1984 (22 percent), was well above the percentage of elderly persons in poor households headed by men and married couples (8 percent).[10] (See Table 8.8.) The percentage of persons aged 65 and over in households with black householders, either men or women, having incomes below the poverty level (32 percent), was three times greater than the percentage for white householders (11 percent). When the householders are black females, the poverty ratio rises sharply (44 percent). The extent of poverty among elderly persons in Hispanic households (22 percent) is about midway between that for whites and for blacks.

Poverty is more likely to occur among elderly individuals living alone or with nonrelatives, especially if they are female, black, or Hispanic, than among elderly individuals in families: In 1984, 1 in 5 of white, 1 in 2 of black, and 2 in 5 of Hispanic unrelated individuals aged 65 and over were poor (Table 8.9). For black elderly women living alone or with nonrelatives, the proportion in poverty rises to 57 percent. All these

---

[10]Includes all householders in married-couple households; about 97 percent of such households report male householders.

480

TABLE 8.8

Percentage of Persons Aged 65 and Over Below the Poverty Level, by Family Status and Race: 1959–1984 (numbers in thousands)

Family Status and Race/Spanish Origin	Number, 1984	Percent			
		1984	1980	1970	1959
All Races					
All Persons Aged 65 and					
Over	3,330	12.4	15.7	24.6	35.2
In families	1,205	6.7	8.5	14.8	NA
Unrelated individuals	2,123	24.2	30.6	47.2	NA
Male	401	20.8	24.4	38.9	NA
Female	1,722	25.9	32.3	49.8	NA
In female-headed households[a]	2,001	22.1	27.8	41.2	49.2
In all other households[b]	1,329	7.5	9.5	16.8	30.2
Black					
All Persons Aged 65 and					
Over	710	31.7	38.1	47.7	62.5
In families	293	20.3	26.2	36.9	NA
Unrelated individuals	417	52.4	59.5	72.3	NA
Male	109	43.4	45.1	58.5	NA
Female	308	56.6	66.5	78.2	NA
In female-headed households[a]	418	43.5	52.5	63.5	69.9
In all other households[b]	292	22.9	28.0	38.6	59.2
Spanish Origin					
All Persons Aged 65 and					
Over	176	21.5	30.8	NA	NA
In families	90	15.0	23.3	NA	NA
Unrelated individuals	86	39.8	56.9	NA	NA
Male	30	c	c	NA	NA
Female	55	39.0	64.1	NA	NA
In female-headed households[a]	79	31.2	51.6	NA	NA
In all other households[b]	97	17.1	23.7	NA	NA

SOURCE: U.S. Bureau of the Census, *Current Population Reports*, series P-60, no. 152 (June 1986), Tables 1 and 3.

NOTES: Persons as of April 1960, March 1971, March 1981, and March 1985. NA = not available.

[a] No husband present; includes female unrelated individuals.
[b] Includes male unrelated individuals.
[c] Base less than 75,000.

TABLE 8.9

Percentage of Unrelated Individuals Aged 65 and Over Below the Poverty Level, by Living Arrangements and Race: 1984

Sex and Living Arrangements	All Races	White	Black
Total, Both Sexes	24.2	21.4	52.4
Living Alone	23.6	20.9	52.9
Living with Nonrelatives	32.2	28.1	50.1
In households	32.8	27.8	50.1
In group quarters	29.6	29.2	a
Total, Male	20.8	17.3	43.4
Living Alone	19.5	16.5	42.1
Living with Nonrelatives	27.5	22.3	a
In households	28.2	21.8	a
In group quarters	a	a	a
Total, Female	25.2	22.5	56.6
Living Alone	24.6	22.0	56.9
Living with Nonrelatives	36.6	33.2	a
In households	37.1	32.8	a
In group quarters	a	a	a

SOURCE: U.S. Bureau of the Census, *Current Population Reports,* series P-60, no. 152 (June 1986), Table 16.

[a]Base less than 75,000.

figures are in sharp contrast to the 7 percent for all elderly persons in families.

The poverty level of elderly families was well below the poverty level of younger families in 1985, as indicated by the poverty ratio of 7 percent for elderly families and 11 percent for all families (Table 8.10). One quarter of families with black female householders aged 65 and over were poor, but this record was far better than that of all families headed by black females, half of which were poor. This pattern of age variation is a recent development. As with individuals, it was not until after 1980 that elderly families had less poverty than all families. We see here again the effect of the shift in relative public support away from the young and in favor of the elderly in the 1960s, 1970s, and 1980s.

Poverty, Near-Poverty, and Descent into Poverty

Data on the proportion of the elderly population below 125 percent of the poverty level in 1985 suggest considerable bunching around the official poverty level. While only 13 percent of the elderly population

TABLE 8.10

Percentage of Families with Householders Aged 65 and Over Below the Poverty Level, by Race/Spanish Origin: 1959–1985

| Race/Spanish Origin | 1985 | | 1980 | 1970 | 1959 |
	All Families	Families with Female Householder[a]			
Householder Aged 65 and Over					
All races	7.0	13.3	9.1	16.5	30.0
White	5.6	10.6	7.3	14.1	26.8
Black	22.0	24.9	28.3	40.8	NA
Spanish origin[b]	16.6	c	23.6	NA	NA
Householder Aged 15 and Over					
All races	11.4	34.0	10.3	10.1	18.5
White	9.1	27.4	8.0	8.0	15.2
Black	28.7	50.5	28.9	29.5	NA
Spanish origin[b]	25.5	53.1	23.2	NA	NA

SOURCES: U.S. Bureau of the Census, *Current Population Reports*, series P-60, no. 154 (August 1986), Table 19; and series P-60, no. 152 (June 1986), Table 4.

NOTE: NA = not available.

[a] No husband present.
[b] May be of any race.
[c] Base less than 75,000.

fell below the official poverty level, some 21 percent fell below 125 percent of it (Table 8.11). The additions for near-poverty are greater for blacks and Hispanics. While 35 percent of persons in families with elderly female householders who are of Spanish origin fell below the official poverty level in 1985, some 50 percent of such persons fell below 125 percent of it. The corresponding figures for blacks are 43 percent and 59 percent. Regardless of race/Spanish origin or family status, the relative increment, over the proportion of the population below 100 percent of the poverty level, of the proportion below 125 percent of the poverty level exceeded 25 percent by a considerable amount. Even if we accept the official measure of poverty—and the measure is arguable—it is clear that a substantial share of the overall elderly population and a major share of elderly persons in some black and Hispanic family groups are living below or nearly below the poverty level.

There is much movement into and out of poverty, even on the part of the elderly. The annual ratio (monthly average) showed only 1 in 8 elderly persons to be poor in 1984, but 1 in 5 elderly persons was poor at some time in the year. The annual ratio in turn will appear to give an exaggerated impression of the extent of poverty among the elderly since the percentage of the elderly who were poor all 12 months of the year was only about half the annual percentage. The pattern for all persons was similar to that for the elderly, but reflects more movement into and out of poverty.

Duration of Poverty	Ages 65 and Over	All Persons
Annual Ratio		
(monthly average)	12.1	13.7
Poor All 12 Months	6.8	5.9
Poor in Any Month	18.5	26.2

SOURCE: Calculated from a 1984 SIPP extract by Patricia Ruggles of the Urban Institute.

Cross-sectional and cohort data on poverty show a progressive increase in the extent of poverty with advancing age in later life. CPS figures for the percentage in poverty in 1985 for the age groups 65 and above reflect this progression in simple cross-sectional form.

Age	Percent	Age	Percent
55–59	9.8	75–79	14.8
60–64	11.3	80–84	16.3
65–69	9.4	85 and Over	18.7
70–74	12.1		

In these terms persons aged 85 and over have twice as great a chance of being poor as those aged 65–69.

The life course pattern by which the extent of poverty changes with advancing age has been analyzed by Ross, Danziger, and Smolensky on the basis of decennial census data for 1950–1980, and by Burkhauser, Holden, and Feaster on the basis of the SSA Retirement History Study for 1969–1979.[11] The Ross et al. study examined the poverty ratios for cohorts differentiated by retirement status and marital status. They found that poverty ratios tended to remain rather constant within retirement and marital categories and that the characteristic life cycle pattern of poverty resulted from the mix of retirement and marital status groups.

[11]C. M. Ross, S. Danziger, and E. Smolensky, "Interpreting Changes in the Economic Status of the Elderly, 1949–1979, *Contemporary Policy Issues* 5 (2) (1989):98–112; R. V. Burkhauser, K. C. Holden, and D. Feaster, "Incidence, Timing, and Events Associated with Poverty: A Dynamic View of Poverty in Retirement," *Journal of Gerontology* 43 (2) (1988):42–52.

TABLE 8.11

Percentage of Persons Aged 65 and Over Below the Poverty Level and Below 125 Percent of the Poverty Level, by Family Status and Race/Spanish Origin: 1985

Poverty Level and Family Status	Race/Spanish Origin			
	All Persons Aged 65 and Over	White	Black	Spanish Origin
Below Poverty Level				
All persons	12.6	11.0	31.5	23.9
In families with female householders[a]	23.2	20.8	42.9	35.0
In all other families[b]	7.3	6.1	23.2	18.0
Below 125 Percent of Poverty Level				
All persons	20.9	18.8	44.9	34.8
In families with female householders[a]	36.6	34.0	58.7	50.4
In all other families[b]	12.9	11.2	34.8	26.7
Ratio $\frac{\text{125 Percent of Poverty Level}^c}{\text{100 Percent of Poverty Level}}$				
All persons	66	71	43	46
In families with female householders[a]	58	63	37	44
In all other families[b]	77	84	50	48

SOURCE: U.S. Bureau of the Census, *Current Population Reports*, series P-60, no. 154 (August 1986), Tables 16 and 17.

[a] No husband present; includes female unrelated individuals.
[b] Includes male unrelated individuals.
[c] Ratio shown as percent excess.

The Burkhauser et al. study also showed that retirement and marital status were the important dynamic factors in increased poverty in later life. Few married couples with pension income fell into poverty following retirement, but loss of a husband without a survivor's pension pulled many widows into poverty at an early date. Couples that retired with a pension and remained intact for the 10 years of the study had a poverty ratio of 2.3 percent in the first year of retirement and even lower ratios in subsequent years (Table 8.12). On the other hand, if the husband died and the wife had no pension, 9.2 percent of the widows became poor in the first year and the risk tended to increase in later years.

Only about 5 percent of couples with a pension *ever* fell into poverty over the 10 years (Table 8.12). At the other extreme, about 28 percent of the widows without pensions fell into poverty *at some point* during the decade. Couples without pensions and widows with pensions had intermediate risks of ever becoming poor. The nonpensioned group had more than a 2-to-1 greater risk of ever becoming poor compared

TABLE 8.12

Percentage of the Nonpoor Who Fell into Poverty in Each Period of Retirement, by Marital Status of the Wife and Pension Status of the Husband: 1969–1979

Period of Retirement	Intact Couples			Wife Eventually Widowed		
	Total	No Pension	With a Pension	Total	No Pension	With a Pension
1	5.5	10.5	2.3	5.2	9.2	2.4
2	4.2	7.8	2.2	5.7	7.1	4.8
3	2.1	4.2	1.0	7.8	11.6	5.4
4	1.3	1.4	1.2	8.0	10.5	6.8
5	0.9	1.1	0.8	4.3	4.9	4.3
Ever Poor	10.5	17.9	5.4	20.5	27.7	15.4

SOURCE: Adapted from R. V. Burkhauser, K. Holden, and D. Feaster, "Incidence, Timing, and Events Associated with Poverty: A Dynamic View of Poverty in Retirement," *Journal of Gerontology* 43 (2) (March 1988): S46–52. Copyright © The Gerontological Society of America. Reprinted by permission.

NOTE: Interviews repeated every two years.

with the pensioned group, while the widowed group had a 2-to-1 greater risk of ever becoming poor compared with intact couples. It is evident that lack of a pension and widowhood are important risk factors and that the first descent into poverty following retirement among those who were not poor before retirement is more closely associated with the event of widowhood and nonreceipt of a pension than with the mere passage of time and the slow erosion of income.

Sources of Income

The single most important (i.e., common) source of income for the elderly is Social Security benefits. Over 90 percent of the elderly receive Social Security benefits (Table 8.13). Few elderly depend solely on Social Security benefits, however; analysis of the income data for 1984 reveals that only 5 percent of elderly families and 14 percent of elderly unrelated individuals live exclusively on Social Security benefits. The vast majority of families and unrelated individuals have income from other sources, although many of these obtain a large share of their income from Social Security benefits. Since most persons receiving only Social Security benefits or mainly Social Security benefits as income had low earnings when they worked, such persons are receiving benefits near or below the poverty line. A large share of the 21 percent of the elderly who reported incomes below 125 percent of the poverty level were living wholly or mainly on Social Security benefits.

Earnings (i.e., wages, salaries, and self-employment income) were received by many elderly families (44 percent) and represent a substantial proportion of the total income received by them.[12] Nearly all elderly families with earnings also had incomes from sources other than earnings, commonly transfer payments (e.g., Social Security, SSI, other public assistance, veterans' payments), private pensions, property income, and related sources. Accordingly, 43 percent of elderly families received incomes from both earnings *and* sources other than earnings, a mere 1 percent had incomes from earnings only and 56 percent had incomes only from other sources. On the other hand, among *all* families 72 percent had incomes from both earnings *and* other sources, and 14 percent each had incomes from earnings only, and from other sources only. In other words, a large majority of nonelderly families had both earned and unearned income, but most elderly families depended on unearned income only.

Elderly unrelated individuals depended almost wholly on income other than earnings. About 12 percent in this group had income from both earnings *and* sources other than earnings, less than 1 percent had incomes from earnings only, and 87 percent had incomes only from other sources (Table 8.13). On the other hand, 46 percent of *all* unrelated individuals received income from both earnings *and* other sources. In sum, among unrelated individuals also, a much larger share of the nonelderly than of the elderly had both earned and unearned income, and the elderly received unearned income only for the most part.

It is evident also that the distribution of money income by source for families with elderly householders differs sharply from that for elderly unrelated individuals. Although only a minute share of both groups were likely to be receiving income from earnings only, unrelated individuals were much more likely to be receiving income only from other sources. Since income from Social Security and related sources is generally smaller than that from earnings, the total money income of elderly unrelated individuals tends to be much smaller than that of families with elderly householders.

In 1984 median incomes from all sources (including earnings) for families with elderly householders ($18,236) and for elderly unrelated individuals ($7,349) were notably higher than the corresponding median incomes from sources other than earnings ($12,188 and $6,750). Yet, the relative excess of income from all sources for families with elderly

[12]S. Grad and K. Foster, "Income of the Population Aged 55 and Older, 1976," *Social Security Bulletin* 42 (7) (July 1979).

TABLE 8.13

Percentage of Total Income Recipients and Relative Median Income, by Type of Income, for Families with Householders Aged 65 and Over and Unrelated Individuals Aged 65 and Over: 1984

| | Percentage of Total Recipients | | | |
| | Families | | Unrelated Individuals | |
Type of Income	Householders Aged 65 and Over	All Householders	Individuals Aged 65 and Over	All Individuals
Total Number	9,794[a]	62,544[a]	8,720[a]	29,684[a]
Total Percent or Ratio	100.0	100.0	100.0	100.0
Earnings Only[c]	0.6	14.0	0.3	19.1
Other Income Only	56.3	14.5	87.3	34.4
Earnings and Other Income	43.2	71.5	12.5	46.5
Total Percent or Ratio	100.0[b]	100.0[b]	100.0[b]	100.0[b]
Earnings[c]	43.7	85.5	12.7	65.6
Wage and salary income	39.0	82.2	11.0	62.1
Total Property Income[d]	76.3	67.7	66.6	60.2
Interest	74.6	65.7	64.6	58.2
Earnings and property income	33.2	59.2	9.6	40.0
Social Security (including Railroad Retirement income)	94.0	23.2	93.6	32.2
Social Security and retirement income[e]	44.9	9.6	27.2	9.2
Social Security without retirement income[e]	49.1	13.5	66.4	23.0
Social Security only	4.9	1.1	13.6	5.0
Total Retirement Income[f]	46.7	13.6	29.6	12.0
Retirement income without Social Security[e]	1.8	3.9	2.4	2.8
Social Security or Retirement Income	95.9	27.1	96.0	35.1
Social Security or Supplemental Security or Both	94.9	24.3	95.5	34.0
Government Transfer Payments[g]	96.4	41.8	97.8	43.6
Government transfer payments only	9.9	4.7	26.3	11.9

SOURCE: U.S. Bureau of the Census, *Current Population Reports*, series P-60, no. 151 (April 1986), Table 25.

[a] Numbers in thousands.
[b] Percentages do not sum to total because most categories overlap.
[c] Wage and salary income and self-employed income.
[d] Interest, dividends, net rent, and estates or trusts.
[e] Estimated by author.
[f] Private pensions or annuities, military retirement pensions, federal employee pensions, and state or local employee pensions.
[g] Social Security, Supplemental Security Income, public assistance or welfare income, and veterans', unemployment, and workers' compensation income.

488

TABLE 8.13 (*continued*)

Ratio to Median Income for Total Recipients			
Families		Unrelated Individuals (per 100)	
Householders Aged 65 and Over	All Householders	Individuals Aged 65 and Over	All Individuals
$18,236	$26,491	$7,349	$11,448
100.0	100.0	100.0	100.0
100.0	100.0	100.0	100.0
136.6	110.5	167.4	131.4
137.5	111.8	168.5	131.9
115.9	121.8	132.5	130.2
117.0	122.6	134.5	131.2
150.8	130.8	186.3	158.2
98.5	72.9	99.9	63.4
118.5	94.9	160.1	106.8
99.2	79.4	100.7	65.4
97.8	71.6	98.8	61.6
98.4	74.3	99.4	64.8
43.2	22.5	61.9	38.3

householders (50 percent) and for elderly unrelated individuals (9 percent) was less pronounced than for *all* families and *all* unrelated individuals. The median incomes from all sources for *all* families ($26,491) and *all* unrelated individuals ($11,448) were more than twice as great as the corresponding median incomes from sources other than earnings only.

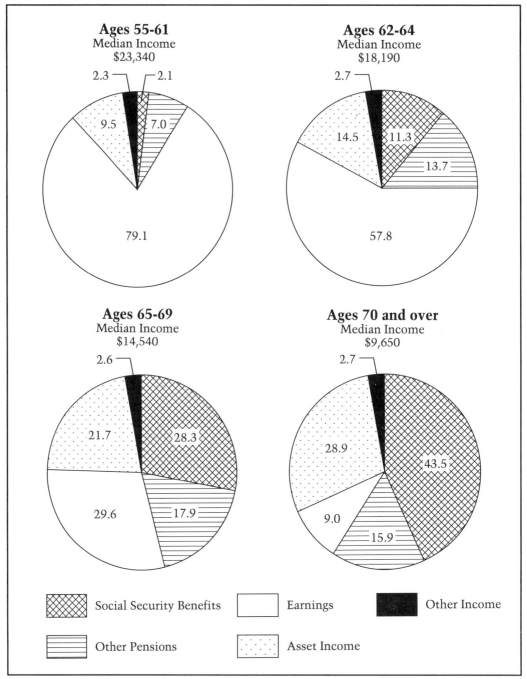

FIGURE 8.2

Type of Income of the Older Population, by Age of Recipient: 1986

Ages 55-61
Median Income
$23,340

2.3 — ⌐2.1
9.5   7.0
79.1

Ages 62-64
Median Income
$18,190

2.7 ⌐
14.5   11.3
13.7
57.8

Ages 65-69
Median Income
$14,540

2.6 ⌐
21.7   28.3
29.6   17.9

Ages 70 and over
Median Income
$9,650

2.7 ⌐
28.9   43.5
9.0
15.9

▨ Social Security Benefits   ☐ Earnings   ■ Other Income

▤ Other Pensions   ⸬ Asset Income

SOURCE: U.S. Social Security Administration, *Social Security Bulletin*, Annual Statistical Supplement (1987), p. vi.

NOTE: Income data based on aged unit. The unit is either a married couple living together, with one or both persons aged 55 or older, or a person aged 55 or older who does not live with a spouse. For the noninstitutionalized population.

This comparison shows that elderly families and unrelated individuals tend to have much smaller additions to their incomes from earnings than nonelderly families and unrelated individuals.

Nearly all elderly families had *either* Social Security *or* other retirement income, that is, pensions (96 percent), or Social Security in combination with some other income (94 percent). Less than half had both Social Security *and* other retirement income (45 percent), and about half had Social Security *without* other retirement income (49 percent). Very few families received other retirement income without Social Security (less than 2 percent).

Although many elderly families had income from earnings (44 percent), they were much more likely to have property income (76 percent), especially interest income (75 percent). Considering *all* families, without regard to the age of the householder, 86 percent received earnings income and 68 percent received property income. Thus, a much smaller proportion of families aged 65 and over received earnings income than families under 65, but the proportion receiving property income was substantially larger.

Elderly families which had earnings income received 37 percent more income, on the average, than all elderly families taken as a group (Table 8.13). The largest income went to families which received both earnings income and property income (51 percent more). Elderly families on Social Security or other retirement income, or on government transfer payments, often accompanied by other income, received about the same income, on the average, as all elderly families. The median income of those which depended *only* on government transfer payments, however, was quite low in comparison with the median income of all elderly families (57 percent less).

The shares of income received by the older population from various sources shift sharply with advancing age. In 1986, earnings made up nearly four fifths of the income of married couples and other persons aged 55–61 but only one eleventh at ages 70 and over (Figure 8.2). Asset income rose from less than 10 percent to nearly 30 percent. At the earlier ages Social Security benefits made up a negligible part of income but by ages 70 and over two fifths of income came from this source. As age increased, Social Security benefits, other pension income, and asset income made up a larger and larger share of the total, while the share from earnings dropped sharply. Note that the shares of various types of income received are strikingly different from the shares of persons receiving various types of income.

Some Geographic and Socioeconomic Variations in Income and Poverty

Metropolitan-Nonmetropolitan Areas

Median incomes are much lower, and poverty is much more common, among the elderly in nonmetropolitan areas than in metropolitan areas. In 1979, the median income of elderly families in nonmetropolitan areas was only three quarters of the median income of elderly families in metropolitan areas. Median individual incomes were only four-fifths as great.

According to a regression analysis carried out by Glasgow,[13] the lower individual median income of the nonmetropolitan elderly is explained more by the population's personal demographic characteristics—such as the high proportion female, low educational attainment, low occupational status, and high proportion not working—than by metropolitan-nonmetropolitan residence per se. That is, the lower income of elderly persons in nonmetropolitan areas is accounted for by the fact that a higher proportion of the elderly with these personal characteristics reside in nonmetropolitan areas.

The record on poverty is parallel. In 1979, nonmetropolitan elderly persons were much more likely (21 percent) than metropolitan elderly persons (13 percent) to have incomes below the poverty level. Moreover, in 1979, poverty in rural areas was more common among the elderly (21 percent) than among persons under age 65 (15 percent), as it was in urban areas. One half of the elderly poor, but only three eighths of the nonelderly poor, lived in rural areas.[14]

There has been considerable progress in recent years in reducing poverty among the elderly in nonmetropolitan areas—more progress than for the elderly in metropolitan areas or for persons under age 65 in nonmetropolitan areas—partly because similar ameliorative programs tend to be more productive where the need is greater. For example, the nonmetropolitan poverty ratio for the elderly fell from 21 percent in 1979 to 18 percent in 1985, while the poverty ratio of the nonmetropolitan population under age 65 rose in this period from 15 percent to 18 percent.

Poverty among the elderly in nonmetropolitan areas is excessively high in the South and among blacks, women, and the aged. In 1979 the

[13]U.S. Department of Agriculture, "The Nonmetropolitan Elderly: Economic and Demographic Status," by N. Glasgow, *Rural Development Research Report*, no. 70 (June 1988).

[14]U.S. Department of Agriculture, "Rural Elderly in Demographic Perspective," by N. Glasgow and L. Beale, *Rural Development Perspectives*, vol. 2 (October 1985).

poverty ratio of elderly persons in the nonmetropolitan South (28 percent) was nearly twice that in the remainder of the country (15 percent). Incomes below the poverty level are alarmingly common among elderly blacks in nonmetropolitan areas (47 percent), but they are also quite common among nonmetropolitan elderly women (25 percent) and nonmetropolitan persons aged 75 and over (27 percent) as well as metropolitan elderly blacks (30 percent).

Sex, Race, and Age	Metropolitan	Nonmetropolitan
Total	12.7	21.3
Male	8.9	16.7
Female	15.3	24.7
White	10.9	19.0
Black	30.0	47.2
65–74	10.8	18.2
75–84	15.4	26.0
85 and Over	18.2	30.1

SOURCE: U.S. Bureau of the Census, Public Use Microdata Sample, 1980; data provided in U.S. Department of Agriculture (1988).

The combination of advanced age, living alone, and nonmetropolitan residence affects the economic status of the elderly very adversely; 41 percent of the elderly aged 75 and over living alone in nonmetropolitan areas have incomes below the poverty level.

Age	Metropolitan	Nonmetropolitan
60–74		
In Families	7.0	15.2
Living Alone	22.5	33.9
75 and Over		
In Families	7.0	15.2
Living Alone	27.0	41.4

SOURCE: U.S. Bureau of the Census, 1980 Census of Population, *U.S. Summary: General Social and Economic Characteristics*, PC80-1-C-1, Table 98.

According to Glasgow's multivariate regression analysis, living alone or with nonrelatives is the major factor associated with poverty among a series of personal demographic characteristics and place-of-residence categories. Low educational level and living in rural areas have a lesser but significant influence.

The poorer economic condition of nonmetropolitan areas exacerbates the problems of planning for and providing adequate housing, transportation, and health and other local services for a dispersed and often isolated elderly population. This is in sharp contrast to the situation for the elderly in metropolitan areas.

Labor Force Participation

As expected, continuing to work at the older ages means higher income. The income of retired persons aged 65 and over is much lower than the income of persons aged 65 and over still working. Family income is augmented progressively insofar as the householder works, works year round (50 or more weeks), and works full time (35 or more hours per week). The median income in 1984 of families with elderly householders who worked year round full time was 2.4 times as high ($39,700) as that of families with elderly householders who did not work year

TABLE 8.14

Median Income of Families with Householders Aged 65 and Over, by Type of Family, and of Unrelated Individuals Aged 65 and Over, by Sex, According to Work Experience of Householder or Unrelated Individual: 1984
(numbers rounded to nearest hundred dollars)

Type of Family and Sex of Unrelated Individual	Total	Year-Round Full-Time Worker		Not Year-Round Full-Time Worker[a]
		Median	Ratio to Total	
Total Families	$18,200	$39,700	2.2	$16,600
Total married-couple families	18,600	40,200	2.2	16,800
Wife employed full time in paid labor force	30,100	54,400	1.8	24,500
Male householder, no wife present	19,500	b	c	c
Female householder, no husband present	15,900	b	c	c
Total Unrelated Individuals	7,300	16,800	2.3	7,000
Male	8,000	20,200	2.5	7,200
Female	7,100	16,000	2.3	6,900

SOURCE: U.S. Bureau of the Census, *Current Population Reports*, series P-60, no. 151 (April 1986), Tables 16 and 17.

[a] Estimated by the author.
[b] Base less than 75,000.
[c] Not calculated.

round full time ($16,600) (Table 8.14). The highest family incomes were those of husband-wife families in which the wife was employed full time in the paid labor force ($30,100), especially if the husband was a year-round full-time worker ($54,400). Among families with elderly householders working year round full time, only 22 percent had incomes below $15,000. By contrast, among all families with elderly householders, including those who did not work year round full time, 39 percent had incomes below $15,000.

The same relation applies to elderly nonfamily householders. Among all types of household units, nonfamily households with male householders gained the greatest income advantage by working year round full time. Families maintained by women aged 65 and over had a median income ($15,900) below that of every other type of elderly family, even married-couple families in which neither the husband nor wife worked.

Educational Level

Education in early life pays off in income in later life. It is hardly surprising that the median incomes of elderly persons and families rise as the educational level of the person or householder rises. For example, families with elderly householders who have had some college education received 50 percent more income in 1984 than families with elderly householders who have had only some high school education ($28,800 vs. $19,200) and 116 percent more income than families with elderly householders who have had only some elementary education ($13,300) (Table 8.15). Furthermore, family incomes are from 62 percent to 112 percent greater at different school levels if the elderly householder is a year-round full-time worker. Incomes of elderly men and women vary in relation to school level like those of elderly families.

The association between income and education is a strong causal one since additional education is a common requirement for jobs demanding special skills and offering higher pay. Education's influence on the income of elderly persons arises partly from the relation of earnings as a source of income to educational level. As has been stated, the mean annual income of those with earnings is much greater than the mean annual income of those without earnings; and the share of elderly persons with earnings rises with increased education. In 1979 the mean annual incomes of elderly male earners and nonearners were $17,600 and $7,900, respectively, and the percentage with earnings increased steadily from 20 percent for elderly men with less than an eighth grade education to 53 percent for those with seven years or more of college.

TABLE 8.15

Median Income of Families with Householders Aged 65 and Over and of Persons Aged 65 and Over, by Sex, According to Years of School Completed and Work Experience of Householder or Person: 1984
(numbers rounded to nearest hundred dollars)

| Years of School Completed | Householders | | | Persons | | | | | |
| | | | | Male | | Female | | Ratio, Female/Male | |
	Total	Year-Round Full-Time Worker	Ratio, Year-Round Full-Time Worker/Total	Total	Year-Round Full-Time Worker	Total	Year-Round Full-Time Worker	Total	Year-Round Full-Time Worker
All Levels	$18,200	$39,700	2.18	$10,500	$26,500	$6,000	$15,200	.58	.58
Total Elementary School	13,300	21,500	1.62	7,300	16,400	4,800	a	.65	b
Less than 8	11,900	a	b	6,400	a	4,400	a	.69	b
8	15,200	a	b	8,400	a	5,200	a	.62	b
Total High School	19,200	37,300	1.94	11,400	24,200	6,400	15,400	.56	.63
1–3	16,700	a	b	9,700	20,500	5,600	a	.58	b
4	21,100	38,600	1.83	12,500	25,800	6,900	15,900	.55	.62
Total College	28,800	61,100	2.12	17,600	38,600	10,600	18,800	.60	.49
1–3	23,700	a	b	14,100	34,200	8,600	a	.61	b
4	31,900	a	b	20,600	37,100	11,800	a	.57	b
5 or more	35,500	63,300	1.79	21,500	48,100	16,100	a	.75	b

SOURCE: Based on U.S. Bureau of the Census, *Current Population Reports*, series P-60, no. 151 (April 1986), Tables 23 and 33.

a Base is less than 75,000.
b Not calculated.

Men with earnings secured a large share of their income from earnings on the average, and they often worked full time. For men with earnings, the percentage of income derived from earnings was about 60 percent regardless of educational level. About half of elderly men with earnings worked full time (i.e., at least 35 hours per week), again with little variation by educational level. The rewards in the form of higher income in later life which additional education brings result in part from workers' continuing to work at the older ages, in part from their working longer hours during the week, and in part from their receiving a larger share of income from earnings at the younger and older ages, the last factor being the principal one.

I have noted that the median income of elderly women is well below (42 percent in 1984) that of elderly men. A similarly large gap remains (42 percent) even when the comparison is restricted to year-round full-time workers (Table 8.15). The differences in the educational level, general work experience, and work interruptions of men and women over the life course have been held largely responsible for the male-female gap in income received in later life. In fact, tabulations of median income according to educational level show that women receive far less income than men even when they have the same education (Table 8.15). Furthermore, there is little variation with education in the relative size of the male-female income gap. The gap in median income is 38 percent for elementary school graduates, 45 percent for high school graduates, and 40 percent for college graduates. The sparse data on the variations in the income of elderly year-round full-time workers according to educational level also show large male-female gaps. For example, elderly year-round full-time female workers who have graduated from high school receive 38 percent less income than their male counterparts.

The data suggest that additional education and more continuous work experience of women will not, in and of themselves, reduce the male-female income gap in older age. Since we are considering elderly persons, however, the differences we observe reflect previous earning history to a large extent. We need, therefore, to analyze earnings, work experience, and work interruptions over a lifetime.

Effect of Education and Work Experience on Lifetime Earnings

Estimates of lifetime earnings could shed further light on male-female differences in economic status in later life, particularly if these estimates take account of educational level and continuity of work experience. Cross-sectional data on age and income, as well as educational

TABLE 8.16

Various Comparative Measures of Expected Lifetime Earnings in 1979, by Sex, Years of School Completed, and Work Experience

			College		
Measure	Less Than 12 Years	High School, 4 Years	1 to 3 Years	4 Years	5 Years or More
Ratio, Female to Male					
All persons					
18 years	0.35	0.44	0.48	0.44	0.54
55 years	0.25	0.34	0.33	0.31	0.38
Year-round, full-time workers					
18 years	0.59	0.61	0.62	0.61	0.64
55 years	0.58	0.60	0.55	0.58	0.56
Ratio to High School					
Male, 18 years					
All persons	0.70	1.00	1.11	1.38	1.51
Year-round full-time workers	0.81	1.00	1.11	1.34	1.44
Female, 18 years					
All persons	0.55	1.00	1.21	1.37	1.83
Year-round, full-time workers	0.79	1.00	1.13	1.33	1.51
Ratio, Year-Round Full-Time Workers to All Persons					
Male, 18 years	1.41	1.21	1.21	1.17	1.16
Female, 18 years	2.37	1.66	1.56	1.62	1.37

SOURCE: Based on U.S. Bureau of the Census, "Lifetime Earnings Estimates for Men and Women in the United States: 1979," by D. L. Burkhead, *Current Population Reports*, series P-60, no. 139 (February 1983), text table, p. 3.

NOTES: Based on expected earnings from age 18 to 64 or from age 55 to 64 in 1981 dollars, assuming a discount rate and productivity growth rate of 0.0 percent. Ratios expressed per 100.

level and work experience, can be merged so as to derive synthetic estimates of lifetime earnings for men and women varying according to education and work experience. Such estimates were generated for 1979 by the U.S. Bureau of the Census by summing the product of (1) the mean earnings at each age from 18 to 64, averaged for the years 1978–1980, separately for various educational levels; (2) the survival rate from age 18 to each successive age; and (3) the projected employment ratio at each age.[15]

[15]U.S. Bureau of the Census, "Lifetime Earnings Estimates for Men and Women in the United States: 1979," by D. L. Burkhead, *Current Population Reports*, series P-60, no. 139 (February 1983).

According to these estimates, women earn only about two fifths as much as men in their lifetime (Table 8.16). The prospect is improved substantially by increased education, but even with postgraduate education women earn only about half as much as men in their lifetime. Advanced education makes a great deal of difference in how much one earns in a lifetime, for both men and women, however. College graduates earn two fifths more than high school graduates and high school graduates earn three fifths more than those who did not complete high school. Additional education is more income-productive for women than men. Year-round full-time workers earn considerably more than workers in general (from 16 percent to 137 percent more, depending on educational level and sex). Because of the frequent work interruptions of women for family reasons, the increase in income for year-round full-time workers was far greater for women than for men at every level of school completed.

The difference in the continuity of work experience for men and women has been cited as a leading reason for the fact that women earn less than men and that women's income in later life is less than that of men. To explore this factor as a possible basis for the lower income of older women, we examine data on the relation between lifetime work experience and earnings from the 1979 Income Survey Development Program conducted by the U.S. Bureau of the Census.[16] The data from the survey show that there are very large differences between the sexes in the frequency of work interruptions and in the numbers of years spent outside the labor force over a lifetime. Work interruptions were experienced by one quarter of the men and about three quarters of the women aged 21–64. Work interruptions occurred mainly for familial reasons; these tended to be longer than work interruptions for other reasons (i.e., inability to find work and illness or disability). A few of the men and two thirds of the women experienced work interruptions due to familial reasons alone. Expressed in terms of time, the mean proportion of potential work years spent away from work was about 3 percent for men and about 31 percent for women.

The study concluded that work interruptions (i.e., periods spent away from work) and general work experience (full-time year-round or not) account for only a small part of the difference in the earnings of men and women aged 21–64 who ever worked. Furthermore, work interruption is less important than either general work experience or education as determinants of earnings. The mean hourly earnings of women were

[16]U.S. Bureau of the Census, "Lifetime Work Experience and Its Effect on Earnings," by J. J. Salvo and J. M. McNeil, *Current Population Reports*, series P-23, no. 136 (June 1984), esp. Tables A, B, C, and G.

only about 63 percent of the mean hourly earnings of men in 1979. If women are assigned the mean work experience and work interruptions of men, the earnings gap would be reduced by only 12 percent. If women are assigned the mean work experience, work interruptions, and education of men, the earnings gap would be reduced by only 15 percent. The mean hourly earnings of women would then be only about 69 percent of the mean hourly earnings of men. Much of the difference in male-female earnings is due then to other factors, such as sex discrimination in the labor market, the choice of relatively low-paying jobs by some women taken in order to permit them to pursue familial responsibilities, and response errors in the survey.

These general findings were confirmed by a more recent analysis of the male-female earnings gap carried out at the Census Bureau on the basis of data from the 1984 SIPP.[17] Data on labor force attachments, education, occupations, and earnings were obtained from persons aged 21–64 with wage or salary income for the period since they were 21. As expected, women are more likely to have experienced work interruptions. Women spent 15 percent of their potential work years away from work while men spent only 2 percent of their potential work years away from work.

Mean earnings per hour for female wage and salary workers were well below those for male workers, implying a female-to-male earnings ratio of .68. Work interruption did not affect this ratio. Even when the worker had 20 years of experience or more with 10 years of job tenure, the male-female hourly earnings ratio was .68. Males and females work in occupations that are, to some degree, segregated by sex. Working in an occupation that has a high proportion of women has a negative effect on earnings. A multivariate analysis of the male-female earnings gap yielded the finding that approximately 35–41 percent of the earnings gap was not accounted for by measured differences in work experience, education, or occupational structure. Other factors were deemed to be responsible for this part of the male-female earnings gap.

Limitations of Income Data

We can obtain a more realistic picture of the economic status of elderly persons and families by adjusting the data on money income

---

[17]U.S. Bureau of the Census, "Male-Female Differences in Work Experience, Occupation, and Earnings: 1984," by J. M. McNeil and E. Lamas, *Current Population Reports,* series P-70, no. 10 (August 1987).

reported by the Census Bureau for various limitations. These limitations include the failure to allow for variations in the size of the family, the exclusion of noncash benefits, the omission of the income of persons not enumerated in the census or survey, and the underreporting of income by enumerated persons. Comparability with income received at other ages is also improved by examining after-tax income (i.e., disposable income).

Reported money income understates the total income received by the elderly as well as other age segments of the population. One major source of understatement is the exclusion of noncash benefits. This exclusion is purposeful in the basic data: Census and CPS data on income are restricted to money income. Still another limitation of reported income data, affecting particularly the income of the elderly, is the underreporting of certain types of money income, especially transfer payments (e.g., Social Security benefits, AFDC, veterans' payments, and SSI), private pension income, and income from assets (e.g., interest, dividends, rents). As noted earlier, much of the income of the elderly consists of transfer payments and income from assets. Some unreported income is illegal and unrecorded ("underground") money income. In addition, it is apparent that the income of persons omitted from the census or CPS is omitted from the income reported in the census or CPS. This income is of all types, but given our knowledge of who is omitted from the census and CPS, it is probably concentrated in wages and salaries, AFDC, and other public assistance. Census and CPS omissions are concentrated among males, particularly black males in the age range 25–54. Many of those omitted, including numerous unemployed, have rather low incomes.

We can make a confident inference, therefore, that the actual money income and, especially, the actual total income of the elderly are substantially higher than reported. Largely because of the difference in the sources of income of elderly and nonelderly persons, it is plausible to reason that the income of the latter is not understated to the same extent as the income of the former. Hence, reported money income tends to understate the *relative* income of the elderly and overstate that of the nonelderly. Adjustment for size of family alone brings the median figures for these two age segments nearly together, however.

Size of Family

Because the size of families maintained by persons aged 65 and over is, on the average, smaller than that of families maintained by younger persons, the family income of older persons is required to support fewer persons. A comparison of the per person median income of families with householders aged 65 and over with the per person median income of all families provides a more favorable picture of the relative income of elderly families than a comparison based on the total median income of families.[18] In 1985, the per person income of families with householders aged 65 and over was about 6 percent below the corresponding figure for all families, whereas the total income of families with householders aged 65 and over was 31 percent below that of all families (Tables 8.17 and 8.4). (See also Figure 8.1.)

The adjustment to a per-person basis has a favorable effect independent of the sex and race of the householder. Consequently, the relative advantage of families maintained by elderly women, noted earlier, is increased by this adjustment. In 1985, families maintained by women aged 65 and over had a per person median income 36 percent greater than all families maintained by women, whereas the excess was only 26 percent before the adjustment.

As a result of the adjustment of family income to a per person basis, the income gap between elderly families and all families among blacks drops from 29 percent to 17 percent (Tables 8.6 and 8.17). On the other hand, the adjustment magnifies the existing gap between the incomes of elderly white and elderly black families. The per person income of elderly black families was about one half that of elderly white families in 1985 compared with a pre-adjustment ratio of three fifths. The adjusted black-white gap was equally large for families maintained by elderly women as for married-couple families—about one half. As recently as 1970 the income ratio was as low as two fifths. In spite of this improvement, the effective difference in black-white family incomes among the elderly remains massive.

The same picture emerges from an examination of the Hispanic data although the adjustments and differences are not as extreme. Hispanic elderly families have a per person median income about equal to that of all Hispanic families. Yet, Hispanic adjusted elderly family income is nearly two fifths below the corresponding white figure. This gap is almost twice that of the unadjusted numbers.

---

[18]Per person median income of families for a given population category is computed as the median family income for that population category divided by the mean size of family in the category. Per person family income does not exactly reflect the comparative income status of elderly persons, however. Because of economies of scale, each additional member in a family requires smaller additions to family income. As a result, the per person income figures for elderly families tend to overstate slightly their income levels in comparison with younger families, which tend to be larger in size. Furthermore, the age, sex, and relationship of family members vary and exert an important influence on family needs and expenses.

TABLE 8.17

Median Family Income per Person for Families with Householders Aged 65 and Over, by Type of Family and Race of Householder: 1960–1985

Race and Year	Total	Married Couples	Male Householder	Female Householder
All Races				
Householder Aged 65 and Over				
1985	$8,051	$8,519	$7,313	$6,084
1980	5,505	5,705	4,649	4,671
1970	2,088	2,131	2,263	2,004
1960	a	1,141	a	a
Ratio, Householder Aged 65 and Over to All Families [b]				
1985	93.8	89.8	89.5	135.8
1980	85.9	82.1	72.4	138.2
1970	76.6	74.6	74.1	129.5
1960	a	73.2	a	a
Black				
Householder Aged 65 and Over				
1985	$3,888	$4,420	c	$3,147
1980	2,881	3,039	c	2,570
1970	1,049	1,183	a	834
Ratio, Householder Aged 65 and Over to All Families [b]				
1985	83.4	67.1	a	117.7
1980	83.4	61.5	a	125.3
1970	72.0	66.1	a	98.5

SOURCES: Based on Tables 8.4 and 8.6; and U.S. Bureau of the Census, *Current Population Reports*, series P-20, no. 411 (September 1986), Table 3.

[a] Not available or not computed.
[b] Ratios per 100.
[c] Base less than 75,000.

Noncash Benefits

To obtain a more complete picture of the income status of the elderly, income in kind or noncash benefits should be considered in addition to money income received. Noncash benefits consist of goods or services obtained without any expenditure or at a rate below the market value of the goods or services. The most important public noncash benefits received currently by the elderly are Medicare, Medicaid, Food

Stamps, and public or subsidized renter-occupied housing.[19] In addition, various noncash benefits are provided by employers or unions (e.g., pension plans and group health insurance plans) and by private businesses (e.g., discounts on prescriptions, bus fares, and theater seats). Relatives and friends substantially supplement the incomes of older persons with noncash benefits (e.g., gifts and services) as well as money.

Nearly all elderly persons are covered by Medicare; 97 percent of households with elderly householders included one or more members who were covered by Medicare in 1984 (Table 8.18). Participation in the other programs is relatively low. Many of the same households participated in more than one of the other programs along with Medicare and received cash public assistance in addition.

Only 13 percent of elderly households were covered by Medicaid— about the same proportion as for all households (10 percent). Nearly all of these were also covered by Medicare. Only 6 percent of elderly households and 8 percent of all households participated in the Food Stamp program. A large share of the elderly households receiving Food Stamps were also covered by Medicare and Medicaid. We could speculate that many of the elderly households were not well informed about the Food Stamp program or felt that participation in the program stigmatized them. Similarly, only 6 percent of elderly households, as of all households, resided in public or subsidized housing. The low participation could result from the scarcity of such housing, the unpopularity of the program, or lack of knowledge about the program, but the relative importance of these reasons is unknown.

[19]The Medicare program is designed to provide adequate medical care for the elderly and disabled. It is financed through monthly premium payments made by each person enrolled and is subsidized by general federal funds. A separate trust fund is maintained for the Medicare program by the U.S. Health Care Financing Administration. The Medicaid program is designed to provide medical assistance to needy families with dependent children and to elderly, blind, and disabled individuals whose incomes or resources are insufficient to pay for necessary medical care. This program is administered by state agencies through grants from the U.S. Health Care Financing Administration.

The major purpose of the Food Stamp program is to aid low-income households in securing a nutritious diet. Persons participating in the program receive coupons to purchase food in retail stores. The value of the coupons received depends on both the income of the recipient and the number of persons in the family. The Food Stamp program is federally funded and is administered by the Food and Nutrition Service of the U.S. Department of Agriculture.

Public or subsidized housing programs are designed to assist low-income families and individuals in securing safe and sanitary housing. Partial financing is provided by the state or the U.S. Department of Housing and Urban Development. Participation in public housing is determined by the family's eligibility for the program and the availability of housing.

Whether the household was poor or not made no difference in the use of Medicare by elderly households since nearly all elderly households were enrolled. Poverty greatly affected the resort to Medicaid, Food Stamps, and subsidized or public housing, however, as might be expected (Table 8.18). Two fifths of elderly poor households benefited from Medicaid compared with only one eighth of all elderly households. Over one quarter of elderly poor households received Food Stamps compared with only one sixteenth of all elderly households. The comparable figures for subsidized housing were one sixth and one sixteenth.

Elderly poor households took much less advantage of the Food Stamp program than younger poor households, however (29 percent vs. 43 percent). There were hardly any differences between elderly and younger poor households in the use of Medicaid and subsidized housing.

Only a modest share of elderly households benefited from group health insurance plans or employer or union pension plans. (A very large share of these have the advantage of the broader health coverage afforded by Medicare.) On the other hand, roughly half of *all* households belonged to such plans. On the basis of this difference between the coverage of elderly households and younger households, we may expect that the elderly households of the future will be better covered by these plans than are those of today.

It is difficult to assign cash values to noncash benefits, especially insurance and retirement plans. Recent studies by the U.S. Bureau of the Census suggest that public noncash benefits, mainly Medicare, would raise the median income of elderly householders by 24 percent in 1990.[20] Perhaps a more significant question is whether the incremental value of noncash benefits is relatively greater for elderly than younger households. This does appear to be the case since the comparable increment for all households is only 5 percent.

After-Tax Money Income

After-tax income is a better measure of disposable income or household purchasing power than before-tax income since the money paid in taxes is not available for private use. For the most part, tax money serves to benefit society as a whole. If a particular group is also favored by the tax laws, it receives a double advantage. Data on after-tax income for 1985 published by the Census Bureau suggest that elderly households are relatively favored by the tax laws compared with households overall.

[20] U.S. Bureau of the Census, *Current Population Reports,* Series P-60, no. 176–RD, August 1991, Table 1.

TABLE 8.18

Percentage of Elderly Households Receiving Specified Noncash Benefits, by Type of Benefit: 1984

Type of Benefit	All Households		Below Poverty Level	
	Householders Aged 65 and Over	Householders Aged 15 and Over	Householders Aged 65 and Over	Householders Aged 15 and Over
Total Number (in thousands)	18,155	86,789	2,683	11,887
Total Percent	100.0	100.0	100.0	100.0
Means-Tested Noncash Benefits				
Receiving at least one benefit	19.0	16.8	53.1	61.1
Food Stamps	6.0	8.1	29.0	43.0
Free or reduced-price school lunch	1.0	6.5	3.5	25.1
Medicaid	13.1	9.6	40.1	42.3
Public or subsidized renter-occupied housing	6.4	4.1	16.5	16.2
Non–Means-tested Noncash Benefits				
Regular-price school lunch	0.9	12.8	NA	NA
Medicare	97.2	24.6	NA	NA
Group health insurance plan	12.8	57.2	NA	NA
Employer or union pension plan	9.8	43.7	NA	NA

SOURCE: Based on U.S. Bureau of the Census, *Current Population Reports*, series P-60, no. 150 (November 1985), Tables 1, 10, and 21.

NOTES: Households as of March 1985. Households are classified according to the poverty status of the primary family or individual. Percentages are not additive since households may receive more than one type of benefit. NA = not available.

After taxes the mean income of elderly households was nearly three quarters as great as the mean income of all households, while the ratio was nearly two thirds before taxes.[21] A comparison on the basis of income per household member is more appropriate and convincing. In 1985,

[21]To estimate after-tax income, the Census Bureau deducted four types of taxes from total money income: federal income taxes, state income taxes, FICA and federal retirement payroll taxes, and property taxes on owner-occupied housing.

after taxes, members of elderly households had about 8 percent more income, on the average, than members of households overall, compared with a relative deficit of a small percentage before taxes. The following table summarizes these differences:

Measure	Householders Aged 65 and Over	All Householders	Ratio per 100
Mean Income			
Before taxes	$18,800	$29,066	64.7
After taxes	16,198	22,646	71.5
Income per Household Member			
Before taxes	10,622	10,884	97.6
After taxes	9,152	8,480	107.9

SOURCE: Based on U.S. Bureau of Census, *Current Population Reports*, series P-23, no. 151 (1987), Table 3.

If we compare poor elderly households with all elderly households, we note a moderate tax advantage for poor households. Taxes were 6 percent of the mean income of poor households and about 14 percent of the mean income of all households. Still, over one half of all poor elderly households pay one or more taxes, most commonly property taxes.

The Understatement of Money Income

Money income as reported in the decennial census and the CPS is understated as a result of the omission of the income of persons who were not enumerated in the census or represented in the CPS and of the underreporting of income by persons who were enumerated. In addition, the number of recipients of money income among those enumerated is understated. Depending on the magnitude and "age distribution" of the income of persons omitted from the census or CPS, or of the unreported income of respondents who underreported their income or did not report receipt of income, the median or mean income and the distribution of income for age groups would be biased.

Evidence on the extent of understatement of income is derived from a comparison of CPS income for 1983 with estimates from independent sources, such as the Bureau of Economic Analysis, Social Security Administration, and Veterans Administration. Estimates of understatement of aggregate income in 1983 for various types of income are as follows:

Type of Income	CPS as Percentage of Independent Estimate
Total	90.1
Wages and Salaries	99.0
Self-Employment	115.5
Social Security	91.7[a]
Supplementary Security Income	84.9[a]
Aid to Families with Dependent Children	76.0
Interest, Dividends, and Rental Income	45.0[a]
Veterans' Payments	63.3[a]
Unemployment Compensation	75.5
Workers' Compensation	47.0
Private, Government, and Military Pensions	72.4[a]

SOURCE: U.S. Bureau of the Census, *Current Population Reports*, series P-60, no. 151 (April 1986), Table A-2.

[a] Particularly applicable to elderly persons.

These estimates presumably cover all forms of income understatement, including omission of income of persons not enumerated and underreporting of income by persons enumerated.

Understatement tends to be more pronounced for income such as asset and property income (interest, dividends, and rental income), public assistance, veterans' payments, unemployment compensation, workers' compensation, and pensions. Income from wages and salaries, self-employment income, and Social Security benefits appear to be rather completely reported. Several types of income that are most subject to understatement are important types of income received by older persons (e.g., asset and property income and pensions).

On the basis of these estimates of income understatement, it may reasonably be inferred that the money income of elderly persons is relatively more understated, and poverty among elderly persons is relatively more overstated, than the money income and poverty of persons of working age. The reported money income is biased downward at all ages, but especially so at the older ages because of the particular sources of income of older persons. On the basis of the estimates of total money income shown by the independent sources, the author estimates that the median money income of elderly persons in the CPS is understated by one fifth or more, while the median money income of the population aged 15 and over is understated by at least one tenth.

Asset Ownership and Net Worth

In addition to receiving income, many of the elderly own assets that contribute directly to income through interest, dividends, and rents, serve as financial reserves for special or emergency needs, and provide services, such as transportation and housing. Assets accumulated during the working years may provide income to supplement a retired person's earnings and other income. Thus, measurement of asset ownership is important in analyzing the financial position of the elderly. Financial position can be even more appropriately measured in terms of net worth, which represents the excess of the value of assets over liabilities. Liabilities include debts secured by any asset, credit card loans or store bills, bank loans, and other unsecured debts. Comprehensive data on household wealth and asset ownership were obtained in 1984 in a supplement to the SIPP conducted by the Census Bureau.[22]

Age Variations in Median Net Worth

The distribution of median net worth by age of owner shows a characteristic life cycle pattern such that, like income, asset holdings increase during the work years and decline after retirement (Table 8.19). Graphically we have a skewed bell-shaped curve. In 1984 median net worth rose with increasing age to $73,700 at ages 55–64 and then declined to $55,200 at ages 75 and over. For ages 65 and over as a whole, median net worth was $60,300. Elderly householders owned nearly 28 percent of total net worth, while constituting only 21 percent of all householders.

[22]These data were published in U.S. Bureau of the Census, "Household Wealth and Asset Ownership: 1984," *Current Population Reports,* series P-70, no. 7 (July 1986). The information was collected in September–December 1984, and the data are averages of balances held and owned at the end of August, September, October, and November 1984. Persons living in group quarters are excluded from the results. (Group quarters are living quarters occupied by several unrelated individuals and consist of separate rooms with common facilities such as dining halls.) Assets included in net worth are interest-earning assets, regular checking accounts, stocks and mutual fund shares, home equity, rental property, other real estate, vehicles, equity in a business or profession, U.S. savings bonds, IRA or Keogh accounts, and other financial investments. The survey did not cover equity in pension plans, cash-surrender value of life insurance policies, or the value of jewelry and home furnishings.

Assets may be classified into three categories: liquid assets, illiquid assets, and home equity. Liquid assets include cash and savings or checking accounts. Illiquid assets consist of stocks and bonds, equity in a business or profession, real estate, insurance policies, and annuities. Ownership of a home constitutes home equity.

TABLE 8.19

Median Net Worth, by Age of Householder and Monthly Household Income: 1984 (in thousands of dollars)

Monthly Household Income	Total	Under Age 35	Ages 35–44	Ages 45–54	Ages 55–64	Ages 65 and Over			
						Total	65–69	70–74	75 and Over
Total Net Worth									
All households	$ 32.7	$ 5.8	$35.6	$ 56.8	$ 73.7	$ 60.3	$ 66.6	$ 60.6	$ 55.2
Less than $900	5.1	0.9	2.1	6.7	23.6	25.9	23.3	23.6	29.0
$900 to $1,999	24.6	4.7	16.5	28.7	60.2	74.8	68.5	75.2	80.0
$2,000 to $3,999	46.7	15.3	44.4	63.2	88.5	162.9	151.3	164.0	175.9
$4,000 or more	123.5	44.4	92.7	139.0	197.6	344.5	247.1	410.3	[a]
Net Worth Excluding Home Equity									
All households	7.8	3.0	7.6	12.7	22.1	18.8	21.5	18.5	17.0
Less than $900	1.4	0.6	0.7	0.9	2.5	3.7	2.5	3.5	4.6
$900 to $1,999	6.3	2.5	3.7	5.3	15.0	29.8	22.4	27.7	41.3
$2,000 to $3,999	11.4	5.9	9.4	13.1	30.5	80.3	73.6	81.1	97.1
$4,000 or more	44.9	18.2	32.6	45.7	88.4	212.7	156.8	268.5	[a]

SOURCE: U.S. Bureau of the Census, *Current Population Reports*, series P-70, no. 7 (1986), Table E.

NOTE: Excludes group quarters.

[a] Base less than 200,000 households.

The pattern of variation of median net worth by age was essentially similar for each of the asset-owning categories. The ages corresponding to the peak for net worth varied from one type of asset to another, however. Median home equity reached a peak of $54,000 at ages 55–64 and then fell to $44,000 at ages 75 and over. The median value of interest-earning assets reached a much lower peak at a later age—$14,600 at ages 70–74.

Home equity was, by far, the single most valuable type of asset held by the elderly as well as by younger householders (Table 8.20): Home equity accounted for 39 percent of net worth owned by elderly householders while interest-earning assets accounted for 30 percent. Home equity accounted for more than one third to nearly one half of total net worth at every age. This large share was maintained through the age groups 65 and over.

Age of Householder	Total	Home Equity	Other Assets
65 and Over	100	39	61
65–69	100	36	64
70–74	100	40	60
75 and Over	100	40	60

SOURCE: Estimated from data in U.S. Bureau of the Census, *Current Population Reports*, series P-70, no. 7 (1986), Tables 1 and 3.

Elderly homeowners held 26 percent of total home equity while constituting 24 percent of all homeowners.

The skewed bell-shaped relation between the age of the householder and median net worth persisted even when home equity was excluded from net worth. Median net worth excluding home equity, for householders aged 65 and over, as well as for householders of all other age groups 35 and over, fell below one third of the median total net worth (i.e., including home equity). (See Table 8.19.)

On the other hand, median net worth increased steadily with advancing age, even through the older ages, when monthly household income was held constant (i.e., when net worth was examined at each income level), whether home equity is included or not (Table 8.19). The relationship is bell-shaped for all households (i.e., combining all income categories), but unidirectional in each income category, because the percentage of households with a low monthly income is greatest among the elderly and net worth has a strong positive relationship with monthly income at every age.

An analysis by Radner based on the 1979 Income Survey Development Program, in which he jointly examines income and wealth of elderly households, concludes that while elderly households as a group

TABLE 8.20

Distribution of Net Worth by Type of Asset, by Age of Householder: 1984

Type of Asset	Total	Ages Under 35	Ages 35–44	Ages 45–54	Ages 55–64	Ages 65 and Over
Total Net Worth	100.0	100.0	100.0	100.0	100.0	100.0
Interest-Earning Assets[a]	18.1	14.4	11.3	11.6	17.5	30.3
Stocks and Mutual Funds	6.8	5.2	5.3	4.7	8.9	8.6
Own Home	41.3	46.0	47.0	42.3	44.1	38.6
Rental Property and Other Real Estate	13.4	9.8	12.7	16.1	16.1	11.2
Motor Vehicle	6.0	16.6	7.4	6.0	4.6	3.4
Own Business or Profession	10.3	7.4	14.1	16.0	7.9	4.5
U.S. Savings Bonds	0.5	0.3	0.2	0.4	0.6	0.8
IRA or Keogh Accounts	2.2	1.6	2.0	2.8	3.3	2.6

SOURCE: U.S. Bureau of the Census, *Current Population Reports*, series P-70, no. 7 (1986), Table F.

NOTE: Excludes group quarters.

[a] Includes checking accounts.

have relatively low income (i.e., in comparison with the income for all households), they have relatively high net worth.[23] Moreover, median income for the elderly is below that of any other age group while median net worth for the elderly is above that for all age groups below 45 and about the same as for the 45–54 age group. When an adjustment is made for household size, relative median income and net worth of elderly households are raised by about 25 percent. Elderly householders with low income (lowest quartile) and low net worth (two lowest quartiles) include a high percentage of female householders, one-person households, and widowed householders; about half of this group consists of widowed female householders living alone.

Age Variations in Percentage of Households Owning Assets

The pattern of variation by age for the percentages of householders owning the various types of assets is essentially similar to that for median net worth of each type of asset. The percentage owning a particular type of asset almost always increased with the age of the house-

[23] D. B. Radner, "The Wealth and Income of Aged Households," paper presented at the annual meeting of the American Statistical Association, Philadelphia, August 13–16, 1984.

holder up to a peak in midlife and then declined. As with median net worth, the peak ages varied from one asset type to another. According to the 1984 SIPP supplement, it was most often ages 55–64 (6 of 13 asset types).

Ownership of interest-earning assets reached a peak of 79 percent at ages 65–69 and remained at or near that level thereafter (Table 8.21). A peak of 80 percent for home ownership was reached at ages 55–64, and by ages 75 and over the percentage had receded to 69. Ownership of a business or profession reached a peak of 20 percent at ages 45–54 and dropped to 7 percent at ages 65–69. From one half to four fifths of the elderly had interest-earning assets, had regular checking accounts, or owned homes.

The age patterns for median net worth and percentage owning assets, characteristic of all households, do not apply to the individual types of households—husband-wife households, male-headed households, and female-headed households. These show steady increases in net worth and percentage owning assets with increasing age. The shift in the distribution of household types according to age—particularly the increase in the share of female-headed households at the older ages—accounts for the decline in net worth and percentage owning assets at the older ages for all households combined. The following data on median net worth reflect the differences between household types:

Type of Household and Age of Householder	Median Net Worth (in thousands)	
	Total	Excluding Home Equity
Married-Couple Householders	$50.1	$12.3
Under 35	14.7	4.8
35–54	63.1	15.9
55–64	91.2	32.8
65 and over	90.3	37.8
Female Householder	13.9	3.0
Under 35	1.3	0.9
35–54	13.2	2.1
55–64	35.9	6.3
65 and over	42.9	10.2
Male Householder	9.9	4.5
Under 35	3.7	2.8
35–54	18.3	6.2
55–64	37.2	9.5
65 and over	41.2	12.6

SOURCE: U.S. Bureau of the Census, *Current Population Reports*, series P-70, no. 7 (1986), Table I.

TABLE 8.21

Percentage of Households Owning Selected Assets, by Age of Householder: 1984

Type of Asset	Total	Ages Under 35	Ages 35–44	Ages 45–54	Ages 55–64	Ages 65–69	Ages 70–74	Ages 75 and Over
Number of Households (thousands)	86.8	25.7	17.4	12.6	12.9	5.7	5.0	7.5
Interest-Earning Assets	72	65	73	73	77	79	76	79
Regular Checking Accounts	54	51	59	60	55	49	50	47
Stocks and Mutual Funds	20	13	23	23	26	23	19	21
Own Business or Profession	13	10	18	20	15	7	6	3
Own Home	64	40	69	78	80	79	72	69
Rental Property	10	4	10	14	15	12	10	10
IRA or Keogh Accounts	20	10	22	31	39	18	6	4

SOURCE: U.S. Bureau of the Census, Current Population Reports, series P-70, no. 7 (1986), Table 1.

NOTE: Excludes group quarters.

The percentages owning the particular types of assets and median net worth, for husband-wife households, were consistently (i.e., for all 13 asset types reported) higher than those in which the householder had no spouse. This tells us that the married state is favorable for asset ownership, as it has proven to be in many other economic and demographic ways.

Cohort Analysis

I turn next to some findings of the Retirement History Study conducted between 1969 and 1979 by the Social Security Administration (SSA). It is of interest because of the abundance of data collected concerning the economic status of the elderly, including asset holdings, by use of a longitudinal design. This study affords an examination of changes that occurred in the asset holdings of a sample cohort as the members of the cohort approached retirement, retired, and then lived into the postretirement years. The sample consisted of married men, nonmarried men, and nonmarried women all of whom were aged 58–63 at the time of the first interview in 1969. These men and women were interviewed biennially through 1979. During the 1969–1975 period a majority of the respondents retired.

Two reports based on the data on assets obtained in the Retirement History Study were published, one prepared by S. R. Sherman and the other by Friedman and Sjogren.[24] Sherman found that asset ownership was common among those approaching retirement age, but that the value of the assets owned was low, especially when home equity was excluded. Only a small proportion of respondents, mainly those with high incomes, had substantial asset wealth.

Friedman and Sjogren found that at the start of the study, in 1969, 86 percent of study participants owned some assets. As the respondents aged and retired, the proportion owning assets shifted upward slightly (89 percent in 1975). In 1975, the proportion of participants owning illiquid assets was relatively small (24 percent) compared with the proportion owning either liquid assets (81 percent) or a home (69 percent).

Variations among the three marital-sex groups identified give further indications of the advantaged status of married persons among the older population. The proportion of married men owning any of the three types of assets in 1975 (94 percent) was higher than the proportion for

[24]U.S. Social Security Administration, Office of Research and Statistics, "Assets on the Threshold of Retirement," by S. R. Sherman, in L. Irelan et al., *Almost 65: Baseline Data from the Retirement History Study* (Research Report no. 49) (1976); and J. Friedman and J. Sjogren, "Assets of the Elderly as They Retire," *Social Security Bulletin* 44 (1) (January 1981):1–16.

nonmarried men or women (about 80 percent). The difference between married men (82 percent), on the one hand, and nonmarried men (51 percent) and women (46 percent), on the other, was especially large with respect to home ownership. There was much less difference in the proportions owning liquid assets, the respective figures being 86 percent, 75 percent, and 73 percent.

Liquid assets ($10,700) and home equity ($11,700) constituted the largest components of the mean total assets portfolio of the survey respondents ($27,600) and represented approximately equal shares of total assets. For homeowners, equity in their home was the most important asset. Illiquid assets were the smallest component of the mean total assets of the survey respondents ($5,200). Few survey respondents owned appreciable amounts of illiquid assets.

Mean total assets showed little net decline as the cohort aged between 1969 and 1975. The share for illiquid assets declined substantially over this period, while home equity increased substantially. The proportion of mean total assets represented by home equity rose from 39 percent to 42 percent, the growth being particularly notable for nonmarried women homeowners (Figure 8.3).

An indication of the long-term growth in assets is given by data for newly retired workers in 1941–1942 and 1982 presented by Ycas and Grad. The median net worth (1982 dollars) of married couples jumped from $11,230 in 1941–1942 to $68,000 in 1982, and the median home equity for those married couples with home equity jumped from $17,300 to $48,000.

Measure and Marital Status	1941–1942	1982	Percent Increase[a]
Median Net Worth (1982 dollars)			
Married couples	$11,230	$68,000	506
Nonmarried males	910	17,300	1768
Nonmarried females	2,840	30,100	960
Percentage Owning Their Own Homes			
Married couples	54	87	33
Nonmarried males	23	47	24
Nonmarried females	23	58	35
Median Home Equity for Those with Home Equity (1982 dollars)			
Married couples	$17,300	$48,000	177
Nonmarried males	17,270	35,000	103
Nonmarried females	13,180	38,000	188

SOURCE: M. Ycas and S. Grad (July 1987), Tables 14 and 15.

[a] Increase in percentage points for "percentage owning their own homes."

FIGURE 8.3

Mean Assets and Type of Asset of Retirement History Study Respondents, by Marital Status and Sex: 1975, 1971, and 1969

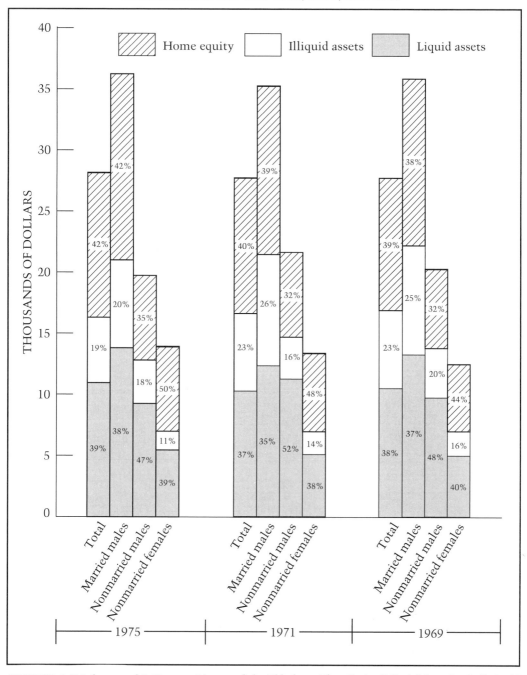

SOURCE: J. Friedman and J. Sjogren, "Assets of the Elderly as They Retire," *Social Security Bulletin* 44 (1) (January 1981).

Increase in home equity among the elderly was rapid during this period, particularly in the 1970s.

The lifetime wealth of successive cohorts has been increasing. This is partly a result of the long-term growth in real earnings and other income[25] and partly a result of the transfer of assets between one cohort and another through bequest.[26] Substantial wealth is transferred from one cohort to another by bequest as a result of the reluctance to spend off assets. Assets tend to fall off in the later years, not because any significant dissaving occurs after age 65, but because they are not replaced by income at the same rate as earlier. This is to say that the life cycle hypothesis of saving-dissaving is not supported by the evidence.

Expenditures

According to the Bureau of Labor Statistics Consumer Expenditure Survey (CES), average annual expenditures for consumer items made by elderly households are well below those at the peak ages.[27] The pattern of expenditures according to the age of the householder has a considerable degree of symmetry. In 1984, for example, in comparison with average expenditures for all consumer units (100), expenditures for age groups rose to a relative peak of 128 at ages 35–44 and 131 at ages 45–54, and then declined in subsequent age groups (Table 8.22). At ages 25–34 and 55–64 the figures were 101 and 107, and at ages under 25 and 65 and over they approximated 62–64. Symmetry in expenditures according to age of householder was evident in the early 1970s as well.

The age pattern of expenditures roughly parallels the age pattern of annual incomes; people *do* spend money according to their incomes. In

---

[25]See R. L. Clark and D. T. Barker, *Reversing the Trend Toward Early Retirement* (Washington, DC: American Enterprise Institute for Public Policy Research, 1981), pp. 45 and 51; and R. L. Clark and D. A. Sumner, "Inflation and the Real Income of the Elderly: Recent Evidence and Expectations for the Future," *Gerontologist* 25 (2) (April 1985):146–152, esp. p. 150.

[26]M. H. David and P. L. Menchik, "Changes in Cohort Wealth Over a Generation," *Demography* 25 (3) (August 1988):317–335.

[27]The CES informs us about spending patterns of the U.S. population. It was conducted at 10-year intervals until 1972–1973, but since 1980 it has been conducted on a continuing basis. The survey is composed of two independent surveys, an Interview Survey and a Diary Survey. The results discussed here are from the Interview Survey. The CES uses national probability samples designed to be representative of the U.S. civilian population. The rural population was covered for the first time in 1984. The survey is described in detail in *BLS Handbook of Methods* (1982), Chapter 6. Consumer units in the CES correspond to households. Consumer units are classified by age according to the age of the reference person or householder.

TABLE 8.22

Relative Annual Expenditures for Consumer Units, by Age of Householder: 1984 and 1972–1973

Age of Householder	1984		1972–1973
	All Units	Urban Units	Urban Units
Total Expenditures	$20,862	$21,788	$9,421
Index, All Ages	100.0	100.0	100.0
Under 25	61.6	60.5	68.1
25–34	101.0	98.7	101.9
35–44	127.5	127.1	127.2
45–54	131.1	131.4	129.7
55–64	106.7	105.6	100.9
65–74	72.1	72.9	NA
75 and Over	51.4	51.4	NA
65 and Over	63.8	64.2	60.2

SOURCES: Based on U.S. Bureau of Labor Statistics, "Consumer Expenditure Survey: 1984 Results for Both Urban and Rural Population," *News*, no. 86-451 (November 20, 1986), Table 3; *Consumer Expenditure Survey: Interview Survey, 1984*, Bulletin no. 2267 (August 1986), Table 4; *Consumer Expenditure Survey: Interview Survey, 1980–81*, Bulletin no. 2225 (April 1985), Table C-2.

NOTES: Base of index is total expenditures by householders of all ages. Total expenditures are annual averages. NA = not available.

TABLE 8.23

Ratio of Expenditures to Income for Urban Consumer Units, by Age of Householder: 1984, 1980–1981, and 1972–1973

Age of Householder	After-Tax Income, 1984	Before-Tax Income		
		1984	1980–1981	1972–1973
All Consumer Units	.99	.89	.86	.76
Under 25	1.24	1.05	.98	.94
25–34	.99	.87	.86	.78
35–44	.96	.86	.86	.77
45–54	1.00	.89	.82	.70
55–64	.96	.85	.78	.69
65–74	1.01	.94	NA	NA
75 and over	.97	.90	NA	NA
65 and over	1.00	.93	.99	.84

SOURCES: Based on U.S. Bureau of Labor Statistics, *Consumer Expenditure Survey: Interview Survey, 1980–81*, Bulletin no. 2225 (April 1985), Table C-2; and *Consumer Expenditure Survey: Interview Survey, 1984*, Bulletin no. 2267 (August 1986), Table 4.

1984, at every age the expenditure/income ratio was relatively high, but at ages 65 and over the ratio was especially high (.93). (See Table 8.23.) At ages 25–64 consumers are in a savings and investment mode, but at ages 65 and over, as at ages under 25, with much lower incomes and new areas of expense, they are pressed to spend all or nearly all of their income. Comparison of the expenditure/income ratios for 1972–1973 and 1984 reflects a declining tendency to save and invest during this period on the part of all age segments, but the change was smaller than average at ages 65 and over, partly because little income was available for this purpose at the outset.

According to the 1984 CES, the leading items in household budgets for elderly households were housing, food, transportation, and health in

TABLE 8.24

Percent Distribution of Annual Expenditures by Budget Item, for All Consumer Units, for Selected Householder Ages: 1984 (numbers rounded to nearest hundred dollars)

Budget Item	All Consumer Units	Ages Under 25	Ages 35–44	Ages 55–64	Ages 65–74	Ages 75 and Over
Average Annual Expenditures	$20,900	$12,800	$26,600	$22,300	$15,000	$10,700
All Items	100.0	100.0	100.0	100.0	100.0	100.0
Food	15.7	15.5	15.8	16.2	18.0	17.4
At home[a]	10.9	9.2	10.9	11.3	13.2	13.8
Away from home[a]	4.9	6.3	5.0	4.9	4.8	3.6
Housing	30.1	28.0	31.1	27.8	30.3	35.1
Shelter	16.7	17.8	18.1	14.0	14.6	17.4
Other	13.4	10.2	13.0	13.8	15.7	17.7
Transportation	20.4	25.5	19.0	19.9	19.5	13.1
Vehicles	8.7	12.7	7.5	8.1	7.5	3.4
Other	11.7	12.8	11.5	11.8	12.0	9.7
Health care	4.3	2.5	3.0	4.8	9.0	13.6
Entertainment	4.7	5.1	5.4	4.5	3.5	2.5
Apparel and services	5.3	5.9	5.8	5.1	4.4	3.1
Cash contributions	3.4	0.8	3.7	3.9	4.5	7.5
Personal insurance and pensions	9.2	6.3	9.8	11.1	4.7	2.1
Other[b]	6.9	10.4	6.4	6.7	6.1	5.6

SOURCE: Based on U.S. Bureau of Labor Statistics, "Consumer Expenditure Survey: 1984 Results for Both Urban and Rural Population," *News*, no. 86-451 (November 20, 1986), Table 3.

[a] Estimated on basis of distribution of food total, "at home" and "away from home," for urban consumer units, Interview Survey, 1984.
[b] Includes alcoholic beverages, personal care, reading, education, tobacco, and miscellaneous.

TABLE 8.25

*Percent Distribution of Average Annual Expenditures by Budget Item,
for Urban Consumer Units, for Householders Aged 65 and Over:
1972–1973, 1980–1981, and 1984*

Budget Item	1984	1980–1981	1972–1973
All Items	100.0	100.0	100.0
Food	17.6	20.6	20.8
At home	13.2	16.2	17.4
Away from home	4.4	4.4	3.4
Housing	32.1	33.3	31.2
Shelter	16.0	16.5	17.4
Other	16.1	16.8	13.8
Transportation	17.2	15.9	14.4
Vehicles	6.5	4.4	4.3
Other	10.6	11.5	10.1
Health care	10.0	9.7	8.0
Apparel and services	4.0	3.9	6.2
Entertainment	3.4	2.9	2.7
Cash contributions	5.8	4.7	8.4
Personal insurance and pensions	4.0	3.0	3.6
Other[a]	5.9	6.0	4.7

SOURCES: Based on U.S. Bureau of Labor Statistics, *Consumer Expenditure Survey: Interview Survey, 1980–81*, Bulletin no. 2225 (April 1985), Table C-2; and *Consumer Expenditure Survey: Interview Survey, 1984*, Bulletin no. 2267 (August 1986), Table 4.

[a]Includes alcoholic beverages, personal care, reading, education, tobacco, and miscellaneous.

that order (Table 8.24). Together, these four categories constituted over three quarters of the total expenditures of elderly households, and each exceeded or equaled 10 percent of the total. Apparel and services, entertainment, cash contributions, and personal insurance and pensions each made up 3–6 percent of the budget. The shares of other items (e.g., education, personal care, alcoholic beverages, etc.) were even smaller. The pattern of the budget of elderly householders was essentially the same in the early 1970s.

The expenditures on housing constituted the largest component of the budget for consumer units of every age. However, the proportion of the budget spent on housing by elderly consumer units (32 percent) was higher than for consumer units in general (30 percent). (See Tables 8.24 and 8.25.) This is not, so far as the elderly are concerned, because of large mortgage payments, since most elderly persons own their homes.

Rather, it is because the homes of the elderly are generally old and often in need of repairs and because of fixed utility and insurance costs.

Families and other consumer units with householders aged 65 and over also spent a somewhat higher proportion of their budget on food (18 percent) than all units on the average (16 percent). The rise in older age was confined to food at home, however. (See Table 8.24.) The elderly spend a large share of their income on food at home mainly because when income is relatively low, as it is for most elderly families, expenditures for basic necessities take precedence in the budget. A possible additional reason is the smaller size of elderly families. As family size decreases, there is some loss of economy of scale and the per person expenditure of a family for various budget items tends to increase.

Expenditures for transportation, the next most important item in the budget of elderly persons (17 percent), are relatively less important at the upper ages than at the younger ones (Table 8.24)—partly because retirement reduces or eliminates the costs of going to and from work and declining health and disability associated with aging tend to reduce the demand for transportation. Recreational travel may increase, particularly among the higher-income groups, however.

Elderly households spend a much smaller proportion of their budgets on health care (10 percent) than transportation, except at the highest ages because, although the total costs of health care are considerably higher for the elderly than the costs of transportation, the major part of the health bill is covered by Medicare or Medicaid payments. The percentage of total expenditures that went for health care was two and a half times greater for elderly units (10.0 percent) than for all consumer units (4.3 percent), however.

In a number of respects the pattern of expenditures according to categories of consumption is strikingly different for the elderly and the other age segments. Elderly consumers have larger relative expenditures for food at home, housing other than shelter, and cash contributions, far larger relative expenditures for health care, and smaller relative expenditures for transportation, entertainment, apparel and services, and personal insurance and pensions.

The estimates for 1984 also reveal differences in the expenditure levels and patterns of younger and older persons within the larger group of persons aged 65 and over.[28] These underline again the heterogeneity of the elderly population. Consumer units in the 75-and-over age group spend 17 percent less on housing than those in the 65–74 age group (Table 8.26). This difference may be accounted for by the greater expen-

---

[28]See also B. Harrison, "Spending Patterns of Older Persons," *Monthly Labor Review* 109 (10) (October 1986), pp. 15–17.

TABLE 8.26

*Relative Annual Expenditures by Budget Item, for Consumer Units,
for Householders Aged 65 and Over: 1984*

Budget Item	Ages 65 and Over to All Ages	Ages 75 and Over to 65–74
All Items	.64	.71
Food	.72	.69
Housing	.68	.83
Transportation	.54	.48
Health care	1.55	1.07
Apparel and services	.48	.50
Entertainment	.44	.50
Cash contributions	1.03	1.17
Personal insurance and pensions	.27	.32
Other[a]	.55	.67

SOURCE: Based on U.S. Bureau of Labor Statistics, "Consumer Expenditure Survey: 1984 Results for Both Urban and Rural Population," *News*, no. 86-451 (November 20, 1986), Table 3.

[a]Includes alcoholic beverages, tobacco, reading, education, personal care, and miscellaneous.

ditures for property taxes and mortgages, and, in general, the higher level of home ownership at the younger ages. Expenditures for transportation were only half as great for the 75-and-over age group as for the 65–74 group because of the higher level of vehicle ownership and the greater use of motor vehicles on the part of the younger group. Expenditures for health care are only moderately higher for the 75-and-over age group than for the 65–74 group. Overall expenditures for the older age group are nearly one third lower than for the younger age group.

The first-ranked item in the budget, housing, constitutes a much larger share of the budget for those aged 75 and over (35 percent) than for those aged 65–74 (30 percent). (See Table 8.24.) The second-ranked item, transportation, accounted for 19 percent of total expenditures for the young elderly and 13 percent for the aged, while the third-ranked item, food, accounted for about the same share of the budget for the two groups (17–18 percent). As expected, the share of total expenditures spent for health care was much higher for the older group (14 percent) than for the younger one (9 percent). As a result of these age differences in expenditures, the rank order of the items shifted between ages 64–74 and ages 75 and over. Transportation moved into fourth place at ages 75 and over from its second position at ages 65–74 (i.e., housing, food, health care, and transportation).

Summary

Economic status in later life is a cumulative product of a life history of economic experiences, involving earning, saving and spending, and participation in pension, health insurance, and public assistance plans. Cumulative economic advantages and disadvantages through the life course contribute to a wide economic inequality among the elderly, particularly among the aged.

Cross-sectional reported total money income has a skewed bell-shape over the age scale: Median income tends to reach a peak in midlife and to drop sharply in later life, particularly at retirement. However, cross-sectional data exaggerate the drop-off experienced by actual cohorts, which tend to reach a peak at a later age and to fall off more moderately. Cohort data at the later ages reflect the lower incomes, skills, education, and productivity of earlier years. Even with cross-sectional data, adjustment for size of household, underreporting of income, tax advantages, and noncash benefits would bring the median income of the elderly much closer to the median income of the nonelderly.

The income replacement ratio is higher for women than for men, but their retirement income is much lower. Women receive far less income than men throughout life and, in spite of the many federal programs to bolster income in later life, women show a marked income deficit at the older ages. Given the large excess of women among the elderly, it is reasonable to speak of the feminization of low income in later life. Blacks and Hispanics also show a large income deficit compared with whites, but the feminization of low income is more marked throughout the life course than its racialization. A substantial part of the difference between the income of men and women cannot be explained by differences in education, work experience, or work interruptions, and some part of it must be attributed to discrimination in hiring, wage and salary scales, promotions, and occupational options.

Between 1950 and 1985, and especially between 1970 and 1985, the economic condition of the elderly improved dramatically, far more rapidly than that of the general population. This general conclusion is supported by independent and combined analysis of data on income, poverty, and net worth. Currently the official percentage of elderly persons who are poor is slightly below that for the nonelderly population, although a few decades ago the percentage was far greater for the elderly. The striking excess of child poverty over elderly poverty has led to charges of favoritism toward the elderly in benefit programs and of neglect of children.

Elderly women have excessive poverty compared with elderly men, and elderly men and elderly women who live alone or with nonrelatives have excessive poverty compared with all elderly men and women, respectively. Elderly women have experienced sizable declines in poverty ratios since 1960 but, in spite of favorable legislation, their poverty ratios fell more slowly than those of men. The marked changes in living arrangements between 1950 and 1985, in particular the increased tendency to live alone, could have influenced the downward trend in poverty at the older ages in this period.

Poverty among the elderly should be a matter of great public concern because of the several special groups among them who have very high levels of poverty. Women and racial minorities in nonmetropolitan areas are notable in this regard. Blacks and Hispanics, black and Hispanic women, and black and Hispanic women who live alone, in ascending order, have excessive poverty ratios. Poverty among the elderly is distinctive also because of the great concentration of elderly persons, particularly elderly blacks and Hispanics, just above the official poverty line. For this and other reasons, there is much movement into and out of poverty on the part of the elderly. If widowhood occurs and the survivor does not receive an employer or union pension directly or as survivor, she—and it is very likely to be a woman—has a good chance of descending into poverty rapidly and remaining there. These two factors, widowhood and nonreceipt of a pension, are leading determinants of the risk of descent into poverty.

Nearly all elderly persons receive Social Security benefits and most receive income from another source. Dependence on Social Security benefits only or mainly leaves a substantial share of the elderly in poverty or just above the poverty line. In general, the elderly are much more likely to receive transfer payments (Social Security, SSI), pensions, and asset income than earnings, the type of income mainly supporting the nonelderly. The most affluent elderly receive pensions and asset income in addition to Social Security benefits, if not earnings, while the least affluent depend only or mostly on Social Security benefits and SSI.

Median net worth (the difference between assets and liabilities), like median income, drops in later life. Yet within income categories median net worth rises steadily. The decline is accounted for by the fact that low net worth is associated with low income and a large share of the elderly have relatively low incomes. Elderly householders have a substantially larger share of total net worth than they constitute of all householders because of the large proportion of elderly persons with home equity and accumulated assets. The principal component of the net worth of householders at older ages as well as at the younger ages is home equity, although even home equity constitutes less than half of total net worth at each age. The median net worth of the elderly has increased markedly since World War II, more rapidly than the median net worth of the general adult population.

Elderly householders as a group spend much less for most consumer items than householders at midlife, in consonance with their smaller incomes. Expenditures continue to fall for most budget items through the older ages. The principal items in the budgets of elderly householders are housing, food, transportation, and health care, in the order given. Elderly householders spend a larger proportion of their incomes than younger householders for these items, except transportation. The shares of the budget spent on housing and health care continue to rise among the aged, while the shares spent on most other items fall. The shifts in the budget after midlife reflect the greater importance of necessities and the smaller importance of amenities at the older ages, in the face of the reduced incomes of later life.

9

HOUSING CHARACTERISTICS

THIS CHAPTER deals with the housing conditions of older persons and the changes in the housing conditions of people as they get older. It also deals with the relationship between the characteristics of older householders and their housing. Housing characteristics include the value, tenure, costs, and quality of the unit,[1] while householder characteristics include the age, race/Hispanic origin, income, type of residence, and region of residence of the householder, and the type of household.

The analysis presented here will generally be based on 1980 census data and relate to housing units maintained by persons aged 65 and over. As noted elsewhere in this volume, there is great diversity in the characteristics of the elderly population in relation to age, and the diversity of elderly housing with respect to the age of the householder will be noted when data for the detailed age groups 65 and over are available. Reference will also be made to data from earlier censuses and to data from the American Housing Survey and the Current Population Survey (CPS).[2] In the census as well as in these surveys the population living in

---

[1] Discussion of the neighborhood characteristics of the elderly is omitted. This would involve consideration of the availability of essential services and amenities, including security and safety, crime victimization, and nuisances.

[2] The data from the American Housing Survey of 1987 became available after the draft of this monograph was completed; as a result, they are, for the most part, discussed independently of the various substantive topics.

housing units excludes the population living in group quarters of various types. Accordingly, the material in this chapter is restricted to occupied housing units and excludes group quarters.

It should be the goal of housing programs for the elderly to promote the provision of housing of good quality, at a cost that is not excessive in relation to income, and with sufficient space to avoid overcrowding and to afford minimal privacy. Where necessary, provision should be made for structural modifications in the unit and for support services that meet the needs of functionally limited persons and the requirements for long-term care. The design of the housing unit (i.e., number and arrangement of rooms), its structural condition, and its location (vis-à-vis other units and the neighborhood), considered in combination with the social support that is available, affect the way the unit can serve the needs of the elderly occupants. Housing programs for the elderly that aim to implement the goals stated must take into account current demographic realities: for example, the large and growing share of women and widows as age advances, the relatively small size of elderly households, the increase in physical limitations that accompany old age, the trend of a rising share of elderly women living alone, and the decline in income in later life. It is useful to bear in mind the goals noted and the demographic characteristics of the elderly in the discussion that follows.

Housing Tenure

Home ownership is strongly desired by the vast majority of families and is achieved by most. Since 1940, home ownership has increased greatly. In that year, 44 percent of the nonfarm dwelling units were owner-occupied. By 1950, the proportion had climbed to 53 percent, and by 1974 the proportion of homeowners, both farm and nonfarm, had risen to 65 percent, where it essentially remained through the 1980s (64 percent in 1987).[3]

The older population has led the upward trend toward a greater proportion of homeowners. In large part, this frontline position is an indirect result of the length of time during which older persons have had the opportunity to accumulate savings and purchase a home. In 1950, the share of elderly homeowners was 65 percent for nonfarm units. By 1960, the figure had climbed to 69 percent, where it essentially re-

[3]Alternative figures for 1940–1980, based on census Public Use Microdata Samples for these years, are presented in A. Chevan, "The Growth of Home Ownership: 1940–1980," *Demography* 26 (2) (May 1989):249–266.

mained through 1974. In 1987, after a decade of renewed increases, about 75 percent of housing units maintained by persons aged 65 and over were owner-occupied (Table 9.1). The proportion of owners at ages 45–64 has shown a similar rise since 1960, while the proportion at the younger ages, 15–44, has risen slowly or not at all, and then, in the 1980s, reversed direction sharply.

In each of the years of the 1970s for which data are available the percentage of persons owning their homes tended to rise from ages 15–24 to a peak at ages 45–54 and then to fall back at ages 65 and over to just below the level at ages 35–44. In the years of the 1980s, however, the percentage of ownership rose to a peak at later ages, 55–64, and then tended to fall back at ages 65 and over to just below the level of ages 45–54. Further examination shows that the peak reached at ages 55–64 in the 1980s was maintained at ages 65–74 before a sharp decline set in at ages 75 and over.

Age Group	Percentage Owner-Occupied, 1987
55–64	80.0
65 and Over	74.9
65–74	79.1
75 and Over	68.8
All Ages	64.0

SOURCE: American Housing Survey, 1987.

The large falloff between ages 55–64 and ages 65 and over observed in the cross-sectional data mostly disappears when the data are examined according to birth cohorts. We would expect home ownership to be cumulative through all or most of the lifetime of a cohort[4] and, in fact, the data bear this expectation out. As Table 9.1 shows, the percentage of homeowners rises, or falls only slightly, between ages 45–54, ages 55–64, and ages 65 and over (proxy for ages 65–74), tracked as a cohort in 1960, 1970, and 1980, or in 1964, 1974, and 1984.

A rough estimate of the generalized pattern for the age cycle of home ownership in recent decades can be developed from the data in Table 9.1. The cohort age-to-age percent changes for 10-year age groups for four periods—1960–1970, 1970–1980, 1964–1974, and 1974–1984—were calculated from the data in Table 9.1 and averaged. Similarly, the period age-to-age percent changes[5] for 10-year age groups for six years—1960,

---

[4]This expectation assumes that the relation between home ownership and the probability of survival is not negative.

[5]That is, changes limited to a particular calendar year.

TABLE 9.1

Home Ownership, by Age of Householder: 1960–1987

Age of Householder	1960	1964	1970	1974	1977	1980	1984	1987
Total, 15 and Over	61.9	NA	62.9	64.6	64.8	65.6	64.6	64.0
15–24	20.1	20.3	21.5	22.9	21.4	21.5	17.6	16.7
25–29	40.5 ⎫	48.2	41.7	43.1	42.6	43.2	38.4	37.5
30–34	57.2 ⎬		57.4	61.8	62.3	61.0	54.4	52.4
35–44	65.5	66.6	69.2	71.6	71.4	72.4	68.9	66.6
45–54	68.2	69.8	73.3	76.4	77.6	77.7	77.4	75.4
55–64	68.1	67.9	71.4	76.3	77.1	79.1	79.4	80.0
65 and Over	68.9	67.6	67.4	69.7	70.7	72.2	75.3	74.9

SOURCES: Unpublished data provided by D. Dahman, U.S. Bureau of the Census: 1960 and 1970, Census of Housing microdata files; 1974, 1977, and 1980, Annual Housing Survey microdata files; 1984, CPS microdata files; 1964, estimated by interpolation; 1987, American Housing Survey.

NOTES: Percentages of households owning the housing unit in which they reside. NA = not available.

1970, 1980, 1964, 1974, and 1984—were calculated and averaged. The four sets of cohort age-to-age percent changes, the six sets of period age-to-age percent changes, and the corresponding averages of the changes for each pair of ages are shown in Table 9.2.

To continue the derivation of a generalized cohort age cycle for home ownership, the average cohort age-to-age percent changes were applied sequentially to the average percentage of home ownership at ages 35–44. (See Appendix 6A for further explanation.) The generalized period "age cycle" was derived in a similar way. The resulting generalized cohort and period age cycles for the percentage of home ownership are as follows:[6]

Age	Cohort	Period
15–24	20.7	20.7
25–34	49.0	49.9
35–44	69.4	69.4
45–54	77.6	74.2
55–64	82.6	74.0
65 and Over	83.0	70.6

The generalized cohort cycle for home ownership rises in older age while the generalized period cycle falls. The average cohort change from ages 55–64 to ages 65 and over is +0.5 percent, while the average period change is −4.6 percent. Hence, we conclude that home ownership in the actual life course hardly changed between these ages even though the period data for these ages indicate a substantial drop in recent decades. A decrease in the proportion of homeowners for the older population in a given year reflects the behavior of earlier cohorts rather than current movement into rental housing. As the 1984 middle-agers, 55–64, move into the higher age group, 65–74 in 1994, we would expect the proportion of homeowners for ages 65 and over as a group to equal or exceed the 1984 level of home ownership for the 55–64 age group even though the cross-sectional data in 1994 show a drop between these ages.

---

[6]The generalized age cycle would not change substantially if the anchor ages selected were 15–24 or 25–34.

TABLE 9.2

Comparison of Period and Cohort Age-to-Age Shifts in Percentage of Home Ownership: 1960–1984

Initial Age	Terminal Age	Period Change (Percent)						
		1960	1964	1970	1974	1980	1984	Average
15–24	25–34	+147.8	+137.4	+129.3	+128.8	+142.8	+163.6	+141.6
25–34	35–44	+31.5	+38.2	+40.4	+36.6	+39.0	+48.5	+39.0
35–44	45–54	+4.1	+4.8	+5.9	+6.7	+7.3	+12.3	+6.9
45–54	55–64	−0.1	−2.7	−2.6	−0.1	+1.8	+2.6	−0.2
55–64	65 and Over[a]	+1.2	−1.2	−5.6	−8.7	−8.7	−5.2	−4.7

Initial Age	Terminal Age	Cohort Change (Percent)				
		1960–1970	1964–1974	1970–1980	1974–1984	Average
15–24	25–34	+145.3	+158.1	+142.8	+102.6	+137.2
25–34	35–44	+39.0	+48.5	+46.9	+31.5	+41.5
35–44	45–54	+11.9	+14.7	+12.3	+8.1	+11.8
45–54	55–64	+4.7	+9.3	+7.9	+3.9	+6.5
55–64	65 and Over[a]	−1.0	+2.7	+1.1	−1.3	+0.4

SOURCE: Table 9.1.

[a] Not fully cohort-compatible, but adequate for this comparison.

Regional Variations

The proportion of the older population owning their homes varies greatly according to geographic area of residence, race, living arrangements, and sex and age of the householder. Older persons living in the South are more likely to be homeowners than older persons living in other regions. Three quarters of the elderly households (i.e., occupied housing units with householders aged 65 or over) in the South are owner-occupied compared with only three fifths of those in the Northeast (Table 9.3). Home ownership among the elderly is nearly as high in the Midwest as in the South. The larger share of blacks in the South (blacks having lower ownership rates) tends to pull down the overall figure for the South, even though black home ownership in the South is much greater than black home ownership in the Midwest (Table 9.4).

Within each region of the country, there is a similar pattern of variation in the extent of home ownership according to the type-of-residence area or degree of population concentration (Table 9.3). Regardless of region, older persons living in suburban areas (urban fringe), urban places outside urbanized areas, and rural areas are much more likely to be homeowners than older persons living in central cities of urbanized areas. The proportion of rural elderly housing units occupied by home-owners is consistently very high (83–85 percent). In general, regional variations in home ownership for the urban fringe, urban places outside urbanized areas, and rural areas are smaller than those for central cities and even entire regions. For example, the figure for home ownership among elderly suburban householders in the Northeast region, 66 percent, is much closer to the highest suburban figure—that in the South (77 percent)—than the total figure for the Northeast is to the total figure for the South. Home ownership is very low only in the older central cities of the Northeast.

Racial/Ethnic and Other Variations

Equally great variation in home ownership can be found among the elderly of various race groups and the Hispanic group. For elderly whites the extent of home ownership in 1980 was 72 percent while the proportions for blacks, Asian and Pacific Islanders (API), and persons of Spanish origin were in the fifties (Table 9.4). The same general pattern of racial and ethnic differences occurred at the ages below 65, as suggested by a comparison of the figures for ages 65 and over and all ages; but as expected, smaller proportions had achieved home ownership at the younger ages.

TABLE 9.3

Home Ownership for Households Maintained by Persons Aged 65 and Over, by Urban-Rural and Metropolitan Residence and Region: 1980

		Urban						Rural				
			Inside Urbanized Areas			Outside Urbanized Areas						
Region	Total	Total	Total	Central City	Urban Fringe	Places of 10,000 or More	Places of 2,500–10,000	Total[a]	Places of 1,000–2,500	Rural-Farm	Inside SMSAs	Outside SMSAs
Ages 65 and Over												
United States	71	66	64	58	72	71	74	84	79	91	67	79
Northeast	60	56	54	42	66	60	69	84	77	89	57	76
Midwest/North Central	74	68	67	62	73	72	74	86	79	92	70	80
South	76	72	71	66	77	72	76	83	80	90	73	79
West	70	67	66	60	71	73	76	85	81	88	67	80
All Ages												
United States	64	59	58	49	68	62	68	80	74	82	62	73
Northeast	59	54	53	36	68	56	64	81	72	84	57	73
Midwest/North Central	69	64	63	54	72	65	71	82	76	82	66	75
South	67	61	60	54	68	61	68	79	74	85	64	73
West	60	58	57	51	62	61	65	75	69	77	59	69

SOURCE: U.S. Bureau of the Census, 1980 Census of Housing, *U.S. Summary: Detailed Characteristics,* HC80-1-B1, Tables 81, 94, 107, 120, and 133.

NOTE: Percentages of households owning the housing unit in which they reside.

[a] Places under 1,000 not shown.

TABLE 9.4

Home Ownership for Households Maintained by Persons Aged 65 and Over, by Region and Race/Spanish Origin: 1980

Race/Spanish Origin	Ages 65 and Over					All Ages				
	United States	Northeast	Midwest/North Central	South	West	United States	Northeast	Midwest/North Central	South	West
All Races	71	60	74	76	70	64	59	69	67	60
White	72	62	75	78	71	68	63	72	71	63
Black	58	41	53	64	54	44	31	44	50	40
Asian and Pacific Islander	56	33	52	63	60	51	37	50	51	56
American Indian/Eskimo/Aleut	67	54	57	72	70	52	42	47	59	52
Spanish Origin [a]	55	23	59	62	60	43	20	43	54	47

SOURCE: U.S. Bureau of the Census, 1980 Census of Housing, *U.S. Summary: Detailed Characteristics*, HC80-1-B1, Tables 81, 83–86, 94, 96–100, 107, 109–113, 120, 122–126, 133, and 135–139.

NOTE: Percentages of households owning the housing unit in which they reside.

[a] Also included in racial categories shown.

Table 9.5 reflects the heterogeneity of the extent of home ownership within the API and Hispanic groups. Elderly Chinese, Puerto Ricans, and Cubans show relatively low percentages of home ownership, and elderly Japanese and Mexicans show relatively high percentages. Chinese and Cubans are notable exceptions to the general record among the race/ethnic groups of higher average ownership for persons aged 65 and over than for persons under age 65.

Low percentages of home ownership for Puerto Ricans and Chinese are consistent with the low percentages in the urban Northeast, where these groups are concentrated. Low home ownership among older Cubans may be due to the recency of their arrival or their continuing plans to return to Cuba.

The influence of geographic area on home ownership cuts across racial and ethnic categories. Older persons of each major racial/ethnic group living in the Northeast have the lowest proportions of home ownership and, conversely, older members of each group living in the South have the highest proportions (Table 9.4).

Relatively high shares of white, black, and Hispanic owners live in the South and relatively high shares of Asian and Pacific Islander and American Indian owners live in the West. If we consider the regional distribution of owners and renters at the same time, we find that renters are concentrated in the same areas as the owners. This reflects the basic regional distribution of the population of the racial/ethnic groups.

Home ownership also varies with the living arrangements of older persons (Table 9.6). Persons who live alone, whether male or female, are much less likely to own their homes than persons having other living arrangements. At every age, except the most advanced ages, those living with a spouse are the most likely to be homeowners, and older male householders are more likely to be homeowners than older female householders. Female householders account for 60 percent of the elderly renters and about 16 percent of all elderly households. Older females are as likely to be renters as homeowners.

Housing Values

The inflationary trend in housing prices during the 1960s and 1970s has been advantageous for older homeowners. Close to half of all homeowners aged 65 and over in 1980 moved into their current dwelling before 1960 and about another quarter bought their homes between 1960 and 1970. Two facts have worked to the economic advantage of the older homeowning population. First, many older homeowners purchased their home at a time when their earning power was at its peak. Second, in many areas, mid-level-priced homes increased the most in value.

Inflation and other economic forces nearly doubled the median value of homes between 1970 and 1980 regardless of year built. In 1950 the median value for all homes was $7,750, in 1970 it was $26,600, and in 1980 it was $47,200.

Year Structure Built	Median Value		
	1980	1970	1950
Total, All Years	$47,200	$26,600[a]	$7,750
1960–1969	53,700	27,806	X
1950–1959	46,200	21,000	X
1940–1949	37,100	17,700	8,965
1939 or Earlier	32,300	16,000	7,227

[a] Total includes housing units built in 1970–1979. X = not applicable.

In 1980, homes owned by the elderly tended to have much lower values than homes of persons under age 65. For married couples, the median value was $39,500 for homes owned by persons aged 65 and over compared with $51,300 for homes owned by persons aged 45–64 (Table 9.7). Only 35 percent of the homes owned by married-couple families with a householder aged 65 and over were estimated to be worth $50,000 or more, while about 51 percent of all homes owned by married-couple families were estimated to be worth $50,000 or more.

In 1980, housing values differed greatly within the older population depending on the type of household. Elderly married couples lived in housing units with the highest median value, $39,500, as previously noted, while elderly female householders (no spouse present) lived in housing units with the lowest median value, $30,700 (Table 9.7). Elderly male householders (no spouse present) lived in dwellings with an intermediate median value, $35,500. This pattern also applied to the housing occupied by younger householders. The variation in housing values for elderly householders according to type of household has increased greatly since 1950, when the median values for the household types were quite similar to one another.

Such statistics of housing values do not tell us anything directly about the quality of housing, specifically the likelihood of a group of elderly householders living in substandard housing, as we would expect, but the proportions of households living in low-valued homes are suggestive of variations in this regard. Male householders (no wife present) and female householders (no husband present) lived in low-valued homes in greater proportions than married couples. About 31 percent of

TABLE 9.5

Home Ownership for Households Maintained by Persons Aged 65 and Over, by Detailed Race/Spanish Origin of Householder: 1980

Race/Spanish Origin	Owner-Occupied Units, Householders Ages 65 and Over[a]	Percentage Owned	
		Householders Ages 65 and Over[b]	Householders All Ages[c]
Total All Races	11,919,000	71	64
White	10,920,800	72	68
Black	835,700	58	44
Total Asian and Pacific Islander	67,000	56	51
Japanese	19,800	68	59
Chinese	13,600	47	55
Filipino	16,000	58	56
Asian Indian	11,800	55	50
American Indian/ Eskimo/Aleut	38,300	67	52
Total Spanish Origin	227,100	55	43
Mexican	142,700	65	49
Puerto Rican	9,300	23	20
Cuban	13,300	27	43
Other	61,900	60	64

SOURCE: U.S. Bureau of the Census, 1980 Census of Housing, HC80-1-B1, Tables 81, 83, 84, 86, and 87.

NOTE: Percentage of households owning the housing unit in which they reside.

[a] Rounded to nearest hundred.
[b] Owner elderly households as percentage of all elderly households of a specified race/origin.
[c] Owner households of all ages as percentage of households of all ages of a specified race/origin.

the elderly male householders and 28 percent of the elderly female householders lived in housing valued at less than $20,000 in 1980 compared with about 17 percent of the elderly married couples (Table 9.7). Although some of this variation can be attributed to the age and size distribution of the older households (e.g., married-couple families are more concentrated in the young-old—65–74—age group than other household types), even when allowance is made for this fact, a smaller percentage of married couples live in low-valued units. We surmise from these data that elderly married couples live in housing units of better quality than elderly male and female householders.

TABLE 9.6

Home Ownership for Older Householders, by Sex, Age, and Living Arrangements of Householder: 1980

Sex and Age of Householder	Total Householders	Living Alone	Living with Spouse[a]	Living with Sibling[b]	Living with Children[b]	Living with Other Relative[b]	Living with Nonrelative[b]
Male							
55–59	80	36	86	67	66	63	43
60–64	79	40	84	69	68	65	41
65–69	77	44	82	67	71	60	44
70–74	74	46	80	66	69	63	48
75–79	70	49	76	67	73	66	48
80–84	67	51	72	67	76	69	57
85 and Over	65	52	70	62	79	76	66
25–64	70	28	78	45	54	54	28
Female							
55–59	59	52	82	66	62	60	58
60–64	59	53	83	66	66	63	58
65–69	57	53	83	65	69	63	59
70–74	56	52	80	66	69	63	65
75–79	53	49	78	62	70	63	65
80–84	51	47	76	64	72	63	64
85 and Over	51	46	71	65	72	66	66
25–64	43	37	71	48	42	56	31

SOURCE: U.S. Bureau of the Census, 1980 Census of Population and Housing, Public Use Microdata Sample; special tabulations prepared for U.S. Senate Special Committee on Aging, Committee Print, serial no. 99-D (October 1985).

NOTE: Percentages of households owning the housing unit in which they reside.

[a] Married-couple households.
[b] No spouse present.

TABLE 9.7
Value of Owner-Occupied Housing Units, by Type of Household and Age of Householder: 1980

Household Type and Age of Householder	Total Units		Percentage of All Units								
	Number (in thousands)	Percent	Less Than $10,000	$10,000–$19,999	$20,000–$29,999	$30,000–$39,999	$40,000–$49,999	$50,000–$59,999	$60,000–$99,999	$100,000 or More	Median[a] (dollars)
Married-Couple Families											
All ages[b]	29,615	100.0	2.1	6.7	11.2	14.3	14.8	12.7	27.3	10.9	$50,600
45–64	11,708	100.0	2.1	6.8	11.2	13.7	14.3	12.4	27.1	12.3	51,300
65 and over	4,400	100.0	4.7	12.6	16.9	16.5	14.3	10.7	17.9	6.4	39,500
Male Householder, No Wife Present											
All ages[b]	2,778	100.0	6.8	13.0	15.5	15.0	13.0	10.1	19.2	7.4	39,800
45–64	848	100.0	7.4	14.1	15.8	14.3	12.3	9.6	18.3	8.2	38,800
65 and over	739	100.0	11.7	19.4	19.6	15.3	11.3	7.7	11.3	3.7	35,500
Female Householder, No Husband Present											
All ages[b]	7,036	100.0	6.8	15.2	18.3	16.6	13.4	9.3	15.6	4.8	35,500
45–64	2,430	100.0	6.0	14.1	17.4	16.2	13.6	10.0	17.2	5.5	37,600
65 and over	3,058	100.0	9.2	18.9	20.6	16.3	12.2	8.1	11.4	3.3	30,700

SOURCE: U.S. Bureau of the Census, 1980 Census of Housing, *U.S. Summary: Detailed Characteristics*, HC80-2-1, Table A-1.

[a] Rounded to nearest hundred dollars.
[b] Ages 15 and over.

Like elderly white homeowners, elderly black homeowners benefited from the recent economic trends which increased housing values,
but they are still much less likely to own the more expensive homes.
According to the 1979 Annual Housing Survey, 32 percent of elderly
white homeowners owned a home worth $50,000 or more and a scant 4
percent owned a home worth less than $10,000. In contrast, only 11
percent of the blacks aged 65 and over owned a home worth $50,000 or
more in 1979 and 19 percent owned a home worth less than $10,000.
Historically, blacks have had neither the financial resources nor the residential options that whites have had. Although this situation may be
changing, a number of years will have to pass before a substantial share
of blacks own the more expensive homes.

The enormous diversity in the economic status of the elderly Spanish-origin population is reflected in the wide variation in the value of
homes owned by them. While about 13 percent of the homeowners of
Spanish origin owned a home worth less than $10,000 in 1979, 52 per-
cent owned a home worth $35,000 or more. In fact, a slightly higher
proportion of elderly Hispanics (35 percent) than elderly whites[7] (32 percent) owned a home worth $50,000 or more in 1979. (Note that the
value of homes owned by Hispanics is affected by their geographic concentration in the West, where property values are higher.)

Reverse-annuity mortgage programs that allow homeowners access
to accumulated financial equity in their homes have emerged as a means
of supplementing current incomes of elderly homeowners. Although in-
novative income programs for the elderly as for others should be encouraged, it is important to recognize that the main beneficiaries of this
particular type of program are middle-class and upper-class whites. Few
older blacks own property which has enough value to provide a reasonable income over a substantial period of time or is located in neighborhoods of interest to bankers and investors capable of providing a reverse-
annuity mortgage plan.

Housing Costs

Housing Costs of Owners as a Percentage of Income

While older persons usually own their own home, the house is likely
to be old and require substantial maintenance. As a result, the costs of
maintenance may be high and consume a large share of the income of
the homeowner. More than half of the housing owned by the elderly is

---

[7]"Whites" includes Hispanics who are white.

over 30 years old. If the homeowners have lived in a residence long enough to pay off a 30-year mortgage, the homeowners and the home have grown old together. At this stage the house is likely to need major repairs and the owners are not likely to be physically able to do the work. The houses of the elderly are also often large and occupied by only a single older person. Hence, just when the houses may have expensive repair costs, the homeowners may be dependent on a single source of income. As a consequence, a much larger share of income is often expended on housing by older owners than by younger owners.

A mortgage payment is a major housing cost for homeowners. Data for 1980 show that older homeowners without a mortgage on their house spend a much smaller proportion of their income for housing costs than do older renters (Table 9.8). On the other hand, older homeowners with a mortgage on their home spend a slightly higher proportion of their income on housing than do older renters, except at the young-old ages and the lowest annual income level (i.e., under $2,500). Owners without a mortgage dominate among elderly householders, however. Less than one fifth of elderly *homeowners* live in a mortgaged home and less than one third of elderly *householders* are renters. As a result, nearly three fifths of all elderly householders own their home "free and clear."

Within each income group, older male homeowners with a mortgage were likely to be paying nearly the same proportion of their income

TABLE 9.8

Median Housing Costs as a Percentage of Household Income for Older Householders, by Age and Sex of Householder and Housing Tenure: 1980

	Male			Female		
Age	Owner Without Mortgage	Owner with Mortgage	Renter	Owner Without Mortgage	Owner with Mortgage	Renter
55–59	7.0	13.9	16.2	12.8	22.8	25.9
60–64	8.1	15.6	17.8	14.6	26.1	27.2
65–69	10.9	20.5	21.7	17.5	33.1	29.8
70–74	12.5	24.0	23.5	19.1	36.5	30.8
75–79	13.5	27.6	24.6	20.5	37.4	31.4
80–84	14.6	30.5	25.5	21.6	38.4	31.7
85 and Over	15.6	33.4	25.8	22.3	39.3	31.8
25–64	7.2	18.1	18.4	13.1	24.7	27.2

SOURCE: U.S. Bureau of the Census, 1980 Census of Population and Housing, Public Use Microdata Sample; special tabulations prepared for U.S. Senate Special Committee on Aging, Committee Print, serial no. 99-D (October 1985).

NOTE: Married-couple households may be classified as either male- or female-headed households, but were reported almost entirely as having male householders.

542

for housing as older female homeowners with a mortgage, irrespective of age (Table 9.9). For example, males aged 75–79 with an annual income of $7,500–$9,999 in 1979 were spending 32 percent of their income for housing compared with 34 percent for the females in the same age and income bracket. However, a larger proportion of females fell in the lowest income bracket so that, for each age group, the median proportion of income paid by females for housing expenses was higher than the median proportion paid by males (Table 9.8; Figure 9.1).

The shares of income paid for housing expenses by elderly householders who own their home free and clear were slightly higher for female householders for most age and income categories than for male householders. Like female homeowners with a mortgage, female homeowners without a mortgage fell in the lower income groups in greater proportions; thus, at each age, irrespective of income, female homeowners without a mortgage paid a higher median amount for housing costs as a share of income than male homeowners without a mortgage. In addition, for both female and male householders, the proportion of income paid rose substantially with age. For example, male owners without a mortgage aged 85 and over paid about 16 percent, compared with 11 percent for male owners without a mortgage aged 65–69 (Table 9.8; Figure 9.1). The corresponding percentages for females also rose by 5 points.

Great differences in shares of income paid for mortgaged housing compared with nonmortgaged housing for different age groups and at different income levels are shown by the data in Tables 9.8 and 9.9. For example, male (including married-couple) householders aged 65–69 with a mortgage paid 20 percent of their income in annual housing costs compared with only 11 percent for the corresponding householders without a mortgage. At income level $7,500–$9,999, the respective shares were 33 percent and 16 percent, and these figures applied approximately at all higher ages at this income level.

Owner householders not in married couples were more likely to be living in the less costly units than married-couple households, as indicated by annual owner costs for elderly households (Table 9.10). The median annual cost in 1979 was $1,318 for the former and $1,520 for the latter, for nonmortgaged units. Mortgaged units had a similar difference.

Gross Rent of Renters as a Percentage of Income

Older renters are often in a less financially stable residential situation than older homeowners. Their rent may be raised periodically or irregularly, with the result that their budget may experience financial

TABLE 9.9

*Median Housing Costs as a Percentage of Household Income, for Male
and Female Elderly Householders, by Selected Householder Ages,
Household Income, and Housing Tenure: 1980*

Housing Tenure and Household Income	Male			
	Ages 65–69	Ages 75–79	Ages 85 and Over	Ages 25–64
Owner, Without Mortgage				
Total	10.9	13.5	15.6	7.2
Under $2,500	40.7	40.3	39.6	41.5
$2,500–$4,999	29.5	28.0	28.3	31.9
$7,500–$9,999	15.8	15.9	15.6	15.4
$15,000–$17,499	9.7	9.0	9.5	8.7
25,000–$29,999	5.9	6.0	6.1	5.7
$40,000–$49,999	5.3	5.5	5.2	5.2
$75,000 and over	5.2	5.3	5.3	5.2
Owner, with Mortgage				
Total	20.5	27.6	33.4	18.1
Under $2,500	42.5	42.5	42.5	42.5
$2,500–$4,999	42.0	41.8	42.0	42.3
$7,500–$9,999	33.4	32.0	35.4	37.7
$15,000–$17,499	20.5	21.0	20.2	24.1
$25,000–$29,999	12.9	13.5	15.0	17.3
$40,000–$49,999	9.4	9.0	7.9	11.8
$75,000 and over	9.1	9.1	8.2	10.6
Renter				
Total	21.7	24.6	25.8	18.4
Under $2,500	53.7	52.0	51.4	60.2
$2,500–$4,999	39.7	34.7	35.0	53.2
$7,500–$9,999	26.7	26.9	26.7	29.0
$15,000–$17,499	18.1	18.9	21.1	18.8
$25,000–$29,999	11.2	13.0	10.9	12.0
$40,000–$49,999	8.4	8.9	8.7	8.8
$75,000 and over	7.5	7.5	7.5	7.5

SOURCE: U.S. Bureau of the Census, 1980 Census of Population and Housing, Public Use Microdata Sample; special tabulations prepared for U.S. Senate Special Committee on Aging, Committee Print, serial no. 99-D (October 1985).

NOTE: Married-couple households may be classified as either male- or female-headed households, but were reported almost entirely as having male householders.

havoc, particularly if their income is fixed or nearly fixed. The entire building in which they live may be sold and demolished or converted to condominiums or cooperatives. In addition, older renters, like renters in general, receive none of the financial benefits that are gained from home

TABLE 9.9 (*continued*)

	Female			
	Ages 65–69	Ages 75–79	85 and Over	Ages 25–64
Owner, Without Mortgage				
Total	17.5	20.5	22.3	13.1
Under $2,500	40.8	40.3	40.3	41.7
$2,500–$4,999	32.1	31.0	32.1	34.7
$7,500–$9,999	16.3	15.8	15.9	16.6
$15,000–$17,499	9.5	9.7	9.0	10.1
$25,000–$29,999	6.1	6.1	6.2	6.1
$40,000–$49,999	5.4	5.3	5.2	5.4
$75,000 and over	5.3	5.2	5.4	5.4
Owner, with Mortgage				
Total	33.1	37.4	39.3	24.7
Under $2,500	42.4	42.5	42.5	42.5
$2,500–$4,999	42.1	41.9	42.3	42.3
$7,500–$9,999	32.3	33.9	36.3	37.2
$15,000–$17,499	20.5	20.4	22.0	24.1
$25,000–$29,999	12.8	15.8	13.1	16.8
$40,000–$49,999	9.9	10.2	10.7	11.5
$75,000 and over	9.5	9.4	9.4	10.3
Renter				
Total	29.8	31.4	31.8	27.2
Under $2,500	54.4	52.4	50.2	60.2
$2,500–$4,999	42.0	38.2	37.8	55.0
$7,500–$9,999	29.1	30.1	29.1	31.2
$15,000–$17,499	18.3	18.9	18.9	20.5
$25,000–$29,999	10.4	12.0	12.6	13.1
$40,000–$49,999	8.2	8.5	8.8	8.8
$75,000 and over	7.5	7.5	7.5	7.5

ownership, such as accrual of equity in the home, income tax deductions, participation in reverse-annuity mortgage programs, and reduced interest on home-secured loans. Moreover, they are dependent on the building owner or management firm for repairs and maintenance.

The amount paid for rent may be considered a rough measure of housing quality, with very low rents suggesting poor housing quality. Units for which no rent is paid may be of good quality, however; they may be occupied by the managers of a rental complex or provided free to certain tenants for services rendered. For this and other reasons, the

FIGURE 9.1

Median Housing Costs as a Percentage of Household Income, for Older Households, by Age and Sex of Householder and Housing Tenure: 1980

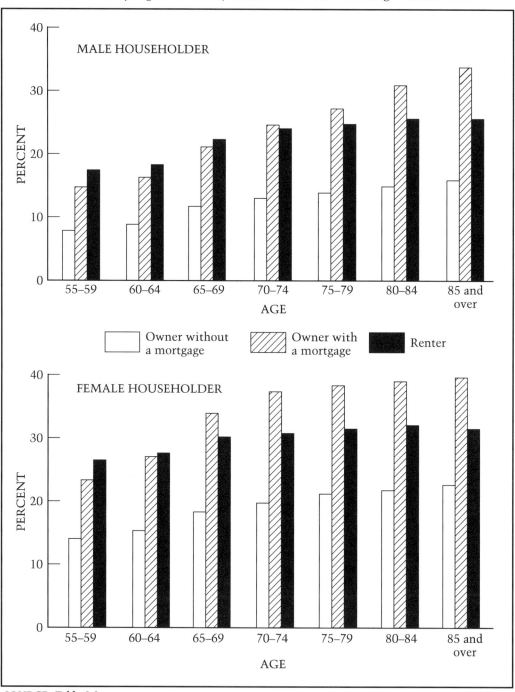

SOURCE: Table 9.8.

NOTE: Married-couple households may be classified as having either male or female householders, but were reported almost entirely as having male householders.

amount paid for rent must be used cautiously as an indicator of housing quality; it should preferably be used in combination with other indicators, taking into account the type of housing and the number of rooms.

By this criterion—payment of higher rents—older married couples who rent live in housing units of better quality than older renters who are not in married couples. In 1980, older persons not in married couples who rented were about four times as likely as married couples who rented to be living in units where the annual rent is less than $1,200 (Table 9.11). About an equal proportion of elderly men (21 percent) and elderly women (22 percent) not in married couples who rented lived in units valued at the lowest end of the rental fee scale (less than $1,200 annually). Because there are far more elderly female renters, however, there were four times as many elderly unmarried female householders as elderly unmarried male householders living in units renting for less than $1,200 annually in 1980. For renter householders in general—that is, including the nonelderly renters—the situation between the sexes is rather different; female renters not in married couples were twice as likely as male renters not in married couples to be living in low-valued rental housing and there were three times as many such females as males.

If housing costs as a percentage of income are compared for homeowners with a mortgage, homeowners without a mortgage, and renters, then older persons with a mortgage allocate the highest proportion of income to housing of all three renter-owner groups. Elderly persons with a mortgage constitute such a small proportion of all elderly homeowners (only 18 percent), however, that the effect of including them is not apparent when housing costs are examined for all elderly homeowners combined. In spite of the low absolute amount spent on rent by many older persons, older renters spend proportionately much more of their total annual household income on housing than do older homeowners without mortgages (Table 9.8).

The share of income spent on gross rent by elderly renters is substantially higher than for nonelderly renters. In 1980, elderly renters spent about 28 percent of their income on rent or maintenance compared with about 23 percent for younger persons. The proportion of income spent by older renters for housing increases with advancing age, albeit only slightly after age 75, just like the situation with older homeowners (Table 9.8). This rise reflects mainly the decline in income with age rather than a rise in rents.

For the elderly renter population, according to 1980 census data, the proportion of income paid for rent is greatest for those elderly renters with an annual income of $2,500 or less. Regardless of the sex or age of the renter, this income group spent at least $1,250, or half of its income, on rent, leaving only $104 or less per month for food, medical care,

TABLE 9.10

Annual Owner-Costs Distribution of Owner-Occupied Housing Units, by Type of Household and Age of Householder: 1980

Type of Household and Age of Householder	Number (in thousands)	Percent	Total Units								Median[a] (dollars)
			Less Than $600	$600– $899	$900– $1,199	$1,200– $1,499	$1,500– $1,799	$1,800– $2,399	$2,400– $2,999	$3,000 or More	
			Nonmortgaged Units								
Married-Couple Families											
All Ages[b]	8,682	100.0	1.7	7.2	15.0	18.4	16.9	22.0	10.0	8.8	1,630
45–64	4,182	100.0	1.0	5.0	12.4	17.6	17.5	24.5	11.7	10.3	1,740
65 and over	3,424	100.0	2.0	9.5	17.8	19.5	16.3	19.3	8.3	7.3	1,520
Male Householder, No Wife Present											
All Ages[b]	1,178	100.0	7.7	14.9	19.1	17.6	13.3	15.4	6.6	5.4	1,340
45–64	385	100.0	6.7	13.2	17.9	17.8	14.2	16.9	7.3	6.0	1,400
65 and over	614	100.0	8.2	16.0	19.6	17.6	12.8	14.5	6.1	5.2	1,310
Female Householder, No Husband Present											
All Ages[b]	4,086	100.0	4.4	13.8	20.0	18.9	14.4	16.2	6.8	5.5	1,390
45–64	1,246	100.0	2.8	10.1	17.8	19.2	16.0	19.1	8.3	6.7	1,500
65 and over	2,613	100.0	5.2	15.9	21.3	18.7	13.5	14.6	6.0	4.8	1,320

TABLE 9.10 (continued)

Type of Household and Age of Householder	Number (in thousands)	Percent	Less Than $600	$600–$899	$900–$1,199	$1,200–$1,499	$1,500–$1,799	$1,800–$2,399	$2,400–$2,999	$3,000 or More	Median[a] (dollars)
					Mortgaged Units						
Married-Couple Families											
All Ages[b]	20,933	100.0	8.1	10.7	12.6	12.4	11.4	17.8	11.2	15.8	4,520
45–64	7,526	100.0	10.9	14.0	14.9	13.0	10.7	15.0	8.7	12.8	4,070
65 and over	977	100.0	26.4	18.7	15.6	11.4	8.2	9.6	4.6	5.5	3,190
Male Householder, No Wife Present											
All Ages[b]	1,600	100.0	13.6	11.9	12.4	11.7	10.4	15.7	9.9	14.3	4,220
45–64	463	100.0	18.6	15.4	14.3	11.7	9.4	12.6	7.4	10.6	3,680
65 and over	125	100.0	38.9	17.0	13.2	9.2	6.6	7.8	3.5	3.8	2,800
Female Householder, No Husband Present											
All Ages[b]	2,950	100.0	19.9	16.1	15.4	12.7	9.9	12.6	6.4	7.0	3,540
45–64	1,184	100.0	22.6	18.5	16.4	12.2	9.0	10.8	5.1	5.4	3,320
65 and over	445	100.0	41.9	17.5	13.0	8.8	5.9	6.8	3.0	3.1	2,680

SOURCE: U.S. Bureau of the Census, 1980 Census of Housing, *U.S. Summary: Detailed Characteristics*, HC80-2-1, Tables A-5, and A-6.

[a] Rounded to nearest ten dollars.
[b] Ages 15 and over.

TABLE 9.11

Annual Gross Rent Distribution of Renter-Occupied Housing Units, by Type of Household and Age of Householder: 1980

Type of Household and Age of Householder	Total Units		Less Than $1,200	$1,200–$2,399	$2,400–$3,599	$3,600–$4,799	$4,800 or More	No Cash Rent	Median[a] (dollars)
	Number (in thousands)	Percent							
Married-Couple Families									
All ages[b]	9,955	100.0	2.3	20.0	37.0	21.3	12.9	6.5	$3,180
45–64	2,004	100.0	2.7	19.6	31.9	20.7	16.0	9.1	3,260
65 and over	1,154	100.0	5.7	27.7	31.3	16.1	9.8	9.4	2,830
Male Householder, No Wife Present									
All ages[b]	6,441	100.0	5.7	27.0	37.4	17.1	9.1	3.7	2,870
45–64	1,204	100.0	9.1	34.2	31.6	12.8	6.8	5.5	2,530
65 and over	720	100.0	21.2	38.1	21.6	6.9	3.6	8.6	1,930
Female Householder, No Husband Present									
All ages[b]	10,856	100.0	10.5	27.6	36.2	15.5	6.7	3.5	2,710
45–64	2,196	100.0	10.0	31.5	34.5	14.1	5.9	4.0	2,590
65 and over	2,775	100.0	22.5	33.2	25.1	8.5	3.8	6.9	2,080

SOURCE: U.S. Bureau of the Census, 1980 Census of Housing, U.S. Summary: Detailed Characteristics, HC80-2-1, Table A-2.

[a] Rounded to nearest ten dollars.
[b] Ages 15 and over.

clothing, and amenities. For elderly renter households in the other income groups also, the proportion of income paid for rent did not vary with increasing age of the renter. For example, at income level $7,500–$9,999, male renters aged 65–69 paid about 27 percent of their annual income for rent, as did male renters aged 85 years and over (Table 9.9).

Again, elderly females are likely to be paying a higher proportion of their annual income for rent than elderly males. For example, males aged 65–69 spent 22 percent while females spent 30 percent; males aged 85 and over spent 26 percent while females spent 32 percent. The less favorable income distribution of older females accounts for these differences since housing costs as a share of income were generally similar for the sexes at each income level.

Housing costs for all older renters are becoming a more critical factor in their monthly budgets. Within the older renter population, females who rent and particularly the oldest females who rent, have the least amount of expendable income for budget items other than rent. Lower incomes, coupled with the rise in the proportion of income spent for housing as age increases, and the upward secular trend in costs, are bringing more older persons to the point of having too few dollars left over to cover basic food and health costs. The older renter cannot look forward to the day when the mortgage is paid and housing costs drop. Renters live each day anticipating that the rent may increase and that it may consume proportionately more and more of their income. This prospect or its reality may cause them to seek cheaper living quarters of poorer quality or perhaps abandon their home altogether for the street.

Density of Occupancy and the Overhousing Issue

We next consider household size in relation to the characteristics of the housing unit, particularly variations by ownership, cost, and number of rooms. There is particular interest in the density of occupancy—that is, the issues of overhousing and crowding.

Several generalizations can be made regarding household size in relation to housing tenure at the older ages. First, owners have larger households than renters at all older ages of the householder. Second, households headed by males (including married-couple households) are larger than households headed by females at all older ages of the householder for the three tenure categories, and there is little variation in the male-female difference as age of householder rises. Third, the number of persons per household declines with the age of the householder for all tenure categories at the *older* ages, but the changes among the *elderly* are slight.

Owner-occupied households may be larger than renter-occupied households because they more often include additional adults, such as a spouse. The dependents formerly living in these households have left them to establish their own households as they got older. The larger size of male-headed households may be explained by the fact that nearly all married-couple households tend to be reported as male-headed (even though they can be assigned to *either* the male-headed *or* female-headed categories) and that relatively few men live alone.

There is a modest association between size of household of the elderly and their economic status as represented by monthly housing costs. The median number of persons per household for elderly households increases slightly and irregularly with an increase in monthly housing costs. This is true for male and female householders and for each tenure category. In addition, median size at every level of monthly housing costs is higher for male-headed households than for female-headed households, for each tenure category. Average size never gets very high, however, the maximum figure being only 2.2 persons for housing units with male householders who owned their homes with a mortgage and who had monthly costs between $250 and $750 in 1980.

It is often observed that many elderly people are "overhoused," that is, that they occupy more housing space than they need. This is a subjective judgment, but it is a reasonable inference from the data. I have previously noted that most of the elderly live alone or with a spouse only, that the size of elderly households is smaller than that of younger households, that many elderly persons "age in place," and that most own their home. Elderly householders who own their home would be expected, therefore, to have more housing space than younger householders who own their home. In fact, the same should apply to all elderly householders, not just owners.

These expectations are borne out. Moreover, this relationship appears to be independent of the number of persons in the household or inversely related to it. For households with female householders (no husband present) aged 65 and over, the number of *persons per room* in 1980 was 0.89 for a 3-room unit and 0.30 for a 4-room unit and remained at about the lower level of density for larger housing units. The number of *persons per unit* in such households hardly varied from 1-to-4-room units (1.22 to 1.26), but then rose gradually to 1.82 persons per unit for units with 8 rooms or more. The housing units of younger householders (e.g., those aged 25–34 and 35–44) were much more densely occupied, with persons per unit ranging from 2.20 for 1-room units to 3.86 for 7-room units.

Elderly persons often live alone in large housing units, aging-in-place after other family members have died or moved away. In 1980, over two thirds of the female householders living alone occupied units of 5 rooms or more. The median age of homeowners living alone in 3-to-6-room units is over 65 and the median age of homeowners living alone in 7-room and 8-room-or-more units is over 60. Renters living alone tend to be much younger—that is, between 45 and 50—and live in smaller units. Two-person owned units have householders nearly as old as one-person owned units, with a median age exceeding 60 for units of 3, 4, or 5 rooms. Householders in units with 3 persons or more tend to be younger.

The overhousing of the elderly as a common situation seems to be substantiated. It means more housing space but not necessarily more housing value. In fact, overhousing is associated with less housing value, higher maintenance costs, and probably lower housing quality.

Housing Quality

It is virtually self-evident that the quality of the home environment influences the psychological and physical well-being of its occupants. If we accept this premise, the home environment becomes increasingly important for the occupants as the amount of time spent in the home increases. This notion is particularly applicable to the elderly because, as might be expected, the amount of time spent at home increases in later life as a result of retirement, a decrease in expendable income, and the onset of physical limitations. The quality of the home environment affects the psychological and physical well-being of the occupants more and more as they get older, particularly if money or energy is not available to maintain the home in good physical condition and to modify it to meet the changing needs of the aging occupants. For example, the elderly have increased risks of respiratory infection if they live in units that are improperly heated or that lack humidification, and increased risks of serious falls and injuries in units that are badly lit.

The census does not provide sufficient information to establish whether a unit is of substandard quality on the basis of its structural soundness. Hence, a number of proxy indicators must be used to provide information on the quality of housing. These include the age of the structure (or alternatively the year the occupants moved in or purchased the unit) and the presence of certain facilities and amenities. Age and structural soundness have been shown to be correlated. In the discussion below, there is an underlying assumption that the age of the housing unit is associated with its physical condition, and hence with its quality as a residence.

Age of Housing

Because older persons tend to age in place, their housing tends to age along with them. This is especially true for older homeowners, many of whom live in old homes. In general, older renters are more likely to live in newer units than older homeowners, even for the corresponding sex-age groups.

The older the householder, the older the unit he/she occupies is likely to be. In 1980, only one quarter of male householders aged 55–59 and just less than one third of female householders at these ages lived in housing units that were built in 1939 or earlier (Table 9.12). The proportion of the population living in units built in those years rises with increasing age of the householder to nearly half for all householders aged 85 years and over. Conversely, the proportion living in units built in 1970 or later decreases steadily for both male and female householders between ages 55–59 and 85 and over.

The pattern of a much older age for the housing of elderly owners than elderly renters applies to the separate race/Hispanic origin groups.

TABLE 9.12

Distribution by Year Structure Built of Occupied Housing Units, for Householders Aged 55 and Over, by Sex and Age: 1980

Sex and Age of Householder	Total Percent	1939 or Earlier	1940– 1949	1950– 1959	1960– 1969	1970– 1980
Male						
55–59	100	26	11	24	21	18
60–64	100	28	13	23	19	17
65–69	100	32	14	20	17	17
70–74	100	36	14	18	16	16
75–79	100	40	13	16	17	14
80–84	100	44	12	15	16	13
85 and over	100	48	12	15	14	11
Female						
55–59	100	31	14	21	18	16
60–64	100	35	14	19	16	16
65–69	100	37	14	17	16	16
70–74	100	39	14	15	16	16
75–79	100	43	13	14	16	14
80–84	100	46	12	13	15	14
85 and over	100	51	11	12	13	12

SOURCE: U.S. Bureau of the Census, 1980 Census of Housing, Public Use Microdata Sample; special tabulations prepared for U.S. Senate Special Committee on Aging, Committee Print, serial no. 99-D (October 1985).

In 1980 30 percent of elderly white homeowners lived in homes that were purchased over 30 years earlier (1949 or earlier). On the other hand, only 8 percent of elderly white renters had moved into their home by 1950. Conversely, 25 percent of elderly white homeowners and 65 percent of elderly white renters in 1980 moved into their current residence in 1970 or later.

The pattern is similar for older blacks and Hispanics. Older owners and renters of these groups also show a tremendous disparity in the number of years they had lived in their home or the age of their housing. As of 1980, 32 percent of elderly black owners and 22 percent of elderly Hispanic owners had lived in the same unit since 1949 or earlier. The corresponding figures for renters are 6 percent for each group. Conversely, a much larger share of elderly black and Hispanic renters than homeowners had moved into their current residence since 1970. The figures are 60 percent for elderly black renters and 80 percent for elderly Hispanic renters compared with 18 percent for elderly black owners and 27 percent for elderly Hispanic owners.

Although the age of the housing unit is only a rough indicator of housing quality, older dwellings are more likely to have structural deficiencies resulting from inadequate original construction, progressive deterioration, or subsequent neglect. Moreover, while a residential move in itself does not ensure that the quality of a later-model home environment will be better than the quality of the earlier-model home environment, the later model is somewhat more likely to be better than the earlier one. Older homes, for example, are more likely to contain older heating systems. If the system fails, the homeowner alone is responsible for the cost of repair or replacement. Few older homeowners have the benefit of a maintenance contract for heating equipment. Although such a contract does not insure the homeowner against equipment failure, it may increase the likelihood that a small problem will be taken care of before it becomes major, and it may reduce the costs of repair in the long term.

Housing Structure and Facilities

The extent to which housing lacks certain facilities or suffers from certain defects represents a fairly direct basis of measuring its quality. According to the Department of Housing and Urban Development, inadequate or substandard housing is characterized by one or more of the following conditions: incomplete plumbing, incomplete kitchen facilities, lack of or insufficient heating equipment (except in the South); certain maintenance defects (e.g., a leaking roof, holes in the floor, holes in the walls or ceilings); electrical defects (e.g., exposed wiring, rooms without a working wall outlet); and lack of independent access to a flush toilet.[8] In addition, the lack of air conditioning and the absence of a telephone in the unit are indirect indicators of housing quality.[9] The 1980 census provides data for some of these indicators of housing quality, cross-tabulated variously by the age, sex, and race of the householder and the tenure and mortgage status of the unit.

On the whole, older persons do not occupy housing of poorer quality than younger persons, if we judge by the availability or lack of the facilities enumerated above. However, some subgroups of the older population, particularly the older aged and the elderly in rural areas, do occupy housing of poorer quality; and certain racial/ethnic groups, such as blacks and American Indians/Eskimos/Aleuts, occupy housing of poorer quality regardless of age. We consider these and other variations below.

Persons aged 85 and over, regardless of the sex of the householder or the tenure of the housing unit, are slightly more likely to live in housing that lacks a complete kitchen than younger persons (Table 9.13). Otherwise, there is little variation in the lack of a complete kitchen by age among elderly householders. Elderly male renters, even those under age 85, are more likely to live in housing with incomplete kitchen facilities than elderly male owners or elderly female renters or owners (Table 9.13). Elderly female renters are the next most likely group to live in housing without a complete kitchen, but the proportion is low and about the same as for ages below 65 (2.3 percent in 1980).

About 21 percent of housing units occupied by elderly households, compared with 17 percent of all housing units, lacked a central heating system in 1980 (Table 9.14). Close to half (47 percent) of all elderly households across the country lacked air conditioning, but this percentage was not much above that for all housing units. In part, this may be due to the relatively recent introduction of central air conditioning and the physical difficulties associated with installing window/wall units. This amenity is probably tied more closely to the age of the housing unit than is central heating, the mechanics of which are much older.

As persons age, they accommodate less satisfactorily to extreme external temperatures, and without proper heating and cooling devices, the risks to health increase. The lack of adequate home heating poses the threat of hypothermia (i.e., subnormal body temperatures) and even

---

[8] Complete kitchens contain an installed sink with piped water, a range or cookstove, and a mechanical refrigerator. Complete plumbing facilities include hot and cold piped water inside the structure as well as a flush toilet, and a bathtub or a shower inside the structure for the exclusive use of the household occupants.

[9] Air conditioning includes both central systems and individual refrigeration units.

TABLE 9.13

Percentage of Older Persons in Occupied Housing Units Lacking a Telephone and Complete Kitchen Facilities, by Sex and Age of Householder and Housing Tenure: 1980 (number in thousands)

Sex of Householder, Housing Tenure, and Measure of Quality	Age						
	60–64	65–69	70–74	75–79	80–84	85 and over	25–64
Male							
Renter-Occupied							
Total persons	778	696	560	401	230	139	13,251
Percent without telephone	14.8	14.5	13.0	12.0	11.1	12.2	14.7
Percent incomplete kitchen	4.7	5.0	4.9	4.8	4.9	6.0	3.2
Owner-Occupied with Mortgage							
Total persons	1,199	654	334	163	75	52	21,934
Percent without telephone	1.5	1.8	2.0	2.5	2.2	2.7	1.4
Percent incomplete kitchen	0.6	0.8	0.9	1.2	0.9	1.0	0.6
Owner-Occupied without Mortgage							
Total persons	1,578	1,534	1,197	762	400	233	6,734
Percent without telephone	2.3	2.5	2.8	3.1	3.4	4.1	3.6
Percent incomplete kitchen	1.1	1.2	1.3	1.6	1.6	2.1	1.7
Female							
Renter-Occupied							
Total persons	1,128	1,156	1,060	867	555	346	14,347
Percent without telephone	7.8	6.7	5.6	5.3	4.8	6.2	11.3
Percent incomplete kitchen	2.5	2.4	2.3	2.3	2.8	3.6	2.3
Owner-Occupied with Mortgage							
Total persons	1,092	675	412	260	159	118	22,615
Percent without telephone	1.3	1.4	1.5	1.8	1.7	1.4	1.3
Percent incomplete kitchen	0.7	0.9	0.9	0.9	0.9	1.1	0.6
Owner-Occupied without Mortgage							
Total persons	1,975	1,897	1,529	1,063	623	415	8,273
Percent without telephone	1.8	1.9	2.0	2.3	2.4	2.9	2.7
Percent incomplete kitchen	1.1	1.1	1.3	1.4	1.4	1.7	1.4

SOURCE: U.S. Bureau of the Census, 1980 Census of Housing, Public Use Microdata Sample; special tabulation prepared for U.S. Senate Special Committee on Aging, Committee Print, serial no. 99-D (October 1985).

TABLE 9.14

Percentage of Occupied Housing Units Maintained by Persons Aged 65 and Over Lacking Selected Facilities, by Type of Residence: 1980 (numbers in thousands)

			Urban			
			Inside Urbanized Areas		Outside Urbanized Areas	
Facility Lacking	Total	Total	Total	Central City	Urban Fringe	Places of 10,000 or More	Places of 2,500–10,000
Units of Persons Aged 65 and Over							
Occupied Housing Units	16,888	12,547	9,979	5,431	4,547	1,163	1,406
Incomplete plumbing	3.0	1.5	1.3	1.6	1.0	1.9	2.3
Incomplete kitchen	2.4	1.4	1.3	1.6	0.9	1.5	1.8
No central heating	20.9	15.1	12.7	15.3	9.5	23.1	26.0
No air conditioning	47.2	43.3	43.0	46.0	39.3	42.7	46.2
No telephone	5.0	3.9	3.6	4.6	2.3	4.6	5.5
All Units							
Occupied Housing Units	80,390	60,557	50,550	25,276	25,274	4,838	5,169
Year-Round Units[a]	86,759	64,666	53,824	27,143	26,681	5,210	5,633
Incomplete plumbing	3.3	2.1	2.0	2.8	1.2	2.5	3.0
Incomplete kitchen	2.5	1.6	1.5	2.0	1.0	1.9	2.3
No central heating	17.2	12.7	11.0	14.2	7.9	19.2	22.3
No air conditioning	45.0	41.6	40.9	45.0	36.6	42.7	47.1
No telephone	7.1	6.2	5.8	8.0	3.6	8.2	9.0

SOURCE: U.S. Bureau of the Census, 1980 Census of Housing, *U.S. Summary: Detailed Characteristics,* HC80-1-B1, Tables 78 and 81.

[a] Percentages based on year-round units.

death. Excessive heat poses a special threat for older persons, particularly those with heart conditions and respiratory diseases.

For older persons living alone, the telephone is an especially important link with the outside world. Access to a telephone can be critical during an emergency. In general, it can serve to reduce the isolation of the elderly and, in particular, it can serve as a means by which housebound older persons maintain continuing social contact with others. Although lack of a telephone is not a structural feature, it is generally associated with lower housing quality.

Telephone availability for the older population varies in accordance with the sex and age of the householder and housing tenure (Table 9.13). Males living in rented housing are far less likely to have a telephone than males living in owned housing. Over 1 in 8 male renters in the age

TABLE 9.14 (*continued*)

| | Rural | | | Inside | Outside |
Total	Places of 1,000–2,500	Rural-Farm	SMSAs	SMSAs
4,340	731	457	11,888	5,010
7.2	2.8	6.4	1.8	5.6
5.2	2.1	4.5	1.6	4.2
37.8	27.9	41.8	15.1	34.8
58.4	51.3	55.6	44.7	53.1
8.1	8.0	4.4	3.9	7.4
19,832	2,551	1,821	60,498	19,892
22,092	2,806	1,821	64,632	22,127
6.6	3.5	4.5	2.3	6.1
4.9	2.6	2.8	1.7	4.6
30.5	24.5	33.5	12.7	30.3
55.2	52.4	51.9	42.3	52.9
9.5	9.2	4.6	6.0	10.4

group 65 and over do not have a telephone. This group of older social isolates may be easily overlooked because they make up such a small proportion of all older householders. Older males have higher proportions of "phonelessness" than older females regardless of tenure. Older females living in renter-occupied households have less than half the proportion of phonelessness (i.e., about 1 in 16) of older male renters, but because of the far greater number of older females, the numbers of phoneless females and phoneless males in the renter group are roughly similar in all age groups aged 65 and over.

The availability of automobiles and of television sets in the homes of older persons would also affect their degree of social isolation. About 3 in 4 elderly households (2 in 3 "aged" households) have access to a motor vehicle. The decrease in the ability of older persons to drive automobiles as they age adds to their possible isolation as does any reluctance they might have to leave their home because of concern about their safety outside.

TABLE 9.15

Percentage of Occupied Housing Units Maintained by Persons Aged 65 and Over Lacking Selected Facilities, by Region and Type of Residence: 1980
(numbers in thousands)

| Region and Facility Lacking | Total | Urban | | | | | |
| | | Total | Inside Urbanized Areas | | | Outside Urbanized Areas | |
			Total	Central City	Urban Fringe	Places of 10,000 or More	Places of 2,500– 10,000
Northeast							
Occupied Housing Units	3,929	3,247	2,901	1,449	1,452	140	206
Incomplete plumbing	2.2	1.8	1.8	2.3	1.2	2.1	1.9
Incomplete kitchen	1.4	1.2	1.2	1.6	0.8	1.0	1.1
No telephone	3.7	3.7	3.7	5.3	2.1	3.5	3.2
No central heating	7.1	5.7	5.4	6.6	4.3	8.4	8.2
No air conditioning	59.8	55.8	53.6	57.3	49.9	74.7	74.0
Midwest/North Central Region							
Occupied Housing Units	4,429	3,118	2,298	1,338	960	382	438
Incomplete plumbing	2.6	1.4	1.3	1.6	0.9	1.7	4.4
Incomplete kitchen	1.9	1.1	1.1	1.3	0.8	1.1	1.3
No telephone	3.4	2.8	2.7	3.6	1.6	2.8	3.3
No central heating	11.8	7.1	5.7	6.9	4.1	9.5	12.5
No air conditioning	46.2	41.2	41.2	45.6	35.1	39.7	42.7
South							
Occupied Housing Units	5,676	3,785	2,772	1,599	1,173	458	555
Incomplete plumbing	4.6	1.6	1.2	1.2	1.1	2.4	3.3
Incomplete kitchen	3.7	1.7	1.4	1.6	1.2	2.3	2.8
No telephone	7.4	5.3	4.4	5.3	3.3	6.6	8.2
No central heating	38.3	28.9	24.1	29.4	17.0	40.0	43.6
No air conditioning	32.8	24.4	21.4	25.5	15.7	30.6	34.7
West							
Occupied Housing Units	2,853	2,397	2,007	1,044	963	182	207
Incomplete plumbing	1.3	1.0	1.0	1.4	0.5	1.0	0.9
Incomplete kitchen	1.7	1.5	1.5	2.0	1.0	1.2	1.2
No telephone	4.2	3.4	3.2	4.1	2.2	4.1	4.9
No central heating	19.7	16.5	15.2	16.7	13.5	20.4	25.4
No air conditioning	59.9	58.8	59.4	62.4	56.1	54.8	56.6

SOURCE: U.S. Bureau of the Census, 1980 Census of Housing, *U.S. Summary: Detailed Characteristics*, HC80-1-B1, Tables 94, 107, 120, and 133.

[a] Places under 1,000 not shown.

TABLE 9.15 *(continued)*

| Total[a] | Rural | | Inside SMSA | Outside SMSA |
	Places of 1,000–2,500	Rural-Farm		
682	122	20	3,288	641
4.1	2.0	5.5	2.0	3.4
2.2	1.1	2.5	1.3	1.9
3.9	3.3	3.3	3.7	3.8
13.7	8.9	19.4	6.0	12.9
78.7	77.0	87.0	56.2	78.4
1,311	272	217	2,812	1,617
5.2	2.0	6.2	1.7	4.0
3.7	1.4	4.6	1.3	2.8
4.9	3.9	3.1	2.9	4.4
23.0	15.2	26.5	7.4	19.5
58.1	46.2	59.3	44.2	49.8
1,891	261	180	3,479	2,197
10.7	4.3	7.6	2.4	8.2
7.9	3.4	5.1	2.2	6.3
11.8	9.5	6.3	5.4	10.7
57.0	48.4	63.6	28.8	53.2
49.6	40.4	45.4	25.3	44.8
457	76	40	2,299	555
3.3	1.4	2.7	1.0	2.7
3.0	1.4	2.0	1.5	2.6
8.0	6.0	4.1	3.4	7.5
36.7	32.9	37.1	16.7	32.3
65.5	65.4	65.6	58.3	66.4

Variations by Type-of-Residence Area and Geographic Region

One notable exception to the generalization that, on the whole, older persons do not occupy housing units of poorer quality than younger persons is the housing situation of the elderly living in rural areas. Older persons living in rural areas are more likely than younger persons living in rural areas to be occupying deficient housing, as measured by the lack of complete plumbing, complete kitchen facilities, air conditioning, and central heating (Table 9.14). Older persons in rural areas are a little more likely to have access to a telephone, however, than younger persons in rural areas.

Considering specific type-of-residence categories, elderly persons living in places of fewer than 1,000 inhabitants and on farms are the most likely to experience the housing deficiencies mentioned above. For example, 8.3 percent and 6.4 percent of the elderly in these two residence categories, respectively, lack complete plumbing, and about 40 percent in each category lack central heating. The next most inadequately housed groups are the elderly living in places of 1,000–2,500 persons and then the elderly living in places of 2,500–10,000 persons. As expected, older persons living in the suburbs are the least likely to reside in homes with one of the five housing deficiencies. Yet, nearly 10 percent of the elderly here lack central heating.

Housing quality for older householders varies somewhat depending on the region of the country in which they reside (Table 9.15). If we examine the data only for the three indicators of quality not influenced by the temperature of the region—that is, incomplete plumbing, incomplete kitchen, and no telephone—then elderly persons residing in the South are slightly more likely to live in housing that is deficient than elderly persons residing in other regions. Elderly persons living on farms and in rural villages in all regions, but especially in the South, continue to be the most likely to live in homes with the types of deficiencies noted. Elderly persons living in the central cities exhibit no clear regional variation in the extent of deficient housing.

Variations by Race/Spanish Origin

If housing quality is examined for race groups and the Spanish-origin population, some wide differences between these groups appear.

The American Indian/Eskimo/Aleut is the most likely of all racial groups to be living in housing without a complete kitchen. According to 1980 census data, 14 percent of housing units headed by elderly American Indians/Eskimos/Aleuts are deficient in this regard (Table 9.16).

TABLE 9.16

Percentage of Occupied Housing Units Maintained by Persons Aged 65 and Over Lacking Selected Facilities, by Detailed Race/Spanish Origin of Householder: 1980

Race/Spanish Origin	Ages 65 and Over				All Ages		
	Incomplete Kitchen Facilities	Incomplete Plumbing Facilities	No Central Heating[a]	No Air Conditioning	Incomplete Kitchen Facilities	Incomplete Plumbing Facilities	No Air Conditioning
All Races	2.4	3.0	20.9	47.2	2.5	3.3	45.0
White	1.8	2.4	18.4	44.9	1.4	2.2	41.9
Black	7.3	18.4	43.5	67.0	4.8	6.4	57.3
Total Asian and Pacific Islander	3.1	3.6	36.3	67.5	2.3	3.8	56.0
Japanese	1.5	1.7	55.8	75.5	1.6	2.1	63.6
Chinese	4.8	5.4	23.8	65.1	2.6	5.5	52.9
Filipino	3.6	4.0	39.0	75.1	2.2	3.0	61.4
Asian Indian	2.0	2.4	17.6	64.7	1.7	2.7	37.9
American Indian/Eskimo/Aleut	13.7	14.2	47.9	63.9	8.6	10.0	59.7
Total Spanish Origin	3.8	4.8	39.4	57.6	3.0	4.8	55.1
Mexican	4.6	5.7	49.9	61.1	3.2	4.9	55.2
Puerto Rican	2.5	4.4	13.6	76.1	3.3	6.4	72.8
Cuban	2.5	2.8	33.6	28.0	2.1	3.1	22.3
Other	3.3	3.9	29.8	57.2	2.7	4.3	53.1

SOURCE: U.S. Bureau of the Census, 1980 Census of Housing, U.S. Summary: Detailed Characteristics, HC80-1-B1, Tables 81 and 83–87.

[a] No comparable data available for all ages.

They fare moderately worse than younger American Indian/Eskimo/Aleut households, but much worse than all elderly households. In 1980, only 2.4 percent of all elderly households lacked complete kitchens.

Blacks are the next most likely of the racial groups to lack complete kitchen facilities. Seven percent of households headed by elderly blacks lacked a complete kitchen in 1980. However, because there are far more black households, many more elderly black households (over 100,000) than elderly American Indian/Eskimo/Aleut households (about 7,500) lack one or more of the three required kitchen features. On the other hand, because elderly blacks themselves constitute only 8 percent of the total elderly population, their housing problems are not readily reflected in the total population figures.

The same general pattern of racial variation in the degree of substandard housing for elderly persons is evidenced with respect to plumbing facilities and central heating systems as with respect to kitchen facilities. Blacks (18 percent) and American Indians/Eskimos/Aleuts (14 percent) lead again in lack of complete plumbing facilities. American Indians (48 percent) and blacks (44 percent) are the most likely to live in dwellings that lack a central heating system. If detailed racial/ethnic subgroups are considered separately, elderly Japanese households (56 percent) and elderly Mexican households (50 percent) are the most likely to lack a central heating system. All these figures are to be evaluated in comparison with the figures for all races combined—3 percent for complete plumbing facilities and 21 percent for central heating systems.

The pattern differs somewhat from region to region (Table 9.17). In the Northeast and Midwest, areas where an efficient heating system would be most critical, elderly American Indians/Eskimos/Aleuts most often lived in housing units lacking this feature in 1980 (17 percent and 30 percent). In the West, elderly Asians (47 percent) were almost as likely as elderly American Indians (55 percent) to live without central heating. In the South, 64 percent of elderly black households lacked central heating in the unit. Most Hispanics of Mexican origin and most American Indians live in the Southwest, where central heating is not considered necessary.

There are very few geographic areas in the country that do not need air conditioning in the summer for one reason or another (i.e., humidity, temperature). Unfortunately, not all older persons can afford to go to Maine for the summer. According to the 1980 census, elderly whites (73 percent) and elderly Asian and Pacific Islanders (72 percent) in the South are most likely to be living in dwellings with some type of air conditioning, while elderly blacks are the least likely to have access to this facility of any of the race/Spanish origin groups in this region (37 percent). (See Table 9.17.)

TABLE 9.17

Percentage of Occupied Housing Units Maintained by Persons Aged 65 and Over Lacking a Central Heating System or Air Conditioning, by Race/Spanish Origin of Householder and Region: 1980

Race/Spanish Origin	United States	Northeast	Midwest/ North Central	South	West
Lacking Central Heating					
All races	20.9	7.1	11.8	38.3	19.7
White	18.4	6.9	11.7	33.4	17.9
Black	43.5	10.6	12.7	64.0	25.6
Asian and Pacific Islander	36.3	6.4	11.2	30.6	47.1
American Indian/ Eskimo/Aleut	47.9	17.1	29.5	54.5	54.6
Spanish origin	39.4	8.2	19.6	57.9	35.8
Lacking Air Conditioning					
All races	47.2	59.8	46.2	32.8	59.9
White	44.9	58.7	44.9	27.2	58.2
Black	67.0	74.7	66.9	63.5	79.1
Asian and Pacific Islander	67.5	58.5	45.3	27.8	78.2
American Indian/ Eskimo/Aleut	64.7	72.7	71.0	45.4	76.8
Spanish origin	57.6	72.8	57.7	41.2	68.8

SOURCE: U.S. Bureau of the Census, 1980 Census of Housing, *U.S. Summary: Detailed Characteristics*, HC80-1-B1, Tables 81, 83–86, 94, 96–100, 107, 109–113, 120, 122–126, 133, and 135–139.

As with the other facilities noted, elderly American Indian and black households are much less likely to have access to a telephone in the home than elderly white and Asian and Pacific Islander households (Table 9.18). It is also common for Hispanics of Puerto Rican and Mexican origin to lack a telephone. Twelve percent or more of the groups cited unfavorably lack a telephone. Unlike the case with other facilities, here the elderly fare better than the rest of the population.

The housing problems of the older members of racial minorities may not be the result mainly of being old, but rather of being members of racial minorities. Older members of racial minorities faced many forms of discrimination while growing up and establishing themselves in the community. Older blacks and American Indians in particular faced discriminatory practices that affected their opportunity and ability to accumulate property. It is reasonable to infer from reviewing the differences in housing characteristics of older whites and older racial minorities

TABLE 9.18

Percentage of Occupied Housing Units Maintained by Persons Aged 65 and Over Lacking a Telephone, by Detailed Race/Spanish Origin of Householder: 1980

Race/Spanish Origin	Units Lacking Telephone,[a] Householder Aged 65 and Over	Percentage of Units Lacking Telephone	
		Ages 65 and Over[b]	All Ages[c]
All Races	839,400	5	7
White	621,800	4	6
Black	177,500	12	16
Total Asian and Pacific Islander	6,700	6	5
Japanese	1,000	3	3
Chinese	1,500	5	4
Filipino	2,400	8	5
Other	1,800	5	7
American Indian/ Eskimo/Aleut	14,400	27	27
Total Spanish Origin	49,600	12	17
Mexican	28,800	13	17
Puerto Rican	8,000	20	28
Cuban	3,400	7	6
Other	9,500	9	12

SOURCE: U.S. Bureau of the Census, 1980 Census of Housing, *U.S. Summary: Detailed Characteristics*, HC80-1-B1, Tables 81 and 83–87.

[a] Rounded to nearest hundred.
[b] Elderly households lacking telephones as percentage of all elderly households of a specified race/origin.
[c] Households of all ages lacking telephones as percentage of households of all ages of a specified race/origin.

that some of the variation in the extent of home ownership, in housing values, and especially in housing quality is attributable to patterns of race relations that were established earlier.

Variations by Living Arrangements

The quality of the housing occupied by the elderly also varies according to type of household and living arrangements. According to Soldo's analysis of survey data for 1979, elderly married-couple households occupy housing of better quality than other elderly households.[10] Married couples are more likely to own their home and owner-occupied units tend to be in better structural condition than renter-occupied units. A similar difference in the quality of units occupied by various types of households applies to rental units separately even though rental units as a group have more structural problems than owner-occupied units.

The elderly who live alone tend to live in housing units with more structural deficiencies since they are more likely to be renters and to be of limited means. Women living alone fare better in the quality of their housing than men living alone since the women are more resourceful in securing necessary assistance. When the housing unit is shared by the elderly person with another person (e.g., a nonelderly relative), it is less likely to be defective than when the elderly person lives alone, largely because the more adequate housing of the younger "host" is available.

American Housing Survey of 1987: Summary

Tenure, Costs, and Value of Housing Units in 1987

The American Housing Survey of 1987 provides more recent data on the housing situation with respect to tenure, costs, value, and quality than the 1980 census.[11] These data are briefly summarized here. About 75 percent of the elderly own their home compared with only 61 percent of the nonelderly. Among the elderly, home ownership rises to a peak in the 55–69 age range and then declines steadily with advancing age. By ages 75 and over, the percentage of homes owned drops to 69. Between 1960 and 1987 home ownership rose more rapidly among the elderly than the nonelderly. Home ownership is relatively highest in the South and relatively lowest in the Northeast.

Elderly owners spend only half as much for housing (in the form of mortgage payments, real estate taxes, utilities, property insurance, etc.) than the nonelderly because most (4 in 5) elderly owners do not have a mortgage and most (7 in 10) younger owners do. Most elderly owners in 1987 have lived in their home long enough to have paid off the loan. Because of their lower income, however, elderly owners spend about the

---

[10]B. J. Soldo, "Household Types, Housing Needs, and Disability," in R. J. Newcomer, M. P. Lawton, and J. O. Byerts, eds., *Housing for an Aging Society—Issues, Alternatives, and Policy* (New York: Van Nostrand Reinhold, 1986).

[11]U.S. Bureau of the Census and U.S. Department of Housing and Urban Development, *The American Housing Survey, United States, 1987*, H150-87 (December 1989).

same percentage of their income for housing as younger owners (19 percent vs. 18 percent). Elderly renters spend a substantially higher percentage of their income on housing (36 percent) than younger renters (28 percent).

By 1987 the value of the homes owned by the elderly had increased to a median of $59,000 compared with $71,000 for younger owners. The difference in age, size, and initial cost of the homes of the elderly account in large part for the difference in current values.

Physical Problems of Housing Units in 1987

The American Housing Survey of 1987 provided data on the quality of housing in that year based on the existence of any of several physical deficits. The data are not fully comparable with 1980 census data or with the 1979 Annual Housing Survey data. The survey reports about the same proportion of housing units with physical problems for the elderly as for the general population—6.5 percent and 7.0 percent. There is no deterioration in housing quality with increasing age of householder among the elderly. The percentage of housing units with severe physical problems approximates 1.2 percent and the percentage with moderate physical problems approximates 5–5.5 percent, whether for the elderly or nonelderly. Elderly married-couple householders show substantially fewer problems, both severe and moderate (0.7 percent and 3.5 percent) than other household types. In addition, slightly fewer elderly owner-occupied units show physical problems than elderly renter-occupied units.

Residential Mobility and Racial Succession in Housing Units

Residential mobility patterns among older persons, as among younger persons, are related to their housing situation. The characteristics of one's housing and one's neighborhood have an effect on the degree of residential satisfaction and, consequently, on the propensity to move.[12] Housing tenure and duration of residence in a community, in particular, are directly related to the propensity to move.[13] For these "reasons" and because of the effect of life cycle influences and community ties on long-

[12] A. Speare, S. Goldstein, and W. H. Frey, *Residential Mobility, Migration, and Metropolitan Change* (Cambridge, MA: Ballinger, 1975).

[13] K. E. McHugh, P. Cohen, and N. Reid, "Determinants of Short- and Long-Term Mobility for Home Owners and Renters," *Demography* 27 (1) (February 1990):81–95.

term moving expectations, renters tend to move more than owners. This is true for renters at the younger ages even if they are satisfied with their present housing. At the older ages, however, tenure makes little difference; older renters and owners have similarly low expectations of moving. Long-term moving expectations decline steadily with age for owners; for renters, the decline begins at the older ages. The residential stability of older renters as of older owners suggests that they tend to view their current residence as permanent. Both are influenced in this decision by such factors as their financial condition, housing preferences, and health status, as well as the availability of alternate housing.[14]

Racial succession in the occupancy of housing units is one of the residential mobility patterns among the older population that are related to its housing situation. The latest pertinent data, compiled by Long and Spain, refer to the period 1967–1971.[15] During this period, only about 3 percent of whites vacating a housing unit were replaced by a black household, but over 29 percent of the black households who moved into a previously occupied housing unit replaced whites (Table 9.19). These figures arithmetically reflect merely the relative difference in the size of the white and black populations. Logically they indicate that the probability of racial succession from white to black is relatively low for white out-movers, but relatively high for black in-movers.

A consistent difference between the black in-mover households and white out-mover households for the 1967–1971 period was the higher age of the white out-movers. The median age of white out-movers was 45 and the median age of black in-movers was 36. The whites who were replaced by blacks tended to be older white couples with lower incomes and levels of education than other white movers who were not replaced by blacks. The percentage of whites replaced by blacks tended roughly to rise with the age of the white out-mover, while the percentage of blacks who replaced whites tended roughly to fall with the age of the black in-mover. For example, the percentage of blacks who replaced whites at ages 65 and over (21 percent) was well below the peak percentage at ages 35–54 (53 percent). Even though the overall mobility rate of older households is far below that of younger households, small differences between in-mover households and out-mover households can rapidly change the character of city neighborhoods, including its racial makeup.

Information regarding the age of the householder is not available in more recent studies of racial residential succession, but the conclusions

[14]McHugh et al. (1990).
[15]U.S. Bureau of the Census, "Racial Succession in Individual Housing Units," by L. H. Long and D. Spain, *Current Population Reports*, series P-23, no. 71 (1978).

TABLE 9.19

Percentage of White Out-Movers Who Were Replaced by Blacks and Percentage of Black In-Movers Who Replaced Whites, by Age of Householder: 1967–1971 (numbers in thousands)

	White Out-Movers		Black In-Movers	
Age of Householder	Total	Percentage Who Were Replaced by Blacks	Total	Percentage Who Replaced Whites
Total 15 and Over	8,400	3.4	988	29.3
15–24	1,472	2.2	202	24.8
25–29	1,549	1.6	171	34.6
30–34	1,107	3.1	142	32.4
35–44	1,511	3.4	218	51.4
45–54	1,082	5.2	120	53.8
55–64	778	5.5	71	44.9
65 and Over	901	5.2	64	20.8

SOURCE: U.S. Bureau of the Census, "Racial Succession in Individual Housing Units," by L. H. Long and D. Spain, *Current Population Reports*, series P-23, no. 71 (September 1978).

of one study may be suggestive of potential changes in age composition of neighborhood populations accompanying changes in racial composition. According to a study by Lee and Wood, the residential succession model of racial neighborhood change (i.e., rapid white-to-black transition in urban neighborhoods that are racially mixed) fit most census tracts in large cities between 1970 and 1980, but a sizable number of racially mixed tracts remained interracially stable, particularly in the West, or experienced a shift toward greater white residency.[16] In 58 cities of 250,000 or more, 3 in 5 census tracts in this decade showed a substantially larger share of black households in 1980 than in 1970. It is a reasonable hypothesis that the process of racial succession in this decade generally contributed to a younging of the population in many parts of large cities, if not in the cities as a whole.

Special Housing Arrangements

Mobile Homes

Older householders increasingly turned to mobile homes as a housing arrangement during the 1970s, following the trail of younger house-

[16]B. A. Lee and P. B. Wood, "Is Neighborhood Racial Succession Place-Specific?" *Demography* 28 (1) (February 1991):21–40.

holders. In 1970, 96,000 elderly households, or 1 percent of all elderly households, lived in mobile homes. By 1980, an estimated 800,000 elderly households, or about 5 percent of all elderly households, lived in mobile homes. In that year the proportion of elderly households living in mobile homes was about the same as for younger households. The trend among older persons to choose this type of housing arrangement continues to grow. About 17 percent of all new mobile homes were purchased by elders in 1980; at that time mobile homes represented only 9 percent of all new housing units purchased. The American Housing Survey of 1987 recorded that 6 percent of elderly households lived in mobile homes.

Retirement Facilities

The 1980 census did not categorize housing units as to whether or not they were retirement housing. Those older persons living in active retirement communities, such as life care centers,[17] were classified in the same manner as their counterparts living in age-integrated neighborhoods. Estimates of the number of retirement households vary widely, and none is considered to be the accepted figure. According to an inventory taken in 1981, there were then about 2,400 retirement communities in the United States.[18]

Retirement facilities for older persons commonly resemble private homes or standard structures with apartments. The residents of these structures maintain an independent lifestyle while having the added assurance of prompt health care or personal support when needed. The characteristic feature of life care communities, for example, is that health care for life is provided. Often the services covered in the monthly fee include one or more communal meals daily as well as a variety of planned social, cultural, and recreational activities, both within and outside the residential community. Supportive services, such as transportation and housekeeping and linen services, are often provided for an additional fee.

There are other types of retirement facilities besides those in retirement communities. "Sheltered housing," "congregate housing," "house sharing," "owner-renter match-ups," "accessory apartments," and "granny flats" represent other types of housing arrangements adapted especially for the retired elderly and varying in the extent of supportive services. Some residential hotels, including single-room occupancy hotels, are also

---

[17] Also called continuing care retirement communities.
[18] M. F. Riche, "Retirement's Lifestyle Pioneers," *American Demographics* 8 (1) (January 1986):42–44, 50–56.

considered to be retirement facilities. Another type of retirement facility, assisted living facilities, consists of rooms or semi-independent apartments with common facilities. They are designed for elderly persons who need some form of assistance with activities of daily life, such as bathing, dressing, or preparing meals, but who are basically well.

In the 1980 census those retirement facilities without kitchens in each unit and with a common dining area were classified as group quarters.[19] As expected, the higher the age group, above age 40 or so, the greater was the percentage of the population living in this type of housing arrangement.

Financially Assisted Housing

One type of financially assisted housing refers to federally funded housing in private residential developments. The federal funding permits private management to offer housing within the means of lower-income households. Another federal program provides rent supplements to enable lower-income households to afford private-market housing which these households locate for themselves. Assisted housing programs offer an alternative to publicly owned, low-rent housing developments that are known as public housing projects. All types of assisted housing units may be earmarked exclusively for older or handicapped persons. The future of federally assisted housing programs is now uncertain.

Homelessness of the Elderly

Among the several million poor and near-poor elderly in the United States are some tens of thousands who are homeless. Many of the homeless occupy unconventional quarters (garages, shacks, abandoned buildings), some occupy community shelters, and some live mostly on the streets. We have little data regarding this segment of the population. The Census Bureau tried to include the homeless population in the 1980 census count through its enumeration of transient and unconventional quarters and its "casual count," but presumably did not count many in this group. In any case, they were not identified as such in the records. The Census Bureau does not count homeless persons in the current sur-

---

[19]Group quarters encompasses small structures housing several unrelated individuals (e.g., small group homes, board and care facilities) as well as large institutional facilities, such as homes for the aged and nursing homes. Group quarters are not considered housing units in the U.S. census. They are treated in more detail in Chapter 6.

veys, which are limited to residents of conventional housing units. A more intensive effort to count them will be made as part of the 1990 census.

Since estimates of the total number of homeless vary widely, no readily acceptable estimate of the elderly who are homeless is available.[20] A study issued by the National Bureau of Economic Research (NBER) gave an estimate of 350,000 homeless of all ages in 1985. The NBER study found that the homeless are largely men aged 30–60. According to a summary analysis of various studies of the homeless population made by Rossi, their median age has dropped sharply over the last three decades from 54 in 1958 to 37 in 1985 and, in sharp contrast to the earlier situation, practically none are now over age 60 or are receiving pensions.[21] In contrast, the Aging Health Policy Center of the University of California, San Francisco, estimated, largely on the basis of shelter reports from eight cities in 1985, that as many as 27 percent of the homeless are aged 60 and over.[22] A disproportionate share of the elderly homeless would be found in the shelters, however. It appears that at mid decade the elderly made up a smaller share of all homeless persons than of the general population.

The scarcity of affordable housing, exacerbated by the sharp reduction in federally subsidized housing, is commonly viewed as a leading cause of homelessness. Like the poor or near-poor in general, the elderly poor or near-poor are vulnerable to being displaced from low-rent units when rents are raised or units are converted to condominiums. At the same time they experience difficulty in securing new housing because the demand for low-rent housing exceeds the supply and federal support for public housing has been cut sharply.

Summary

Among the several interrelated issues associated with the housing of the elderly are its cost, the quality of the housing and the neighborhood, and the use of housing space, particularly the question of overhousing of the elderly. These issues often play out differently according to the tenure of the housing unit, the social support available, and other factors.

[20] Population Reference Bureau, "Counting the U.S.'s Homeless," *Population Today* 14, (10) (October 1986), pp. 3 and 8.
[21] P. Rossi, "Homeless," an address before the Washington Academy of Sciences, October 15, 1987.
[22] Reported in C. I. Cohen et al., "Survival Strategies of Older Homeless Men," *Gerontologist* 28 (1) (February 1988):58–65, esp. p. 58.

Some elderly housing units are rented; but the great majority are owned, and few of these are still mortgaged. Housing costs absorb a disproportionate share of the income of the elderly, particularly if the units are rented or owned with a mortgage, or household income is low. The housing units of the elderly are often large, and housing space is underutilized, as measured by the number of persons per room or persons per unit. This is usually the result of the fact that a spouse or parent has died and younger members have left. The great majority of older people age in place, continuing to occupy the same housing unit from age 60 through most or all of their later years. A small share move to another housing unit in the same neighborhood, and an even smaller share move to a housing unit in a retirement community a considerable distance away.

Much of the housing occupied by the elderly, particularly owned units, is old, but it only occasionally needs major repairs (e.g., leaking roof, holes in walls or floor) or lacks basic facilities (i.e., complete plumbing, complete kitchen, central heating). The age or value of the housing unit suggests a relative deficiency in housing quality more than the reported lack of facilities or structural defects. Lack of facilities is more common in rural areas than in urban areas (even the central cities of urbanized areas), among particular racial/ethnic minorities than among whites, and among the older aged than among other elderly. In general, however, elderly housing suffers from severe or even moderate deficiencies no more frequently than the housing of the general population.

Neighborhood conditions may be in decline, as measured by inaccessibility to essential services, poor government services, neighborhood nuisances, crime victimization, and fear of victimization. Many essential services, such as professional services and specialized retail outlets, have moved from central cities to suburban shopping areas, and many elderly cannot travel to secure the services and goods they need because of lack of public transportation or a transportation disability. Some elderly lack telephones, and even TV sets and automobiles, and hence they may be socially isolated as well.

Lack of funds, inertia, attachment to friends, and fear of leaving familiar surroundings are factors discouraging or preventing older persons from moving to better housing or better neighborhoods. Older persons, both owners and renters, resist moving. When the elderly, especially the poor elderly, do move, they move often for reasons beyond their control, such as neighborhood redevelopment (gentrification), urban renewal, or condemnation orders. Then they move from sections of the city where the rent is relatively low, even minimal, to sections where the rent is relatively high, and affordable housing may not be available.

574

Most elderly persons living in the community (i.e., not in group quarters) occupy housing units little different in basic design from those occupied by younger persons, in spite of the fact that many have one or more chronic health conditions that restrict them in their activities. However, a large share of the elderly do occupy housing that accommodates in one way or another for diminished levels of functioning. The accommodations may be social (e.g., shared housing) or physical (e.g., additional lights, single-level units). Housing conditions become most circumscribed for the small percentage of the elderly confined to their homes because of a mobility problem.

In spite of the long history of plans for older persons to take advantage of low-rent public housing, subsidized housing, or government-guaranteed mortgages, older persons still generally live under the same housing arrangements as they did in the past. The number of elderly households living in retirement communities, congregate housing, and other retirement facilities is growing rapidly, but these still cover only a minority of the elderly.

Projections of the age distribution of the population, and especially the population with functional impairments, foreshadow a growing need to accommodate housing structures and home services to the special requirements of the functionally impaired elderly, including the demands for long-term care. Structural modifications of the housing unit may be a way of reducing the burden on caregivers, particularly family caregivers. Alternatively, relocation of the older person to another housing unit that has been appropriately redesigned, to a planned retirement community, to congregate housing, or even to an institution may be preferable.

10

SUMMARY, PROSPECTS, AND IMPLICATIONS

Reprise of Selected Topics

Status of Elderly Women

THE MAJORITY of elderly persons, especially of those aged 75 and over, are women. The characteristics of the elderly population, particularly the aged population, are mainly, therefore, the characteristics of elderly women, as are the health, social, and economic problems of the elderly. Elderly women have many problems that are usually more severe than those of elderly men or younger women. In large part because the elderly are mostly women, a disproportionate share of the elderly are widowed, live alone, are isolated, have low incomes or are poor, live in substandard housing, suffer from certain chronic, non-disabling diseases, and are institutionalized. Married women generally maintain their physical, social, and economic independence longer than unmarried women, but the proportion married at the older ages is low. For women aged 75 and over living in the community, less than one quarter are married and live with husbands, about one quarter live with other relatives or nonrelatives, and about one half live alone.

The decades from 1950 to 1980 have been noted for tremendous progress in the economic security of older women. Yet, the economic situation of older women remains relatively unfavorable compared with older men and younger women. Older women usually pay a larger percentage of their income for housing than younger women. Older women are more likely to be poor or nearly poor than older men or younger women. This is especially true for women living alone or with persons other than a husband, and for black and Hispanic women. In addition to low earnings in their working years—partly a result of unequal pay and limited occupational options—a major reason for the relatively unsatisfactory economic situation of elderly women is that many have not been regular participants in the paid labor force and no pecuniary reward is given for home management, housework, and childcare. Retirement systems do not set a value on the contribution of women to the management of the home, nor do they recognize the need for interrupting work in the paid labor force for childrearing. Irregular and truncated labor force participation reduces sharply the likelihood of receiving a pension from a particular job and increases sharply the likelihood of receiving only minimal Social Security benefits or none at all.

Variations Among the Elderly by Age

The demographic diversity of the elderly population has been noted frequently in this monograph, as has the fact that its characteristics are steadily changing. There are distinct variations in the characteristics of the component ages, a rapid turnover from year to year, and substantial shifts in the characteristics of new entrants.

To emphasize further the range and degree of the diversity of the older population, I present a comparison of two widely separate age bands among the elderly, 65–69 and 85 and over in 1970 and 1980, with respect to a broad spectrum of demographic, social, and economic characteristics, based on a study by Rosenwaike (Table 10.1). Only basic or single variables are listed, and it is quite possible that cross-classifications of these and other variables would show larger or smaller differences over the elderly age span. In comparison with the population aged 65–69, the population aged 85 and over has a far lower ratio of men to women, a higher proportion of foreign-born, and a higher proportion of persons who changed residence in the preceding five years. A member of the older group is much more likely to be widowed and far less likely to be married. He or she is far less likely to be living with a relative and more likely to be living alone or with nonrelatives, or in an institution. Finally, he or she is much less likely to have finished elementary school or high school and to be economically active and much more likely to have had less than eight years of schooling, to be receiving only a small retirement income, and to be poor.

TABLE 10.1

Selected Characteristics of Persons Aged 65–69 and 85 and Over: 1970 and 1980

	1970			1980		
Characteristic	Ages 65–69	Ages 85 and Over	Difference	Ages 65–69	Ages 85 and Over	Difference
Sex ratio (Males/100 Females)	80.7	53.3	−27.4	80.0	43.7	−36.3
Percent Foreign-born	12.8	18.6	+5.8	7.8	18.6	+10.8
Percent Movers[a]	27.8	35.7[b]	+7.9	22.9	29.3	+6.4
Percent Married						
Male	80.6	42.4	−38.2	83.0	48.4	−34.6
Female	52.0	9.9	−42.1	54.8	8.4	−46.4
Percent Widowed						
Male	8.8	47.0	+38.2	7.3	43.8	+36.5
Female	36.5	79.0	+42.5	33.8	81.8	+48.0
Percent in Families						
Male	83.9	60.4	−23.5	85.4	58.9	−26.5
Female	67.2	47.9	−19.3	66.8	36.7	−30.1
Percent Living Alone or with Nonrelatives						
Male	13.8	24.2	+10.4	12.9	24.1	+11.2
Female	30.5	29.0	−1.5	31.5	35.6	+4.1
Percentage in Institutions						
Male	1.8	14.3	+12.5	1.4	16.1	+14.7
Female	1.6	21.9	+20.3	1.3	26.3	+25.0
Years of School Completed Percent high school						
graduates	30.5	23.0	−7.5	45.1	30.0	−15.1
Percent 8 or more	70.9	60.1	−10.8	81.2	66.6	−14.6
Percent less than 8	29.1	39.9	+10.8	19.8	33.4	+13.6
Percent in labor force						
Male	39.0	6.8	−32.2	29.2	4.2	−25.0
Female	17.2	3.4	−13.8	15.0	1.5	−13.5
Median Income (Previous Year)						
Male	$3,616	$1,668	−$1,948	$8,584	$4,797	−$3,787
Female	1,558	1,171	−387	3,819	3,284	−535
Percent Below Poverty Level	21.6	37.1	+15.5	11.6	21.3	+9.7

SOURCES: U.S. Bureau of the Census, 1970 and 1980 Censuses of Population and Public Use Microdata Samples. Adapted from I. Rosenwaike, "A Demographic Portrait of the Oldest Old," *Milbank Memorial Fund Quarterly* 63 (2) (Spring 1985): 187–205, Table 2. Reprinted with permission of the *Milbank Memorial Fund Quarterly.*

[a] 1970 data are for 1965–1970 and hence for the cohorts aged 60–64 in 1965 (65–69 in 1970) and 80 and over in 1965 (85 and over in 1970); 1980 data are for 1975–1980 and hence for the cohorts aged 60–64 in 1975 (65–69 in 1980) and 80 and over in 1975 (85 and over in 1980).
[b] Excludes ages 100 and over.

The differences in most characteristics between the older age groups increased between 1970 and 1980. While the age difference in the percentage below the poverty level diminished during the decade, the difference in median income, particularly for men, increased sharply. There were striking adverse changes in the age variation of the living arrangements of women—namely, the increased tendency for women aged 85 and over to be widowed, to live alone or with nonrelatives, or to reside in an institution, and not to live as a member of a married couple or a family.

Geographic Variations Among the Aged

We have seen that the older aged—85 and over—have very different demographic, social, and economic characteristics from the population under age 85 as a whole and from the younger elderly and aged, those 65–74 and 75–84. Even so, the older aged themselves show a considerable degree of variation in their characteristics, as reflected in the differences in 1980 between the high and low states for a wide range of demographic, social, and economic characteristics compiled by Longino (Table 10.2). Much geographic variation would be expected for the shares of the older aged who belong to one racial/ethnic group or another since they would mirror the wide geographic variation in the residence patterns of these groups. The variation in shares of other characteristics would mirror the settlement patterns of immigrant groups—for example, naturalized citizens and non-English speakers.

Variation in the percentages/medians/means for most characteristics would be largely independent of these influences, however. We note particularly, among the demographic and social characteristics, the state variation in the percentage of women, from 61 percent (Hawaii) to 76 percent (Delaware); in the percentage of persons widowed, from 61 percent (Alaska) to 79 percent (Delaware); and in the mean years of school completed, from 6 years (Hawaii) to 10 years (Utah). Even greater state variations occur for living arrangements and health—for example, in the percentages living alone, in an institution, with a public transportation disability, and in the status of householder or spouse of householder. State variations are impressively large for certain economic characteristics. There is a 3-to-1 difference, for example, for mean household income between Hawaii and Arkansas, and for the percentage below the poverty level between Mississippi and California. Home ownership ranges from 42 percent in New York to 67 percent in West Virginia. There is a very wide variation in the share of the older aged population receiving different types of income, particularly public assistance and pension income.

TABLE 10.2

State Variations in the Demographic, Social, and Economic Characteristics of Persons Aged 85 and Over: 1980

Characteristic	U.S. Average	High		Low	
		Value	State	Value	State
Sex, Race, and Ethnicity					
Female	69.2	75.6	Delaware	60.8	Hawaii
Black	7.1	46.6	District of Columbia	—	[a]
American Indian/Eskimo/					
Aleut	0.3	46.4	Alaska	—	[b]
Asian and Pacific Islander	0.7	70.4	Hawaii	—	[c]
Spanish origin	2.1	28.8	New Mexico	—	[d]
Naturalized citizen	16.0	36.7	Massachusetts	1.0	Mississippi
Non-English-speaking	4.5	48.5	Hawaii	0.2	Kentucky
Social Characteristics					
Married	20.7	28.6	Alaska	10.3	Delaware
Widowed	70.7	78.6	Delaware	60.7	Alaska
Never married	7.2	12.8	Maine	3.6	[e]
Average (mean) years of					
schooling	8.6	10.2	Utah	5.6	Hawaii
Economic Characteristics					
Homeowner	53.1	67.4	West Virginia	41.5	New York
Self-employed	2.2	6.4	Iowa	—	Alaska
Receiving					
Wage or salary income	3.7	9.3	District of Columbia	1.7	Maine
Interest, dividends, rental					
income	34.4	45.1	Iowa	15.6	Mississippi

SOURCE: C. F. Longino, Jr., "A State by State Look at the Oldest Americans," *American Demographics* 8 (11) (November 1986); 38–42. Based on Public Use Microdata Sample, 1980 census. Reproduced with permission of *American Demographics*.

NOTES: Percentage of relevant total except where indicated. Dash denotes that figure rounds to 0.0.

[a] Alaska, Hawaii, Idaho, Montana, New Hampshire, North Dakota, South Dakota, and Vermont.
[b] Connecticut, District of Columbia, Hawaii, Illinois, Maine, New Hampshire, Ohio, Pennsylvania, South Carolina, Vermont, and West Virginia.
[c] Alaska, Delaware, New Mexico, North Dakota, Ohio, Rhode Island, South Dakota, and Vermont.
[d] Alaska, Delaware, North Dakota, and South Dakota.
[e] Alaska and Oklahoma.
[f] 1979 income in 1985 dollars, inflated using Consumer Price Index.
[g] Alaska and Wyoming.
[h] With public transportation disability.

It is evident that the characteristics of the older aged vary widely among the states. Heterogeneity abounds among the elderly, not only along the age cycle but also in space as well. Accordingly, the states face very different situations in providing services to their older aged residents.

TABLE 10.2 *(continued)*

Characteristic	U.S. Average	High		Low	
		Value	State	Value	State
Social Security income	74.7	81.2	West Virginia	60.2	District of Columbia
Public assistance	12.5	32.1	Mississippi	5.8	Nebraska
Pension or other income	20.2	42.9	Alaska	8.8	North Dakota
Per capita income (1985)	$8,089	$13,053	District of Columbia	$5,660	Mississippi
Average (mean) household income[f]	$20,161	$37,754	Hawaii	$13,099	Arkansas
Below the poverty level	16.2	30.8	Mississippi	9.6	California
Below twice the poverty level	34.5	56.2	Hawaii	17.9	South Dakota
Living Arrangements and Disability					
Householder or spouse of householder	54.3	62.6	Idaho	35.8	Hawaii
Parent of householder	16.4	37.7	Hawaii	6.2	Iowa
Sibling of householder	1.6	2.6	Delaware	— [g]	
Other relative of householder	2.1	3.8	Mississippi	0.5	Minnesota
Not related to householder	1.2	3.7	District of Columbia	—	Wyoming
In institution	24.4	37.2	South Dakota	13.3	New Mexico
In home for the aged	22.2	35.1	South Dakota	10.6	Florida
Living alone	29.7	37.7	Wyoming	13.1	West Virginia
Disabled,[h] living alone	9.3	14.4	Vermont	3.6	Alaska
Disabled[h]	47.8	53.7	Mississippi	28.1	Maine

Authenticity of Cross-sectional Variations by Age

For many topics covered in this mongraph, I have compared the variations with age observed on a calendar-year, or cross-sectional, basis with the variations with age observed on a cohort basis. Such comparisons were made, for example, for migration, life expectancy, marital status, educational level, income, labor force participation, and home ownership. We have seen repeatedly that cross-sectional data tend to give a misleading impression as to the lifetime experience of real cohorts. In the case of educational level, approximate constancy, with advancing age, of the proportions graduating from high school for cohorts stands in sharp contrast to the steady decrease in the proportion seen in the cross-sectional data. This difference has important implications for the interpretation of the educational level of the elderly and for the prospective changes in their educational level. Each successive cohort in fact shows a pronounced rise in educational level at the older ages. I have incorporated these findings in developing a new set of projections of high school graduates for the older population.

In the case of income, we have seen how cross-sectional data give a greatly exaggerated impression as to the drop-off in income in the older ages. Data for real cohorts show a much more gradual reduction in income with advancing age and suggest the prospect for substantially increased income levels for the elderly in the next few decades. Similarly, in the case of the proportion married, cross-sectional data exaggerate the falloff in the older ages; the current data for the older ages reflect the much lower marriage rates (and higher widowing rates) of the early decades of this century. Proportions widowed at the older ages in cross-sectional data are "too high" because they reflect the higher death rates of earlier decades. Widowhood ratios actually rise less rapidly with increasing age. Compared with cross-sectional data, cohort data on lifetime migration highlight the fact that much interstate migration occurs at the younger ages and that older people are relatively immobile. Once they have reached the older ages, older persons commonly age in place and, whether owners or renters, tend not to move.

I conclude, then, by noting that older persons are quite diverse in their demographic, social, and economic characteristics; that the characteristics of older persons as individuals and as a group are rapidly changing; and that late-life characteristics are strongly influenced by the events affecting the same individuals in earlier years of the life course. This diversity of the characteristics of older persons, their dynamic nature, and the influence of the earlier life course on older age should be recognized explicitly in the development of public policy relating to the elderly.[1]

Prospects for the Elderly Population and Some Implications

Short-Term and Intermediate-Term Prospects

Between 1985 and 2010 the elderly population as a whole will grow much more slowly than it did in the prior quarter century. This expectation applies, in fact, only to the segment aged 65–74 since the group aged 75–84 will continue to increase rapidly and the group aged 85 and over will continue its explosive rise. As a result of the more rapid growth of the elderly population than the total population, its share in the total

---

[1] R. H. Binstock, "The Oldest Old: A Fresh Perspective or Compassionate Ageism Revisited?" *Milbank Memorial Fund Quarterly* 63 (2) (Spring 1985):421–451.

population will continue to rise. By 2010, it is expected that about 14 percent of the population will be aged 65 and over compared with 12 percent in 1987. As a result of the more rapid growth of the older aged than of all the elderly, the proportion of the older aged among the elderly will increase sharply between 1985 and 2010.

The black elderly population will increase more rapidly than the total black population in the next quarter century. As a result, the proportion of the elderly among blacks is expected to rise moderately in this period, from 8 percent in 1987 to 9 percent in 2010. A much sharper rise, from 5 percent to 8 percent, is envisaged for the Hispanic population.

The total age dependency burden will change little in the decades to come because of the opposing trends of the two dependent age categories. The total dependency ratio (i.e., persons under age 18 and 65 and over per 100 persons aged 18–64) is expected to decline from 62 in 1987 to 58 in 2010. The elderly component will make up a steadily increasing share of the total dependency burden, and the child component will constitute a steadily decreasing share. The ratio of child to elderly dependency is expected to shift from 2 to 1 in 1987 to 3 to 2 in 2010.

The great mass of elderly persons will be living in metropolitan areas in 2010, as will the population in general, but whether or not the share of the elderly population that is metropolitan will rise or fall in the next quarter century is not clear. It is expected that, like the general population, the share of the elderly population living in the South and West will continue to increase.

The prospects are that an increasing proportion of households will be headed by elderly persons, that an increasing share of the elderly will be living independently (i.e., in their own home and alone), and that a decreasing share will be living in the homes of relatives (other than spouses) or nonrelatives. The median age of becoming widowed will continue to rise, but the increasing longevity of survivors will maintain or extend the period of solitary living of survivors.

The labor force will gradually get older as the baby-boom cohorts move into their late 40s and 50s, after decades during which the labor force has been getting younger. By 1985, after persistent declines in worker ratios at ages 65 and over, only 18 percent of the men and 8 percent of the women at these ages were in the labor force. It is expected that, in spite of continued inflation, increased longevity, disincentives in recent Social Security legislation to retire early, and growing industry support for flexible work programs, labor force participation at the older ages will continue to fall to the early part of the next century, albeit much more slowly than it did in the past. Increased economic security gained mainly through the Social Security program, employer and union pension programs, and public and private health insurance programs, as well as the emergence of an ethic of leisure and new public and private programs to enjoy it (e.g., gerontic recreation centers, "Leisure World"), will militate against an early reversal of the labor force trend.

The educational level of the elderly is expected to continue rising rapidly. At mid decade, less than one half of the elderly had completed high school, but by the end of the century almost two thirds will be high school graduates.

Most elderly persons will continue to live in a home they own and have occupied for much of their adult lives. Home ownership of the elderly may rise very little in the decades until 2010 because of the financial barriers to home ownership during the 1970s and the inability of many elderly in recent years to sell their old homes profitably so as to move to retirement areas. Changes in age structure will influence the problems of providing suitable housing for the population, including the elderly. We may anticipate a shift in demand from large detached units to small, one-story or two-story attached units or to apartments. Occupancy of rental and owned units in multi-unit structures, and of mobile homes, is expected to increase, therefore. The demand for smaller housing units by the elderly is related in large part to the diminution in the size of households maintained by elderly persons, a result of the trend toward independent living and the reduction in fertility since the early 1960s. Finally, there may be serious problems in maintaining the quality of the housing inventory, particularly the large segment of older housing occupied by the elderly.

Long-Term Prospects

A dominant characteristic of the U.S. population during the first half of the next century is expected to be the very large share of elderly persons and the high and rising median age.[2] These will be associated with continuing low fertility and low mortality. Since the future level of fertility will largely determine the shape of the population distribution and hence influence the degree of population aging, it is important to note that there is considerable agreement among demographers that the general long-term outlook is for low fertility in the United States. In all three series of fertility projections of the Census Bureau, fertility is assumed to conform to historically low levels or fall below them. Not only is the population expected to continue aging in the three principal

---

[2]The first part of this section is adapted from material in J. S. Siegel and C. Taeuber, "Demographic Dimensions of an Aging Population," in A. Pifer and L. Bronte, eds., *Our Aging Society: Paradox and Promise* (New York: Norton, 1986).

population series, but in the lowest and middle series the population will reach zero population growth (ZPG) and then decline some time in the next century—early in the century in the lowest series and just before the middle of the century in the middle series.

These population changes will effect a significant transformation in the demographic characteristics of American society. A description of the Census Bureau's middle population series in 2050 provides an outline of the probable demographic situation in that year. This projection scenario and others are summarized in Table 10.3 in terms of the broad age distribution, the median age of the population and of deaths, dependency ratios, and similar parameters.

In the middle series the total population would amount to 309 million in 2050, by which year it will have ceased growing. Among the 67 million people aged 65 and over, some 60 percent would be women. They would outnumber men by 45 percent. The proportion of the population aged 65 and over would be about twice as great as in the mid 1980s (22 percent vs. 12 percent), and the proportion under age 20 would be three quarters as great (23 percent vs. 31 percent). The median age of the population would be 42, 11 years higher than at mid decade. The elderly dependency ratio (persons aged 65 and over per 100 persons aged 20–64) would be double (40) its recent level (20), but the total dependency ratio (including persons under age 20) of 82 would be only 12 percent greater than the recent figure of 73.

The median age at death in 2050 would be 84, 11 years higher than in the mid 1980s. Eighty-three percent of deaths would occur to persons aged 65 and over in 2050 compared with 68 percent in the recent past, and 43 percent of deaths would occur to persons aged 85 and over compared with 20 percent at mid decade. The death rate, at 12.8 per 1,000 population, would be about 50 percent greater than it is today; and there would be twice as many deaths annually as now, with a 13 percent excess of deaths over births. Hence, death will be a very common occurrence, but it will occur at almost predictable occasions, mostly when people have lived out their full lives.

On the assumption that no major medical breakthroughs would occur, but only sustained, gradual progress in medicine, the average ages of onset of the major chronic illnesses would remain unchanged and the number of chronically ill persons in the population would be far greater than today. However, the number of persons limited in their major activity as a result of chronic illness may not be much greater than today if the degree of limitation can be reduced or the average age of onset of limitation of activity can be raised as a result of progress in the management and treatment of the principal chronic illnesses.

Suppose, instead, that fertility, mortality, and net immigration all fall to the low levels of the Census Bureau projection. (See the column

TABLE 10.3

Demographic Parameters of the U.S. Population in 2050 Under Various Assumptions of Fertility, Mortality, and Net Immigration (numbers in thousands)

Parameter	Current Data, 1982	High Fertility, High Mortality, and High Immigration	Middle Fertility, Middle Mortality, and Middle Immigration	Low Fertility, Low Mortality, and Low Immigration	Low-Middle Fertility[a] Extremely Low Mortality, and Middle Immigration	Low Fertility, Extremely Low Mortality, and Low Immigration
Total Fertility Rate	1,831	2,300	1,900	1,600	1,750	1,600
Life Expectancy at Birth	74.6	76.7	79.6	83.3	100.0	100.0
Net Immigration (per Year)	480	750	450	250	450	250
Population	232,057	402,687	309,488	253,603	331,972	287,960
Age (total percent)	100.0	100.0	100.0	100.0	100.0[b]	100.0[b]
Under 20	30.7	29.5	23.3	18.1	18.4	16.1
20–44	38.6	33.2	30.9	27.7	26.2	24.8
45–64	19.2	21.7	24.0	24.9	22.5	22.9
65 and over	11.6	15.6	21.8	29.3	32.9	36.2
Median Age	31	35	42	49	51	53
Dependency Ratios						
Total[c]	73	83	82	90	105	110
Child[d]	53	54	42	34	38	34
Elderly[e]	20	29	40	56	67	76
Net Growth Rate (per 1,000)	+9.5	+6.2	0.0	−4.7	+2.0	−0.9
Birth Rate	16.1	15.4	11.4	8.2	8.8	7.3
Death Rate	8.6	11.1	12.8	13.9	8.2	9.1

TABLE 10.3 (continued)

Parameter	Current Data, 1982	High Fertility, High Mortality, and High Immigration	Middle Fertility, Middle Mortality, and Middle Immigration	Low Fertility, Low Mortality, and Low Immigration	Low-Middle Fertility[a], Extremely Low Mortality, and Middle Immigration	Low Fertility, Extremely Low Mortality, and Low Immigration
Immigration Rate	2.1	1.9	1.5	1.0	1.4	0.9
Net Change	+2,199	+2,500	+10	−1,198	+653	−265
Births	3,731	6,206	3,517	2,089	2,917	2,101
Deaths	1,986	4,455	3,957	3,537	2,714	2,615
Median Age of Deaths	73	77	84	91	ca. 102	ca. 105

SOURCES: Based on, or estimated from data in, reports of the U.S. Census Bureau, esp. *Current Population Reports*, series P-25, no. 952. Projections assuming "extremely low mortality" were prepared in collaboration with Gregory Spencer of the U.S. Census Bureau. Reproduced from Table 4, "Demographic Dimensions of an Aging Population," by Jacob S. Siegel and Cynthia M. Taeuber, *Our Aging Society: Paradox and Promise*, edited by Alan Pifer and Lydia Bronte. Copyright © 1986 by Carnegie Corporation of New York; by permission of the publisher, W. W. Norton and Company, Inc.

[a] Intermediate between middle and low fertility.
[b] Age distribution estimated by short-cut methods from available Census Bureau population projections.

[c] $\dfrac{\text{Population under age 20} + \text{population aged 65 and over}}{\text{Population aged 20–64}} \times 100.$

[d] $\dfrac{\text{Population under age 20}}{\text{Population aged 20–64}} \times 100.$

[e] $\dfrac{\text{Population aged 65 and over}}{\text{Population aged 20–64}} \times 100.$

"Low Fertility, Low Mortality, and Low Immigration" in Table 10.3.) Such a series would tend to maximize the proportion of elderly persons and minimize the proportion of children. The population would reach ZPG at a somewhat earlier date than in the middle series, about 2023, and then decline. The median age of the population in 2050 would be 49, about 18 years higher than in the mid 1980s. Some 29 percent of the population would be aged 65 and over and only 18 percent would be below age 20. The elderly dependency ratio would be nearly three times its present level, but the total dependency ratio would be only one quarter greater because of the decline of the child population. There would be nearly 45 percent fewer births and nearly 80 percent more deaths; as a result, deaths would be more than two thirds more frequent than births.

To appreciate better the transformations that would occur in the structure of the population as a result of future possible changes in mortality, consider now the effects of an extreme assumption of mortality decline. This scenario of the population in the middle of the next century is based on projected mortality trends leading to a life expectancy at birth of 100 in 2050. This assumption corresponds roughly to the level of mortality obtained by projecting current age-specific death rates for females to 2050 at the rates of decline recorded in the decade and a half from 1968 to 1983, or, alternatively, by reducing the best-country age-specific death rates for females on record in 1980 by some 70 percent. Such sharp future declines in mortality would contribute greatly to the aging of the population inasmuch as their effect would necessarily be concentrated at the older ages.

A life expectancy of 100 is technically consistent with an extension of the human life span to 115 or even 120. Whether such a new lead-lag relationship will be achieved will depend in part on whether the life span can be extended at all. The survival curve may become sharply rectangular at about age 100 if life span remains around 100, but if life span shows a significant extension, as is possible, the squaring of the survival curve may be only approximately achieved.

The special scenario combines low fertility and low net immigration with the extremely low mortality assumption just described. Under these conditions, one half of the population would be aged 53 and over and more than one third of the population would be aged 65 and over! Only 1 in 6 persons would be under age 20; that is only about half of today's proportion. In spite of the sharp decline in the share of children, the overall dependency ratio would be well over the current figure because of the nearly threefold increase in the elderly dependency ratio.

Under the demographic conditions described for 2050 in the two scenarios based on the Census Bureau's projections, and especially under those assumed in the third scenario, the nature of American society would be very different from what it is today. Very high proportions of elderly persons and very high dependency ratios, associated with continuing low fertility, low or very low mortality, and slow population growth or population decline, would have profound social and economic consequences. All areas of social life, including education, health care, housing, recreation, religion, and worklife, would be greatly affected by the changes in the age structure and by the pattern of population changes. There are possible implications, for example, for the size, character, and productive capacity of the labor force and the growth of the economy, the patterning of education, work, retirement, and leisure in the life course, the structure of the family and family relationships, the nature of support services, the funding of the Social Security system, and the capacity of the health care system to serve the population, especially the oldest segment of it.

A large and growing proportion of old people has been associated for several years with low fertility, low mortality, and slow, zero, or declining population growth in various western European countries. Yet, analysis of the ways in which ZPG, population stationarity (i.e., zero growth with a fixed age structure), and declining population affect the social and economic conditions of older persons and society as a whole has only recently been undertaken on an intensive scale.[3] I offer here some general speculations on possible consequences of increased longevity and further aging of our society.

Education, family life, work, retirement, and leisure, as components of the life course, will be combined in a variety of ways, varying with respect to their sequence or contemporaneity and their duration in the

---

[3]A. Pifer and L. Bronte, eds., *Our Aging Society: Paradox and Promise* (New York: Norton 1986); K. Davis, M. S. Bernstam, and R. Ricardo-Campbell, eds., "Below-Replacement Fertility in Industrial Societies: Causes, Consequences, Policies," *Population and Development Review* 12 (supplement) (1986); W. J. Serow, "Some Implications of Changing Age Compositions of Low Fertility Countries. Empirical Evidence: An Assessment, in Particular, of Its Practical Significance," *International Population Conference, Manila, 1981*, vol. 3 (Liège: International Union for the Scientific Study of Population); J. van den Boomen, "Age-Cost Profiles: A Common Denominator?" *International Population Conference, Manila, 1981*, vol. 3 (Liège, Belgium: International Union for the Scientific Study of Population); H. Wander, "Short, Medium, and Long Term Implications of a Stationary or Declining Population on Education, Labour Force, Housing Needs, Social Security and Economic Development," *International Population Conference, Mexico City, 1977*, vol. 3 (Liège: International Union for the Scientific Study of Population); T. Espenshade and W. Serow, eds., *The Economic Consequences of Slowing Population Growth* (New York: Academic Press, 1978); K. Schwarz, "Public Health Implications of Stationary and Declining Populations," *World Health Statistics Report* 30, no. 4 (1977):340–354; J. S. Spengler, *Toward Zero Population Growth: Reactions and Interpretations, Past and Present* (Durham, NC: Duke University Press, 1978); G. W. Leeson, "Some Economic Consequences of an Aging and Declining Population in Denmark," *European Demographic Information Bulletin* 14 (3) (1983):81–85.

life course. The education-work-retirement sequence will still be the underlying structure on which variations will be imposed. Periodic retraining to maintain effectiveness in the workplace will become necessary and pursuance of multiple careers in tandem will become commonplace. The educational level of the elderly will be much higher than it is today not only because of the rise in the educational achievement of the more recent cohorts in youth, but also because of these cohorts' increased pursuit of education as older adults.

The prospects for maintaining a marriage to the same partner for a lifetime will become increasingly dim, and it is likely that each marrying person will have two marriage partners in his or her lifetime on the average. The total marriage rate for women, representing the average number of marriages per woman in a lifetime, may not reflect the tendency to multiple marriages fully because of more frequent nonmarriage. This pattern of marriage obsolescence will result partly from the individualistic character of postindustrial life, partly from the conflict between mates associated with personality changes occurring in a long life, and partly from the difference in the longevity of marriage partners. Unmarried parenthood, unmarried cohabitation, and sequential marriage and divorce will be established elements of U.S. culture. For many women, childbearing will come early, before marriage; for many others, biological parenthood will be irrevocably postponed and parenthood will come through adoption, if at all. "Families" will be typically composed of three to four generations, with many families containing five generations. Family relationships will become more complex because of the increased number of generations, the increased number of marriage partners, relatives, and step-relatives, and the great variety of types of families, including many single-parent male-headed families and same-sex couple "families." The practice of living independently will be more commonplace as each nuclear family and each unmarried adult seeks to have a separate housing unit and as management of chronic illness in later life improves.

A huge increase in the number of elderly persons, particularly of nonworking elderly persons, is expected between 1985 and 2030. Extremely large additions of nonworking elderly persons may have an adverse effect on the economy, even if they result from reductions in death rates and are accompanied by reductions in morbidity rates. The problem will be greatly aggravated by an increase in the ratio of older persons not in the labor force to persons in the labor force—an increase that will become massive after 2010. Possible economic consequences of this development include a reduction in per capita output and income, and a decline in consumer demand, resulting in depressed living levels. A rise in the economic activity of older persons, which is a reasonable possibility after the early years of the next century, and an increase in the economic activity of persons of working age, especially women aged 25–54, could help reduce the negative effects. These effects may also be offset by savings in the cost of health care resulting from reductions in morbidity rates, at least up to the most advanced ages, and the introduction of a system of national health insurance, and by savings in the aggregate costs of rearing children resulting from the reduced child dependency burden.

The aging of society will require increasingly larger financial contributions to the federal treasury by workers on behalf of older nonworkers as the older-nonworker/worker ratio continues to rise. Grave funding problems could result for the Social Security system under the demographic conditions envisioned for the years after 2010. Vast expenditures will have to be made for the maintenance of the burgeoning numbers of elderly persons. Tax rates could become oppressively high and serve as a disincentive to work. The possible crisis arising from the unfavorable ratio of elderly dependents to workers can be obviated in a variety of ways, implemented perhaps in combination, for example, a sharp rise in the age of eligibility for Social Security benefits (a rise beyond that now required by the 1983 Amendments to the Social Security Act), by the elimination of early retirement with reduced benefits, and especially by a rise in the age of eligibility for private retirement benefits.

Although we cannot depend on a large voluntary rise in the typical age of retirement, much depends on the success of methods for sustaining or even increasing the productive vigor of older persons and for inducing them to remain in or return to the labor force. Society would especially benefit if elderly persons continued to practice their professional and technical skills, particularly when many years had to be devoted to developing them. Society would benefit also if it could find socially useful roles, apart from paid work, for the many nonworking elderly.

The work force will very probably be older in 2050 than it is today, even though labor force participation at the older ages may be lower and a larger proportion of women under age 50 may be in the labor force. Like the general population, the labor force will grow very slowly or not at all by that year. These changes in themselves should have little effect on productivity, but labor mobility, both within organizations and between regions, is likely to decrease. As a result, imbalances between labor supply and demand would increase and opportunities for promotion within organizations would be reduced.

The most significant questions relate to the health of the future elderly population. We have seen that the health needs of older persons and their utilization of health services are greater than those of younger people. The need for health services is likely to grow even if the health status of the elderly generally improves. The increased need resulting from the growth in the number and proportion of older persons will be magnified by the growth in the number and proportion of persons of extreme age.

Changes in the age structure of the population will cause a pronounced shift in the age distribution of patients and hence in the types of illnesses. These changes in turn will affect the delivery of health care, particularly for the population in the extreme ages, and will cause serious problems in the availability of health manpower, particularly for the geriatric specialties.

It is possible only to conjecture whether the elderly of the future will be healthier than they are today. More elderly will probably have chronic conditions, be disabled, require assistance in carrying out the activities of daily living, and require institutionalization. Under such circumstances, there will be a need, in particular, for additional health services and facilities for extended care among the older aged. The percentage of the elderly population having chronic conditions, and the percentage disabled, however, may rise or fall, depending mainly on the opposing influences of changes in the age distribution of the elderly and progress in the treatment and management of chronic diseases. The relative extent of illness and physical dependency among the elderly will rise, according to Manton, both because of the inertia of the ages of onset of the chronic conditions and because of the aging of the older population.[4] The extent of health conditions will almost certainly rise even if death and morbidity rates among the younger elderly fall, as persons saved from death at an earlier age accumulate at the older ages. The social and economic impact of the chronic conditions is uncertain, however, since this will depend on the prevailing life style, technological developments in the home and workplace, medical progress in the management of chronic conditions, and health care delivery practices, as well as on the social acceptability of, and accommodation to, disability.

We may state the principal health issues in the following series of questions. Will the period of active (functional) life, the years of inactive (dysfunctional) life, or both, be extended as life expectancy is increased? Will the various disabling nonfatal illnesses, such as arthritis and osteoporosis, have an increased average duration if life expectancy continues

[4]K. G. Manton, "Past and Future Life Expectancy Increases at Later Ages: Their Implications for the Linkage of Chronic Morbidity, Disability, and Mortality," *Journal of Gerontology* 41 (5) (September 1986):672–681.

to rise? Similarly, will the various chronic, fatal illnesses and the associated disabling conditions simply be experienced longer? Can improvements in the treatment and management of chronic diseases, postponing death from them, be matched by a postponement of the average ages of onset of these conditions? Will the added years of healthy life allow an extension of worklife and thus help reduce, if not obviate, the burden of the massive costs of the Social Security system and long-term care programs that will confront us in the next century?

The consequences described above will probably result simply from a moderate extension of life expectancy. If, however, life expectancy resumes its earlier sharp upward pace and maintains it and if life span is extended to age 120 or so, the consequences could be enormous.[5] Because of the range and complexity of possible consequences, I can suggest no more than a few of them. Normal aging will be postponed and the ages of onset of chronic illness and disability will be delayed. Diseases of old age will dominate a smaller proportion of one's lifetime than now. The relationship between chronological age and functional age as we know it will, very probably, be completely changed. For example, under the new regime persons aged 75 may be able to function like 65-year-olds today. Retirement age will be postponed and the period of working life will be extended. Retirement may come, on the average, at age 75 instead of age 62, as at present, and the average age at death will be around 100 rather than 75. There may be pronounced changes in the ratio of nonworkers to workers that could have a major impact on per capita output. The childbearing period could be lengthened, with a resulting increase in options for individual family planning and the possibility of having a career before parenthood.[6] An extension of the childbearing period could be a "younging" experience psychologically as well as physically. Both major technological innovations and institutional adjustments will be required to deal with the population changes described. We may anticipate a revolution in our values and interpersonal relations as well as in our social institutions.

Implications for Public Programs and Policies
Implications Related to Age Structure

The current and prospective demographic developments set forth in the previous chapters and in earlier sections of this chapter provide a

---

[5]See Alexander Leaf, *Youth in Old Age* (New York: McGraw-Hill, 1975), chap. 9.
[6]R. Walford, *Maximum Life Span* (New York: Norton, 1983).

basis for identifing many of the issues that will confront policymakers and program administrators concerned with the status of the elderly in the next half century. These developments are associated often with the changes in the age structure of the population or with the progressive aging of the population. Major public issues arise from the relative rapidity of the growth of the elderly population, especially the older aged, and other age segments: the rise in the relative numbers of elders and children, of elders and the working-age population, and of elders and the total population; and the increase in the share of the older aged among the elderly.

The prospective changes in age structure impose especially difficult tasks of planning for the needs of the elderly and have major implications for a wide array of planning and policy issues relating to the economy, the family, housing, and health. These implications are important for society and the general welfare of the elderly because the elderly, particularly the older aged, require a disproportionate level of services and account for a disproportionate share of the public budget.[7] The demographic trends described and the attendant issues occur in the social context of limited public resources and pressures for budgetary restraint, differing philosophies as to the role of the government in private life and as to the share of public and private resources to be allocated to the elderly, divergent views as to the population group requiring principal support (e.g., children or the elderly), and even differing opinions among professionals as to the basis for government support (e.g., age or need).

A major policy issue associated with the shifting balance in the numbers of elders and children is the relative allocation of public resources to the two groups of dependents. This issue is intensified by their disproportionate needs, differences in political power, and the necessarily limited resources available. Some social scientists and advocacy groups focus so sharply on the unmet needs of the elderly population as to denigrate the sometimes opposing needs of the larger society, including those of children.[8] Other social scientists hold the view that an excessive share of public resources is already being allocated to the elderly and that the needs of children are neglected.[9]

---

[7]W. F. Laurie and P. A. Iler, "Graying of the National Budget: the Year 2020," paper presented at the annual meeting of the American Statistical Association, Philadelphia, August 13–16, 1984.

[8]This appeared to be the prevailing view, for example, of the Gerontological Society of America until the mid 1980s, although it was not explicitly promulgated.

[9]H. A. Richman and M. W. Stagner, "Children: Treasured Resource or Forgotten Minority?" in A. Pifer and L. Bronte, eds., Our Aging Society: Paradox or Promise (New York: Norton, 1986), esp. pp. 174–178. S. Preston, "Children and the Elderly: Divergent Paths for America's Dependents," Demography 21 (4) (November 1984):435–458. J. Axinn and M. J. Stern, "Age and Dependency: Children and the Aged in American Social Policy," Milbank Memorial Fund Quarterly 63 (4) (Fall 1985):648–670.

This policy issue is closely linked to another—namely, the relative allocation of public and private resources to the elderly. Children and the elderly have traditionally been almost wholly supported by private family resources. Since the start of the Social Security program in 1935, however, the balance has shifted sharply toward public responsibility for, if not public support of, the elderly. Many factors have contributed to a larger role of government. They include major changes in the structure of the family, excessive poverty of the elderly and the recognition of the need for income support programs, the increased costs of health care, and the nature and degree of care required by chronically ill but long-lived very old persons. The slower growth of the child and teenage population than of the elderly population in the next few decades should permit the transfer of additional resources to the support of the elderly. However, the support costs for older persons are probably greater than for children and, as suggested, have tended to become public responsibilities compared with the support costs for children, which have tended to remain private family responsibilities. Having the advantage of a great array of public programs, the elderly have made considerable economic progress, while children, having largely remained the responsibility of their parents, have become increasingly poor.[10]

The combination of a burgeoning elderly population, a relatively small working-age population, and continuing low fertility means that only a relatively small number of persons of working age will be available to provide the services and funds the elderly need. Variations over time in age dependency ratios indicate the periods when the age structure of the population is likely to contribute most to supporting the needs of the elderly (i.e., providing health and social services, adequate housing, and satisfactory work) as well as when the possibility of tension between the elderly and children for social support will be greatest.[11]

The demographic changes anticipated have implications for the administration of the Social Security Trust Fund, other entitlement programs covering the older population, private pension programs, and, in general, the structure and financing of programs for the elderly. The concentration of persons in the ages where chronic health problems are most common, in combination with the rise in the ratio of older dependents to workers, has problematic consequences for the funding of health and social services and the supply of health and social service workers. The rise in the elderly dependency ratio makes more difficult the support of and provision of services to the elderly through programs such

[10]Axinn and Stern (1985); Richman and Stagner (1986).
[11]E. A. Wynne, "Will the Young Support the Old?" in A. Pifer and L. Bronte, eds., *Our Aging Society: Paradox or Promise* (New York: Norton, 1986).

as Social Security and Medicare. This is already a problem in several more developed countries, such as Germany and Japan.[12] In Germany the ratio of retired persons to workers is the highest in the world, and Japan is now experiencing the most rapid increases in this regard. These countries face the prospect of allocating an increasing portion of their budget to Social Security benefits at a time when the competing demands for use of public and private funds already will be considerable.

The burden on the working-age population to support the older population has been intensified by the rapid and continuous decline in labor force participation of men at the older ages and the general stagnation in labor productivity. It has been mitigated by the steady, sharp rise in the labor force participation of women at the principal working ages brought about mainly by the demand on the part of women for economic independence and security. The slow increase in the relative size of the older population expected in the next few decades will ease the problem of maintaining the solvency of pension funds briefly, but the advent of the baby-boom cohorts after 2010 will sorely challenge their viability.

Implications Related to Other Demographic Changes

The primary fact to be dealt with regarding old age is failing health and the consequent loss of the ability to take care of oneself. The basic needs of the elderly, even the older aged, are quite similar to those of other adults in general but diverge sharply when the elderly become dysfunctional. Then their needs—whether in the area of health services, finances, housing, or social and psychological support—change radically and drastic adjustments are required, particularly in living arrangements. It is the numbers with impaired functioning who form the basis for costly public programs and the expenditure of huge amounts of money and resources, both public and private. More emphasis is given in this monograph to the characteristics of persons aged 85 and over than is seemingly justified by their small numbers precisely because of the large proportion of them with impaired functioning, and the resulting need for expensive long-term care.

We are moving toward a crisis in the familial support of the elderly with impaired functioning. At the same time as the proportion of women

---

[12]Bundesrepublik Deutschland, *Bericht über die Bevölkerungsentwicklung in der Bundesrepublik Deutschland*, Teil 2 (Population Development in the Federal Republic of Germany, pt. 2) (1984). T. Kuroda, "Aging of the Population of Japan: Prospects and Challenges," in *Population Aging in Japan: Problems and Policy Issues in the 21st Century*, International Symposium on an Aging Society: Strategies for 21st Century Japan, Tokyo, November 24–27, 1982.

who work has been rising sharply, longevity has been increasing greatly. The extension of human life has been causing an increase in the number of generations in families. As a result, an increasing number of families now include two generations of elderly members requiring assistance at a time when there are strong financial and other inducements for the middle-aged children of the aging parents to work.

Poverty in old age is a second major concern to be dealt with. While the proportion of elderly people who are officially poor is only slightly higher than that for the general adult population, the proportion who are poor or near-poor (i.e., under 125 percent of the poverty line) is greater than for the general adult population, and for certain categories of elderly people (e.g., black women, especially those living alone), the proportion in poverty or close to poverty is extremely high. Income inequality is greater for the elderly than for the general population. The elderly remain, therefore, a group for which programs of economic support are essential.

A third major concern is the preponderance of women. Older women have special needs and problems, and public policy should be directed to meet these needs. In particular, public policy and programs should be designed to maintain the economic, social, and physical independence of women as long as possible. The problems would be mitigated greatly, as we have seen, if a much larger proportion of older women were married. It is not to be expected, however, that public policy can do much to bring this about—except by supporting programs designed specifically to reduce the excessive mortality of men. Men have commonly already made the "supreme sacrifice." From a philosophical and ethical point of view, we may, therefore, also see the problems of older women as an issue of prevention versus treatment. In fact, the locus of the main problem is a legitimate matter of debate. I note simply that an important part of the solution of the problems of older women may be the preservation of the lives of men. The same goal may be achieved indirectly by a major cultural revolution in the age-selection of marriage partners, especially in remarriages. Increasingly, however, the growing economic independence of women makes their being married and saving the men seem less necessary and important!

Epilogue

This demographic analysis of the older population and aging in the United States concludes with some suggestions and admonitions regarding the directions of thinking about the older population. The immense diversity of the older population suggests a greater focus on older adults as individuals rather than as members of a class and on the potential for positive change in the later years of life. The need to focus on the individual and the potential for positive change should be construed as applying broadly—that is, in the areas of work, income, housing, health, living arrangements, and other aspects of daily life. Furthermore, the focus should be on the specific characteristics of the individual that imply a problem—for example, unemployment or underemployment, poverty, or ill health—rather than on age itself. As the Neugartens have written, "Perhaps the most constructive way of adapting to an aging society will emerge by focusing, not on age at all, but on more relevant dimensions of human needs, human competencies, and human diversity."[13]

With respect to work status, for example, attention should be given to the individual's capacity for work based on skills, work experience, and health. In the area of income, we should recognize the general principle of individual need, that is, the right of all members of society to receive a minimum adequate income and minimum adequate retirement benefits. At the same time, we should recognize the general principle that returns to labor, including benefits in old age, should bear a reasonable relation to the amount and kind of work performed and retirement tax contributions made by the individual.

We need to reconsider regarding the elderly as dependent. It is true that a large share of older workers retire from their primary job, and hence become dependent, as early as age 62, but if we consider their capacity for regular work in the workplace, part time as well as full time, and volunteer work as well as paid work, we would not deem most older persons dependent until some age well beyond 70. From the point of view of health, few elderly persons are dependent by age 80, and even at age 85 many are fully able to take care of themselves. We might better think of ages 65–74 merely as part of the "third quarter of life," as Pifer and Bronte have suggested, and ages 75–84 as part of the fourth quarter.[14]

Finally, we need to think more in terms of mutual rights and obligations among the generations than in terms of the grounds for intergenerational conflict. In other words, we need to recognize the transgenerational nature of our aging society.

The major policy implication of these ways of thinking is that we should move away from the categorical programs that are based on tra-

[13]B. L. Neugarten and D. A. Neugarten, "Age in the Aging Society," *Daedalus* 115 (1) (Winter 1986):31–49, esp. p. 47.

[14]A. Pifer and L. Bronte, "Introduction: Squaring the Pyramid," *Daedalus* 115 (1) (Winter 1986):1–11, especially pp. 9–10.

ditional ideas as to what people can and should do at particular stages of life.[15] We need a new set of assumptions as to when to support and help individuals. Some illustrations of possible shifts in policy are offered. The role of public policy with respect to work should be to provide opportunities for work designed to maximize the use of human resources. Government's role should be to make or support changes that will permit the elderly to continue to be economically productive. Frequent, if not continuous, opportunities for retraining of workers as they grow older and flexible work programs are needed to maintain the productivity of workers and, hence, their retainability in the workplace as they reach the later ages. Ways must be found to make the transitions from job to job, required because of technological changes, international competition, and other factors, more manageable and less traumatic. Social Security should be gradually converted to a true insurance savings-investment scheme, wherein housework is viewed as having economic value, but it will need to be supplemented by a program to assure minimum adequate benefits for everyone, including nonworkers.[16]

Finally, we need to reform our health care delivery system, including health insurance programs, so as to assure basic health services for everyone and make the coverage of long-term care (including necessary home care services), as well as coverage of major acute episodes, available to all members of our society. A comprehensive system of national health insurance, paralleling our system of national economic insurance, is an urgent need.

[15]Neugarten and Neugarten (1986), esp. pp. 43–47.
[16]V. L. Fuchs, *How We Live* (Cambridge, MA: Harvard University Press, 1983), chap. 7.

Bibliography

Aaron, H. J., and G. Burtless "Introduction and Summary," in Henry J. Aaron and Gary Burtless, eds. *Retirement and Economic Behavior.* Washington, DC: Brookings Institution, 1984.

Adamchak, D. J., and E. A. Friedman "Societal Aging and Generational Dependency Relationships: Problems of Measurement and Conceptualization." *Research on Aging* 5 (3) (September 1983):319–338.

Arriaga, E. "Measuring and Explaining the Change in Life Expectancies." *Demography* 21 (1) (February 1984):83–96.

Atkins, G. L. "The Economic Status of the Oldest Old." *Milbank Memorial Fund Quarterly* 63 (2) (Spring 1985):395–419.

Avorn, J. L. "Medicine, Health, and the Geriatric Transformation." *Daedalus* 115 (1) (Winter 1986):211–225.

Axinn, J., and M. J. Stern "Age and Dependency: Children and the Aged in American Social Policy." *Milbank Memorial Fund Quarterly* 63 (4) (Fall 1985):648–670.

Baer, W. C. "Empty Housing Space: An Overlooked Resource." *Policy Studies Journal* 8 (2) (Special 1) (1979):220–227.

Barsby, S. L., and D. R. Cox *Interstate Migration of the Elderly: An Economic Analysis.* Lexington, MA: Heath, 1975.

Bartlema, J. D. *Developments in Kinship Networks for the Aged in the Netherlands.* Recks Sociale Zekerheids Wetenschap, Katholieke Universiteit Brabant, Tilburg, 1987.

Becker, G. S. *A Treatise on the Family.* Cambridge, MA: Harvard University Press, 1981.

Belloc, N. B. "Personal Behavior Affecting Mortality." In Samuel H. Preston, ed. *Biological and Social Aspects of Mortality and the Length of Life.* International Union for the Scientific Study of Population. Liège: Ordina Editions, 1982.

———, **and L. Breslow** "Relationship of Physical Health Status and Health Practices." *Preventive Medicine* 1 (3) (August 1972):409–421.

Bennett, N. G. "The Roots of Crossover Mortality: Imperfect Data vs. Heterogeneity of Frailty." Paper presented at the Workshop on Methodologies of Forecasting Life Expectancy and Active Life Expectancy, National Institutes of Health, Bethesda, MD, June 1985.

———, **and L. K. Garson** "Extraordinary Longevity in the Soviet Union: Fact or Artifact." *Gerontologist* 26 (4) (August 1986):358–361.

Berg, S.; D. Mellstrom; G. Perrson; and A. Svanborg "Loneliness in Swedish Aged." *Journal of Gerontology* 36 (3) (May 1981):342–349.

Biggar, J. C. "Who Moved Among the Elderly, 1965–1970: A Comparison of Types of Older Movers." *Research on Aging* 2 (1) (March 1980):73–92.

—— "The Graying of the Sunbelt: A Look at the Impact of Elderly Migration." *Population Trends and Policy Series.* Washington, DC: Population Reference Bureau, 1984.

—— "Reassessing Elderly Sunbelt Migration." *Research on Aging* 2 (2) (June 1980):177–190.

Binstock, R. H. "The Elderly in America: Their Economic Resources, Income Status, and Costs." In W. Brown and L. Olson, eds. *Aging and Public Policy: The Politics of Growing Old in America.* Westport, CT: Greenwood Press, 1983.

—— "The Oldest Old: A Fresh Perspective or Compassionate Ageism Revisited?" *Milbank Memorial Fund Quarterly* 63 (2) (Spring 1985):421–451.

Blum, A., and R. Plessat "Une nouvelle table de mortalité pour l'URSS (1984–85)." *Population* (Paris) 42 (6) (November–December 1987):843–862.

Boaz, R. F. "The 1983 Amendments to the Social Security Act: Will They Delay Retirement? A Summary of the Evidence." *Gerontologist* 27 (2) (April 1987):151–156.

Bourgeois-Pichat, J. "Essai sur la mortalité 'biologique' de l'homme." *Population* (Paris) 7 (3) (July–September 1952):381–394.

—— "Future Outlook for Mortality Decline in the World." In *Prospects of Population: Methodology and Assumptions* (Papers of the Ad Hoc Group of Experts on Demographic Projections), Population Studies, series A, no. 67. New York: United Nations, 1979.

—— "La transition démographique: Vieillissement de la population." In *Population Science in the Service of Mankind,* Conference on Science in the Service of Life, sponsored by the Institute of Life and the International Union for the Scientific Study of Population, Vichy, France, 1979.

Branch, L. G. "Continuing Care Retirement Communities: Self-Insuring for Long-Term Care." *Gerontologist* 27 (1) (February 1987):4–8.

Branch, L. G., and A. M. Jette "A Prospective Study of Long-Term Care Institutionalization Among the Aged." *American Journal of Public Health* 72 (1982):1373–1379.

—— "Personal Health Practices and Mortality Among the Elderly." *American Journal of Public Health* 74 (10) (October 1984):1126–1129.

Brody, E. M. "Parent Care as a Normative Family Stress." *Gerontologist* 25 (1) (February 1985):19–29.

——; **W. Poulshock; and C. F. Masciocchi** "The Family Care Unit: A Major Consideration in the Long-Term Support System." *Gerontologist* 18 (5) (October 1978):556–561.

Brody, J. A. "Length of Life and the Health of Older People." *National Forum* 62 (Fall 1982):4–5.

Brookdale Institute on Aging and Adult Development, Columbia University, and International Exchange Center on Gerontology, University of South Florida. *Returning from the Sunbelt: Myths and Realities of Migratory Patterns Among the Elderly.* Proceedings of a Symposium, March 15, 1985.

Bumpass, L. L. "What's Happening to the Family? Interactions Between Demographic and Institutional Change." *Demography* 27 (4) (November 1990):483–498.

Bundesrepublik Deutschland *Bericht über die Bevölkerungsentwicklung in der Bundesrepublik Deutschland,* Teil 2 (Population Development in the Federal Republic of Germany, pt. 2) (1984).

Burkhauser, R. V.; K. C. Holden; and D. Feaster "Incidence, Timing, and Events Associated with Poverty: A Dynamic View of Poverty in Retirement." *Journal of Gerontology* 43 (2) (1988):S46–52.

Burney, S. W. "Morbidity and Mortality in a Healthy Aging Male Population: 10-Year Survey." *Gerontologist* 12 (1) (February 1972):49–54.

Burt, B. A. "The Oral Health of Older Americans." *American Journal of Public Health* 76 (1986):1133–1134.

Butz, W. T., and M. P. Ward "Will U.S. Fertility Remain Low? A New Economic Interpretation, *Population and Development Review* 5 (1979):663–688.

Cain, L. D. "The Growing Importance of Legal Age in Determining the Status of the Elderly." *Gerontologist* 14 (2) (April 1974):167–174.

——— "Aging and the Law." In R. H. Binstock and E. Shanas, eds. *Handbook of Aging and the Social Sciences.* New York: Van Nostrand Reinhold, 1976.

——— "Counting Backward from Projected Death. An Alternative to Chronological Age in Assigning Status to the Elderly." Paper presented at Syracuse University, March 22, 1978.

Cantrell, R. S., and R. L. Clark "Retirement and Promotional Prospects." *Gerontologist* 20 (5) (October 1980):575–580.

Carp, F. M. "Housing and Living Environments of Older People." In R. Binstock and E. Shanas, eds. *Handbook of Aging and the Social Sciences.* New York: Van Nostrand Reinhold, 1976.

Chen, Y.-P. "Economic Status of the Aging." In R. H. Binstock and E. Shanas, eds. *Handbook of Aging and the Social Sciences,* 2nd ed. New York: Van Nostrand Reinhold, 1985.

Chevan, A. "Age, Housing Choice, and Neighborhood Structure." *American Journal of Sociology* 87 (1982):1133–1149.

——— "The Growth of Home Ownership: 1940–1980." *Demography* 26 (2) (May 1989):249–266.

———, **and L. R. Fischer** "Retirement and Interstate Migration." *Social Forces* 57 (6) (1979):1365–1380.

Clark, R. L., and D. T. Barker *Reversing the Trend Toward Early Retirement.* Washington, DC: American Enterprise Institute for Public Policy Research, 1981.

Clark, R. L.; G. L. Maddox; R. P. Schrimper; and D. A. Sumner *Inflation and the Economic Well-Being of the Elderly.* Baltimore: Johns Hopkins University, 1986.

Clark, R. L., and J. J. Spengler "Changing Demography and Dependency Costs: The Implications of Future Dependency Ratios and Their Composition." In B. R. Herzog, ed. *Aging and Income: Programs and Prospects for the Elderly.* New York: Human Sciences Press, 1978.

——— "Dependency Ratios: Their Use in Economic Analysis." In J. L. Simon and J. DaVanzo, eds. *Research in Population Economics,* vol. 2. Greenwich, CT: JAI Press, 1980.

——— *The Economics of Individual and Population Aging.* Cambridge: Cambridge University Press, 1980b.

Clark, R. L., and D. A. Sumner "Inflation and the Real Income of the Elderly: Recent Evidence and Expectations for the Future." *Gerontologist* 25 (2) (April 1985):146–152.

Coale, A. J. "The Effects of Changes in Mortality and Fertility on Age Composition." *Milbank Memorial Fund Quarterly* 34 (1) (January 1956):79–114.

———, and E. Kisker "Mortality Crossovers: Reality or Bad Data?" *Population Studies* 40 (3) (November 1986):389–401.

Coale, A. J., and N. W. Rives, Jr. "A Statistical Reconstruction of the Black Population of the United States, 1880–1970: Estimates of True Numbers by Age and Sex, Birth Rates, and Total Fertility." *Population Index* 39 (1) (January 1973):3–36.

Coale, A. J., and M. Zelnik *New Estimates of Fertility and Population in the United States.* Princeton, NJ: Princeton University Press, 1963.

Cohen, C. I., et al. "Surviving Strategies of Older Homeless Men." *Gerontologist* 28 (1) (February 1988):58–65.

Cohen, J. "Competing Risks, Without Independence." Paper presented at the annual meeting of the Population Association of America, Boston, March 28–30, 1985.

Colvez, A., and M. Blanchet "Disability Trends in the United States Population, 1966–76: Analysis of Reported Causes." *American Journal of Public Health* 71 (5) (May 1981):464–471.

Colvez, A.; J. M. Robine; et al. "Life Expectancy Without Incapacity in France in 1982." *Population* (Paris) 4 (6) (November/December 1986):1025–1042.

Cowgill, D. O. "The Future Location of the Elderly Population Within Metropolitan Areas." In *Consequences of Changing U.S. Population: Demographics of Aging.* Joint Hearings before the Select Committee on Population and the Select Committee on Aging, U.S. House of Representatives, May 24, 1978.

——— "Residential Segregation by Age in American Metropolitan Areas." *Journal of Gerontology* 33 (3) (May 1978):446–453.

Crimmins, E. M. "Life Expectancy and the Older Population: Demographic Implications of Recent and Prospective Trends in Old Age Mortality." *Research on Aging* 6 (4) (December 1984):490–514.

——— "Are Americans Healthier as Well as Long Lived?" *Journal of Insurance Medicine* 22 (3) (Summer 1990): 89–92.

———; Y. Saito; and D. Ingegneri "Changes in Life Expectancy and Disability-Free Life Expectancy in the United States." *Population and Development Review* 15 (2) (June 1989):235–267.

———, and D. Igegneri "Interaction and Living Arrangements of Older Americans and Their Adult Children: Past Trends, Present Determinants, and Future Implications." *Research on Aging* 12 (1) (1990):3–35.

Crown, W. H. "Some Thoughts on Reformulating the Dependency Ratio." *Gerontologist* 25 (2) (April 1985):166–171.

Crystal, S. F. *America's Old Age Crisis: Public Policy and the Two Worlds of Aging.* New York: Basic Books, 1982.

——— "Measuring Income and Inequality Among the Elderly." *Gerontologist* 26 (1) (February 1986):56–59.

David, M. H., and P. L. Menchik "Changes in Cohort Wealth Over a Generation." *Demography* 25 (3) (August 1988):317–335.

Davis, K. "Equal Treatment and Unequal Benefits: The Medicare Program." *Milbank Memorial Fund Quarterly* 53 (4) (1975):449–488.

Davis, K.; M. S. Bernstam; and R. Ricardo-Campbell, eds. "Below Replacement Fertility in Industrial Societies: Causes, Consequences, Policies." *Population and Development Review* 12 (supplement) (1986).

Davis, M. A.; S. P. Murphy; and J. M. Neuhaus "Living Arrangements and Eating Behaviors of Older Adults in the United States." *Journal of Gerontology* 43 (3) (May 1988):S96–98.

Denton, N. A. "Differences in Residential Segregation of the Elderly in the United States: Whites, Blacks, Hispanics, and Asians, 1970–1980." Paper presented at the annual meeting of the Population Association of America, Chicago, April 29–May 2, 1987.

Durand, J. D. *The Labor Force in Economic Development.* Princeton, NJ: Princeton University Press, 1975.

Dwyer, T., and B. S. Hetzel "A Comparison of Trends of Coronary Heart Disease Mortality in Australia, England and Wales and U.S.A. with Reference to Three Major Risk Factors—Hypertension, Cigarette Smoking and Diet." *International Journal of Epidemiology* 9 (1980):65–71.

Easterlin, R. A. "What Will 1984 Be Like? Socioeconomic Implications of Recent Twists in Age Structure," *Demography* 15 (4) (1978):397–432.

Espenshade, T., and W. Serow, eds. *The Economic Consequences of Slowing Population Growth.* New York: Academic Press, 1978.

Farley, R. *Blacks and Whites: Narrowing the Gap?,* Cambridge, MA: Harvard University Press, 1986.

Feldman, J. J. "Work Ability of the Aged Under Conditions of Improving Mortality." *Milbank Memorial Fund Quarterly* 61 (3) (Summer 1983):430–444.

Fields, G. S., and O. S. Mitchell *Retirement, Pensions, and Social Security.* Cambridge, MA: MIT Press, 1984.

Fienberg, S. E., and W. M. Mason "Identification and Estimation of Age-Period-Cohort Models in the Analysis of Discrete Archival Data." In K. F. Schuessler, ed. *Sociological Methodology.* San Francisco: Jossey-Bass, 1979.

Fisher, C. F. "Differences by Age Groups in Health Care Spending." *Health Care Financial Review* 1 (4) (Spring 1980):65–90.

Fitzpatrick, K. M., and J. R. Logan "The Aging of the Suburbs, 1960–1980." *American Sociological Review* 50 (1) (February 1985):106–117.

Flynn, C. B.; C. F. Longino; R. F. Wiseman; and J. C. Biggar "The Redistribution of America's Older Population: Major National Migration Patterns for Three Census Decades." *Gerontologist* 25 (3) (June 1985):292–296.

Foner, A., and K. Schwab *Aging and Retirement.* Monterey, CA: Brooks/Cole, 1981.

Frankenhaueser, M. "Psychoneuroendocrine Sex Difference in Adaptation to the Psychosocial Environment." Paper presented at the Sereno Symposium, Siena, Italy, 1976.

———; M. Von Wright; A. Collins; J. Von Wright; G. Sedvall, and C. Swahn "Sex Differences in Psychoneuroendocrine Reactions to Examination Stress." *Psychosomatic Medicine* 40 (1978):334–343.

Frey, W. H. "Lifecourse Migration and Distribution of the Elderly Across U.S. Regions and Metropolitan Areas." *Economic Outlook USA* 13 (2) (2nd quarter, 1986):10–16.

Friedman, J., and J. Sjogren "Assets of the Elderly as They Retire." *Social Security Bulletin* 44 (1) (January 1981):1–16.

Fries, J. F. "Aging, Natural Death, and the Compression of Morbidity." *New England Journal of Medicine* 303 (3) (July 17, 1980):130–135.

——— "The Compression of Morbidity." *Milbank Memorial Fund Quarterly* 61 (3) (1983):397–419.

———, and L. M. Crapo *Vitality and Aging: Implications of the Rectangular Curve.* San Francisco: Freeman, 1981.

Fuchs, V. L. *How We Live.* Cambridge, MA: Harvard University Press, 1983.

Fuguitt, G. V., and S. J. Tordella "Elderly Net Migration: The New Trend of Nonmetropolitan Change." *Research on Aging* 2 (2) (June 1980):191–204.

Fullerton, H. N., Jr. "Labor Force Projections: 1988 to 2000." *Monthly Labor Review* 110 (9) (September 1987): 19–29.

——— "The 1995 Labor Force: BLS' Latest Projections." *Monthly Labor Review* 108 (11) (November 1985):17–25.

———**, and J. Tschetter** "The 1995 Labor Force: A Second Look." *Monthly Labor Review* (November 1983):3–10.

———**, and J. J. Byrne** "Length of Working Life for Men and Women, 1970." *Monthly Labor Review* 99 (2) (February 1976).

Garfinkle, S. H. "The Length of Working Life for Males, 1900–60." In C. B. Nam, ed. *Population and Society*. Boston: Houghton Mifflin, 1968.

Gelfand, D. E. *Aging: The Ethnic Factor*. Boston: Little-Brown, 1982.

———**, and A. J. Kutzik, eds.** *Ethnicity and Aging: Theory, Research, and Policy*. New York: Springer, 1979.

Gibson, R. C. "Blacks in an Aging Society." *Daedalus* 115 (1) (Winter 1986):349–371.

——— *Blacks in an Aging Society*. Report of a conference sponsored by the Aging Society Project, Carnegie Corporation of New York, July 1986.

——— "Reconceptualizing Retirement for Black Americans." *Gerontologist* 27 (6) (December 1987):691–698.

Gist, J. R., ed. *Social Security and Economic Well-Being Across Generations*. Public Policy Institute, American Association of Retired Persons, Washington, DC, 1988.

Glenn, N. D. *Cohort Analysis*. Beverly Hills, CA: Sage, 1977.

Glick, P. C. "The Future Marital Status and Living Arrangements of the Elderly." *Gerontologist* 19 (3) (June 1979):301–309.

Golant, S. M. "The Residential Location and Spatial Behavior of the Elderly." Department of Geography Research Paper No. 143, University of Chicago, 1972.

——— "The Housing Tenure Adjustments of the Young and the Elderly and Policy Implications." *Urban Affairs Quarterly* 13 (1) (September 1977):95–108.

——— "The Metropolitanization and Suburbanization of the U.S. Elderly Population: 1970–1988." *Gerontologist* 30 (1) (February 1990):80–85.

——— "Post-1980 Regional Migration Patterns of the U.S. Elderly Population." *Journal of Gerontology* 45 (4) (July 1990):S135–140.

———**, ed.** *Location and Environment of Elderly Population*. Washington, DC: Winston, 1979.

Goldman, L., and E. F. Cook "The Decline of Ischemic Heart Disease Mortality Rates: An Analysis of the Comparative Effects of Medical Intervention and Changes in Lifestyle." *Annals of Internal Medicine* 101 (6) (December 1984):825–836.

Goldman, N.; C. F. Westoff; and C. Hammerslough "Demography of the Marriage Market in the United States." *Population Index* 50 (1) (Spring 1984):5–25.

Gordon, T. T. "Prospects for Aging in America." In M. W. Riley, ed. *Aging from Birth to Death: Interdisciplinary Perspectives*. Boulder, CO: Westview Press, 1979.

Gordus, J. P. *Leaving Early: Perspectives and Problems in Current Retirement Practice and Policy*. Kalamazoo: W. E. Upjohn Institute for Employment Research, 1980.

Government of Sweden SOV, Pensionnar. *The Pensioner Survey, 1977*, 75, Norstedts, Stockholm, 1977.

Grad, S., and K. Foster "Income of the Population Aged 55 and Older, 1976." *Social Security Bulletin* 42 (7) (July 1979).

Grimaldi, P. L. "Measured Inflation and the Elderly, 1973 to 1981." *Gerontologist* 22 (4) (August 1982):347–353.

Gruenberg, E. M. "The Failure of Success." *Milbank Memorial Fund Quarterly* 55 (1) (1977):3–24.

Gustman, A. L., and T. L. Steinmeier "Modeling the Retirement Process for Policy Evaluation and Research." *Monthly Labor Review* 107 (7) (July 1984):26–33.

Gutowski, M., and T. Feild *The Graying of Suburbia.* Washington, DC: Urban Institute, 1979.

Hagestad, G. O. "The Aging Society as a Context for Family Life." *Daedalus* 115 (1) (Winter 1986):77–117.

Hammel, E. A.; K. W. Wachter; and C. K. McDaniel "The Kin of the Aged in A.D. 2000: The Chickens Come Home to Roost." In S. B. Kiesler, J. M. Morgan, and V. K. Oppenheimer, eds. *Aging: Social Change.* New York: Academic Press, 1981.

Handler, B. *Housing Needs of the Elderly: A Quantitative Analysis.* Ann Arbor: National Policy Center on Housing and Living Arrangements for Older Americans, 1983.

Harrington, C.; R. J. Newcomer; and C. L. Estes, and Associates *Long-Term Care of the Elderly.* Beverly Hills, CA: Sage, 1985.

Harrison, B. "Spending Patterns of Older Americans." *Monthly Labor Review* 109 (10) (October 1986):15–17.

Haug, M. R. "Age and Medical Care Utilization Patterns." *Journal of Gerontology* 36 (1) (January 1981):103–111.

Havlik, R. J. and M. Feinleib, eds. *Proceedings of the Conference on the Decline in Coronary Heart Disease Mortality.* NIH Pub. No. 79-1610, U.S. Government Printing Office, Washington, DC, 1979.

Hayflick, L. "The Strategy of Senescence." *Gerontologist* 14 (1) (February 1974):37–45.

————— "Biological Aspects of Aging." In S. Preston, ed. *Biological and Social Aspects of Mortality and the Length of Life.* International Union for the Scientific Study of Population. Liège: Ordina Editions, 1982.

Hayward, M. D.; W. R. Grady; and S. D. McLaughlin "Changes in the Retirement Process Among Older Men in the United States: 1972–1980." *Demography* 25 (3) (August 1988):331–378.

Heaton, T. B. "Recent Trends in the Geographical Distribution of the Elderly Population." In M. W. Riley, B. B. Hess, and K. Bond, eds. *Aging in Society.* Hillsdale, NJ: Lawrence Erlbaum, 1983.

—————; **W. B. Clifford; and G. V. Fuguitt** "Changing Retirement Patterns of Retirement Migration Movement Between Metropolitan and Nonmetropolitan Areas." *Research on Aging* 2 (1) (March 1980):93–104.

Hermalin, A. I. "The Effect of Changes in Mortality Rates on Population Growth and Age Distribution in the United States." *Milbank Memorial Fund Quarterly* 44 (4) (October 1966):451–469.

Herzog, B. R., ed. *Aging and Income: Programs and Prospects for the Elderly.* New York: Human Sciences Press, 1978.

Hobcraft, J.; J. Menken; and S. Preston "Age, Period, and Cohort Effects in Demography: A Review." *Population Index* 48 (1) (Spring 1982):4–43.

Horowitz, A. "Sons and Daughters as Caregivers to Older Parents: Difference in

Role Performance and Consequences." *Gerontologist* 25 (6) (December 1985):613–617.

Houston, M.; R. G. Klamer; and J. M. Barrett "Female Predominance of Immigration to the United States Since 1930: A First Look." *International Migration Review* 18 (4) (1984):908–963.

Ingegneri, D. G., and E. G. Crimmins "Demographic, Social, and Economic Determinants of Health Status among the Older Population." Paper presented at the annual meeting of the Gerontological Society of America, Chicago, November 1986.

Ingram, D. K., and J. R. Barry "National Statistics on Deaths in Nursing Homes: Interpretations and Implications." *Gerontologist* 17 (3) (June 1977):303–308.

International Labor Office *World Labor Report* 1. Geneva, 1984.

—— *World Summary*, 3rd ed. Economically Active Population, Estimates and Projections, 1950–2025, vol. 5. Geneva, 1986.

Jackson, J. *Minorities and Aging*. Belmont, CA: Wadsworth, 1980.

Kastenbaum, B. "The Measurement of Early Retirement." *Journal of the American Statistical Association* 80 (389) (March 1985):38–45.

Kastenbaum, R., and S. Candy "The 4-Percent Fallacy: A Methodological and Empirical Critique of Extended Care Facility Population Statistics." *International Journal of Aging and Human Development* 4 (1973):15–21.

Katz, S.; L. G. Branch; et al. "Active Life Expectancy." *New England Journal of Medicine* 309 (20) (November 17, 1983):1218–1224.

Keith, V. M., and D. P. Smith "The Current Differential in Black and White Life Expectancy." *Demography* 25 (4) (November 1988):625–632.

Kennedy, J. M., and G. F. DeJong "Aged in Cities: Residential Segregation in 10 U.S.A. Central Cities." *Journal of Gerontology* 32 (1) (January 1977):197–202.

Keyfitz, N. "What Difference Would It Make If Cancer Were Eradicated? An Examination of the Taeuber Paradox." *Demography* 14 (4) (November 1977):411–418.

——, and J. Gomez de Leon "Considérations démographiques sur les systèmes de retraite." *Population* (Paris) 35 (4–5) (July–October 1980):815–836.

Kii, T. "A New Index for Measuring Demographic Aging." *Gerontologist* 22 (4) (August 1982):438–442.

Kingston, E. R.; B. A. Hirshorn; and J. M. Cornman *Ties That Bind: The Interdependence of Generations*. Cabin John, MD: Seven Locks Press, 1986.

Kitagawa, E. "On Mortality." *Demography* 14 (4) (November 1977):381–389.

——, and P. M. Hauser *Differential Mortality in the United States: A Study in Socioeconomic Epidemiology*. Cambridge, MA: Harvard University Press, 1973.

Kleinman, J. C.; M. Gold; and D. Makiec "Use of Ambulatory Medical Care by the Poor: Another Look at Equity." *Medical Care* 19 (10) (October 1981):1011–1029.

Kobrin, F. E. "The Fall of Household Size and the Rise of the Primary Individual in the United States." *Demography* 13 (1) (February 1976):127–138.

—— "Family Extension and the Elderly: Economic, Demographic, and Family Cycle Factors." *Journal of Gerontology* 36 (3) (May 1981):370–377.

Koizumi, A. "Health Problems of the Year 2000 and Beyond." *Health Policy* 4 (1985):307–319.

Kovar, M. G. "Health of the Elderly and Use of Health Services." *Public Health Reports* 42 (1) (February 1977):9–19.

Kovar, M. G., and L. A. Fingerhut "Recent Trends in U.S. Mortality Among the Aged." *Consequences of a Changing Population: Demographics of Aging.* Joint Hearings Before the Select Committee on Population, U.S. House of Representatives, and the Select Committee on Aging, May 24, 1978, Washington, DC.

Kuroda, T. "Aging of the Population of Japan: Prospects and Challenges." In *Population Aging in Japan: Problems and Policy Issues in the 21st Century.* International Symposium on an Aging Society: Strategies for 21st Century Japan, November 24–27, 1982.

LaGory, M.; R. A. Ward, and M. Mucatel "Patterns of Age Segregation." *Sociological Focus* 14 (1) (January 1981):1–13.

LaGory, M.; R. A. Ward; and T. Juravich "Explanations of the Age Segregation Process in American Cities." *Urban Affairs Quarterly* 16 (1) (1980):59–80.

Lane, T. S., and J. D. Feins "Are the Elderly Overhoused? Definitions of Space Utilization and Policy Implications." *Gerontologist* 25 (3) (June 1985):243–250.

Laurie, W. F. "Employing the Duke OARS Methodology in Cost Comparisons: Home Services and Institutionalization." Duke University Center for the Study of Aging and Human Development. *Advances in Research* 2 (2) (1978).

———, **and P. A. Iler** "Graying of the National Budget: the Year 2020." Paper presented at the annual meeting of the American Statistical Association, Philadelphia, August 13–16, 1984.

Lawton, M. P. *Environment and Aging.* Monterey, CA: Brooks/Cole, 1980.

——— "Housing and Living Environments of Older People." In R. H. Binstock and E. Shanas, eds. *Handbook of Aging and the Social Sciences,* 2nd ed. New York: Van Nostrand Reinhold, 1985.

———; **M. H. Kleban; and D. Carlson** "The Inner-City Resident: To Move or Not to Move." *Gerontologist* 13 (4) (August 1973):443–448.

Lawton, M. P.; M. Moss; and M. H. Kleban "Marital Status, Living Arrangements, and the Well-Being of Older People." *Research on Aging* 6 (3) (September 1984):323–345.

Leaf, A. *Youth in Old Age.* New York: McGraw-Hill, 1975.

Lee, B. A., and P. B. Wood "Is Neighborhood Racial Succession Place-Specific?" *Demography* 28 (1) (February 1991):21–40.

Lee, R. D.; W. B. Arthur; and G. Rodgers, eds. *Economics of Changing Age Distributions in Developed Countries.* Oxford: Clarendon Press, 1989.

Leeson, G. W. "Some Economic Consequences of an Aging and Declining Population in Denmark." *European Demographic Information Bulletin* 14 (3) (1983):81–95.

——— "Aging and Economic Welfare." *Genus* 41 (3–4) (December 1985):157–169.

Liang, J., and E. Jow-Ching Tu "Estimating Lifetime Risk of Nursing Home Residency: A Further Note." *Gerontologist* 26 (5) (October 1986):560–563.

Lichter, D. T.; G. V. Fuguitt; T. B. Heaton; and W. B. Clifford "Components of Change in the Residential Concentrations of the Elderly Population: 1950–1975." *Journal of Gerontology* 36 (4) (July 1981):480–489.

Litwak, E., and C. F. Longino, Jr. "Migration Patterns Among the Elderly: A Developmental Perspective." *Gerontologist* 27 (3) (1987):266–272.

Liu, K., and K. G. Manton "The Characteristics and Utilization Patterns of Admission Cohorts of Nursing Home Patients." *Gerontologist* 19 (1) (February 1979):53–55.

Liu, K., and Y. Palesch "The Nursing Home Population: Different Perspectives and Implications for Policy." *Health Care Financing Review* 3 (2) (December 1981):15–23.

Logan, J. R., and G. Spitze "Suburbanization and Public Services for the Aging." *Gerontologist* 28 (5) (October 1988):644–647.

Longino, C. F., Jr. "Changing Aged Nonmetropolitan Migration Patterns, 1955 to 1960 and 1965 to 1970." *Journal of Gerontology* 37 (2) (March 1982):228–234.

—— "Returning from the Sunbelt: Myths and Realities of Migratory Patterns Among the Elderly." In *Proceedings of Symposium on Returning from the Sunbelt, March 15, 1985.* Brookdale Institute, Columbia University, and International Exchange on Gerontology, University of South Florida.

—— "A State by State Look at the Oldest Americans." *American Demographics* 8 (11) (November 1986):38–42.

——, **and J. C. Biggar** "The Impact of Population Redistribution on Service Delivery." *Gerontologist* 22 (2) (April 1982):153–159.

Longino, C. F., Jr., and D. J. Jackson, eds. "Migration and the Aged." *Research on Aging* 2 (2) (June 1980): special issue.

Luloff, A. E.; L. E. Swanson; and R. H. Warland "Reconceptualizing Age and Retirement Status." *Sociological Focus* 18 (3) (August 1985):273–278.

Madigan, F. C. "Are Sex Mortality Differentials Biologically Caused?" *Milbank Memorial Fund Quarterly* 35 (2) (1957):202–203.

Magnum, W. P. "Housing for the Elderly in the United States." In A. M. Warnes, ed. *Geographical Perspectives on the Elderly.* London: Wiley, 1982.

Manton, K. G. "Sex and Race Specific Mortality Differentials in Multiple Cause of Death Data." *Gerontologist* 20 (4) (August 1980):480–493.

—— "Changing Concepts of Mortality and Morbidity in the Elderly Population." *Milbank Memorial Fund Quarterly* 60 (2) (Spring 1982):183–244.

—— "Past and Future Life Expectancy Increases at Later Ages: Their Implications for the Linkage of Chronic Morbidity, Disability, and Mortality." *Journal of Gerontology* 41 (5) (September 1986):672–681.

—— "A Longitudinal Study of Functional Change and Mortality in the United States." *Journal of Gerontology* 43 (5) (1988):S153–161.

Manton, K. G., and K. Liu "The Future Growth of the Long-Term Care Population: Projections Based on the 1977 National Nursing Home Survey and the 1982 Long-Term Care Survey." Presented at the Third National Leadership Conference on Long-Term Care Issues, Washington, DC, March 7–9, 1984.

Manton, K. G.; C. H. Patrick; and K. W. Johnson "Health Differentials Between Blacks and Whites: Recent Trends in Mortality and Morbidity." *Milbank Memorial Fund Quarterly* 65 (Supplement 1) (1987):129–199.

Manton, K. G., and S. S. Poss "Effects of Dependency Among Causes of Death for Cause Elimination of Life Table Strategies." *Demography* 16 (2) (May 1979):313–327.

Manton, K. G., and B. J. Soldo "Dynamics of Health Changes in the Oldest Old: New Perspectives and Evidence." *Milbank Memorial Fund Quarterly* 63 (2) (Spring 1985):206–285.

Manton, K. G.; M. A. Woodbury; and K. Liu "Life Table Methods for Assessing the Dynamics of U.S. Nursing Home Utilization: 1976–77." *Journal of Gerontology* 39 (1) (January 1984):79–87.

Manton, K. G., and E. Stallard "Methods for Evaluating the Heterogeneity of Aging Processes Using Vital Statistics Data: Explaining the Black/White Mortality Crossover by a Model of Mortality Selection." *Human Biology* 53 (1981):47–67.

Manton, K. G.; H. D. Tolley; and S. S. Poss "Life Table Techniques for Multiple Cause Mortality." *Demography* 13 (4) (November 1976):541–564.

Manton, K. G.; S. S. Poss; and S. Wing "The Black/White Mortality Crossover: Investigation from the Perspective of the Components of Aging." *Gerontologist* 19 (3) (June 1979):291–300.

Markides, K. S., and C. H. Mindel *Aging and Ethnicity.* Beverly Hills, CA: Sage, 1986.

Massey, D. S. "Residential Segregation and Spatial Distribution of a Non–Labor Force Population: The Needy Elderly and Disabled." *Economic Geography* 56 (3) (1980):190–200.

Massey, D. S., and N. S. Denton "The Dimensions of Residential Segregation." Unpublished paper, Population Studies Center, University of Pennsylvania, 1986.

McCarthy, K. F. *The Elderly Population's Changing Spatial Distribution.* Santa Monica, CA: Rand, 1983.

McConnel, C. E. "A Note on the Lifetime Risk of Nursing Home Residency." *Gerontologist* 24 (2) (April 1984):193–198.

McHugh, K. E.; P. Cohen; and N. Reid "Determinants of Short- and Long-Term Mobility for Home Owners and Renters." *Demography* 27 (1) (February 1990):81–95.

McFarland, D. "The Aged in the 21st Century: A Demographic View." In L. F. Jarvik, ed. *Aging into the 21st Century: Middle-Agers Today.* New York: Gardner Press, 1978.

McMillan, M. M., and C. Nam "Mortality Crossovers by Cause of Death and Race in the U.S. in the 1970's." Paper presented at a meeting of the International Union for the Scientific Study of Population, Florence, 1985.

McMillan, M. M., and H. M. Rosenberg "New Research Directions on Socio-Economic Differential Mortality in the United States of America." *Socio-Economic Differential Mortality in Industrialized Societies* 3, United Nations Population Division, World Health Organization, and Committee for International Cooperation in National Research in Demography, 1984.

McNeely, R. L., and J. N. Colen, eds. *Aging in Minority Groups.* Beverly Hills, CA: Sage, 1983.

Menken, J. L. "Age and Fertility: How Late Can You Wait?" *Demography* 22 (4) (November 1985):469–484.

Miller, A. R. "Changing Work Life Patterns: A Twenty-Five Year Review." *Annals of the American Academy of Political and Social Science* 435 (January 1978):83–101.

Mindell, C. N. "Multigenerational Family Households: Recent Trends and Implications for the Future." *Gerontologist* 19 (5) (October 1979):456–463.

Minkler, M., and R. Stone "The Feminization of Poverty and Older Women." *Gerontologist* 25 (4) (August 1985):351–357.

Moon, M. *The Measurement of Economic Welfare: Its Application to the Aged Poor.* New York: Academic Press, 1977.

Mor, V.; S. Sherwood; and C. Gutkin "A National Study of Residential Care for the Aged." *Gerontologist* 26 (4) (August 1986):405–417.

Morris, R., and S. A. Bass "The Elderly as Surplus People: Is There a Role for Higher Education?" *Gerontologist* 26 (1) (February 1986):12–18.

Morrison, M. H. "Work and Retirement in the Aging Society." *Daedalus* 115 (1) (Winter 1986):269–323.

Nam, C. B., and K. A. Ockay "Factors Contributing to the Mortality Crossover Pattern: Effects of Development Level, Overall Mortality Level, and Causes of Death." *Proceedings of the 18th General Conference of the International Union for the Scientific Study of Population*, Mexico City, August 8–13, 1977.

Nam, C. B.; N. L. Weatherby; and K. A. Ockay "Causes of Death Which Contribute to the Mortality Crossover Effect." *Social Biology* 25 (4) (Winter 1978):306–314.

National Academy of Sciences *The Aging Population in the Twenty-First Century: Statistics for Health Policy*. Washington, DC: National Academy Press, 1988.

Neugarten, B. L. "The Future and the Young-Old." In L. F. Jarvik, ed. *Aging into the 21st Century: Middle-Agers Today*. New York: Gardner Press, 1978.

———. ed. *Age or Need? Public Policies for Older People*. Beverly Hills, CA: Sage, 1982.

Neugarten, B. L., and R. T. Havighurst, eds. *Extending the Human Life Span: Social Policy and Social Ethics*. Committee on Human Development, University of Chicago. Washington, DC: U.S. Government Printing Office, 1977.

———, **and D. A. Neugarten** "Age in the Aging Society." *Daedalus* 115 (1) (Winter 1986):31–49.

Newcomer, R. J.; M. P. Lawton; and T. O. Byerts, eds. *Housing an Aging Society: Issues, Alternatives, and Policy*. New York: Van Nostrand Reinhold, 1986.

Nightingale, E. "Prospects for Reducing Mortality in Developed Countries by Changes in Day-to-Day Behavior." *International Population Conference, Manila, 1981*. Liège: International Union for the Scientific Study of Population, 1981.

Omran, A. R. "Epidemiologic Transition in the United States: The Health Factor in Population Change." *Population Bulletin* 32 (2) (May 1977).

Palmer, J. L., and S. G. Gould "The Economic Consequences of An Aging Society." *Daedalus* 115 (1) (Winter 1986):295–323.

Palmer, J. L., and B. B. Torrey "Health Care Financing and Pensions Programs." In G. B. Mills and J. L. Palmer, eds. *Federal Budget Policy in the 1980s*. Washington, DC: Urban Institute Press, 1984.

Palmore, E. B. "Trends in the Health of the Aged." *Gerontologist* 26 (3) (June 1986):298–302.

Pampel, F. C. "Changes in the Propensity to Live Alone, Evidence from Consecutive Cross-Sectional Surveys." *Demography* 20 (4) (October 1983):433–449.

———, **and H. Choldin** "Urban Location and Segregation of the Aged: A Block-level Analysis." *Social Forces* 56 (4) (1978):1121–1139.

Pampel, F. C., and J. A. Weiss "Economic Development, Pension Policies, and the Labor Force Participation of Aged Males: A Cross-National Longitudinal Approach." *American Journal of Sociology* 89 (2) (September 1983):350–372.

Patrick, C. H. "Health and Migration of the Elderly." *Research on Aging* 2 (2) (June 1980):233–241.

———; **Y. Y. Palesch; M. Feinleib; and J. A. Brody** "Sex Differences in Declining Cohort Death Rates from Heart Diseases." *American Journal of Public Health* 72 (2) (February 1982):161–166.

Pifer, A., and L. Bronte "Introduction: Squaring the Pyramid." *Daedalus* 115 (1) (Winter 1986):1–11.

———, **eds.** *Our Aging Society: Paradox and Promise*. New York: Norton, 1986.

Population Reference Bureau "Counting the U.S.'s Homeless." *Population Today* 14 (10) (October 1986):3, 8.

Poterba, J. M., and L. H. Summers "Public Policy Implications of Declining Old-Age Mortality." Paper prepared for the Brookings Conference on Retirement and Aging, Washington, DC, May 2, 1985.

Preston, S. "Older Male Mortality and Cigarette Smoking: A Demographic Analysis." *Population Monograph Series,* No. 7, University of California, Berkeley, 1970.

―――― *Mortality Patterns in National Populations, with Special Reference to Recorded Causes of Death.* New York: Academic Press, 1976.

―――― "Children and the Elderly: Divergent Paths for America's Dependents." *Demography* 21 (4) (November 1984a):435–458.

―――― "Children and the Elderly in the United States." *Scientific American* 251 (6) (1984b):44–49.

―――― "The Demography of Public Transfers to Dependents: Analytic Issues." Paper presented at the annual meeting of the American Sociological Association, New York, September 2, 1986.

――――; **C. Himes; and M. Eggers** "Demographic Conditions Responsible for Population Aging." *Demography* 26 (4) (November 1989):691–704.

Preston, S.; N. Keyfitz; and R. Schoen *Causes of Death: Life Tables for National Populations.* New York: Seminar Press, 1972.

Pullum, T. W. "The Eventual Frequencies of Kin in a Stable Population." *Demography* 19 (2) (November 1982):549–565.

Radner, D. B. "The Wealth and Income of Aged Households." Paper presented at a meeting of the American Statistical Association, Philadelphia, August 13–16, 1984.

Ragan, P. K., ed. *Work and Retirement: Policy Issues.* Ethel Percy Andrus Gerontology Center, Los Angeles: University of Southern California Press, 1980.

Ralls, K.; R. L. Brownell, Jr.; and J. Ballon. "Differential Mortality by Sex and Age in Mammals, with Specific Reference to the Sperm Whale." In *Sperm Whales: Special Issue,* Reports of the International Whaling Commission, Cambridge, MA. 1980.

Ramey, E. R. "The Natural Capacity for Health in Women." In P. W. Berman and E. R. Ramey, eds. *Women: A Developmental Perspective.* National Institutes of Health, April 1982.

Reeves, J. H. "Projection of Number of Kin." In J. Bongaarts et al., eds. *Family Demography.* New York: Oxford University Press, 1987.

Reimers, C. "Is the Average Age at Retirement Changing?" *Journal of the American Statistical Association* 71 (355) (September 1976):552–558.

Retherford, R. D. "Tobacco Smoking and the Sex Mortality Differential." *Demography* 9 (2) (1972):203–216.

―――― *The Changing Sex Differential in Mortality.* Westport, CT: Greenwood Press, 1975.

Rhine, S. H. *Older Workers and Retirement.* New York: Conference Board, 1978.

Rice, D. P., and M. La Plante "The Burden of Multiple Chronic Conditions." Paper presented at the annual meeting of the American Public Health Association, November 1984.

―――― "Chronic Illness, Disability, and Increasing Longevity." In S. Sullivan and M. E. Lewis, eds. *The Economics and Ethics of Long-Term Care and Disability.* Washington, DC: American Enterprise Institute, 1988.

Riche, M. F. "Retirement's Lifestyle Pioneers." *American Demographics* 8 (January 1986):42–44, 50–56.

Richman, H. A., and M. W. Stagner "Children: Treasured Resource or Forgotten Minority." In A. Pifer and L. Bronte, eds. *Our Aging Society: Paradox or Promise.* New York: Norton, 1986.

Riley, J. C. "The Risk of Being Sick: Morbidity Trends in Four Countries." *Population and Development Review* 16 (3) (September 1990):403–432.

Riley, M. W., and K. Bond "Beyond Ageism: Postponing the Onset of Disability." In M. W. Riley, B. B. Hess, and K. Bond, eds. *Aging in Society: Selected Reviews of Recent Research,* Hillsdale, NJ: Lawrence Erlbaum, 1983.

Riley, M. W.; M. E. Johnson, and A. Foner, eds. *Aging and Society. A Sociology of Age Stratification,* vol. 3. New York: Russell Sage Foundation, 1972.

Rives, N., Jr., and W. J. Serow "Interstate Migration of the Elderly: Demographic Aspects." *Research on Aging* 3 (2) (June 1981):259–278.

Rix, S., and P. Fischer *Retirement-Age Policy: An International Perspective.* Washington, DC: American Institutes for Research, 1981.

Robinson, J. G. "Labor Force Participation Rates of Cohorts of Women in the United States: 1890–1979." Paper presented at the annual meeting of the Population Association of America, Denver, Colorado, April 11, 1980.

Robinson, P. K.; S. Coberly, and C. E. Paul "Work and Retirement." In R. H. Binstock and E. Shanas, eds. *Handbook of Aging and the Social Sciences,* 2nd ed., Van Nostrand Reinhold Co., New York, 1985.

Rogers, A. "Age Patterns of Elderly Migration: An International Comparison." *Demography* 25 (3) (August 1988):355–370.

Rogers, A.; R. G. Rogers; and A. Belanger "Active Life Among the Elderly in the United States: Multistate Life Table Estimates and Population Projections." *Milbank Memorial Fund Quarterly* 67 (3–4) (1989):370–411.

————; R. G. Rogers; and A. Belanger "Longer Life But Worse Health? Measurement and Dynamics." *Gerontologist* 30 (5) (October 1990):640–649.

Rones, P. L. "Older Men—The Choice Between Work and Retirement." *Monthly Labor Review* 101 (11) (November 1978):3–10.

———— "The Labor Market Problems of Older Workers." *Monthly Labor Review* 106 (5) (May 1983):3–12.

Root, L. S., and J. E. Tropman "Income Sources of the Elderly." *Social Service Review* 58 (3) (September 1984):384–403.

Rosenfeld, C., and S. C. Brown "The Labor Force Status of Older Workers." *Monthly Labor Review* 102 (11) (November 1979):12–18.

Rosenwaike, I. "A New Evaluation of United States Census Data on the Extreme Aged." *Demography* 16 (2) (May 1979):279–288.

———— *The Extreme Aged in America: A Portrait of an Expanding Population.* Westport, CT: Greenwood Press, 1985a.

———— "A Demographic Portrait of the Oldest Old." *Milbank Memorial Fund Quarterly* 63 (2) (Spring 1985b):187–205.

————, and A. Dolinsky "The Changing Determinants of the Growth of the Extreme Aged." *Gerontologist* 27 (3) (June 1987):275–280.

Ross, C. M.; S. Danziger; and E. Smolensky "Interpreting Changes in the Economic Status of the Elderly, 1949–1979." *Contemporary Policy Issues* 5 (2) (1989):98–112.

Rossi, A. S. "Sex and Gender in an Aging Society." *Daedalus* 115 (1) (Winter 1986):141–169.

Rossi, P. "Homeless." Address before the Washington Academy of Sciences, October 15, 1987.

Rothschild, H., ed. *Biocultural Aspects of Disease.* New York: Academic Press, 1981.

Rowles, G. D.; R. Q. Hanham; and J. R. Bohland "Explaining Changes in the Regional Concentration of the Elderly in the U.S.A." Paper presented at the International Congress of Gerontology, New York, July 15, 1985.

Rubinstein, R. L. "Never Married Elderly as a Social Type: Re-Evaluating Some Images." *Gerontologist* 27 (1) (February 1987):108–113.

Ruggles, P. "The Economic Status of the Low-Income Elderly: New Evidence from the SIPP." Paper presented at the annual meeting of the Gerontological Society of America, Washington, DC, November 20, 1987.

—— Chapter 6 in *Drawing the Line: Alternative Poverty Measures and Their Implications for Public Policy.* Washington, DC: Urban Institute Press, 1990.

Ruggles, S. "The Demography of the Unrelated Individual." *Demography* 25 (4) (November 1988):521–536.

Ruhm, C. J. "Why Older Americans Stop Working." *Gerontologist* 29 (3) (1989):294–299.

Ryder, N. B. "The Process of Demographic Transition." *Demography* 1 (1964):74–82.

—— "The Cohort as a Concept in the Study of Social Change." *American Sociological Review* 30 (6) (December 1965):843–861.

—— "Notes on Stationary Populations." *Population Index* 14 (1) (January 1975):3–28.

Santi, L. L. "Household Headship Among Unmarried Persons in the United States, 1970–1985." *Demography* 27 (2) (May 1990):219–232.

Schneider, E. L., and J. A. Brody "Aging, Natural Death, and the Compression of Morbidity: Another View." *New England Journal of Medicine* 309 (14) (October 6, 1983):854–856.

Schoen, R.; W. Urton; K. Woodrow; and J. Baj "Marriage and Divorce in Twentieth Century American Cohorts." *Demography* 22 (1) (February 1985):101–114.

Schulz, J. H. *The Economics of Aging,* 3rd ed. New York: Van Nostrand Reinhold, 1985.

Schwarz, K. "Public Health Implications of Stationary and Declining Populations." *World Health Statistics Report* 30 (4) (1977):340–354.

Semler, N. J., and A. Tella "Inflation and Labor Force Participation." In *Stagflation: The Causes, Effects, and Solutions,* vol. 4. Studies prepared for the use of the Special Study on Economic Change of the Joint Economic Committee, Congress of the United States, December 17, 1980.

Serow, W. J. "Return Migration of the Elderly in the USA: 1955–1960 and 1965–1970." *Journal of Gerontology* 33 (2) (March 1978):288–295.

—— "Determinants of Interstate Migration: Differences Between Elderly and Nonelderly Movers." *Journal of Gerontology* 42 (1) (January 1987):95–100.

—— "Some Implications of Changing Age Compositions of Low Fertility Countries. Empirical Evidence: An Assessment, in Particular, of Its Practical Significance." *International Population Conference, Manila, 1981,* vol. 3. Liège: International Union for the Scientific Study of Population, 1981.

Shanas, E. "Health Status of Older People: Cross-National Implications." *Journal of the American Public Health Association* 64 (3) (March 1974):261–264.

—— "The Family as a Social Support System in Old Age." *Gerontologist* 19 (2) (April 1979):169–174.

Shapiro, E., and R. Tate "Who Is Really at Risk of Institutionalization?" *Gerontologist* 28 (2) (April 1988):237–245.

Sheldon, H. D. *The Older Population of the United States.* New York: Wiley, 1958.

Sheppard, H. L., and S. E. Rix *The Graying of Working America: The Coming Crisis of Retirement-Age Policy.* New York: Free Press, 1977.

Sherman, S. R. "Reported Reasons Retired Workers Left Their Last Job: Findings from the New Beneficiary Survey." *Social Security Bulletin* 48 (3) (March 1985):25–26.

Shiloh, A., and I. C. Selavan, eds. *The Jews.* Ethnic Groups of America: Their Morbidity, Mortality, and Behavior Disorders, vol. 1. Springfield, IL: Thomas, 1974.

————, **eds.** *The Blacks.* Ethnic Groups of America: Their Morbidity, Mortality, and Behavior Disorders, vol. 2. Springfield, IL: Thomas, 1975.

Shryock, H. S., Jr.; J. S. Siegel; and Associates, U.S. Bureau of the Census *The Methods and Materials of Demography.* Washington, DC: U.S. Government Printing Office, 1980.

Siegel, J. S. "Demographic Background for International Gerontological Studies." *Journal of Gerontology* 36 (1) (January 1981):93–102.

————, **and S. L. Hoover** "Demographic Aspects of the Health of the Elderly to the Year 2000 and Beyond." *World Health Statistics Quarterly* 35 (3-4) (1982):134–202.

Siegel, J. S., and J. S. Passel "New Estimates of the Number of Centenarians in the United States," *Journal of the American Statistical Association* 71 (355) (September 1976):559–566.

Siegel, J. S., and C. Taeuber "Demographic Dimensions of an Aging Population." In A. Pifer and L. Bronte, eds. *Our Aging Society: Paradox and Promise.* New York: Norton, 1986.

Smeeding, T. M. "Nonmoney Income and the Elderly: The Case of the 'Tweeners'." Discussion Paper no. 759-784, Institute for Research on Poverty, University of Wisconsin, Madison, 1984.

Smith, B. W., and J. Hiltner "Intra-urban Location of the Elderly." *Journal of Gerontology* 30 (4) (July 1975):473–478.

Soldo, B. J. "Household Types, Housing Needs, and Disability." In R. J. Newcomer, M. P. Lawton, and J. O. Byerts, eds. *Housing for an Aging Society— Issues, Alternatives, and Policy.* New York: Van Nostrand Reinhold, 1986.

————, **and C. F. Longino, Jr.** "Social and Physical Environments for the Vulnerable Aged." In Institute of Medicine/National Research Council, *The Social and Built Environment in an Older Society.* Washington, DC: National Academy Press, 1988.

Soldo, B. J., and J. Myllyuoma "Caregivers Who Live with Dependent Elderly." *Gerontologist* 23 (6) (December 1983):605–611.

Spanier, G. B.; P. A. Roos; and J. Shockey "Marital Trajectories of American Women: Variations in the Life Course." *Journal of Marriage and the Family* 47 (November 1985):993–1003.

Speare, A.; S. Goldstein; and W. H. Frey *Residential Mobility, Migration, and Metropolitan Change.* Cambridge, MA: Ballinger, 1975.

Speare, A. "Home Ownership, Life Cycle State, and Residential Mobility." *Demography* 7 (4) (November 1970):449–458.

Spence, D. A., and J. Wiener "Nursing Home Length of Stay Patterns: Results from the 1985 National Nursing Home Survey." *Gerontologist* 30 (1) (February 1990):16–25.

Spengler, J. J. *Toward Zero Population Growth: Reactions and Interpretations, Past and Present.* Durham, NC: Duke University Press, 1978.

Spitze, G., and J. Logan "Gender Differences in Family Support: Is There a Payoff?" *Gerontologist* 29 (1) (February 1989):108–112.

Sternlieb, G., and J. W. Hughes "Demographics and Housing in America." *Population Bulletin* 41 (1) (January 1986), Population Reference Bureau, Washington, DC.

Stone, R.; G. L. Cafferata; and J. Sangl "Caregivers of the Frail Elderly: A National Profile." *Gerontologist* 27 (5) (October 1987):616–626.

Storey, J. R. "Financial Disincentives for Continued Work by Older Americans." Paper presented at the annual meeting of the Gerontological Association of America, San Diego, November 23, 1980.

Struyk, R. J. "The Housing Situation of Elderly Americans." *Gerontologist* 17 (2) (April 1977):130–139.

———— "Housing Adjustments of Relocating Elderly Households." *Gerontologist* 20 (1) (February 1980):45–55.

———— "Current and Emerging Issues in Housing Environments for the Elderly." In Institute of Medicine/National Research Council, *The Social and Built Environment in an Older Society.* Washington, DC: National Academy Press, 1988.

————, **and B. J. Soldo** *Improving the Elderly's Housing.* Cambridge, MA: Ballinger, 1980.

Susser, M. "Industrialization, Urbanization, and Health: An Epidemiological View." In *International Population Conference, Manila, 1981.* Liège: International Union for the Scientific Study of Population, 1981.

Suzman, R., and M. W. Riley, eds. *Milbank Memorial Fund Quarterly* 63 (2) (Spring 1985): special issue, *The Oldest Child.*

Tierney, J. P. "A Comparative Examination of the Residential Segregation of Persons 65 to 75 and Persons 75 and Above in 18 United States Metropolitan Areas for 1970 and 1980." *Journal of Gerontology* 42 (1) (January 1987):101–106.

Torres-Gil, F. "The Latinization of a Multigenerational Population: Hispanics in an Aging Society," *Daedalus* 115 (1) (Winter 1986):325–348.

———— *Hispanics in an Aging Society.* Report of a conference sponsored by the Aging Society Project, Carnegie Corporation of New York, August 1986b.

Torrey, B. B. "Sharing Increasing Costs on Declining Income: The Visible Dilemma of the Invisible Aged." *Milbank Memorial Fund Quarterly* 63 (2) (Spring 1985):377–394.

Townsend, P. "The Emergence of the Four-Generation Family in Industrial Society." In B. L. Neugarten, ed. *Middle Age and Aging.* Chicago: University of Chicago Press, 1968.

Tracy, M. B. "Trends in Retirement." *International Social Security Review* 31 (2) (1979):131–159.

Treas, J. "Family Support Systems for the Aged: Some Social and Demographic Considerations." *Gerontologist* 17 (6) (1977):486–491.

———— "The Great American Fertility Debate: Generational Balance and Support of the Aged." *Gerontologist* 21 (1) (February 1981a):98–103.

———— "Women's Employment and Its Implications for the Status of the Elderly of the Future." In B. Kiesler, J. Morgan, and V. K. Oppenheimer, eds. *Aging and Social Change.* New York: Academic Press, 1981b.

————, **and A. Van Hilst** "Marriage and Remarriage Rates Among Older Americans." *Gerontologist* 16 (2):132–136.

Uhlenberg, P. "Demographic Change and Problems of the Aged." In M. W. Riley, ed. *Aging from Birth to Death: Interdisciplinary Perspectives.* Boulder: Westview Press, 1979.

————, and **M. A. P. Myers** "Divorce and the Elderly." *Gerontologist* 21 (3) (June 1981):276–282.

United Nations *Determinants and Consequences of Population Trends.* Population Studies, series A, no. 50. New York: United Nations, 1973.

———— *Levels and Trends of Mortality Since 1950,* Population Studies, series A, no. 74. New York: United Nations, 1982.

———— *World Population Trends: 1983 Monitoring Report,* Population and Development Interrelations and Population Policies, vol. 2. New York: United Nations, 1985.

———— *Global Estimates and Projections of Population by Sex and Age: 1988 Revision.* New York: United Nations, 1989.

U.S. Bureau of the Census "Marital Status and Living Arrangements: March 1977." *Current Population Reports,* series P-20, no. 323 (April 1978).

———— "1976 Survey of Institutionalized Persons: A Study of Persons Receiving Long-Term Care." *Current Population Reports,* series P-23, no. 69 (1978).

———— "Racial Succession in Individual Housing Units," by L. H. Long and D. Spain. *Current Population Reports,* series P-23, no. 71 (September 1978).

———— "Lifetime Earnings Estimates for Men and Women in the United States: 1979," by D. L. Burkhead. *Current Population Reports,* series P-60, no. 139 (February 1983).

———— "Labor Force Status and Other Characteristics of Persons with a Work Disability: 1982," by J. McNeil. *Current Population Reports,* series P-23, no. 127 (July 1983).

———— "Projections of the Population of the United States, by Age, Sex, and Race: 1983 to 2080," by G. Spencer. *Current Population Reports,* series P-25, no. 952 (May 1984).

———— "Lifetime Work Experience and Its Effect on Earnings," by J. J. Salvo and J. M. McNeil. *Current Population Reports,* series P-23, no. 136 (June 1984).

———— "Demographic and Socioeconomic Aspects of Aging in the United States," by J. S. Siegel and M. Davidson. *Current Population Reports,* series P-23, no. 138 (August 1984).

———— "Household Wealth and Asset Ownership: 1984." *Current Population Reports,* series P-70, no. 7 (July 1986).

———— "Marital Status and Living Arrangements: March 1985." *Current Population Reports,* series P-20, no. 410 (November 1986).

———— "Male-Female Differences in Work Experience, Occupation, and Earnings: 1984," by J. M. McNeil and E. Lamas. *Current Population Reports,* series P-70, no. 10 (August 1987).

———— "Pensions: Worker Coverage and Retirement Income: 1984." *Current Population Reports,* series P-70, no. 12 (September 1987).

———— "Educational Attainment in the United States: March 1982 to 1985." *Current Population Reports,* series P-20, no. 415 (November 1987).

———— "Who's Helping Out?" *Current Population Reports,* series P-70, no. 13 (October 1988).

———— Projections of the Population of the United States by Age, Sex, and Race: 1988 to 2080." *Current Populaton Reports,* Series P-25, no. 108 (January 1989).

———— "Health Insurance Coverage: 1986–1988." *Current Population Reports,* series P-70, no. 17 (September 1990).

———— *The American Housing Survey, United States, 1987,* H150-87 (December 1989).

———— **and U.S. Department of Housing and Urban Development** "The Coverage of Population in the 1980 Census," by R. E. Fay, J. S. Passel, and J. G. Robinson. *Evaluation and Research Reports*, series PHC80-E4 (February 1988).

U.S. Bureau of Labor Statistics *Tables of Working Life for Women, 1950*, by S. H. Garfinkle. Bulletin no. 1204. Reprinted from *Monthly Labor Review* (June, August, and October 1956).

—— *Length of Working Life for Men and Women, 1970*, by H. N. Fullerton, Jr., and J. J. Byrne. Special Labor Force Report no. 187. Reprinted from *Monthly Labor Review* (February 1976).

—— *BLS Handbook of Methods*. 1982.

—— *Worklife Estimates: Effects of Race and Education*, by S. Smith. Bulletin no. 2254 (February 1986).

—— *Tables of Working Life: The Increment-Decrement Model*, by S. Smith. Bulletin no. 2135 (November 1982).

—— "Consumer Expenditure Survey: 1984 Results for Both Urban and Rural Population." *News*, no. 86-451 (November 20, 1986).

U.S. Congress Congressional Budget Office. *Profile of Health Care Coverage: The Haves and the Have-Nots* (1979).

U.S. Council of Economic Advisors *Economic Report of the President*. Transmitted to the Congress, February 1985; reproduced in part in *Population and Development Review*, vol. 11, no. 2 (June 1985).

U.S. Department of Agriculture "Net Migration of the Population, 1950–60, by Age, Sex, and Color," by G. K. Bowles and J. D. Tarver. *Population-Migration Report*, vol. 1 (May 1965).

—— "Rural Elderly in Demographic Perspective," by N. Glasgow and C. L. Beale. *Rural Development Perspectives*, vol. 29 (October 1985).

—— "The Nonmetropolitan Elderly: Economic and Demographic Status," by N. Glasgow. *Rural Development Research Report*, no. 70 (June 1988).

U.S. Department of Agriculture et al. "Net Migration of the Population, 1960–70, by Age, Sex, and Color," by G. K. Bowles and E. S. Lee. *Population-Migration Report* (December 1975), parts 1–6.

U.S. Department of Housing and Urban Development, Office of Policy Development and Research "How Well Are We Housed? No. 4. The Elderly," by A. Yezer. Washington, DC, May 1979.

U.S. General Accounting Office *Retirement Before Age 65: Trends, Costs, and National Issues*. Report to the Chairman, Select Committee on Aging, July 1986.

U.S. House of Representatives *Consequences of Changing U.S. Population: Demographics of Aging*. Joint Hearings before the Select Committee on Population and the Select Committee on Aging, May 24, 1978.

U.S. National Commission on Employment Policy *Restructuring Social Security: How Will Retirement Ages Respond?* by G. S. Fields and O. S. Mitchell. Washington, DC: U.S. Government Printing Office, 1983.

U.S. National Center for Health Statistics "U.S. Life Tables by Causes of Death, 1959–61," by T. N. E. Greville. *U.S. Life Tables, 1959–61*, vol. 1, no. 6 (1968).

—— "U.S. Life Tables by Causes of Death, 1969–71," by T. N. E. Greville, F. Bayo, and R. S. Foster. *U.S. Life Tables, 1969–71*, vol. 1, no. 5 (May 1975).

—— "Limitation of Activity Due to Chronic Conditions, United States, 1974," by C. S. Wilder. *Vital and Health Statistics*, series 10, no. 111 (June 1977).

—— "A Comparison of Nursing Home Residents and Discharges from the 1977 National Nursing Home Survey: United States." *Vital and Health Statistics*, Advance Data, no. 28 (1978).

—————— "The National Nursing Home Survey, 1977, Summary for the United States." *Vital and Health Statistics,* series 13, no. 43 (1979).

—————— "Acute Conditions: Incidence and Associated Disability, United States, July 1977–June 1978," by P. W. Ries. *Vital and Health Statistics,* series 10, no. 132 (September 1979).

—————— "Nursing Home Utilization in California, Illinois, Massachusetts, New York and Texas: 1977 National Nursing Home Survey." *Vital and Health Statistics,* series 13, no. 48 (1980).

—————— "Current Estimates from the National Health Interview Survey, United States, 1979," by S. S. Jack. *Vital and Health Statistics,* series 10, no. 136 (April 1981).

—————— "Social and Economic Implications of Cancer in the United States," by D. P. Rice and T. A. Hodgson. *Vital and Health Statistics,* series 3, no. 20 (March 1981).

—————— "Americans Needing Help to Function at Home," by B. Feller. *Vital and Health Statistics,* Advance Data, series 10, no. 92 (September 1983).

—————— "U.S. Life Tables Eliminating Certain Causes of Death," by R. Armstrong and L. R. Curtin. *U.S. Decennial Life Tables, 1979–81,* vol. 1, no. 2 (1986).

—————— "Advance Report of Final Marriage Statistics, 1982." *Monthly Vital Statistics Report,* vol. 34, no. 3, supplement (June 28, 1985).

—————— *Vital and Health Statistics,* series 3, no. 25 (1986).

—————— "Aging in the Eighties, Age 65 Years and Over and Living Alone, Contacts with Family, Friends, and Neighbors, Preliminary Data from the Supplement on Aging to the National Health Interview Survey: United States, January–June 1984," by M. G. Kovar, *Vital and Health Statistics,* Advance Data, no. 116 (May 1986).

—————— *Proceedings of the 1987 Public Health Conference on Records and Statistics: Data for an Aging Population.* DHHS pub. no. (PHS) 88-1214 (December 1987).

—————— "The Prevalence of Comorbidity and Its Association with Disability," by J. M. Guralnik, A. Z. LaCroix, D. F. Everett, and M. G. Kovar, *Vital and Health Statistics,* Advance Data, no. 170 (May 1989).

—————— "Health of Black and White America, 1985–87," by Peter Ries. *Vital and Health Statistics,* Series 10, No. 171, 1990 (PHS):90–1599.

—————— **and National Center for Health Services Research** "Elderly People: The Population 65 Years and Over," by M. G. Kovar. *Health. United States, 1976–77,* pt. A, chap. 1 (1978).

U.S. National Institute on Aging and the National Heart, Lung, and Blood Institute *Proceedings of the Second Conference on the Epidemiology of Aging, March 28–29, 1977,* edited by S. G. Haynes and M. Feinlieb, July 1980.

U.S. National Institute of Child Health and Human Development *Epidemiology of Aging,* edited by A. M. Ostfeld and D. C. Gibson, proceedings of a research conference on the Epidemiology of Aging, June 1972.

U.S. National Institute of Neurological and Communicative Disorders and Stroke *The Dementias: Hope Through Research.* Publication no. 83-2252, June 1983.

U.S. Senate, Special Committee on Aging *Developments in Aging: 1985,* vol. 3. Washington, DC: U.S. Government Printing Office, 1985.

U.S. Social Security Administration, Office of the Actuary "Life Tables for the United States, 1900–2050," by J. F. Faber. *Actuarial Study,* no. 87 (September 1982).

—————— "Life Tables for the United States, 1900–2050," by J. F. Faber and A. H. Wade. *Actuarial Study,* no. 89 (December 1983).

—————— "Social Security Area Population Projections, 1984," by A. Wade. *Actuarial Study*, no. 92 (May 1984).

—————— "Social Security Area Population Projections, 1985," by A. H. Wade. *Actuarial Study*, no. 95 (October 1985).

U.S. Social Security Administration, Office of Research and Statistics "Economic Value of a Housewife," by W. H. Brody. *Research and Statistics Note*, DHEW pub. no. (SSA) 75-11701 (August 28, 1975).

—————— "Assets on the Threshold of Retirement," by S. R. Sherman. In L. Irelan et al. *Almost 65: Baseline Data from the Retirement History Study*. Research Report no. 49 (1976).

U.S. Social Security Administration, Office of Research, Statistics, and International Policy "Changes in the Money Income of the Aged and Nonaged, 1967–1983," by D. B. Radner. *Studies in Income Distribution*, no. 14 (September 1986).

van de Kaa, D. J. "Europe's Second Demographic Transition." *Population Bulletin* vol. 42, no. 1 (March 1987). Population Reference Bureau, Washington, DC.

van den Boomen, J. "Age-Cost Profiles: A Common Denominator?" *International Population Conference, Manila, 1981*, vol. 3. Liège, Belgium: International Union for the Scientific Study of Population.

Varady, D. P. "Housing Problems and Mobility Plans Among the Elderly." *Journal of the American Planning Association* 46 (1980):301–314.

Verbrugge, L. M. "Sex Differentials in Morbidity and Mortality in the United States." *Social Biology* 23 (4) (Winter 1976):275–296.

—————— "Women and Men: Mortality and Health of Older People." In M. W. Riley, B. B. Hess, and K. Bond, eds. *Aging in Society: Selected Reviews of Recent Research*. Hillsdale, NJ: Lawrence Erlbaum, 1983.

—————— "Longer Life But Worsening Health? Trends in Health and Mortality of Middle-Aged and Older Persons." *Milbank Memorial Fund Quarterly* 62 (3) (Summer 1984):475–519.

—————— "Sex Differences in Health Behavior, Morbidity, and Mortality." Paper presented at the NIH Conference on Gender and Longevity, Bethesda, MD, September 17–18, 1987.

——————, **and J. H. Madens** "Social Roles and Health Trends of America Women." *Milbank Memorial Fund Quarterly* 63 (4) (Fall 1985):691–735.

Vincente, L.; J. Wiley; and R. A. Carrington "The Risk of Institutionalization Before Death." *Gerontologist* 19 (1) (February 1979):52–55.

Waite, L. J. "U.S. Women at Work." *Population Bulletin* 36 (2) (May 1981).

Waldo, D., and H. C. Lazenby "Demographic Characteristics and Health Care Use and Expenditures by the Aged in the United States, 1977–1984." *Health Care Financing Review* 6 (1) (Fall 1984):1–29.

Waldron, I. "Why Do Women Live Longer Than Men." *Journal of Human Stress* 2 (1) (March 1976):2–13.

—————— "Sex Differences in Human Mortality: The Role of Genetic Factors." *Social Science Medicine* 17 (6) (1983):321–333.

—————— "The Contribution of Smoking to Sex Differences in Mortality." Paper presented at the annual meeting of the Population Association of America, Boston, March 1985.

——————, , **and S. Johnston** "Why Do Women Live Longer Than Men." *Journal of Human Stress* 2 (2) (June 1976):19–29.

Walford, R. *Maximum Life Span*. New York: Norton, 1983.

—————— *The 120 Year Diet: How to Double Your Vital Years*. New York: Simon & Schuster, 1987.

Wander, H. "Short, Medium, and Long Term Implications of a Stationary or Declining Population on Education, Labour Force, Housing Needs, Social Security and Economic Development." *International Population Conference, Mexico City, 1977,* vol. 3. Liège: International Union for the Scientific Study of Population, 1977.

———. "Zero Population Growth Now: The Lessons from Europe." In T. J. Espenshade and W. J. Serow, eds. *The Economic Consequences of Slowing Population Growth.* New York: Academic Press, 1978.

Ward, R. A. "The Implications of Neighborhood Age Structure for Older People." *Sociological Symposium* 26 (1) (Spring 1979a):42–63.

——— "The Never Married in Later Life." *Journal of Gerontology* 34 (6) (November 1979b):861–869.

Watkins, S. C.; J. A. Menken, and J. Bongaarts "Demographic Foundations of Family Change." *American Sociological Review* 52 (June 1987):346–358.

Westoff, C. F. "Some Speculations on the Future of Marriage and Fertility," *Family Planning Perspectives* 10 (2) (March–April 1978):79–83.

——— "Fertility Decline in the West: Causes and Prospects," *Population and Development Review* 9 (1) (March 1983):99–105.

Wiley, J. A., and T. C. Camacho "Life Style and Future Health: Evidence from the Alameda County Study." *Preventive Medicine* 9 (1) (January 1980):1–21.

Wilkin, J. C. "Recent Trends in the Mortality of the Aged." *Transactions of the Society of Actuaries* 33 (1) (January 1981):53–86.

Wing, S.; K. G. Manton; E. Stallard; C. G. Haines; and H. A. Tyroler "The Black/White Mortality Crossover: Investigation in a Community-based Study." *Journal of Gerontology* 40 (1) (January 1985):78–84.

Wiseman, R. F. "Why Older People Move: Theoretical Issues." *Research on Aging* 2 (2) (June 1980):141–154.

Wolf, D. A. "Kin Availability and the Living Arrangements of Older Women." *Social Science Research* 13 (1) (March 1984):72–89.

———, **and B. J. Soldo** "Household Composition Choices of Older Unmarried Women." *Demography* 25 (3) (August 1988):387–403.

Wulf, D. "Low Fertility in Europe: A Report from the IUSSP Meeting." *International Family Planning Perspectives* 8 (2) (June 1982):63–69.

Wynne, E. A. "Will the Young Support the Old?" In A. Pifer and L. Bronte, eds. *Our Aging Society: Paradox or Promise.* New York: Norton, 1986.

Ycas, M. A. "Recent Trends in Health Near the Age of Retirement: New Findings from the Health Interview Survey." *Social Security Bulletin* 50 (2) (February 1978):9–12.

———, **and S. Grad** "Income of Retirement-Aged Persons in the United States." *Social Security Bulletin* 50 (7) (July 1987).

Yeats, D. E.; J. C. Biggar; and C. F. Longino, Jr. "Distance Versus Destination: Stream Sensitivity of Elderly Interstate Migrants." *Journal of Gerontology* 42 (3) (May 1987):288–294.

Yvert-Jalu, H. "Les personnes âgées en Union Soviétique." *Population* (Paris) 40 (6) (November–December 1985):829–853.

Zais, J., and T. G. Thibodeau *The Elderly and Urban Housing.* Washington, DC: Urban Institute Press, 1983.

Zick, C. D., and K. R. Smith "Immediate and Delayed Effects of Widowhood on Poverty: Patterns from the 1970s." *Gerontologist* 26 (6) (December 1986):669–675.

Name Index

Boldface numbers refer to figures and tables.

Subject Index

Boldface numbers refer to figures and tables.

M

malignant neoplasms: cause of death, 206–209, 211, 213, 218, 223, 230–231; lifestyle influences, 293; morbidity, 247; obesity and, 293

marital distribution: nursing home care, 284

marital status: age cycle, **308;** age variations, 300–306, **301, 303–305;** institutionalized population, 351, **353,** 359; labor force participation, 409–410, **410,** 452; mortality and, **314;** poverty, **486;** race differences, 302; sex differences, 300–306, **301, 303–305,** 307–311, **308,** 360. *See also* divorce; widowhood

marriage: age of, 344; asset ownership and net worth, 515; dissolution, 334; family size and income, 502; forecasting, 590; living arrangements and marital composition, 325–326, 340–341; rates, 344; remarriage, 309–311, 317, 590

Massachusetts: net interstate and interregional migration, 130; number and proportion of elderly, 103

MDC. *See* More Developed Countries

mean age: childbearing, 344; population, **7;** retirement, 428; Social Security benefits, 447

median age: childbearing, 338n; of death, 208–209, **209,** 585; forecasting, 584–585; homelessness, 573; homeowners, 553; households, 327; labor force, 437, 437n; population, **7;** retirement, 422, 424

median income: age groups, **461–462,** 461–464, **466;** age, race and sex differences, **476–477;** elderly families, 467; families, **468–470;** interstate exchanges, migration, 156, **157–160;** labor force participation, **494;** nonmetropolitan areas, 492; peak ages, 524; statistics, **488–489;** unrelated individuals, 487; women, 473

median net worth, 509–512, **510–512,** 513, **513,** 525

Medicaid: cost of health care, 288; coverage, 504, 504n, 505; death rates, decline of, 194; expenditures and, 522; hospital care, 278; mental hospital patients, decrease in, 354; nursing home care, 280, 357

medical care. *See* health care

medical intervention: life expectancy, 208

medical technology: life expectancy, 222

Medicare: cost of health care, 288, 289; coverage, 504, 505; death rates, 194, 204; elderly dependency ratio, 596; expenditures and, 522; hospital care, effect on, 277, 279; labor force participation ratios, 452; mental hospital patients, decrease in, 354; nursing home care, 280; olderaged (85 and over), **16;** qualification for, 4; solvency of, 431

memory and aging, 5

mental illness: institutionalization, 354, 359; morbidity, 247

metropolitan areas (SMSA): age-restricted environments, 176; age-specific net migration rates, **173;** forecasting, 583; health care, 256; index of dissimilarity, 175; intergenerational relations, 177; intergroup contract, 175; key elderly SMSAs, 175–76; morbidity, 256; physical characteristics, 170; residential clustering, 163, **164–167,** 173–177; school taxes, support for, 177

Mexicans: housing, 536, 565

Mexico: immigration to U.S., 84; migration, 181

Michigan: geographic variations, counties, 114; interstate exchanges, migration, 156; migration, 122; number and proportion of elderly, 99

middle-aged: baby boom cohorts, 339, 340, 583; death rate, 336; family life cycle, 361; family support by, 338; gross interstate and interregional migration, 143n; interstate migration, 143; parents, support of, 597

Middle Atlantic Division states, 114, 116; gross interstate and interregional migration, 147; interstate exchanges, migration, 156; life expectancy, 219; migration, 122, 181; net interstate and interregional migration, 123–127

middle-series projections of Census Bureau, 2, 92

Midwestern states: central cities, 179; geographic variations, counties, 114; gross interstate and interregional migration, 145; housing, regional variations, 533; interstate migration, 141, 141n; life expectancy, 219; migration, 181; residen-